The Fight Against Hunger and Malnutrition

The Fight Against Hunger and Malnutrition

The Role of Food, Agriculture, and Targeted Policies

Edited by
David E. Sahn

OXFORD
UNIVERSITY PRESS

OXFORD
UNIVERSITY PRESS

Great Clarendon Street, Oxford, OX2 6DP,
United Kingdom

Oxford University Press is a department of the University of Oxford.
It furthers the University's objective of excellence in research, scholarship,
and education by publishing worldwide. Oxford is a registered trade mark of
Oxford University Press in the UK and in certain other countries

First Edition published in 2015

Impression: 1

Published in the United States of America by Oxford University Press
198 Madison Avenue, New York, NY 10016, United States of America

British Library Cataloguing in Publication Data
Data available

Library of Congress Control Number: 2015933186

ISBN 978–0–19–873320–1

Printed and bound by
CPI Group (UK) Ltd, Croydon, CR0 4YY

Preface

Per Pinstrup-Andersen, to whom we dedicate this book, has been a tireless and effective advocate for the poor and hungry throughout his luminous career as a scholar, teacher, policy advisor, and advocate. For more than 50 years, Dr. Pinstrup-Andersen has inspired and motivated his students in his role as a revered professor, provided leadership in building and strengthening institutions dedicated to food and nutrition policy, and influenced policymakers throughout the world through his understanding and compelling articulation of knowledge and ideas that advance the cause of fighting malnutrition and ameliorating poverty through enlightened policy. Dr. Pinstrup-Andersen's passion and the efficacy of his efforts to promote technological, scientific, and policy advances has only been equaled by his humanity and the strength of his enduring friendships and relationships among the myriad people who have come to know Dr. Pinstrup-Andersen during his long and illustrious career.

Recounting Dr. Pinstrup-Andersen's professional accomplishments is far beyond the scope of this preface. Nonetheless, his roles as Babcock Professor of Food and Nutrition Policy at Cornell University and Director General of the International Food Policy Research Institute exemplify his accomplishments, and are the culmination of numerous important positions that he has held, including at the Centro Internacional de Agricultura Tropical in Cali, Colombia, as the chairman of the Science Council of the Consultative Group on International Agricultural Research, as a professor at the Royal Veterinary and Agricultural University and the University of Copenhagen in Denmark, and as past president of the American Agricultural Economics Association. He was recognized as the 2001 recipient of the World Food Prize and the Charles A. Black Award, as well as the 2002 Agricultural Economics Association Distinguished Policy Contribution Award.

This book, which is a product of a Festschrift that I organized in honor of Dr. Pinstrup-Andersen, is intended to carry forward his research and commitment to the poor and malnourished throughout the world, for whom he has been such a powerful voice. It has been my privilege to have worked on this volume with so many colleagues, all of whom are not only exceptional scholars, but share in common a close personal connection to Per. While I have worked with Per for more than 30 years, going back to my days in graduate school when he was an inspirational mentor, some contributors to this volume have known him far longer, and others include his recent PhD students. My goal as convener of the Festschrift and editor of this book thus aspires to several principles that have been key to Per Pinstrup-Andersen's illustrious career. These include the importance of sound technological advances and scientific research, the dissemination of knowledge, the exchange of information, policy dialogue, and emphasis on policy implementation. Dr. Pinstrup-Andersen's work is not yet finished, and we look forward to his continued leadership and scientific contributions for years to come.

Finally, both the Festschrift and this book were made possible by the efforts of several people that deserve special acknowledgment. First and foremost is Birgit Andersen, a truly amazing friend and inspirational figure. Those who have been privileged to know Birgit Andersen fully appreciate that she has been Per's indispensible partner for all his accomplishments. We all salute Birgit Andersen along with Per Pinstrup-Andersen in this book.

Patrick Stover, the Director of the Division of Nutritional Sciences at Cornell University, made the Festschrift and this volume possible with his generous encouragement and financial support. I also want to thank Mary-Catherine French for her extraordinary efforts in organizing and providing administrative support in planning and carrying out the Festschrift. And as those who contributed to this book can testify, it has been my privilege to once again work with Patricia Mason, whose editorial support and communication and organizational skills contributed to the timeliness and excellence of this book. All three of these wonderful people also have close ties with Dr. Pinstrup-Andersen, which has helped make this book project so thoroughly rewarding and fun.

Contents

Contents

List of Figures

List of Tables

List of Abbreviations

ADRA	Adventist Development and Relief Agency
AEI	Agroecological intensification
AGRA	Alliance for a Green Revolution in Africa
ASF	Animal-source foods
AU	African Union
BMGF	Bill & Melinda Gates Foundation
BMI	Body mass index
BRAC	Bangladesh Rural Advancement Committee
CARE	Cooperative for Assistance and Relief Everywhere
CAADP	Comprehensive Africa Agriculture Development Programme
CCS	Carbon capture and storage
CCT	Conditional cash transfer program
CDC	Centers for Disease Control and Prevention, US
CGIAR	Consultative Group on International Agricultural Research
CFS	Committee on World Food Security (UN)
CI	Confidence interval
CIMMYT	CGIAR's International Maize and Wheat Improvement Center
CNI	Child Nutrition Initiative
CONSEA	National Council on Food and Nutritional Security, Brazil
CSO	Civil society organization
CSPI	Center for Science in the Public Interest
DALYs	Disability-adjusted life years
DES	Dietary energy supply
DFID	Department for International Development, UK
DHS	Demographic and Health Surveys
DRC	Democratic Republic of the Congo
DSB	Dispute Settlement Body
EAR	Estimated Average Requirement (of dietary intake)

List of Abbreviations

EE	Eastern Europe
ESSP	Ethiopia Strategy Support Program
FAO	Food and Agriculture Organization of the United Nations
FEWS NET	Famine Early Warning Systems Network
FMC	Food market chains
FSNM	Food Security and Nutrition Monitoring
FSU	Former Soviet Union
G8	Group of 8—Governments of Canada, France, Germany, Italy, Japan, Russia, United Kingdom, and United States, with representation also from European Union
G20	Group of 20—Governments of Argentina, Australia, Brazil, Canada, China, France, Germany, India, Indonesia, Italy, Japan, Mexico, Russia, Saudi Arabia, South Africa, Korea, Turkey, United Kingdom, United States, European Union
GATT	General Agreement on Tariffs and Trade
GDP	Gross domestic product
GHG	Greenhouse gas
GIEWS	Global Information and Early Warning System on Food and Agriculture
GIS	Geographic Information Systems
GIVAS	Global Impact and Vulnerability Alert System
GM	Genetically modified
GMFS	Global Monitoring for Food Security
GMO	Genetically modified organism
GNI	Global national income
GNP	Gross national product
GR	Green Revolution
GVP	Gross value of production
HANCI	Hunger and Nutrition Commitment Index
IBRD	International Bank for Reconstruction and Development (World Bank)
ICN	International Conference on Nutrition
IDD	Iodine deficiency disorder
IFAD	International Fund for Agricultural Development
IFPRI	International Food Policy Research Institute
IGC	International Growth Centre
IGO	Intergovernmental organization
IMF	International Monetary Fund
INCRA	National Institute for Colonization and Agrarian Reform

INGO	International non-governmental organization
IPCC	Intergovernmental Panel on Climate Change
IPG	International public good
IPM	Integrated pest management
IRRI	International Rice Research Institute
LNS	Lipid-based nutrient supplements
MCLCP	Mesa de Concertacíon para la Lucha Contra la Pobreza
MDGs	Millennium Development Goals
MFP	Multi-factor productivity
MICS	Multiple Indicator Cluster Surveys
MST	Movement of Rural Landless Workers (Movimento dos Trabalhadores Rurais Sem Terra)
NASS	National Agricultural Statistics Service, US
NEPAD	The New Partnership for Africa's Development (African Union)
NEWS	National Early Warning Systems
NCHS	National Center for Health Statistics, US
NGO	Non-governmental organization
NPK	Nitrogen-phosphorus-potassium (fertilizer rating)
NRM	Natural Resource Management
ODI	Overseas Development Institute
OECD	Organisation for Economic Co-operation and Development
OSP	Orange-Fleshed Sweet Potatoes
PAHO	Pan American Health Organization
PAN	Pesticide Action Network
PI	Probability interval
PNSAN	National Food and Nutritional Security Plan of Brazil
PPP	Public–private partnerships
PROGRESA	Programa de Educación, Salud, y Alimenación (Oportunidades)
PRSP	Poverty Reduction Strategy Program
RCP	Representative Concentration Pathway
RCT	Randomized controlled trial
RDA	Recommended Dietary Allowance
SADC	South African Development Community
SCN	Standing Committee on Nutrition (United Nations System)
SDGs	Sustainable Development Goals
SEC	US Securities and Exchange Commission

SES	Social and economic status
SINESAN	Guatemala's National System of Food and Nutrition Security
SOFA	State of Food and Agriculture
SOWC	State of the World's Children
SSA	Sub-Saharan Africa
SSB	Sugar-sweetened beverage
SSP	Strategy Support Program
TFP	Total factor productivity
TFR	Total fertility rates
UCT	Unconditional cash transfer
UNDP	United Nations Development Programme
UNECA	United Nations Economic Commission for Africa
UNESCO	United Nations Educational, Scientific, and Cultural Organization
UNICEF	United Nations Children's Fund
UPOV	International Union for the Protection of New Varieties of Plants
USAID	United States Agency for International Development
USDA	United States Department of Agriculture
USDHHS	United States Department of Health and Human Services
VARHS	Vietnam Access to Resources Household Survey
VHLSS	Vietnam Household Living Standards Survey
WFP	UN World Food Programme
WHO	World Health Organization
WTO	World Trade Organization
ZM	Zero Malnutrition Program

Notes on Contributors

Harold Alderman has a Master's degree in nutrition (Cornell) and a PhD in economics (Harvard)—where Per Pinstrup-Andersen served as an outside member on his thesis committee. He has gravitated to research on the economics of nutrition and food policy. He spent 10 years at the International Food Policy Research Institute (IFPRI) prior to joining the World Bank in 1991. He rejoined IFPRI in 2012. While at the World Bank, he divided his time between the Development Research Group and the Africa region, where he advised on social protection policy. His current research has focused on the linkages between nutrition and early child development and the means by which nutrition and social protection programs contribute to long-term economic growth.

Julian M. Alston is a Professor in the Department of Agricultural and Resource Economics of the University of California at Davis, where he teaches graduate and undergraduate classes in microeconomic theory and the analysis of agricultural markets and policies. At UC-Davis, Alston is a member of the Giannini Foundation of Agricultural Economics and serves as the Director of the Robert Mondavi Institute Center for Wine Economics and as Associate Director for Science and Technology Policy at the University of California Agricultural Issues Center. He is a Fellow of the American Agricultural Economics Association, a Distinguished Fellow and Past President of the Australian Agricultural and Resource Economics Society, a Distinguished Scholar of the Western Agricultural Economics Association, and a Fellow of the American Association of Wine Economists.

Suresh Chandra Babu is a Senior Research Fellow and a Program Leader for the Capacity Strengthening Program at the International Food Policy Research Institute in Washington, DC. He has published more than 65 peer-reviewed journal papers and 13 books and monographs. Over the years, he has trained more than 2,000 people in food policy research and analysis. He has held visiting honorary professorships at American University, Washington, DC; Indira Gandhi National Open University, India; University of Kwazulu-Natal, South Africa; and Zhejiang University, China. He currently serves on several academic journals, including *Food Security, Agricultural Economics Research Review, African Journal of Agricultural and Resource Economics, Journal of Sustainable Development, Food and Nutrition Bulletin,* and *African Journal of Food, Nutritional and Development.* Dr. Babu received his PhD and MS in Economics from Iowa State University. He completed his MSc and BSc in Agriculture at the Agricultural Universities in Tamil Nadu, India.

Christopher B. Barrett is the David J. Nolan Director, Stephen B. and Janice G. Ashley Professor of Applied Economics and Management and International Professor of Agriculture in the Charles H. Dyson School of Applied Economics and Management, as well as Professor in the Department of Economics and Fellow of the David R. Atkinson Center for a Sustainable Future (ACSF), all at Cornell University, where he also serves as the Director of the Cornell Institute for International Food, Agriculture and Development's initiative on Stimulating Agricultural and Rural Transformation, and served as the founding Associate Director for Economic Development programs for the ACSF. He holds degrees from Princeton, Oxford, and the University of Wisconsin-Madison. He has held visiting professorships at Monash University and the University of Melbourne and directed summer seminar programs at Calvin College. Professor Barrett has published or has in press 14 books and more than 260 journal articles or book chapters. He has served on a variety of boards; has won several university, national, and international awards for teaching, research, and public outreach; and is an elected Fellow of both the Agricultural and Applied Economics Association and the African Association of Agricultural Economists.

Leah E. M. Bevis is a fifth year PhD candidate in the Dyson School of Applied Economics and Management, and a Fellow of the Food Systems and Poverty Reduction IGERT program at Cornell University. She obtained her undergraduate degree from Middlebury College in Vermont, where she majored in geography and minored in economics. She has been living and working in East Africa for about 10 years now, including a year spent in eastern Uganda running village-level health programs for a nonprofit organization called Uganda Village Project. Leah is interested in the problem of persistent poverty at the household level in Africa and the ways in which food systems and human capital accumulation affect persistent poverty. She is also particularly focused on childhood micronutrient malnutrition. Her dissertation research focuses on soil-to-human micronutrient transmission and soil degradation-based poverty traps in Uganda.

Shenggen Fan (樊胜根) has been Director General of the International Food Policy Research Institute (IFPRI) since 2009. Dr. Fan joined IFPRI in 1995 as a research fellow, conducting extensive research on pro-poor development strategies in Africa, Asia, and the Middle East. He led IFPRI's program on public investment before becoming the Director of the Institute's Development Strategy and Governance Division in 2005. He now serves as the Vice-Chairman of the World Economic Forum's Global Agenda Council on Food and Nutrition Security, after serving as Chair of the Council from 2012 to 2014. In 2014, Dr. Fan received the Hunger Hero Award from the World Food Programme in recognition of his commitment to and leadership in fighting hunger worldwide. Dr. Fan received a PhD in applied economics from the University of Minnesota and Bachelor's and Master's degrees from Nanjing Agricultural University in China.

Edward A. Frongillo is Professor and Chair of the Department of Health Promotion, Education, and Behavior at the University of South Carolina. He has a PhD in biometry and an MS in human nutrition and child development from Cornell University. He studies how to solve undernutrition and overnutrition in populations globally, especially children and families living in poverty, using qualitative and quantitative methods. His research interests are growth, development, and feeding of infants and young children; family stress and parenting; household and child food insecurity; policy advancement and programs for improving nutrition and development; and design and analysis of longitudinal studies. He has designed, with others, large longitudinal studies, including the World Health Organization's *Multicentre Growth Reference Study* and the *Maternal and Infant Nutrition Interventions in Matlab* study in Bangladesh.

Sinafikeh Gemessa, an Ethiopian national, joined IFPRI in July 2012, as a Senior Research Assistant in the Director General's Office. Sinafikeh received a BS in Statistics and a MS in Economics from Addis Ababa University and a Masters in International Development from Harvard University. He first joined IFPRI, in late 2008, as a research officer in the Ethiopia Strategy Support Program, before he left for his graduate study at Harvard. He has experience working in agricultural development and food security and nutrition issues. In fall 2014, he enrolled in the PhD program in Applied Economics at the University of Minnesota.

Jean-Pierre Habicht, MD (Zurich), PhD (MIT), MPH (Harvard) is a Cornell Professor Emeritus. In retirement, he continues to work as Graduate Professor of Epidemiology in the Division of Nutritional Sciences at Cornell University. In 1969, he went to Guatemala to the Institute of Nutrition of Central America as a WHO medical officer in charge of primary healthcare and epidemiological studies, and then he worked for the US National Center for Health Statistics on nutritional surveillance. He came to Cornell University in 1977 to develop a program of research and training in nutritional epidemiology. This research aimed at elucidating nutritional determinants and their impacts on the health, performance, and survival of mothers and their children. His first experience in bringing epidemiologically derived knowledge to bear programmatically was in developing a Timely Warning and Intervention System to prevent famines in Indonesia. These recurring famines occurred in spite of an excellent food supply system that effectively prevented food scarcity. At this time, Per Pinstrup-Andersen became director of the Cornell Nutrition Surveillance Program, which he transformed into the Cornell Food and Nutrition Policy Program (CFNPP). Jean-Pierre continued working with him as he developed nutrition surveillance systems for policy development in Indonesia and in the People's Republic of China. These experiences led Jean-Pierre to appreciate the importance of translating and utilizing knowledge about the determinants of malnutrition to design nutrition delivery interventions. Per Pinstrup-Andersen's work was a trailblazer for the development of effective policies for the delivery of nutrition. Understanding these delivery systems has become a major focus of Jean-Pierre's present work.

Peter B. R. Hazell trained as an agriculturalist in England before completing his MS and PhD degrees in Agricultural Economics at Cornell University and a postdoctoral assignment at the University of Newcastle upon Tyne, England. From 1972 to 2005, he held various research positions at the World Bank and the International Food Policy Research Institute, including serving as Director of the Environment and Production Technology division (1992–2003) and the Development Strategy and Governance division (2003–05) at IFPRI. After returning to the UK in 2005, he became a Visiting Professor at Imperial College London and a Professorial Research Associate at the

School of Oriental and African Studies, University of London. Peter's extensive and widely cited publications include works on mathematical programming; risk management; insurance; the impact of technological change on growth and poverty; the rural non-farm economy; sustainable development strategies for marginal lands; the role of agriculture in economic development; and the future of small farms. Peter is an elected Fellow of the Agricultural and Applied Economics Association and of the African Association of Agricultural Economists. He currently lives in Santa Barbara, California, from where he undertakes consulting assignments for IFPRI, the World Bank, and the Bill & Melinda Gates Foundation.

Anna Herforth is a consultant specializing in nutrition as a multisectoral issue related to agriculture and the environment. She consults for the World Bank, the UN Food and Agriculture Organization (FAO), and USAID's SPRING (Strengthening Partnerships, Results, and Innovations in Nutrition Globally) project, among others. She has worked with universities, nonprofit organizations, agencies of the United Nations, and CGIAR on nutrition policy and programs in Africa, South Asia, and Latin America. In each region, she has spent considerable time working with agricultural and indigenous communities. Anna is a founding member of the Agriculture-Nutrition Community of Practice, an active online community with members from over 80 countries. She holds a PhD from Cornell University in International Nutrition with a minor in International Agriculture, a MS in Food Policy from Tufts Friedman School, and a BS in Plant Science from Cornell University.

Tina Andersen Huey received her PhD from the University of Pennsylvania's Annenberg School for Communication in Philadelphia, PA. Her dissertation concerned the legitimization of knowledge in discourse about genetically modified (GM) food. Her research interests focus on the meaning people ascribe to food and in popular food movements (e.g., Slow Food, organics, anti-GMO). Dr. Huey is Per Pinstrup-Andersen's daughter.

Andrew D. Jones is a public health nutritionist, interested in understanding the influence of agriculture and food systems on the food security of households and the nutritional status of women, young children, and adolescents in low-income settings. He is especially interested in understanding the pathways through which macro socio-environmental trends, including climate change, urbanization, and globalization, interact with food systems to impact nutrition outcomes. His research includes a strong focus on the evaluation of programs and policies that aim to improve maternal and child nutrition, especially through agriculture and food systems-based approaches. Andrew currently holds the position of Assistant Professor in the School of Public Health at the University of Michigan. Prior to this appointment, Andrew worked as a Research Associate in the Division of Nutritional Sciences at Cornell University. He has also worked as a consultant for several institutions, including the World Bank, the International Food Policy Research Institute, and UNICEF. He received his PhD in International Nutrition from Cornell University and holds BA degrees from the Pennsylvania State University in Geography and Film Production.

Jef L. Leroy is a Senior Research Fellow in IFPRI's Poverty, Health, and Nutrition Division. At IFPRI, he studies the impact of two large-scale integrated food and nutrition programs in Burundi and Guatemala on maternal and child nutrition and health. He also conducts research on how aflatoxin exposure may contribute to child growth faltering and on the valid measurement of child linear growth retardation. Before joining IFPRI in 2009, he was a research associate at the Center for Evaluation Research and Surveys at the National Institute of Public Health in Mexico, where he worked on the impact evaluation of large-scale programs, including the impact of the urban and rural Oportunidades programs on child nutrition and health, and the impact of the Programa de Apoyo Alimentario (an in-kind transfer program) on household food consumption and women's weights. He also conducted research on child mortality. Jef has a PhD in International Nutrition (Cornell University) and a MSc in Agricultural and Applied Biological Sciences (Ghent University, Belgium).

Andy McKay is Professor of Development Economics at the University of Sussex, where he has worked since 2006; he acted as department chair from 2009 to 2012. Prior to Sussex, he worked at the University of Nottingham for 11 years, as well as shorter periods at the University of Bath and the Overseas Development Institute (ODI). He works on issues relating to poverty and inequality in low-income countries, including how these issues are impacted by different policies. From 2000 to 2010, he was an active participant in the Department for International Development (DFID) UK-funded Chronic Poverty Research Centre, working on issues of poverty dynamics, assets, and poverty traps; he also acted as Associate Director of the Centre from 2005 to 2010. Additionally, he has worked on agricultural and labor issues in low-income countries. His main geographic foci are East Africa, West Africa, and Vietnam. He supervises and has supervised many PhD students on a range of applied development topics. He has been actively and closely involved with the African Economic Research Consortium (AERC), acting as a resource person at every biannual workshop since 2005; and acted as co-coordinator of a recent collaborative AERC project on the growth–poverty nexus in Africa. He is widely published in leading journals on these themes; he has one co-edited book and two forthcoming, and has written many book chapters. Additionally, he has extensive experience providing policy advice to developing country governments, DFID, World Bank, the European Commission, and others.

Malden C. Nesheim is Professor of Nutrition Emeritus and Provost Emeritus. He joined the Cornell faculty in 1959. In 1974, he was named Director of the Division of Nutritional Sciences, a post that he held until the summer of 1987. Prior to becoming Provost of Cornell University in September 1989, he held the position of Vice President for Planning and Budgeting. He has received the Conrad A. Elvehjem Award for Public Service from the American Institute of Nutrition. He was elected a Fellow of the American Academy of Arts and Sciences in 1995 and a Fellow of the American Society of Nutritional Sciences in 1997. He earned a BS in Agricultural Science and an MS in Animal Nutrition from the University of Illinois, followed by a PhD in Nutrition from Cornell. His research interests have been aspects of nutritional biochemistry and the relationship of parasitic infections to nutritional status, along with other aspects of human nutrition. His most recent book, with Marion Nestle, *Why Calories Count—From Science to Politics*, was published by the University of California Press in 2012.

Marion Nestle is the Paulette Goddard Professor in the Department of Nutrition, Food Studies, and Public Health at New York University, which she chaired from 1988 to 2003. She is also Professor of Sociology at NYU and Visiting Professor of Nutritional Sciences at Cornell. She earned a PhD in Molecular Biology and an MPH in Public Health Nutrition from the University of California, Berkeley. Previous faculty positions were at Brandeis University and the University of California San Francisco School of Medicine. From 1986 to 1988, she was senior nutrition policy advisor in the Department of Health and Human Services and editor of *The Surgeon General's Report on Nutrition and Health*. Her research examines scientific and socioeconomic influences on food choice, emphasizing the role of food marketing. She is the author or co-author of five prize-winning books: *Food Politics: How the Food Industry Influences Nutrition and Health; Safe Food: The Politics of Food Safety; What to Eat*; and, with Malden Nesheim, *Why Calories Count*; and *Eat, Drink, Vote: An Illustrated Guide to Food Politics*. She also has written two books about pet food, *Pet Food Politics: The Chihuahua in the Coal Mine* and *Feed Your Pet Right* (also with Malden Nesheim). Her most recent book is *Soda Politics: Taking on Big Soda (and Winning)*. She blogs at www.foodpolitics.com.

Tolulope Olofinbiyi is a Senior Program Manager in the Director General's Office at the International Food Policy Research Institute. Tolu has worked with Development Alternatives, Inc. in Bethesda, MD, and has an extensive background working in the agribusiness sector in Nigeria. She received her Bachelor of Agriculture (BA) degree in Agricultural Economics from University of Agriculture, Abeokuta in Nigeria; Master of Agribusiness (MAB) degree from Texas A&M University; and a Masters of Arts in Law and Diplomacy (MALD) degree in International Affairs (development economics) from the Fletcher School, Tufts University. She is also a PhD candidate, studying development economics and political economy at the Fletcher School.

Robert Paarlberg is the B. F. Johnson Professor of Political Science at Wellesley College and Adjunct Professor of Public Policy at the Harvard Kennedy School. He has also been a Visiting Professor of Government at Harvard University and is an Associate at Harvard's Weatherhead Center for International Affairs. Paarlberg received his BA in Government from Carleton College in 1967 (which honored him in 2012 with a distinguished alumni achievement award), and his PhD in International Relations from Harvard University in 1975. Paarlberg's central research interest is international food and agricultural policy. He has been the author of academic books on food and agricultural policy published by Cornell University Press, Johns Hopkins University Press, the University of Chicago Press, and Harvard University Press. His 2008 Harvard Press book, *Starved for Science*, included a foreword by Norman E. Borlaug and Jimmy Carter. His most recent book is from Oxford University Press in 2015, and is entitled *The United States of Excess: Gluttony and the Dark Side of American Exceptionalism.*

Philip G. Pardey is a Professor in the Department of Applied Economics, University of Minnesota, where he also directs the University's International Science and Technology Practice and Policy (InSTePP) center. Prior to joining the university in 2002, he was a Senior Research Fellow at the International Food Policy Research Institute, Washington, DC, and previously a senior research officer at the International

Service for National Agricultural Research in The Hague, Netherlands. His research deals with the finance and conduct of R&D globally and its economic consequences, the bio-economics of agricultural production and productivity worldwide, and the economic and policy (especially intellectual property) aspects of genetic resources and the biosciences. He is a Fellow of the American Agricultural Economic Association, a Distinguished Fellow and Past President of the Australian Agricultural and Resource Economics Society, and was awarded the Siehl Prize for excellence in agriculture.

Prabhu Pingali is a Professor in the Charles H. Dyson School of Applied Economics and Management and the Founding Director of the Tata–Cornell Agriculture and Nutrition Initiative (TCi). Prior to joining Cornell in June 2013, he was the Deputy Director, Agriculture Development Division of the Bill & Melinda Gates Foundation, based in Seattle, Washington, from 2008 to May 2013. Pingali was elected to the US National Academy of Sciences as a Foreign Fellow in May 2007, a Fellow of the American Agricultural Economics Association (AAEA) in 2006, and a Fellow of the International Association of Agricultural Economists (IAAE) in 2009. He served as the President of IAAE from 2003 to 2006, and was named the 2010 Outstanding Alumnus of North Carolina State University. He has received several international awards for his work, including the Research Discovery Award from the AAEA. Pingali has over three decades of experience working with some of the leading international agricultural development organizations as a research economist, development practitioner, and senior manager. He was the Director of the Agricultural and Development Economics Division of the Food and Agriculture Organization of the United Nations from 2002 to 2007, and the Director of the Economics Program at the Center for International Maize and Wheat Improvement Center (CIMMYT), Mexico, from 1996 to 2002. Prior to joining CIMMYT, he worked at the International Rice Research Institute at Los Banos, Philippines, from 1987 to 1996, as an Agricultural Economist, and at the World Bank's Agriculture and Rural Development Department from 1982 to 1987, as an Economist. Professor Pingali has written 10 books and over 100 referred journal articles and book chapters on food policy, technological change, productivity growth, environmental externalities, and resource management in the developing world.

Mitch Renkow has been a Professor of Agricultural and Resource Economics at North Carolina State University since 1991. Prior to that time, he worked at the International Crops Research Institute for the Semi-Arid-Tropics (ICRISAT) and at CIMMYT. His research focuses on technology adoption, determinants of market participation, and the aggregate and distributional impacts of agricultural research. His work on the impact of agricultural research includes a study of the impacts of CGIAR research since 2000 (as part of the 2010 External Review of the CGIAR); assessments of policy-oriented research on less-favored areas and on pro-poor public investment; work for the Standing Panel on Impact Assessment (SPIA) on the environmental impacts of CGIAR research; and most recently, an assessment of IFPRI's cumulative research in Ethiopia since 1995.

Katie Ricketts is a Research Associate with Cornell University and Cornell Cooperative Extension. She was previously the Program/Research Manager for the Tata–Cornell Agriculture and Nutrition Initiative, where she offered strategic guidance and support for project implementation, evaluation, and overall program development. On the research front, Katie's work has analyzed the impact of global and domestic food value chains and food retailing on the affordability and availability of micronutrient-dense food in rural communities. This has included streamlining and improving methodologies for obtaining information on dietary diversity and nutrition for use in large-scale agriculture surveys. Katie has also worked extensively on understanding the evolution of and opportunities for public and private extension systems across a variety of crops and commodities, including fresh and frozen produce, cocoa, and coffee throughout Africa, Asia, and Latin America. Prior to working for Cornell, Katie was with the International Center for Tropical Agriculture (CIAT) in Colombia, researching and evaluating business models for integrating rural communities into higher-value agriculture opportunities. Katie holds undergraduate and graduate degrees in International Development and Applied Economics and Management from the University of California Los Angeles (UCLA) and Cornell University, respectively.

Marie T. Ruel has been Director of IFPRI's Poverty, Health and Nutrition Division since 2004. From 1996 until her current appointment, she served as Senior Research Fellow and Research Fellow in that division. Dr. Ruel has worked for more than 30 years on policies and programs to alleviate poverty, food insecurity, and malnutrition in developing countries. She has published extensively on topics such as maternal and child nutrition; agriculture and food-based strategies to improve diet quality and micronutrient nutrition; and urban livelihoods, food security, and nutrition, with a focus on program evaluation and delivery science. Her current research focuses on the evaluation and strengthening of a wide range of integrated, multisectoral development programs in the areas of agriculture, social protection, and health; and at building the evidence on their role in reducing maternal and child malnutrition globally. Prior to IFPRI, she was head of the Nutrition and Health Division at the Institute of Nutrition of Central America and Panama/Pan American Health Organization (INCAP/PAHO) in Guatemala. Dr. Ruel received her PhD in International Nutrition from Cornell University and her Masters in Health Sciences from Laval University in Canada.

David E. Sahn is an International Professor of Economics in the Division of Nutritional Sciences and the Department of Economics at Cornell University. He is also an IZA Research Fellow at the Institute for the Study of Labor (IZA) in Bonn, Germany. From 2011 to 2013, he was a Professor, holding the Chaire d'Excellence at Centre d'Etudes et de Recherches sur le Développement International (CERDI), l'Université d'Auvergne, France. He has a PhD from the Massachusetts Institute of Technology and a Masters of Public Health from the University of Michigan. His main academic interest is in identifying the solutions to poverty, malnutrition, and disease in developing countries, as well as the determinants of human capital and the role of education and skills in labor market and other social outcomes. In addition to teaching and mentoring of graduate students, he devotes considerable efforts to training and capacity building of research institutions in Africa and working with government officials and international organizations to integrate research findings into policy. Before coming to Cornell in 1988, Professor Sahn was an Economist at the World Bank, and prior to that, a Research Fellow at the International Food Policy Research Institute. He has been a Visiting Scholar at the International Monetary Fund, a visiting Distinguished Professor at l'Université d'Auvergne, visiting researcher at both the Département et Laboratoire d'Economie Théorique et Appliquée, École Normale Superieure (DELTA) and Laboratoire d'Économie Appliquée de Paris, Institut National de la Recherche Agronomique in Paris, as well as a Visiting Professor at Kenyatta University in Nairobi. He has also worked extensively with numerous international organizations, such as the Hewlett Foundation, the African Development Bank, Organisation for Economic Co-operation and Development (OECD), and several UN agencies such as UNICEF, the UN Development Program, the Food and Agricultural Organization, the United Nations University, and the World Health Organization. He has also worked as a consultant for various governments in Asia, Africa, and transition economies in Eastern Europe.

Roger Slade holds undergraduate and graduate degrees from the London School of Economics and the College of St Gregory and St Martin at Wye (University of London). He has nearly 50 years' experience in development as an economist, researcher, evaluator, and manager, including periods of residence in southern and western Africa and Southeast Asia. He is a former trustee and Director of Africa Now, past Director and Treasurer of the International Development Evaluation Association, and a long-time advisor to Farm Africa. From 1975 to 1999, he held progressively senior appointments in the World Bank. His published work spans technology adoption, agricultural research and extension, regional growth, dairy development, and monitoring and evaluation. Since retiring from the World Bank, he has worked as a consultant economist, most recently leading a global study of FAO's role in fostering investment in agriculture and studies for IFAD and IFPRI.

Finn Tarp holds the Chair in Development Economics at the Department of Economics at the University of Copenhagen. He founded the Development Economics Research Group (DERG) in 1996, and in 2009 was appointed Director of the United Nations University World Institute for Development Economics Research (UNU-WIDER), Helsinki, Finland. In this capacity, Professor Tarp leads and manages an internationally recognized multidisciplinary and policy-relevant development economics research program; and UNU-WIDER is widely recognized as a top international development think tank that has contributed effectively to development thinking and practice for 30 years. Finn Tarp has a total of more than 35 years of experience in academic and applied development economics, including 20 years of work experience in some 35 countries across Africa and the developing world, including longer-term assignments in Swaziland, Mozambique, Zimbabwe, and Vietnam. Finn Tarp is a leading international expert on issues of development strategy and foreign aid, and he is a member of a large number of international committees and advisory bodies. They include academic journals, the European Union Development Network (EUDN), and the African Economic Research Consortium (AERC). Special honors include the Vietnamese Government Merit "Medal for the Cause of Science and Technology" and the Vietnamese Government "Medal of Honour for Contributions to the Cause of Planning and Investment." Professor Tarp was appointed member of the Council of Eminent Persons (CEP), advising the Chief Economist of the World Bank in early 2013.

Erik Thorbecke is the H. E. Babcock Professor of Economics Emeritus and Graduate School and International Professor at Cornell University and one of the creators of the Foster-Greer-Thorbecke (FGT) metric for measuring poverty. Professor Thorbecke is also former Director of the Program on Comparative Economic Development at Cornell, and he is a longstanding member of the Advisory Board for the Cornell Institute for African Development. His past positions include Chairman of the Department of Economics at Cornell, a professorship at Iowa State University, and associate assistant administrator for program policy at the Agency for International Development. In 1981, Professor Thorbecke was awarded an honorary doctorate degree by the University of Ghent. He has made contributions in the areas of economic and agricultural development, the measurement and analysis of poverty and malnutrition, the Social Accounting Matrix and general equilibrium modeling, and international economic policy. The Foster-Greer-Thorbecke poverty measure (*Econometrica*, 1984) that he developed (with James Foster and Joel Greer) has been adopted as the standard poverty measure by the World Bank and many UN agencies and is widely used by researchers doing empirical work on poverty. A variant of the FGT was adopted by the Mexican government and used to allocate federal government funds to educational, health, and nutrition programs benefiting the poor. Since the early 1990s, he has been closely associated with the African Economic Research Consortium, a "public, not-for-profit organization devoted to the advancement of economic policy research and training." He serves as the Chairman of the Thematic Research Group on Poverty, Income Distribution and Food Security. Over the past several years (2005–10), Professor Thorbecke has been co-directing (with Machiko Nissanke) a large-scale research project on "The Impact of Globalization on the World's Poor" under the auspices of the United Nations University's World Institute for Development Economics Research. He is the author or co-author of more than 25 books and over 150 articles.

Barbara Boyle Torrey has been a Visiting Fellow at the Population Reference Bureau. She was previously Executive Director of the Division of Behavioral and Social Sciences at the National Research Council. She was also Chief of the Center for International Research at the Census Bureau and an economist at the Office of Management and Budget. She edited *Population and Land Use Change* for the National Academy Press, as well as two other books and has published a number of articles on international population and income trends. She did her undergraduate and graduate work at Stanford University's Food Research Institute. She is a member of the National Research Council's Committee on Population.

E. Fuller Torrey, MD, is the former Executive Director of the Stanley Medical Research Institute in Chevy Chase, Maryland (he has recently stepped down and is now Associate Director), and Professor of Psychiatry at the Uniformed Services University of the Health Sciences. He received an AB from Princeton University, an MD from McGill University, and a Master's in Anthropology and training in Psychiatry at Stanford University. He spent two years as a Peace Corps physician in Ethiopia and has returned there several times. He has published more than 200 professional papers and 20 books, including *Beasts of the Earth: Animals, Humans, and Disease* with Robert

Yolken. *The Roots of Treason*, his biography of Ezra Pound, was nominated as one of the five best biographies of 1983 by the National Book Critics Circle. He is married to Barbara Boyle Torrey, an economist.

Joachim von Braun is an economist with a Doctoral degree in Agricultural Economics from University of Göttingen, Germany. He joined the Center for Development Research (*Zentrum für Entwicklungsforschung*) of the University of Bonn (ZEF) as Professor and Director of the Department for Economic and Technological Change in December 2009. He was also Director of ZEF during its foundation phase, 1997–2002. Professor von Braun was Director General of the International Food Policy Research Institute in Washington, DC, from 2002 to 2009. His research addresses international and development economics topics, including markets and trade, poverty, health and nutrition, agriculture, and science and technology. Professor von Braun was President of the International Association of Agricultural Economists (IAAE). He is a member of the Academy of Science of North-Rhine Westphalia, the German Academy of Science and Engineering (acatech), and the Pontifical Academy of Sciences of the Vatican, as well as Fellow of the American Association for the Advancement of Sciences; he is Vice-President of the NGO "Welthungerhilfe" and Chair of the Bioeconomy Council of the German Federal Government. Among awards received by von Braun are an honorary Doctoral degree from University of Hohenheim, the Bertebos Prize of the Swedish Academy of Agricultural Sciences for his research on food security, and the Justus von Liebig Prize for his research on international nutrition.

Marygold Walsh-Dilley is an Assistant Professor of Social and Behavioral Sciences in the Honors College at the University of New Mexico. She holds a BA in International and Comparative Policy Studies from Reed College and an MS in Applied Economics and Management and a PhD in Development Sociology from Cornell University. Her research focuses on the political economy of rural development, peasant and indigenous farming systems, and the lived experiences and local negotiations of global social and agrarian change, primarily in the Bolivian Andes.

Wendy Wolford is the Robert A. and Ruth E. Polson Professor of Development Sociology at Cornell University. She received a BA in Economics and International Development from McGill University, and an MS and PhD in Geography from University of California at Berkeley. She has worked with one of the largest grass-roots social movements in Brazilian history, the Landless Workers' Movement, for over two decades. In 2010, she helped to found the Land Deals Politics Initiative and also joined the faculty at Cornell. In 2012, she became Faculty Director for Economic Development programs in Cornell's Atkinson Center for a Sustainable Future. Dr. Wolford has published widely in the areas of development studies, social movements, agrarian societies, political ecology, land use, land reform, and critical ethnography, all with regional concentrations in Brazil, Ecuador, and Mozambique.

Sivan Yosef is a Senior Program Manager with the International Food Policy Research Institute. She works under IFPRI's 2020 Vision Initiative, as well as the Poverty, Health and Nutrition Division. During her time at IFPRI, she has led work on the Institute's

2013–18 strategy, helped organize two 2020 conferences ("Leveraging Agriculture for Improving Nutrition and Health" in New Delhi and "Building Resilience for Food and Nutrition Security" in Addis Ababa), and has supported the publication of numerous books and papers on food and nutrition security. Prior to joining IFPRI in 2008, she co-founded an international development organization operating in Africa, Asia, and the Caribbean.

Introduction

David E. Sahn

Over nearly 50 years, Per Pinstrup-Andersen, who we honor with this book, has tirelessly promoted and conducted research with an overriding goal of combatting the global scourge of hunger and malnutrition. He has focused on the objectives of increasing food supplies to keep pace with a growing population; promoting a sustainable food system that contributes to the availability and accessibility of a low-priced, diverse, and safe supply of foods to consumers; and exploring consumer behavior and intervention programs that are designed to ensure household-level access to an adequate and healthy diet. In this volume, we bring together a truly exceptional group of scholars to formulate and begin to address the major challenges, controversies, and opportunities in combatting hunger and malnutrition in the years ahead. Contributors include distinguished professors and pre-eminent researchers in the fields of economics, nutrition, and agriculture and food systems, and directors and leaders of some of the most important international think tanks and institutes concerned with sustainable initiatives designed to alleviate hunger and malnutrition, with years of experience in Africa, Asia, and Latin America.

Specifically, the first part of this book explores the future of nutrition programs and policies. The second part examines the challenges of agricultural and supply side policies to sustainably feed the world's growing population. The third part concerns globalization and political economy. The chapters cover a wide range of controversies and policy considerations in these three domains.

One immutable fact that underlies this book is that there have been amazing advances in science and policy during the past 50 years that have contributed to preventing global food shortages and that have forestalled the threat of rising global hunger—despite the fact that the world's population soared in the latter half of the 20th century. Indeed, today, the number of undernourished people is smaller than it has been in decades, even though the population is nearly five times larger than it was in 1900. Furthermore, the share of malnourished individuals is lower than at any point since reliable statistics became available. There are numerous explanations for this tentative success. These begin with the simple fact that economic growth has accelerated in countries and regions, particularly in Southeast Asia, but increasingly in other regions of the world such as in Africa, putting more money into the pockets of a larger number of households. A decline in poverty, however, is only part of the story. Additionally, the decline in global hunger is in large measure attributable to the dynamism of the agricultural sector where food production and markets have kept pace with growing demand, thus contributing to a plentiful supply of food at moderate prices that are within reach of an increasing share of the world's population. Technological change in agriculture has enabled the world's farmers to raise food output to levels that were unforeseen a half-century ago. The Green Revolution, of course, is now recognized as one of the great scientific advances of the latter part of the 20th century; and opportunities from biotechnology hold the promise of being equally transformative, despite the very active discourse that surrounds the role of genetically modified crops. It is in this context, however, that new controversies emerge, such as the sustainability of the global food system that has witnessed dramatic changes in concert with scientific and technology advances: whether it be concerns over climate change, the environmental and health impact of genetically modified foods, or even the marginalization of small farmers.

While supply side advances have been at the nexus of the successes of efforts to prevent and reduce malnutrition, the evolution of global and regional markets and advances in the efficiency of the food system, in general, have been integral to progress in combatting undernourishment. The importance of food markets and value chain in providing a plentiful and safe food supply is not only increasingly better understood, but in practice has evolved in ways that are almost the equal of the agricultural sector in these efforts.

Advances in the food system have also been complemented with a vastly improved understanding of household behavior that focuses more on patterns of demand and choices of households, and the implications for health and nutrition outcomes. This includes understanding food acquisition behaviors, but also a range of other considerations such as intrahousehold decision-making and food allocation, as well as choices regarding nurturing and care behaviors that directly impact the nutritional intake and well-being of vulnerable groups. This knowledge, in turn, has contributed to the design of effective programs and policies that focus on raising demand for and access to food. Likewise, interventions focused on improving the quality and utilization of foods and related behaviors, such as breastfeeding promotion, the use of oral rehydration therapy, and public health measures to improve water and sanitation, have been integral to the fight against hunger and malnutrition.

Despite all the scientific advances and the growth of evidence to guide policymakers in their efforts to design policies and programs to alleviate hunger, the fact remains that progress is uneven; certain regions, particularly South Asia and much of Africa, show far more modest success in this endeavor. And even in regions where noteworthy reductions in hunger and malnutrition have been recorded, inequalities have left large shares of the population in many countries still at high risk of hunger and malnutrition. The reasons are many and range from a lack of scientific advances in some areas to a paucity of understanding of the true causes of malnutrition in its multiple and complex dimensions. The challenge extends beyond science and knowledge itself, however, and includes the paramount issue of commitment, particularly political will and prioritizing the alleviation of hunger in government policy, something that remains elusive.

Thus, although there is a need to better understand the nature of the progress in the fight against hunger and malnutrition to date, there is even more urgency to look ahead at the evolving landscape and challenges in addressing the persistence of suffering, which afflicts a large share of the world's population. It is that imperative that motivates this book, and the role of research and policy to mitigate hunger and malnutrition is the thread that runs through the chapters in this volume.

More specifically, this book focuses on the future, and particularly, the opportunities to help the poor and malnourished. We do so ever cognizant that we live in a new era of globalization, where change in technology, markets, and social programs are not done in isolation, but rather in a context where problems and suffering may be local, as are many solutions, but both the challenges and the responses inevitably have an increasingly global dimension. This requires a better appreciation of not only the opportunities and choices of farmers and traders, but also the labor market and income-earning prospects of those residing in growing urban settlements. It requires better understanding of the options for consumers of where to buy food and the quality, diversity, and prices of food in traditional markets and new outlets, such as supermarkets—choices that reflect changes in the value chain or the related rapidly changing consumer tastes and preferences. Overlaying all these issues are concerns, such as sustainability and climate change, which will inevitably condition the behavior of local and global institutions and the opportunities and constraints facing policymakers in their efforts to assist those in need. Quite simply, with the progress and change of the past decades come new challenges and concerns that have broad implications for agriculture, food, and nutrition. These are, perhaps, nowhere more obvious than with issues such as (1) how to make production systems sustainable, in terms of promoting high output agriculture while preserving natural resources and promoting conservation; (2) how to ensure the economic sustainability of farmers and the role of agriculture as a sector of economic growth and employment; and (3) how to foster a competitive environment in which farmers and traders contribute to an efficient and low-cost food system that meets the needs of urban and rural consumers and takes into account other issues such as energy costs and efficiencies in the food supply chain.

The first section of the book takes a microeconomic focus on some critical debates on the future of nutrition programs and policies. In recent years, there has been an emerging consensus that the first 1,000 days of an individual's life, from conception to 2 years of age, is the most critical period for health, and that malnutrition during this period will have long-term consequences over the entire life course of the individual, and even across generations. Consequently, nutrition policy and intervention programs have increasingly targeted women of childbearing age and children less than 24 months of age. However, like all ideas in good currency, there remain a number of uncertainties in terms of the long-term consequences of early childhood malnutrition. One of the most active debates is the opportunity for "catch-up growth" among young children, or in other words, whether programs and policies that are targeted to stunted or chronically malnourished children, will contribute to their catching up to norms. This is a crucial question: the ability, or lack thereof, to catch-up or recover from early nutritional deficits has formidable implications for the timing of and potential benefits from nutritional interventions. Thus, the first chapter of the book, jointly authored by Jef Leroy, Marie Ruel, Jean-Pierre Habicht, and Edward Frongillo, tackles this issue using an innovative methodological approach. Here the authors report their finding of an absence of catch-up growth between 2 and 5 years of age, adding to the support for the critical need of investing in improving nutrition during the first 1,000 days. Their research reinforces the imperative of preventing rather than reversing stunting, and more generally, supports the current programmatic focus on the first 1,000 days, as well as the health of women of childbearing age.

In light of these findings, the second chapter, authored by Harold Alderman, is particularly salient in examining the role of transfer programs in reducing hunger and malnutrition. Alderman's comprehensive and critical review begins by examining the role of income generally in determining nutrition outcomes, and more specifically, how transfer programs can respond to specific shocks or serve to raise consumption over an extended period. Beyond the consumption objectives of transfer programs, many are intended to influence the price of human capital investments, as well as incentivize a shift in the family's resource allocation through the imposition of conditions. Thus, Alderman focuses on services that accompany transfer programs and broadly concludes that there is limited evidence that such programs reduce malnutrition. A variety of reasons may explain this disappointing outcome, ranging from design of the intervention, such as the failure to focus on the most vulnerable groups, to issues concerning the evaluation methods employed.

The next two chapters of the book, by Chris Barrett and Leah Bevis, and Malden Nesheim and Marion Nestle, respectively, confront two other emerging challenges: the need to go beyond merely addressing chronic malnutrition and wasting, which has traditionally been the focus of programs such as the types of conditional cash transfers discussed in the previous two chapters. Barrett and Bevis address what is often referred to as "hidden hunger" in the form of micronutrient deficiencies. There is some irony in the fact that micronutrient malnutrition is given far less attention than other forms of malnutrition, such as wasting, despite the fact that iron deficiency anemia, for example, is the most prevalent form of malnutrition, affecting approximately 1.6 billion people. The key question that the authors raise is why are micronutrient deficiencies so much less responsive to income growth than other indicators of malnutrition? They explore the causation of micronutrient malnutrition and the implications for structuring policies and programs in the future to address this enormous problem, using a food systems approach that looks at a range of considerations from production-related issues such as soil deficiencies and the role of biofortification, to the role of markets and the value chain in terms of the availability of diverse, low-cost foods that contain requisite levels of minerals and vitamins.

The chapter by Nesheim and Nestle focuses on the growing epidemic of chronic disease that is linked to dietary excesses, including the intake of refined carbohydrates and sugar that contribute to obesity and related chronic diseases such as diabetes. The magnitude of the obesity epidemic is staggering: more than one in three adults in the United States are overweight or obese, and in parts of Europe, the Middle East, and Latin America, more than 60 percent of adults over the age of 15 are classified as overweight or obese. Nesheim and Nestle examine the changing behavior of consumers, and more specifically, the marketing behavior of corporations—especially, the messages directed toward children encouraging consumption of unhealthy foods and large portions. While the chapter focuses on the role of beverage companies, it is clear that that there are general lessons that emerge. These include encouraging more responsible marketing behavior by corporations, while considering the role of public policies such as tax initiatives and public information dissemination—including labeling, media campaigns about healthy eating, and public education—more broadly to promote skills for changing the food environment and personal behavior.

In combination, the first four chapters of the book imply a relatively clear agenda for nutrition policy and programs with the well-defined needs: (1) to focus on the first 1,000 days; (2) to place transfer programs at the center of government strategies to reach nutritionally vulnerable groups; (3) to address hidden hunger in the form of micronutrient deficiencies, too long given far too little attention, as the central part of efforts to reduce malnutrition; and (4) to confront the formidable challenge of how the changing food system and patterns of consumer behavior are contributing to new risks of chronic disease, hardly even discussed just a few years ago outside of developed countries, as governments and the international community continue to focus on problems of undernutrition. Although this agenda for action is compelling and scientifically grounded, translating it into action is another matter altogether, and this is, then, the subject of the next two chapters of this part of the book.

Suresh Chandra Babu looks at the challenges in encouraging and improving evidence-based policymaking, particularly in response to emerging food and nutrition crises. He focuses on the development and implementation of food security and nutrition monitoring systems to identify policy, institutional, organizational, and system capacity challenges. He presents lessons that could be useful to overcome these challenges at the global, regional, and national levels. A wide range of lessons are distilled from the review of how governments respond to food crises, and specifically, the role of information systems that are characteristically weak and poorly integrated into the decision-making apparatus of governments and international organizations, who must lead the response to prevent and mitigate the consequences of events such as price shocks and drought. For example, there is a need to improve the accuracy, geographic-specificity, cost-effectiveness, reliability, and availability of timely information, always recognizing that the more precise the information, the more costly it is likely to be. Information systems need to be designed not just to monitor the emergence of crises, but also to understand the efficacy of the response of programs and policies to protect the nutritionally vulnerable.

Although the emphasis on designing and implementing food and nutrition monitoring systems is well supported in Suresh Babu's chapter, one important question left unanswered is how to define the appropriate indicators of food security and nutritional well-being, from the local to the global level. It is this question that motivates the chapter by Anna Herforth. Herforth attempts to answer the question of who will make decisions based on food security indicators, and what are the major information gaps that, if filled, could inform better action to improve food security? In addressing these questions, it becomes clear that relative to what is now available from traditional data sources, generated by governments and international organizations, new food security indicators are needed that can more effectively guide actions to improve availability of and access to healthy diets. Suggestions are made for how new food indicators can be mainstreamed in the nutrition and agriculture data sets and parlance, to shift the generalized construction of "food" from one of caloric adequacy to one of complete food security: safe, sufficient, and nutritious food for a healthy and active life.

The second part of the book examines the critical challenges of agricultural and supply sides policies to provide healthy and sufficiently available food to feed the world's growing population. Specifically, we focus on several major debates that will condition success in this regard over the decades ahead. The first chapter of this part begins with a focus by Prabhu Pingali, Katie Ricketts, and David Sahn on a general framework to understand the pathways between agricultural interventions and nutritional outcomes. Their chapter presents a typology of agricultural systems that capture the different stages of agricultural development and how they impact nutritional outcomes. The typology includes small-scale and subsistence agriculture systems, such as those prevalent in sub-Saharan Africa; intensive cereal crop systems, primarily found in Asia; and commercial/export-oriented systems, typically seen in Latin America. The main thrust of the chapter is a discussion of how agricultural policy and interventions can be oriented to address the types of nutritional problems that tend to be most pronounced in areas with different types of agricultural systems. The chapter goes further, however, to consider more broadly the role of agricultural and rural development efforts, in terms of a range of goals, including employment generation, access to clean water and sanitation, and education. Efforts to influence behavioral change and intra-household allocation are also discussed with respect to their importance in alleviating malnutrition. Thus, the authors conclude that although the past 50 years has been a period of extraordinary food crop productivity growth, there is still a great deal of work needed to orient policy and programs driven by nutritional goals, particularly with a focus on rural women and children.

The next chapter, by Peter Hazell, expands on this framework, but focuses on small farm-led development. Small farm-led development has been the dominant agricultural development paradigm among agricultural economists since its remarkable success in driving Asia's Green Revolution during the 1960s and 1970s. Despite its proven success, the small farm development paradigm is widely challenged today, and there is considerable debate about its continuing relevance for Asia and Africa. Critics argue that because of rural population growth on a fixed land base, the onslaught of globalization and market liberalization policies, and the emergence of new types of farm technologies, the economic context for small-scale farming has changed, and small may no longer be as beautiful as before. This chapter considers these arguments and their implications for agricultural development and small farm assistance strategies. Although Hazell concludes that there will be a diminished role for small farms in the future, a range of complementary investments, in terms of markets, financial services, and research and development, are paramount to both ensure the sustainability of small farms and their transition to more commercialized enterprises.

In the next chapter, Julian Alston and Philip Pardey take up the issue of the role of agricultural research and development (R&D) as the cornerstone of efforts to alleviate hunger and malnutrition in the decades ahead. As a point of departure, Alston and Pardey extoll the remarkable historical success of public and private agricultural R&D in increasing output, meeting the dramatic growth in demand, and raising productivity that has improved welfare and health and provided cheap wage goods for a rapidly urbanizing population. They point out, though, that all is not well: productivity growth is declining, with a slowdown in R&D spending especially in developed countries, despite the high rates of return from such investments. The authors show how this is a short-sighted policy in terms of the need to accelerate production to keep pace with global growing demand and increase the abundance of food.

Agricultural science R&D, in terms of increasing commodities for the consumer, does not capture the entirety of the role and considerations that underlie the future investment needs of what Joachim von Braun refers to as the "bioeconomy"—the emerging cross-cutting economic sector that produces, transforms, and uses bio-based materials and products. Professor von Braun, in his contribution to this volume, makes a persuasive argument that R&D in agriculture must be viewed in a larger context of the need of the growing population for not only a future with a secure and safe source of food, but also in terms of a source of energy and industrial raw materials, and these, too, should be considered in the larger context of the need to protect renewable resources, such as water. This puts the bioeconomy at the nexus of the discussion on sustainability, especially as food for human consumption competes with other aspects of the bioeconomy, such as demand for biomass. In taking a holistic view, focusing not only on competing claims on agriculture, but also on synergies between technologies and the creation of new links in and between value chains (e.g., production of biochemicals alongside production of biofuels, use for waste products of other bio-based products in chemical and building material industries), von Braun argues for increased investment, including for biotechnologies.

And it is precisely the role of biotechnology that motivates the next chapter in this part of the book, which deals explicitly with the contentious issue of genetically modified foods. The use of genetically modified organisms (GMOs) in food is portrayed by science-driven development organizations as beneficial, while social movements that share a tangential, if not central, concern with poverty and hunger portray them as undesirable. This has set up a dramatic confrontation and left consumers and policymakers both confused and uncertain as to the potential and risk associated with GMOs. Tina Andersen Huey, whose research interests focus on the meaning people ascribe to food in popular movements, explores this issue of GMOs from a critical angle: the role of communications research in understanding what kind of information is received by food-related social movements, how the information is shared, and how it is acted upon in a policy context. While she focuses on a case study from Connecticut, which was the first state in the United States that required labels on any product containing GMOs, the findings are put into the broader political context through comparison with other states such as California and food labeling movements in other countries. Although the chapter focuses specifically on the GM food controversy, more broadly speaking, it can be seen as a prism through which to view globalization's discontents—that is, the central problem of how to determine the future of the planet absent institutions answerable to citizens.

In the last chapter in this part of the book, Barbara Torrey and Fuller Torrey review the issue of the race between population growth and food production from the perspective of the broad sweep of history, bringing that discussion to a contemporary focus on present-day Africa. As the authors point out, the race between agricultural productivity and population dates back 11,000 years to a period when increasing Neolithic fertility and mortality rates led inexorably to an increasing world population. It was during the 19th century, however, when populations in industrializing countries continued to grow and their fertility and mortality rates began to slowly fall, that the demographic transition began in earnest. It was only in the 1960s, however, with the beginning of the demographic transition in non-industrial countries, that the race between agriculture and population growth accelerated. Fortunately, the agricultural sciences produced one of the most important scientific success stories in the world, especially in many of the developing countries. That being said, Africa remains the one major continent that is not yet feeding its population. This chapter thus concentrates on describing the varieties of sub-Saharan Africa's demographic transitions and the stall observed in a number of them. This, in turn, has placed greater demands on what is often a faltering agricultural sector. Thus, the clear lesson is that we must consider population policy as a necessary adjunct to the types of research and development efforts that need to be accelerated in Africa and other lagging regions.

The final part of this book deals with issues of globalization and political economy, and specifically, how the changing global context and response of governments and international institutions have and will condition the ability of countries to feed their populations and provide for their nutritional well-being. The chapter that leads off this part is by Shenggen Fan,

Director General of IFPRI since 2009, and Chairman of the World Economic Forum's Global Agenda Council on Food Security and Nutrition, and his co-authors, Tolulope Olofinbiyi and Sinafikeh Gemessa, who provide a compelling case that ending hunger by 2025 is not only of paramount importance in terms of the human and economic costs, but more importantly, that this is a goal that is realistic and within reach. More specifically, they draw upon the success of a wide range of countries from Asia and Latin America to inform the way forward, emphasizing the role of technological, policy, and institutional innovations to date that put us in a better position to spur even greater successes in reducing hunger and undernutrition. The chapter outlines a typology of strategies that have been successful, including agricultural growth-led policies and social protection-led strategies. Recalling the earlier chapters in the book by Babu and Herforth, they also emphasize the role of building institutional capacity to collect and analyze more timely data and information for decision-making, as key to fostering evidence-based policymaking. Similarly, they emphasize the role of experimentation as a means to provide vital information on the proper design, sequencing, and implementation of reforms. Policymakers must foster a culture that values adaptation and change by creating the legal and political space for local experimentation.

In the next chapter, Erik Thorbecke also takes a broad look at the experience and the keys to success, in terms of the broader goal of economic growth and poverty alleviation. His chapter focuses on Africa. His main findings, described here, are that: (1) a quantum jump in GDP growth per capita occurred around 2000; (2) income inequality remained stubbornly very high; and (3) absolute poverty declined significantly since 2000. The more interesting issue is his analysis of the interrelationship among growth, inequality, and poverty. Looking back, he argues that the majority of sub-Saharan African countries between 1960 and 2000 underwent a flawed structural transformation, characterized by a stagnating per capita income and a dramatic fall in the share of agriculture in the labor force. This meant that the migration that occurred was not pulled by rising incomes outside agriculture but pushed by lack of income opportunities within it, resulting in stagnant rural incomes. Again, in keeping with the forward-looking theme of this book, Thorbecke addresses the issue of how structural transformation can be further accelerated. He concludes that the two most important elements of a development strategy are the reduction of inequality and the creation of productive jobs. The evidence presented in this chapter suggests that the recent structural changes in Africa have contributed to more inclusive growth and improvements in the well-being of the poor, and that the two key interventions in this regard are investment in infrastructure and integrated rural development to improve small farmers' productivity.

In the next two chapters, there is also a regional focus: Marygold Walsh-Dilley and Wendy Wolford examine the role of civil society and its interactions with government on food security and nutrition in Latin America; and then, Andy McKay and Finn Tarp consider the case of Vietnam and its response to the world food price shocks in 2008. Both chapters emphasize the critical importance of government policy in the fight against hunger and malnutrition, but draw upon very different experiences and methodological approaches to do so.

Wolford has worked for over 15 years with one of the most important grassroots social movements in Latin American history, the *Movimento dos Trabalhadores Rurais Sem Terra* (the Movement of Rural Landless Workers, or the MST). In the case study here of the contemporary experience in Latin America, Wolford and her co-author Walsh-Dilley highlight the role of civil society and how it can influence the nature and extent of a government's actions in combatting malnutrition. They point to the central role that civil society groups have played in pressuring governments to implement legislation and alleviate hunger and malnutrition—in essence, giving voice to vulnerable groups that are often excluded from the political process.

Finn Tarp and Andy McKay take a different approach in examining the political economy of food and nutrition policy in their case study of how the Vietnamese government responded to the price fluctuations during the period 2006 to 2012. They specifically focus on the impact, on both consumers and producers, of the government's response to the dramatic doubling of rice prices that occurred in 2008. Globally, much attention was accorded the deleterious impact of the 2008 price increase, including predictions by the World Bank that as many as 700,000 deaths would result. The overall conclusion of their chapter is that the Vietnamese government responded effectively by imposing an export ban and reducing its export quota. They did so despite widespread criticism, both at home and internationally, that this would have adverse global and domestic results. In fact, the analysis in the chapter indicates that the poorer households, who are often net producers, were the main beneficiaries, while the losers were the wealthier non-producers. The effectiveness of government intervention in Vietnam contrasts with other countries, including those in the region, which were far less successful in buffering their economy from world price instability. McKay and Tarp thus provide some broader lessons, and interestingly, some that depart from the normal policy wisdom that is prevalent, in terms of how governments should intervene in the food system and agricultural economy.

These chapters in this part of the book all emphasize the importance of the decisions that governments make on the productivity of key sectors such as agriculture, and that affect the nutritional status and general well-being of the population. The role of knowledge and research in the policymaking process is also underscored. This is done with the understanding that there is an important interaction between those institutions charged with generating evidence and the political considerations of government policymakers. Furthermore, there are other institutions, particularly in civil society, that often demand or seek input into the decision-making process. It is in this context that the contribution by Roger Slade and Mitch Renkow to this book is so important. They discuss how institutions conducting research, in their search for relevance, seek close collaboration with a target audience—typically a government or its agents. A review of the germane literature shows that pay-offs to different forms of collaboration is under-researched, and the inherent risks of close collaboration—especially the explicit or implicit trade-offs between independence in choosing and analyzing research questions on the one hand, and the likelihood of influencing policy adoption and implementation on the other—are largely disregarded. These trade-offs often reflect the extent to which policy research agendas are captured by host governments or special interests. They are also influenced by the openness of the policy environment. To examine this issue more fully, the authors conduct a case study of the policy research of the International Food Policy Research Institute (IFPRI) in Ethiopia in support of the government's development of its national agricultural strategy. They find that this relationship gave IFPRI an important role in the policymaking apparatus; but at the same time, this close relationship had large impacts on the composition and nature of IFRPI's research. Not surprisingly, the analysis in this chapter raises some very important questions about the politics of external institutions working in support of government policy analysis, even if their main role is purportedly providing information to support evidence-based policymaking. And, more generally, Slade and Renkow inform the science of policy research in terms of the conceptual basis for how to design, undertake, and learn from this discipline and ensure its relevance.

Looking at the issue of the role of international institutions in an even broader context is the domain of the chapter by Robert Paarlberg, who argues that researchers should focus on the behavior of national governments and try to better understand why, unlike in the case of Vietnam discussed above, governments act in ways that seem ill-advised or inconsistent with economic and social ideals. This question is particularly salient since, according to Paarlberg, public policy remains the responsibility—and firmly under the control—of national and local government, and thus local political considerations. This is despite the global reach and influence of transnational corporations and inter-governmental and international organizations, including non-governmental organizations. Focusing on the same 2008 food price shocks as discussed in the chapter by McKay and Tarp, for example, Paarlberg concludes that despite a robust rhetorical response by inter-governmental organizations, including convening meetings, creating task forces, and founding new institutions to address the problem, in the end, all these initiatives had "no measurable impact on anybody's food production or consumption." This lack of external authority and influence is also applicable to actors such as the World Bank, and, perhaps most surprisingly, transnational corporations. For example, this chapter debunks the myth that private corporations have disproportionate control over global food and farming incomes, and instead, shows that their influence is far less than commonly understood.

The analysis by Paarlberg about authority and influence is particularly relevant in considering the topic of the final chapter of this part, the particularly contentious issue of climate change. Andrew Jones and Sivan Yosef argue that climate change is the most transformative force that will affect the pattern and possibilities for global development in the future. This is indeed a hefty assertion, but one that the authors support by considering the changes in precipitation patterns, global temperatures, and the frequency and severity of extreme weather events. The important contribution of this chapter is that it identifies the principal linkages between climate change and nutrition. They make the case that increases in temperatures in many regions of the world—especially in developing countries where most of the malnourished live—lead to greater rainfall volatility, extreme seasonal heat, and more frequent and severe droughts that will adversely affect nutrition through three principal intermediate outcomes: (1) the quality and quantity of crop and livestock production; (2) the stability of ecosystems; and (3) the distribution and survival of disease vectors. The chapter explores measures to both mitigate and adapt to climate change, and the potential role to be played by governments, industry, and civil society. In the case of mitigation, the strategies to reduce global greenhouse gas emissions are largely the domain of the developed and transition economies, although the chapter points out that agriculture contributes to climate in an important way, and in turn has great potential to mitigate the negative impacts on nutrition outcomes that are predicted from climate change. Strategies such as reducing fossil fuel use and improving energy efficiency in agriculture, adapting techniques such as reduced- or no-till agriculture, promoting agroforestry, and improved irrigation technologies are all discussed. And in terms of adaptation, the authors suggest that the actions required are largely the same as those needed for sustainable development broadly, although they emphasize specific actions such as agroecological intensification.

In its totality, this book addresses emerging challenges, both scientific and at the level of formulating and implementing policies, to alleviating hunger and malnutrition in the years ahead. Many of the issues and problems faced by researchers and policymakers today remain similar to those of years past. These include the widespread stunting and undernutrition that has proven so intractable; the perennial food policy dilemma of remunerative prices for farmers and low food prices for consumers; and the distributional consequences of technological change. There are also new challenges, some of which have long existed but received relatively little attention, and others that have emerged in the last decade. The former includes the household and health-related problems that have been accorded far too little attention, such as micronutrient deficiencies, as well as more supply side questions such as how to promote and incentivize diversity in production systems. Likewise, among the newly recognized problems at the household level are issues such as the burgeoning prevalence of overweight and chronic disease, while on the production side, is the issue of sustainability as environmental stress and agricultural systems are increasing at the nexus of the discussion of sustainable food systems. What is unambiguously true, however, is that the search for solutions will take place in a dramatically different global landscape from decades past. Globalization, revolutions in information and the biotechnology sectors, changes in the food value chain, issues of sustainability, and the changing political environment—ranging from the realignment of north–south interests and priorities to forms of governance internationally and domestically—have reshaped the thinking on how to address both traditional and newly emergent nutrition, food, and agricultural challenges. By bringing together three intertwined issues—the role of food and nutrition policies at the microeconomic level, the role of agricultural research and development and food systems approaches, and the global scope and political economy of food and nutrition policy—this volume makes it clear that coordinated efforts at the local level must be complemented by a global agenda for action that enables policymakers and stakeholders to work collaboratively to address the vulnerabilities of the poor. And in that context, it is clear that while old prescriptions for success are still relevant—even if sometimes ignored, such as investing more in agricultural research and development—these efforts must be undertaken in a far more complex global economic environment. Whether it be the challenges of dealing with misgivings and misperceptions about genetically modified organisms, the global reach of multinational corporations that have an enormous role on the value chain, the competition of other sectors such as energy with the food sector, or the new realities of the triple burden of malnutrition that includes "hidden hunger" in terms of micronutrients and the scourge of chronic disease, the way forward is far more complicated, despite the progress of the past. Similarly, with more emphasis on evidence-based policymaking and with the raising of the standard of proof, in terms of causal inference and evaluation of impact, the microeconomic-level interventions, traditionally so widely embraced, have come under increased scrutiny. For example, what can really be expected of cash transfer programs with respect to nutritional improvement, and what should be the target groups of these interventions?

And overlaying all of these interventions are the political and social considerations and constraints that need to be taken into account when trying to translate knowledge and information into practice. These factors, too, are highlighted in numerous chapters in the volume. What emerges is a greater understanding and appreciation of the crucial role of government, international organizations, and a range of civil society stakeholders in incorporating and translating the scientific knowledge highlighted in the volume into action. We see, for example, how the public debate over GMOs is of equal or greater importance than the technology itself in effecting adoption of new seeds and agricultural varieties; or how despite the labors and pronouncements of intergovernmental agencies, their influence is receding relative to the state, even with their increased visibility and purported global constituency with shared transnational goals.

The experience of the contributors in research and policymaking, and shared and often long engagement, in the fight to alleviate hunger—albeit often from very different disciplinary and institutional perspectives—provides a way forward in addressing these multiple policy challenges and dimensions.

Part I
Nutrition Policy and Programs

1

Using Height-for-Age Difference Instead of Height-for-Age Z-Scores for the Meaningful Measurement of Catch-Up Growth in Children under 5 Years of Age

Jef L. Leroy, Marie T. Ruel, Jean-Pierre Habicht, and Edward A. Frongillo

Introduction

Chronic malnutrition in children remains an important global problem, with an estimated 165 million children under 5 years old being stunted (Black et al. 2013). Evidence suggests that the most effective way to reduce stunting globally is to scale up interventions to *prevent* (rather than *treat* or *reverse*) stunting, and that children should be exposed to these interventions during the full first 1,000 days of life (from conception to the child's second birthday) (Black et al. 2008, 2013; Ruel et al. 2008). This period is now universally recognized as the "window of opportunity for preventing undernutrition," and nutrition programs increasingly target women and children during this critical period. This programmatic shift from the earlier focus on children under 5 years of age has been implemented not only because of the recognition that this is the period of most rapid growth failure (Victora et al. 2010), but also because there is some evidence, albeit mostly from one country (Guatemala), that interventions beyond this age have little or no impact on child linear growth (Ruel 2010). Thus, a common view among the nutrition community is that stunting is largely irreversible after 2 years of age, when the window of opportunity for preventing undernutrition has closed.

Despite the general consensus achieved about the importance of the first 1,000 days, the verdict on the potential for catch-up in linear growth during mid- or later childhood or at adolescence remains open. The term *catch-up growth* was first used to describe the reversal of linear growth retardation in children treated for secondary growth disorders, such as renal disease, Cushing's syndrome, celiac disease, and hypothyroidism (Prader et al. 1963; Boersma and Wit 1997). Catch-up growth has been defined as "rapid linear growth that allowed the child to accelerate toward and, in favorable circumstances, resume his/her pre-illness growth curve" (Boersma and Wit 1997, p. 646). Adoption studies have also shown that malnourished children, adopted into wealthier households during their first few years of life, experience substantial catch-up growth. Little or no catch-up growth has been found, however, in children who remained in the same deprived settings in which growth retardation had occurred in the first place (Martorell et al. 1994).

Notwithstanding these earlier findings, the possibility that linear growth retardation can be reversed, even if only partially, has continued to intrigue researchers. A number of recent studies document catch-up growth after 2 years of age in children exposed to standard of care practices typical of developing country contexts, but in the absence of interventions specifically aimed at improving linear growth (Crookston et al. 2010; Outes and Porter 2013; Prentice et al. 2013). In contrast with earlier studies, which mostly used reductions in the absolute height deficit (Martorell et al. 1994), this new body of research is entirely based on the use of height-for-age Z-scores (HAZ) to define catch-up growth (e.g., improvements in HAZ or the reversal of stunting).

The main objective of this study was to assess whether there is evidence of catch-up growth in children between 2 and 5 years old, when catch-up growth is defined as it was originally—as *a reduction in the deficit in height* (compared with standards) between two points in time. We use absolute height-for-age difference (HAD: child's height compared to standards, expressed in centimeters) and compare with findings using HAZ. The rationale for this comparison is that HAZ, which is constructed from cross-sectional data, is useful to assess children's attained height at a given age, but inappropriate to evaluate changes in height over time. We first show mathematically that using HAD to assess catch-up growth is fundamentally different from defining catch-up growth using HAZ. We then use data from select developing countries and compare changes in linear growth and evidence of catch-up growth in children between 2 and 5 years old when estimated using HAD versus HAZ.

Study Scope and Definition

Most recent studies that documented catch-up growth have looked at changes in HAZ between childhood and either adolescence or adulthood (Adair 1999; Coly et al. 2006; Hirvonen 2013; Prentice et al. 2013). Others have looked at changes in HAZ between early infancy (first 2 years of age) and mid-childhood (e.g., 5–6 years) (Crookston et al. 2010; Outes and Porter 2013; Prentice et al. 2013). Our analysis focuses on the latter; therefore, our research addresses the question of whether or not catch-up in linear growth is achieved between 2 and 5 years of age.

We define catch-up growth as population-level reductions in mean linear growth deficit with age. For simplicity, throughout this chapter, we use the terms height, HAZ, and HAD, irrespective of the child's age, despite the fact that supine length, rather than standing height, is usually measured in children less than 2 years old and that the terms "length" and "length-for-age" are normally used for these children.

Theoretical Background

Since infants and young children from diverse ethnic groups grow similarly for the first 5 years of life when their nutrition, health, and care needs are met (Habicht et al. 1974; WHO Multicentre Growth Reference Study Group 2006a), a single international growth standard is used to quantify the growth deficit for the first 5 years of life. The mean growth trajectory of a population of healthy children is expected to be at the median of the growth standards. Growth deficits in height for groups of children are thus expressed as the mean of the individual deficits. These are calculated as the difference between the measured height and the median sex- and age-specific height obtained from the growth standards. This HAD can be used in absolute terms (as proposed here), or be used relative to the sex- and age-specific standard deviation (SD) (i.e., standardized by dividing HAD by the SD from the growth standards to calculate HAZ as is traditionally done; see Equation 1.1). Catch-up growth is defined as a reduction in the absolute deficit as groups of children age.

Mathematical Background

HAZ is calculated as the age- and sex-specific absolute deficit in height (measured height minus age- and sex-specific median obtained from the growth standards) divided by the age- and sex-specific SD:

$$HAZ = \frac{observed\ height - median\ height\ growth\ standards}{SD}$$
$$= \frac{height\text{-}for\text{-}age\ difference}{SD} = \frac{HAD}{SD} \tag{1.1}$$

The SDs for height are not constant over time—they increase substantially from birth to 5 years of age (see Figure 1.1).

Therefore, if HAD is negative but remains constant with age, the Z-score will increase with age (suggesting catch-up growth), for the simple mathematical reason that the denominator (SD) increases, and not because the numerator (the height deficit) has decreased over time. Likewise, HAZ can remain constant with age or even improve, even while HAD decreases with age.

As noted earlier, most of the recent studies that found evidence of catch-up growth based their conclusions on the observation that population mean HAZ increased after 2 years of age. These studies define population-level catch-up growth as an increase in mean HAZ over time (see Equation 1.2).

$$HAZ_{t=2} > HAZ_{t=1}$$
$$\Leftrightarrow \Delta HAZ > 0$$

(1.2)

The interpretation of Equation 1.2 is that, if HAZ is higher at time 2 than at time 1, there is catch-up growth in this population during the time period studied. Note that the definition based on the reversal of stunting (being stunted (HAZ < −2 SD) at time 1 and not stunted (HAZ > −2 SD) at time 2) used in some studies (e.g., Crookston et al. 2010) is mathematically equivalent. The validity of this definition of catch-up growth is questionable. HAZ is

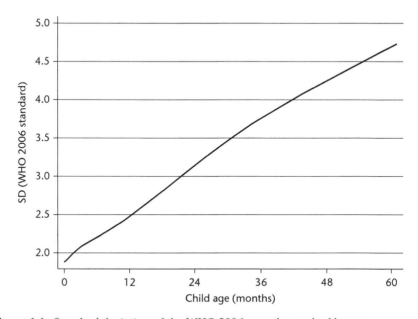

Figure 1.1. Standard deviation of the WHO 2006 growth standard by age

Source: Authors' calculations using WHO child growth standards (<http://www.who.int/childgrowth/standards/height_for_age/en/>).

constructed from cross-sectional data, and thus provides a tool for the assessment of attained growth at one point in time. HAZ is inappropriate, however, to assess changes in height over time or across ages. Furthermore, changes in HAZ with age can be a consequence of changes in the numerator (the magnitude of the difference, HAD) or in the denominator (the SD increasing with age, see Figure 1.1), making changes in HAZ across ages difficult to interpret.

A more meaningful definition of catch-up growth is a reduction in the mean absolute HAD of a population as children age:

$$HAD_{t=2} > HAD_{t=1} \tag{1.3}$$
$$\Leftrightarrow \Delta HAD > 0$$

The *Z-score criterion* (Equation 1.2) and the *absolute difference criterion* (Equation 1.3) are fundamentally different and have no one-to-one correspondence, as is shown below. Following from Equation 1.2, the *Z-score criterion* can be written as:

$$\frac{HAD_2}{SD_2} > \frac{HAD_1}{SD_1}$$

(subscripts 1 and 2 refer to $t = 1$ and $t = 2$, respectively). We now define $\Delta SD = SD_2 - SD_1$. We then get:

$$\Leftrightarrow \frac{HAD_1 + \Delta HAD}{SD_1 + \Delta SD} > \frac{HAD_1}{SD_1}$$
$$\Leftrightarrow SD_1(HAD_1 + \Delta HAD) > HAD_1(SD_1 + \Delta SD) \tag{1.4}$$
$$\Leftrightarrow SD_1 \Delta HAD > HAD_1 \Delta SD$$
$$\Leftrightarrow \Delta HAD > HAD_1 \frac{\Delta SD}{SD_1}$$

The *Z-score criterion* (Equation 1.4) is thus different from the *absolute difference criterion*, $\Delta HAD > 0$. The last equation also shows that the *Z-score criterion* will lead to the (erroneous) conclusions of population-level catch-up growth when the *absolute difference criterion* does not. The reason is that $HAD_1 \frac{\Delta SD}{SD_1} < 0$, since HAD_1 is always negative (HAD_1 is a deficit relative to the growth standards) and $\frac{\Delta SD}{SD_1}$ is always positive (SD increases with age).

Motivated by these theoretical considerations, we compared patterns of growth obtained for children from selected developing countries, using changes in mean HAZ versus HAD.

Methods

Data Sets

Our analyses used three different types of data. First, we used data from six purposefully selected Demographic and Health Surveys (DHS) from Latin America (Guatemala, Peru), Africa (Benin, Ethiopia), and South Asia (India and Bangladesh). The countries were selected based on the availability of data sets with large sample sizes. Our second source of data is from the Young Lives study which has collected data since 2002 on cohorts of children in Peru, Ethiopia, India, and Vietnam, with the intent to track the children for 15 years (Barnett et al. 2013). We used data for children at the time of enrollment, when children were between 6 and 18 months of age, and at first follow-up, when they were between 4.5 and 6 years old. Finally, we redrew Figure 1 from the COHORTS (Consortium on Health-Orientated Research in Transitional Societies) study presented in Stein et al. (2010), using HAD instead of HAZ.

Data Analyses

For about 17 percent of all children in the DHS data sets used, their days (but not the months or years) of birth were missing. To maximize the number of observations that could be included, a random day of birth was generated for these children. After creating the age in days for all children, we calculated the HAZ scores using the WHO 2006 growth standards (WHO Multicentre Growth Reference Study Group 2006b). The HAD, reported in cm, was calculated by subtracting the age- and sex-specific WHO 2006 growth standard's median height from the child's actual height. Any observation with an absolute HAZ value larger than 5 was dropped from the analyses.

Two types of analyses were conducted using the DHS data. First, we assessed how HAD changed with age as compared with HAZ. We graphed the means of both variables by completed month and the smoothed values using the kernel-weighted local polynomial smoothing algorithm in Stata (version 13.1). Using the smoothed values, we then calculated the change in HAZ and HAD by year, that is, the change from birth to 11 months of age, from 12 to 23 months of age, and other yearly intervals up to 60 months of age.

Analyses of the Young Lives data were limited to children who were younger than 60 months of age at follow-up and had valid HAZ values (same criterion as above) in both surveys. Observations with an absolute change in HAZ between rounds larger than 4 SD were dropped also. As we did for the DHS data, we graphed the HAZ and HAD at baseline and follow-up and tabulated the absolute change in these deficits over time.

In our final set of analyses, we estimated HAD at different ages using published summary statistics from five cohort studies conducted in low- and middle-income countries (see Stein et al. [2010]). HAD could not be calculated at mid-childhood for children in the Philippines (96 months is outside the range of the WHO 2006 international growth standards) and South Africa (implausible reported HAZ/height of children 60 months of age).

Results

The survey country, year, type, age range, total sample size, and number of children included in the analyses are shown in Table 1.1 for the DHS and Young Lives data sets. Nearly all surveys were conducted since 2000. The percentage of observations that could be included in the analyses varied from around 75 percent in Benin to 96 percent in Peru.

Figure 1.2A shows that substantial growth faltering was present in all six DHS countries according to the HAZ. The magnitude of the linear growth retardation, however, differed considerably between countries. Except for Ethiopia, mean HAZ started below the standard with deficits ranging from −0.5 Z-scores in India to large deficits of around −1.3 Z-scores in Guatemala. Mean Z-scores then dropped up to the age of 18 to 24 months in all countries, after which they stabilized and slightly increased in some of the countries. The largest drop (around −2 Z-scores) was seen in Ethiopia. Even though children in Peru started with the second largest deficit at birth (around −0.8 Z-scores), the subsequent drop was the smallest of the six countries studied (less than 0.5 Z-scores), resulting in the highest mean Z-score after 2 years of age. Children in Benin, Bangladesh, and India followed a similar growth pattern: starting with a mean Z-score of roughly −0.50 to −0.75, children stabilized at around −1.8 Z-scores after 24 months. Children in Guatemala were by far the worst off, with Z-scores well below the other countries at all ages, with a mean HAZ after 24 months close to −2.5 Z-scores.

Like the HAZ curves, the HAD curves (see Figure 1.2B) showed that the absolute height deficit at birth varied considerably across countries: from no deficit in Ethiopia to a massive deficit of nearly −3 cm in Guatemala. Also similar to the HAZ curves, the most pronounced faltering (i.e., the steepest slope) was found between 6 and 18 months of age. In sharp contrast with what the HAZ curves suggested, however, substantial growth faltering continued after 24 months of age in all countries, with total accumulated deficits ranging from −5.2 cm in Peru to −10.7 cm in Guatemala. The slopes of the curves indicate that the process of growth faltering decelerated only slightly, which suggests that growth faltering might continue beyond 5 years of age. Note that "bumps" in Figures 1.2A and 1.2B just after 24, 36, and 48 months

Table 1.1. DHS and Young Lives data sets analyzed

Type of survey and country	Survey	Age range	Observations included in the analyses	
	(Year)	(Months)	(n)	(Proportion of total)
DHS				
Bangladesh	2011	0–59	7635	0.87
Benin	2006	0–59	12126	0.75
Ethiopia	2003	0–59	9450	0.81
Guatemala	1999	0–59	3860	0.78
India	2006	0–59	41327	0.80
Peru	2012	0–59	9219	0.96
Young Lives				
Ethiopia	2002	6–15	520	0.90
	2006	55–59		
India	2002	6–18	240	0.93
	2006	55–59		
Peru	2002	5–12	393	0.95
	2006	53–59		
Vietnam	2002	4–15	332	0.94
	2006	50–59		

Source: Authors' calculations using DHS (<http://www.dhsprogram.com/>) and Young Lives data (<http://www.younglives.org.uk/>).

were due to age rounding and heaping, that is, the tendency to report age in completed years rather than in exact months.

The magnitude of the change in HAZ and in HAD during each of the first 5 years is shown in Figure 1.3, by yearly age intervals. As would be expected from the previous results, the significant drops in HAZ were limited to the first 2 years of life, and larger in the first compared with the second year for all countries except Guatemala. After 2 years, there were either no changes, or very small increases in HAZ. These small increases, however, have led to some of the recent claims of catch-up growth after 2 years of age described in the literature (see, for example Prentice et al. 2013). The change in HAD by year showed a different picture. First, children lost ground with respect to the standard during every single year of the first 5 years of life, with the largest drops occurring before 24 months of age, and even more importantly, during the second year in all six countries (drops in absolute height during the second year of life ranged from –1.2 cm in Peru to –3.2 cm in Ethiopia).

Child HAZ and absolute height deficit in the four Young Lives country cohorts are shown in Figure 1.4. At baseline, when children were on average 8 months old, mean HAZ ranged from –0.81 Z-scores in Vietnam to –1.33 in Peru. At follow-up (children on average 58 months old), HAZ had dropped further in all countries to reach values ranging from –1.38 to –1.99 Z-scores in Ethiopia and Peru, respectively. The absolute deficits at baseline were around –2 cm

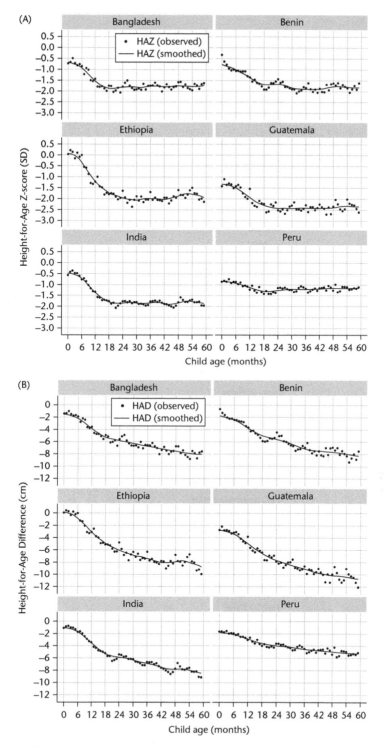

Figure 1.2 Mean height-for-age Z-scores (A) and height-for-age difference (B) relative to the WHO standard (1 to 59 months) by completed month and kernel-weighted local polynomial smoothed values for 6 DHS surveys

Source: Authors' calculations using DHS data (<http://www.dhsprogram.com/>).

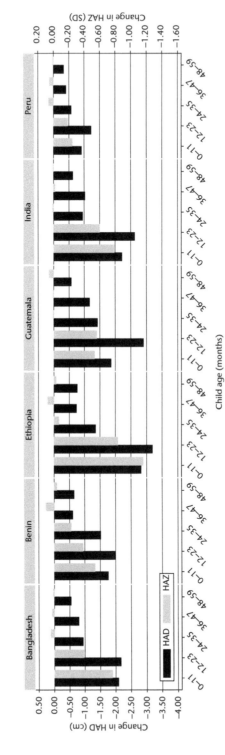

Figure 1.3 Mean changes in HAD and HAZ by year for 6 DHS surveys (1 to 59 months)

Source: Authors' calculations using DHS data (<ttp://www.dhsprogram.com/>).

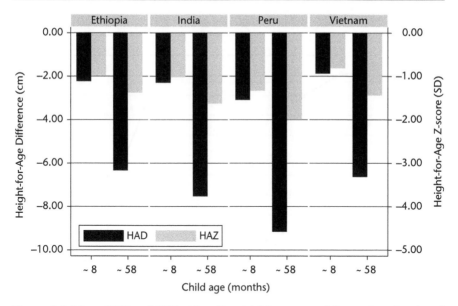

Figure 1.4 Mean HAD and HAZ at baseline (children around 8 months of age) and follow-up (around 58 months of age) of the Young Lives 4 country cohort study
Source: Authors' calculations using Young Lives data (<http://www.younglives.org.uk/>).

Table 1.2. Change in the absolute height deficit and HAZ from baseline (children around 8 months of age) to follow-up (around 58 months of age) in the Young Lives 4 country cohort study by catch-up growth (using the Z-score criterion)

		Change from baseline to follow-up in	Ethiopia	India	Peru	Vietnam
All children		Height deficit (cm)	−4.1	−5.2	−6.1	−4.8
		HAZ	−0.40	−0.61	−0.66	−0.62
		n	*520*	*240*	*393*	*332*
By catch-up according to Z-score criterion	No	Height deficit (cm)	−6.3	−6.9	−7.3	−5.8
		HAZ	−1.27	−1.2	−1.01	−0.92
		n	*324*	*167*	*308*	*267*
	Yes	Height deficit (cm)	−0.5	−1.5	−1.7	−0.5
		HAZ	1.03	0.75	0.61	0.61
		n	*196*	*73*	*85*	*65*

Source: Authors' calculations using Young Lives data (<http://www.younglives.org.uk/>).

for Ethiopia, India, and Vietnam and −3 cm in Peru. At follow-up, the total absolute height deficit had approximately tripled in all four countries. The changes in HAZ and HAD between baseline and follow-up are shown in Table 1.2. For instance in Ethiopia, the mean deficit increased 4.1 cm from baseline to follow-up. Children categorized as not experiencing catch-up growth according to the Z-score criterion accrued an additional deficit of 6.3 cm; children in

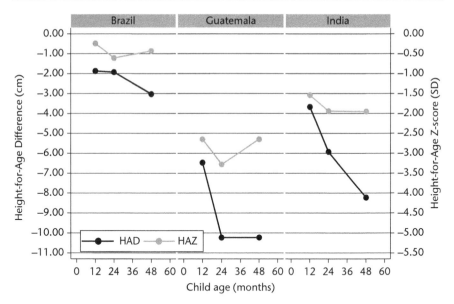

Figure 1.5 Mean HAD and HAZ at 12 months, 24 months, and 48 months in 3 birth cohort studies

Source: Authors' calculations on data obtained from Stein et al. (2010).

the catch-up group (again according to the Z-score criterion) accumulated an additional 0.5 cm in deficit. In line with our hypothesis, even groups of children classified as having experienced catch-up growth using the HAZ criterion accrued additional height deficit from baseline to follow-up in all countries.

For the three COHORTS countries for which HAD could be calculated at mid-childhood, it was confirmed that there was no evidence of catch-up growth when using HAD (see Figure 1.5). The height deficit worsened significantly from 24 to 48 months in Brazil and India and remained stable (but very large, >10 cm) in Guatemala.

Discussion

Using data from some of the same cohort studies that recently claimed catch-up growth using the Z-score (HAZ) criterion (4 from Young Lives and 3 from COHORTS), we show not only an absence of population-level catch-up growth between 2 and 5 years of age, but continued deterioration reflected in an increase in height deficit relative to growth standards. We explain algebraically why using HAZ leads to a perception about catch-up that is contradicted by using HAD. We also demonstrate, using cross-sectional data from six DHS surveys, the different patterns of growth observed in children between birth and 5 years of age when using HAZ versus HAD. As documented globally (Victora et al. 2010), growth patterns based on HAZ for the six countries analyzed show a steep decline in linear growth during the first 18–24 months of age, followed by a leveling off of the curves and an absence of further deterioration up to 60 months of age. By contrast, the HAD curves show a continued deterioration from birth to 60 months of age (with a steeper slope in the first 2 years), and no sign of improvement or flattening of the curve between 24 and 60 months of age. Based on our analyses of absolute deficits in height from both cross-sectional and longitudinal data, we conclude that there is no linear catch-up growth in the data sets we analyzed.

Changes in the absolute deficit in height, rather than changes in HAZ, should be used for the meaningful assessment of catch-up growth. As noted above, HAZ has been used to assess and compare the attained growth of groups of children with different age and sex composition at a given point in time; it was not designed and should not be used to assess *changes* in attained height as a population ages. In addition, the definition of HAZ makes it impossible to identify whether changes in HAZ with age are due to changes in the numerator (the magnitude of the deficit) or to changes in the denominator (the increasing SD with age).

Our results do not challenge the assumption that catch-up growth in height is possible; however, they confirm findings from earlier reviews that linear catch-up growth does not usually occur among children who remain in the same impoverished environments and are exposed to the same standards of healthcare, nutrition, and hygiene practices that led to growth faltering in the first place (Martorell et al. 1994). Given that none of the data sets we used (except for the Guatemala COHORTS data) were from studies that tested the impact of specific nutrition and health interventions among children exposed at different ages, our analysis does not answer the question of whether catch-up growth beyond 2 years of age in response to successful programs is possible. This question has been answered authoritatively in the Guatemala study, which consistently showed greater benefits from a nutrition and health intervention, including a protein-energy supplement, on a series of outcomes—including physical, cognitive, and economic outcomes in adulthood—among individuals who were exposed to the intervention before 2–3 years of life, as compared with those exposed when they were older (Martorell et al. 2010). This study, however, has not been reproduced in other countries, and it could be that Guatemala is a special case.

Our finding showing that the accrual of deficits in height continues well into childhood—and possibly beyond—raises an important question related to the timing of the window(s) of opportunity for improving nutrition. Although there is no doubt that the first 1,000 days is a critical period for preventing undernutrition, the question of whether something can be done to prevent further deterioration beyond 2 years of life remains unanswered. The curves derived from the DHS data are descriptive and do not provide information on the potential to benefit from interventions; the cohort studies (except for the Guatemalan study) also were not designed to answer this question. It is possible that the continued increase in the magnitude of height deficit between 2 and 5 years is a long-term consequence of inadequate health, nutrition, and care experienced during the first 1,000 days, and may or may not be reversible with interventions after 2 years of age. As noted above, the continued deterioration may also be due to the sustained poor health, nutrition, and care environment that children between 2 and 5 years of age continue to be exposed to.

Many of the recent studies that documented catch-up growth using HAZ or stunting definitions have focused on changes between early childhood and adolescence or adulthood (Adair 1999; Coly et al. 2006; Hirvonen 2013; Prentice et al. 2013). This requires a different approach than comparing children at different ages within the period of 0–5 years. The reason is that, for children less than 5 years of age, international growth standards have been developed based on evidence that infants and young children from diverse ethnic groups grow similarly for the first 5 years of life if their nutrition, health, and care needs are met (Habicht et al. 1974; WHO Multicentre Growth Reference Study Group 2006a). This evidence, however, does not exist for older children and during adolescence. For the latter, a particular challenge is that malnourished children tend to have a delayed pubertal growth spurt when compared to the healthy children included in growth standards (see, for instance, Kulin et al. 1982 and Parent et al. 2003); this makes comparisons with references to quantify height deficits during adolescence difficult or impossible to interpret. Other approaches must therefore be developed to measure catch-up growth during periods such as adolescence, when growth references do not accurately reflect growth potential. We suggested previously that the possibility of catch-up growth in this age group should be evaluated through experimental studies in which the absolute linear growth of children or adolescents receiving a growth-promoting intervention is compared with that of a comparable non-intervention group (Leroy et al. 2013).

Child linear growth is the best available summary measure of chronic malnutrition. It predicts a host of important outcomes throughout the life cycle, including mortality, cognitive development, behavioral outcomes, school achievement, economic productivity, and risks of chronic diseases (Black et al. 2013). The importance of these functional correlates, and the potential reversibility of stunting and related negative functional outcomes, has motivated many of the studies on catch-up growth. Whether linear growth retardation is part of the biological causal pathway linking the determinants of malnutrition to these outcomes, however, is not known, nor is the extent to which interventions aimed at improving population-level growth—and possibly achieving catch-up growth—can also successfully remedy the functional correlates of growth retardation.

Conclusion

Our analyses using HAD find no catch-up growth in cohort studies and reveal substantial deterioration in height deficit beyond 2 years of age, in both cohort and cross-sectional studies. The findings do not challenge the current focus on the first 1,000 days as the critical window to improve nutrition. The findings, however, highlight the need for research (1) to better understand whether preventing stunting during the first 1,000 days can also help prevent further deterioration in linear growth during mid-childhood and beyond; and (2) to identify the types of nutrition inputs that may be needed beyond 2 years of age to at least stabilize, if not reduce, the magnitude of height deficit.

Another important question that remains unanswered is whether catch-up growth past 2 years of age, if possible, results in meaningful reversal of some of the functional consequences of undernutrition in early childhood. New research aimed at elucidating the potential of catch-up growth beyond 2 years of age and its consequences on other outcomes, however, should not distract from the current programmatic focus on the first 1,000 days and the growing commitment of countries to scale up nutrition interventions (SUN initiative, see <http://scalingupnutrition.org/>) specifically targeted to mothers and children during the first 1,000 days. Research and programming aimed at improving nutrition among adolescent girls and young women before pregnancy and identifying platforms to deliver these interventions at scale also remain important. Preventing undernutrition, rather than reversing it, should continue to be the key goal for tackling the global burden of malnutrition.

Acknowledgments

We thank Lilia Bliznashka, senior research assistant at the International Food Policy Research Institute (IFPRI), for excellent research support to compile the data sets and prepare them for analyses. The study was funded by the CGIAR Research Program on Agriculture for Nutrition and Health (A4NH), led by IFPRI. The funders had no role in study design, data collection and analysis, the decision to publish, or preparation of the manuscript.

References

Adair, L. S. 1999. "Filipino Children Exhibit Catch-up Growth from Age 2 to 12 Years." *Journal of Nutrition* 129 (6): pp. 1140–1148.

Barnett, Inka, Proochista Ariana, Stavros Petrou, Mary E. Penny, Le Thuc Duc, S. Galab, Tassew Woldehanna, Javier A. Escobal, Emma Plugge, and Jo Boyden. 2013. "Cohort Profile: The Young Lives Study." *International Journal of Epidemiology* 42 (3): pp. 701–708.

Black, Robert E., Lindsay H. Allen, Zulfiqar A. Bhutta, Laura E. Caulfield, Mercedes de Onis, Majid Ezzati, Colin Mathers, Juan Rivera, for the Maternal and Child Undernutrition Study Group. 2008. "Maternal and Child Undernutrition: Global and Regional Exposures and Health Consequences." *Lancet* 371 (9608): pp. 243–260.

Black, Robert E., Cesar G. Victora, Susan P. Walker, Zulfiqar A. Bhutta, Parul Christian, Mercedes de Onis, Majid Ezzati, Sally Grantham-McGregor, Joanne Katz, Reynaldo Martorell, Ricardo Uauy, and the Maternal and Child Nutrition Study Group. 2013. "Maternal and Child Undernutrition and Overweight in Low-income and Middle-income Countries." *Lancet* 382 (9890): pp. 427–451.

Boersma, B., and J. M. Wit. 1997. "Catch-up Growth." *Endocrine Reviews* 18 (5): pp. 646–661.

Coly, A. N., J. Milet, A. Diallo, T. Ndiaye, E. Bénéfice, F. Simondon, S. Wade, and K. B. Simondon. 2006. "Preschool Stunting, Adolescent Migration, Catch-up Growth, and Adult Height in Young Senegalese Men and Women of Rural Origin." *Journal of Nutrition* 136 (9): pp. 2412–2420.

Crookston, B. T., M. E. Penny, S. C. Alder, T. T. Dickerson, R. M. Merrill, J. B. Stanford, C. A. Porucznik, and K. A. Dearden. 2010. "Children Who Recover from Early Stunting and Children Who Are Not Stunted Demonstrate Similar Levels of Cognition." *Journal of Nutrition* 140 (11): pp. 1996–2001.

Habicht, J.-P., R. Martorell, C. Yarbrough, R. M. Malina, and R. E. Klein. 1974. "Height and Weight Standards for Preschool Children. How Relevant Are Ethnic Differences in Growth Potential?" *Lancet* 1 (7858): pp. 611–614.

Hirvonen, K. 2013. "Measuring Catch-up Growth in Malnourished Populations." *Annals of Human Biology* 41 (1): pp. 67–75.

Kulin, Howard E., Nimrod Bwibo, Dominic Mutie, and Steven J. Santer. 1982. "The Effect of Chronic Childhood Malnutrition on Pubertal Growth and Development." *American Journal of Clinical Nutrition* 36 (3): pp. 527–536.

Leroy, J. L., M. Ruel, and J.-P. Habicht. 2013. Letter re: "Critical Windows for Nutritional Interventions against Stunting." *American Journal of Clinical Nutrition* 98 (3): pp. 854–855.

Martorell, R., L. K. Khan, and D. G. Schroeder. 1994. "Reversibility of Stunting: Epidemiological Findings in Children from Developing Countries." *European Journal of Clinical Nutrition* 45 (Suppl. 1): pp. S45–S57.

Martorell, Reynaldo, Paul Melgar, John A. Maluccio, Aryeh D. Stein, and Juan A. Rivera. 2010. "The Nutrition Intervention Improved Adult Human Capital and Economic Productivity." *Journal of Nutrition* 140 (2): pp. 411–414.

Outes, I. and C. Porter. 2013. "Catching Up from Early Nutritional Deficits? Evidence from Rural Ethiopia." *Economics and Human Biology* 11 (2): pp. 148–163.

Parent, A.-S., G. Teilmann, A. Juul, N. E. Skakkebaek, J. Toppari, and J. P. Bourguignon. 2003. "The Timing of Normal Puberty and the Age Limits of Sexual Precocity: Variations around the World, Secular Trends, and Changes after Migration." *Endocrine Reviews* 24 (5): pp. 668–693.

Prader, A., J. M. Tanner, and G. von Harnack. 1963. "Catch-up Growth Following Illness or Starvation. An Example of Developmental Canalization in Man." *Journal of Pediatrics* 62 (5): pp. 646–659.

Prentice, A. M., K. A. Ward, G. R. Goldberg, L. M. Jarjou, S. E. Moore, A. J. Fulford, and A. Prentice. 2013. "Critical Windows for Nutritional Interventions against Stunting." *American Journal of Clinical Nutrition* 97 (5): pp. 911–918.

Ruel, M. T. 2010. "The Oriente Study: Program and Policy Impacts." *Journal of Nutrition* 140 (2): pp. 415–418.

Ruel, M. T., P. Menon, J.-P. Habicht, C. Loechl, G. Bergeron, G. Pelto, M. Arimond, J. Maluccio, L. Michaud, and B. Hankebo. 2008. "Age-based Preventive Targeting of Food Assistance and Behaviour Change and Communication for Reduction of Childhood Undernutrition in Haiti: A Cluster Randomised Trial." *Lancet* 371 (9612): pp. 588–595.

Stein, A. D., M. Wang, R. Martorell, S. A. Norris, L. S. Adair, I. Bas, H. S. Sachdev, S. K. Bhargava, C. H. Fall, D. P. Gigante, C. G. Victora, and Cohorts Group. 2010. "Growth Patterns in Early Childhood and Final Attained Stature: Data from Five Birth Cohorts from Low- and Middle-income Countries." *American Journal of Human Biology* 22 (3): pp. 353–359.

Victora, C. G., M. de Onis, P. C. Hallal, M. Blössner, and R. Shrimpton. 2010. "Worldwide Timing of Growth Faltering: Revisiting Implications for Interventions." *Pediatrics* 125 (3): pp. e473–e480.

WHO Multicentre Growth Reference Study Group. 2006a. "Assessment of Differences in Linear Growth among Populations in the WHO Multicentre Growth Reference Study." *Acta Paediatrica* 95 (Suppl. 450): pp. 56–65.

WHO Multicentre Growth Reference Study Group. 2006b. "WHO Child Growth Standards." *Acta Paediatrica* 95 (Suppl. 450): pp. 5–101.

2

Can Transfer Programs Be Made More Nutrition Sensitive?

Harold Alderman

Introduction

In 2013, a camel herder in northern Kenya could take her identification card, embedded with her fingerprint and photo, to designated shopkeepers and, within minutes, receive 2,700 Kenyan shillings of income support on a monthly basis. This example illustrates recent changes both in the willingness of governments and donors in low- and middle-income countries to provide support to low-income households, and in their use of technology to do so effectively. This shift has been prompted, in part, by the accumulated evidence on the contribution of transfer programs to both equity and to asset creation (Das et al. 2005; Alderman and Yemtsov 2014). Thus, in the wake of the sequence of food price and financial shocks in 2007 and 2008, between 0.75 billion and 1.0 billion people in low- and middle-income countries were recipients of cash support (DFID 2011).

With relatively minor changes in labor supply and private transfers documented in most programs, the impact on recipients' total consumption is largely determined by the targeting efficiency and the generosity of the transfer program. However, the public value of any increase in aggregate consumption by low-income households is difficult to measure for the basic reason that although the welfare benefit from improved equity is real, it is hard to quantify. On the other hand, an extensive range of studies quantifies changes in specific investments and behaviors attributable to eligibility for transfer programs. Prominent among the outcomes studied is the impact of transfers on nutrition. Still, despite reasonable expectations—indeed, despite design features included in some programs to increase the nutritional impact—there is far less evidence from low- and middle-income settings that transfers influence the nutritional status of young children than evidence that specific underlying health-seeking behaviors have increased (Manley et al. 2013; Ruel and Alderman 2013).

This chapter explores the interplay of transfer programs and child nutrition. Because the potential for transfer programs to influence nutrition starts with the role of income in the production of nutrition, this chapter begins with this topic. Moreover, because transfer programs may be designed as a response to specific shocks or as predictable contributions to household resources, this discussion distinguishes the goal of raising consumption over an extended period from the objective of enhancing resilience during times of crisis. However, many transfer programs—particularly, but not only, conditional cash transfers (CCTs)—aim to influence the price of human capital investments and also to shift a family's resource envelope. Therefore, this chapter next looks at the services that accompany transfer programs. Whether conditional or not, increasingly such transfers provide cash rather than food to households. Yet, in some circumstances in-kind transfers are still preferred. Accordingly, we then review recent evidence on this mode of delivery. The concluding section offers suggestions for enhancing the nutritional impacts of transfers programs.

The Relationship of Income and Malnutrition

As incomes increase—through either earnings or transfers—low-income consumers increase both the quantity and quality of the food they purchase. Moreover, they are usually able to obtain more health services as their income increases. Furthermore, at the national level as overall resources increase, governments are able to increase the services provided in addition to funding the transfer programs studied here. What, then, is the empirical record linking gross domestic product (GDP) growth or household income with malnutrition?

Using country-level data from the 1970s, 1980s, and 1990s, Haddad et al. (2003) found that the Millennium Development Goals indicator of rates of underweight children less than 5 years old declined at half the rate that GDP grew. The authors observed an overall pattern of similar magnitude using household data from 12 household surveys, all of which were collected in the 1990s, although there was appreciable heterogeneity in country-specific results. More recent analysis of current cross-country data found a somewhat larger response to income change, with underweight declining by 7 percent and stunting declining by 6 percent for every 10 percent increase in GDP (Ruel and Alderman 2013; see Table 2.1).[1] These findings contrast with Ruel and Alderman's (2013) findings for income poverty, which declined at the

37

Table 2.1. Estimated elasticity of nutrition indicators relative to economic growth

Dependent variable	Poverty (<$1.25/day)	Child stunting (HAZ <-2)	Child underweight (WAZ<-2)	Low birthweight (<2.5 kg)	Maternal low BMI (<18.5 kg/m²)	Maternal high BMI(>=25 kg/m²)
GDP per capita (β)	-1.102***	-0.587***	-0.703***	-0.228***	-0.403**	0.7***
Standard error	0.12	0.09	0.09	0.07	-0.17	0.15
Constant	11.369***	7.901***	8.132***	4.137***	5.256***	1.18
Standard error	1.0	0.68	0.69	0.58	1.26	0.37
Number of observations	438	233	317	575	110	182
R-square	0.57	0.48	0.49	0.23	0.48	0.62

Notes: BMI = body mass index; GDP = gross domestic product; HAZ = height-for-age Z-score; WAZ = weight-for-age Z-score. * $p < 0.10$; ** $p < 0.05$; *** $p < 0.01$.

The models use country fixed-effects regressions, except the maternal low-BMI regression, which estimates regional fixed effects because of the smaller sample size. Dependent variables are all specified in logarithms. Thus, the parameters can be interpreted as elasticities. All regressions are run on a sample of countries with GDP per capita of less than $12,500 in 2005 international dollars. The inclusion of higher-income countries substantially reduces all elasticity estimates. GDP per capita is measured in an international currency (2005 purchasing power parity dollars) to better account for international price differences. Poverty is defined according to the World Bank's $1.25 household poverty head count, measured in 2005 international dollars.

Sources: Adapted from the online appendix to Ruel and Alderman (2013). Anthropometric data for stunting, underweight, and maternal BMI are drawn from WHO (2013) and MEASURE Demographic and Health Surveys (DHS). Low birthweight data are drawn from UNICEF's *State of the World's Children* reports and Childinfo, and from DHS.

same rate as the increase in gross national product (GNP) per capita, based on cross-country data. From one perspective, such results, as well those of a similar study showing that anemia declines half as fast as does stunting (Alderman and Linnemayr 2009), indicate the likely time frame for reducing malnutrition in the absence of specific interventions. Even with equitable growth, the time frame for, say, halving undernutrition is measured more in terms of a generation rather than in a few years.

From another perspective, however, the results also imply that transfer programs might have a more rapid impact than GDP growth alone on the nutritional status of beneficiaries. Although the magnitude of transfers varies appreciably across countries—ranging from transfers that increase total income marginally to those that boost income by as much as one-third for the poorest recipients—it is not uncommon for a program to augment consumption in low-income households by 20 percent. The expected decline in stunting from a transfer of this size—around 12 percent using the relationship between income and stunting reported above—should be measurable among recipient households in comparison with similar households in a well-designed household survey. Whether this improvement is observable on a national scale is a somewhat different issue. Evidence on program impacts often comes from pilot phases or donor-funded projects, not all of which go to scale. On the other hand, some current transfer programs have wide coverage; transfers in Brazil and Mexico reach 25 percent of the population, and a program in Ecuador assisted 40 percent of the population (Fiszbein and Schady 2009). Ethiopia's productive safety net—the largest transfer program in Africa south of the Sahara, with the exception of South Africa's—covers 10 percent of the population (World Bank 2012). Using an average income elasticity of stunting of –0.6, the increment to household resources attributable to programs at this scale may reduce the national stunting rate by 1–5 percent from the period prior to implementation to the time the program is rolled out to full nationwide coverage. This is appreciable and appreciated, but possibly overshadowed by other trends and thus not easily identified.

Is transfer income used differently than other income? Based on studies of household decisions with regard to food expenditure, it is plausible that this would be the case. Evidence from cash transfers in Colombia, Ecuador, Mexico, and Nicaragua reported by Attanasio et al. (2012), as well as from the food stamp program in the United States (Breunig and Dasgupta 2005), indicates that households commonly spend more on food and health out of transfer income than from general sources of income even when the transfers are only indirectly linked to nutrition and health. One possible explanation for this is labeling (Kooreman 2000), whereby participation in a program influences a household's spending patterns.[2] Labeling is also raised as a possible reason that take-home rations in a food-for-education program in Burkina Faso had a substantially larger impact on the weight-for-age of younger siblings (6 to 60 months old) of girls eligible for these rations, compared with the estimated impact of an income transfer of similar value (Kazianga et al. 2014).[3]

Other studies attribute changes in expenditure patterns to a combination of gender control—many transfer programs earmark women as recipients—and social marketing. That women generally spend differently than men has been shown in a variety of settings, with the identification often coming from exogenous differences in earnings and assets or from inheritance and alimony legislation (see the recent review by Doss [2013]). Moreover, an analysis of differences in expenditure patterns following an increase in child benefits financed from wage taxes in the United Kingdom (Lundberg et al. 1997) provided evidence closer to the current theme of transfer programs. Similarly, studies of food expenditures in Mexico's CCT program, PROGRESA (Programa de Educación, Salud y Alimentación), have found that the recipients' expenditures on food increased more than would be expected due to income effects alone (Attanasio and Lechene 2002; Hoddinott and Skoufias 2004; Bobonis 2009). The papers by Attanasio and Lechene (2002) and by Bobonis (2009) attributed the increased food expenditures to female control of income, a hypothesis that was explicitly tested in the studies, whereas the paper by Hoddinott and Skoufias (2004) found that the increased food expenditures reflected increased diet quality rather than increased calorie consumption, inferring that this was due to the nutrition education that was provided to program participants. These two interpretations are not mutually exclusive. Although these analyses were based on a random assignment into the transfer program, I am not aware of any studies that have looked at nutritional outcomes (as opposed to educational outcomes) using a random assignment to male and female recipients within the same intervention.

The majority of studies, which use exogenously assigned eligibility for a transfer program to avoid biases that stem from the possibility that female control of resources reflects household preferences and labor choices, have looked at expenditures as the outcome to be studied. Duflo (2003), however, directly measured differences in the anthropometry of the grandchildren of recipients of South Africa's relatively generous pension program. This study found that pensions received by women had a significant impact on the nutritional status of their grandchildren, an outcome that was not found for relatives of male pensioners. While this result clearly supports the view that women and men have different patterns of investment, it does not imply that a pension transfer is necessarily a good vehicle for improving child nutrition. In fact, only 46 percent of pensioners—either male or female—lived with their grandchildren, and the positive nutritional impact was observed only if the woman's grandchild was a girl.

Abstracting from any targeting errors in transfer programs, their impact on nutrition depends, in part, on the proportion of the beneficiary population that is in the nutritionally vulnerable population. This core group consists of pregnant women and children less than 2 years of age, often referred to as children in the first 1,000 days from conception. Because transfer programs often have equity motives as well as explicit nutrition goals—many poor households do not contain individuals who are in the vulnerable 1,000 days—there are clear trade-offs that need to be considered in allocating any transfer budget. Ruel and Alderman (2013) surmised that one reason for the limited observed impact of transfer programs on nutrition is that the measurement of nutritional impact is often over a broader group of children included in transfer programs rather than those in the most responsive age group. With heterogeneity of nutritional outcomes, this approach would likely dilute and possibly mask overall changes in the treated population that could be attributable to a transfer program.

Still, even when transfers are used to augment diet quality for the most vulnerable household members, they are unlikely to have a major impact on other inputs into improved nutrition, such as the supply and quality of health and sanitation services, which are largely public goods.[4] Similarly, although an increase of purchasing power similar to what is provided in a transfer program may encourage health-seeking behavior, larger investments and behavioral changes are needed to reduce the exposure to pathogens in the community in which a child plays (Spears 2013; Ngure et al. 2014).

Transfers and Resilience

There is almost a cottage industry producing studies that show the vulnerability of children to short-term crises. For example, Alderman et al. (2006) showed that drought and civil unrest (independently as well as jointly) contributed to increased stunting in Zimbabwe and subsequently, this stunting led to reduced schooling. Akresh et al. (2011) also showed that both drought and conflict—tested separately but not jointly—contributed to persistent stunting in Rwanda.[5] In extreme cases, such as the massive policy-induced famine in China between 1957 and 1961, observed stunting may be an underestimate of the nutritional insult, because extremely high mortality may selectively remove stunted children from subsequent measurement (Gørgens et al. 2012). However, Maccini and Yang (2009) showed that a rain shortfall does not have to be substantial to result in reduced linear growth and schooling. Nor are these human capital crises confined to conflict- and drought-affected economies; Cruces et al. (2012) found that the incidence of low birthweight increased with the economic contraction in Argentina in

2001–02, with both GDP contraction and reduced health expenditures per capita independently explaining this outcome.

To drill down into mechanisms, it is useful to draw upon more general models of human capital, covering education and mortality as well as nutritional status. Ferreira and Schady (2009) pointed out that economic downturns influence relative prices as well as overall resources and thus induce substitution effects as well as income effects. In developed countries, substitution effects (in addition to changing fertility patterns) may, paradoxically, result in improved human capital outcomes during economic downturns, especially with regard to schooling, because the opportunity cost of education declines when employment contracts. Baird et al. (2011), however, documented that in low-income countries mortality is countercyclical; that is, infant mortality increases when GNP declines.

One notable exception to this pattern is a study by Miller and Urdinola (2010) that reported a procyclical pattern with coffee prices in Colombia. The authors attributed this result to the cost of labor, and thus, of childcare, which declines when coffee prices fall and rise during a price spike.[6] This outcome contrasts with estimates for India, where countercyclical mortality was explained, in part, by the need for additional income sources when rainfall is inadequate; Bhalotra (2010) observed increased female labor supply and decreased time for childcare in times of stress.

The issue of childcare may be part of the answer to the puzzle as to why negative economic shocks seem to have a larger impact in absolute terms than does an increase in income, as shown in the cross-country results of Baird et al. (2011), a result that is echoed in the relative point estimates of Cruces et al. (2012). The issue of childcare may also be behind the fact that many studies— including those of Baird et al. (2011), Akresh et al. (2011), and Maccini and Yang (2009)—have found that girls are affected more than boys in times of stress. This finding differs from the results of most cross-sectional regressions, which have shown the nutritional status of girls to be generally the same as or better than boys in the same environment; recent analysis of 20 DHS data sets undertaken at the International Food Policy Research Institute (IFPRI) found that in all of the surveys the odds ratio for the probability of stunting was less than 1 for girls, and significantly so for all but two of the countries. This pattern, which implies a lower risk for girls, is apparent even in analysis of surveys from countries such as India and Bangladesh, which on the basis of other forms of gender bias (including mortality in Bhalotra's [2010] study) are occasionally incorrectly assumed to have a nationwide pattern of gender discrimination with regard to nutrition.

An additional reason that shocks may have a negative influence on health and nutrition that is greater in absolute value than the improvement in health from increases in income may have to do with stock-out of assets; a household cannot draw down financial assets (including credit and social exchanges) indefinitely, but it can increase them to the degree desired with income growth. Thus, in the wake of a shock, a poor household may be forced to trade off current consumption against assets, reducing the former in order to protect the household's long-term productive capacity, while households with more assets are able to smooth consumption (Kazianga and Udry 2006; Carter and Lybbert 2012).[7] Reducing food consumption, however, is not merely a welfare loss; it also may influence current productivity and, as documented, the future earning capacity of the next generation. Thus, the absence of liquidity not only constrains consumption smoothing but forces households to forgo potential earnings in order to protect current assets, as Hoddinott (2006) argued occurred in Zimbabwe in 1994–95. Hoddinott's (2006) underlying behavioral model is similar to that elaborated by Carter and Lybbert (2012), with the major difference being that Hoddinott disaggregated the impact of shocks over individuals within the household.

As mentioned, Cruces et al. (2012) found that the incidence of low birthweight increased when provincial public health expenditures declined, and this increase was at a greater rate when the economy was also in decline. However, this incidence was not associated with changes in *total* public expenditures—that is, government outlays summed over all sectors. Paxson and Schady (2005) gave a similar explanation in terms of public expenditures in their study of changes in mortality in Peru during a severe economic contraction. Moreover, Ferreira and Schady (2009) contrasted the increased mortality in Peru with the absence of severe health consequences in the wake of the 1997–98 economic crisis in Indonesia, and they used this example to bolster the suggestion that one strategy to protect children during economic downturns is to protect public expenditures.

For this reasonable proposition to be valid, however, these expenditures must be on services that can be shown to protect health; where the public health system is sparsely present or ineffective, protecting the system is unlikely to contribute to resiliency. Alternatively—or additionally—a government can protect private expenditures by introducing new safety net programs or by expanding the coverage or increasing the level of support in existing programs, the latter being administratively the easier option in the short run if such a program is available. For example, Ethiopia increased wages in its public works program in 2008, in the wake of rapidly rising food prices, and in the same year Brazil increased the cash grant in the Bolsa Família CCT, in addition to increasing minimum wages. Ferreira et al. (2013) noted that the combination of these measures in Brazil, as well as general equilibrium effects on producer incomes and rural wages attributed to higher food prices, mitigated the effects of the price increases on purchasing power. This protection was largely confined to the poorest two deciles of rural residents and the poorest decile in urban areas, while middle-income consumers had the largest proportional losses in welfare.

Ferreira et al. (2013), however, did not have the data to take the analysis one step further and measure the impact of transfers on nutrition or other dimensions of child health. There are particular research obstacles to such an investigation. For example, randomized trials among shock-affected populations are largely incompatible with research ethics; moreover, comparisons between recipients and nonrecipients need to take into account the endogeneity of the heightened requirements for assistance. Yamano et al. (2005) addressed the problem of endogeneity by first modeling program placement as a function of rainfall shortages and then measuring the impact of food aid conditional on its allocation to the community (not the household itself). The study replicated the common finding that drought leads to a reduction in the rate of linear growth for children but also found that the food aid allocation offset this risk, largely mitigating the effects of the drought where the aid was provided.

Giles and Satriawan (2015) also addressed program placement and its duration, in their study of supplementary feeding provided to children 6 to 60 months old by the government of Indonesia as a specific response measure in the wake of the 1998 economic crisis in that country. They noted benefits for children 12–24 months old, but did not observe a similar impact on stunting for either younger children or older children, reflecting both age-specific health risks and differences in daily food allocation. The overall effect was a reduction in the likelihood of stunting by 15 percent. The examples in Ethiopia and Indonesia, both in response to relatively slow-onset disasters (relative to, say, a typhoon), are examples of in-kind transfers, an issue that is explored further later in this chapter.

Also relevant to the role of transfer programs in protecting health in the wake of a financial shock in Uruguay is a study by Amarante et al. (2012). This research found a 15–17 percent reduction in low birthweight, attributable to an unconditional transfer program implemented between April 2005 and December 2007 on an emergency basis in response to a contraction in GNP of 10 percent. The study used administrative microdata matched to longitudinal vital statistics on the universe of births. The authors also indicated that the transfer increased household income by at least 25 percent, implying income elasticity for low birthweight of approximately –0.6. This is nearly three times the magnitude of the elasticity for the reduction in low birthweight (–0.228) reported in Table 2.1. Amarante et al. (2012) did not report the attendant changes in purchases financed by this transfer or in health services demanded, although they ruled out the possibility that the improvement in birthweight was due to significant changes in health-seeking behavior. They flagged both reduced stress and reduced labor supply as possible contributors to the outcomes measured, implying a role of the transfer beyond that of earned income.

An important policy issue related to transfers and shocks is the potential for catch-up growth. Although in general, stunting at age 2 has consequences that persist over a lifetime—with some risk of increased obesity when programs attempt to increase growth on a small frame after that age—there is some debate as to whether this generality holds when conditions that contributed to the stunting are removed. Singh et al. (2014), for example, found that school feeding in India apparently reversed the impact of a severe drought on stunting. Few studies, however, have similar results that can point to safety net programs that negate the impact of undernutrition on physical growth, although targeted stimulation programs may offset the consequences for cognitive development (Ruel and Alderman 2013).

Linking Transfers and Health Services

Transfer programs are frequently aimed at increasing investments in human capital. This goal is often fostered by adding a requirement that the beneficiary household members participate in schooling or designated healthcare activities (Fiszbein and Schady 2009). In effect, such requirements change the relative price of investments in addition to increasing the budget envelope. These requirements are motivated, in part, by the assumption that poor households underinvest relative to a social optimum (Das et al. 2005). The evidence from careful studies of CCTs indicates that these programs virtually always augment household food consumption and dietary diversity while increasing participation in preventive healthcare.[8] Some trials of CCTs have also found improved anthropometry (Behrman and Hoddinott 2005; Maluccio and Flores 2005). However, on average, the impact of CCTs on anthropometric measures of nutritional status is small (Manley et al. 2013; Ruel and Alderman 2013).[9] Similarly, a significant improvement in anemia was found in only one of the three country programs in which that outcome was studied (Leroy et al. 2009).

This pattern of limited observed impact on nutritional outcomes is partially explained by the nature of the studies, some of which include in their focus individuals outside the first 1,000 days who are not expected to be as responsive to nutrition interventions as younger individuals. Additionally, nutritional impacts are cumulative, and some studies risk a bias toward limited impact if they cover too short a time frame (King and Behrman 2009). Moreover, with the exception of recent preliminary results from the Philippines—which have not yet been included in any meta-analysis—all published studies of the impact of CCT programs on nutritional outcomes have explored interventions in Latin America rather than Africa or Asia,[10] where malnutrition rates are, in general, much higher. The recent evidence from the Philippines comes from two related studies of the Pantawid Pamilya program, which covered more than three million people by 2012. These studies used both a randomized trial and a regression discontinuity design to assess the impact of the program on health and education and found reductions of 10–16 percentage points in stunting in the two samples (Chaudhury et al. 2012; Onishi et al. 2013).

Yet another reason hypothesized for the observed increase in health service participation, with limited corresponding improvement in outcomes, is the quality of services received (Gaarder et al. 2010). Conversely, one study (Barber and Gertler 2010) found an improvement in the birthweight of children born to women eligible for Oportunidades (a successor to PROGRESA in Mexico), but did not find an increase in attendance at prenatal centers. This outcome, according to the authors, stemmed entirely from an improvement in the quality of services—an improvement they attributed not to additional financial resources provided to the clinics but rather to the empowerment of the recipient women who demanded better services.

The insignificant pooled results of the impact of CCT programs in Latin America on nutrition also masks program heterogeneity. For example, Fernald et al. (2009) saw a larger impact of PROGRESA on children who were in the program 18 months longer than a comparison group of participants. In another study of PROGRESA, Behrman and Hoddinott (2005) found no overall impact on nutritional status when looking at program eligibility but did observe that, after controlling for unobserved heterogeneity correlated with actual access to the program's supplementary food—not all eligible children had such access—there was a significant positive and fairly substantial reduction in stunting among children 12–36 months old who received the supplements. The reduction was greatest among the poorest families with functionally literate women present. An analysis of the improvement in anemia from PROGRESA[11] that aimed to uncover the impact pathway attributed the improvement to increased dietary intake from the food supplements rather than other aspects of improved home diets of the young children within the household (Ramírez-Silva et al. 2013). This analysis was not confined to iron intakes; the group that received supplements also consumed more retinol and zinc. The study, however, did not analyze the reasons why one group of participants consumed the supplements and another did not.

Ultimately, it may be argued that, similar to the various studies that attempt to unpack the causal chain to better nutrition, increased weights and heights, themselves, are part of an expanded pathway toward reduced mortality and better cognitive abilities of the survivors. In this regard, two recent studies showing that CCTs reduced mortality in Latin America are important. In one,

Rasella et al. (2013) linked CCT coverage in Brazil with municipal mortality data using fixed-effects regressional analysis and observed that as coverage increased, under-5 mortality declined. Similarly, a drop in deaths attributed to malnutrition was associated with the program's availabilty. The analysis also accounted for the rollout of a program to provide free community-based healthcare and found that the reduction in overall mortality was greatest where both programs had widespread coverage. In a similar study using municipal data, Barham (2011) found that PROGRESA reduced infant mortality as program coverage increased; mortality declined by 17 percent in rural areas with full coverage and by 8 percent overall. Moreover, the subset of deaths attributed to nutritional deficiencies was found to decline significantly, even though this trend contributed less to overall reductions in infant mortality than did the changes in intestinal infections or respiratory diseases. The study, however, did not find a statistically significant reduction in neonatal mortality.[12]

The most detailed study of indicators of cognitive development in a CCT program—albeit one in which the actual monitoring of health-seeking behaviors as a condition of participation was minimal—showed that young Nicaraguan children eligible for the emergency program Atención a Crisis had improved measures of child development two years after the program ended (Macours et al. 2012). The authors presented evidence supporting the view that this improvement was not merely due to the income effect, although they could not link the outcome to any specific program element. Fernald and Hidrobo (2011) also showed improved cognitive development in a transfer program in Ecuador. Both the Ecuadoran and the Nicaraguan programs, however, did not show improvements in height-for-age. Thus, the transfer programs may have an impact on the subsequent economic outcomes for the children of families currently receiving benefits, even if this is not apparently mediated via a nutritional pathway.[13]

Turning the causal pathway around, there may be a link from cognitive states to improved nutrition mediated through transfer programs. There is new evidence that poverty raises stress levels in a manner that reduces an individual's cognitive functioning and, in effect, leads to a negative feedback loop (Mani et al. 2013). This mechanism may be due to a tying up of mental resources or attention (Shah et al. 2012) or to increased cortisol levels associated with stress (Chemin et al. 2013). In either case, chronically poor individuals would be more susceptible to the effects of a crisis. This dimension of cognitive capacity and poverty has just begun to be studied in detail. A few studies have indicated that transfer programs can reduce symptoms of stress. For example, Fernald and Gunnar (2009) observed lower cortisol in women with highly depressive symptoms after they participated in Oportunidades; and Baird et al. (2013) found that cash transfers in Malawi reduced psychological stress, which accounted for a sizable portion of the overall program impact on schooling and consumption.[14] While this nascent field has not yet traced this psychological link as part of the causal pathway from transfer programs to evidence on nutritional outcomes, there is an association between depression and stunting (Surkan et al. 2011), and, thus, it is plausible that transfers may prevent malnutrition in economically stressful environments by reducing attendant psychological stress. Interdisciplinary research on depression and health may find this a productive area for investigation.

In-Kind Transfers

Until relatively recently, governments were more likely to support consumption by low-income households through price supports and in-kind transfers than through cash assistance. Despite the well-known economic arguments favoring income transfers as less distortive of preferences than price subsidies or in-kind assistance, price supports were favored in many circumstances due to logistical advantages. Moreover, food assistance was advocated, in part, due to a distrust of markets as well as an explicit goal of shifting consumption patterns (Pinstrup-Andersen 1988). Political concerns and the availability of food aid (itself, a dimension of the political concerns) also contributed to the predominance of in-kind support programs. As mentioned in the introduction, however, cash transfers have recently taken center stage. Where, if at all, might there be exceptions to the advantages of cash support?

One domain in which in-kind assistance still predominates is disaster relief, particularly in response to sudden-onset emergencies such as earthquakes and hurricanes, because these emergencies often disrupt normal market channels. Such situations may render the logistical advantages of cash transfers less advantageous, although cash vouchers were a component of the post-tsunami response in 2004 (Harvey 2007). Although food aid deliveries overall have declined from 15 million metric tons in 1999 to 5.4 million metric tons in 2009, emergency deliveries remained more or less constant, so that they now comprise more than two-thirds of total food aid (Barrett et al. 2012). Two related trends are apparent: the World Food Programme (WFP) now provides 70 percent of global food aid flow, including assistance purchased locally or regionally. Such purchases have also risen, becoming close to half the total flow.

Disaster relief usually takes the form of general assistance to the family. As indicated in the discussion of Yamano et al. (2005) earlier, emergency support to the household may be sufficient to prevent deterioration of nutritional status in crises. However, the impact may be diluted not only because the food is often shared among all household members, but also because assistance is not designed to meet the dietary needs of the most vulnerable children. Thus, nutritional impacts of emergency deliveries can be enhanced by including lipid-based nutrient supplements (LNS) in the packages of assistance to families; these products have ample shelf life and can be specially formulated for nutritionally at-risk children (Chaparro and Dewey 2010). One recent trial that added LNS to general food distribution in an emergency situation in the Democratic Republic of the Congo (DRC) found improvement in linear growth and hemoglobin but not in wasting (Huybregts et al. 2012). Another trial in Niger with a similar formulation, and also in the context of general household rations, found reduced wasting but no impact on linear growth (Grellety et al. 2012). More crucial, however, may be the reduction in mortality that was observed, combined with the fact that many of the observed deaths were of children who had not exhibited signs of wasting. While many of the current issues in regard to LNS for emergency or other contexts are biological (Dewey and Arimond 2012)—such as the potential stimulation to growth from milk powders—other topics highlighted in these recent studies have to do with program administration and targeting procedures, themes that closely overlap with economics.

One advantage of in-kind programs is that the items distributed retain their real value in the face of price fluctuations and inflation. To be sure, cash transfers can be adjusted administratively, as Brazil did in 2008. However, doing so depends on an executive decision—one that is politically awkward to reverse if food prices retreat. In contrast, in-kind transfers are intrinsically protected from devaluation. Sabates-Wheeler and Devereux (2010) documented the extensive temporal and spatial differences in the value of cash and in-kind public work wages in Ethiopia between 2006 and 2008, a period of extensive food price volatility. Although the authors did not track these differences to their impact on nutrition, they did show that participants, who received wages wholly or partially as food, subsequently reduced their food deficits more than those who received wages in cash, despite an increase in nominal cash wages in 2008.

An infusion of cash into a remote community may also put pressure on local food prices. In a randomized trial in Mexico, Cunha et al. (2011) found that cash transfers led to higher prices locally and thus, a purchasing power loss for program participants amounting to 11 percent relative to those who received an in-kind transfer of similar value. It is not clear, however, how generalizable these results are because the study was conducted in remote villages. Indeed, their inaccessibility was the main reason these communities were not included in PROGRESA. Moreover, the commodities offered were largely processed food items and, perhaps, less competitively marketed in these communities than basic grains.[15] Other randomized trials such as that of Aker et al. (2011) have not found cash transfers to inflate food prices. More generally, the impact of an infusion of cash on local prices is expected to be modest where markets function well. Similarly, whether food aid depresses producer prices depends critically on the degree of market integration.

Cunha (2014) noted that the in-kind distribution program in Mexico was largely inframarginal. The commodities received in-kind substituted for others that would otherwise have been purchased. Nevertheless, the in-kind distribution increased micronutrient consumption—likely a general result in any program in which a fortified commodity is provided if the alternative foods obtained from the market are not similarly enriched. Cunha (2014), however, also noted that these foods cost substantially more to distribute than cash transfers, and questioned whether the benefits in terms of micronutrient intake justified these costs.

A series of randomized experiments designed to assist the World Food Programme in understanding modalities of assistance sheds further light on the relative impacts of cash and in-kind programs and also verifies that cash transfers can be substantially less expensive to administer than food assistance. For example, Hidrobo et al. (2014) compared cash, vouchers, and in-kind food assistance in Ecuador. Each program arm delivered the equivalent of US$40 in assistance per household monthly, with all participants also receiving nutrition education. As expected, each program increased food expenditures relative to the control group, with no statistical difference among the arms. Food transfers, however, had a larger impact on calorie consumption than did cash, and the voucher program had a larger impact on dietary diversity than either of the other treatments.[16] On the other hand, a related trial in Niger, comparing cash and food, found that the latter increased dietary diversity more than did cash, possibly because cash was used for large seasonal purchases of grain (Hoddinott et al. 2013). While the experiment in Niger included pulses and oil as well as grain, a similar program in Yemen (Schwab 2013) provided only flour and oil, and found that the cash arm of the trial led to greater dietary diversity, while the in-kind program increased calorie consumption more than the cash assistance did.

A similar experiment (though not part of the World Food Programme set of trials) compared cash and vouchers in the Democratic Republic of the Congo (Aker 2013). While there were differences in terms of expenditure patterns—for example, the group that received cash saved more of the transfers—there were no differences in dietary diversity or food security between the two groups. This was explained, in part, by the fact that resale was possible for voucher households. However, cash transfers were clearly less costly to deliver and administer.

These four studies tracked changes in consumption but did not document impacts on health or child development. A randomized controlled trial (RCT) in Uganda, however, did compare the provision of cash and food (valued at US$12 over a six-week period) to families with children in preschool programs (Gilligan and Roy 2013). The children aged 3 to 5 years in the group that received cash showed improved performance on a set of measures of cognitive development relative to the control group, while those receiving food did not. This result was attributed to a combination of improved diet quality (mainly meat and dairy) and a substantial increase in attendance at preschool as well as higher payments to the staff of these centers, which likely improved motivation. Despite the short period of observation, the group that received cash also saw a reduction in anemia. This was not observed in the food treatment arm, even though the corn-soy blend that this group received was fortified with 99 percent of iron requirements for young children.

These studies were not designed to assess whether nutrition education enhances the impact of in-kind or cash distributions. In contrast, one of the earliest RCTs exploring the joint impact of food pricing and education on nutrition (Garcia and Pinstrup-Andersen 1987) found that the positive and significant impact of a subsidy of rice and cooking oil on household food expenditures and preschool weight gain in the Philippines was enhanced when nutrition education was also included.[17]

In-kind distribution of food or food subsidies does not always lead to marked improvements in dietary intake. One randomized experiment with subsidized rations in China found no increase in nutrient intakes (Jensen and Miller 2011). In this case, the rations were capped at 750 g of grain per individual and were valued between US$0.02 and US$0.06 a day per person, depending on the random assignment. With typical household consumption in this poor urban population reported as lying between US$0.41 and US$0.82 per day, the ration was worth at most 15 percent of consumption, and generally, far less. Similarly, the subsidy was at most a 30 percent reduction of the price of the staple grain. The participants in this particular experiment exhibited a unique reduction in grain consumption with lower prices.

However, even with a more commonly observed increase of consumption with lower prices, the impact of a price subsidy is often modest. This may be because the value of the transfer is small due to the limitations imposed by the ration quotas. Moreover, the price response will be limited when the ration is inframarginal. Additionally, when one considers a full range of cross-price effects, the net increase of nutrients consumed with a subsidy on a single commodity is often less than the change in intake of the subsidized good alone (Pinstrup-Andersen et al. 1976; Pitt 1983; Alderman and del Ninno 1999). Thus, unlike situations in which global or localized shocks lead to broad spikes in a number of food commodities, a subsidy on a single commodity is unlikely to translate into observable changes in nutritional outcomes. Clearly, a full subsidy—that is, free distribution—would have a greater impact, as might a subsidy accompanied by nutrition education.

Conclusion

Many of the world's poor benefit from direct cash transfer programs. These clearly increase overall consumption and welfare. Moreover, the bulk of evidence shows that both conditional and unconditional transfers increase utilization of healthcare service (with mixed results as to the added value of conditions). Nevertheless, meta-analysis shows little impact of such programs on stunting or anemia. This may reflect the fact that many evaluations have covered children outside of the most vulnerable—and most responsive—age brackets. Additionally, since impacts on stunting are cumulative over a period of years, some studies have been too short to assess the full impact of a sustained program. Moreover, to date, the majority of impact evaluations for transfer programs have been in Latin America; these results may not be fully valid for programs in Africa or Asia, where malnutrition rates are higher and where the underlying conditions of malnutrition reflect more extreme poverty. This situation suggests not only obvious research gaps but also a potential for improved nutrition should programs be more finely tuned to focus resources on the population most at risk of malnutrition.

Still, the main challenge for enhanced impact of transfer programs that are formally or informally linked to healthcare services or to nutritional education remains the same as the challenge for improving the quality of health services delivered in other contexts, including issues of worker training and incentives. From the standpoint of the demand for these services, however, the role of cash provision interacts with the time constraints of the caregiver, an issue that is widely acknowledged but, nevertheless, difficult to address. The need to more fully acknowledge these time costs when designing programs is underscored when one considers that programs aimed at improving nutrition are potentially synergistic with programs to improve caregiving for child stimulation (Ruel and Alderman 2013).

As the ability to deliver cash in an accountable manner has improved, the role of in-kind transfers has diminished. Still, there are settings where cash is less effective, because either markets are not functioning adequately or programs are not sufficiently flexible to accommodate major swings in food prices. It is not clear, however, whether reported examples of isolated markets are widely representative, and the food-versus-cash debate remains nuanced; as is often the case, context matters. Moreover, some cash transfer and emergency relief programs have had enhanced nutritional impacts, attributed to the inclusion of child-specific rations, particularly lipid-based supplements. Thus, there remains a research agenda focused on when to include in-kind transfers, which ones, and at what cost. Moreover, if these programs are to address the acute crises that particularly harm young children, they need to be designed to scale up rapidly and, given the need to hold resources available for long-term investments, also to scale back when appropriate.

Appendix: A Caveat in Regard to Obesity

The programs reviewed in this chapter are designed to transfer income to low-income families. They are intended to address both equity and poverty traps, including underinvestment in both health and education. But, in fact, the poor are also at risk of overnutrition, in part, because low birthweight and stunting are associated with increased body mass index (BMI) and chronic illness (Alderman 2012). In fact, in the short term, transfer programs can exacerbate overnutrition while aiming to reduce undernutrition.

For example, Fernald et al. (2008) found that Oportunidades participation led to higher BMIs as well as higher blood pressure measurements, and Forde et al. (2012) found a similar risk for BMI in Colombia's transfer program. Following up on the results of Fernald et al. (2008), Leroy et al. (2013) compared the impact of cash and food distribution on the obesity of women in the same Mexican program studied by Cunha et al. (2011). Both forms of support led to increased weight gain relative to the control group. The point estimate of the transfer was larger for recipients of food relative to those who received cash. The difference, however, was not statistically significant. The study also found that women with higher body mass at the start of the two-year program had the largest increase in weight. Indeed, those with a BMI of less than 25 showed no gain during the study. Thus, while this program has been able to increase dietary diversity, and thereby the consumption of micronutrients (Leroy et al. 2010), there are both gains and risks associated with the intervention. Leroy et al. (2013) also reported that a nutrition education component was included with the food distribution. However, the implementation was flawed, and no impact was noted.

Acknowledgments

The author is indebted to Melissa Hidrobo, Esther Duflo, and Stephen Younger for their comments on earlier drafts. The preparation of this chapter was supported by the CGIAR Research Program on Policies, Institutions, and Markets at the International Food Policy Research Institute (IFPRI).

Notes

1. While largely outside of the theme of this chapter, this recent study also observed that maternal obesity increased by 7 percent for a 10 percent increase in GDP.
2. Labeling may affect education choices as well (Benhassine et al. 2013).
3. This result was not observed for school meals of the same value in this randomized controlled trial.

4. Estimates of the impact of GNP on nutrition are larger in absolute value when infrastructure is allowed to vary, compared with holding it constant (Haddad et al. 2003).
5. That conflict affects health outcomes is not surprising and is regularly reported. See, for one example, Minoiu and Shemyakina (2012). It is not clear, however, that the mechanisms of impact or the policy responses of the transfer programs discussed in this paper are widely applicable to conflict situations.
6. Ferreira and Schady (2009) claimed that this result is so large as to be implausible.
7. This model of poverty traps and differences in intertemporal choices has not, to my knowledge, been applied to leisure or to time allocation for childcare. However, it may offer insights relevant to the work of Bhalotra (2010).
8. Unconditional cash transfers (UCTs) generally also achieve increased food consumption but may have smaller impacts on healthcare. However, despite the strong views in the literature about the relative values of CCTs and UCTs, direct comparisons of CCTs and UCTs are rare and are more likely to be concerned with education. One such comparison found that only CCTs increased visits to preventive health services in Burkina Faso (Akresh et al. 2012). Note that a full policy-relevant comparison of programs should also study costs of delivery, including the resource costs to households of meeting the conditions, including time allocation.
9. Manley et al. (2013) included UCTs in their meta-analysis, so their conclusions are not restricted to CCTs.
10. A range of studies of CCTs from Africa and Asia do show, however, that these programs influence decisions on healthcare as well as schooling.
11. The study was funded by Oportunidades, but the data used for the study were collected under the earlier PROGRESA program.
12. This was tentatively attributed to underreporting, although plausibly, it could reflect the fact that CCTs have a smaller effect on behaviors that influence neonatal mortality than on those associated with subsequent health risks.
13. A cost-effectiveness analysis, in terms of nutritional outcomes, then, might lead to different conclusions than a multidimensional benefit–cost assessment.
14. They also noted an increase in stress among nonparticipants, possibly reflecting increased inequality.
15. Moreover, the value (in local terms) and the frequency of delivery differed between the two program modes.
16. In each arm, the majority of households indicated a preference for the modality in which they were participating.
17. In a different context, Ruel (2001) also argued that increasing the availability of nutritious foods—including through increased home production—has limited impact on nutrition without concurrent nutritional messaging.

References

Aker, Jenny. 2013. "Cash or Vouchers? The Relative Impacts of Cash and Vouchers in the Democratic Republic of Congo." Unpublished, Department of Economics, Tufts University, Medford, MA.

Aker, Jenny, Rachid Boumnijel, Amanda McClelland, and Niall Tierney. 2011. "Zap It to Me: The Short-Term Impacts of a Mobile Cash Transfer Program." Working Paper #268, Center for Global Development, Washington, DC.

Akresh, Richard, Damien De Walque, and Harounan Kazianga. 2012. "Alternative Cash Transfer Delivery Mechanisms: Impacts on Routine Preventative Health Clinic Visits in Burkina Faso." Policy Research Working Paper #5958, World Bank, Washington, DC.

Akresh, Richard, Philip Verwimp, and Tom Bundervoet. 2011. "Civil War, Crop Failure, and Child Stunting in Rwanda." *Economic Development and Cultural Change* 59 (4): pp. 779–810.

Alderman, Harold. 2012. "The Response of Child Nutrition to Changes in Income: Linking Biology with Economics." *CESifo Economic Studies* 58 (2): pp. 256–273.

Alderman, Harold, and Carlo del Ninno. 1999. "Poverty Issues for Zero Rating VAT in South Africa." *Journal of African Economies* 8 (2): pp. 182–208.

Alderman, Harold, John Hoddinott, and William Kinsey. 2006. "Long Term Consequences of Early Childhood Malnutrition." *Oxford Economic Papers* 58 (3): pp. 450–474.

Alderman Harold, and Sebastian Linnemayr. 2009. "Anemia in Low-Income Countries Is Unlikely to Be Addressed by Economic Development without Additional Programs." *Food and Nutrition Bulletin* 30 (3): pp. 265–270.

Alderman, Harold, and Ruslan Yemtsov. 2014. "How Can Safety Nets Contribute to Economic Growth?" *World Bank Economic Review* 28 (1): pp. 1–20.

Amarante, Verónica, Marco Manacorda, Edward Miguel, and Andrea Vigorito. 2012. "Do Cash Transfers Improve Birth Outcomes? Evidence from Matched Vital Statistics, Program and Social Security Data." CEGA Working Papers WPS-004, Center for Effective Global Action, University of California-Berkeley.

Attanasio, Orazio, Erich Battistin, and Alice Mesnard. 2012. "Food and Cash Transfers: Evidence from Colombia." *The Economic Journal* 122 (559): pp. 92–124.

Attanasio, Orazio, and Valerie Lechene. 2002. "Test of Income Pooling in Household Decisions." *Review of Economic Dynamics* 5 (4): pp. 720–748.

Baird, Sarah, Jacobus de Hoop, and Berk Ozler. 2013. "Income Shocks and Adolescent Mental Health." *Journal of Human Resources* 48 (2): pp. 370–403.

Baird, Sarah, Jed Friedman, and Norbert Schady. 2011. "Aggregate Income Shocks and Infant Mortality in the Developing World." *Review of Economics and Statistics* 93 (3): pp. 847–856.

Barber, Sarah, and Paul Gertler. 2010. "Empowering Women: How Mexico's Conditional Cash Transfer Programme Raised Prenatal Care Quality and Birth Weight." *Journal of Development Effectiveness* 2 (1): pp. 51–73.

Barham, Tania. 2011. "A Healthier Start: The Effect of Conditional Cash Transfers on Neonatal and Infant Mortality in Rural Mexico." *Journal of Development Economics* 94 (1): pp. 74–85.

Barrett, Christopher, Andrea Binder, and Julia Steets, eds. 2012. *Uniting on Food Assistance: The Case for Transatlantic Cooperation.* Abingdon and New York: Routledge.

Behrman, Jere, and John Hoddinott. 2005. "Programme Evaluation with Unobserved Heterogeneity and Selective Implementation: The Mexican *PROGRESA* Impact on Child Nutrition." *Oxford Bulletin of Economics and Statistics* 67 (4): pp. 547–569.

Benhassine, Najy, Florencia Devoto, Esther Duflo, Pascaline Dupas, and Victor Pouliquen. 2013. "Turning a Shove into a Nudge? A 'Labeled Cash Transfer' for Education." NBER Working Paper No. 19227, National Bureau of Economic Research, Cambridge, MA.

Bhalotra, Sonia. 2010. "Fatal Fluctuations? Cyclicality in Infant Mortality in India." *Journal of Development Economics* 93 (1): pp. 7–19.

Bobonis, Gustavo. 2009. "Allocation of Resources within the Household Efficient? New Evidence from a Randomized Experiment." *Journal of Political Economy* 117 (3): pp. 453–503.

Breunig, Robert, and Indraneel Dasgupta. 2005. "Do Intra-household Effects Generate the Food Stamp Cash-Out Puzzle?" *American Journal of Agricultural Economics* 87 (3): pp. 552–568.

Carter, Michael, and Travis Lybbert. 2012. "Consumption Versus Asset Smoothing: Testing the Implications of Poverty Trap Theory in Burkina Faso." *Journal of Development Economics* 99 (2): pp. 255–264.

Chaparro, Camila, and Kathryn Dewey. 2010. "Use of Lipid-based Nutrient Supplements (LNS) to Improve the Nutrient Adequacy of General Food Distribution Rations for Vulnerable Sub-groups in Emergency Settings." *Maternal and Child Nutrition* 6 (Supp. s1): pp. 1–69.

Chaudhury, N., J. Friedman, and J. Onishi. 2012. *Philippines Conditional Cash Transfer Program Impact Evaluation 2012*. Washington, DC: World Bank.

Chemin, Matthieu, Joost de Laat, and Johannes Haushofer. 2013. "Negative Rainfall Shocks Increase Levels of the Stress Hormone Cortisol Among Poor Farmers in Kenya." Unpublished, Massachusetts Institute of Technology, Cambridge, MA.

Cruces, Guillermo, Pablo Glüzmann, and Luis Felipe López Calva. 2012. "Economic Crises, Maternal and Infant Mortality, Low Birth Weight and Enrollment Rates: Evidence from Argentina's Downturns." *World Development* 40 (2): pp. 303–314.

Cunha, Jesse. 2014. "Testing Paternalism: Cash Versus In-kind Transfers." *American Economic Journal: Applied Economics* 6 (2): pp. 195–230.

Cunha, Jesse, Giacomo De Giorgi, and Seema Jayachandran. 2011. "The Price Effects of Cash Versus In-Kind Transfers." NBER Working Paper 17456, National Bureau of Economic Research, Cambridge, MA.

Das, Jishnu, Q. Do, and B. Özler. 2005. "Reassessing Conditional Cash Transfer Programs." *World Bank Research Observer* 20 (1): pp. 57–80.

Dewey, Kathryn, and Mary Arimond. 2012. "Lipid-Based Nutrient Supplements: How Can they Combat Malnutrition?" *PLOS Medicine* 9. e1001314.

DFID (UK Department for International Development). 2011. *DFID Cash Transfers Evidence Paper*. London: Policy Division, DFID.

Doss, Cheryl. 2013. "Intrahousehold Bargaining and Resource Allocation in Developing Countries." *World Bank Research Observer* 28 (1): pp. 52–78.

Duflo, E. 2003. "Grandmothers and Granddaughters: Old-Age Pensions and Intra-household Allocation in South Africa." *World Bank Economic Review* 17 (1): pp. 1–25.

Fernald, Lia, Paul Gertler, and Xiaohui Hou. 2008. "Cash Component of Conditional Cash Transfer Program Is Associated with Higher Body Mass Index and Blood Pressure in Adults." *Journal of Nutrition* 138 (11): pp. 2250–2257.

Fernald, Lia. Paul Gertler, and Lynnette Neufeld. 2009. "10-Year Effect of Oportunidades, Mexico's Conditional Cash Transfer Programme, on Child Growth, Cognition, Language, and Behaviour: A Longitudinal Follow-up Study." *The Lancet* 374 (9706): pp. 1997–2005.

Fernald, Lia, and Megan Gunnar. 2009. "Poverty-alleviation Program Participation and Salivary Cortisol in Very Low-income Children." *Social Science and Medicine* 68 (12): pp. 2180–2189.

Fernald, Lia, and Melissa Hidrobo. 2011. "Effect of Ecuador's Cash Transfer Program (*Bono de Desarrollo Humano*) on Child Development in Infants and Toddlers: A Randomized Effectiveness Trial." *Social Science and Medicine* 72 (9): pp. 1437–1446.

Ferreira, Francisco, Anna Fruttero, Phillippe Leite, and Leonardo Lucchetti. 2013. "Rising Food Prices and Household Welfare: Evidence from Brazil in 2008." *Journal of Agricultural Economics* 64 (1): pp. 151–176.

Ferreira, Francisco, and Norbert Schady. 2009. "Aggregate Economic Shocks, Child Schooling, and Child Health." *World Bank Research Observer* 24 (2): pp. 147–181.

Fiszbein, Ariel, and Norbert Schady. 2009. *Conditional Cash Transfers for Attacking Present and Future Poverty*. Washington, DC: The World Bank.

Forde, Ian, Tarani Chandola, Sandra Garcia, Michael Marmot, and Orazio Attanasio. 2012. "The Impact of Cash Transfers to Poor Women in Colombia on BMI and Obesity: Prospective Cohort Study." *International Journal of Obesity* 36 (9): pp. 1209–1214.

Gaarder, Marie, Amanda Glassman, and Jessica Todd. 2010. "Conditional Cash Transfers and Health: Unpacking the Causal Chain." *Journal of Development Effectiveness* 2 (1): pp. 6–50.

Garcia, Marito, and Per Pinstrup-Andersen. 1987. "The Pilot Food Price Subsidy Scheme in the Philippines: Its Impact on Income, Food Consumption and Nutritional Status." Research Report #61, International Food Policy Research Institute, Washington, DC.

Giles, John, and Elan Satriawan. 2015. "Protecting Child Nutritional Status in the Aftermath of a Financial Crisis: Evidence from Indonesia." *Journal of Development Economics* 114 (May): pp. 97–106.

Gilligan, D., and S. Roy. 2013. "Resources, Stimulation, and Cognition: How Transfer Programs and Preschool Shape Cognitive Development in Uganda." Paper presented at annual meeting of Agricultural & Applied Economics Association, Washington, DC, August 4–6.

Gørgens, Tue, Xin Meng, and Rhema Vaithianathan. 2012. "Stunting and Selection Effects of Famine: A Case Study of the Great Chinese Famine." *Journal of Development Economics* 97 (1): pp. 99–111.

Grellety, Emmanuel, Susan Shepherd, Thomas Roederer, Mahamane Manzo, Stephane Doyon, Eric-Alain Ategbo, and Rebecca Grais. 2012. "Effect of Mass Supplementation with Ready-to-Use Supplementary Food during an Anticipated Nutritional Emergency." *PloS one* 7: e44549.

Haddad, Lawrence, Harold Alderman, Simon Appleton, Lina Song, and Yisehac Yohannes. 2003. "Reducing Child Malnutrition: How Far Does Income Growth Take Us?" *World Bank Economic Review* 17 (1): pp. 107–131.

Harvey, Paul. 2007. "Cash-Based Response in Emergencies." Humanitarian Policy Group Report #24, Overseas Development Institute, London.

Hidrobo, Melissa, John Hoddinott, Amber Peterman, Amy Margolies, and Vanessa Moreira. 2014. "Cash, Food, or Vouchers? Evidence from a Randomized Experiment in Northern Ecuador." *Journal of Development Economics* 107 (1): pp. 144–156.

Hoddinott, John. 2006. "Shocks and their Consequences Across and Within Households in Rural Zimbabwe." *Journal of Development Studies* 42 (2): pp. 301–321.

Hoddinott, John, Susanna Sandström, and Joanna Upton. 2013. "The Impact of Cash and Food Transfers: Evidence from a Randomized Intervention in Niger." Paper presented at annual meeting of Agricultural & Applied Economics Association, Washington, DC, August 4–6.

Hoddinott, John, and Emmanuel Skoufias. 2004. "The Impact of PROGRESA on Food Consumption." *Economic Development and Cultural Change* 53 (1): pp. 37–61.

Huybregts, Lieven, Freddy Houngbé, Cecile Salpéteur, Rebecca Brown, Dominique Roberfroid, Miriam Ait-Aissa, and Patrick Kolsteren. 2012. "The Effect of Adding Ready-to-use Supplementary Food to a General Food Distribution on Child Nutritional Status and Morbidity: A Cluster-randomized Controlled Trial." *PLoS Medicine* 9: e1001313.

Jensen, Robert, and Nolan Miller. 2011. "Do Consumer Price Subsidies Really Improve Nutrition?" *Review of Economics and Statistics* 93 (4): pp. 1205–1223.

Kazianga, Harounan, Damien de Walque, and Harold Alderman. 2014. "School Feeding Programs, Intrahousehold Allocation and the Nutrition of Siblings: Evidence from a Randomized Trial in Rural Burkina Faso." *Journal of Development Economics* 106: pp. 15–34.

Kazianga, Harounan, and Christopher Udry. 2006. "Consumption Smoothing? Livestock, Insurance and Drought in Rural Burkina Faso." *Journal of Development Economics* 79 (2): pp. 413–446.

King, Elizabeth, and Jere Behrman. 2009. "Timing and Duration of Exposure in Evaluations of Social Programs." *World Bank Research Observer* 24 (1): pp. 55–82.

Kooreman, Peter. 2000. "The Labeling Effect of a Child Benefit System." *American Economic Review* 90 (3): pp. 571–583.

Leroy, Jef, Paola Gadsden, Teresa González de Cossío, and Paul Gertler. 2013. "Cash and In-kind Transfers Lead to Excess Weight Gain in a Population of Women with a High Prevalence of Overweight in Rural Mexico." *Journal of Nutrition* 143 (3): pp. 378–383.

Leroy, Jef, Paola Gadsden, Sonia Rodríguez-Ramírez, and Teresa González de Cossiío. 2010. "Cash and In-kind Transfers in Poor Rural Communities in Mexico Increase Household Fruit, Vegetable, and Micronutrient Consumption But Also Lead to Excess Energy Consumption." *Journal of Nutrition* 140 (3): pp. 612–617.

Leroy, Jef, Marie Ruel, and Ellen Verhofstadt. 2009. "The Impact of Conditional Cash Transfer Programmes on Child Nutrition: A Review of Evidence Using a Programme Theory Framework." *Journal of Development Effectiveness* 1 (2): pp. 103–129.

Lundberg, Shelly, Robert Pollak, and Terence Wales. 1997. "Husbands and Wives Pool Their Resources? Evidence from the United Kingdom Child Benefit." *Journal of Human Resources* 32 (3): pp. 463–480.

Maccini, Sharon, and Dean Yang. 2009. "Under the Weather: Health, Schooling, and Economic Consequences of Early-Life Rainfall." *American Economic Review* 99 (3): pp. 1006–1026.

Macours, Karen, Norbert Schady, and Renos Vakis. 2012. "Cash Transfers, Behavioral Changes, and Cognitive Development in Early Childhood: Evidence from a Randomized Experiment." *American Economic Journal: Applied Economics* 49 (2): pp. 247–273.

Maluccio, John, and Rafael Flores. 2005. "Impact Evaluation of a Conditional Cash Transfer Program: The Nicaraguan Red de Proteccion Social." Research Report 141. International Food Policy Research Institute, Washington, DC.

Mani, Anandi Sendhil Mullainathan, Eldar Shafir, and Jiaying Zhao. 2013. "Poverty Impedes Cognitive Function." *Science* 34 (6149): pp. 976–980.

Manley, J., S. Gitter, and V. Slavchevska. 2013. "How Effective Are Cash Transfer Programmes at Improving Nutritional Status?" *World Development* 48: pp. 133–155.

MEASURE DHS. 2013. Demographic and Health Surveys. Calverton: ICF International. <http://www.measuredhs.com/>.

Miller, Grant, and Piedad Urdinola. 2010. "Cyclicality, Mortality, and the Value of Time: The Case of Coffee Price Fluctuations and Child Survival in Colombia." *Journal of Political Economy* 118 (1): pp. 113–155.

Minoiu, Camelia, and Olga Shemyakina. 2012. "Child Health and Conflict in Côte d'Ivoire." *American Economic Review* 102 (3): pp. 294–299.

Ngure, Francis, Brie Reid, Jean Humphrey, Mduduzi Mbuya, Gretel Pelto, and Rebecca Stoltzfus. 2014. "Water, Sanitation and Hygiene (WASH), Environmental Enteropathy, Nutrition, and Early Child Development: Making the Links." *Annals of the New York Academy of Sciences* 1308 (Special issue entitled "Every Child's Potential: Integrating Nutrition and Early Childhood Development Interventions"): pp. 118–128.

Onishi, Junko, Eeshani Kandpal, Nazmul Chaudhury, Deon Filmer, and Jed Friedman. 2013. "Evaluating *Pantawid Pamilya* Using Regression Discontinuity Design: Key Results and Lessons." Unpublished, World Bank, Washington, DC.

Paxson, Christina, and Norbert Schady. 2005. "Child Health and Economic Crisis in Peru." *World Bank Economic Review* 19 (2): pp. 203–223.

Pinstrup-Andersen, Per, ed. 1988. *Consumer-Oriented Food Subsidies: Costs, Benefits, and Policy Options for Developing Countries*. Baltimore, MD: Johns Hopkins University Press.

Pinstrup-Andersen, Per, Norha Ruiz de Londoño, and Edward Hoover. 1976. "The Impact of Increasing Food Supply on Human Nutrition: Implications for Commodity Priorities in Agricultural Research and Policy." *American Journal of Agricultural Economics* 58 (2): pp. 133–142.

Pitt, Mark. 1983. "Food Preferences and Nutrition in Rural Bangladesh." *Review of Economics and Statistics* 65 (1): pp. 105–114.

Ramírez-Silva, Ivonne, Juan Rivera, Jef Leroy, and Lynette Neufeld. 2013. "The Oportunidades Program's Fortified Food Supplement, But Not Improvements in the Home Diet, Increased the Intake of Key Micronutrients in Rural Mexican Children Aged 12–59 Months." *Journal of Nutrition* 143 (5): pp. 656–663.

Rasella, Davide, Rosana Aquino, Carlos Santos, Romulo Paes-Sousa, and Maurico Barreto. 2013. "Effect of a Conditional Cash Transfer Programme on Childhood

Mortality: A Nationwide Analysis of Brazilian Municipalities." *The Lancet* 382 (9886): pp. 57–64.

Ruel, Marie. 2001. *Can Food-based Strategies Help Reduce Vitamin A and Iron Deficiencies? A Review of Recent Evidence.* Food Policy Review 5, International Food Policy Research Institute, Washington, DC.

Ruel, Marie, and Harold Alderman. 2013. "Nutrition-Sensitive Interventions and Programs: How Can They Help Accelerate Progress in Improving Maternal and Child Nutrition?" *The Lancet* 382 (9891): pp. 536–551.

Sabates-Wheeler, Rachel, and Stephen Devereux. 2010. "Cash Transfers and High Food Prices: Explaining Outcomes in Ethiopia's Safety Net Programme." *Food Policy* 25 (3): pp. 274–285.

Schwab, Benjamin. 2013. "In the Form of Bread? A Randomized Comparison of Cash and Food Transfers in Yemen." Paper presented at annual meeting of Agricultural & Applied Economics Association, Washington, DC, August 4–6.

Shah, Anuj, Sendhil Mullainathan, and Eldar Shafir. 2012. "Some Consequences of Having Too Little." *Science* 338 (6107): pp. 682–685.

Singh, Abhijeet, Albert Park, and Stefan Dercon. 2014. "School Meals as a Safety Net: An Evaluation of the Midday Meal Scheme in India." *Economic Development and Cultural Change* 62 (2): pp. 275–306.

Spears, Dean. 2013. "How Much International Variation in Child Height Can Sanitation Explain?" Policy Research Working Paper #6351, World Bank, Washington, DC.

Surkan, Pamela, Caitlin Kennedy, Kristen Hurley, and Maureen Black. 2011. "Maternal Depression and Early Childhood Growth in Developing Countries: Systematic Review and Meta-analysis." *Bulletin of the World Health Organization* 89 (8): pp. 608–615.

UNICEF (United Nations Children's Fund). Various Years. *State of the World's Children.* New York: UNICEF.

WHO (World Health Organization). 2013. Global Database on Body Mass Index. <http://www.who.int/bmi/>

World Bank. 2012. *Managing Risk, Promoting Growth: Developing Systems for Social Protection in Africa. The World Bank's Africa Social Protection Strategy 2012–2022.* Washington, DC: World Bank.

Yamano, Takashi, Harold Alderman, and Luc Christiaensen. 2005. "Child Growth, Shocks, and Food Aid in Rural Ethiopia." *American Journal of Agricultural Economics* 87 (2): pp. 273–288.

3

The Micronutrient Deficiencies Challenge in African Food Systems

Christopher B. Barrett and Leah E. M. Bevis

Introduction

Per Pinstrup-Andersen was among the first to call attention to the "triple burden" of malnutrition that transcends insufficient dietary energy supply to encompass problems of overweight/obesity and micronutrient deficiencies as well (Pinstrup-Andersen 2005, 2007). He has also been among the most articulate analysts of the complex linkages between producers, consumers, and marketing intermediaries in food systems in developing countries (Pinstrup-Andersen 2007, 2010; Pinstrup-Andersen and Watson 2011; Gómez et al. 2013). In this chapter, we celebrate Per's insights in both of these dimensions with a review of the oft-overlooked role of micronutrient deficiencies and their relation to nutrition-related poverty traps, with an emphasis on the many entry points within food systems where micronutrients deficiencies might originate and be remedied.

"Hidden hunger" due to micronutrient (mineral and vitamin) deficiencies is widespread. Iron deficiency is one of the most common nutritional disorders worldwide (McDowell 2003). About 1.6 billion people (25 percent of the global population and almost 50 percent of children worldwide) suffer from anemia, of which half is iron-deficiency anemia, while iron deficiency without anemia is equally common (Horton and Ross 2003; WHO 2008). One-third of school age children and a similar share of the global population suffer from insufficient iodine intake and are, therefore, at risk of iodine deficiency disorder (IDD), even though over half of the world's population has access to iodized salt (WHO 2004). Vitamin A deficiency affects up to 21 percent of children under 5 (WHO 2009). Food availability data suggest that at least one-third of the global population suffers from zinc deficiency (Hotz and Brown 2004).

Widespread micronutrient malnutrition is particularly problematic, given the potential irreversibility of its effects. Even short periods of severe micronutrient malnutrition in utero or during early childhood can permanently damage a child's future physical ability, cognitive capacity, and civic and economic productivity. For example, severe iodine deficiency is the most common cause of preventable mental defects worldwide, and even mild iodine deficiency, which also falls under the broad category of IDD, reduces cognitive abilities (Hetzel 1990; Hetzel and Wellby 1997). Severe selenium deficiency in utero is associated with cretinism, and even mild selenium deficiency in pregnant women can have lifelong health impacts for their unborn children through miscarriage, preeclampsia, and pre-term labor (Mistry et al. 2012). Vitamin A deficiency is a leading cause of acquired blindness in children (WHO 2009). Zinc deficiency causes abnormal labor and fetal abnormalities in pregnant women, retards physical growth and cognitive capacity in children, and delays sexual maturity in adolescents (Prasad 2003; Hotz and Brown 2004). Micronutrient deficiencies can thereby lead to permanent impairment, especially among young children who neither understand the consequences of insufficient intake nor have much agency over their diets. And by degrading human capital, such irreversible cognitive and physical impairment may readily lead to poverty traps (Barrett 2010; Barrett and Carter 2013).

The widespread prevalence and stubborn persistence of micronutrient deficiencies is illustrated in Figure 3.1, which depicts the association between global national income (GNI) per capita and the national-scale prevalence of wasting (weight-for-height Z-score < –2), several micronutrient deficiency indicators, and stunting (height-for-age Z-score < –2). This relationship depicted reflects a simple univariate logarithmic regression, using the most current indicators available in reasonably consistent form.[1] Note that the prevalence of wasting, characterized by extremely low weight-for-height and caused primarily by insufficient macronutrient (mainly calorie and protein) consumption, poor sanitation, and early childhood infections, starts relatively low and falls rapidly with growth in a country's GNI. This suggests that people increase macronutrient intake fairly immediately with a rise in income.

By contrast, stunting (characterized by extremely low height-for-age) and indicators of micronutrient deficiency appear much less responsive to growth in GNI. Stunting reflects the cumulative impact of all insults to health, including macro- and micronutrient deprivation, and particularly in early childhood (Thomas et al. 1991; Fogel 2004). The primary clinical indicator for zinc deficiency, for example, is stunting (Hotz and Brown 2004), and iron deficiency is also associated with stunting (Yip 2001).

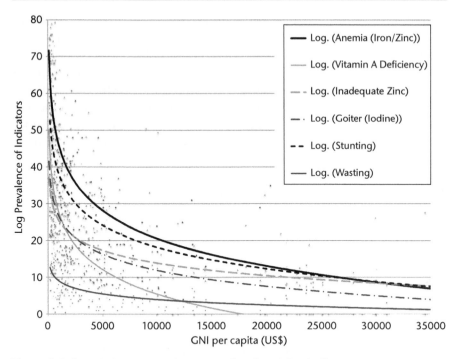

Figure 3.1 Associations among income and malnutrition indicators

Data sources:

GNI data from World Bank (2014).

Anemia, vitamin A, and zinc indicators from United Call to Action (2009).

Goiter data from World Health Organization's *Iodine Status Worldwide 2004* (WHO 2004).

Stunting and wasting data from UNICEF (2013).

With the exception of vitamin A deficiency, which declines at a faster rate than wasting, micronutrient deficiencies and stunting appear much less responsive to growth in GNI per capita than does wasting. The average prevalence of each micronutrient indicator is higher than the average prevalence of wasting at all levels of GNI and remains at unacceptably high levels of 30 percent or more throughout the low-income range and above 10 percent throughout the middle-income range.[2]

Figure 3.1 strongly suggests that while dietary energy intake increases as income rises, leading to reasonably rapid improvements in the undernourishment measure that serves as the United Nations' Food and Agricultural Organization's (FAO's) central indicator of hunger and food insecurity, micronutrient intake does not always increase at the same rate.

This pattern is somewhat counterintuitive, as economists commonly believe that the income elasticity of dietary diversity, the main source of dietary minerals and vitamins, is greater than one, meaning dietary diversity increases faster than income. So why are micronutrient deficiencies so much less responsive to income growth than are the wasting or undernourishment indicators that guide most popular and high-level policy and popular discussions of hunger and food insecurity? There are multiple prospective reasons for the apparent slow response of micronutrient deficiencies to income growth, each related to different, important features of food systems. Knowing where within the food system these problems originate, and why, is essential to targeting and prioritizing among candidate policy and technology interventions. It is therefore important to begin integrating the disparate research findings that exist on the etiology and effective treatment of micronutrient deficiencies into a more holistic food systems perspective. That is the central aim of this chapter.

Is this primarily a downstream problem due to inadequate consumer understanding of micronutrient deficiencies, and dietary transitions associated with income growth and urbanization, as well as consumer response to changing relative prices among food groups? In such circumstances, consumer education and outreach, and perhaps subsidies for micronutrient-rich foods and/or "sin taxes" on unhealthy foods that too often substitute for mineral- or vitamin-dense ones, may be policy instruments of choice.

Or maybe the problem originates mainly—or is most cost-effectively addressed—within the marketing channel that delivers food from farmers to consumers. This would be especially true if supply chain intermediaries fail to preserve micronutrients in perishable or processed products or to fortify foods with minerals and vitamins where feasible and affordable. Addressing micronutrient deficiencies along the value chain may require improved fortification, processing, and storage technologies, along with, potentially, food quality certification.

Alternatively, the problem might originate primarily at the upstream end, either in cropping patterns and practices that limit the mineral and vitamin content of harvested foods, or in micronutrient deficiencies in the soils and water from which edible plants extract essential minerals. In the former case, research and extension, improved marketing arrangements, or other interventions to induce greater production of micronutrient-rich foods may be a policy priority. If the problem is micronutrient deficiencies in the natural resources used to produce food, however, then minerals must be added, either as nutrient amendments in fertilizers or irrigation water, or by advancing new, micronutrient-dense cultivars (biofortified crops) that can be grown in the appropriate setting, or through post-harvest fortification.

Where should policymakers invest in order to accelerate the reduction of micronutrient deficiencies during the process of economic development and income growth? Unfortunately, the scientific community presently lacks compelling, integrated evidence to inform clear prioritization of the limited resources that governments, non-profits, and agri-food firms have to address the widespread micronutrient deficiencies that plague the low- and middle-income world. While we know something about where in the food system micronutrient deficiencies originate, this knowledge is not being integrated, in the sense of being able to assess comparatively sources of micronutrient deficiencies. Nor do we know much about the relative effectiveness of alternative policies or technologies to remedy these problems. Moreover, it seems highly likely that problems exist at multiple points along the food value chain, that the relative balance among them varies sharply among distinct sub-populations, and that policymakers lack guidelines to steer communities through this intrinsic heterogeneity.

In this chapter we examine a few specific reasons why micronutrient deficiencies might not decline quickly with rising GNI per capita. We nest this within a food systems perspective, in an effort to make a small step towards a more holistic approach to diagnosing and treating the serious challenge of micronutrient deficiencies. We focus primarily on African food systems, as this is the world region in which micronutrient deficiencies are most severe.

Consumer Demand Patterns

As incomes grow from a very low level, the elasticity of macronutrient (calorie and protein) intake with respect to income growth appears to decrease rapidly (Deaton 1997). Beyond some rather low level of food expenditure at which energy and protein intake becomes sufficient to transcend the physical discomfort of hunger, consumers' non-nutritional preference for variety, taste, appearance, convenience, and social status of foods—and demand for non-food goods and services—seems to predominate (Strauss and Thomas 1998; Barrett 2002). By contrast, micronutrient malnutrition is often called "hidden hunger" because, unlike the physical sensations of stomach pain or fatigue that commonly signal energy or protein deficiency and trigger food consumption to take in macronutrients, mineral and vitamin deficiencies rarely manifest themselves in obvious sensory ways until the condition becomes severe. Thus, individuals are often unaware that they lack essential minerals and vitamins.

The difference in the sensory feedback loop between macro- and micronutrients could help explain the apparent income elasticity differential between micronutrient deficiencies and more palpable forms of protein-energy malnutrition as an information problem. If true, then educating consumers and cooks, especially mothers who commonly make food choices on behalf of their children, about micronutrients would seem a logical strategy. Indeed, efforts to promote breastfeeding and appropriate complementary feeding practices for young children aim in part to reduce child micronutrient malnutrition (Isabelle and Chan 2011). However, little empirical evidence exists on the linkage between information/education and micronutrient deficiency. Existing studies that do evaluate nutrition education interventions tend to focus on macronutrient rather than micronutrient intake, to be located within the developed rather than developing world, and to evaluate interventions using potentially biased, self-reported outcomes rather than objective, measured outcomes such as biomarkers (Abood et al. 2004; Kroeze et al. 2011; Poelman et al. 2013). Until more research is done, the linkage between nutrition knowledge and micronutrient deficiency will remain a largely untested hypothesis.

Information gaps are just one of the candidate explanations at the downstream, consumer end of the food system. Across the developing world, rising GNI is associated with a "nutritional transition" as consumer diets naturally evolve with increasing disposable income. This transition differs across regions, but is generally characterized by a diversification away from traditional staples of coarse grains, legumes, and roots and tubers, and accompanied by increasing consumption of finer grains like rice and wheat, of animal-source foods, of temperate fruit and vegetables, and of "Western" processed foods high in sugars and fats (Regmi 2001; Pingali 2006).[3] This dietary transition can either accelerate or decelerate micronutrient intake. We review a few potential impacts next.

Rising income is almost always accompanied by greater consumption of animal-source foods (Regmi and Dyck 2001). Not only does this decrease wasting in places where children suffer from hunger and protein deficiency, it should also increase intake of iron, zinc, selenium, vitamin B12, and other micronutrients commonly found in animal-source foods. Zinc, for instance, is primarily found in animal-source foods, particularly in meat and shellfish but to a lesser extent in eggs and dairy products (Dibley 2001; Hotz and Brown 2004).[4] While the majority of iron intake comes in the form of plants and dairy products, the bioavailability of iron found in animal flesh is much higher. Additionally, consuming even small amounts of meat along with other foods increases the iron absorption from the non-meat foods by a factor of around four (Yip 2001). Selenium is most bioavailable in cereals, but is also found in high—though slightly less bioavailable—levels in meat, poultry, and milk (Mistry 2012). Animal organs, such as kidney or liver, hold particularly high levels of selenium. Vitamin B12 is found almost solely in animal-source foods, including milk, honey, and eggs, though an animal's ability to synthesize B12 is dependent on sufficient cobalt in their feed, and thus in soils (Graham et al. 2007).

The nutritional transition is also characterized by a shift in staple foods. Often this includes reduced consumption of coarse grains, such as millet and sorghum, and of roots and tubers, and increased consumption of wheat flour, particularly in the form of breads, and polished rice (Regmi 2001; Pingali 2006; Dapi et al. 2007). There is, of course, considerable variation in such patterns. For example, estimates of the income elasticity of demand for cassava are routinely very low, sometimes negative, in contrast to relatively robust income elasticity of demand for potato in most developing countries and to highly variable elasticity estimates for sweet potatoes and yams (Scott et al. 2000).

One reason the shift in staple foods matters is that the mineral and vitamin content differs considerably among staple foods. Table 3.1 compares selected micronutrient and vitamin levels in a number of unprocessed grains and roots and tubers commonly eaten in Africa. The common roots and tubers typically contain less minerals, but considerably more of certain essential vitamins, than do grains. And among the cereals there are important differences in, for example, iron, zinc, or beta-carotene content. The nutritional transition, therefore, often implies some reduction in micronutrient density of staple foods, which may or may not be compensated for by an increase in the volume of staples consumed or increased consumption of non-staple foods as dietary diversity increases.

Like the rest of the developing world, Africa is urbanizing rapidly. Urban residents typically face especially high opportunity costs to their time, as they increasingly work away from home and spend extended periods commuting to and from jobs. Multiple studies show that increased opportunity cost of women's time, specifically, increases demand for convenient "food away from home," often from street vendors, and for foods that are faster to prepare (Regmi 2001; Regmi and Dyck 2001; Pingali 2006). For example, Dapi et al. (2007) note that urban youth in Cameroon, and particularly those from poorer families, consume high quantities of fried dough because "it is always around."

Without context-specific information, the relationship between increased reliance on fast food/street food and micronutrient consumption is ambiguous. It seems, however, that a high proportion of street food relies on wheat flour and/or rice, as well as fats, oils, salts, and sugars (Regmi and Dyck 2001; Pingali 2006; Dapi et al. 2007). Thus, if income and urbanization are associated with increased consumption of time-saving street food, this may exacerbate a more general shift towards processed wheat and rice consumption and anti-nutrients, i.e., to foods offering "empty calories" rather than essential minerals and vitamins.

Consumer choice among foods responds to relative prices. Food supply growth has been concentrated disproportionately in cereals for the past half century, resulting in falling relative prices for grains and products made from processed cereals—flours, corn syrup, etc. Ironically, then, crop productivity growth, a primary mechanism for achieving success in reducing

Table 3.1. Vitamin and mineral quantities found in 100 g of West African raw food items

Foods (all raw)	Iron (mg)	Zinc (mg)	Vit C (mg)	RAE*/ Vit A (mcg)	B-carotene equiv/Vit A (mcg)	Thiamin/Vit B1 (mg)	Riboflavin/Vit B2 (mg)	Niacin/Vit B3 (mg)	Vit B6 (mg)
Daily EAR for adult males	6	8.5–9.4	75	625	NA	1	1.1	12	1.1
Daily EAR for adults females	8.1	7.3–6.8	60	500	NA	0.9	0.9	11	1.1
Maize flour: whole-grain, yellow	3	1.73	0	28	366	0.44	0.13	1.9	0.3
Maize flour: whole-grain, white	3.8	1.73	0	0	1	0.5	0.12	1.4	0.37
Maize flour: degermed, white	1	0.51	0	0	0	0.13	0.04	0.8	0.08
Wheat grains: whole-grain	4.7	1.7	0	0	3	0.47	0.1	5.6	0.29
Wheat flour: white	2	1.8	0	0	1	0.28	0.1	1.2	0.2
Pearl millet: whole-grain	[7.6]	2.83	0	0	[3]	0.32	0.27	2.4	0.74
Pearl millet: flour without bran	[5.8]	2.91	0	0	[3]	0.18	0.14	1.3	NA
Rice: whole-grain	1.9	2.02	0	0	0	0.38	0.07	5	0.51
Rice: white, polished	0.7	1.1	0	0	0	0.07	0.03	0.4	0.13
Sorghum: whole-grain	3.7	1.79	0	1	[17]	0.36	0.16	3.3	0.25
Sorghum: degermed flour	3.8	2.14	0	0	1	0.18	0.12	1.4	0.25
Cassava tuber	0.7	0.34	30	1	15	0.04	0.05	0.7	0.09
Cocoyam tuber	0.6	0.38	8	NA	NA	0.1	0.03	0.8	0.24
Sweet potato (pale yellow)	1.1	0.39	22.3	3	39	0.09	0.04	0.6	0.27
Irish potato	0.9	0.35	17.3	1	14	0.08	0.12	1.2	0.27

Notes:

Table 3.1, Rows 3–17

Data from the *West Africa Food Composition Table* (FAO 2012).

[] indicates an alternative analytical method or expression, or low-quality data.

NA indicates that no data was available.

* RAE—Retinol activity equivalent, a measure of vitamin A activity based on the capacity of the body to convert provitamin carotenoids into retinol.

The foods in Table 3.1 represent average values of the collected compositional data from nine countries (Benin, Burkina Faso, Gambia, Ghana, Guinea, Mali, Niger, Nigeria, and Senegal). Data sources for rows 3–17 included scientific papers, theses, university reports, as well as food composition databases. These data were supplemented by other sources of food composition data (mostly from outside Africa) to complete the missing values, especially minerals and vitamins. For some vitamins, especially vitamins A and E, data were not available and no sources were found from which to derive reliable data.

Table 3.1 Rows 1–2

Estimated Average Requirement (EAR) is the nutrient intake value that is estimated to meet the requirement defined by a specified indicator of adequacy in 50 percent of a population defined by gender and age. The exact age of reference in the EARs listed above changes according to micronutrient: 19–50 years for iron and zinc, 19–70 years for vitamin C, >18 years for vitamin A, and 18–30 years for all B vitamins.

All EAR data are taken from the latest USDA Dietary Reference Intake reports, which can be found at USDA (2014).

Recommended Daily Allowance (RDA) is often used alongside EAR when discussing adequate levels of micronutrient intake. RDA is defined as the nutrient intake value that will meet the requirement of most (97–98 percent) individuals in a given population. When the standard deviation of EAR (SD) is known, RDA is calculated by allowing RDA = 2*SD + EAR. When the distribution of EAR is unknown, RDA is calculated using RDA = 1.2*EAR.

macronutrient deficiencies manifest in hunger and undernourishment estimates, may have inadvertently attenuated advances against micronutrient deficiencies, by increasing the relative prices of more micronutrient-dense foods and thereby discouraging price-sensitive poor consumers from buying such foods (Pinstrup-Andersen 2005; Gómez et al. 2013).

All of the consumer patterns associated with income growth and urbanization in Africa (and elsewhere in the developing world) point to the prospective role of information and education in efforts to decrease micronutrient deficiency rates. Policy instruments such as commodity-specific subsidies (for micronutrient-dense foods) or taxes (on foods offering few micronutrients) could accelerate micronutrient intake within income growth, relative to what might occur in the absence of policy interventions.

Micronutrients along the Food Value Chain

Another central feature of income growth and the structural transformation of economies is the rise of commercial food market intermediation, as people exit farming for the non-farm economy and migrate from rural areas to cities and towns. In the food market chains (FMCs) in traditional agrarian societies, traders buy primarily from smallholder farmers and sell fresh, recently harvested food in primarily local markets (Gómez and Ricketts 2013). As households decrease autoconsumption of foods produced at home and rely increasingly on store and market purchases, the nature of FMCs changes considerably. "Modern" FMCs rely more heavily on domestic and multinational food manufactures and commercial farmers, and more often sell food through supermarket outlets (Gómez and Ricketts 2013). As a transition from traditional FMCs to modern FMCs occurs, the post-harvest functions of preservation, processing, storage, and transport clearly grow in importance. This makes food market intermediaries a natural focus of attention for understanding the slow response of micronutrient deficiencies to income growth.

There are at least three different ways in which the food value chain affects micronutrient intake. First, perishable foods naturally lose vitamins over time, so the speed with which fresh foods are delivered and the means by which foods are preserved matters fundamentally to their micronutrient content. Second, the technology of processing of grains, tubers, and so on, often shifts with a transition from household-scale to bulk milling, and that change often carries implications for the minerals and vitamins retained in staple foods. Third, unlike individual households, food manufacturers and processors can often cost-effectively add micronutrients through fortification in processing.

69

Urban residents often enjoy higher availability of many processed food items, while suffering lower availability of fresh food items (Regmi 2001; Pingali 2006; Gómez and Ricketts 2013). In many low- and middle-income countries, fruits and vegetables, especially, are either less available to poor urban residents or at least less fresh. This has clear implications for micronutrient intake, as it is well known that the vitamin content of fruit and vegetables declines over time after harvest. For example, the content of vitamin C, one of the most unstable vitamins within food, declines by 20–60 percent in broccoli, carrots, green beans, and peas within one week of storage at an ambient temperature, and by even more in spinach (Favell 1998; Hunter and Fletcher 2002; Rickman et al. 2007). B vitamins, especially thiamin (vitamin B1) and riboflavin (vitamin B2), degrade similarly over time after harvest. Losses are reduced significantly when vegetables are stored at colder temperatures, but cold chains are not readily available in most of Africa.

So the micronutrient content of vegetables and fruits is likely compromised by longer-distance FMCs, with exceptions perhaps for the highest-end supermarket chains that charge better-off consumers higher prices to cover the costs of refrigeration along the supply chain. In Africa, the "garden fresh" vegetables consumed in rural areas are almost certainly optimal when it comes to micronutrient intake, with frozen or refrigerated vegetables the best alternative. On the other hand, "garden fresh" is often only seasonally available in rural areas, as micronutrient-rich foods typically become scarce in lean seasons. Thus, modern FMCs could actually boost micronutrient intake for some urban consumers, if the compromised levels of micronutrients in their food is offset by their year-long food availability thanks to imports (Gómez and Ricketts 2013). The real losers are likely to be the urban poor and working class, who have neither access to seasonally available "garden fresh" food nor constantly available, higher-end food available in supermarkets or particularly efficient markets.

A different form of micronutrient loss occurs due to changes in post-harvest processing technologies as grains, legumes, and tubers shift from home-based artisanal processing to industrial milling (Welch 2001). For example, before the advent of large-scale mechanical milling machines in villages, rice was processed for cooking mainly by pounding or parboiling. Now, rice is most commonly eaten after "polishing," a process which removes the bran, or outer layers, of the rice grain. This bran includes the pericarp, seed coat, testa, and the nutrient-rich aleurone layer; the germ of the grain is often removed along with the bran. Thus, much of the iron, zinc, calcium, vitamins, and some of the protein are lost to polishing (Lauren et al. 2001). Similarly, wheat is usually milled before use. In semi-subsistence rural settings, this is typically done by stone grinding, which retains all components of the wheat, including the aleurone layer and the germ, in the final product (Welch 2001). As with rice, however, modern milling removes both the bran and the germ of the wheat grain, shearing away the vitamins, most of the minerals, and most of the healthy oils carried in wheat grain (Pollan 2013).

Welch and Graham (1999) show that rice and wheat lose 69 and 67 percent of their iron contents to milling, respectively, as well as 39 and 73 percent of their respective zinc contents. Even more dramatic effects were found on the iron and zinc reductions in sorghum and maize due to milling. Table 3.1 similarly compares micronutrient levels of both processed and unprocessed wheat, rice, maize, sorghum, and pearl millet from West Africa. Processed cereals of all types have lower levels of both minerals and vitamins.[5] Insofar as larger-scale, longer-distance market intermediation induces a switch in processing technologies that strips the bran and germ from the milled grain, the mineral content of the food degrades.

Food fortification aimed at increasing micronutrient intake has been widely implemented in the developed world. Oils, sugar, and cereal flours are commonly fortified with vitamin A; iodized salt is now consumed across much of the globe; milk is often fortified with vitamin D; and polished rice, white bread, and other processed staples and cereals are commonly fortified with iron and even zinc. Food fortification is most feasible where there exist large, centralized food processors capable of fortifying, packaging, and labeling the relevant food items. Food fortification is most likely to be effective if implemented among a population of well-educated consumers who are (1) aware of the value of added micronutrients in their food and (2) willing to pay for that value addition (Dary and Mora 2002). Both of these conditions slow the development of commercially viable post-harvest fortification of foods by processors in Africa, although there has been some progress over the past decade or so.

It is also necessary, in any given setting, to consider which food(s), once fortified, will be the most effective vehicle(s) for any given micronutrient with respect to a particular target population (Mora et al. 2000). Utilizing nationwide consumption data for Uganda, for example, Fiedler and Afidra (2010) found that vitamin A fortification of vegetable oil is 4.6 times more cost effective than vitamin A fortification of sugar, but that the Ugandans most at risk of vitamin A deficiency would benefit disproportionately from the introduction of sugar rather than oil fortification.

The effectiveness of food fortification preparation relies on a few issues. To begin with, fortification methods must be appropriate to local food preparation practices. Rice "dusting" for instance, which entails dusting polished rice grains with a powdered form of micronutrient premix, is not appropriate in countries where rice is washed and rinsed before cooking (Alavi et al. 2008). Quality control is also key and requires government monitoring. Such monitoring may be difficult for cash-strapped countries, or for countries where processing occurs at many small facilities rather than a few larger facilities (Alavi et al. 2008).

The Production End of the Food System

The central role of food production to address nutrient deficiencies is well known. The Green Revolution of the 1960s–1980s aimed to reduce malnutrition, understood then as protein and energy deficiencies. It largely succeeded in that task, significantly expanding the per capita supply of both calories and protein (Evenson and Gollin 2003). It failed, however, to similarly expand the per capita supply of minerals and vitamins. Thus, the agricultural technological change associated with the Green Revolution may have inadvertently shifted relative profitability and prices, by decreasing per capita micronutrient supplies and driving up the relative prices of micronutrient-rich foods, thereby discouraging price-sensitive poor consumers from buying such foods (Gómez et al. 2013). Today, as the world has come to appreciate that improving nutrition requires more than just rapidly increasing the global production of calories and protein, attention is slowly shifting away from calorie-dense staple grains toward micronutrient-rich fruits, legumes, vegetables, and animal-source foods.

The upstream, production end of the food system impacts micronutrient intake through at least four distinct pathways. First, the soils and water that farmers use are the primary source of minerals in the plants that humans eat or feed to livestock (Allaway 1986). Thus, if the soil of a region is low in particular minerals, families who rely only on locally produced foods will typically suffer from a deficiency of the locally scarce nutrient.

Iodine exemplifies this rule. It is rare in the earth's crust and found primarily in seawater. Thus, mountainous areas or inland areas, where wind and rain are unable to carry iodine in trace amounts from the sea, are most likely to have iodine-deficient soils (McDowell 2003). These are precisely the areas where iodine deficiency and goiter—the most prevalent clinical manifestation of iodine deficiency—are most widespread. For example, in the High Atlas Mountains of Morocco, far from the ocean with soils severely lacking in iodine, a large majority of households suffer iodine deficiency. The likelihood of such deficiency was explained largely by how much purchased fish a family consumed, since ocean fish imported from the coast was the only source of dietary iodine available in the valley, which did not have iodized salt available (Oldham et al. 1998).

The linkage between soils and plants is particularly strong for certain micronutrients. Zinc, nickel, iodine, and selenium are all nutrients that are clearly transmitted from soils to crops to humans; iron levels in soils, however, do not correlate well with iron levels in plants or humans (Bouis and Welch 2010; Graham et al. 2012). Scientists first realized the importance of soil micronutrients to animal and human health when they noticed that certain animal "diseases" (those associated with micronutrient deficiencies) occurred consistently in particular grazing areas, but disappeared once animals were relocated to a different grazing ground (Allaway 1986). Not all soils that are productive in terms of crop yields (product weight per unit area) produce micronutrient-rich food for man and animals.

Farmers can supplement the natural availability of micronutrients with fertilizers, but there has thus far been relatively little attention paid to micronutrients amid the burgeoning interest in fertilizers in African food systems. This is a pity, as soil has been shown to be a highly effective entry point for reducing micronutrient malnutrition in various areas of the world. For example, iodine deficiency was widespread in Xinjiang, the westernmost province of China, until policymakers decided to try increasing soil iodine levels via irrigation water (Cao et al. 1994). Subsequent results were startling: measurements of soil, crops, livestock, and human urine indicated that added iodine persisted in the soil for more than four years, continuing to elevate levels of iodine in plants, animals, and humans (Ren et al. 2008). What is more, infant mortality declined by 50 percent, with similar rates of decline for neonatal mortality, and children born after treatment had larger heads and taller statures (Delong et al. 1997; Ren et al. 2008). Ren et al. (2008) wrote that soil proved an efficient entry point for iodine into the food system, since this intervention did not require any medical expertise or knowledge on the part of local families, and it improved livestock production as well as human health.

Similarly, certain regions have soils low in selenium, and thus produce both crops and humans with low selenium status. In Finland, for example, selenium added to fertilizers and applied to soils increased the selenium status of the entire Finnish population from below WHO deficiency levels to above them (Mäkelä et al. 1993). In Malawi, Chilimba et al. (2011) measured widespread deficiencies in soil levels of selenium across the country, and calculated that mean dietary intake of selenium was at 40 and 60 percent of recommended values in two particular districts, respectively. Because maize is so heavily consumed in Malawi, it contributed the bulk of all selenium intake for most families. Later field trials showed that applying selenium-enriched fertilizers to maize fields could likely raise the selenium intake of households into the recommended intake levels (Chilimba et al. 2012).

Similar examples can be found for soil-to-human zinc transmission. In rural Bangladesh, Mayer et al. (2007) showed that soil pH, rice variety, and soil zinc status affect the zinc content of rice, and that the zinc content of rice is strongly and statistically significantly associated with zinc levels in human hair. They concluded that zinc-enriched fertilizers, as well as a few other soil management techniques, may significantly improve human zinc status in rural Bangladesh. Similarly, Tidemann-Andersen et al. (2011) found that zinc intake was low in Ugandan populations, primarily due to staples being low in zinc. They suggested that the low zinc content of Ugandan staples, as compared to Kenyan and Malian staples, stems from differences in soil zinc content or soil zinc availability.

The most serious micronutrient deficiencies commonly arise in rural areas of developing countries where families depend heavily on locally grown food crops and have little access to processed foods that are subject to post-harvest mineral or vitamin fortification. In such situations, income growth that leads to increased food consumption might lessen hunger or wasting rates, yet does little to decrease the prevalence of micronutrient deficiencies that stem from the soils. Farmers, and even agriculture ministries and local researchers, rarely know the micronutrient status of soils in rural Africa, however, because soil testing is expensive, and macronutrient analysis to increase crop yields, and thereby farm incomes, typically takes priority. While micronutrient-enriched fertilizers may increase crop yield in highly deficient soils, this is not always the case. For instance, Cakmak (2002) explained that while foliar application of zinc and application of zinc-enriched fertilizer often increased zinc content in grain, there was no direct economic motivation for such application, since grain yield does not increase along with zinc density. Thus, appropriately targeted micronutrient fertilizer regimes, such as those implemented in some high-income countries that have focused specifically on health benefits rather than yield increase, remain largely unknown in Africa.

The second pathway through which production practices affect micronutrient availability and intake arises through crop choice patterns. The Green Revolution prioritized high-yielding cereal varieties—especially, rice and wheat—and encouraged widespread use of fertilizer, irrigation, and other yield-increasing technologies, substantially expanding dietary energy supply. In doing so, however, it also inadvertently decreased the production—and thereby, increased prices and decreased consumption—of micronutrients across much of the developing, resource-poor world (Tontisirin et al. 2002; Graham et al. 2012).

One major trend, the induced shift toward cereal monocropping and away from varied, intercropping or rotation agricultural systems, meant that lower micronutrient crops became more prominent in diets (Welch 2001). In South Asia, the introduction of "modern" rice and wheat production practices resulted in a 200 percent increase in rice production and a 400 percent increase in wheat production over 30 years. Over the same period, however, production of iron-rich legumes decreased; iron density in South Asian diets (mg iron per kcal) declined dramatically; and the percentage of anemic women increased (ACC/SCN 1992; Welch 2001). Similarly, in West Africa, high rates of micronutrient malnutrition are believed to occur in large part because cereals are becoming increasingly important sources of dietary protein, while production of legumes and animal products has been declining, resulting in reduced iron and zinc in the diet (Lopriore and Muehlhoff 2003). Legumes, including beans and pulses, are a richer source of micronutrients than grains, both because most legumes are simply higher in micronutrients than are cereals and because legumes are generally consumed whole, while many cereals are processed in such a way that their micronutrient-rich husks are removed.

The third pathway concerns the use of new and "improved" agronomic practices, which—irrespective of crop choice—may have inadvertently reduced micronutrient availability in harvested crops. Of particular concern, given the current high-level emphasis on promoting inorganic fertilizer use in African agriculture, fertilizer use can increase, decrease, or leave unchanged the micronutrient content of crops (Welch 2001). For example, excessive nitrogen fertilization can adversely affect the accumulation of vitamin C in various horticulture crops such as lettuce, beets, kale, endive, or Brussels sprouts, and also in fruit crops such as oranges, lemons, mandarins, cantaloupes, and apples (Nagy and Wardowski 1988; Salunkhe and Desai 1988; Welch 2001). Harris (1975) wrote that the negative effect of nitrogen on vitamin C accumulation, in fruits at least, could be due to increased acid metabolism.

Similarly, nitrogen fertilization often causes a marked decrease in grain iron content or grain iron uptake (Speirs et al. 1944; Solimon et al. 1992). Panda et al. (2012) found that excessive application of NPK (nitrogen-phosphorus-potassium) fertilizer decreases the iron content of high-yielding tropical rice. Solimon et al. (1992) found that at high levels of sulfur application, application of nitrogen is positively related to corn uptake of manganese, but negatively related to corn uptake of iron and zinc. They discuss a number of other studies that find similar effects with rice, oats, barley, and soybeans. The inverse relationship between manganese and iron/zinc reflects their competition for uptake by plant roots.

Many commercial fertilizers mix phosphorus and/or potassium with nitrogen, and the effect of these additional macronutrients on crop vitamin content appears mixed. Potassium fertilizer usually increases the accumulation of vitamin C in horticulture and fruit (Ijdo 1936; Welch 2001), although phosphorus application to citrus fruits can either increase or decrease vitamin C content (Salunkhe and Deshpande 1988). Application of potassium has sometimes been found to increase beta-carotene content in sweet potatoes (George et al. 2002; Abd El-Baky et al. 2010; Laurie et al. 2012), though not always

(Swanson et al. 1933; Samuels and Landrau 1952), while the effect on horticulture is varied (Fellers et al. 1934; Whittemore 1934; Ijdo 1936). Maynard and Beeson (1943) reviewed a number of studies on the effect of phosphorus application to horticulture and concluded that very little effect could be found of phosphorus fertilizers on crop beta-carotene content. Gao et al. (2011) wrote that potassium chloride fertilization generally decreased zinc in 15 different types of wheat, across a variety of environments. Both grain zinc and grain cadmium were inversely related to grain yield—more grain usually meant less zinc and cadmium per volume. This is not surprising, given that an increase in grain yield is often driven by larger grain size, which comes with a smaller bran to grain interior ratio (R. M. Welch, personal communication[6]). Application of phosphorus fertilizer seems to lower zinc uptake in certain cereals and results in phytate-to-zinc ratios that are less favorable for the bioavailability of zinc to humans (Robson and Pitman 1983; Cakmak 2002). For example, Moraghan (1994) found that applied phosphorus acts as an antagonist to zinc in navy beans, lowering both zinc content and zinc concentration in all areas of the plant.

A longstanding body of agronomic evidence thus suggests that NPK fertilizers are likely to negatively affect the iron, zinc, and vitamin C content of various crops, at least if used in excess. Most interactions between fertilizer application and crop micronutrient levels, however, are context specific. Thus, fertilization has the power to greatly increase micronutrient production if utilized carefully, but also to negatively impact micronutrient production if used without care or without knowledge of these potential interactions.

Fourth, the rise of new crop varieties bred specifically to increase the plant's production of bioavailable micronutrients—a process known as "biofortification"—offers a new mechanism for expanding micronutrient supplies from specific farming systems. Biofortification is designed to target resource-poor, rural, usually agrarian populations in the developing world, who would be unlikely to purchase most fortified foods, even if fortification was feasible in their country (Miller and Welch 2013). So far, biofortified foods have targeted vitamin A, iron, and zinc; and crops developed or under development include sweet potato, maize, cassava, rice, wheat, pearl millet, beans, cowpeas, lentils, sorghum, pumpkin, Irish potato, and banana (Saltzman et al. 2013).

Biofortified foods are primarily meant to be produced and consumed at the household level, rather than purchased (Miller and Welch 2013). In Uganda, for example, HarvestPlus introduced beta-carotene rich Orange-Fleshed Sweet Potatoes (OSP) by distributing 20 kg of free OSP vines to all target households as planting materials, and providing training to farmers' groups on planting techniques (Hotz et al. 2012). As OSP intake increased, the prevalence of inadequate beta-carotene intake fell, and the vitamin A status of children seemed to improve. It is possible, however, that some of the increase in OSP intake was due to families purchasing OSP locally from their neighbors, rather than producing it themselves.

This question of marketability will always be important in gauging the potential impact of biofortified foods. Rates of adoption and disadoption are also clearly important, as is the rate of product failure, or the "breeding out" of increased micronutrient content.[7] Visibly identifiable characteristics of biofortified foods may be useful in differentiating them from similar, non-biofortified foods, though characteristics viewed as undesirable might reduce marketability. Introducing iron-rich beans to Uganda may prove more challenging than introducing OSP, given that no visible marker differentiates their seeds for planting or their pods for sale (Anna-Marie Ball, personal communication[8]). Crop yields are also clearly important; farmers are unlikely to adopt a biofortified cultivar if its yields are lower than those more typically found at market (Saltzman et al. 2013).

Some of these production-level concerns regard variation in micronutrient levels across crops, such as the iron density of grains as compared to legumes. Others regard variation in micronutrient levels within a particular crop but across different settings (high nutrient soil vs. low nutrient soil), or across various cultivars (traditional crops vs. biofortified crops). It may be hard to know a priori which type of variation is most important in any given setting. For some communities food diversification, or the introduction of new foods, may be the only way to significantly increase micronutrient intake. For others, increasing the micronutrient density of one particular food through biofortification, or a particular set of foods via nutrient-enriched fertilizers, may be equally effective and more feasible.

Added Complexity due to Cross-Complementarities

Micronutrient status suffers (or benefits) from cross-complementarities between nutrients; deficiency in one micronutrient may inhibit absorption of another nutrient or worsen the effects of another deficiency. Selenium deficiency, for example, exacerbates the harmful effects of iodine deficiency on the thyroid (Arthur et al. 1999). In a longitudinal study carried out by Zimmermann et al. (2000) in Côte d'Ivoire, selenium deficiency decreased the thyroid response to iodine supplementation in goitrous patients. In the Democratic Republic of the Congo (DRC) where both iodine and selenium deficiencies are common, a combination of these deficiencies exacerbates hypothyroidism and may manifest itself as myxoedematous cretinism (Vanderpas et al. 1990). Myxoedematous cretinism is one of three forms of cretinism—the other two are called neurological cretinism and Keshan's disease. Foster (1995) wrote that although neurological cretinism is clearly associated with iodine deficiency, and Keshan's disease is clearly caused by selenium deficiency, it seems likely that myxoedematous cretinism stems from a deficiency in both micronutrients.

Similarly, Graham et al. (2012) argued that much of the current iron deficiency in the world may be due to underlying zinc deficiency. Iron status depends both on iron consumption and on iron uptake—how much iron a human body absorbs from consumed foods that contain iron. Graham et al. (2012) explained that iron absorption is partially regulated by a molecule called hepcidin. For example, injections of hepcidin decreased iron absorption both in iron-deficient and iron-adequate mice populations (Laftah et al. 2004). Hepcidin synthesis is induced by infection and inflammation, and zinc deficiency aggregates oxidative stress in cells, causing systematic intestinal inflammation. Thus, it is possible that zinc deficiency contributes to reduced iron absorption by inducing hepcidin synthesis.

Graham et al. (2012) also supported their argument geographically. Much of the world's iron-deficient populations live on the acidic soils of the wet Asian and African tropics, where iron deficiency in crops is rare but soils are often zinc deficient. Should this connection between iron deficiency and zinc deficiency prove true, zinc deficiency would be all the more crucial a public health issue, given that 1.6 billion people are anemic across the globe (WHO 2008). The hypothesis is still new, however, and more research is necessary to uncover whether zinc deficiency truly plays a role in driving iron deficiency.

Zinc deficiency has potential implications not only for iron status, but for vitamin A status also. The metabolism of vitamin A depends on zinc-containing enzymes (Welch 1997). Zinc-deficient populations cannot utilize vitamin A efficiently, and may therefore become vitamin A deficient. Giving such populations vitamin A supplements, however, without first treating the underlying zinc deficiency, will have little effect (Shrimpton 1993). Similar interrelationships have been shown for iron, because the metabolic activation of provitamin A carotinoids depends on an iron-containing enzyme (National Research Council 1989).

Micronutrient malnutrition that stems from multiple, interacting mineral and/or vitamin deficiencies will clearly be harder to treat than forms of malnutrition that merely require more food, more protein, or more of one particular micronutrient. Such complementarities in micronutrients lead to diseases like myxoedematous cretinism, which stems from both iodine and selenium deficiency. In areas where this disease is prevalent, iodine prophylaxis alone will not prevent widespread depression of IQ (Foster 1995), nor will selenium supplementation alone. Rather, both underlying deficiencies must be addressed to reduce these severe manifestations of micronutrient malnutrition. Recent research supports the hypothesis that many micronutrient deficiencies are at least nominally impacted by the status of multiple micronutrients. If true, micronutrient malnutrition is inherently more difficult to treat than more classic forms of protein-energy malnutrition that result in wasting or stunting. Not only are more inputs required in order to reduce deficiency levels, but more "expert" knowledge is necessary in order to choose the appropriate inputs.

Conclusions

Can we begin to draw any conclusions as to why micronutrient deficiencies stubbornly persist in the face of income growth? By analyzing the challenge throughout the food system, it quickly becomes apparent that at each level—the upstream producer end, the downstream consumer end, and the market intermediation in the middle—there exist factors that both ameliorate and aggravate micronutrient deficiencies in diets. Because severe micronutrient deficiencies are associated with a range of irreversible cognitive and physical effects that can cause chronic conditions of ill health and poverty, the returns are high to improving our understanding of how and where to intervene in food systems in order to address persistent micronutrient deficiencies.

At the upstream end of the food system, soil deficiencies seem a very real problem, which points both to the prospect of fertilizers (and irrigation) and post-harvest fortification as paths to augment supply, as at least 90 percent of the food consumed in Africa is grown on the continent. Current debates about fertilizer policy are strikingly silent on the topic of fertilizers' micronutrient content, however. Biofortified foods hold promise for increasing certain micronutrient levels, but it remains to be seen how rates of adoption and disadoption, as well as marketability of adopted foods, shape their impact on human health. Increased attention to these micronutrient issues in agricultural technology development is, however, a promising improvement on the Green Revolution era.

Farm-level solutions, however, may be less cost-effective for an increasingly urban population. Improvements in market intermediation hold considerable promise, especially refrigeration and improved storage to preserve perishable foods' mineral and vitamin content, as well cost-effective fortification of nutrients that are difficult to get into foods through fertilizers or biofortified crop varieties. The tremendous success of salt iodization in sharply reducing cretinism, as well as milder forms of IDD, offers encouragement that low-cost interventions can remedy dietary nutrient shortfalls that stem fundamentally from minerals lacking in native soils.

But with the continent urbanizing rapidly and enjoying much faster economic growth than before, managing consumers' nutritional transition is equally important. Consumer education and simple policy instruments for nudging consumers toward healthy food choices (e.g., using subsidies or taxes to change relative prices, school meal menus) offer possible solutions, albeit inconclusively tested in Africa.

The lack of any integrated assessment of alternative intervention options to combat mineral and vitamin deficiencies is one of the main stumbling blocks to mounting a serious effort to accelerate the reduction of micronutrient deficiencies as incomes grow in Africa and other low-income regions. The research and donor communities must come together to begin a more systematic assessment of (1) where micronutrient deficiencies are severe and widespread; (2) the root sources of those deficiencies for distinct subpopulations—especially those most vulnerable to falling into nutritional poverty traps: pregnant and lactating women, infants, and young children; (3) the comparative cost-effectiveness of alternative approaches to remedy those deficiencies; and (4) appropriate targeting rules for interventions to assist priority subpopulations. This sort of systematic, integrative, cost-effective solutions-oriented approach to addressing the micronutrient deficiency challenges of African food systems would fit with and honor the laudable policy-oriented research tradition of Per Pinstrup-Andersen.

Acknowledgments

The authors thank Joanna Barrett for excellent research assistance and Anne-Marie Ball, Miguel Gómez, Dennis Miller, Per Pinstrup-Andersen, and Ross Welch for helpful conversations that have helped shape this chapter, as well as David Sahn and two anonymous reviewers for helpful comments on an earlier draft. All remaining errors are solely our responsibility.

Notes

1. For each indicator, log prevalence is regressed on log GNI via ordinary least squares, and then predicted log prevalence is graphed over GNI. GNI data are either for 2000 or 2009, as appropriate to the time period of the indicator.
2. The World Bank currently classifies countries as low income if annual GNI per capita is $1,035 or less, and middle income if annual GNI per capita is $1,036–$12,615.
3. Relatedly, the nutrition transition is also associated with an epidemiological transition characterized by decreasing levels of infectious diseases and a rise in chronic (non-communicable) diseases (Delisle et al. 2011). The four primary types of non-communicable diseases are cardiovascular diseases (like heart attacks and stroke), cancers, chronic respiratory diseases (such as chronic obstructive pulmonary disease and asthma), and diabetes.

4. Zinc content is also fairly high in nuts, seeds, legumes, and whole-grain cereals.

5. While Table 3.1 displays only the minerals iron and zinc, the FAO food composition table from which these data are drawn contains many other minerals: copper, manganese, calcium, etc. Processing reduces levels of the other minerals, just as it reduces iron and zinc content.

6. Until his retirement, Ross Welch worked as a plant pathologist and the Lead Scientist at the US Department of Agriculture's Agriculture Research Service (USDA-ARS), the Robert W. Holley Research Center for Agriculture and Health, located on the Cornell University campus. He was also a Professor of Plant Nutrition within the Department of Crop and Soil Sciences at Cornell University. Dr. Welch was one of the first scientists in the United States to study human-to-soil micronutrient transmission, beginning work on the topic in the 1960s. He is still one of the leading experts on the phenomenon today.

7. Biofortified foods are theoretically designed to be stable across many generations, unlike hybrid seeds that must be purchased afresh each season in order to maintain desired qualities.

8. Anne-Marie Ball is the country manager for HarvestPlus in Uganda. She joined HarvestPlus in 2006 to lead the Reaching End Users Orange Sweet Potato Project, which introduced biofortified sweet potatoes to farmers across Uganda between 2006 and 2009.

References

Abd El-Baky, H. M. M., A. A. Ahmed, M. A. El-Nemr, and M. F. Zaki. 2010. "Effect of Potassium Fertilizer and Foliar Zinc Application on Yield and Quality of Sweet Potato." *Research Journal of Agriculture and Biological Sciences* 6 (4): pp. 386–394.

Abood, Doris A, David R. Black, and Rachel D. Birnbaum. 2004. "Nutrition Education Intervention for College Female Athletes." *Journal of Nutrition Education and Behavior* 36 (3): pp. 135–139.

ACC/SCN. 1992. 2nd Report on the World Nutrition Situation—Volume 1: Global and Regional Results. Administrative Committee on Coordination/Subcommittee on Nutrition, United Nations, Geneva.

Alavi, Sajid, Betty Bugusu, Gail Cramer, Omar Dary, Tung-Ching Lee, Luann Martin, Jennifer McEntire, and Eric Wailes. 2008. *Rice Fortification in Developing Countries: A Critical Review of the Technical and Economic Feasibility.* A2Z Project, Academy for Educational Development, Washington, DC.

Allaway, W. H. 1986. "Soil-Plant-Animal and Human Interrelationships in Trace Element Nutrition." In *Trace Elements in Human and Animal Nutrition*, edited by W. Mertz, 5th edition, pp. 465–488. Orlando, San Diego, New York, Austin, London, Montreal, Sydney, Tokyo, Toronto: Academic Press, Inc.

Arthur, J. R., G. J. Beckett, and J. H. Mitchell. 1999. "The Interactions between Selenium and Iodine Deficiencies in Man and Animals." *Nutrition Research Reviews* 12 (1): pp. 55–73.

Barrett, Christopher B. 2002. "Food Security and Food Assistance Programs." In *Handbook of Agricultural Economics*, Vol. 2, Part B, edited by B. L. Gardner and G. C. Rausser, pp. 2103–2190. Amsterdam: Elsevier.

Barrett, Christopher B. 2010. "Food Systems and the Escape from Poverty and Hunger Traps in Sub-Saharan Africa." In *The African Food System and Its Interaction with Human Health and Nutrition*, edited by P. Pinstrup-Andersen, pp. 242–260. Ithaca, NY: Cornell University Press.

Barrett, Christopher B., and Michael Carter. 2013. "The Economics of Poverty Traps and Persistent Poverty: Policy and Empirical Implications." *Journal of Development Studies* 49 (7): pp. 976–990.

Bouis, H. E., and R. M. Welch. 2010. "Biofortification—A Sustainable Agricultural Strategy for Reducing Micronutrient Malnutrition in the Global South." *Crop Science* 50 (Suppl. 1): S20–S32.

Cakmak, I. 2002. "Plant Nutrition Research: Priorities to Meet Human Needs for Food in Sustainable Ways." *Plant Soil* 247: pp. 3–24.

Cao, X. Y., X. M. Jiang, A. Kareem, Z. H. Dou, M. R. Rakeman, M. L. Zhang, T. Ma, K. O'Donnell, N. DeLong, and G. R. DeLong. 1994. "Iodination of Irrigation Water as a Method of Supplying Iodine to a Severely Iodine-deficient Population in Xinjiang, China." *Lancet* 344 (8915): pp. 107–110.

Chilimba, A. D. C., S. D. Young, C. R. Black, K. B. Rogerson, E. L. Ander, M. Watts, J. Lammel, and M. R. Broadley. 2011. "Maize Grain and Soil Surveys Reveal Suboptimal Dietary Selenium Intake Is Widespread in Malawi." *Scientific Reports* 1 (72). doi: 10.1038/srep00072.

Chilimba, Allan D. C., Scott D. Young, Colin R. Black, Mark C. Meacham, Joachim Lammel, and Martin R. Broadley. 2012. "Agronomic Biofortification of Maize with Selenium (Se) in Malawi." *Field Crops Research* 125: pp. 118–128.

Dapi, Leonie N., Cecile Omoloko, Urban Janlert, Lars Dahlgren, and Lena Haglin. 2007. "'I Eat to Be Happy, to Be Strong, and to Live.' Perceptions of Rural and Urban Adolescents in Cameroon, Africa." *Journal of Nutrition Education and Behavior* 39 (6): pp. 320–329.

Dary, Omar, and Jose O. Mora. 2002. "Food Fortification to Reduce Vitamin A Deficiency: International Vitamin A Consultative Group Recommendations." *Journal of Nutrition* 132 (9 Suppl.): 2927S–2933S.

Deaton, Angus. 1997. *The Analysis of Household Surveys: A Microeconometric Approach to Development Policy*. Washington, DC: The World Bank.

Delisle, H., V. Agueh, and B. Fayomi. 2011. "Partnership Research on Nutrition Transition and Chronic Diseases in West Africa—Trends, Outcomes and Impacts." *BMC International Health and Human Rights* 11 (Suppl 2): S10.

Delong, G. Robert, Paul W. Leslie, Shou-Hua Wang, Xin-Min Jiang, Ming-Li Zhang, Murdon Abdul Rakeman, Ji-Yong Jiang, Tai Ma, and Xue-Yi Cao. 1997. "Effect on Infant Mortality of Iodination of Irrigation Water in a Severely Iodine-deficient Area of China." *Lancet* 350 (9080): pp. 771–773.

Dibley, Michael J. 2001. "Zinc." In *Present Knowledge in Nutrition*, 8th ed., edited by Barbara A. Bowman and Robert M. Russel, pp. 329–343. Washington, DC: International Life Sciences Institute, Nutrition Foundation.

Evenson, R. E., and D. Gollin, eds. 2003. *Crop Variety Improvement and its Effect on Productivity.* Wallingford: CABI International.

FAO. 2012. *West African Food Composition Table.* Rome: Food and Agricultural Organization of the United Nations. <http://www.fao.org/docrep/015/i2698b/i2698b00.pdf>.

Favell, D. J. 1998. "A Comparison of the Vitamin C content of Fresh and Frozen Vegetables." *Food Chemistry* 62 (1): pp. 59–64.

Fellers, C. R., R. E. Young, P. D. Isham, and J. A. Clague. 1934. "Effect of Fertilization, Freezing, Cooking, and Canning on the Vitamin C and A Content of Asparagus." *Proceedings of the American Society for Horticultural Science* 31: pp. 145–151.

Fiedler, John L., and Ronald Afidra. 2010. "Vitamin A Fortification in Uganda: Comparing the Feasibility, Coverage, Costs, and Cost-effectiveness of Fortifying Vegetable Oil and Sugar" *Food and Nutrition Bulletin* 31 (2): pp. 193–205.

Fogel, Robert. 2004. "Health, Nutrition, and Economic Growth." *Economic Development and Cultural Change* 52 (3): pp. 643–658.

Foster, H. D. 1995. "Cretinism: The Iodine-Selenium Connection." *Journal of Orthomolecular Medicine* 10 (3&4): 139–144.

Gao, Xiaopeng, Ramona M. Mohr, Debra L. McLauren, and Cynthia A. Grant. 2011. "Grain Cadmium and Zinc Concentrations in Wheat as Affected by Genotypic Variation and Potassium Chloride Fertilization." *Field Crops Research* 122 (2): pp. 95–103.

George, M. S., G. Lu, and W. Zhou. 2002. "Genotypic Variation for Potassium Uptake and Utilization Efficiency in Sweet Potatoes." *Field Crops Research* 77 (1): pp. 7–15.

Gómez, Miguel I., and Katie D. Ricketts. 2013. "Food Value Chain Transformations in Developing Countries: Selected Hypotheses on Nutritional Implications." *Food Policy* 42: pp. 139–150.

Gómez, Miguel I., Christopher B. Barrett, Terri Raney, Per Pinstrup-Andersen, Janice Meerman, André Croppenstedt, Brian Carisma, and Brian Thompson. 2013. "Post-Green Revolution Food Systems and the Triple Burden of Malnutrition." *Food Policy* 42 (1): pp. 129–138.

Graham, R. D., R. M. Welch, D. A. Saunders, I. Ortiz-Monasterio, H. E. Bouis, M. Bonierbale, S. de Haan, G. Burgos, G. Thiele, R. Liria, C. A. Meisner, S. E. Beebe, M. J. Potts, M. Kadian, P. R. Hobbs, R. K. Gupta, and S. Twomlow. 2007. "Nutritious Subsistence Food Systems." *Advances in Agronomy* 92: pp. 1–74.

Graham, Robin D., Marija Knez, and Ross M. Welch. 2012. "How Much Nutritional Iron Deficiency in Humans Globally Is Due to an Underlying Zinc Deficiency?" *Advances in Agronomy* 115: pp. 1–40.

Harris, R. S. 1975. "Effects of Agricultural Practices on the Composition of Foods." In *Nutritional Evaluation of Food Processing*, 2nd ed., edited by R. S. Harris and E. Karmas, pp. 34–57. Westport, CT: Avi Publishing Company, Inc.

Hetzel, B. S. 1990. "Iodine Deficiency: An International Public Health Problem." In *Present Knowledge in Nutrition*, edited by M. L. Brown, pp. 308–313. Washington, DC: International Life Sciences Institute, Nutrition Foundation.

Hetzel, B. S., and M. L. Wellby. 1997. "Iodine." In *Handbook of Nutritionally Essential Mineral Elements*, edited by B. L. O'Dell and R. A. Sunde, pp. 557–582. New York: Marcel Dekker, Inc.

Horton, S., and J. Ross. 2003. "The Economics of Iron Deficiency." *Food Policy* 28 (1): pp. 51–75.

Hotz, C., and K. H. Brown, eds. 2004. International Zinc Nutrition Consultative Group (IZiNCG) Technical Document #1—Assessment of the Risk of Zinc Deficiency in Populations and Options for its Control. *Food and Nutrition Bulletin* 25 (Suppl. 2) (March): pp. S91–S203.

Hotz, C., C. Loechl, A. de Brauw, P. Eozenou, D. Gilligan, M. Moursi, B. Munhaua, P. van Jaarsveld, A. Carriquiry, and J. V. Meenakshi. 2012. "A Large-scale Intervention to Introduce Orange Sweet Potato in Rural Mozambique Increases Vitamin A Intakes among Children and Women." *British Journal of Nutrition* 108 (1): pp. 163–176.

Hunter, Karl J., and John M. Fletcher. 2002. "The Antioxidant Activity and Composition of Fresh, Frozen, Jarred and Canned Vegetables." *Innovative Food Science and Emerging Technologies* 3 (4): pp. 399–406.

Ijdo, J. B. H. 1936. "The Influence of Fertilizers on the Carotene and Vitamin C Content of Plants." *Biochemical Journal* 30 (12): pp. 2307–2312.

Isabelle, Mia, and Pauline Chan. 2011. "Seminar on Young Child Nutrition: Improving Nutrition and Health Status of Young Children in Indonesia." *Asia Pacific Journal of Clinical Nutrition* 20 (1): pp. 141–147.

Kroeze, Willemieke, Pieter C. Dagnelie, Martijn W. Heymans, Ake Oenema, and Johannes Brug. 2011. "Biomarker Evaluation Does Not Confirm Efficacy of Computer-tailored Nutrition Education." *Journal of Nutrition Education and Behavior* 43 (5): pp. 323–330.

Laftah, Abas H., B. Ramesh, R. J. Simpson, N. Solanky. S. Bahram, K. Schümann, E. S. Debnam, and S. K. Srai. 2004. "Effect of Hepcidin on Intestinal Iron Absorption in Mice." *Blood* 103 (10): pp. 3940–3944.

Lauren, J. G., R. Shrestha, M. A. Sattar, and R. L. Yadav. 2001. "Legumes and Diversification of the Rice-Wheat Cropping System." In *The Rice-Wheat Cropping System of South Asia: Trends, Constraints, Productivity and Policy*, edited by P. K. Kataki, pp. 67–102. New York: Food Products Press.

Laurie, S. M., M. Faber, P. J. van Jaarsveld, R. N. Laurie, C. P. Plooy, and P. C. Modisane. 2012. "β-Carotene Yield and Productivity of Orange-Fleshed Sweet Potato (*Ipomoea batatas* L. Lam.) as Influenced by Irrigation and Fertilizer Application Treatments." *Scientia Horticulturae* 142: pp. 180–184.

Lopriore, Cristina, and Ellen Muehlhoff. 2003. "Food Security and Nutrition Trends in West Africa—Challenges and the Way Forward." Conference Paper—2nd International Workshop on Food-based Approaches for a Healthy Nutrition, Ouagadougou, Burkina-Faso.

Mäkelä, A.-L., V. Näntö, P. Mäkelä, and W. Wang. 1993. "The Effect of Nationwide Selenium Enrichment of Fertilizers on Selenium Status of Healthy Finnish Medical Students Living in South Western Finland." *Biological Trace Element Research* 36 (2): pp. 151–157.

Mayer, Anne-Marie, Michael Latham, John Duxbury, Nazmul Hassan, and Edward Frongillo. 2007. "A Food-Based Approach to Improving Zinc Nutrition through Increasing the Zinc Content of Rice in Bangladesh." *Journal of Hunger and Environmental Nutrition* 2 (1): pp. 19–39.

Maynard, L. S., and K. C. Beeson. 1943. "Some Causes of Variation in the Vitamin Content of Plants Grown for Foods." *Nutrition Abstracts and Reviews* 13: pp. 155–164.

McDowell, L. R., ed. 2003. *Minerals in Animals and Human Nutrition*, 2nd ed. Amsterdam: Elsevier Science B.V.

Miller, Dennis D., and Ross M. Welch. 2013. "Food System Strategies for Preventing Micronutrient Malnutrition." *Food Policy* 42: pp. 115–128.

Mistry, Hiten D., Fiona Broughton Pipkin, Christopher W. G. Redman, and Lucilla Posten. 2012. "Selenium in Reproductive Health." *American Journal of Obstetrics & Gynecology* 206 (1): pp. 21–30.

Mora, J. O., O. Dary, D. Chinchilla, and G. Arroyave. 2000. "Vitamin A Sugar Fortification in Central America: Experience and Lessons Learned." MOST/US Agency for International Development, Arlington, VA.

Moraghan, J. T. 1994. "Accumulation of Zinc, Phosphorus, and Magnesium by Navy Bean Seed." *Journal of Plant Nutrition* 17 (7): pp. 1111–1125.

Nagy S., and W. F. Wardowski. 1988. "Effects of Agricultural Practices, Handling, Processing, and Storage on Vegetables." In *Nutritional Evaluation of Food Processing*, 3rd edition, edited by E. Karmas, and R. S. Harris, pp. 73–100. New York: Avi Book, Van Nostrand Reinhold Co.

National Research Council. 1989. *Recommended Dietary Allowances*. National Academy Press, Washington, DC.

Oldham, Elizabeth, Christopher B. Barrett, Sabah Benjelloun, Brahim Ahanou, and Pamela J. Riley. 1998. "An Analysis of Iodine Deficiency Disorder and Eradication Strategies in the High Atlas Mountains of Morocco." *Ecology of Food and Nutrition* 37 (3): pp. 197–217.

Panda, Binyay Bhusan, Srigopal Sharma, Pravat Kumar Mohapatra, and Avijit Das. 2012. "Application of Excess Nitrogen, Phosphorus and Potassium Fertilizers Leads to Lowering of Grain and Iron Content in High-Yielding Tropical Rice." *Communications in Soil Science and Plant Analysis* 43: pp. 2590–2602.

Pingali, Prabhu. 2006. "Westernization of Asian Diets and the Transformation of Food Systems: Implications for Research and Policy." *Food Policy* 32 (3): pp. 281–298.

Pinstrup-Andersen, Per, ed. 2010. *The African Food System and Its Interaction with Human Health and Nutrition*. Ithaca, NY: Cornell University Press.

Pinstrup-Andersen, Per. 2005. "Agricultural Research and Policy to Achieve Nutrition Goals." In *Poverty, Inequality and Development: Essays in Honor of Erik Thorbecke*, edited by Alain de Janvry and Ravi Kanbur, pp. 353–370. Amsterdam: Kluwer.

Pinstrup-Andersen, Per. 2007. "Agricultural Research and Policy for Better Health and Nutrition in Developing Countries: A Food Systems Approach." *Agricultural Economics* 37 (Suppl. 1): pp. 187–198.

Pinstrup-Andersen, Per, and Derrill D, Watson II. 2011. *Food Policy for Developing Countries: The Role of Government in Global, National, and Local Food Systems*. Cornell University Press, NY.

Poelman, Maartje P., Ingrid H. M. Steenhuis, Emely de Vet, and Jacob C. Seidell. 2013. "The Development and Evaluation of an Internet-Based Intervention to Increase Awareness about Food Portion Sizes: A Randomized, Controlled Trial." *Journal of Nutrition Education and Behavior* 45 (6): pp. 701–707.

Pollan, Michael. 2013. *Cooked: A Natural History of Transformation.* New York: The Penguin Press.

Prasad, Ananda. 2003. "Zinc Deficiency Has Been Known of for 40 Years but Ignored by Global Health Organisations." *British Medical Journal* 326 (7386): pp. 409–410.

Regmi, Anita. 2001. "Changing Structure of Global Food Consumption and Trade: An Introduction." In *Changing Structure of Global Food Consumption and Trade*, edited by Anita Regmi, pp. 23–30. Washington, DC: Market and Trade Economics Division, Economic Research Service, US Department of Agriculture, Agriculture and Trade Report. WRS-01-01.

Regmi, Anita, and John Dyck. 2001. "Effects of Urbanization on Global Food Demand," In *Changing Structure of Global Food Consumption and Trade*, edited by Anita Regmi, pp. 1–3. Washington, DC: Market and Trade Economics Division, Economic Research Service, US Department of Agriculture, Agriculture and Trade Report. WRS-01-01.

Ren, Q., F. Fan, Z. Zhang, X. Zheng, and G. R. DeLong. 2008. "An Environmental Approach to Correcting Iodine Deficiency: Supplementing Iodine in Soil by Iodination of Irrigation Water in Remote Areas." *Journal of Trace Elements in Medicine and Biology* 22 (1): pp. 1–8.

Rickman, Joy C., Diane M. Barrett, and Christine M. Bruhn. 2007. "Nutritional Comparison of Fresh, Frozen and Canned Fruits and Vegetables. Part 1. Vitamins C and B and Phenolic Compounds." *Journal of the Science of Food and Agriculture* 87 (6): pp. 930–944.

Robson, A. D., and M. G. Pitman. 1983. "Interactions between Nutrients in Higher Plants." In *Encyclopedia of Plant Physiology*, New Series, Vol. 15 A. edited by A. Lauchli, and R. L. Bieleski, pp. 147–180. Berlin and New York: Springer-Verlag.

Saltzman, A., E. Birol, H. E. Bouis, E. Boy, F. F. De Moura, Y. Islam, and W. H. Pfeiffer. 2013. "Biofortification: Progress towards a More Nourishing Future." *Global Food Security* 2 (1): pp. 9–17.

Salunkhe, D. K. and B. B. Desai. 1988. "Effects of Agricultural Practices, Handling, Processing, and Storage on Vegetables," In *Nutritional Evaluation of Food Processing, Edition,* Vol. 3, edited by E. Karmas, and R. S. Harris, pp. 23–71. New York: Avi Book, Van Nostrand Reinhold Co.

Samuels, George, and Pablo Landrau, Jr. 1952. "The Influence of Fertilizers on the Carotene Content of Sweet Potatoes." *Agronomy* 44 (7): pp. 348–352.

Scott, G. S., M. W. Rosegrant, and C. Ringler. 2000. "Roots and Tubers for the 21st Century: Trends, Projections, and Policy for Developing Countries." Food, Agriculture, and Environment Discussion Paper No. 31, International Food Policy Research Institute (IFPRI), Washington, DC.

Shrimpton, R. 1993. "Zinc Deficiency—Is It Widespread but Under-Recognized?" *SCN News* 9: pp. 24–27.

Solimon, M. F., S. F. Kostandi, and M. L. van Beusichem. 1992. "Influence of Sulfur and Nitrogen Fertilizer on the Uptake of Iron, Manganese and Zinc by Corn Plants Grown in Calcareous Soil." *Communication in Soil Science and Plant Analysis* 23 (11–12): pp. 1289–1300.

Speirs, M., W. S. Anderson, M. Gieger, L. McWhirter, O. A. Sheets, R. Reder, J. B. Edmond, E. J. Lease, J. H. Mitchell, G. S. Fraps, J. Whitacre, S. H. Yarnell, W. B. Eilet, R. C. Moore,

H. H. Zimmerley, L. Ascham, and H. L. Cochran. 1944. "Effect of Fertilizer and Environment on the Iron Content of Turnip Greens." *Southern Cooperative Series Bulletin* No. 2, Southern Association of Agricultural Experiment Station Directors.

Strauss, J., and D. Thomas. 1998. "Health, Nutrition, and Economic Development." *Journal of Economic Literature* 36 (2): pp. 766–817.

Swanson, P. A., P. M. Nelson, and E. S. Haber. 1933. "Vitamin A Content of Sweet Potatoes of the Prolific Variety Grown with Varying Known Fertilizer Treatments." Report on Agricultural Research, Iowa Agricultural Experiment Station, p. 119.

Thomas, Duncan, John Strauss, and Maria-Helena Henriques. 1991. "How Does Mother's Education Affect Child Height?" *Journal of Human Resources* 26 (2): pp. 183–211.

Tidemann-Andersen, Ida, Hedwig Acham, Amund Maag, and Marian K. Malde. 2011. "Iron and Zinc Content of Selected Foods in the Diet of Schoolchildren in Kumi District, East of Uganda: A Cross-Sectional Study." *Nutrition Journal* 10: pp. 81–92.

Tontisirin, K., G. Nantel, and L. Bhattacharjee. 2002. "Food-based Strategies to Meet the Challenges of Micronutrient Malnutrition in the Developing World." *Proceedings of the Nutrition Society* 61, pp. 243–250.

UNICEF (United Nations Children's Fund). 2013. Statistics and Monitoring. <http://www.unicef.org/statistics/index_step1.php>.

United Call to Action. 2009. *Investing in the Future: A United Call to Action on Vitamin and Mineral Deficiencies.* Data and Statistics. Annex A: Selected Micronutrient Indicators by Country. Micronutrient Initiative, Ottawa. <http://www.unitedcalltoaction.org/documents/Investing_in_the_future_AnnexA.pdf>.

USDA. 2014. United States Department of Agriculture. National Agricultural Library. Dietary Guidance. Dietary Reference Intakes. <http://fnic.nal.usda.gov/dietary-guidance/dietary-reference-intakes/dri-reports>.

Vanderpas J. B., B. Contempré, N. L. Duale, W. Goossens, N. Bebe, R. Thorpe, K. Ntambue, J. Dumont, C. H. Thilly, and A. T. Diplock. 1990. "Iodine and Selenium Deficiency Associated with Cretinism in Northern Zaire." *American Journal of Clinical Nutrition* 52 (6): pp. 1087–1093.

Welch, R. M. 1997. "Agronomic Problems Related to Provitamin A Carotenoid-Rich Plants." *European Journal of Clinical Nutrition* 51 (Suppl. 4): pp. S34–S38.

Welch, R. M. 2001. "Micronutrients, Agriculture and Nutrition; Linkages for Improved Health and Well Being." In *Perspectives on the Micronutrient Nutrition of Crops*, edited by K. Singh, S. Mori, and R. M. Welch, pp. 247–289. Jodhpur: Scientific Publishers.

Welch, R. M., and Robin D. Graham. 1999. "A New Paradigm for World Agriculture: Meeting Human Needs Productive, Sustainable, Nutritious." *Field Crop Research* 60 (1–2): pp. 1–10.

Whittemore, M. 1934. "The Influence of Fertilizer Treatment on the Vitamin A Content of Spinach." *Rhode Island Agricultural Experiment Station Bulletin* 29: pp. 94–97.

WHO. 2004. *Iodine Status Worldwide, WHO Global Database on Iodine Deficiency.* Edited by Bruno de Benoist, Maria Andersson, Ines Egli, Bahi Takkouche, and Henrietta Allen. Geneva: World Health Organization. <http://whqlibdoc.who.int/publications/2004/9241592001.pdf>.

WHO. 2008. *Worldwide Prevalence of Anaemia 1993–2005, WHO Global Database on Anaemia*. Edited by Bruno de Benoist, Erin McLean, Ines Egli, and Mary Cogswell. Geneva: World Health Organization.

WHO. 2009. *Global Prevalence of Vitamin A Deficiency in Populations at Risk 1995–2005, WHO Global Database on Vitamin A Deficiency*. Geneva: World Health Organization.

World Bank. 2014. Data: GDP per capita (current US$). <http://data.worldbank.org/indicator/NY.GDP.PCAP.CD?page=2>.

Yip, Ray. 2001. "Iron." In *Present Knowledge in Nutrition*, 8th ed., edited by Barbara A. Bowman, and Robert M. Russel, pp. 329–328. Washington, DC: International Life Sciences Institute, Nutrition Foundation.

Zimmermann, M. B., P. Adou, T. Torresani, C. Zeder, and R. F. Hurrell. 2000. "Effect of Oral Iodized Oil on Thyroid Size and Thyroid Hormone Metabolism in Children with Concurrent Selenium and Iodine Deficiency." *European Journal of Clinical Nutrition* 54 (3): pp. 209–213.

4

The Internationalization of the Obesity Epidemic

The Case of Sugar-Sweetened Sodas

Malden C. Nesheim and Marion Nestle

Introduction

The prevalence of overweight and obesity in the US population increased markedly from the late 1970s to the early 2000s. Whereas surveys in 1976–80 found 15 percent of the adult population to be obese on the basis of body mass index (BMI), they identified 31 percent as obese in 1999–2000.[1] The most recent figures from 2009–10 suggest that 36 percent of the adult population, men and women, meet BMI criteria for obesity, and another third is overweight (Fryar et al. 2012). During these same years, the prevalence of obesity tripled among children, such that 17 percent of children and adolescents are now classified as obese (Ogden et al. 2012). Overall, national surveys find about two-thirds of the US population to be overweight or obese.

The United States is not alone in experiencing a rising prevalence of obesity. The most recent data from the Food and Agriculture Organization (FAO) reveal overweight and obesity to be a global problem, rising from a combined prevalence of 25 percent in 1980 to 34 percent in 2008 (Stevens et al. 2012). Nearly all countries have experienced this rise in prevalence, even those in which undernutrition and micronutrient deficiencies—and their consequent stunting and wasting—remain common. In parts of Europe, the Middle East, and Latin America, more than 60 percent of adults over the age of 15 are classified as overweight or obese. In Mexico, for example, the proportion of the population considered obese now exceeds that of the United States (FAO 2013).

Concerns about obesity would not be so serious if this condition were only a matter of appearance (Bray 2004). Obesity, however, raises risks for a number of diseases and conditions, such as coronary heart disease, Type 2 diabetes, high blood pressure, stroke, certain cancers, liver and gallbladder disease, osteoarthritis, sleep apnea and other respiratory problems, and various gynecological disorders, particularly abnormal menses and infertility. Obesity and its consequences affect quality of life and can lead to disability and premature mortality. In addition to the personal costs for individuals, the societal costs for medical care and lost productivity are estimated at upwards of $150 billion dollars annually in the United States alone (Finkelstein 2009).

Although obesity results from habitual consumption of more calories than are expended, and thus is a matter of personal action, many factors in society influence dietary choices. Obesity is closely linked to economic development and the replacement of traditional food systems with Westernized diets that provide more meat, fats, and refined carbohydrates and, therefore, more calories. This obesity-promoting shift in dietary patterns occurs so commonly in emerging economies that it has been given its own designation, the "nutrition transition" (Popkin et al. 2012).

The societal changes that promote dietary transitions are well identified in the United States. From the early 1900s to about 1980, the US food supply provided an average of 3,200 calories per day per capita. From 1980 to 2000, per capita calorie availability had increased to 3,900 calories per day (USDA 2014). Even when adjusted for wastage, per capita calories per day increased by 400 from 1980 to 2010. Calorie availability represents food produced in the United States, plus exports less imports, and is likely to overestimate average calorie intake. In contrast, surveys of reported food consumption tend to underestimate actual intake. Even so, they report increases of 200 to 300 calories per day for both men and women since the early 1980s (Kant and Graubard 2006).

Increases in calorie availability and intake are the result of an "eat more" food environment, spurred by aggressive food-industry marketing. Beginning in the early 1980s, food availability became ubiquitous. Food and drinks are now available in retail stores selling clothing, office supplies, and books—places where they had never been sold before. Spending on foods away from home increased from about one-third of total food expenditures to about one-half, and the proportion of calories obtained away from home increased from less than 20 percent to more than 30 percent, much of it in the form of fast food. The changes have been especially dramatic for children, who now get more of their calories from fast-food outlets than they do from schools (Nestle and Nesheim 2012). United States Department of Agriculture (USDA) nutritionists have estimated that the average meal eaten away from home by an adult adds 134 calories to daily intake, and that one meal a week eaten at a restaurant can account for an annual weight gain of 2 pounds (Mancino et al. 2009).

Since the 1980s, the portion sizes of food and beverages offered to consumers by restaurants, fast-food outlets, and major food companies have increased substantially in an effort to attract customers. Larger portions contain more calories and contribute more calories to the diet. They are also cheaper on a per-calorie basis. During this period, the relative prices of fruits and vegetables increased by about 40 percent, whereas the relative prices of desserts, snack foods, and sodas have declined by 20 to 30 percent. To expand sales, food companies have developed new products aimed at convenience, but these new offerings are often high in salt, sugar, fat, and calories. These foods are designed to be consumed as snacks, readily available at relatively low cost. Together, these market-driven changes have fueled an increase in overall calorie intake and the rise in obesity in large segments of the US population (Nestle and Nesheim 2012).

Internationally, the growth of obesity as a public health problem in low-income countries follows a similar pattern. Diets everywhere are becoming sweeter and more energy dense. As economies improve, portion sizes increase, and eating away from home and snacking become more frequent. In many countries, consumption of edible oils and animal products increases (Popkin 2006). The World Health Organization (WHO) reports that non-communicable diseases—especially cardiovascular disease, diabetes, cancer, and chronic respiratory diseases—are likely to be responsible for as many deaths as those caused by infectious, maternal, perinatal, and nutritional diseases by 2020. WHO scientists suggest that behavioral risk factors such as smoking, inactivity, and diet are responsible for as much as 80 percent of worldwide deaths from cardiovascular disease. The global rise in obesity is also accompanied by a rise in the prevalence of Type 2 diabetes, creating a further burden on healthcare systems (WHO 2011). Designing public health interventions to counter such trends presents great challenges.

The Role of Sugar-Sweetened Beverages

Sugar-sweetened beverages (SSBs) constitute an excellent case study for understanding the difficulties of devising public health policies to decelerate or reverse the rise in worldwide obesity. Increasing evidence suggests that consumption of SSBs (or sodas) contributes significantly to development of overweight and obesity, particularly among children and adolescents. Also, some evidence suggests that physiological controls of food energy do not function well when calories from sugars are consumed in liquid rather than solid form (CSPI 2009).

Since the early 2000s, studies of trends in SSB intake among schoolchildren have shown that the addition of even one soda to the daily diet of a child increases the likelihood of the child becoming overweight (Ludwig et al. 2001). Similarly, reducing soda consumption decreases the prevalence of overweight (James et al. 2004). Although not all studies have reported such results (see Newby et al. [2004]), most have identified at least a small correlation between consuming sodas and higher calorie intakes and body weights among children (Striegel-Moore et al. 2006). Furthermore, clinical trials of soda reduction have demonstrated lower rates of weight gain in young children (de Ruyter et al. 2012). One clinical trial of adolescents also reported reduced weight gain (Ebbeling et al. 2006), although that benefit disappeared after the second year (Ebbeling et al. 2012). When such studies are subjected to systematic reviews, the overall results show impressive correlations between soda intake and weight gain in the young (Pérez-Morales et al. 2013). One recent meta-analysis concludes that SSB consumption is associated with weight gain in both children and adults (Vasanti et al. 2013).

Soda Consumption, United States

Sugar-sweetened beverages, unlike candy, are typically consumed in large amounts. Recent reports derived from national surveys in the United States suggest several conclusions (Bleich et al. 2009; Ogden et al. 2011; Han and Powell 2013; Hsiao and Wang 2013):

- Only half the population over the age of 2 years drinks sodas; the other half reports drinking no sodas at all.
- One-quarter of the population consumes at least 16 ounces a day.
- 5 percent of the population consumes 48 ounces a day, or more.
- Men drink nearly twice as many sodas as women, 14 ounces as compared to 8 ounces a day.
- Children of ages 2 to 5 years drink an average of 6 ounces a day.
- Boys of ages 12 to 19 years are the highest consumers of sodas; 70 percent drink sodas on any given day for an average consumption of 22 ounces.
- The elderly consume the fewest sodas (males, 6 ounces per day; females, 4 ounces).
- Blacks and Hispanics report drinking more sodas than other racial and ethnic groups.
- Soda consumption is higher among low-income Americans; the lower the income, the more soda consumed.

- All age groups report drinking less soda than they did in the late 1990s, reflecting replacement of carbonated SSBs with sports drinks, pre-sweetened teas, and diet drinks.

- Sugar consumption from sodas has declined by 15 g a day since the late 1990s, consistent with the decline in SSB consumption (Popkin and Nielsen 2003; Nielsen and Popkin 2004; Welsh et al. 2011; Ervin and Ogden 2013).

- Sodas, along with energy drinks and sweetened waters, are the fourth leading source of calories in the diets of adults and the third leading source for children; they account for one-third of total reported sugar intake (USDA and USDHHS 2010; National Cancer Institute 2014).

So many independently funded studies and reviews associate habitual consumption of SSBs to childhood obesity, and so few do not, that many researchers are confident that the evidence justifies public health efforts to reduce children's soda intake (James and Kerr 2005). In contrast, studies sponsored by Coca-Cola tend to come to conclusions favorable to soda intake (Lesser et al. 2007; Forshee et al. 2008). Such views have led to attempts to eliminate sodas from vending machines in schools, educate the public about reducing soda consumption, restrict portion sizes, and to impose taxes on soft drinks. The soda industry strongly resists such measures, and few have been implemented successfully in the United States.

International Soda Consumption

As consumption of SSBs declines in industrialized countries, soda companies have shifted marketing efforts to international countries. Such markets have long been recognized as growth opportunities. In 1991, for example, Roberto Goizueta, then chief executive of Coca-Cola, explained to a reporter from the *New York Times* why his company was focusing efforts on selling sodas outside the United States: "Willie Sutton used to say he robbed banks because that is where the money is. Well, we are increasingly global because 95 percent of the world's consumers are outside this country. It's that simple" (Cohen 1991). By that year, Coca-Cola's international sales already accounted for 80 percent of its profits. Profit margins, sales growth, and growth potential were much greater in international markets than in the United States, and competition from Pepsi Cola was much weaker. The president of Coca-Cola, Donald Keough, told the *New York Times* reporter: "Our single and relentless focus has been internationalizing this business. ... To do so, we have become the most pragmatic company in the world. ... When I think of Indonesia—a country on the Equator with 180 million people, a median age of 18, and a Moslem ban on alcohol—I feel I know what heaven looks like" (Cohen 1991).

Coca-Cola intended to enter foreign markets from its onset. The company made its first foreign sale in 1899 to a merchant in Cuba. Within the next decade, Coca-Cola began selling syrup in Mexico, Puerto Rico, and the Philippines, and established its first international bottling plant in Cuba in 1906. For the next 20 years, the company added foreign franchises and established foreign subsidiaries to 76 countries by 1930, China among them. By today's standards, however, its foreign presence was quite limited. The limitations were overcome during World War II, when the company pledged to supply a bottle of Coca-Cola for 5 cents to every American in the armed forces anywhere in the world. By the end of the war, it provided 95 percent of the soft drinks served to the US military and was supplying 155 international bottling plants—as compared to just one for Pepsi. After the war, its global investments grew even more rapidly (Giebelhaus 1994).

Today, international sales continue to account for large percentages of soda company profits. Coca-Cola claims sales in more than 200 countries, with 81 percent of revenues coming from outside the United States, especially from Mexico, China, Brazil, and Japan (Coca-Cola Company 2012a). Its leading market is Latin America: Mexico, Chile, Panama, Argentina, and Bolivia are among the ten highest consumers of Coca-Cola drinks (Coca-Cola Company 2012b). In 2013, the United States lifted decades-old trade sanctions imposed against the military junta in Myanmar, thereby leaving just two countries with US trade embargoes that block soda sales: North Korea since 1950, and Cuba since 1962. The Cuba situation is particularly ironic in the light of Coca-Cola's early sales in that country. The company left Cuba when Fidel Castro's government seized private assets, and it is unlikely to return until the Cuban government changes. As one Coca-Cola executive explained, "The moment Coca-Cola starts shipping is the moment you can say there might be real change going on... Coca-Cola is the nearest thing to capitalism in a bottle" (Hebblethwaite 2012).

PepsiCo also says it sells products in more than 200 countries, but international sales account for only 35 percent of profits. To expand market share, PepsiCo, too, is investing in emerging and developing markets. It claims to be the leading food and beverage business in Russia, India, and the Middle East; the second leading business in Mexico; and among the top five in Brazil and Turkey (PepsiCo 2012a).

Both Coca-Cola and PepsiCo especially want to expand sales in the countries listed in Table 4.1 (Mullaney 2013). China and India are obvious targets for soda marketing; their populations exceed 1 billion, and their soda consumptions are extremely low. Both companies have pledged to invest billions of dollars in both countries over the next several years. Although Mexico is currently the top soda consumer, it still has potential for slow but steady sales growth—unless concerns about obesity affect sales. The

Table 4.1. Top 10 emerging markets for beverages, per capita carbonated soda availability, and prevalence of obesity

Rank[a]	Country[a]	% estimated sales growth, 2012–2017[a]	Availability, 8-ounce servings per capita, 2012[b]	% obese 2008[c]
1	China	8	37	6
2	India	5	12	2
3	Russia	4	128	27
4	Brazil	2	358	19
5	Indonesia	4	15	5
6	South Korea	4	114	8
7	Malaysia	3	74	14
8	Mexico	2	617	32
9	South Africa	3	280	31
10	Turkey	2	199	28

Sources:
[a] Mullaney (2013).
[b] Euromonitor International (2013). Note: includes diet and regular carbonated sodas.
[c] Central Intelligence Agency (n.d). The World Factbook.

prevalence of obesity tends to be higher in countries with higher soda consumption. Countries with low soda consumption—most notably China, India, Indonesia, and South Korea—still experience a low prevalence of obesity. The prevalence is expected to rise with an increase in average soda consumption.

Marketing Methods

Although the populations of emerging and developing markets have relatively little money to spend, small increases in soda consumption among enormous numbers of people quickly add up. Soda advertising is ubiquitous in developing countries and has become an expected, but largely unnoticed, part of the environment.

Billboards and advertisements, however, constitute only a minor part of soda companies' marketing strategies. Coca-Cola and PepsiCo both invest substantial thought and effort in identifying ways to sell sodas to people of widely different cultures who may never have consumed such drinks before, and in creating effective business partnerships in each country. Coca-Cola, for example, was an early user of cell phone technology to advertise to young, tech-savvy Japanese customers (Terhune and Kahn 2003). This company especially focuses on the use of music and sports to connect with its multicultural customers. Coca-Cola supports local concerts and sports teams, as well as international sporting events such as the Tour de France, the soccer World

Cup, and the Olympics. It also supports student scholarships and health programs, offers emergency relief in natural disasters, and supports environmental causes.

Coca-Cola is particularly adept in using philanthropy to neutralize potential critics. In 2012, for example, a Reuters investigative team discovered that the Pan American Health Organization (PAHO), the Latin American arm of WHO, had accepted a $50,000 gift from Coca-Cola. One of the company's top officials sits on the steering committee of WHO's Pan American Forum for Action on Non-Communicable Diseases, a group that determines efforts to counter obesity in Latin America (Wilson and Kerlin 2012).

PepsiCo also emphasizes sports as a leading marketing strategy. In 2013, it announced a strategic partnership with the Asian Football Development Project (AFDP) with lofty goals that go well beyond games. AFDP uses football (soccer) as a tool to promote health, social development, and the empowerment of women in 40 countries, but with a focus on the Middle East and India (PepsiCo and AFDP 2013).

The efforts of these companies to reach international markets are stunningly comprehensive. Whenever a potential opening appears, they quickly move in. Both use innovative methods to sell sodas in developing and emerging economies in Asia, the Indian subcontinent, the Middle East, and Africa. In Table 4.2, we give just a few recent examples of soda marketing activities in selected countries—in the form of advertising, philanthropy, sponsorship, and social responsibility. No doubt as a result of such efforts, Coca-Cola scores high in international surveys of public views of corporations. Among 60 admired companies, Coca-Cola ranked second in the Philippines, fourth in India and South Korea, fifth in Thailand, seventh in Myanmar, and eighth in China (Consultant Survey 2013).

The Marketing Challenges: Political

Soda companies engage in such actions not only to promote products, but also to reduce the considerable economic and political risks of selling products in cultures decidedly different from that of the United States. Any company doing business overseas must confront fluctuations in the value of the dollar, political instability, trade restrictions, and cultural misunderstandings (Cohen 1991). In 2013, for example, Coca-Cola conducted a marketing campaign in Israel involving placement of 150 popular first names on its cans. Although about 1.5 million Arabs live in Israel, no Arab names appeared on the cans. The result: Mideast controversy (Bouckley 2013).

Coca-Cola and PepsiCo also must confront, however, a particular source of political opposition: views of sodas as emblems of American cultural and economic domination. Although many people in developing countries hold

Table 4.2. Selected examples of Coca-Cola and PepsiCo international marketing, 2012–13

Country	Marketing event
China	Pepsi CEO opens new bottling plant in Zhengzhou; opens new food and beverage center in Shanghai; donates $1 million earthquake aid to Sichuan. Coca-Cola will invest $4 billion to establish new bottling plants in central and western regions.
India	Pepsi spends $72 million to sponsor cricket tournament. Coca-Cola recruits Bollywood stars to promote "Share Happiness" campaign in films, digital media, merchandise, and on-ground initiatives in 1,000 communities; launches online store for product delivery. Coca-Cola and PepsiCo commit about $5 billion each to market expansion.
Indonesia	Coca-Cola intends to spend $700 million on marketing among other "big plans."
Kenya	Coca-Cola partnership sells solar power to rural kiosks.
Laos	Coca-Cola announces joint venture to open bottling operation by 2014.
Mexico	A former president of Coca-Cola, Vicente Fox, was president of Mexico from 2000–2006. Coke is still involved in Mexican politics.
Myanmar	Coca-Cola discovers its products are seen as expensive and elitist; keeps messages simple ("delicious, refreshing"); distributes free samples; puts price on bottle. Pepsi signs with United Nations Educational, Scientific, and Cultural Organization (UNESCO) to develop vocational training initiatives. Its CEO says, "We believe we can build a strong business in Myanmar and play a positive role in the country's continued development."
Pakistan	Coca-Cola creates "happiness without borders" campaign to share drinks with Indians and reduce political tensions between the two countries.
Philippines	More than 6,000 women attend Coke-sponsored International Women's Day celebration.
Singapore	Coca-Cola pilots "phenomenally successful" cans that split in two for sharing.
Vietnam	Pepsi forms bottling and marketing partnership; considers Vietnam "linchpin" of campaign to expand in emerging markets.

Sources: Current newspapers, magazines, and Internet reports.

images of Coca-Cola or Pepsi as symbols of freedom and the most enviable aspects of American society, others see these companies as cultural and economic intruders intent on exploiting the local population—"Coca-Colonization," as the French called it in the 1950s. In the 1990s, boycotts were organized in Guatemala to protest the company's alleged violence against union organizers, and similar problems in Colombia led to creation of a "Killer Coke" campaign, which still continues (Blanding 2010).

In 2003, demonstrators in Thailand poured Coca-Cola onto the streets in protest against the American invasion of Iraq (Coca-Cola Company 2012a). More recently, the president of Iran threatened to ban Coca-Cola in retaliation for economic sanctions imposed against his country (LaFranchi 2010), and the late president of Venezuela, Hugo Chávez, called on supporters to boycott foreign imports such as Coca-Cola or Pepsi (Associated Press 2012). A boycott campaign in Vietnam accused Coca-Cola of tax evasion and lack of social responsibility to its customers (Iyer 2013).

The Marketing Challenges: Obesity

Obesity may incur costs to individuals and to society, but it also poses a threat to soda companies. Obesity rates are rising in emerging economies in parallel with increasing soda consumption. Concerns about the health consequences of promoting sodas to vulnerable populations in developing countries have led to calls for restrictions on soda marketing, taxes, and bans on sales. As early as 2003, investment analysts were warning food companies that obesity posed a threat to their profits (Streets et al. 2002; Langlois 2006). Soda companies were well aware of this threat. In 2007, a Coca-Cola marketing executive gave an interview to *Advertising Age*, in which she said, "Our Achilles heel is the discussion about obesity... It's gone from a small, manageable U.S. issue to a huge global issue. It dilutes our marketing and works against it. It's a huge, huge issue" (Thompson 2007).

The US Securities and Exchange Commission (SEC) requires corporations to describe factors that pose risks to profits. Coca-Cola lists obesity as the most important threat that might reduce demand for its products. PepsiCo, however, does not list obesity as a risk factor in its SEC filings, although it says obesity "represents a significant challenge to our industry" (PepsiCo 2012b). Coca-Cola explains how the company is countering this threat:

> All of our beverages can be consumed as part of a balanced diet. Consumers who want to reduce the calories they consume from beverages can choose from our continuously expanding portfolio of more than 800 low- and no-calorie beverages, nearly 25 percent of our global portfolio, as well as our regular beverages in smaller portion sizes. We believe in the importance and power of "informed choice," and we continue to support the fact-based nutrition labeling and education initiatives that encourage people to live active, healthy lifestyles. (Cohen 1991)

Anti-Obesity Campaigns

Soda companies have good reason to be concerned about the effects of anti-obesity campaigns. American and international consumer advocacy groups have created global "Dump Soda" campaigns in countries such as India, Japan, Malaysia, and Mexico. The goal of these campaigns is to induce soda companies to:

- stop marketing to children under age 16;
- stop selling sodas in schools;
- stop promoting physical activity or health programs unless they do so without featuring their corporate logos or brands; and
- sell sodas in smaller portions (CSPI and IACFO 2007).

Such campaigns are supported by WHO policy statements. In 2010, WHO recommended that its member nations reduce the marketing of high-sugar foods to children and the exposure of children to such marketing (WHO 2010a). Although these recommendations did not specify soft drinks, an accompanying resolution urged countries to reduce the marketing of non-alcoholic beverages (translation: sodas) to children, and "to cooperate with civil society and with public and private stakeholders in implementing [these recommendations]. . . in order to reduce the impact of that marketing, while ensuring avoidance of potential conflicts of interest" (WHO 2010b).

More recently, the WHO identified key global strategies related to obesity prevention, among them community-based and policy interventions to limit the consumption and marketing of unhealthy beverages to children (WHO 2012). To implement these recommendations, the United Nations Special Rapporteur on the Right to Food, Olivier De Schutter, observed that the most effective way to reduce consumption of high-sugar foods is through regulation: "Impose taxes on soft drinks (sodas)" (De Schutter 2011).

Many governments and non-governmental organizations (NGOs) have responded to WHO recommendations, especially those directed at children. One study identified more than 30 countries with national and or regional policies to restrict the availability of sodas in schools (Hawkes 2008, 2010). A coalition of NGOs, the Sweet Enough Network, has called for bans on all food products in schools, particularly soft drinks (Thai Health Promotion Foundation 2010). In Mexico, 47 organizations called for higher taxes on soft drinks as part of a national "Crusade against Hunger" (Versa 2013). In 2013, despite intense soda industry lobbying, Mexico passed a tax of 1 peso per liter on SSBs—and a tax of 8 percent on snack foods—as part of an effort to reduce obesity trends (Villegas 2013). Tax initiatives may be as much about raising revenue as they are about obesity prevention, but advocates in many countries expect the revenues to be used for health and other social purposes.

In 2013, the WHO surveyed member countries on their anti-obesity initiatives. The survey found most countries to have instituted policies to reduce obesity and diet-related diseases, but only one-third regulated the marketing of sodas to children, and with about half of these countries reporting restrictions on marketing sodas in schools. Despite what seem like major efforts (by American standards), the WHO report lamented that most countries considered obesity to be a problem of personal responsibility rather than a public health matter of governmental concern, as indicated by the most common policies reported: educating individuals through dietary guidelines, food labels, and media campaigns about healthy eating (WHO 2013).

Conclusion

From the standpoint of soda companies, such obesity prevention efforts must be of intense concern. Efforts to reduce soda consumption are having an effect. In India, for example, sales of Pepsi and Coca-Cola are not growing as fast as they once did, a problem attributed to increasing preferences for drinks that seem healthier—fruit drinks, nectars, juices, and energy drinks (Natti 2013). Soda companies are responding by redoubling marketing in target countries and by creating social responsibility campaigns and voluntary "responsible marketing" campaigns, such as the one developed for schools by PepsiCo (PepsiCo [n.d.], "Advertising"). PepsiCo says it will not sell its full-sugar drinks in schools. It pledges "not to engage in product advertising or marketing communications directed to students in primary schools, except if requested by, or agreed with, the school administration for specific educational purposes." But, it says, "this restriction does not apply to signage at the point of sale" (PepsiCo [2014], "Policy on Responsible Advertising to Children"). It is difficult to know what such promises mean in practice, especially in light of Pepsi's other marketing efforts.

In this light, the Global Dump Soft Drinks campaign makes an important point. It calls on soda companies to stop marketing to children in *any* form: print and broadcast advertising, product placement, Internet advertising, cell phone messages, athletic event sponsorship, signage, packaging promotions, merchandising, and other means.

In 2013, the international food policy analyst, Corinna Hawkes, produced a background paper for FAO in which she reviewed international policies for promoting healthier eating and what existing programs reveal about their effectiveness. Advocacy, she finds, is likely to be most effective when it involves multiple components—not only education, but also information and skills for changing the food environment as well as personal behavior. Soda companies do both when they back product reformulations with advertising campaigns. Governments do both when they combine policies on nutrition labels with public information about how to use them, and when they insist that school nutrition standards be accompanied by classroom instruction. Advocacy is more likely to succeed when it backs up policy initiatives with public education (Hawkes 2013).

Acknowledgment

Much of this chapter is drawn from M. Nestle, *Soda Politics: Taking on Big Soda (and Winning)*. New York: Oxford University Press, September, 2015.

References

Associated Press. 2012. "Hugo Chávez Tells Venezuelans to Drink Juice Not Coke." *The Guardian*, July 23, 2012. <http://www.guardian.co.uk/world/2012/jul/23/hugo-chavez-venezuelans-drink-juice>.

Blanding, M. 2010. *The Coke Machine: The Dirty Truth behind the World's Favorite Soft Drink*. New York: Avery.

Bleich, S. N., Y. C. Wang, Y. Wang, and S. L. Gortmaker. 2009. "Increasing Consumption of Sugar-sweetened Beverages among US Adults: 1988–1994 to 1999–2004." *American Journal of Clinical Nutrition* 89 (1): pp. 372–381. doi:10.3945/ajcn.2008.26883.

Bouckley, B. 2013. "Bittersweet Coke Taste in Israel as Personalized Cans Stoke Controversy." Beverage Daily.com newsletter, May 24, 2013. <http://www.beveragedaily.com/Markets/Bittersweet-Coke-taste-in-Israel-as-Personalized-cans-stoke-controversy>.

Bray, G. A. 2004. "Medical Consequences of Obesity." *Journal of Clinical Endocrinology & Metabolism* 89 (6): pp. 2583–2589.

Central Intelligence Agency. n.d. The World Factbook. Country Comparison: Obesity—Adult Prevalence. <https://www.cia.gov/library/publications/the-world-factbook/rankorder/2228rank.html?countryName=China&countryCode=ch&regionCode=eas&rank=152#ch>.

Coca-Cola Company. 2012a. United States Security and Exchange Commission, Washington, DC. Form 10-K, December 31, 2012. <http://assets.coca-colacompany.com/c4/28/d86e73434193975a768f3500ffae/2012-annual-report-on-form-10-k.pdf>.

Coca-Cola Company. 2012b. "Per Capita Consumption of Company Beverage Products, 2012." <http://www.coca-colacompany.com/annual-review/2012/pdf/2012-per-capita-consumption.pdf>.

Cohen R. 1991. "Coke's World View—A Special Report: For Coke, World Is Its Oyster." *New York Times*, November 21, 1991. <http://www.nytimes.com/1991/11/21/business/coke-s-world-view-a-special-report-for-coke-world-is-its-oyster.html>.

"Consultant Survey Finds Coke's Brand Image in Top 10 in 6 Markets." 2013. The Nation, June 14, 2013. <http://www.nationmultimedia.com/business/Consultant-survey-finds-Cokes-brand-image-in-top-1-30208242.html>.

CSPI (Center for Science in the Public Interest). 2009. "In the Drink: When It Comes to Calories, Solid is Better than Liquid." *Nutrition Action Healthletter*, November 2009: pp. 7–9.

CSPI (Center for Science in the Public Interest) and IACFO (International Association of Consumer Food Organizations). 2007. "The Global Dump Soft Drinks Campaign." <http://www.dumpsoda.org>.

de Ruyter, J. C., M. R. Olthof, J. C. Seidell, and M. B. Katan. 2012. "A Trial of Sugar-free or Sugar-sweetened Beverages and Body Weight in Children." *New England Journal of Medicine* 367 (15): pp. 1397–1406.

De Schutter, O. 2011. Report submitted by the Special Rapporteur on the Right to Food. United Nations General Assembly, Human Rights Council, December 26, 2011. <http://www.ohchr.org/Documents/HRBodies/HRCouncil/RegularSession/Session19/A-HRC-19-59_en.pdf>.

Ebbeling, C. B., H. A. Feldman, V. R. Chomitz, T. A. Antonelli, S. L. Gortmaker, S. K. Osganian, and D. S. Ludwig. 2012. "A Randomized Trial of Sugar-sweetened Beverages and Adolescent Body Weight." *New England Journal of Medicine* 367 (15): pp. 1407–1416.

Ebbeling, C. B., H. A. Feldman, S. K. Osganian, V. R. Chomitz, S. J. Ellenbogen, and D. S. Ludwig. 2006. "Effects of Decreasing Sugar-sweetened Beverage Consumption on Body Weight in Adolescents: A Randomized, Controlled Pilot Study." *Pediatrics* 117 (3): pp. 673–680.

Ervin, R. B., and C. L. Ogden. 2013. "Consumption of Added Sugars among U.S. Adults, 2005–2010." NCHS Data Brief No. 122, May, National Center for Health Statistics. <http://www.cdc.gov/nchs/data/databriefs/db122.htm>.

Euromonitor International. 2013. "Total Volume Carbonates, 2013." <http://www.euromonitor.com/carbonates>.

FAO (Food and Agricultural Organization). 2013. *The State of Food and Agriculture: Food Systems for Better Nutrition, 2013*. <http://www.fao.org/docrep/018/i3300e/i3300e.pdf>.

Finkelstein, E. A., J. G. Trogdon, J. W. Cohen, and W. Dietz. 2009. "Annual Medical Spending Attributable to Obesity: Payer and Service Specific Estimates." *Health Affairs* 28 (5): pp. w822–w831.

Forshee, R. A., P. A. Anderson, and M. L. Storey. 2008. "Sugar-Sweetened Beverages and Body Mass Index in Children and Adolescents: A Meta-Analysis." *American Journal of Clinical Nutrition* 87 (6): pp. 1662–1671.

Fryar, C. D., M. D. Carroll, and C. L. Ogden. 2012. "Prevalence of Overweight, Obesity, and Extreme Obesity among Adults: United States, Trends 1960–1962 through 2009–2010." Centers for Disease Control and Prevention, National Center for Health Statistics, NCHS Health E-Stat. <http://www.cdc.gov/nchs/data/hestat/obesity_adult_09_10/obesity_adult_09_10.htm#table2>.

Giebelhaus, A. W. 1994. "The Pause that Refreshed the World: The Evolution of Coca-Cola's Global Marketing Strategy." In *Adding Value: Brands and Marketing in Food and Drink*, edited by G. Jones and N. J. Morgan, pp. 191–214. London: Routledge.

Han, E., and L. M. Powell. 2013. "Consumption Patterns of Sugar-Sweetened Beverages in the United States." *Journal of the Academy of Nutrition and Dietetics* 113 (1): pp. 43–53.

Hawkes, C. 2013. "Promoting Healthy Diets through Nutrition Education and Changes in the Food Environment: An International Review of Actions and Their Effectiveness." Rome: Food and Agricultural Organization (FAO).

Hawkes, C. 2008. "Regulations, Guidelines and Voluntary Initiatives on Soft Drink Availability in Schools around the World." Unpublished report, World Heart Federation, Geneva. <http://www.dumpsoda.org/hawkeswhffinaldec2008.pdf>.

Hawkes, C. 2010. "The Worldwide Battle against Soft Drinks in Schools." *American Journal of Preventive Medicine* 38 (4): pp. 457–461.

Hebblethwaite, C. 2012. "Who, What, Why: In Which Countries Is Coca-Cola Not Sold?" *BBC News Magazine*, September 11, 2012. <http://www.bbc.co.uk/news/magazine-19550067>.

Hsiao, A., and Y. C. Wang. 2013. "Reducing Sugar-Sweetened Beverage Consumption: Evidence, Policies, and Economics." *Current Obesity Reports* 2 (3): pp. 191–199. doi: 10.1007/s13679-013-0065-8.

Iyer, B. 2013. "Why Consumers in Vietnam Are Calling for a Ban on Coke." *Campaign Asia-Pacific Magazine* (e-magazine), May 28, 2013. <http://www.campaignasia.com/Article/344805,why-consumers-in-vietnam-are-calling-for-a-ban-on-coke.aspx>.

James, J., and D. Kerr. 2005. "Prevention of Childhood Obesity by Reducing Soft Drinks." *International Journal of Obesity* 29: pp. S54–S57.

James, J., P. Thomas, D. Cavan, and D. Kerr. 2004. "Preventing Childhood Obesity by Reducing Consumption of Carbonated Drinks: Cluster Randomised Controlled Trial." *BMJ* 328 (7450): p. 1237. doi: 10.1136/bmj.38077.458438.EE.

Kant, A. K., and B. I. Graubard. 2006. "Secular Trends in Patterns of Self-Reported Food Consumption of American Adults: NHANES 1971–1975 to NHANES 1999–2002. *American Journal of Clinical Nutrition* 84 (5): pp. 1215–1223.

LaFranchi, H. 2010. "Iran Sanctions Kick In, and Ahmadinejad Says He'll Ban Coca-Cola." *Christian Science Monitor*, July 1, 2010. <http://www.csmonitor.com/USA/Foreign-Policy/2010/0701/Iran-sanctions-kick-in-and-Ahmadinejad-says-he-ll-ban-Coca-Cola>.

Langlois, A. 2006. *Obesity: Re-shaping the Food Industry*. London: JP Morgan Global Equity Research.

Lesser, L. I., C. B. Ebbeling, M. Goozner, David Wypij, and D. S. Ludwig. 2007. "Relationship between Funding Source and Conclusion among Nutrition-Related Scientific Articles." *PLoS Medicine* 4 (1): p. 41. January 9, 2007. doi: 10.1371/journal.pmed.0040005.

Ludwig, D. S., K. E. Peterson, and S. L. Gortmaker. 2001. "Relation between Consumption of Sugar-Sweetened Drinks and Childhood Obesity: A Prospective, Observational Analysis." *Lancet* 357 (9255): pp. 505–508.

Mancino, L., Todd, J., and B.-H. Lin. 2009. "Separating What We Eat from Where: Measuring the Effect of Food away from Home on Diet Quality." *Food Policy* 34 (6): pp. 557–562.

Mullaney, L. 2013. "Top 10 Emerging Markets for Food and Drink Manufacturers." *Food Manufacture*, May 28, 2013. <http://www.foodmanufacture.co.uk/Business-News/Top-10-emerging-markets-for-food-and-drink-manufacturers>.

National Cancer Institute. 2014. "Sources of Beverage Intakes among the US Population, 2005–06." Applied Research: Cancer Control and Population Sciences website: Monitoring Risk & Health Behaviors/Food Sources/Beverages. Last modified: April 11, 2014. <http://riskfactor.cancer.gov/diet/foodsources/beverages>.

Natti, S. 2013. "India Thinks Healthy, Drinks Healthy." *The New Indian Express*, June 9, 2013. <http://newindianexpress.com/business/news/India-thinks-healthy-drinks-healthy/2013/06/09/article1626493.ece>.

Nestle, M., and M. Nesheim. 2012. *Why Calories Count: From Science to Politics*. Berkeley, CA: University of California Press.

Newby, P. K., K. E. Peterson, C. S. Berkey, J. Leppert, W. C. Willett, and G. A. Colditz. 2004. "Beverage Consumption Is Not Associated with Changes in Weight and Body

Mass Index among Low-Income Preschool Children in North Dakota." *Journal of the American Dietetic Association* 104 (7): pp. 1086–1094.

Nielsen, S. J., and B. M. Popkin. 2004. "Changes in Beverage Intake between 1977 and 2001." *American Journal of Preventive Medicine* 27 (3): pp. 206–210.

Ogden, C. L., M. D. Carroll, K. K. Brian, and K. M. Flegal. 2012. "Prevalence of Obesity in the United States, 2009–2010." Centers for Disease Control and Prevention, National Center for Health Statistics, NCHS data brief No. 82, January. <http://www.cdc.gov/nchs/data/databriefs/db82.htm>.

Ogden, C. L., B. K. Kit, M. D. Carroll, and S. Park S. 2011. "Consumption of Sugar Drinks in the United States, 2005–2008." NCHS Data Brief, No 17, August 2011, National Center for Health Statistics. <http://www.cdc.gov/nchs/data/databriefs/db71.htm>.

PepsiCo, Inc. 2012a. Annual Report. <http://www.pepsico.com/Uploads/Documents/Investors/AnnualReports/PEP_Annual_Report_2012.pdf>.

PepsiCo, Inc. 2012b. United States Security and Exchange Commission, Washington, DC. Form 10-K, December 29, 2012. <http://www.pepsico.com/investors/sec-filings.html>.

PepsiCo. 2014. "PepsiCo Policy on Responsible Advertising to Children." <http://www.pepsico.com/docs/album/policies-doc/pwp/pepsico_policy_responsible.pdf?sfvrsn=2>.

PepsiCo. n.d. "Advertising." <http://www.pepsico.com/Purpose/Human-Sustainability/Responsible-Marketing.html>.

"PepsiCo and the Asian Football Development Project (AFDP) Sign Strategic Partnership Agreement." 2013. *Al Bawaba Business*, April 8, 2013. <http://www.albawaba.com/business/pr/pepsico-asian-football-development-project-482844>.

"PepsiCo Expects Center to Speed Innovation in China." 2012. *Beverage* Daily Newsletter, November 13, 2012. <http://www.beveragedaily.com/Markets/PepsiCo-expects-center-to-speed-innovation-in-China>.

Pérez-Morales, E., M. Bacardí-Gascón, and A. Jiménez-Cruz. 2013. "Sugar-sweetened Beverage Intake before 6 Years of Age and Weight or BMI Status among Older Children; Systematic Review of Prospective Studies." *Nutrición Hospitalaria* 28 (1): pp. 47–51.

Popkin, B. M. 2006. "Global Nutrition Dynamics: The World Is Rapidly Shifting toward a Diet Linked with Non-Communicable Diseases." *American Journal of Clinical Nutrition* 84 (2): pp. 289–298.

Popkin, B. M., L. S. Adair, and S. W. Ng. 2012. "Global Nutrition Transition and the Pandemic of Obesity in Developing Countries. *Nutrition Reviews* 70 (1): pp. 3–21. doi: 10.1111/j.1753-4887.2011.00456.x.

Popkin, B. M., and S. J. Nielsen. 2003. "The Sweetening of the World's Diet." *Obesity Research* 11 (11): pp. 1325–1332. doi:10.1038/oby.2003.179.

Stevens, G. A., G. M. Singh, Y. Lu, G. Danaei, J. K. Lin, M. M. Finucane, A. N. Bahalim, R. K. McIntire, H. R. Gutierrez, M. Cowan, Christopher J. Paciorek, F. Farzadfar, L. Riley, M. Ezzati, and the Global Burden of Metabolic Risk Factors of Chronic Diseases Collaborating Group. 2012. "National, Regional and Global Trends in Adult Overweight and Obesity Prevalences." *Population Health Metrics* 10(1): 22. doi: 10.1186/1478-7954-10-22.

Streets, J., C. Levy, A. Erskine, and J. Hudson. 2002. *Absolute Risk of Obesity*. London: UBS Warburg Global Equity Research.

Striegel-Moore, R. H., D. Thompson, S. G. Affenito, D. L. Franko, E. Obarzanek, B. A. Barton, G. B. Schreiber, S. R. Daniels, M. Schmidt, and P. B. Crawford. 2006. "Correlates of Beverage Intake in Adolescent Girls: The National Heart, Lung, and Blood Institute Growth and Health Study." *Journal of Pediatrics* 148 (2): pp. 183–187.

Terhune, C., and G. Kahn. 2003. "Coke Lures Japanese Customers with Cellphone Come-Ons." *Wall Street Journal*, September 8, 2003:B1. <http://online.wsj.com/news/articles/SB106297213391315800>.

Thai Health Promotion Foundation. 2010. "Sweet Enough Network Persuades Schools to Avoid Risk of 'Obesity'." December 15, 2010.

Thompson, S. 2007. "Obesity Fear Frenzy Grips Food Industry." Advertising Age, April 23, 2007. <http://adage.com/article/news/obesity-fear-frenzy-grips-food-industry/116233/.>

USDA (US Department of Agriculture). 2014. Food availability (per capita) data system. <http://ers.usda.gov/data-products/food-availability-(per-capita)-data-system/.aspx#>.

USDA (US Department of Agriculture) and USDHHS (US Department of Health and Human Services). 2010. *Dietary Guidelines for Americans, 2010*. 7th ed. Washington, DC: US Government Printing Office. December. <http://www.cnpp.usda.gov/dgas2010-policydocument.htm>.

Vasanti, S. M., A. Pan, W. C. Willett, and F. B. Hu. 2013. "Sugar-sweetened Beverages and Weight Gain in Children and Adults: A Systematic Review and Meta-Analysis." *American Journal of Clinical Nutrition* 98 (4): pp. 1084–1102.

Versa, M. 2013. "The "Coca-Colization" of Mexico, the Spark of Obesity." *Periodismo Humano*, May 3, 2013. <http://english.periodismohumano.com/2013/03/05/the-coca-colization-of-mexico-the-spark-of-obesity/>.

Villegas, P. 2013. "Mexico: Junk Food Tax Is Approved." *New York Times*, October 31, 2013. <http://www.nytimes.com/2013/11/01/world/americas/mexico-junk-food-tax-is-approved.html>.

Welsh, J. A., A. J. Sharma, L. Grellinger, and M. B. Vos. 2011. "Consumption of Added Sugars Is Decreasing in the United States." *American Journal of Clinical Nutrition* 94 (3): pp. 726–734. doi:10.3945/ajcn.111.018366.

WHO (World Health Organization). 2010a. Sixty-Third World Health Assembly. "Prevention and Control of Noncommunicable Diseases: Implementation of the Global Strategy." Report by the Secretariat, April 1, 2010. <http://apps.who.int/gb/ebwha/pdf_files/WHA63/A63_12-en.pdf>.

WHO (World Health Organization) 2010b. "Marketing of Food and Non-Alcoholic Beverages to Children." Resolution WHA63.14. Sixty-third World Health Assembly, Geneva, 17–21 May 2010. <http://apps.who.int/gb/ebwha/pdf_files/WHA63-REC1/WHA63_REC1-P2-en.pdf>.

WHO (World Health Organization). 2011. *Global Status Report on Noncommunicable Diseases, 2010*. April. Geneva: World Health Organization. <http://www.who.int/nmh/publications/ncd_report2010/en/>.

WHO (World Health Organization) 2012. *Population-Based Approaches to Childhood Obesity Prevention*. Geneva: World Health Organization. <http://www.who.int/dietphysicalactivity/childhood/WHO_new_childhoodobesity_PREVENTION_27nov_HR_PRINT_OK.pdf>.

WHO (World Health Organization). 2013. *Global Nutrition Policy Review: What Does It Take to Scale Up Nutrition Action?* Geneva: World Health Organization. <http://www.who.int/nutrition/publications/policies/global_nut_policyreview/en/index.html>.

Wilson, D., and A. Kerlin. 2012. "Special Report: Food, Beverage Industry Pays for Seat at Health-policy Table." Reuters, October 19, 2012. <http://www.reuters.com/article/2012/10/19/us-obesity-who-industry-idUSBRE89I0K620121019>.

5

Evidence-Informed Policymaking

Lessons from Food Security and Nutrition Monitoring Systems during Food Crises

Suresh Chandra Babu

Introduction

> *"Stronger assessment, monitoring, and surveillance systems are needed to better prepare for tomorrow's crises and to ensure that actions taken by governments and the international community are minimizing risks and mitigating the effects of high food prices on the most vulnerable."*
>
> —Comprehensive Framework for Action for Addressing the Food Crisis by the UN Secretary General (UN 2009a, p. 25.)

Food policymaking continues under the veil of a lack of evidence. The policy responses to the recent food crises in many developing countries were typical. Yet there is a poor understanding of the factors contributing to such reactive policy processes (Pinstrup-Andersen 2014). Food policy researchers have long assumed that if they produced adequate evidence on policy alternatives and communicated them effectively, policymakers will adopt them or at least consider them in the decision-making process. Such assumptions no longer seem to be valid. There is increased recognition of the role of political economy issues in decision-making and how knowledge for evidence-informed policymaking is generated, managed, and used (Besley and Burgess 2002; Bates and Block 2010; Birner and Resnick 2010). Strong and sustainable institutions that generate, process, and analyze information are essential for evidence-informed policymaking.

In this chapter, we look at the development and implementation of food security and nutrition monitoring systems over the last 30 years and, more critically, in the context of evidence-based policymaking during the recent food crises to identify policy, institutional, organizational, and system challenges. We present lessons that could be useful to overcome these challenges at the global, regional, and national levels.

The recent global food crisis emphasized the importance of evidence-based policymaking and program design to food policymakers in developing countries. Countries continue to face localized food crises from recurrent drought-related emergencies. For example, the recent famine-like conditions in the Horn of Africa affected 12 million people in 2011 (the fourth such event in the last 10 years), and another major weather-induced food crisis affected 18 million people in the Sahel (the third such event in the last eight years). Reports indicate that such events kill thousands of people and displace millions (UN 2009b). In Somalia, between October 2010 and April 2012, for example, about 258,000 people died due to severe food insecurity and famine, and half of these deaths were children under 5 years of age (FSNAU and FEWS NET 2013). Over the years, food security and nutrition monitoring systems, as part of broader food policy systems, have helped in forewarning policymakers and program managers of impending food crises. Yet the design and implementation of food security and nutrition monitoring (FSNM)[1] systems continue to face a number of constraints and challenges. However, much progress has been made to mainstream the information and knowledge system for food security and nutrition monitoring (WFP-UNICEF RIVAF 2011).

Past experiences show that food crises emerge slowly. Thus, with effective forecasting (using food security and nutrition indicators) and careful monitoring of food prices, rainfall levels, and crop production losses, it is possible to guide policymakers and humanitarian agencies to act early to minimize the impact of the food crisis and to prevent major disasters and human loss. Early action saves both lives and costs. A major challenge that continues to plague the development community is the weak link between information systems and the use of evidence from such systems in designing informed policy and program action. This is largely due to weak capacity to design and implement early actions to prevent a crisis from unfolding. The amount of time taken to gather information and to translate it into action is so large that by the time aid is organized, it is too late to affect results on the ground. Although the food crisis provides context to take a critical look at the existing food security and nutrition monitoring systems, the principles and practice of improving their relevance, design, effectiveness, efficiency, sustainability, and impact also apply to regular short-, medium-, and long-term food policymaking.

The chapter is organized as follows: In the following section, we provide a brief background and history of food security monitoring. Next, we develop a conceptual framework for analyzing the relevance, effectiveness, efficiency, impact, and sustainability of FSNM systems. We then apply this framework to understanding how FSNM systems in select developing countries have responded to recent food crises. In the subsequent section, we draw lessons for overcoming the challenges of effectively implementing FSNM systems. Concluding remarks form the last section.

A Brief History of Food Security and Nutrition Monitoring Systems

Food security and nutrition monitoring systems can play an important role in generating evidence for policy and program interventions by identifying, analyzing, and addressing food security and nutrition challenges. Although there is high recognition of the roles that various components of FSNM systems can play, there is limited understanding of the issues, constraints, and challenges faced in the development and implementation of such systems in developing countries (Pinstrup-Andersen 2009; UN 2009). In this section, we present a brief background and history of FSNM systems in the context of evidence-informed management of food crises.

Defining a Food Security and Nutrition Monitoring System

Definitions of FSNM systems vary, and over the years have evolved depending on the nature and magnitude of the problems at hand. They have also evolved along with the definitions of food security, nutrition security, and famine. How practitioners define food and nutrition security is likely to influence what indicators are monitored, thus affecting the generation of information for policymaking. Recently, the definition of food security has been expanded to include a resilience and stability dimension (Dorwood 2013). Thus, stability indicators, such as those that assess the role of increasing food price volatility on food security and the nutritional status of a population, must also be tracked (Glantz 1996). The spatial and time dimensions of food security issues make the units of indicators complex, especially when looking at aggregated data at the national, regional, and global levels. For the purposes of this chapter, a food security and nutrition monitoring system is defined as "a process of policymaking and program design through generating evidence, monitoring, analysis and the interpretation of indicators and causal factors associated with food security and nutrition, in order to make appropriate decisions that will lead to effective interventions which result in improvements in the food security and nutritional status of the population" (Babu and Quinn 1994, p. 215).

Objectives of Food Security and Nutrition Monitoring Systems

The objectives of FSNM systems have changed over the years. There are usually five main objectives: (1) timely (early) warning and intervention; (2) development planning and policy design; (3) program management and evaluation; (4) problem identification and advocacy; and (5) monitoring impact of special programs and policies. Each objective has particular information needs, yet the information obtained for one objective may be of use to fulfill some of the other objectives as well.

Based on the specific objectives, several FSNM systems could operate simultaneously within a country context. The main purpose of an early warning system is to gather data that monitors people's access to food so as to predict or foresee an imminent food crisis, and therefore to initiate a timely response, particularly in nations regularly burdened by drought and famine (Buchanan-Smith 2000; Devereux 2001). FSNM systems that are intended to serve the needs of development planning and policy design attempt to satisfy the "information needs of planners, policy analysts, and policy decision-makers at the local, regional, and national level" (Babu and Pinstrup-Andersen 1994). Program management and evaluative FSNM systems are generally designed to help program managers, officials, and donors in the implementation and assessment of existing programs, such as determining whether the programs successfully reached the targeted populations (Tucker et al. 1989; Arnauld et al. 1990). A monitoring system for problem identification and advocacy collects and interprets information on nutritional indicators, in order to determine the quantity of resources needed to address a specific problem (Habicht 2000). Special programs and policies that address issues arising from globalization, World Trade Organization (WTO) agreements, or climate change-related weather events can often have negative impacts on different segments of a population. Hence, the consequences of such events on the food security and nutritional conditions of the poor need to be monitored. The information derived from such monitoring systems is important for targeting aid and improving future policies (Babu and Pinstrup-Andersen 1994; Pinstrup-Andersen 2009).

Evolution of Food Security and Nutrition Monitoring Systems

The food emergencies of the 1980s brought the importance of nutritional surveillance to the attention of global decision-makers (Habicht and Pinstrup-Andersen 1990; Babu and Chapasuka 1997; Mock and Mason 1999). At the same time, early warning systems were established at national and regional levels to support food and nutrition policymaking and program interventions (GIEWS 2013). Regional systems were organized to support national systems to produce the information needed by national policymakers in the event of a crisis (UN 2009b).

In the early stages of the development of monitoring systems, there was more focus on improving data collection mechanisms, and little attention was given to the effective conversion of data into information and of information into policy. Although much data were collected, only a portion was analyzed, and only a portion of the analyzed data was used in policy and program design (Babu and Mthindi 1994). Differing sectoral needs for information and a lack of consensus on the purpose, assumptions, and methods of monitoring for various sectors—such as agriculture, food, health, and nutrition—presented additional challenges over the years to the improvement and sustainability of the monitoring systems (FSIN 2014). Finally, weak capacity at the individual, organizational, and system levels has been a chronic challenge in effectively using the monitoring systems for policymaking and program intervention (Pelletier and Jonsson 1994; Babu and Blom 2014).

Following the 1974 World Food Conference, the Food and Agriculture Organization (FAO) created the Global Information and Early Warning System on Food and Agriculture (GIEWS). It is the primary supplier of "information on food production and food security for every country in the world," and consists of a network of numerous governments, NGOs, and research organizations (GIEWS 2013). GIEWS assists in national and regional efforts to improve food security information and early warning systems. The 1980s brought efforts to establish coordinated regional early warning systems. For example, the South African Development Community (SADC) regional system was initiated in 1987 (Belbase and Morgan 1994). As several countries in the SADC region faced common problems such as periodic droughts, conflict, and high population growth, it was acknowledged that "timely, accurate, and reliable" information was crucial to achieving food security (FAO 1998). GIEWS has also helped sub-Saharan African nations launch national early warning systems (NEWS) (FNSWG 2013).

Other examples of monitoring on a regional or global scale include the Famine Early Warning Systems Network (FEWS NET) and the Global Monitoring for Food Security (GMFS 2013). Among the objectives of FEWS NET, a USAID-funded project that conducts integrated food security analysis in 36 developing countries, is to develop "more useful and sustainable" food security information systems in sub-Saharan Africa (FEWS NET 2013). FEWS NET strives to enable the countries in which it operates to determine existing food security problems and to support them in solving these problems themselves, particularly by enhancing their capacity to increase the quality and effectiveness of food security information systems and networks (FEWS NET 2013). FEWS NET also produces a monthly price watch as well as bulletins for the countries in which it operates (FEWS 2014).

Recent Developments

At the global level, in response to the 2007–08 food price crisis, the United Nations' (UN) High Level Task Force on Global Food Security updated its Comprehensive Framework for Action, calling for a strengthening of food security and nutrition assessment systems for informed policymaking. Continuous tracking of the indicators and causal factors of food insecurity and malnutrition was seen as a priority to minimize the impact of high global food prices on vulnerable populations. The agencies that participate in the UN High Level Task Force on Global Food Security responded in different ways to collect and organize information. For example, the FAO's Food Price Data and Analysis Tool was developed to monitor food prices at the country level. The FAO also regularly produces food supply data. The World Food Programme (WFP) responded by conducting vulnerability assessment mappings of hunger and the factors affecting food insecurity. It identified the most vulnerable countries in need of intervention assistance.

In addition, the UN developed the Global Impact and Vulnerability Alert System (GIVAS), "consisting of a Global Impact and Vulnerability Data Platform and a series of Global Alert products, to track developments, and report on the political, economic, social, and environmental dimensions of a crisis." (UN 2009b, pp. 39–40). GIVAS attempts to provide real-time data and analysis for timely response by the international community. However, the quality of the data collected through GIVAS crucially depends on the capacity of the national institutions and their monitoring systems to provide this data. Thus, the global, regional, and national systems depend on the same capacity and infrastructure for generating quality and reliable data for decision-making at various levels.

At the regional level, food security monitoring has moved beyond crisis management to medium- and long-term planning and policymaking. For example, the New Partnership for Africa's Development (NEPAD) developed a peer review mechanism, and the Comprehensive Africa Agriculture Development Programme (CAADP) provided support for national entities contributing to food security and nutrition monitoring systems. The broad goal of CAADP is to increase the income of farming households, reduce poverty and hunger, and increase food and nutrition security. These development goals are seen as indicators of development outcomes. In order to achieve these development outcomes, CAADP countries are supported to achieve 6 percent growth in the agriculture sector by committing 10 percent of the government budget to the agriculture sector. In recent years, the food security and nutrition monitoring process has brought together public, private, and civil society organizations (CSOs), as well as donors, to design policies and programs and to track the progress made while holding stakeholders mutually accountable (CAADP 2010).

At the country level, food security and nutrition monitoring systems have tended to increasingly involve various actors, players, and stakeholders from the public sector, private sector, CSOs, and donor organizations (Babu and Chaura 1997; Babu 2013). Periodic review of the progress made by countries to achieve their food security and nutrition objectives, through food and agriculture strategy development processes, has helped position the monitoring systems as an integral part of policy process (FSIN 2014). For example, in sub-Saharan Africa, sector-level development of investment plans, joint sector reviews, and mutual accountability of donors and governments have helped to increase the demand for FSNM systems (CAADP 2010). Information on the state of household food security and nutritional status—and the factors that influence them—have formed key evidence for the development of sector strategies (Babu and Mthindi 1995a). However, a major challenge, which developing countries continue to face, is the varying degrees of interest that policymakers show in the use of evidence in making food security and nutrition-related decisions. Identifying such challenges and constraints in the functioning and use of FSNM systems could help in increasing their sustainability (Babu 1997; Devereux 2001; NeKSAP 2010).

Understanding the various components of a country's FSNM system and how they come together to contribute to intervention policies and programs requires several related questions to be addressed. How well are the various stakeholders in a country brought together to use evidence in the policy process? What institutional architecture currently exists to address the challenges of FSNM systems and related program challenges? Does the information gathered, analyzed, and reported satisfy information needs? How does the information affect policy decisions, and how does information from policy implementation feed back into the policy process? What demand exists from the policymakers for the information generated by FSNM? Who decides what information is to be collected? What capacity strengthening issues need to be addressed to make the evidence-based policymaking sustainable? Answering these questions requires closer examination of the various components of FSNM systems. Recent food crises in several developing countries provided an opportunity to study the FSNM systems in the context of food security decision-making. In the next section, we develop a conceptual framework for studying and evaluating various FSNM systems in developing countries.

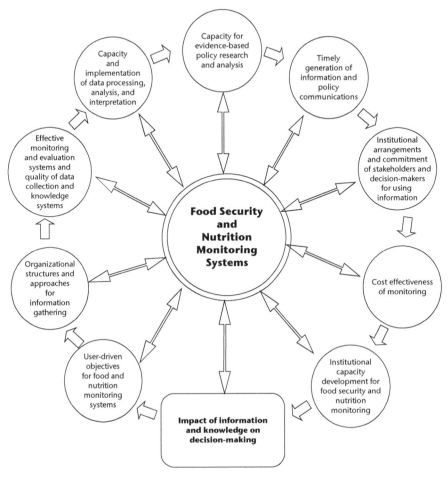

Figure 5.1 A conceptual framework for studying various characteristics of food security and nutrition monitoring systems

Source: Author, adapted from Babu (1997).

A Conceptual Framework for Studying FSNM Systems

Figure 5.1 presents a conceptual framework for studying FSNM systems for their effectiveness in providing evidence for informed decision-making. We view the functioning of the FSNM system as a cycle. A sound food security and nutrition monitoring system is simple, user-driven, and based on existing institutional structures (which increases the capacity for analysis and interpretation). It also has the commitment of the relevant decision-makers who will use the system's outputs in planning and policy design. Tracking deviations of the design and implementation of an

FSNM system from these criteria helps to reorient activities toward the ultimate goal of developing informed food security and nutrition policy decisions.

The sustainability of an FSNM system depends on its user-driven nature. Operational linkages need to be in place between the monitoring system and the institutions using the information generated, in order for the system to be successful in triggering appropriate policy and program response (FAO 1998; Babu and Tashmatov 2000). The quality of data and the speed with which it is generated are determined by the simplicity of the instruments used for gathering information. The use of existing infrastructure for collecting and compiling information has proven to be more successful than the creation of new institutional structures for the purposes of FSNM (Babu and Pinstrup-Andersen 1994). FSNM systems also use information from local communities for early warning purposes (Buchanan-Smith and Cosgrave 2010; ACF 2011).

FSNM systems need to be studied for the quality of the data they produce, as well as their capacity for data processing, analysis, and interpretation. Timeliness of information and the commitment of the policymakers to using the data produced by FSNM systems are critical for the systems' sustainability. The cost of generating information is often small compared to the benefits of the policy or program impacts developed based on the outputs of the monitoring systems, if the information is effectively linked to the decision-making processes (Babu and Mthindi 1995b; Babu and Reidhead 2007). Empirical evidence from Malawi indicates that the internal rate of return to FSNM ranges from 66 to 75 percent (Babu et al. 1996).

External agencies that fund data collection use some of the information collected by the monitoring systems in their planning exercises, hence saving their resources that would otherwise be used for data collection. Monitoring systems that are connected to the policymaking process can be effective in informing the evidence generated.

Monitoring the use of information in designing policies and interventions and evaluating the impact on policy decisions can help in identifying new channels for information dissemination. Information obtained from evaluating the benefits of monitoring systems in influencing policies can be a useful instrument for raising resources and support for sustaining the systems. Monitoring and evaluating the impact of the monitoring systems in influencing policy decisions requires constant follow-up on the information generated and its use at various stages of decision-making. The benefits of such documentation, however, may outweigh the time and costs involved.

In the next section, the characteristics of the FSNM systems described here are studied in relation to the policy responses in eight countries during recent food crises. In addition, the use of information from FSNM systems is analyzed in various decision-making processes, in order to draw lessons for improving the effectiveness and utility of the FSNM systems in developing countries.

Food Security and Nutrition Monitoring during the Food Crisis

In this section, we use the conceptual framework developed above to analyze how countries used their FSNM systems to develop responses to the food price increases. The synthesis presented in this section is based on in-country and regional consultations in selected countries in 2009 and 2010 in South Asia, Southeast Asia, and sub-Saharan Africa. As part of a multi-country project investigating the causes and responses of the food price crisis in developing countries, the institutions and organizations involved in food policy systems were enumerated and studied in terms of their role in the policy process. This was followed by consultative workshops with key policymakers, policy advisors, and policy researchers, in which local collaborators presented selected papers on the causes and the responses to food crises. The presentations were followed by group discussions on the lessons learned in strengthening data, information, and knowledge management systems for addressing future food crises. Key informant interviews were also conducted with a number of professionals involved in the development and implementation of FSNM systems, members of food security task-forces, researchers of policy think tanks, and policymakers in each of the countries to identify the role of FSNM systems in each country's response to the crisis. Additional information on the responses to the food crisis in the study countries was obtained from research reports and published papers on the responses to food crisis in these countries (Pinstrup-Andersen 2014).

We use information gathered from the sources noted above to first look at the responses that the countries developed to address the food crisis; and in the context of information-based decision-making, we then identify the organizational and institutional structures that helped to provide evidence, data, and information for the decision-making process. We next study the characteristics of the FSNM systems that provided evidence and information support for the policy responses, in an effort to draw broader lessons on how to improve the effectiveness of the monitoring systems.

Responses to the Food Crisis

Countries responded differently to the food crisis based on the nature and magnitude of the impact of global food price increases on local prices and the country's food security (Levine and Chastre 2011; Bryan 2013). A brief summary of the responses to the food crisis in the study countries is presented in Table 5.1. Responses to the food crisis varied, depending on the type of policy problem, the resources at the disposal of the governments, and the type of evidence on which the policymakers had to base their decisions.

The developing countries' governments analyzed here chose responses that ranged from increasing incentives for production to market interventions, such as export bans and import tariffs. The responses of these countries can be put into one of two broad categories: supply-oriented responses or demand-oriented responses. Subsidies for production inputs, such as chemical fertilizers and seeds, or for the adoption of modern technologies, were the most common policies to augment food supply. For example, Malawi further strengthened its already well-established fertilizer subsidy program. Other countries, such as India and Kenya, maintained their input subsidy programs to encourage farmers to continue to produce. To meet the domestic demand for food and to bring down the rising food prices, India imposed an export ban on its rice and wheat, Vietnam banned rice exports, and Malawi banned the export of maize to its neighbor Zimbabwe. Ethiopia and Nigeria responded by releasing food stocks in their domestic markets in order to stabilize domestic food prices.

On the demand side, safety net programs were strengthened in India, Bangladesh, and Ethiopia to protect their most vulnerable populations. The efforts were mainly implemented through already existing programs, such as food for work, cash transfer programs, or guaranteed employment programs. For certain essential commodities, such as rice and pulses, Bangladesh and India resorted to selling these commodities at strategic selling points to benefit urban consumers directly.

These policy and program responses were well advertised in the media to increase transparency and to appease the countries' opposition parties (Watson 2013). The use of information and evidence in various policy and program measures varied according to the type of domestic pressures that each country government faced during the food crisis. The nature of the political environment, the level of decentralization, and the sensitivity of the policymakers to the reactions of the consumer and producer groups also affected both the information use and the time taken to respond to the food crisis. Ruling parties in democratic countries, such as India and Bangladesh, responded to avoid criticism from their opposition parties. In Nigeria, the major push for government action came from consumers taking to the streets.

Table 5.1. Summary of policy responses to the food crisis and related policy processes in selected developing countries

Country and policy problem triggered by the food price crisis	Example of food policy responses	Key information needs
Bangladesh:		
Sharp rise in food prices in domestic markets. Significant number of households sliding into poverty. Increased vulnerability of marginalized groups	Long-term food security goals such as price support, fertilizer and fuel subsidies maintained. Net importing, yet fourth largest rice producer in the world. Increased allocation of funds for social safety nets. Built higher food stock and reduced import tariffs on food for open market sales in urban areas. Banned rice exports and eliminated import duty on rice and wheat	Macro level data on production, stocks, imports and distribution, household data on consumption and vulnerability
Ethiopia:		
Chronic food insecurity and low productivity of agriculture accentuated by the food price increase	Imposed export ban on all cereal crops. Released grain stocks to distribution centers and to grain mills. Targeted food distribution to affected population	Production data in various regions, areas affected, food shortage, household level information on food security
India:		
Food price increase at the international level had little direct influence on domestic prices. However, high domestic food inflation was criticized by opposition parties and civil society organizations; structural change in demand for high-value commodities combined with poor supply response	Ban on common rice and wheat exports. Additional procurement of wheat was doubled in 2008–09. Government proactively increased the support price for major cereals, increased the food subsidies, released the food stocks in open markets, and increased the fertilizer subsidy	National level data on production, stocks, imports, internal and external trade, food distribution, micro level information on households below poverty level, consumption of food by food insecure households
Kenya:		
Food prices began steadily increasing from 2007. Policy distortions and under-provision of public goods were identified as major causes of food insecurity and reinforced by high food prices	Policy responses were slow. Policy responses included producer support policies and other supply side interventions. Increased importation of food grains to build up domestic stocks. Reduction of wheat import tariff and suspension of maize import tariff	Food price data in various regions, production and rainfall data based on early warning, food insecurity among vulnerable groups in rural and urban areas
Malawi:		
Export of maize, forging ahead with input subsidies during the crisis. Media criticized the government	Ban on export of maize. Restriction on private domestic trade. Commitment to produce additional maize through fertilizer subsidy. Export commitments not kept; strategic grain reserves	Production shortfall in various localities, household consumption of food and food price, cross-border trade of maize
Mozambique:		
Domestic food prices continued to rise even after the international prices started to decline, resulting in demonstrations on the streets of Maputo by the end of 2010	Reduced import tariffs in early 2008, cut the tariffs of maize, wheat, and rice from 25 percent to 2.5 percent. Trade policy measures were generally effective in reducing the international price shock impact	Food production and availability at provincial levels. Data on food prices, food consumption and poverty levels in urban and rural areas

(Continued)

Table 5.1. Continued

Country and policy problem triggered by the food price crisis	Example of food policy responses	Key information needs
Nigeria: Droughts in some parts of the country; growing food shortages in many parts of the country	Released stocks of food grains and increased rice imports. Emergency meeting of governors. Increased fertilizer subsidy and other subsidies for small-scale machines. Implemented guaranteed minimum price, commercial agricultural credit program, and national food crisis response program	State-level information on production, consumption, trade of food, availability of food in local stocks, food prices in various markets
Vietnam: Although a major rice exporter, increase in international prices was not seen as an opportunity to increase the income of rice farmers. Poor consumers in rural and urban areas became vulnerable to food price increases	Export ban on rice preceded by lowering the rice export quota. Domestic food grain market was fully liberalized. Fulfilling domestic demand for rice became the prime policy objective of the government. Procured rice from farmers and built up food stocks	Data on food consumption among poor and vulnerable households, food price data in various local areas along with production shortfalls during crisis and non-crisis periods

Source: Author.

Although not fully democratic, the Vietnamese government also reacted to avoid the suffering of vulnerable groups due to high food prices.

Implications for Evidence-Based Policymaking

Use of information and evidence in the food policy decision-making processes differed depending on several factors. Large countries such as India, which reacted to higher food prices in global markets by imposing an export ban on rice, acted after quick consultations with local think tanks that are supported by the government. Data on food availability in various states, routinely collected and published by various state and central publications, were used by researchers to alert the policymakers. However, the policy process was so quick, there was little time for researchers and analysts to evaluate the policy options.

In small countries like Malawi, the decision to back maize exports came from a policy announcement by the president to nullify fears that higher food prices would increase informal cross-border trade in food grains, leaving Malawians with no food in their communities. However, in developing the policy measures and program interventions that followed food crises, many countries used the existing information collection infrastructure to assess the food security conditions on the ground. For example, Malawian policymakers frequently used the FEWS NET bulletins in their discussions and for monitoring food availability in various parts of the country. Yet the capacity to produce such information is severely lacking in public institutions.

In the rest of this section, we look at the characteristics of FSNM systems to analyze how various organizational and institutional structures interacted to develop and implement the policy responses identified above.

Characteristics of FSNM Systems during Food Crises

Table 5.2 presents the current status of the FSNM systems in the eight study countries. This provides a snapshot of how the FSNM systems were organized and used when developing responses to the food crisis in each of the countries.

Bangladesh: When the food crisis hit Bangladesh, the necessary infrastructure for information collection was in place. However, the capacity for data analysis and policy decision-making was severely constrained. The Ministry of Food quickly put together a team under the leadership of the Director General of Food to take a crash course on food policy analysis in India. This helped the team to better organize their data and improve the use of it for program targeting and implementation, especially to address the problems of its most vulnerable populations. At the national level, the Ministry of Commerce and the Ministry of Food worked together to identify policy options to ensure an adequate supply of food in the country. The governance of the tendering system was particularly effective in involving the private sector. However, a lack of coordination among the agencies and ministries involved in agriculture, food, commerce, trade, and health to develop food policy responses presented a major challenge (Raihan 2013). Business associations pressured the government to act based on the food price data available in the public domain.

A food crisis task force was commissioned, but it was ineffective due to coordination problems. However, the limited consultations did involve major civil society organizations in discussions and decision-making. Due to a lack of transparency in decision-making, the private sector did not trust government policies and actions. External players, particularly donors, were effective at highlighting the food crisis problem early on using existing data from various information sources. The government used relief measures to protect urban consumers, such as subsidized open market sales of food grains. A major challenge for the government was to provide information to CSOs and donors to guide interventions in vulnerable areas. Household-level data was not available to identify those affected by the crisis, resulting in a blanket distribution of food. Connecting data to knowledge management and dissemination channels, and using it for effective program implementation, remains a challenge in Bangladesh.

Ethiopia: The Disaster Risk Management and Food Security Sector, an agency of the Ethiopian Ministry of Agriculture, played a crucial role in

Table 5.2. Characteristics of FSNM systems in the study countries during the food crisis

Country	Type of monitoring system	Key objectives	Infrastructure for data collection	Capacity for data processing, analysis, and interpretation	Timely generation of information	Commitment of decision-makers	Impact of information on decision-making
Bangladesh	Food policy monitoring system in the Ministry of Food	Monitor food production, prices, and stock levels; food distribution and consumption among poor	Data from the districts, food controllers, and household surveys	At the national level, through externally funded projects	Regular joint sector reviews allow for sharing of information with policymakers	High-level commitment to use data for determining the extent of food emergencies and the need for data	National-level policymaking benefits from macro systems; challenges persist on assessing the impact of various interventions and refining them
Ethiopia	Various systems, both national and international	Monitor food prices, production, vulnerability	Regional offices mandated to collect information	Weak capacity in government; NGOs fill time–capacity gap	Timely information is produced by international agencies	High commitment of decision-making to use information; high role of politics	Information used by donors to guide decision-makers; not clear how government systems of data collection are corroborated with external data sources
India	Various systems in agriculture, food, and nutrition	Monitor food production and consumption; food consumption through intervention programs	Highly developed infrastructure for data collection	High capacity for data processing and analysis	Regular bulletins on price and food availability	High commitment to policy responses but low level engagement with evidence/information use	Analysis of information left to researchers who have limited access to policymakers; vast research policymaking gap exists
Kenya	FEWS NET provided regular information on food prices	Information price and production trends; identifying vulnerable regions and seasons for interventions	Mostly data on price and food products; household-level data collection was maintained	Capacity in government ministries is weak, some capacity in think tanks	Policy research think tanks provided information for decision-making but was not systematic	Opposition party played key role in raising concerns and increasing the commitment of the government	Food security steering groups help in use of information for policymaking; use of data in policymaking is not fully known

(Continued)

Table 5.2. Continued

Country	Type of monitoring system	Key objectives	Infrastructure for data collection	Capacity for data processing, analysis, and interpretation	Timely generation of information	Commitment of decision-makers	Impact of information on decision-making
Malawi	Various approaches, including famine early warning system	Food security vulnerability assessments; food price monitoring in key markets	Good infrastructure to collect data but not fully used	Capacity continues to be limited; external help from technical assistance	Regular collection of data helps update information	Strong commitment and leadership of policymakers; yet focused on fertilizer subsidy as intervention	Donors support groups that regularly met and demanded information for decision-making; data on food prices and fertilizer use was key source of policy debate
Mozambique	No nationally organized monitoring system; FEWS NET	FEWS NET monitors prices and food production	Weak infrastructure for data collection	Some capacity exists but needs strengthening	Information from field delayed due to poor capacity	Policymakers are committed but do not have capacity	Systematic use of information for decision-making
Nigeria	No functioning food security monitoring in place	No well-defined objectives exist for monitoring; not clear as to who is mandated with food security monitoring	Data collection infrastructure exists but is poorly used for monitoring purposes	Capacity for data analysis weak in government agencies—capacity to policy	Policy think tanks generated information, but it was not timely and government did not use it	National food crisis response program but was not successful; coordination challenges at federal and state levels	Implementation challenges faced due to lack of information sharing among agencies; no systematic information on who and how information is used for decision-making
Vietnam	Well established food price monitoring systems in the Ministry of Agriculture	Information on trends and variations in food prices and food availability in the regions	Data collected through the existing channels of regional and district administration	Capacity for regular analysis of the data and connecting the food prices to the household indicators remains low	Food price data was available on time, but sharing with public was limited	Decision-makers were highly committed but overreacted to price increase, hurting small-scale producers	Information was not effectively used, due to limited analysis and political pressure; not clear how senior advisors are consulted and how they use information

Source: Author.

sounding early warnings of the food crisis. The agency, which was originally a response to the frequent droughts and famines of the 1980s, was reorganized in 2009 in response to the food crisis and has developed considerable capacity for the collection and sharing of food security data from various parts of the country. It also works with the Central Statistical Agency to generate information on the food security and nutritional status of the population. In addition, FEWS NET and the GIEWS program produce regular bulletins that share information and which have been used in decision-making. During the food crisis, the national-level response was coordinated by the Ministry of Finance and the Prime Minister's Office, with close consultations with the government-supported Economic Development Research Institute. NGOs were mainly used for food distribution in affected areas. The private sector played a limited role in transporting the food to areas where the prices were high during the food crisis. This was partly due to challenges of sharing information with the private sector and partly due to the infrastructure and transportation costs in shifting food to remote areas of the country.

The response to the food crisis was mainly organized by the public sector. The decision-making process was minimally consultative, and when consultations did occur, the participants were invited to endorse the decisions that were already made by the policymakers (Admassie 2013). This reduced the enthusiasm of the participants who had done their own analysis, using the available data. Although information was produced with the help of external technical assistance, the use of information from the monitoring system was less systematic. NGOs were not permitted to treat food security as a human rights issue. Parliamentary debates were largely concerned with supporting centrally made decisions. Although early warning systems are well developed, the major challenge here is to connect the information generated to the policymaking system in the food and agricultural sectors.

India: A combination of data sources provides information for policy responses to higher food prices in India. Regular national-level food consumption surveys, Demographic and Health Surveys (DHS), and the National Nutrition Monitoring Bureau's FSNM surveys provided data for researchers to analyze and inform policymakers (Ramachandran and Gopalan 2011). Thus, there exists infrastructure for data collection and processing for regular surveys. However, due to limited time to act during the food crisis, the policymaking process involved only selected public institutions for consultation, which had to quickly develop "supporting evidence" for the decisions proposed by the government (personal interviews with the researchers). Although the details of the discussions between the policymakers and the researchers remain confidential, there was some consultation with stakeholder groups on the issues and potential policy options. Yet the use of information from the national monitoring systems was limited, due to the political pressure on the government to quickly develop policies in order to reduce the public's fears. This situation occurred because the opposition parties raised the issue of high food prices in the parliament. Civil society organizations used the opportunity to express their commitment and support for the "Right to Food" agenda.

Policy think tanks provided information for policymaking through internally circulated policy briefs and presentations. India's Planning Commission provided policy advice as well, although it is not clear how much of the information it had disseminated originated from the monitoring system. In addition, the media played an effective role in circulating various groups' policy preferences. Farmers' groups protested for increased support from the government. International organizations provided information about global food prices. Advocacy coalitions of CSOs and farmers' organizations that work toward protecting the poor and vulnerable continued to put pressure on the government. At the same time, market-oriented policy entrepreneurs cautioned the government against intervening too much and condemned the export ban as having the potential to exacerbate the problem (Gulati and Ganguly 2013).

In summary, Indian policymakers relied on selected evidence, and a vast majority of policy researchers and analysts who analyzed household-level information to argue their case were not effectively heard in the policy process. However, the consultative process recently proved to be quite different when the National Food Security Bill was being developed. There were ample opportunities for consultations and discussions on the costs and benefits of the program, and the debate lasted almost three years. In the end, these debates also failed to fully utilize the analysis and research that stemmed from India's data collection and research systems, partly due to the political riskiness of the topic. Additionally, the analyses produced by the Planning Commission and publicly funded institutions were not taken seriously by those who opposed the bill.

Kenya: A food security task force provided the platform for discussion on both emerging and long-term food security issues in Kenya. Since 2000, its famine early warning system provided information through its monthly bulletin about at-risk populations and the vulnerability of various regions to food insecurity. During the food crisis, policy research institutions, such as the Kenya Institute for Public Policy Research and Analysis, regularly published information on food prices (Nzuma 2013). The interministerial price committee and National Cereals and Produce Board (NCPB) used information on food prices and played a key role in determining maize prices. Producer organizations, such as the Kenya Federation of Agricultural Producers and the Cereal Growers Association (CGA), were influential in demanding policy action based on the food price information. In addition, processors' and millers' associations played a crucial role in setting and affecting the maize meal prices that prevailed in the market. However, the use of information for long-term policymaking in Kenya is ad hoc at best. Yet, during the food crisis, members of parliament, particularly in the opposition, raised their voices to protect the poor and the vulnerable. Although the food security task force, comprised of public sector officials from various ministries dealing with food security issues, the private sector, and NGOs, helped in generating evidence for policy decision-making, the generation of FSNM information needs to be mainstreamed in regular food security and nutrition policymaking.

Malawi: The president of Malawi played a direct role in addressing the food crisis in the country. Due to this high-level decision-making, there was little opportunity for policy dialogue based on the FSNM information available. Several factors contributed to the government's speedy policy response: discussion of the problem in the media, pressure from the CSOs related to fertilizer policy and strategic grain reserves, and resistance to domestic trade restrictions from the private sector. Decreasing the domestic price of maize and helping farmers to produce more were seen as the president's major policy objectives. The politically motivated commitment to input subsidies for smallholder farmers drove much of the food policy process in the country (Chirwa and Chinsinga 2013). Global recognition of the country's efforts to address its food security problems in the recent past reinforced these bold yet prudent policy moves. Several insights emerge from Malawi's food crisis experience.

In the early 1990s, Malawi had a sufficiently decentralized infrastructure for data collection and analysis to address food security issues. However, high staff turnover resulted in irregular data collection from the field, and hence, inadequate analysis for designing program and policy interventions. Due to a lack of local capacity, Malawi continues to depend on external technical assistance to generate information about its food and nutrition policy issues. Analysis of policy alternatives continues to be conducted by donor-supported, external researchers, albeit in collaboration with local counterparts. There is a need to connect the FEWS NET that currently provides food security information at the regional level to household- and community-level data systems to design and implement interventions and to monitor the progress against CAADP goals.

Mozambique: An interministerial committee was formed to develop policy responses to the high food prices in Mozambique. A major source of food security information was FEWS NET, which regularly produced a monthly bulletin, both in Portuguese and in English, for more than a decade. The Ministry of Agriculture collected data on food production and agricultural commodities, albeit on an ad hoc basis, producing additional evidence for the development of intervention programs. However, there is no national-level infrastructure for regular data collection on food security and nutrition in the country.

During the food crisis, the implementation responsibilities rested on the Directorate of Economics in the Ministry of Agriculture, which has limited capacity for monitoring and evaluation (M&E), knowledge management, and evidence generation. Despite capacity challenges, the government responded by allowing imports of food grain that were successful in reducing the upward trend of food prices. Due to capacity challenges, a functional monitoring system for addressing food security issues on a regular basis has yet to be developed.

Nigeria: The National Food Reserve Agency, a specialized agency of the Ministry of Agriculture, was initiated in 2007 and entrusted with developing a food security strategy for Nigeria. However, the federal agency has limited capacity to undertake the analysis needed for strategy development. Its linkages with state ministries of agriculture are limited due to poor coordination and the absence of a formal chain of command mandating accountability of state ministries to the federal agency. Poor accountability between the state commissioners of agriculture and the federal ministry has further reduced the possibility of generating a national-level FSNM system.

At the state level, monitoring and evaluation units have inadequate human and physical capacity to handle information generation and processing responsibilities. The Agricultural Development Programs of the State, a project funded by the World Bank in the 1990s and 2000s, continues to generate information on agricultural production. However, their linkages to local development authorities are weak. Additionally, the recent decision to remove the responsibilities of the local government authorities to distribute fertilizer as part of the Agricultural Transformation Agenda reforms has further distanced local knowledge sources from state agencies. However, during the food crisis, members of the Legislative Assembly, the Federal Ministry of Agriculture and Rural Development, state-level ministries of agriculture, the National Food Reserves Agency, the National Food Security Program, the private sector (especially rice millers), CSOs, the Agriculture Research Council of Nigeria, and other agencies were brought together for consultations to discuss the high food prices that the country was facing.

Policy inconsistencies, lack of continuity, and a shift of approaches by successive governments have made it difficult for participants in the policy process to effectively develop a systematic method of integrating information use in policymaking (Olomola 2013). Weak institutional arrangements for program implementation and inadequate feedback mechanisms to identify implementation challenges resulted in the selection of policy interventions with minimal impact. Even at the national level, monitoring and evaluation of federal food security programs continues to suffer from a lack of infrastructure and capacity for data collection, processing, and analysis.

Vietnam: Several committees were established by the government to develop solutions to the increases in food prices in Vietnam. The media, despite being government-controlled, raised the issue of food insecurity in various provinces during the food crisis. This pushed the government to act swiftly. Its reaction was to ban rice exports. Public research organizations in the Ministry of Agriculture collected and disseminated information on prices and production. The food crisis also stimulated the formation of coalitions of NGOs working toward food security. These coalitions have continued to engage in policy discussions after the crisis period. The major food policy decisions are made by the prime minister, in consultation with the sectoral ministries. For example, the quantity of exports was determined in consultation with the Ministry of Agriculture and Rural Development (MARD), the Ministry of Industry and Trade (MOIT), and the Viet Food Association (VFA).

Senior policy advisors close to the government are usually consulted prior to making major policy announcements. Government decision-makers regularly consult researchers who work in public research organizations for advice. However, due to the centralized nature of decision-making in Vietnam, researchers find little room to actually discuss and debate policy options with policymakers. The information collected by monitoring systems is available to government agencies for use in their decision-making processes. However, the public and private sector have to pay for access to this data (Nguyen and Talbot 2013). Thus, even with well-developed data collection infrastructure, analysis and use of information is limited. Further, household-level data on food security is only collected by national surveys, such as the Living Standards Measurement Survey conducted once every several years. Data gaps are filled by ad hoc surveys conducted by NGOs on a small scale and are not connected to policymaking systems.

Table 5.3 summarizes the use of food security and nutrition monitoring systems in responding to food crises in the study countries. The systems for data collection, analysis, and use differed widely among these countries. In Bangladesh, a strong presence of NGOs drove the data collection and dissemination at the local level, although information on food stocks and prices in various regions and markets were monitored by the government agencies. However, sharing of the data publicly was a challenge, as access to data by private traders was seen as a threat to public policy implementation. Low capacity for data analysis and evidence use in policy and program intervention was a major challenge during the food crises. Ethiopian policymakers were proactive in using available information produced by the national systems in responding to food crises. Although better coordination of data collection and its use in program design and implementation is needed,

Table 5.3. Use of FSNM in responding to the food crisis

Country/ Information Use	In national consultative/ policy processes	Policy and program design	Emergency responses	Program M&E/ implementation	Information sharing for advocacy	Food security planning at local levels
Bangladesh	Several consultative meetings of key government ministries were held and used the data and analysis from the Ministry of Food	Interaction between Ministry of Food, which highlighted the food security problem, and the Ministry of Agriculture is not clear	Data from the districts were effectively used in tracking vulnerability and targeting the regions for food distribution	Poor use of available data and information for program design revealed capacity gaps at all levels for policy analysis and program evaluation	International and national NGOs produced information on vulnerability in various districts but not coordinated for dissemination. National information was not effectively shown among stakeholders	Data on food stock and food prices at the district levels were monitored and used in allocation and release of food to various districts
Ethiopia	Ministry of Finance and Prime Minister's office led the national-level consultations. Data and analysis of the disaster management agency was used in policy discussion	Ethiopian Development Research Institute supported evidence generation for policy responses during food crisis. Prime Minister's office provided leadership	NGOs develop emergency responses while working with donor community. Productive food subsidy program was given emphasis by the government	Monitoring of food security through production/food distribution system provided regular feedback on the food security situation	FEWS NET and GIEWS produce regular bulletins which are used in discussions by government agencies and NGOs	Effective use of data collected at lower-most administrative (Woreda) level for identifying vulnerable regions
India	Main source of national debate was the national household survey and Demographic Health Surveys used in policy debate with no direct link to policymaking	Use of information for policy design was at best indirect through researchers from the government-supported think tanks. Right to food approach was strengthened using results reported by studies of food crisis impact	Emergency responses were attempted at state level by further increasing food subsidies. No direct link to information vulnerable groups was observed	Data on food subsidy recipients and leakages in food distribution system helped to lighten the monitoring and reporting of food distribution	No systematic sharing of information on the national level. However, NGOs and support groups used their own evidence to advocate for increased state intervention	State responded based on the information gathered by their interaction programs; increased support of school feeding programs, child development services; streamlined food distribution system
Kenya	Food security task force at the national level provided consultative process for short-term and long-term policy discussion	Use of information and evidence for long-term policymaking is not fully coordinated	Maize price was determined based on food prices prevailing in the market to reduce burden on the consumers	Monitoring systems that help in regular program implementation remain weak and need strengthening for addressing food security	National famine early warning system is well developed to collate and disseminate data on food security	Local action for protecting vulnerable was called for by parliamentarians based on food prices reported in media

Malawi	Little opportunity for policy consultation; president played key role in responding to food crisis. Key policy objective was fertilizer subsidy, which was forged ahead	Fertilizer subsidy, strategic grain reserve, and domestic trade restriction were all guided by food price data collected and published by both government, FEWS NET, and CSO sources	Decreasing the domestic food price became key policy objective in response to food crisis. FEWS NET bulletins played key role in identifying vulnerable regions	Data on fertilizer subsidy, its use and distribution were monitored carefully and effectively used for specific policy agenda. Not fully connected to food security monitoring	Media was active in highlighting the food price increases; Parliamentarians, opposition leaders, and civil society organizations actively used data on food process	Fertilizer subsidy was the overreaching policy and program response. It covered all districts and vulnerable populations. Data on program implementation guided this process at local level
Mozambique	The interministerial committee to develop policy responses used both data collection by FEWS NET and by government departments	The Ministry of Agriculture and Ministry of Finance relied on the statistics collected by the Directorate of Economics. Due to capacity challenges, this effort was not systematic	Emergency responses were mainly driven by donors (such as WFP). The data collection system of donors are not integrated with government decision-making	Low capacity for functional monitoring and evaluation system prevented meaningful tracking of the impact of food price increase	Although FEWS NET was a major source of food security information, government efforts to collect, process, and disseminate information widely faced coordination challenges	At the local levels, food security interventions were mainly handled by the donors and the NGOs funded by them. No regular use of data by government agencies at the local level
Nigeria	National policy processes continue to be externally driven by donors. Use of information on food security and nutrition is limited	Policy formulation during food crisis. In the absence of national-level FSNM and capacity, use of evidence is a serious challenge	Local administrative authorities are the source of knowledge of vulnerability. Yet there is disconnect between information and action	At the state level M&E systems were used to enumerate farmers needing fertilizer subsidies. The systems are connected to federal ministry but need improvement	Information collected by state and federal agencies are not shared effectively with stakeholders	No systematic collection and use of FSNM at local authority level. State level M&E systems partially functional
Vietnam	Several stakeholder groups share information freely. Food and agricultural prices are published and discussed in media, national consultations, and inclusive discussions	Prime Minister's office made use of data produced by sectorial ministries. Policy suggestions were vetted through senior advisors from the Communist Party	Growing number of NGOs collected data at the local levels and responded with emergency interventions. Local governments engaged NGOs in problem-solving	National-level monitoring systems exists for programs and projects which were used to identify food insecurity vulnerable groups and areas during food crisis	Effective coalition of NGOs working towards food security. Effective use of local information to highlight and advocate for food security of vulnerable groups	It is not clear how the data collected from the local levels are used for designing interventions, as much of the policy program directives come from the center

Source: Author.

policymakers in Ethiopia used information from local FSNM systems. Responses to the food crises in India primarily occurred at the state level. Information produced by monitoring the public food distribution system, school feeding programs, and integrated child development services provided support to local responses. National-level data collection systems supported the evidence generation by a variety of research and analytical organizations. However, government policymakers relied solely on information provided by the think tanks they supported. The food crisis, however, was effective in triggering long-term responses, including the National Food Security Bill ensuring food security for all as a human right. Parliamentarians, opposition parties, and the private sector were active in holding the government accountable during the food crises in Kenya. Research think tanks provided regular information on food prices, which was used effectively by the national food security task forces to increase the quality of policy debate. Program monitoring of the fertilizer subsidy intervention along with the early warning system was effective in providing information for programmatic policy interventions in Malawi. Lack of capacity at the national level prevented the data collection system from functioning effectively during the food crisis in Mozambique. Institutional disconnect between federal agencies and state- and local-level authorities reduced the role of information in decision-making in Nigeria. Data generation by both the government and NGOs helped in locating the vulnerable regions and populations in Vietnam. The food crisis also forced government agencies to better organize the data generation and disseminating systems.

Lessons from the Use of Food Security and Nutrition Monitoring Systems in Responding to the Food Crisis

The recent food crisis provided an opportunity to take a hard look at the role of food security and nutrition monitoring systems in enabling evidence-informed decision-making in developing countries. Based on the analysis presented in the above section, some of the lessons for improving the effectiveness and the utility of FSNM systems are given below.

Increasing Information and Decision-Making Linkages

Use of evidence from monitoring systems during the food crisis in the study countries indicates that stronger linkages need to be established between information generation and decision-making. Involving policymakers in the design of monitoring systems improves the relevance and the flow of information for decision-making. For example, in Vietnam the food price data collected by the Ministry of Agriculture was openly available for the public and decision-makers alike, which helped provide better feedback for policymakers from the private sector and the food security-related NGOs. The sustainability of FSNM systems crucially depends on maintaining continuous linkages between information generation and decision-making.

Commitment of Country Governments

Food crises in Vietnam and Ethiopia forced these countries to streamline their monitoring systems. In countries where the monitoring systems are currently funded by the donors (for example, FEWS NET), there is recognition of the need to invest in the locally owned monitoring systems. However, a locally owned FSNM system is not likely to be sustainable without sufficient government commitment and investment. This provides an opportunity for collaboration between the systems run by the donors and those locally owned with national systems to increase the local ownership, which can further increase the use of information for decision-making.

Reorient Donor Funding Toward Capacity Development

Poor capacity to organize and implement FSNM in Mozambique during the food crisis suggests that continued donor funding may be necessary when governments lack the resources to invest in monitoring systems. However, efforts must be made to slowly wean countries off donor support in order to increase local commitment and ownership. This will help the local systems to develop further. For example, during the food crisis the Ethiopian national system produced similar information to the externally funded and run FEWS NET. However, resource constraints resulted in the delayed publication and dissemination of information collected and analyzed by the national institutions. Transferring responsibility to local institutions will require developing capacity for various FSNM activities at all levels. Collaborating with national partners and employing local professionals would be a good start to building such capacity.

Political Economy of Policymaking and Information Use

Experiences during food crises in India and Bangladesh indicate that collecting and analyzing information alone will not lead to successful policy implementation. Political pressures and the power and influence of various stakeholders, who may gain or lose from various policy responses, also matter in the policy process. Successful use of information and evidence from the monitoring systems require better understanding of the political economy of policymaking and the role of various actors and players in the policy process (Babu 2014).

Streamlining the Information Base and Creating Synergy

In countries such as Malawi and Ethiopia, policymakers were given information on the food security conditions from different sources. Multiple sources of information lead to confusion, slowing the decision-making process and often, as a consequence, lead to poor use of evidence by policymakers. Regular consultations among various systems of information generation and reporting can help in streamlining the information availability and reduce duplication of efforts.

Sustained Investment in FSNM Systems

Evidence-based decision-making during the crisis and for long-term policy development requires sound monitoring systems that can provide timely information on the nature of the food security and nutrition problems and their causal factors. Interest and investment in monitoring systems over the last 30 years closely corresponds with the occurrence of the food crises. Policymakers do not give much importance to or use information from monitoring systems during non-crisis periods. For example, group discussions in India and Bangladesh indicated that monitoring systems are expected to operate even if there is no real demand from policymakers. Due to this unintended neglect, monitoring systems deteriorate and when a crisis hits, it is often too cumbersome to organize the monitoring systems. As a result, the responses tend to be reactionary and do not result in effective programs or policies that are based on evidence.

Keeping FSNM Systems Functional

In most of the study countries, although several data collection systems existed, they were dysfunctional when the countries faced the food crisis. Low funding and deployment of staff to other functions during non-crisis periods was observed in most of the countries. Regular assessments of FSNM systems, in terms of their relevance, effectiveness, efficiency, impact, and sustainability, are essential—even in non-crisis periods—for provision of evidence for regular policymaking. Such assessments are also useful for regional and global monitoring systems to be able to refine the quality of the data collected through national systems. Sharing lessons and experiences in monitoring and exchanging innovations via regional networks can help in reducing the deficiencies of national FSNM systems.

Cross-Country Learning

Given the increased frequency of food-related emergencies, regular collection of food security data at the household, community, market, and national levels is important for preventing food-related disasters. During the recent food crisis, countries that had functioning household-level FSNM systems were better able to undertake emergency planning. A steady flow of information on food security and nutrition helped to identify resource needs, and hence, to allocate resources to where they could be most effective. Monitoring the benefits of the intervention programs and the adequacy of delivery of program interventions can help in improving their efficiency. Thus, demonstrating the benefits of FSNM systems to policymakers can improve support and resources. Sharing experiences across countries—for example, how one country effectively used its monitoring systems in decision-making—can help other countries to respect the importance of FSNM systems and value its outputs. Additional case studies are needed to promote such cross-country learning.

Well-Developed National Systems Contribute to Global Information

The recent food crisis also revealed that due to poorly developed national FSNM systems, there is a large information gap in the regional and global systems, even though they are well funded and have adequate infrastructure and capacity (UN 2009b). For example, a recent policy paper identified several key areas that could be strengthened to better track and predict global food security issues and food price changes. These include improving the quality of data on production, input, import tariffs, and policy responses. In addition, by tracking data on various food value chains, from inputs to consumption, future food crises can be better predicted, and hence, more appropriate responses can be developed. Investment is needed to build local capacity to use remote sensing technologies and to track input and output markets, local price information at decentralized markets levels, local wages rates, and tariffs (IFPRI 2010).

Connecting National Systems to Regional and Global Systems

Regional and global collaboration is essential for effective functioning of the FSNM systems during crisis periods. For example, countries in a region with similar agroecological systems face similar food and nutrition security problems. They are also interconnected through increasing regional and global trade in food and face related food safety concerns. Regional and global organizations that depend on national systems for data collection and information on food security have a responsibility to develop, nurture, and maintain a network of researchers and analysts who work on food security and nutrition issues. Regular information sharing and presentation of data to policymakers can increase government commitment to FSNM systems and hence their sustainability. Further, intra-regional cooperation can help nations in recognizing the most pressing food and nutrition security problems, which can help improve demand for FSNM systems and the information they produce.

Concluding Remarks

In this chapter we have studied the functioning of the FNSM systems, during the food crisis, for their use in evidence-based policymaking. FSNM systems have experienced cycles of support and neglect, corresponding to the frequency of food emergencies that countries face. Of the various types of monitoring systems, early warning systems are able to help policy decision-making the most, although they tend to be externally driven and funded. Monitoring food security and nutritional status as part of regular policymaking and program implementation processes has not yet been mainstreamed in many developing countries, and as a consequence, policies continue to be developed and implemented on an ad hoc basis, even during crisis periods, as shown by country examples presented in this chapter.

Each time a food crisis hits a country, either due to natural or manmade disaster, the policy system of a country is shaken. Demand for information to devise policies and programs temporarily increases, and policymakers discuss the need for strengthening data collection and surveillance systems to ensure they address policymaking needs. This is true for regional and global bodies engaged in FSNM as well. As soon as the crisis subsides, however, monitoring systems are forgotten in terms of their use, their capacity, and their funding.

Lessons from the recent food crisis and the increasing frequency of natural disasters seen in recent years call for strategic investment in monitoring systems that will forewarn and reduce the damages caused by food emergencies. Increasing the resilience of food systems is key to preparing countries to face future food crises (Babu and Blom 2014). This in turn requires sound food policy institutions that are capable of designing policy and program interventions for the immediate-, short-, medium-, and long-term. The role of evidence in this process is critical. Strengthening local FSNM systems also strengthens regional and global information systems. The systems operating at different levels cannot be seen as independent, since harmony of data collection and analytical methods is critical to providing credible information to policymakers at all levels to swiftly develop policy solutions and program interventions.

Acknowledgments

The author would like to thank Per Pinstrup-Andersen who introduced him to the field of Food Security and Nutrition Monitoring. The author also thanks David Sahn, Erin Martin, and an anonymous reviewer for their excellent comments and suggestions for improving the content of this chapter. The author takes full responsibility for any remaining errors and omissions.

Note

1. The term "food security and nutrition monitoring" encompasses a wide range of institutional and organizational arrangements at the country, regional, and global levels for evidence-based policymaking. It includes developing and sustaining data and knowledge systems, monitoring and evaluation mechanisms, policy and program development processes, and impact assessment. It has its origins in the data-based information systems that were initiated in the 1980s, both in the food security sector (national early warning systems) and nutrition sectors (nutritional surveillance systems) to inform policy and program design in order to address food security and nutrition challenges. These systems address a wide range of policy and program needs including early warning, program design and evaluation, and policy design and implementation (Babu and Pinstrup-Andersen 1994).

References

ACF International. 2011. *Food Security and Livelihood Monitoring and Evaluation Guidelines: A Practical Guide for Field Workers*. London: ACF (Action Contre la Faim) International.

Admassie, A. 2013. "The Political Economy of Food Price: The Case of Ethiopia." WIDER Working Paper No. 2013/001, UNU-WIDER, Helsinki, Finland.

Arnauld, J., J. A. Alarcón, and M. D. C. Immink. 1990. "Food Security and Food and Nutritional Surveillance in Central America: The Need for Functional Approaches." *Food and Nutrition Bulletin* 12 (1): pp. 26–33.

Babu, S. C. 1997. "Evaluating Food Security Monitoring Systems in Africa: A Case Study and Lessons from Uganda." IFPRI, Outreach Division Discussion Paper No. 20, International Food and Policy Research Institute, Washington, DC.

Babu, S. C. 2013. "Policy Process and Food Price Crisis: A Framework for Analysis and Lessons from Country Studies." WIDER Working Paper No: 2013/070, UNU-WIDER, Helsinki, Finland.

Babu, S. C., and S. Blom. 2014. "Capacity Development for Resilient Food Systems: Issues, Approaches, and Knowledge Gaps." 2020 Resilience Conference Paper 6, Addis Adaba, Ethiopia, May 15–17, 2014. International Food Policy Research Institute, Washington, DC.

Babu, S. C., and E. Chapasuka. 1997. "Mitigating the Effects of Drought through Food Security and Nutrition Monitoring: Lessons from Malawi." *Food and Nutrition Bulletin* 18 (1): pp. 71–83.

Babu, S. C., and B. Chaura. 1997. "Facing Donor Missions with Informed Policy Decisions: Lessons from Food Security and Nutrition Monitoring in Malawi." *Africa Development* 22 (2): pp. 5–24.

Babu, S. C., and G. B. Mthindi. 1994. "Household Food Security and Nutrition Monitoring: The Malawi Approach to Development Planning and Policy Interventions." *Food Policy* 19 (3): pp. 272–284.

Babu, S. C., and G. B. Mthindi. 1995a. "Developing Decentralized Capacity for Disaster Prevention: Lessons from Food Security and Nutrition Monitoring in Malawi." *Disasters* 19 (2): pp. 127–139.

Babu, S. C., and G. B. Mthindi. 1995b. "Costs and Benefits of Informed Food Policy Decisions: A Case Study of Food Security and Nutrition Monitoring in Malawi." *Quarterly Journal of International Agriculture* 34 (3): pp. 292–308.

Babu, S. C., G. B. Mthindi, and D. Ng'Ong'Ola. 1996. "Developing Decentralized Capacity for Development Policy Analysis: Lessons from Food Security and Nutrition Monitoring in Malawi." *African Development Review* 8 (1): pp. 127–145.

Babu, S. C., and P. Pinstrup-Andersen. 1994. "Food Security and Nutrition Monitoring: A Conceptual Framework, Issues, and Challenges." *Food Policy* 19 (3): pp. 218–233.

Babu, S. C., and V. J. Quinn. 1994. "Food Security and Nutrition Monitoring in Africa: Introduction and Historical Background." *Food Policy* 19 (3): pp. 211–217.

Babu, S. C., and W. Reidhead. 2007. "Measuring the Benefits of Development Research: A Case Study of Food Policy Reforms in Bangladesh." *Quarterly Journal of International Agriculture* 46 (2): pp. 159–182.

Babu, S. C., and A. Tashmatov, eds. 2000. *Food Policy Reforms in Central Asia: Setting the Research Priorities.* Washington, DC: International Food Policy Research Institute.

Bates, R. H., and S. Block. 2010. "Political Institutions and Agricultural Trade Interventions in Africa." *American Journal of Agricultural Economics* 93 (2): pp. 317–323.

Belbase, K., and R. Morgan. 1994. "Food Security and Nutrition Monitoring for Drought Relief Management." *Food Policy* 19 (3): pp. 285–300.

Besley, T., and R. Burgess. 2002. "The Political Economy of Government Responsiveness: Theory and Evidence from India." *Quarterly Journal of Economics* 117 (4): pp. 1415–1451.

Birner, R., and D. Resnick 2010. "The Political Economy of Policies for Smallholder Agriculture." *World Development* 38 (10): pp. 1442–1452.

Bryan, Shane. 2013. "A Cacophony of Policy Responses: Evidence from Fourteen Countries during the 2007/08 Food Price Crisis." WIDER Working Paper No. 2013/029, UNU-WIDER, Helsinki, Finland.

Buchanan-Smith, M. 2000. "Role of Early Warning Systems in Decision-making Processes." Overseas Development Institute, London.

Buchanan-Smith, M., and J. Cosgrave. 2010. *Evaluation of Humanitarian Action (EHA) Course Reference Manual.* London: ALNAP (Active Learning Network for Accountability and Performance) and Channel Research. <http://www.alnap.org/resources/guides/training.aspx>.

CAADP (Comprehensive Africa Agriculture Development Programme). 2010. CAADP Policy Process, NEPAD Secretariat, Pretoria.

Chirwa, E. W., and B. Chinsinga. 2013. "Dealing with the 2007/08 Global Food Price Crisis: The Political Economy of Food Price Policy in Malawi." WIDER Working Paper No. 2013/30, UNU-WIDER, Helsinki, Finland.

Devereux, S. 2001. "Food Security Information Systems." In *Food Security in Sub-Saharan Africa*, edited by S. Devereux, and M. Maxwell, pp. 201–230. London: ITDG Publishing.

Dorwood, A. R. 2013. "Agricultural Labor Productivity, Food prices and Sustainable Development Impacts and Indicators." *Food Policy* 39 (1): pp. 40–50.

FAO (Food and Agricultural Organization of the United Nations). 1998. "Development of a Regional Food Security and Nutrition Information System." FAO, Rome. <http://www.fao.org/docrep/field/383975.htm>.

FEWS NET. 2013. Famine Early Warning Systems Network. <http://www.fews.net/about-us>.

FEWS. 2014. Global Price Watch. February 2014. <http://www.fews.net/global/price-watch/fri-2014-02-28>.

FNSWG. 2013. Monthly Update. Issue 3/2013 (August). Food and Nutrition Security Working Group (Southern Africa). <http://reliefweb.int/sites/reliefweb.int/files/resources/FSNWG Update Aug 2013.pdf>.

FSIN. 2014. "Resilience Measurement Principles: Toward an Agenda for Measurement Design." Technical Series No. 1, Resilience Measurement Technical Working Group, Food Security Information Network (FSIN), Rome.

FSNAU and FEWS NET. 2013. "Study Suggests 250,000 Somalis Died Due to Severe Food Insecurity and Famine." Technical Release, United Nations Food and Agriculture Organization's (FAO) Food Security and Nutrition Analysis Unit for Somalia (FSNAU) and the USAID-funded Famine Early Warning Systems Network (FEWS NET). <http://www.fsnau.org/in-focus/technical-release-study-suggests-258000-somalis-died-due-severe-food-insecurity-and-famine->.

GIEWS (Global Information and Early Warning System on Food and Agriculture). 2013. Global Information and Early Warning System on Food and Agriculture (GIEWS), Food and Agricultural Organization (FAO), Rome.

Glantz, M. H. 1996. "Are Famines So Difficult To Predict?" *Internet Journal of African Studies*, April. <http:/www.brad.ac.uk/research/igas>.

GMFS. 2013. Global Monitoring for Food Security (GMFS). World Food Programme, Rome.

Gulati, A., and K. Ganguly. 2013. "The Political Economy of Food Price Policy: The Case Study of India." WIDER Working Paper No. 2013/034, UNU-WIDER, Helsinki, Finland.

Habicht, J. P. 2000. "Evaluation and Monitoring: Who Needs What Information and Why Do They Need It?" *Food and Nutrition Bulletin* 21 (1): pp. 87–90.

Habicht, J. P., and P. Pinstrup-Andersen. 1990. "Principles of Nutritional Surveillance." Pew/Cornell Lecture Series on Food and Nutrition Policy, Cornell Food and Nutrition Policy Program, Cornell University, Ithaca, NY.

IFPRI (International Food Policy Research Institute). 2010. IFPRI 2009 Annual Report. IFPRI, Washington, DC.

Levine, S., and C. Chastre. 2011. "Nutrition and Food Security Response Analysis in Emergency Contexts." HPG Commissioned Paper, Overseas Development Institute (ODI), London.

Mock, N., and J. Mason. 1999. "Nutrition Information Systems for Implementing Child Nutrition Programs." *Asian Development Review* 17 (1, 2): pp. 214–245.

NeKSAP (Nepal Food Security Monitoring System). 2010. Framework Document. Prepared by the Government of Nepal, the UN World Food Programme, and the Food and Agricultural Organization joint mission: <http://documents.wfp.org/stellent/groups/public/documents/ena/wfp224722.pdf>.

Nguyen, M. H., and T. Talbot. 2013. "The Political Economy of Food Price Policy: The Case of Rice Prices in Vietnam." WIDER Working Paper WP/2013/035, UNU-WIDER, Helsinki, Finland.

Nzuma, J. M. 2013. "The Political Economy of Food Price Policy: Kenya Country Case." WIDER Working Paper WP/2013/026, UNU-WIDER, Helsinki, Finland.

Olomola, A. S. 2013. "The Political Economy of Food Price Policy in Nigeria." WIDER Working Paper WP/2013/016, UNU-WIDER, Helsinki, Finland.

Pelletier. D., and U. Jonsson. 1994. "The Use of Information in the Iringa Nutrition Programme: Some Global Lessons for Nutrition Surveillance." *Food Policy* 19 (3): pp. 301–313.

Pinstrup-Andersen, P. 2009. "Food Security: Definition and Measurement." *Food Security* 1: pp. 5–7.

Pinstrup-Andersen, P., ed. 2014. *Food Price Policy in an Era of Market Instability. A Political Economy Analysis.* Oxford: Oxford University Press.

Raihan, S. 2013. "Political Economy of Food Price Policy: The Case of Bangladesh." WIDER Working Paper WP/2013/002, UNU-WIDER, Helsinki, Finland.

Ramachandran, P., and H. S. Gopalan. 2011. "Assessment of Nutritional Status in Indian Preschool Children using WHO 2006 Growth Standards." *Indian Journal of Medical Research* 134 (1): pp. 47–53.

Tucker, K., D. Pelletier, K. Rasmussen, J. P. Habicht. P. Pinstrup-Andersen, and F. Roche. 1989. "Advancement in Nutritional Surveillance: The Cornell Nutritional Surveillance Program 1981–1987." CFNPP Monograph 89-2, Cornell Food and Nutrition Policy Program, Cornell University, Ithaca, NY.

UN (United Nations). 2009a. Comprehensive Framework for Action for Addressing the Food Crisis by the UN Secretary General. UN, New York.

UN (United Nations). 2009b. "Progress Report April 2008–October 2009." High Level Task Force on the Global Security Crisis, UN, New York. <http://www.un.org/en/issues/food/taskforce/pdf/COMPLETED UN HLTF PROGRESS REPORT April 08 to Oct 09.pdf>.

Watson, II, D. D. 2013. "Political Economy Synthesis: The Food Policy Crisis." WIDER Working Paper WP/2013/050, UNU-WIDER, Helsinki, Finland.

WFP-UNICEF RIVAF. 2011. "Food and Nutrition Security Monitoring and Analysis Systems: A Review of Five Countries (Indonesia, Madagascar, Malawi, Nepal, and Zambia)." UN Global Pulse's "Rapid Impact and Vulnerability Assessment Fund" (RIVAF) research project with United Nations Children's Fund (UNICEF) and World Food Program (WFP), New York.

6

Access to Adequate Nutritious Food: New Indicators to Track Progress and Inform Action

Anna Herforth

Introduction

Access to adequate food for all is a globally held vision. The United Nations Zero Hunger Challenge, endorsed in 2013 by the UN secretary-general, includes as one of five goals, "100 percent access to adequate food all year round" (UN 2014). In some form, a food security goal will certainly be part of the post-2015 Sustainable Development Goals as well. These sets of goals succeed the Millennium Development Goals (MDGs), which have shaped the direction of development efforts among governments, donors, and non-profit organizations, for targets spanning the period from 1990–2015.

"Access to adequate food" seems like an obvious, desirable, and foundationally important goal for equity, well-being, and human development. But what, exactly, *is* access to adequate food? And what is the agriculture and food sector—which is by far the largest contributing sector to food—supposed to do about it? How is "access to adequate food" defined and measured in order to enable accountability toward that goal? A precedent was set with the MDGs, in which the only food target is *halving the proportion of people unable to access adequate calories*. The precedent for that particular target and indicator goes back at least 50 years. As the post-2015 development agenda is being debated, it is timely to revisit whether that indicator guides development efforts in a direction appropriate for addressing food problems in the world today.

The Origins of Current Indicators: Half a Century Ago

In the 1960s–1970s, it was clear what was meant by "adequate food," and it was equally clear what agriculture was supposed to do about it. There were famines and fears of mass food shortages, amidst alarm about population growth. The Green Revolution raised yields of major cereals dramatically. The Consultative Group on International Agricultural Research (CGIAR) system was formed in 1971, first with the International Rice Research Institute (IRRI) and the International Center for Improvement of Maize and Wheat (CIMMYT), with the aim of improving productivity of the major staple grains. The concept of "food security" first arose in 1974, defined as "availability at all times of adequate world food supplies" (UN 1975).

At the same time, nutritional concerns were being recognized as contributing to poor national development in addition to human development (Berg 1967, 1973). These concerns led to growing global interest in nutrition.[1] The main nutrition problems were considered to be deficiencies of calories and proteins.[2] With this focus, agriculture's key role was to provide access to adequate calories for all. Interestingly, part of the reason for this focus may have been linked to the data that were available to understand the malnutrition problem. Data on actual malnutrition prevalence were remarkably scarce. Estimates were made based on national per capita food supplies, in the absence of virtually any nationally representative surveys of child anthropometry or micronutrient status.[3] Therefore, increasing food supply would necessarily bring down estimated rates of malnutrition.

Data on Prevalence and Causes of Malnutrition Have Evolved

In the 1980s–1990s, malnutrition rates started being measured directly. Data on child and adult anthropometry have been collected regularly in nearly all countries since the mid-1990s (UNICEF 2006), primarily through the Demographic and Health Surveys (DHS), which started in 1984; UNICEF's Multiple Indicator Cluster Surveys (MICS), started in the mid-1990s; and other nationally representative surveys (for example, India's National Family Health Survey which started in 1992). Biochemical or clinical indicators of micronutrient deficiencies are collected in some of these surveys.

National survey data are compiled in annual United Nations agency reports, which are important sources of information on the prevalence and causes of malnutrition globally and by country. In 1981, UNICEF published the first of what would become its annual flagship publication: *State of the World's Children* (SOWC). Although the initial report contained no data tables, in the years that followed, the UNICEF SOWC statistical annexes became a standard reference compiling the available data on indicators related to child survival and development and child nutrition. Countries' most recent anthropometric data are published annually in UNICEF's *State of the World's Children* report, and periodically in the UN SCN *Reports on the World Nutrition Situation*. FAO has published food supply data in its flagship *State of Food and Agriculture* reports, and in *State of Food Insecurity in the World* reports.

National and global reports provide the basis for surveillance, for tracking progress toward goals, for cross-country comparisons and analyses, and for informing policy to support public well-being. They also provide the basis for advocacy and problem-framing: "In addition to identifying the problems and measuring the number of people affected, information from [food security and nutrition monitoring] is also used for sensitizing the public and the decision makers in the government and donor community" (Babu and Pinstrup-Andersen 1994).

The indicators collected and reported globally started by emphasizing nutrition as a problem of hunger, and then shifted toward nutrition as a problem of inadequate infant and childcare practices, sanitation, and health services. (See Table 6.1.) In the 1970s, the main data available for causal analysis of nutrition problems were only related to food: Dietary Energy Supply (DES) and protein supply.[4] As data on malnutrition prevalence improved in the late 1980s through the mid-1990s, understanding of the causes of malnutrition sharpened as well. The main underlying causes of malnutrition are now understood to be inadequate food, inadequate health services and unhealthy environments, and inadequate care practices; the immediate causes of malnutrition are inadequate dietary intake and disease (UNICEF 1990). Consistent with the theory about causes of malnutrition, the UNICEF SOWC data tables in the 1980s–mid-1990s included several indicators of the *health* situation and indicators of *care practices* (focused on breastfeeding). As for *food* causes of malnutrition, UNICEF and SCN initially published dietary energy supply and undernourishment statistics.[5] In 1998, all food indicators disappeared from the UNICEF SOWC report. Incidentally, that was the first year that the report's theme was "nutrition," seeming to suggest that food—or, at least the indicators available to represent food—were not relevant to a causal analysis of malnutrition.

The *health* and *care practices* indicators have evolved over time with advances in knowledge, data, and research.[6] Even anthropometric indicators have evolved: in 2013, UNICEF SOWC began reporting the prevalence of child obesity, as data become available in more countries (UNICEF 2013). In contrast, the *food* indicators have not fundamentally changed since the 1970s; they still reflect availability and access to calories. Dietary intake data are not available either. While many national surveys collect dietary

Table 6.1. Indicators on the causes of malnutrition published in UN agency flagship reports

	Food	Health	Care
1970s	Dietary Energy Supply Protein supply		
1980s–mid-1990s	Dietary Energy Supply Undernourishment Supply of iron and vitamin A*	Access to safe water Access to health services Immunization	Breastfeeding to 3 months Breastfeeding to 6 months Breastfeeding to 12 months
1998	Dietary Energy Supply Undernourishment	Access to safe water Access to adequate sanitation Immunization ORT use	Exclusive breastfeeding at 0–3 months Breastfeeding and complementary food at 6–12 months Breastfeeding at 20–23 months
2013	Dietary Energy Supply (DES) Undernourishment Protein supply % DES derived from cereals, roots, and tubers	Access to safe water Access to adequate sanitation Immunization ORS use Vitamin A supplementation	Early initiation of breastfeeding Exclusive breastfeeding to 6 months Introduction of solid/semi- solid/soft foods 6–8 months Breastfeeding at age 2 years

Notes: UNICEF SOWC in the 1980s also had indicators of "Index of food production per capita."

UNICEF SOWC 1998, % consuming iodized salt appeared.

FAO SOFI 2013 also includes in the suite of indicators: "% protein from animal origin" and "average value of food production" but what these are supposed to indicate regarding food security is not explained in the report.

Sources: UNICEF SOWC, SCN Reports on the World Nutrition Situation, FAO SOFA and SOFI reports (UNICEF 1987, 1994, 1997, 1998, 2013; UN ACC/SCN 1987, 1992; UNSCN 2010; FAO 1976; FAO 1998; FAO et al. 2013)

* The supply of iron and vitamin A in food was published in the first SCN Reports on the World Nutrition Situation (1987, 1992) only for the purpose of estimating the prevalence of iron and vitamin A deficiencies, since no biochemical data were available.

intake information using diverse methods and indicators, the DHS and MICS surveys do not, and there are no globally comparable indicators of diet quality compiled or published.

The Concept of Food Security Has Evolved

The concept of food security was new in 1974, when at the World Food Summit it was defined as "availability at all times of adequate world food supplies" (UN 1975). In the 20 years that followed, the concept of food security evolved and, in reality, diversified (Pinstrup-Andersen and Herforth 2008; Jones et al. 2013). As some stakeholders continued to place primary importance on world food supplies, new theory and analyses showed that world or even national supplies were not sufficient for the poor to obtain adequate food (Sen 1982; Pinstrup-Andersen 1984). The current most widely used definition of food security emerged from the 1996 World Food Summit, as "physical and economic access to sufficient, safe, nutritious food to meet dietary needs and food preferences for a healthy and active life" (FAO 1996). While in the 1970s, the major concern was world food supply, the concern now is *access* to food—and not just sufficient calories, but *safe and nutritious* food for a healthy and active life. The definition also clarifies that income is not enough to guarantee access to adequate food all year round; inadequate availability and physical access (such as proximity or ease of obtaining food) can be barriers as well.

Why Have Food Indicators Not Evolved?

When the leaders of the world agreed to a new food security definition nearly 20 years ago, no clear indicators or targets accompanied it. Ensuring commitment to "nutritious food to meet dietary needs" would seem to be a major nutrition issue, but advocacy around it was limited. The attention of the nutrition community was not on food at the time, but strongly focused on other causes of malnutrition that were seen as more limiting and on interventions that were considered more cost-effective.[7]

The first UNICEF SOWC report, in 1980, emphasized: "The major lesson of the last 20 years is that reductions in malnutrition cannot be achieved only by increases in food production" (Grant 1981, p. 10).[8] In the 1970s, much effort was put into multisectoral nutrition planning, including a focus on agriculture to increase food access among the poor and nutritionally vulnerable. Political commitment to nutrition beyond basic food supply increases did not materialize, however. The field of nutrition moved away from multisectoral planning, and attention turned elsewhere during a period sometimes referred to as "nutrition isolationism" (Levinson and McLachlan 1999), when the field of nutrition incubated its story, data, and priorities. Research focused on micronutrients, breastfeeding, community-based interventions to treat malnutrition, and on exposing the consequences of malnutrition. The capstone of this coalescing evidence base for nutrition was the 2008 *Lancet Series on Maternal and Child Undernutrition*, which enumerated direct nutrition interventions that had been studied and honed over the previous 20–30 years, strongly supported by a clear storyline on the costly consequences of undernutrition. The prevalence, causes, and consequences of poor diets were not part of the evidence base.

The nutrition community's distant relationship with food issues since the 1970s, though, is perhaps consistent with its earliest roots. Since vitamin deficiencies were discovered around the turn of the 20th century, the main responses were nutrient and food supplementation, food fortification, and nutrition education.[9] Poor *diet quality* has been traditionally treated primarily as a personal affair: either medical (solved by supplementation—or now, bariatric surgery), or behavioral (solved by nutrition education), but rarely systemic (solved by food and economic policy). A case could be made that this tradition is rooted in gendered fields of study and influence: women studied nutrition within home economics departments and could address dietary intakes via nutrition education; agricultural economics, which dealt with agricultural research and policy, was primarily the realm of men and did not often deal with nutrition directly.[10] If nutrition education efforts were the primary tool to improve dietary intake (i.e., attempts to change *care practices*), in conjunction with micronutrient supplements for missing nutrients, then care practices would be the most relevant factor to track. Indeed, the only dietary quality indicator currently collected at global scale is for young children (Minimum Acceptable Diet) and was created to reflect care practices (WHO 2008).[11]

Urban Jonsson has observed that paradigm shifts occur when "the old paradigm increasingly fails to explain phenomena or causes of a problem... Paradigm shifts are most often the result of either new scientific discovery and/or a changing 'ethical climate', influenced by changing political and ideological positions. Sometimes both take place" (Jonsson 2009, p. 2). The field of nutrition may now be on the cusp of a new paradigm that emphasizes food systems. There is renewed emphasis on agriculture as part of the twin-track agenda of nutrition-specific and nutrition-sensitive development introduced with the Scaling Up Nutrition (SUN) movement. And increasingly, the evidence shows that the range of nutrition problems today has a great deal to do with food.

The Nature of Nutrition Problems Has Changed

The prevalence of nutritional problems has shifted over time. The range of nutritional problems today is sometimes referred to as the "triple burden" of malnutrition (Gómez et al. 2013): undernutrition (stunting affects 165 million children), micronutrient deficiencies (estimated to affect 2 billion people), and overweight/obesity (affecting 1.5 billion people), and related non-communicable disease. These coexist in the same countries and even the same households and individuals. Among 80 countries identified as "high stunting-burden" (child stunting rates of 20 percent or higher[12]), over one-third have adult overweight/obesity rates of over 30 percent, and 14 high stunting-burden countries have overweight/obesity rates of 50 percent or greater (Figure 6.1). Sub-Saharan Africa and South Asia—the regions with the highest burden of child undernutrition—are also projected to have the highest increases in diabetes by 2030 (IDF 2011). These statistics show that obesity and related chronic disease are not only problems for wealthy nations or people. In fact, they are more problematic for the poor, since the poor are more likely to develop and die from untreated diet-related chronic disease (such as diabetes) than the wealthy (WHO 2010).

The coexistence of these nutrition problems is unquestionably related to poor diets and the types of food people can access. The most prevalent non-communicable diseases are attributable mainly to diet. The Institute for Health Metrics and Evaluation reports that dietary risks are the top cause of

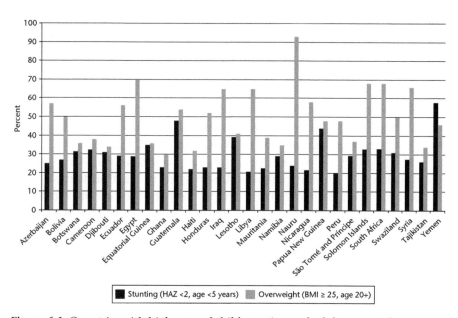

Figure 6.1 Countries with high rates of child stunting and adult overweight

Data source: WHO Global Health Observatory Data Repository, UNICEF Statistics by Area (WHO 2013; UNICEF 2014).

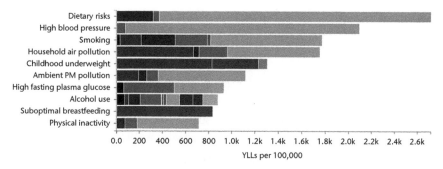

Figure 6.2 Top 10 causes of years of life lost (YLLs); all developing countries, 2010

Data source: Institute for Health Metrics and Evaluation, "GBD Compare" data visualization tool (IHME 2013).

disability-adjusted life years (DALYs) and years of life lost for all developing countries combined (IHME 2013) (Figure 6.2).[13] Among the top contributors to dietary risks are low fruit and vegetables, high sodium, low nuts and seeds, low whole grains, low omega-3 fatty acids, low fiber, and high processed meat (IHME 2013).

Inadequate Access to Nutritious Food

The available data suggest that in many countries it is not possible for most of the population to access adequate nutritious food to meet dietary needs, even if they could afford it. Figure 6.3 shows that, based on food availability data from sub-Saharan Africa, starchy roots and cereals would be expected to dominate diets, as they do. Fruits, vegetables, and pulses are not available enough, let alone affordable enough, for all people to have nutritious diets. There are just 254 g of fruits and vegetables available per capita daily—compared to 400–600 g per day recommended by WHO and FAO (2003; Lock et al. 2004). Only 35 g of pulses are available per capita daily in sub-Saharan Africa, which is well below the amount that would be needed to meet protein needs in combination with starches.[14] These are precisely the food groups lacking in diets associated with greater years of life lost (IHME 2013). Low availability

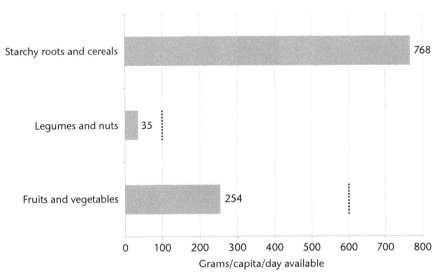

Figure 6.3 Food availability in sub-Saharan Africa

Data source: FAOSTAT, 2009 data (FAO 2014).

Note: Bars represent amounts available for consumption; dotted lines represent estimated nutritional needs.

of non-staples is reflected in high prices. In Bangladesh, consumption and expenditure surveys showed that staple foods made up over 80 percent of energy intake, with non-staple plants accounting for about 15 percent and animal-source foods less than 4 percent, but each of three food groups required approximately one-third of the household food budget (Bouis et al. 2011). If dietary guidelines are believable as evidence-based standards of nutritious diets, and if food availability and price data are believable, then there is clear evidence of inadequate access to food.

Increasing Access to Unhealthy Food

Markets respond to demand signals, and the conventional wisdom says that if incomes are sufficient, the food environment should be a good reflection of the kinds of foods people want to consume. For example, a key message of the FAO SOFA 2013 report, stated in the report's executive summary and on its landing webpage: "Consumers ultimately determine what they eat and therefore what the food system produces" (FAO 2013, p. xii).[15] The relationship is bi-directional, though: while demand undoubtedly influences production, what consumers eat is affected by availability and prices of food. These are in part determined by supply-side factors: for example, policies that provide incentives or disincentives for certain kinds of production, production constraints or risk associated with producing certain crops or livestock, and barriers to entry from one kind of crop/livestock production to another.

It is also worth considering where the demand is coming from. Pinstrup-Andersen has observed that, "In high-income and rapidly growing low-income countries, the agricultural sector has become or is rapidly becoming a supplier of raw materials for the food processing industry, rather than a provider of food for direct consumption" (Pinstrup-Andersen 2013, p. 375). In many contexts, the food processing industry is both scriptwriter and translator between individual consumers and agricultural producers, and it can shape what the food system produces through direct contracts with farmers, its own research and development, and political influence of agri-food policy. Ultra-processed foods are increasingly available and marketed in low- and middle-income countries (Monteiro et al. 2010), demanding increased production of ingredients for these foods (primarily refined starches, oils, and sugars) at the same time as supply of nutritious, minimally processed foods is constrained.

Eating norms and habits can change over time and are influenced by the kinds of food available, affordable, convenient, and marketed. Much of the research documenting what is known as "the nutrition transition" describes a convergence of patterns in disparate places, consistent with availability, convenience, and marketing of less healthy foods (Sobal 1999; Popkin 2003;

Popkin et al. 2005). Research on dietary patterns of immigrants shows a robust trend of acculturation to the norms and types of food available in the new country (Satia-Abouta et al. 2002). These studies of the nutrition transition and dietary acculturation of immigrants offer strong evidence that food environments shape personal choice.

If healthy diets are more expensive and less convenient than unhealthy diets, then diet quality is unlikely to be optimized through the traditional tools of the nutrition community (nutrition education) and agricultural economics (income generation) alone. It is improbable that nutrition education will cause people to spend their income counter to market signals. It is even more improbable if eating habits and food preferences have shifted toward unhealthy ultra-processed foods and away from healthy food preferences present in many traditional diets.

Why Is It Important to Monitor Access to Adequate Nutritious Food and Dietary Quality?

Because the food environment is created not only by consumer preferences, but also by multiple supply-side and demand-side factors, there is a role for policy to influence those factors. Current food data are insufficient for informing actions to improve access to nutritious food and to create incentives (and remove disincentives) for better nutrition. Three main reasons food data need to be expanded include:

1. Consistency with ideals

Simply put, the food indicators collected and reported today do not match the vision for food security of *access to sufficient, safe, nutritious food to meet dietary needs*, set forth by the global community almost 20 years ago (FAO 1996). Using food-based dietary guidelines as a basis, access to "nutritious food to meet dietary needs" should be tracked.

2. Ability to identify major causes of malnutrition

Indicators of access to and consumption of adequate nutritious food are basic data that are, to date, missing in the world's ability to identify causes of malnutrition. Great strides have been made in the monitoring of nutritional status, infant and young childcare practices, and health risk factors; infectious disease prevalence is also well monitored. These data enable analysis of the important causes of malnutrition in a given country or region, and appropriate policy options to address them. Current indicators of food, however, do not allow for understanding food causes of malnutrition beyond lack of calories. Access to calories is not closely correlated with undernutrition,[16] suggesting that either food access is irrelevant to nutrition (improbable), or the way it is measured needs improvement. In addition, dietary quality is the factor probably most synonymous with a layperson's or policymaker's concept of nutrition, but data to describe it are missing. At a time when the triple burden of malnutrition exists in all regions and income levels, and diet quality is a key factor underlying all of these forms of malnutrition, it is an almost unbelievable data gap that no globally comparable indicators of dietary quality are collected.

3. Ability to track progress on nutrition-sensitive agriculture

Addressing nutrition through agriculture is now high on agendas, and substantial investments are being made in nutrition-sensitive agriculture—for example, $19 billion was committed by many donors and governments in 2013 at the G8 meetings (Government of UK 2013). Yet targets and benchmarks in the agriculture sector for improved nutrition are largely absent. Effects of these investments need to be monitored on food—the agriculture and food sector's main, unique contribution to nutrition. A consensus view is that, "Food and agriculture policies can have a better impact on nutrition if they monitor dietary consumption and access to safe, diverse, and nutritious foods" (Agriculture-Nutrition Community of Practice 2013). In the absence of such indicators and targets, it will be difficult to capture how "nutrition-sensitive" investments are contributing to improved nutrition.

Overall, indicators on access to adequate nutritious food and dietary quality would enable better informed policy options to improve food security and nutrition. If collected over time, these indicators would also allow for an improved evidence base of how agriculture and food policies and programs can affect nutrition. Such monitoring data do not guarantee policy solutions; the data could lead to a variety of responses in various sectors, and may not necessarily lead to immediate action. Without basic information on the food situation and what people are eating, however, any efforts to address food insecurity and malnutrition have a major blind spot. The following section proposes examples of indicators that could help to fill the information gaps on food.

Global Monitoring of Access to Adequate Nutritious Food and Diet Quality

Tracking "access to adequate food all year round" is a deceptively simple idea. It is well recognized, though, that no single indicator will be able to capture all aspects of it. In 2013, for the first time, the annual *State of*

Food Insecurity in the World (SOFI) report included a suite of 30 indicators, intended to capture various aspects of food insecurity (FAO et al. 2013). This in itself indicates a movement away from relying only on the undernourishment indicator as a proxy for food security. Still, few indicators in the new suite shed light on the availability, access, and dietary consumption of healthy diets. To fill this information gap, indicators could be monitored at four levels: national-level food availability, local-level food environments, household-level food access, and individual-level diet quality. The following sections explore current and possible indicators at each of these four levels, summarized in Table 6.2.

Table 6.2. Possible indicators of adequate food

Indicators	Notes
National-level food availability	
– % Non-starches	Negatively correlated with stunting (FAO et al. 2013) but not correlated with obesity (Remans et al. 2014)
– Fruit and vegetable availability	Falls below need in most countries in the world (Siegel et al. 2014)
– Sugar availability	Significantly associated with diabetes prevalence (Basu et al. 2013)
– Availability of other food groups	Could be useful if recommended amounts were established
Local-level food environments	
– Cost of healthy diets	Important information but insufficient: would need disaggregation by food group to go beyond status quo policy conclusion (increase incomes and decrease price of food generally)
– Prices of different food groups	Could show which components of the food basket are causing healthy diets to be less affordable
– In some locales: Community-level production diversity	May be useful where a majority of food is produced and consumed locally
– In some locales: Indicators of obesogenic food environments	May be useful where markets are easily accessible
Household-level food access	
– Food Insecurity Experience Scale (FIES)	An informative complement to dietary data; the experience of food insecurity can only be gained from household survey data (Ballard et al. 2013)
Individual-level diet quality	
– Women's dietary diversity (MDD-W)	Validated for micronutrient adequacy (FAO and IRD 2014); can be used as a dichotomous or quasi-continuous indicator
– Botanical dietary variety	May be associated with reduced risk of chronic disease
– Proportion of ultra-processed foods in the diet (Monteiro 2013)	A lower proportion may be associated with improved dietary quality and reduced risk of chronic disease

Source: Author.

National-Level Food Availability

At the national level, data are available that could be used in a more informative way to illustrate the general picture of food availability in a country. Ideally, national-level data could be used to estimate the per capita supply of food groups and to understand whether it is theoretically possible for all people in a country to access adequate food as recommended in dietary guidelines. The data could not explain the reasons for a supply gap or excess, but could show whether there is one. For example, 400–600 g per capita daily of fruits and vegetables are recommended as a minimum intake for healthy diets (WHO and FAO 2003; Lock et al. 2004). Recent analyses show that fruit and vegetable availability falls below dietary need in most countries in the world (Keats and Wiggins 2014; Siegel et al. 2014). WHO also recommends limiting salt to less than 2 g per day (WHO 2012) and has drafted a guideline to limit sugar consumption to 5 percent of dietary energy intake (WHO 2014). National-level sugar availability appears to be significantly associated with diabetes prevalence (Basu et al. 2013). For other food groups, there is currently no international recommendation for amounts needed.[17]

Currently, the national-level food indicators reported in the *State of Food Insecurity in the World 2013* include the traditional indicators—dietary energy supply, protein supply, and undernourishment—as well as two indicators related to the type of food available: share of dietary energy supply derived from cereals, roots, and tubers; and average supply of protein of animal origin (FAO et al. 2013). The latter is difficult to interpret, since there is no defined optimal value, and it is not clear whether increases are positive or negative.[18] The former may reflect nutritious food access to some extent, because as the share of energy supply from starchy staples goes down, the proportion of stunting also goes down (FAO et al. 2013; Remans et al. 2014). It is probably not a sufficient indicator, however, of access to adequate nutritious food for several reasons. First, it could indicate the likelihood of consuming diets excessive in animal-source food, sugar, and fat, because these are all also highly correlated with a lower proportion of energy supply in starchy staples and gross national income (FAO 1998; Popkin 2003; FAO et al. 2013). Indeed, the indicator of energy supply derived from non-staples is not significantly correlated with obesity rates (Remans et al. 2014). Second, appropriate policy responses would be difficult to define, since it does not indicate which parts of the diet are relatively more or less accessible.

National-level indicators of nutritious food availability are highly feasible to report, since FAO collects food availability data annually. Using FAO's food balance sheets, both the per capita supply and estimated prevalence of inadequate consumption (or overconsumption) of the various food groups could be calculated. Furthermore, the same technique used to calculate undernourishment could be adapted to calculate the prevalence of people not able to consume recommended amounts of various food groups. National food availability data cannot provide direct information on dietary quality (which requires survey data), but could provide useful information underlying the food access and dietary consumption patterns.

Local-Level Food Environments

National-level data can mask significant regional and local differences. The local level is most significant for eating behaviors, because it is where households interact with the market—it is where prices, convenience, advertising, and norms have the most influence on consumption behavior. Ideally, local- or community-level data would be collected on availability, affordability, and convenience of various food groups or food types.

A promising type of indicator is of affordability of adequate nutritious diets. On average, healthy diets cost approximately US$10.50 per week more than unhealthy alternatives (Rao et al. 2013).[19] Various tools have been developed that could measure cost of adequate nutritious diets, such as Save the Children's "Cost of Diet" tool which results in an indicator "percent of households who cannot afford a balanced diet" (Chastre et al. 2009). This indicator highlights the issue of access to nutritious diets, although it would likely result in policy implications no different than the status quo: raise incomes and lower overall food prices. In order to know *which* foods are out of reach, any data on the cost of a nutritious food basket should be able to be disaggregated into different food groups of public health significance (e.g., grains and tubers, fruits and vegetables, legumes and nuts, milk, other animal-source foods, and ultra-processed foods).

Currently, local-level data on market prices are regularly compiled and reported only for staple grains on the World Food Programme's VAM website (WFP 2014). The techniques used to gather and report these data might possibly be expanded to other foods as well. Quality of existing market price data collected by ministries of agriculture is probably highly variable. Methods for aggregating data and coming to a price representing the whole food group need to be developed, possibly taking cues from the minimum food basket methodology.

Other community-level food environment indicators have been developed in high-income countries to reflect "obesogenic" food environments (Glanz 2009; Swinburn et al. 2013). These types of indicators may be increasingly relevant globally. In less urban, more agricultural locales, production diversity may be a useful local indicator—one study in Kenya showed that community-level production diversity was associated with greater household dietary diversity (Remans et al. 2011).

Household-Level Food Access

Household survey data is needed for information on food consumption and the direct experience of food insecurity. A limitation of household surveys is that they are usually not done every year, so they cannot be used for yearly monitoring or indices. Ideally, household-level data would be collected on experience-based measures that ask household respondents directly about food insecurity-related feelings or behaviors (such as, "did anyone in the household go to bed hungry in the last month?"). Currently, such an experience-based scale has been validated for all of Latin America (FAO 2012). The Food Insecurity Experience Scale, developed by the FAO Voices of the Hungry project, is based on the Latin American scale and earlier similar scales (Radimer et al. 1990; Coates et al. 2006), and was being piloted in the Gallup World Poll in 2014 (Ballard et al. 2013). Certain indicators of household consumption, such as the Food Consumption Score and Household Dietary Diversity Score, are validated against calorie consumption (Hoddinott and Yohannes 2002; Wiesmann et al. 2009) and have been shown to be correlated with child nutritional status (Tiwari et al. 2013). There may be possibilities to improve household-level consumption data through household consumption and expenditure surveys (HCES), but the best data for dietary quality is at the individual level.

Individual-Level Diet Quality

Dietary intake is closely linked to nutrition, health, and development outcomes. Along with food access data, dietary quality information would be an important indicator to enable targets or benchmarking for nutrition-sensitive policies and programs, particularly in the agriculture sector. Some countries measure dietary quality in national surveys, and FAO is undertaking an effort to create a global database of dietary intake data. Currently, however, there are no globally comparable indicators of diet quality collected.[20] Ideally, diet quality indicators would reflect how closely diets align with dietary recommendations (which are based on both nutrient adequacy and epidemiologic data). Furthermore, ideal diet quality indicators would be easy to collect, analyze, and interpret. Scores with cut-offs for adequate values may be the kind of dietary data most easily interpretable by policymakers.

Individual dietary diversity scores, in particular the minimum dietary diversity for women indicator (MDD-W), aim to reflect nutrient adequacy. They are highly feasible to collect and have been developed and validated against adequacy of micronutrients (FAO 2011; FAO and IRD 2014). A limitation of dietary diversity scores is that although they correlate well with nutrient adequacy, they do not have a strong or meaningful association with overconsumption or chronic disease. As that is increasingly a problem with dietary quality, additional or other indicators are needed. Botanical dietary variety (the number of plant foods consumed over a specified recall period) may be an indicator of present and future chronic disease risk. Another possible indicator, used in research in Brazil where diets are rapidly changing, is the proportion of ultra-processed foods in the diet (Monteiro 2013). The USDA monitors dietary quality in the US with an indicator, the Healthy Eating Index, which is designed to measure how well diets match the Dietary Guidelines for Americans, and measures both "adequacy" (getting enough of certain foods or nutrients) and "moderation" components (not getting too much of certain foods or nutrients) (Kennedy 2008). This sort of indicator could be adapted for global use.

Conclusion

Current global indicators, data, and targets are insufficient to monitor access to adequate food and dietary quality. This data gap results in an inability to analyze major causes of malnutrition, or to track progress related to nutrition-sensitive agriculture investments. Most importantly, it precludes accountability toward a goal of universally agreed importance: that all people, at all times, have access to sufficient, safe, and nutritious food for a healthy and active life (rearticulated in the UN Zero Hunger Challenge as "100 percent access to adequate food all year round") (FAO 1996; UN 2014).

What is monitored at the global scale has consequences. The Millennium Development Goals have shown the importance of well-chosen indicators: "The MDGs have had enormous communicative power. Once the goals were defined and the targets set, they began to shape the way that development was understood" (Fukuda-Parr et al. 2013, p. 19). In the post-2015 development agenda, the global community now has an opportunity to align indicators better with ideals for food access—especially since it is increasingly clear that poor diets are a major cause of all forms of malnutrition, and food access is a major contributor to poor diets.

Current global measurement of food access was made for a different world of 50 years ago. Then, the challenge was *food shortage*. Now, the major problem in most places in the world is *nutritious food shortage* (World Bank 2014). Based on current food availability data, it is theoretically possible for everyone to consume *enough*, but it is impossible for everyone to consume *nutritious diets*. The required data and indicators to reflect this new food challenge are not monitored yet; and some indicators probably need to be developed (see Table 6.2). That, however, should not prevent the inclusion of indicators in global monitoring frameworks now.[21]

One lesson from history is that the core data collected and published can change, resulting in a better understanding over time of the problems that need to be tackled. Thirty years ago, the collection and reporting of data on anthropometry and infant feeding behaviors was a daunting challenge, but one that was overcome, with enormous impact due to how the data have been used.

The challenge now is to update the way "food" is monitored globally. Given the current triple burden of malnutrition, data and indicators need to reflect access to *nutritious* food, along with dietary quality. It may take time to get the ideal indicators, but analogous to how indicators of infant feeding evolved, there are feasible indicators available now (see Table 6.2). Indicators such as women's dietary diversity and the cost of a nutritious diet would already be informative, and they can start to highlight the issue of nutritious food as worthy of global attention. Collecting and reporting better food indicators would give policymakers the necessary information to weigh potential policy and program options to improve nutritious food access, particularly in the agriculture and food sector. Indicators aligned with the vision of "adequate food for all" are vital to action and accountability toward that ideal.

Notes

1. For example, the World Bank created a nutrition unit for the first time in 1973, based on the rationale that malnutrition contributes to poverty.
2. According to a World Bank policy document, "The major nutrition problem in the world today, according to most nutritionists, is insufficient intake of calories, or food energy" (World Bank 1980, p. i). Another report stated, "Although deficiency of vitamins and minerals may cause serious health problems, especially among children, the therapy is now well known and relatively easy to apply so that the magnitude of this problem is almost negligible in relation to the one created by lack of calories and proteins" (Chafkin et al. 1972, p. 7).
3. From the *State of Food and Agriculture 1975*:

   Most of the present knowledge of nutritional problems has had to be derived from national average figures of per caput food supplies, because of the inadequate number of reliable household consumption, budgetary and clinical surveys. While still far from adequate, the limited available information is, however, sufficient to demonstrate some of the broad features of the nutritional situation, the awesome magnitude of the problem, and the urgent need for action. (FAO 1976, p. 75)

   From the *First Report on the World Nutrition Situation*:

   These analyses must be regarded as of a tentative nature because of the scarcity of data on child anthropometry which would provide the basis for a robust assessment of trends. (UN ACC/SCN 1987, p. 6)

4. These indicators were published in the *State of Food and Agriculture* (SOFA) reports, the flagship publication of the UN Food and Agriculture Organization (FAO).

5. These statistics continue to be published yearly in FAO's *State of Food Insecurity in the World* reports. According to the FAO, "Undernourishment refers to the condition of people whose dietary energy consumption is continuously below a minimum dietary energy requirement for maintaining a healthy life and carrying out a light physical activity" (FAO 2014). By using data on income inequality, the undernourishment indicator added an element of "access" to the construct, which had previously only been about national-level supply.

6. For example, indicators of infant feeding shifted to *exclusive* breastfeeding and timely introduction of complementary foods.

7. For a comprehensive review of nutrition priorities over time, see World Bank (2014).

8. This echoed advocates for improving the contribution of agriculture to nutrition, who had said that aggregate food production was not sufficient—that nutritional objectives needed to be explicit, and that agricultural investments needed to target the poor and nutritionally vulnerable (World Bank 1980; Pinstrup-Andersen 1981).

9. The first United States Department of Agriculture (USDA) dietary guidelines, "How to Select Foods" by Caroline Hunt and Helen Atwater, was published in 1917.

10. It was in the 1970s that agricultural economists became involved (e.g., Pinstrup-Andersen and Calcedo 1977), as systemic issues became a focus in nutrition within multisectoral nutrition planning (Berg 1987).

11. This indicator is collected in DHS and MICS surveys.

12. Horton et al. (2010) used a cut-off of stunting rates of 20 percent or higher to identify high stunting-burden countries.

13. The calculation of dietary risks to years of life lost only deals with those related to non-communicable disease, and not undernutrition, so it is likely an underestimate of the overall impact of poor diets.

14. In the absence of an amount specified by dietary guidelines, calculating the amount that would meet protein requirements is one way to estimate need, which may be appropriate since legumes are the primary protein source for the poorest (methodology found in Herforth [2010, 159–160]). Their contribution to dietary quality goes beyond protein, however, due to their fiber and phytonutrient content. Several studies in high-income countries have shown greater consumption of legumes and nuts to be associated with a variety of improved health outcomes, including reduced all-cause mortality (Bao et al. 2013).

15. The same report also states: "... governments, international organizations, the private sector and civil society can all help consumers make healthier decisions... by providing information and ensuring access to diverse and nutritious foods" (FAO 2013, p. xii).

16. "The relationship between the prevalence of undernourishment and the percentage of preschool children who are stunted is quite weak. ($R^2 = 0.28$)" (FAO et al. 2013).

17. There are no recommended amounts of food groups, apart from fruits and vegetables, primarily because the nutrients in various foods are substitutable between food types. The health benefits from plant foods such as fruits and vegetables, however, probably come primarily from their phytonutrient content rather than

micronutrient content, which is why they are not substitutable. Although there is no recommended amount of legumes and nuts, greater consumption of them is associated with reduced all-cause mortality in high-income countries (Bao et al. 2013). There is no recommendation on an optimal amount of animal-source food consumption, which may depend on life-cycle stage, as well as the type of animal-source food (milk, meat, fish, etc.).

18. An increase in animal protein consumption might be consumed disproportionately by the wealthier, for whom increases may be negative for health, instead of by the poor, for whom increases may be positive for health.

19. A majority of studies were from high-income countries, but the authors note that results were similar between high-income and lower-income countries.

20. While indicators of diet quality for young children are very recently collected (e.g., Minimum Acceptable Diet, WHO [2008]), these are primarily reflective of care practices and not reflective of diets in the general population.

21. Reflecting on the inclusion criteria for MDG indicators, which specified that data should be presently available, one scholar has observed that, "It may be the case that issue areas that have been underemphasized or marginalized may be precisely the ones for which data is lacking. To then use this lack of data to exclude these issues from the goal-setting process is to compound the marginalization" (Fukuda-Parr et al. 2013, p. 27).

References

Agriculture-Nutrition Community of Practice. 2013. Key Recommendations for Improving Nutrition through Agriculture. <http://unscn.org/files/Agriculture-Nutrition-CoP/Agriculture-Nutrition_Key_recommendations.pdf>.

Babu, S., and P. Pinstrup-Andersen. 1994. "Food Security and Nutrition Monitoring: A Conceptual Framework, Issues and Challenges." *Food Policy* 19 (3): pp. 218–233.

Ballard, T., A. W. Kepple, and C. Cafiero. 2013. "The Food Insecurity Experience Scale: Development of a Global Standard for Monitoring Hunger Worldwide." FAO Technical Paper, Food and Agricultural Organization of the United Nations (FAO), Rome. <http://www.fao.org/economic/ess/ess-fs/voices/en/>.

Bao, Y., J. Han, F. B. Hu, E. L. Giovannucci, M. J. Stampfer, W. C. Willett, and C. S. Fuchs. 2013. "Association of Nut Consumption with Total and Cause-Specific Mortality." *New England Journal of Medicine* 369 (21): pp. 2001–2011.

Basu, S., P. Yoffe, N. Hills, and R. H. Lustig. 2013. "The Relationship of Sugar to Population-Level Diabetes Prevalence: An Econometric Analysis of Repeated Cross-Sectional Data." PLoS ONE 8 (2): e57873. doi:10.1371/journal.pone.0057873.

Berg, A. 1967. "Malnutrition and National Development." *Foreign Affairs* (October 1). <http://www.foreignaffairs.com/articles/23929/alan-d-berg/malnutrition-and-national-development>.

Berg, A. 1973. The Nutrition Factor: Its Role in National Development. Washington, DC: The Brookings Institute.

Berg, A. 1987. "Nutrition Planning Is Alive and Well, Thank You." *Food Policy* 12 (4): pp. 365–375.

Bouis, H., P. Eozenou, and A. Rahman. 2011. "Food Prices, Household Income, and Resource Allocation: Socioeconomic Perspectives on Their Effects on Dietary Quality and Nutritional Status." *Food and Nutrition Bulletin* 32 (1): pp. S14–S23.

Chafkin, S., J. Pines, A. Berg, and R. Longhurst. 1972. *A Review of Possible World Bank Actions on Malnutrition Problems.* American Technical Assistance Corporation—January 1972, Folder 347351, World Bank Group Archives, Washington, DC.

Chastre, C., A. Duffield, H. Kindness, S. LeJeune, and A. Taylor. 2009. "The Minimum Cost of a Healthy Diet: Findings from Piloting a New Methodology in Four Study Locations." London: Save the Children. <http://www.savethechildren.org.uk/sites/default/files/docs/The_Minimum_Cost_of_a_Healthy_Diet_corrected09_1.pdf>.

Coates, J., A. Swindale, and P. Bilinsky. 2006. *Household Food Insecurity Access Scale (HFIAS) for Measurement of Household Food Access: Indicator Guide* (v. 2). Washington, DC: Food and Nutrition Technical Assistance Project, Academy for Educational Development.

FAO (Food and Agricultural Organization). 1976. *The State of Food and Agriculture 1975.* Rome: Food and Agricultural Organization of the United Nations.

FAO (Food and Agricultural Organization). 1996. "Rome Declaration on World Food Security and World Food Summit Plan of Action." Food and Agricultural Organization of the United Nations, Rome. <http://www.fao.org/docrep/003/w3613e/w3613e00.HTM>.

FAO (Food and Agricultural Organization). 1998. *The State of Food and Agriculture 1998.* Rome: Food and Agricultural Organization of the United Nations.

FAO (Food and Agricultural Organization). 2011. *Guidelines for Measuring Household and Individual Dietary Diversity.* Rome: Food and Agricultural Organization of the United Nations. <http://www.fao.org/docrep/014/i1983e/i1983e00.pdf>.

FAO (Food and Agricultural Organization). 2012. *Escala Lationamericana y Caribena de Seguridad Alimentaria (ELCSA): Manual de Uso y Aplicaciones. Comité Científico de la ELCSA.* Rome: Food and Agricultural Organization of the United Nations.

FAO (Food and Agricultural Organization). 2013. *The State of Food and Agriculture 2013.* Rome: Food and Agricultural Organization of the United Nations.

FAO (Food and Agricultural Organization). 2014. FAOSTAT. <http://faostat.fao.org>.

FAO (Food and Agricultural Organization), IFAD (International Fund for Agricultural Development), and WFP (World Food Programme). 2013. *The State of Food Insecurity in the World 2013: The Multiple Dimensions of Food Security.* Rome: Food and Agricultural Organization of the United Nations.

FAO (Food and Agriculture Organization) and IRD (Institut de Recherche pour le Développement). 2014. *Defining a Standard Operational Indicator of Women's Dietary Diversity: The Women's Dietary Diversity Follow-up Project.* Contributors: Y. Martin-Prével, P. Allemand, D. Wiesmann, M. Arimond, T. J. Ballard, M. Deitchler, M. C. Dop, G. Kennedy, W. T. K. Lee, and M. Moursi. Rome and Montpellier: Food and Agricultural Organization of the United Nations and Institut de Recherche pour le Développement.

Fukuda-Parr, S., A. E. Yamin, and J. Greenstein. 2013. "Synthesis Paper—The Power of Numbers: A Critical Review of MDG Targets for Human Development and Human

Rights." Working Paper Series, Harvard School of Public Health, Harvard University FXB Center for Health & Human Rights, and the New School.

Glanz, K. 2009. "Measuring Food Environments: A Historical Perspective." *American Journal of Preventive Medicine* 36 (4S): pp. S93–S98.

Gómez, M. I., C. B. Barrett, T. Raney, P. Pinstrup-Andersen, J. Meerman, A. Croppenstedt, B. Carisma, and B. Thompson. 2013. "Post-Green Revolution Food Systems and the Triple Burden of Malnutrition." *Food Policy* 42: pp. 129–138.

Government of UK. 2013. Nutrition for Growth Commitments. <https://www.gov.uk/government/uploads/system/uploads/attachment_data/file/207274/nutrition-for-growth-commitments.pdf>.

Grant, J. P. 1981. *The State of the World's Children 1980–81*. New York: UNICEF.

Herforth, A. 2010. "Nutrition and the Environment: Fundamental to Food Security in Africa." In *The African Food System and its Interaction with Human Health and Nutrition*, edited by Per Pinstrup-Andersen, pp. 128–160. Ithaca, NY: Cornell University Press.

Hoddinott, J., and Y. Yohannes. 2002. "Dietary Diversity as a Food Security Indicator." FCND Discussion Paper No 136, International Food Policy Research Institute (IFPRI), Washington, DC.

Horton, S., M. Shekar, C. McDonald, A. Mahal, and J. K. Brooks. 2010. *Scaling Up Nutrition: What Will It Cost?* Washington, DC: World Bank.

IDF. 2011. *Diabetes Atlas* 5th ed. Brussels: International Diabetes Federation (IDF).

IHME (Institute for Health Metrics and Evaluation). 2013. Global Burden of Disease Interactive Tool. Institute for Health Metrics and Evaluation, Seattle, WA. <http://www.healthmetricsandevaluation.org/tools/data-visualizations>.

Jones, A. D., F. M. Ngure, G. Pelto, and S. L. Young. 2013. "What Are We Assessing When We Measure Food Security? A Compendium and Review of Current Metrics." *Advances in Nutrition* 4: pp. 481–505.

Jonsson, U. 2009. "Paradigms in Applied Nutrition." Paper presented at the 19th International Congress of Nutrition (ICN) Bangkok, October 4–9, 2009.

Keats, S., and S. Wiggins. 2014. "Future Diets: Implications for Agriculture and Food Prices." Overseas Development Institute, London.

Kennedy, E. 2008. "Putting the Pyramid into Action: The Healthy Eating Index and Food Quality Score." *Asia Pacific Journal of Clinical Nutrition* 17 (S1): pp. 70–74.

Levinson, F. J., and M. McLachlan. 1999. "How Did We Get Here? A History of International Nutrition." In *Scaling Up, Scaling Down: Overcoming Malnutrition in Developing Countries*, edited by Thomas J. Marchione, pp. 41–48. Amsterdam: Gordon and Breach Publishers.

Lock, K., J. Pomerleau, L. Causer, and M. McKee. 2004. "Low Fruit and Vegetable Consumption." In *Comparative Quantification of Health Risks: Global and Regional Burden of Diseases Attributable to Selected Major Risk Factors*, edited by Ezzati M., A. D. Lopez, A. Rodgers, and C. J. L. Murray, pp. 597–728. Geneva: World Health Organization.

Monteiro, C. 2013. "The New Role of Industrial Food Processing in Food Systems and Its Impact on Nutrition and Health—A Perspective from the South." Presentation at UN-SCN Meeting of the Minds on Nutrition Impact of Food Systems, Geneva, March 25–28, 2013. <http://www.unscn.org/files/Annual_Sessions/UNSCN_Meetings_2013/Monteiro_Geneva_MoM_final.pdf>.

Monteiro, C., F. Gomes, and G. Cannon. 2010. "The Snack Attack." *American Journal of Public Health* 100 (6): pp. 975–981.

Pinstrup-Andersen, P. 1981. "Nutritional Consequences of Agricultural Projects: Conceptual Relationships and Assessment Approaches." World Bank Staff Working Paper No. 456, World Bank, Washington, DC.

Pinstrup-Andersen, P. 1984. "Incorporating Nutritional Goals into the Design of International Agricultural Research—An Overview." In *International Agricultural Research and Human Nutrition*, edited by P. Pinstrup-Andersen, A. Berg, and M. Forman, pp. 13–23. Washington, DC: International Food Policy Research Institute (IFPRI).

Pinstrup-Andersen, P. 2013. "Nutrition-Sensitive Food Systems: From Rhetoric to Action." *The Lancet* 382 (9890): pp. 375–376.

Pinstrup-Andersen, P., and E. Caicedo. 1977. "The Potential Impact of Changes in Income Distribution on Food Demand and Human Nutrition." *American Journal of Agricultural Economics* 60 (3): pp. 402–415.

Pinstrup-Andersen, P., and A. Herforth. 2008. "Food Security: Achieving the Potential." *Environment: Science and Policy for Sustainable Development* 50 (5): pp. 48–60.

Popkin, B. M. 2003. "The Nutrition Transition in the Developing World." *Development Policy Review* 21 (5–6): pp. 581–597.

Popkin, B. M., K. Duffey, and P. Gordon-Larsen. 2005. "Environmental Influences on Food Choice, Physical Activity and Energy Balance." *Physiology & Behavior* 86 (5): pp. 603–613.

Radimer, K. L., C. M. Olson, and C. C. Campbell. 1990. "Development of Indicators to Assess Hunger." *Journal of Nutrition* 120 (11): pp. 1544–1548.

Rao, M., A. Afshin, G. Singh, and D. Mozaffarian. 2013. "Do Healthier Foods and Diet Patterns Cost More than Less Healthy Options? A Systematic Review and Meta-analysis." *BMJ Open* 2013, 3: e004277. doi:10.1136/bmjopen-2013-004277.

Remans, R., D. F. B. Flynn, F. DeClerck, W. Diru, J. Fanzo, K. Gaynor, I. Lambrecht, J. Mudiope, P. K. Mutuo, P. Nkhoma, D. Siriri, C. Sullivan, and C. A. Palm. 2011. "Assessing Nutritional Diversity of Cropping Systems in African Villages." *PLoS ONE* 6 (6): e21235. doi:10.1371/journal.pone.0021235.

Remans, R., S. Wood, N. Saha, T. L. Anderman, and R. DeFries. 2014. "Measuring Nutritional Diversity of National Food Supplies." *Global Food Security*. Available online July 22, 2014. doi: 10.1016/j.gfs.2014.07.001.

Satia-Abouta, J., R. E. Patterson, M. L. Neuhouser, and J. Elder. 2002. "Dietary Acculturation: Applications to Nutrition Research and Dietetics." *Journal of the American Dietetic Association* 102 (8): pp. 1105–1118.

Sen, A. 1982. *Poverty and Famines: An Essay on Entitlement and Deprivation*. Oxford: Oxford University Press.

Siegel, K., M. K. Ali, A. Srinivasiah, R. A. Nugent, and K. M. Venkat Narayan. 2014. "Do We Produce Enough Fruits and Vegetables to Meet Global Health Need?" *PLoS One* 9 (8): e104059. doi:10.1371/journal.pone.0104059.

Sobal, J. 1999. "Food System Globalization, Eating Transformations, and Nutrition Transitions." In *Food in Global History*, edited by Raymond Grew, pp. 171–193. Boulder, CO: Westview Press.

Swinburn, B., G. Sacks, S. Vandevijvere, S. Kumanyika, T. Lobstein, B. Neal, S. Barquera, S. Friel, C. Hawkes, B. Kelly, M. L'Abbé, A. Lee, J. Ma, J. Macmullan, S. Mohan, C. Monteiro, M. Rayner, D. Sanders, W. Snowdon, C. Walker, and INFORMAS. 2013. "INFORMAS (International Network for Food and Obesity/Non-communicable Diseases Research, Monitoring and Action Support): Overview and Key Principles." *Obesity Reviews* 14 (S1): pp. 1–12.

Tiwari, S., E. Skoufias, and M. Sherpa. 2013. "Shorter, Cheaper, Quicker, Better: Linking Measures of Household Food Security to Nutritional Outcomes in Bangladesh, Nepal, Pakistan, Uganda, and Tanzania." Policy Research Working Paper 6584, World Bank, Washington, DC.

UN (United Nations). 1975. Report of the World Food Conference, Rome 5–16 November 1974. United Nations, New York.

UN (United Nations). 2014. "The Challenge: Hunger Can Be Eliminated in Our Lifetimes." Zero Hunger Challenge. United Nations. <http://www.un.org/en/zerohunger/challenge.shtml>.

UN ACC/SCN (United Nations Administrative Committee on Coordination/Subcommittee on Nutrition). 1987. *First Report on the World Nutrition Situation*. Geneva: UN ACC/SCN.

UN ACC/SCN (United Nations Administrative Committee on Coordination/Subcommittee on Nutrition). 1992. *Second Report on the World Nutrition Situation—Vol. I: Global and Regional Results*. Geneva: UN ACC/SCN. Prepared in collaboration with the International Food Policy Research Institute (IFPRI), Washington, DC.

UNICEF (United Nations Children's Fund). 1987. *The State of the World's Children*. New York: Oxford University Press for UNICEF.

UNICEF (United Nations Children's Fund). 1990. *Strategy for Improved Nutrition of Children and Women in Developing Countries*. New York: UNICEF.

UNICEF (United Nations Children's Fund). 1994. *The State of the World's Children*. New York: Oxford University Press for UNICEF.

UNICEF (United Nations Children's Fund). 1997. *The State of the World's Children: Focus on Child Labour*. Oxford and New York: Oxford University Press for UNICEF.

UNICEF (United Nations Children's Fund). 1998. *The State of the World's Children: Focus on Nutrition*. Oxford and New York: Oxford University Press for UNICEF.

UNICEF (United Nations Children's Fund). 2006. *Progress for Children: A Report Card on Nutrition*, No. 4, May 2006. New York: UNICEF.

UNICEF (United Nations Children's Fund). 2013. *The State of the World's Children: Children with Disabilities*. New York: UNICEF.

UNICEF (United Nations Children's Fund). 2014. Statistics by Area/Child Nutrition: Nutritional Status (last updated February 2014). <http://www.childinfo.org/malnutrition_nutritional_status.php>.

UNSCN (United Nations Systems Standing Committee on Nutrition). 2010. *Sixth Report on the World Nutrition Situation: Progress in Nutrition*. Geneva: UNSCN.

WFP (World Food Programme). 2014. VAM Food and Commodity Prices Data Store. Continuously updated: <http://foodprices.vam.wfp.org/>.

WHO (World Health Organization). 2008. *Indicators for Assessing Infant and Young Child Feeding Practices: Conclusions of a Consensus Meeting Held 6–8 November 2007 in*

Washington, DC, USA. Part 1: Definitions. Geneva: WHO. <http://www.unicef.org/nutritioncluster/files/IYCFE_WHO_Part1_eng.pdf>.

WHO (World Health Organization). 2010. *Global Status Report on Noncommunicable Diseases 2010.* Geneva: WHO.

WHO (World Health Organization). 2012. *Guideline: Sodium Intake for Adults and Children.* Geneva: WHO.

WHO (World Health Organization). 2013. WHO. Global Health Data Repository. Non-Communicable Diseases: Risk Factors: Overweight/ Obesity. <http://apps.who.int/gho/data/node.main.A897>.

WHO (World Health Organization). 2014. Draft guideline: Sugars Intake for Adults and Children. <http://www.who.int/nutrition/sugars_public_consultation/en/.>

WHO (World Health Organization) and FAO (Food and Agricultural Organization). 2003. *Diet, Nutrition, and the Prevention of Chronic Diseases.* Report of a Joint WHO/FAO Expert Consultation. WHO Technical Report Series 916. Geneva: WHO.

Wiesmann, D., L. Bassett, T. Benson, and J. Hoddinott. 2009. "Validation of the World Food Programme's Food Consumption Score and Alternative Indicators of Household Food Security." IFPRI Discussion Paper 00870, International Food Policy Research Institute (IFPRI), Washington, DC.

World Bank. 1980. "Nutrition, Basic Needs, and Growth." Population, Health, and Nutrition Department. Washington, DC: World Bank.

World Bank. 2014. "Learning from World Bank History: Agriculture and Food-Based Approaches to Address Malnutrition." Agricultural and Environmental Sciences Discussion Paper 10, World Bank Report No. 88740-GLB, World Bank, Washington, DC.

Part II
Agricultural Development and Research and Technology Policy

7

Agriculture for Nutrition

Getting Policies Right

Prabhu Pingali, Katie Ricketts, and David E. Sahn

Introduction

The past 50 years have been a period of extraordinary food crop productivity growth, despite rising populations and increasing land scarcity, largely due to the Green Revolution (GR). Despite these massive gains in productivity and agricultural development, malnutrition has persisted across the developing world. Undernourishment (insufficient calorie and protein intake) and micronutrient malnutrition continue to plague sub-Saharan Africa and South Asia, while overnutrition (excess calories leading to obesity and overweight) is a major emerging concern in the middle- and higher-income countries. Enlightened agricultural policies, implemented in association with complementary policies for improved health, water and sanitation, and household behavior change, can have significant positive nutritional impacts.

The nutrition community has coalesced around the first 1,000 days of a child's life, from conception through the first 2 years, as the critical window for averting stunting. Many question the role of agriculture in redressing the problems of stunting in the first 1,000 days. This chapter argues that sustainable gains in childhood stunting are inextricably linked to the health, nutritional status, and empowerment of the mother. A society of healthy women of childbearing age—those between 15–45 years of age—will witness significant long-term reductions in the prevalence of child stunting. Rural women—who are overwhelmingly dependent on agriculture for employment, income, and food—draw an undeniable link between agriculture and nutrition.

Rarely, however, are agricultural interventions defined or driven by nutritional goals, particularly with a focus on rural women and children. We introduce a typology of agricultural systems that reflect the particular stage of structural transformation of a country and highlight the necessary agricultural initiatives that can potentially reduce undernutrition and micronutrient malnutrition. Our typology includes low-productive agricultural systems, such as those prevalent in sub-Saharan Africa; modernizing agricultural systems, primarily found in Asia; and commercialized systems, typically found in advanced economies. This chapter focuses on low-productive and modernizing agricultural systems.

Low-productive agricultural systems, predominantly in sub-Saharan Africa, include those that experienced little or none of the staple-crop productivity gains experienced during the Green Revolution. Rapid growth in population makes several parts of sub-Saharan Africa conducive to investments in intensification today. The challenge, however, is to promote sustainable intensification based on crops (and livestock) that are important to the food systems of the poor rather than crowding them out, as happened during the Green Revolution in Asia. Identifying policies that promote crop-neutral intensification, that is, providing the conditions for yield enhancement, while maintaining crop and food system diversity, should be a priority for these countries. Since women are the primary food producers in sub-Saharan Africa, identifying opportunities for reducing the labor burden in pre- and post-harvest operations would contribute significantly to their health. Given the continued importance and the large share of staple crops in the diets of the poor, identifying mechanisms for enhancing the micronutrient density of grains through biofortification can potentially be a high-return strategy.

Countries with modernizing agricultural systems have advanced along the structural transformation pathway by using agriculture as an engine of growth. These countries focused on increasing staple food crop supply and expanding smallholder incomes. However, many of these countries have seen a significant drop in the cultivation of traditional micronutrient-rich crops, such as lentils and pulses. The relative price of fresh fruit and vegetables is high and deters diversification of diets of the poor. Sustained investments in productivity growth and diversification out of staple cereals toward micronutrient-dense foods remain areas of agricultural policy that can have a direct impact on the availability (supply) and affordability of dietary diversity. Much of this diversification away from cereal crops requires policy attention in infrastructure and extension, as well as market access. We highlight the policy opportunities and evidence for pro-poor integration of smallholders to domestic/global markets through modern food value chains and various public–private partnerships. Meanwhile, kitchen gardens and backyard livestock production remain critical areas of policy promotion, and we provide examples of successful implementation in South Asia and elsewhere.

Finally, our chapter emphasizes the need for complimentary development policies that promote clean drinking water, access to toilets, and sanitation education. The importance of equity in intra-house food allocation and behavior change interventions in this regard are also addressed.

Structural Transformation and the Nutrition Transition

There exists a strong connection between the stage of economic transition—the process of structural transformation—and population-level nutrition patterns. Structural transformation refers to the process whereby agriculture, through higher productivity, provides food, labor, and savings to the process of urbanization and industrialization. The four processes outlining a country's movement within structural transformation include a declining share of agriculture in gross domestic product (GDP), a rural-to-urban migration that stimulates the process of urbanization, the rise of a modern industrial service economy, and a demographic transition from high to low rates of birth and death (i.e., rising health standards) (Timmer and Akkus 2008). More recently, there has been recognition of the connection between the stage of structural transformation and nutritional outcomes, particularly the decline in stunting and wasting rates and the rise in obesity rates (Webb and Block 2012).

Cross-country comparisons indicate that there are a large number of developing countries progressing along the structural transformation continuum. However, there are also a large number of countries that have stalled in the transformation process or have yet to "get agriculture moving." These are almost always countries that are classified as the "least developed." They are also ranked extremely low on the United Nations Development Programme's (UNDP) Human Development Index. Even within countries that are well on the pathway toward agricultural transformation, there are significant inter-regional differences (Eastern India, for example). Some of the reasons for poor agricultural performance include the following: low and inelastic demand for agricultural products, poor provision of public goods (including R&D), high share of agroclimatically constrained land resources, institutional barriers, and governance problems (Pingali 2010).

In virtually all underdeveloped countries, agriculture is an existing industry of major proportions. As countries enact policies that contribute to more productive agriculture sectors, generally through improved productivity of staple grains, GDP per capita rises and agriculture's share of GDP falls as other industries begin to expand and become more competitive (Figure 7.1). As these productivity gains in agriculture enable the transfer of wealth and resources (e.g., labor) from agriculture to non-agricultural industries, rises in per capita GDP and food affordability and availability are correlated with declines in stunting

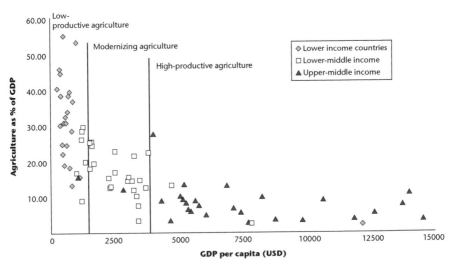

Figure 7.1 Structural transformation, human development, and agricultural performance

Source: Authors' creation from The World Bank, World Development Indicators, 2011. <http://data.worldbank.org>.

and wasting (Webb and Block 2012). However, as Webb and Block (2012) pointed out in a multi-country study on income and nutritional outcomes, increased wealth alone does not predict good nutritional outcomes for a population. The same study shows that, after controlling for income effects, stunting declines at a faster pace for countries supporting and sustaining agricultural development through targeted policies aimed at smallholders, further underscoring the crucial role that agriculture plays in improved nutrition outcomes.

Yet as structural transformation continues and agricultural systems modernize, a different set of nutritional challenges emerge with increased GDP and agricultural productivity. These include, specifically, obesity and other associated conditions with overnutrition. Once again, agricultural policies have a role to play. In modernizing systems, agricultural policies can sustain reductions in stunting but also encourage diversification away from staple-intensive production and into higher-value, micronutrient-dense foods.

The Contribution of Nutrition and Health to Agricultural Productivity and Development

The above discussion is not meant to imply that the relationship between agricultural growth and nutrition outcomes is unidimensional. The relationship goes both ways—food security and good nutrition are important *inputs* into a productive agricultural system, reflecting the role that health plays in human capital development and productive work. That the nutritional well-being of workers is essential to economic growth is a concept that dates back to perhaps the most notable economics treatise ever written: Adam Smith's *The Wealth of Nations*, which first appeared in 1776. In that influential work, Smith discusses how sickness and hunger can be expected to reduce worker productivity (Smith [1776] 1960).

After the 1992 International Conference on Nutrition (ICN), the literature on this relationship really burgeoned. The seminal work of Robert Fogel (1994, 2004a, 2004b), as well as that of other economic historians, have provided persuasive evidence that nutrition and health have contributed in an important way to increases in productivity and economic growth. Fogel showed how inadequacies in diet contributed to disease and early mortality, greatly limiting the possibility for productive work in 18th-century England and France. His estimates indicate that 50 percent of Britain's growth since 1800 is attributable to increases in dietary energy available for work and improvements in the efficiency in the transformation of nutrients, particularly calories, into work (Fogel 2004b).

Our expectation of the paramount importance of food security and nutrition in enabling a healthy agriculture and food sector in developing countries is predicated on several facts. First, agriculture dominates as a source of income and employment in developing countries where nutritional problems are most acute. Second is the simple spatial argument: nutrition problems are most severe and hard physical labor most important in rural areas where agriculture is the predominant sector.

Third, own production and self-provisioning are of particular importance in these same geographic areas; and under such circumstances, reduced levels of output from hunger and malnutrition can contribute to large consumption shortfalls—an outcome less likely to occur in more market-oriented economies. Fourth, the propensity for market failures, such as in credit markets, will also simultaneously contribute to economic inefficiencies, as mediated by the underinvestment in nutrition and agricultural capital. Reinforcing this low-level equilibrium are binding time constraints, in terms of the time available to devote to the production of health, home production (e.g., care of children), and farm production. Thus shocks, whether they are health-related or other exogenous shocks such as pests or adverse weather conditions, jointly have an adverse affect on health and agriculture.

Fifth, the prospect of early mortality related to hunger and disease reduces the incentives for parents to invest in the education of their children, as these factors lower the returns to schooling. Thus, illness or death resulting from poor health and nutrition will not only limit future productivity in the labor market, but also the incentives for parents to care for children, greatly increasing the risk that adverse health events will have long-lasting consequences.

Sixth, there is a related investment story that results from the expectations for a short lifespan. This will reduce saving, and thus investment in physical capital, particularly land and technological advances in agriculture. Like the reduced incentives to invest in children, such failure to invest in land and physical capital will have intergenerational impacts that are only starting to be fully appreciated, in part due to the challenging data and empirical demands of such analysis.

Conceptual Framework

We posit that agricultural policies for enhanced nutrition can be most effectively undertaken when the particular agricultural context (stage of agricultural development) and nutritional challenges of a particular country are understood. In order to recommend such appropriate policies, we put forth (1) a typology of agricultural systems based on the stage of agricultural development, and (2) a conceptual framework useful for thinking about the specific pathways between agriculture and nutrition. This approach offers policymakers the opportunity to think about the consequences that structural transformation has for both poverty and nutrition, and the ways that policy support for agriculture might impact food affordability, availability, diet quality, and rural income growth for improved nutrition.

Agricultural System Typologies

We identify three types of countries, based on the level of agricultural development, that exist along the structural transformation continuum. This classification is useful, given our premise that the stage of agricultural development illuminates specific agricultural policies and programs capable of influencing nutritional outcomes within the agricultural system context. Our classification includes: (1) low-productive agricultural systems, (2) modernizing agricultural systems, and (3) commercialized systems.

LOW-PRODUCTIVE AGRICULTURAL SYSTEMS
Countries in the low-productive agricultural category are invariably low-income, least developed countries, with the major share of their national GDP in small-scale agriculture. Most of the nations in this category are in sub-Saharan Africa. These nations experience some of the highest global prevalence of childhood stunting, wasting, and micronutrient deficiencies (including iron and vitamin A deficiency). Productivity in agriculture remains

hampered by poor nutrition and health, especially for women who assume a predominant role in the production of food crops.

Low-productive agricultural systems face a unique set of agricultural development and nutrition problems. In these systems, large quantities of resources—land and labor—are committed to agriculture and yet are used at very low levels of productivity. Positive income elasticity for staple crop consumption suggests that higher productivity for these crops will be met by an eager market; but without the productivity gains, these agriculture-based countries face low prospects for meeting the Millennium Development Goals of hunger and poverty reduction. Prices of non-staples, including micronutrient-rich fruits and vegetables and macronutrient-rich meat and dairy, remain relatively high, and quantities are limited seasonally or year round. In these systems, agricultural productivity growth is essential for expanding access to staple foods, jumpstarting overall growth, and reducing rural poverty.

MODERNIZING AGRICULTURAL SYSTEMS

Modernizing agricultural systems include many countries in Asia and parts of Latin America, where agriculture-led policies and GR technologies were promoted to increase the availability and supply of cereals and staple grains. These productivity-focused policies promoted agriculture as an engine of growth and sought to expand basic calorie access, elevate producer incomes, reduce real cereal food prices, and utilize scarce resources more efficiently (Scobie and Posada 1978; Stevenson et al. 2013). In addition to lowering food prices and expanding the available supply of calories, staple food productivity growth drove the process of structural transformation and stimulated growth in the non-agricultural sectors (Pingali 2010). Decades later, many of these regions face completely different demand side factors and nutritional realities. Today, negative income elasticity of demand for staples (given the current market supply in these regions), ensures that the policies enacted to "get agriculture moving" must be reimagined for an agricultural system that has moved beyond the conditions that characterized the GR era. Positive demand elasticity for protein and micronutrient-rich food suggests the potential to ignite agriculture once again as a growth sector, link smallholder farmers to new market opportunities, and expand the dietary quality of the food supply in order tackle micronutrient and protein malnutrition (Dorjee et al. 2003; Joshi et al. 2004; Pingali 2010).

COMMERCIALIZED AGRICULTURAL SYSTEMS

The third category, commercialized agriculture—which we spend the least time discussing in this chapter—constitutes the agricultural systems of the developed world. These high-income countries have relatively small rural populations, and agriculture typically accounts for less than 10 percent of GDP (Pingali 2010). However, when we do discuss these systems, we underscore insights that even when agriculture has less of a proportional impact on total GDP and is no longer the primary engine of growth, agricultural policies are still necessary to ensure human nutrition through the promotion of food safety, competitive markets, and obesity prevention.

Pathways Connecting Agriculture to Nutrition

Using this classification, we now present a framework for thinking through specific types of agricultural policies. We premise this discussion by asserting that different stages of agricultural development merit different types of policy approaches for influencing nutritional outcomes. Understanding how these pathways evolve and intersect, based on the stage of agricultural development, is essential for developing and prioritizing policies that respond to the unique nutritional challenges and food supply constraints that occur throughout a country's development process. We identify four interlocking pathways between agriculture and nutrition. These pathways to improved nutrition include: (1) the income pathway, where gains in household income can translate to better food affordability (among other impacts); (2) the food supply pathway, including the availability of quality, quantity, and diversity of food year round and for vulnerable subpopulations; (3) the intra-household access pathway, where interventions attempt to equalize food allocation among individuals within a common household; and finally (4) the health environment pathway, which links access to clean water and improved sanitation/hygiene practices to better nutritional health.

Our framework for understanding the pathways between agriculture and nutrition has, on the one hand, *household food access* and on the other, *individual nutrient uptake and access*. Household food access rests on the ability for a family unit to access the quantity, quality, and diversity of food needed to achieve daily micronutrient, energy, and protein needs. Individual nutrition access demands intra-household food distribution equality and a healthy environment that allows the person to metabolically absorb and utilize the food consumed (Figure 7.2).

On the left side of Figure 7.2, we see that food access is premised on the ability to afford and access an array of nutrient-dense foods. Food affordability requires the expansion of household budgets to allow rural farmers to purchase the quantity, quality, and diversity of food needed. Household incomes are determined by the productivity of smallholder farmer operations and the opportunities available for increased income opportunities (i.e., linking farmers to domestic and global food value chains) and non-farm income

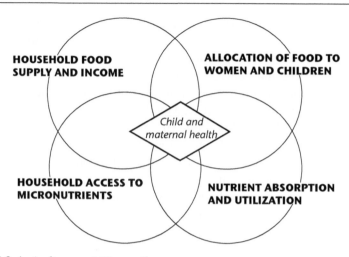

Figure 7.2 Agriculture–nutrition pathways

Source: Adapted from Tata-Cornell Agriculture and Nutrition Initiative (TCi) 2014. <http://tci.cals.cornell.edu>.

opportunities. The seasonality and volatility of these market opportunities are of special consideration and importance.

However, increases in income and expansion of food budgets, must be matched by actual food availability, in particular the availability of diverse, micronutrient-rich food. Micronutrient-rich food availability is determined by the spatial location of the household, its proximity to diverse food retailers, or on-farm diversification and home cultivation of micronutrient-rich food (e.g., kitchen gardens and backyard livestock). Micronutrient-rich food availability may also be increased through policy efforts to increase rural access to food diversity with food and cash transfer programs and safety net programs.

On the right side of Figure 7.2, barriers to individual nutrition access and absorption, including intra-household food allocation and nutrient absorption, are identified. A household is made up of individuals who may differ in terms of individual food intake and individual food needs—even if a household can access and afford food sufficiency and dietary diversity, individual nutrition within a household is not always equal. Distribution within a household may favor men and older boys, allowing them to eat first and select the amount and quality they desire. Women and young children are often left with the food that remains.

Yet even if an individual comes from a household that is able to afford and access a diversity of nutrient-rich food and is distributed enough food for her needs, the environment she lives in can determine her biological ability to absorb energy and nutrients. Drinking water supply and sanitation around the world continues to be inadequate, and intestinal inflammation and infection due to water contaminated with worms, parasites, viruses, and bacteria, lead to partial or complete malabsorption of essential nutrients and calories, in addition to life-threatening dehydration.

Certainly, agricultural policies are only one critical dimension of the policy puzzle for improving nutrition. A number of mediating factors influence household income, micronutrient availability, nutrient absorption and utilization, and household food allocation. The income (Pathway 1) and the food supply (Pathway 2) have the most obvious connections to agriculture, given the dependency of the poor on these activities for income, as well as the ability to influence the quality, quantity, and diversity of the overall food supply. However, improvements along some pathways can create ripple effects for others. For example, improvements in women's income-earning opportunities, say, through investment in agricultural technologies for women, can promote women as decision-makers within the household and lead to more equal access to household resources—including better quality or quantities of food. Similarly, public investments in clean water access can support rural communities to comply with the food quality and safety regulations that are otherwise a barrier to entering higher-value agricultural markets. Nutrition, like agriculture, is multidimensional and capable of promoting and affecting multiple facets of life, and development across these areas must occur simultaneously.

In short, all of these pathways are important to improving nutrition. However, the relevance of a particular agriculture–nutrition pathway, and the types of useful agricultural interventions within that pathway, depend on the stage of agricultural transformation. Thus, in order to understand and use agriculture as a tool for improving nutrition, one needs to understand the role of agriculture in a particular system and adjust policies along the various agriculture–nutrition pathways accordingly. Agricultural policies for improved nutrition are specific to context and should not been seen as a homogeneous set of policies for use in any and every situation. Countries in each of the three typologies we have described interact with the agriculture–nutrition pathways differently, based on production constraints and current supply, as well as demand drivers that influence new market opportunities and future supply potential. The nutritional goals may also differ by the stage of transformation, ranging from reduction in stunting to managing obesity.

Agricultural Policies for Improved Nutrition

Low-Productive Agricultural Systems

Low-productive agricultural systems face a negative cycle: low-productive agriculture in staple crops contributes to widespread hunger (calorie deficiency) and low dietary diversity. Together, these nutrition outcomes translate to inefficient labor investment, and thereby, reduce overall farm productivity. Productivity-focused investments in staple crop production have the ability to reduce widespread hunger by making staple grains more affordable and available in the short term. After agriculture "gets moving" and transitions from a low-productive agricultural system to a modernizing system, policies that invest in non-staple crop diversification can begin to tackle the issue of dietary diversity access. Options to pursue biofortification of staple grains with key nutrients, as we suggest in a later section, offers a chance to address micronutrient malnutrition in the short term.

Low-productive agricultural systems, which are found primarily in low-income countries, exist in a unique economic context. One must consider the role of agriculture in explaining the quantity and quality of the food supplied, *in addition* to explaining the persistence of rural poverty. Both are inextricably tied to nutrition through the income and food supply pathways (Pathways 1 and 2). Given that most smallholder farmers are net food buyers (Barrett and Dorosh 1996), impoverished households generate weak demand for the relatively higher priced micronutrient- and protein-dense food, which further depresses production and reduces diversity in the overall food supply. Under such circumstances, expansions in food supply without simultaneous increases in consumer incomes—most importantly, the incomes of the poor—will contribute relatively little to the elimination of malnutrition (Pinstrup-Andersen and Caicedo 1978).

SYNERGISTIC IMPROVEMENTS IN PATHWAYS 1 AND 2:
AGRICULTURE AS AN ENGINE OF GROWTH THAT IMPROVES
INCOME AND EXPANDS CALORIE ACCESS

Investments that improve agricultural productivity have the potential to both grow producer incomes (Pathway 1) while elevating the quantity of food available (Pathway 2). To achieve this, however, agricultural policies capable of "kick-starting" economic growth through improvements in productivity must be pursued. The world, however, has encountered this problem before: the rapid increase in agricultural output resulting from the Green Revolution (GR) provided impressive staple grain yields for many developing countries in Asia and Latin America, including a 208 percent increase in wheat production, 109 percent in rice production, and 157 percent in maize production (Pingali 2012). This contributed to a significant shift in the food supply function, which, in turn, contributed to a decrease in real food prices and an increase in cereal production (between 12–13 percent) (Hayami and Herdt 1977; Scobie and Posada 1978).

Unfortunately, much of the African continent never reaped the benefits of the GR. Many countries continue to suffer from low-producing agriculture, and some of the highest rates of poverty and malnutrition persist. Downstream issues of governance and marketing, viable input supply systems, and sustained provision of productivity-enhancing seed and fertilizer technologies and market outlets for absorbing surplus production have all contributed to a "GR failure" of increased productivity of staple grains in Africa (Pingali 2012). A new push for cereal-based strategies for improving income and the food supply must be pursued in order to get agriculture to kick-start the engine of economic transformation.

Emerging success stories from Africa that highlight agricultural productivity growth in recent decades show that: (1) the context for agricultural development has shifted; and (2) investments in research to address the crops and constraints relevant to the continent's agriculture are yielding high returns. For example, productivity gains in cassava and improved varieties of sorghum and millet have risen close to 40 percent between 1980 and 2005 (Binswanger-Mkhize and McCalla 2010). For cassava, a major West, Central, and Southern African staple crop, virus and pest issues once nearly eradicated this important locally consumed food. Investments in crop research (by the International Institute of Tropical Agriculture in Nigeria) played a critical role in creating mosaic disease-resistant varieties and establishing mealybug control programs that resulted not only in sustained cassava production, but enabled cassava expansion across Africa into new processing opportunities and industry activities for smallholder producers.

For Africa, reprioritizing investments into productive agricultural development can improve nutrition by increasing farm-level profitability that can ultimately mobilize the process of structural transformation. High rates of return for improvements in crop breeding and genetics, farm management techniques and extension, as well as investments in irrigation and credit infrastructure have been found to extend far beyond the short term and influence both food availability and rural household income (Datt and Ravallion 1998; Gómez et al. 2013). For example, in Asia, significant public investment in the 1960s, and continuing through the 1980s, in irrigation infrastructure and input access laid the foundation for rapid adoption of GR technologies that enabled the proliferation of cereal intensification and calorie access across the region (Pingali 2012).

Today, improvements are being made in Africa, but change must be accelerated and enacted on multiple fronts. In the early 1990s, the Kenyan government launched a series of reforms designed to spur productivity by encouraging private investment in fertilizer distribution and removing fertilizer import restrictions (Ariga and Jayne 2010). Ariga and Jayne (2010) provided evidence showing how the average transit distance from farmer to fertilizer outlet and the average travel distance to hybrid seed retailers declined from 8.1 to 3.4 kilometers and from 5.6 to 3.4 kilometers, respectively. The authors point out the simultaneous improvements in productivity and diets: yield increases rose by roughly 18 percent (1997–2007), and price decreases for critical maize food products like maize meal also occurred.

Despite these positive trends, many countries in sub-Saharan Africa still have very low-productive agricultural systems. In these areas, chronic hunger and poverty continue to be daunting problems; and lack of technology, poor market infrastructure, inappropriate institutions, and a disabling policy environment depress nutrition and stagnate economic growth (Pingali 2012). Exacerbated by poor health, agricultural productivity surely suffers. Renewed private sector interest is combining with a public interest to invest and improve agricultural productivity, especially through public–private extension efforts and institution building. Increasingly, public, public–private, private, and non-governmental organization intervention in extension services are creating new ways to upgrade and assist farmers. These organizations are providing business advising services, agronomy support, and market opportunities, as well as facilitating the distribution and adoption of improved inputs and credit (IFPRI and The World Bank 2010; Ricketts et al. 2013). In addition to improving the quality and quantity of food produced by small-scale farmers, extension can also be enacted to reduce food-borne illnesses, pathogens, and diseases, which complicate individual nutrition uptake, disrupt trading relationships, and reduce smallholder market opportunities.

ENSURING PROGRESS ALONG PATHWAY 1 FOR THE PRIMARY
FOOD PRODUCERS: RURAL WOMEN

Women's vulnerability results from their special role not only as food producers, but also from their unique reproductive roles, and the associated demands of motherhood. Health and nutrition shocks that adversely affect women not only adversely affect their productive role as workers in the agricultural sector, but also impact their joint production role as caregivers for their children, and thus induce a recurrent and intergenerational cycle of crisis and deprivation. In terms of accessing essential inputs for productive agriculture, women face serious barriers in obtaining credit, machinery, education (agricultural knowledge), and improved inputs (Gladwin et al. 1997; Quisumbing and Pandolfelli 2010).

Policies that invest in the expansion of peer-to-peer learning networks, extension systems, and input access can have significant effects on agricultural productivity and profitability, especially for women. Among rural women, the organization, expansion, and support of women's groups can help foster demand for critical agricultural inputs (credit, improved seeds, and inputs), and support entrepreneurial ambition and empowerment. Research has suggested that depressed credit demand and reduced entrepreneurial activity for women exists in many communities because of social norms that prescribe what kinds of market-oriented activities are appropriate (Fletschner and Carter 2008; Fletschner 2009), and because women lack access to collateral, education (literacy), markets and contracts, land and water, among other things (see a review in Quisumbing and Pandolfelli [2010]).

Advancements and investment in extension and infrastructure can be especially important for reducing the barriers that women face in entering higher-value markets and intensifying their land with adequate inputs. A study in 2010 highlighted gains in income and per-acre productivity for participants with new access to extension personnel in Kenya, Tanzania, and Uganda—a finding that was particularly true for women participants (Davis et al. 2012). Despite this success, a 2009 review of women and extension activities (India, Ghana, Ethiopia), undertaken by the International Food and Policy Research Institute (IFPRI), illustrated that extension workers tended to be overwhelmingly male, and that only a fraction of female-headed households had access to extension and livestock services over the previous year (IFPRI and The World Bank 2010).

IMPROVING MICRONUTRIENT-RICH FOOD ACCESS WHILE PURSUING STAPLE GRAIN (CALORIE) PRODUCTIVITY GOALS

In tandem with these staple grain intensification goals, micronutrient and protein interventions can concurrently be pursued in order to ensure that hunger (calorie deficiency) is not addressed at the expense of reducing micronutrient malnutrition. Biofortification of staple grains can enable access to essential micronutrients like iron, vitamin A, and zinc (among others). Biofortification of staples offers an integrated, food system approach aimed at reducing micronutrient deficiency until the longer-term, most sustainable solution (i.e., dietary diversification) can be achieved. A review of biofortification efforts has underscored that this approach is an efficacious and cost-effective strategy in rural areas of several developing countries (Asare-Marfo et al. 2013). In 2012, HarvestPlus technologies enabled trials of vitamin A-biofortified maize in Zambia. In Benin, iron-biofortified pearl millet has been shown to bolster bioavailable iron compared with regular millet (Cercamondi et al. 2013). In addition to enhancing the content of various nutrients, attempts to breed in positive agronomic traits have also been undertaken. Disease resistance, drought tolerance, and acid soil tolerance qualities suggest that improved nutrition can go hand in hand with improved productivity and farm management, and that agronomically competitive varieties are possible (Bouis et al. 2011).

Biofortification of non-cereal staples, like roots and tubers, have also been undertaken. In 2011, HarvestPlus technologies enabled trials of vitamin A-biofortified cassava in Nigeria and the Democratic Republic of the Congo (Bouis et al. 2011). Evidence has shown that vitamin A intake from biofortified orange-fleshed varieties of sweet potato resulted in improved vitamin A intake among trial participants in Uganda (Hotz et al. 2012) and Mozambique (Low et al. 2007). Additional impact and evaluative studies are forthcoming.

Similarly, policies promoting backyard livestock and home garden programs can be ideal for low-productive agricultural systems that are in the early stages of structural transformation. These programs are especially useful in the short term, before demand for dietary diversity triggers a market response (or before technologies, institutions, and inputs *allow* producers to respond). As agriculture "gets moving" with staple productivity gains and household income expansions, smallholder farmers can respond to an evolving market for supplying micronutrient- and protein-dense food. In parts of Africa, the promotion of indigenous plants in home gardens has been advantageous, given that these varieties require minimum inputs, mature quickly, and can be harvested in a short period of time in soils with limited fertility (Faber and van Jaarsveld 2007). In fact, it was found that when comparing agricultural with home gardening interventions, home gardens had a higher success rate for nutritional impact than comparative agricultural interventions—especially if cultivation methods and product selection targeted women (Berti et al. 2004; Faber and van Jaarsveld 2007). Stigma against these garden crops, as a "poor person's food," requires education and a strong promotional campaign from public extension and education agencies, non-governmental organizations, and community leaders. In South Africa, use of demonstration gardens within villages developed understanding and enthusiasm about the potentials for home garden cultivation and household nutrition (Faber et al. 2001).

Modernizing Agricultural Systems

The modernizing agricultural systems of much of Asia and Latin America have experienced significant gains in agricultural productivity, staple crop food supply, and staple food price decreases. These gains were fueled by successful implementation of the GR, which was underpinned by high rates of public investment in crop research, infrastructure, market development, and appropriate policy (Pingali 2012). Gains in cereal yields are not enough to address malnutrition. Despite the intensification of grain production in these regions and the multiplicative effects that the GR had on reducing poverty, it brought these countries only so far. Poverty and food insecurity in some communities have persisted; especially in rain-fed farming areas and for communities that have been isolated due to lack of technology and extension coverage and insufficient access to credit and land. Access to staple grains and the fall in the cost of calories both illuminated and exacerbated the problem of "hidden hunger," or micronutrient malnutrition. Today, micronutrient malnutrition plays a strong role in the elevated instances of childhood stunting, anemia, vitamin A deficiency, and other major deficiencies in South Asia (India, in particular), in Southeast Asia, and across China. Globally, these micronutrient and macronutrient deficiencies contribute significantly to the overall global disease burden for women and children (Black et al. 2008).

During the GR, productivity-focused policies for these previously low-producing agricultural systems succeeded in elevating grain supplies and placing downward pressure on real food prices, a feature that had positive nutrition effects (increased protein and calorie intake) for poor households who were net food consumers (Alston et al. 1995). A study in Bangladesh further showed how savings on food expenditures increased access to non-staple foods, and that this had a significant positive impact on child nutrition status as households changed consumption patterns and spent more on non-rice foods (Torlesse et al. 2003). Of course, the linkages between household dietary diversity, socioeconomic status, and income have long been established (Hoddinott and Yohannes 2002; Arimond and Ruel 2004). This seemingly complicates the connections that can be made between improved dietary diversity and nutrition outcomes, given that these other factors also have an influence. To be sure, socioeconomically higher-level households tend to have greater access to additional positive nutrition pathways (Pathways 3 and 4), which include access to water, sanitation, hygiene, and education. Despite this, an 11-country study on child nutritional status, controlled for these wealth and welfare factors, found dietary diversity was still significantly associated with core nutrition metrics (child height and weight) (Arimond and Ruel 2004).

Additional authors and studies have pointed to the income elasticity of staples and the inelasticity of micronutrient- and protein-dense foods (fruits, vegetables, dairy, and meat, for example), and that households with increased incomes often switch to consuming higher-quality foods (within the same food group) or consume a more diverse set of food groups (Bouis and Haddad 1992; Behrman 1998; Pingali 2004). Although this aspect of the search for diversity and quality may help address nutrient deficits other than calories, for example, proteins and micronutrients, there is also evidence that the increased diversity involves consumption of more refined carbohydrates. Recent evidence has shown that while stunting rates decrease with improvements in per capita income, levels of obesity rise (Webb and Block 2012). Macroeconomic and supply side agricultural policy certainly has a role to play in ensuring that micronutrient- and macronutrient-rich food is both affordable and available.

ENABLING MICRONUTRIENT-RICH FOOD ACCESS
THROUGH TRADITIONAL MARKET UPGRADING AND MARKET
DEVELOPMENT

For modernizing systems, policy emphasis must shift from a focus on cereal intensification to one that encourages broader food supply diversification, by expanding household income via linkages to new and higher-value markets (via Pathway 1) that encourage on-farm diversification and impact the overall diversity of the food supply (impacts through Pathway 2). Non-staple crops, including fresh fruits, vegetables, meats, and dairy products, require a heightened level of infrastructure and support in order for farmers to survive. Policies that focus on market development, as we use the term here, include those that help lower food prices and increase income (Pathway 1) and improve diversity in the overall food supply (Pathway 2). In particular, this includes policies that can (1) encourage production diversification by linking smallholder farmers to new market opportunities in order to diversify out of staple crop production; (2) strengthen demand for non-staples; and (3) upgrade traditional markets.

LINKING FARMERS TO HIGHER-VALUE MARKETS: EXPANDING
INCOMES AND DIVERSIFYING THE FOOD SUPPLY

Linking farmers to higher-value markets has long been of interest to organizations and policymakers looking to spur growth for rural areas where incomes depend on agriculture. By linking rural producers to non-staple, higher-value domestic, export, and retail markets, improvements in income (Pathway 1), as well as access to productive services and inputs have been shown to increase income and welfare (Carter et al. 1996; Kaplinsky and Morris 2001; Dolan and Sorby 2003; Humphrey 2005; Barrett et al. 2011). Critics have been quick to point out, however, that new market linkages can disrupt domestic food security, and that these market opportunities tend to be accessible to farmers who are already relatively "better off." Households that are less reliant on subsistence production and who are more oriented toward market production have been found to have more diverse diets (Jones et al. 2014). These farming households are often marked by advantageous features, including favorable socioeconomic, financial, geographic, or biophysical qualities that can help to characterize participation patterns (Barrett et al. 2011).

Agricultural policies can play a role in ensuring equal participation by developing a more level playing field. Given the connection between market linkages, economic growth, and dietary diversity, investments that can equip a diverse socioeconomic group of farmers to participate is essential. However, it is worth noting that even in instances where the poorest farmers do participate directly, positive spillovers have been shown to accrue to non-members, including poorer farmers in the village or region. Transfers of information from members to non-members and access to productive inputs and assets have been found to reach excluded growers, and thus contribute to wider income and productivity gains (Bernard and Spielman 2009). In terms of diet, recent research continues to show a positive relationship between farm production and diversity (Jones et al. 2014).

Public policies aimed at developing new market opportunities tend to mean working with private companies in order to access and identify market opportunities and creating an "enabling environment" that focuses on developing necessary institutions in order to ensure broad-based participation. The latter includes investments in *connective* infrastructure (paved roads, telecommunication networks, known and widespread networks for distribution), as well as *mediating* infrastructure (providing credit, credit rating agencies, property titles, and other legal and regulatory institutions that can depersonalize exchange transactions and make assets fungible) (De Soto 2000).

In particular, access to finance and land registration can be instrumental in enabling farmers to diversify crops, make longer-term and more efficient production decisions, and manage risk and resources more effectively. Policies supporting household access to finance and land registration have been found to improve profitability (income), ensure greater on-farm productivity, and enable market access (Bliss and Stern 1982; Atwood 1990; Morduch 1994; Zeller et al. 1998; Dercon 2002; Fafchamps 2009). Moreover, policies that succeed in creating an "enabling environment" for agriculture may disproportionally preserve opportunities for those who are the most closely tied to agriculture: those who are very poor, uneducated, recent immigrants, or women, and who tend to be less likely to have access to non-farm employment (Barrett et al. 2001; Vanderpuye-Orgle and Barrett 2009). Additionally, the development of financial markets in rural areas for intermediaries (e.g., small- and medium-sized traders or wholesalers), has been found necessary to ensure that farmers diversify production (Coulter and Shepherd 1995; World Bank 2007; Dalberg 2012).

Public efforts can also be geared toward providing market information that can be essential to harnessing demand and enabling smallholder integration into new markets. Public–private partnerships (PPPs) have been shown to increase information and investment flow, as well as investment into supply chains capable of linking or integrating smallholder farmers. In some cases, evidence for improved efficiencies for smallholder farmers and traders has been identified through greater communications technologies, quality training, inputs, and services (de Silva and Ratnadiwakara 2008; Aker and Fafchamps 2010; Ricketts et al. 2013). Improving the transfer of information about prices and good agricultural practices can help align marketing incentives all along the food value chain. In Tanzania, collaboration between the

Tanzanian government and others developed the *First Mile* project, which aimed to facilitate learning among local groups, improve market linkages, and share locally developed best practices and information on current market supply and demanded product qualities. Information shared via phone text messages and community billboard postings created competition between intermediaries (market "spies"), who eventually began to charge and compete for providing valuable market information (World Economic Forum 2009). Additionally, PPPs can provide opportunities for governments to update and modernize extension services (see Ricketts et al. [2013] for additional examples).

STRENGTHENING DEMAND FOR NON-STAPLES

While supply side policies and institutional investments can expand availability of diverse foods and enable smallholder income gains, agricultural policies for improved nutrition can also aim to strengthen consumer demand for foods rich in micronutrients and protein. This alignment is essential. Broadly, policy investments in market information technologies, product standardization, and food safety regulations can build consumer trust, identify new market demands, and provide meaningful opportunities for farmer response.

When product standardization and labeling initiatives are absent or poorly enforced, consumers are forced to establish their own methods of determining quality; these preferences can be difficult to measure and impossible for market actors to respond to (Jabbar et al. 2010; Gómez and Ricketts 2013). A 2010 review of demands for livestock products in developing countries pointed out that consumer perception of quality, safety, and convenience influenced the price and purchase of livestock products (Grunert 2005, as cited by Jabbar et al. 2010). Jabbar et al. (2010) found that although no official standards for meats existed in Ethiopia and Bangladesh, poor consumers in traditional markets used informal criteria (like color and odor) to determine quality. Similar results were found by Minten (2008) regarding meat product preferences in Madagascar. Generally, however, poorly understood consumer demand ensures that the delivery of products, which could otherwise expand dietary diversity, is either not developed or improperly placed. Especially for protein-dense foods, Jabbar et al. (2010), in a study on livestock food demand in Asia and Africa, found that all consumers are willing to pay a premium price for higher standards of livestock products. For policymakers looking to strengthen demand for micronutrient- and protein-dense products, research into the preferences of the poor and basic product standardization can open up new market opportunities and set baselines for product quality indicators.

Policy support for regulating food safety is critical for sustained access to markets for smallholder farmers, for preserving the quality of the available food supply, and for promoting human health and individual nutrition uptake. However, food safety regulations pose a threat to the participation of smallholder growers who may find compliance difficult or impossible. Policy efforts focused on developing and maintaining producer organizations must keep in mind that some food safety standards require changes to group size and composition, as well as linkages to new sources of market information that can help farmer groups adapt (Narrod et al. 2009). In fact, policies that expand access to entities specializing in food safety training and certification are becoming very important conditions for maintaining competitive producer organizations. Despite this, some developing countries have yet to adapt and update policies, which may leave producer organizations with little incentive to comply or compete on providing superior food safety measures. For example, in some Indian states, laws prohibiting cooperatives from forming external linkages include those that train and provide knowledge on food safety issues (Narrod et al. 2009). Equipping farmers and farmer organizations for commercial success means revisiting policies and public investments that encourage market linkages to essential entities that could support knowledge sharing and training around food safety issues.

UPGRADING TRADITIONAL MARKETS FOR NUTRITIONAL IMPACT

Poor people in developing countries generally rely on traditional food value chains and traditional markets, both in urban and rural areas, for the bulk of their food. Historically, "traditional retail" has been undertaken similarly in different regions around the globe: food from farmers in close proximity is bought and eventually sold in small, "mom and pop" corner stores, wet markets, roadside stands, and vendors through a network of informal farmers, traders, wholesalers, and intermediaries (Ruben et al. 2006; Reardon et al. 2010; Reddy et al. 2010; Gorton et al. 2011). For modern supermarket and retail integration, adequate transportation, proper storage, volume coordination, and assurance of food safety can present insurmountable challenges for the typical smallholder farmer—so, too, can achieving the level of quality demanded by modern retailers. As a result, traditional markets that offer flexibility on price and quality have continued to be a critical marketing opportunity for small-scale producers.

Low margins and production seasonality, combined with lack of post-harvest and distribution infrastructure, however, often reduce the incomes in traditional food value chains and the quality and quantity of food available year round (Gómez and Ricketts 2013). Public investment in these markets to promote and safeguard a diverse supply of micronutrient-rich food, while protecting smallholder incomes, will remain essential to improving health and nutrition.

Public investments that legitimize and expand the availability and transparency of sectors, including entrepreneurial retailers, traders, and wholesalers, can support trade, reduce transaction costs, and improve consumer prices within traditional marketing channels. In Kenya, informal milk markets account for 86 percent of milk supplies to consumers, and many supply chain actors are small-scale producers, milk bar operators, milk transport traders, and other micro-entrepreneurs (Kaitibie et al. 2010; Omore and Baker 2011). Government policies had previously criminalized small-scale producers and traders who could not afford or access the licensing and certification process required. Prior to a policy change in 2004, small-scale dairy producers were often harassed by large, powerful dairy market players who sought to increase their relatively small market share by claiming public health concerns and blaming zoonotic outbreaks on these small producers (Kaitibie et al. 2010). These unsubstantiated threats endangered the livelihoods of more than 1.8 million cattle producers who owned 1–2 dairy cows on areas of less than 2 hectares (Omore and Baker 2011). In 2004, policymakers responded by liberalizing the small-scale dairy sector and investing in a new system for registering and licensing for small-scale farmers. Milk quality was raised, and improvements in handling and hygiene practices changed public perceptions; an average of 9 percent reduction in milk-marketing margins showed improved competition (reflecting reductions in the monopoly that large dairy producers once enjoyed), resulting in *higher* prices for small-scale farmers and *lower* retail prices for consumers (Kaitibie et al. 2010; Omore and Baker 2011).

Policies promoting food safety should be a policy priority for upgrading traditional markets and ensuring that human health is safeguarded. In addition to reducing instances of foodborne illness and disease, food safety policies can make traditional markets a viable place for procurement by modern retailers. This can further improve smallholder incomes. Improvements can include infrastructure investments like the pouring of cement slabs for establishment of stalls and zoning of animal/livestock products away from produce, and the establishment of sanitation stations in wet markets where equipment and products can be washed and waste can be discarded safely.

Conclusion

Remarkable progress has been made in raising agricultural productivity and preventing global food shortages over the past 50 years, a success story made all the more impressive in light of the exploding global population. Malnutrition has declined, especially in Southeast Asia, as the process of structural transformation has occurred, largely reflecting the success of the Green Revolution. The agricultural research underpinning the development of the Green Revolution, in turn, was supported by public investment in infrastructure, markets, and price policies that provided incentives for a range of farmers and entrepreneurs in the food system.

The successes we have witnessed, however, leave no room for complacency. In large regions of South Asia and Africa, hunger and malnutrition continue to afflict large shares of the population; and there is an increasing recognition that micronutrient deficits, in part a reflection of the neglect by policymakers of micronutrient-dense foods, remain a serious global threat. Perhaps more worrisome is the burgeoning global epidemic of overweight and obesity leading to chronic illnesses such as diabetes and cardiovascular disease.

In this chapter, we have focused on the future policy challenges and opportunities in agriculture in terms of a broader supply chain, as well as non-agricultural policies that will help in the fight against malnutrition. We emphasize the need for continued efforts to modernize agricultural systems in large swaths of the world, where the structural transformation has yet to occur. The challenges of investing in productivity growth in these areas remain formidable, especially in regions characterized by low-productive systems primarily found in sub-Saharan Africa and parts of South Asia. Even in countries with modernizing agricultural systems, there is a need to do more in terms of promoting diversity in production and consumption of non-staple food crops, which have until now been largely neglected by agricultural researchers. Additionally, although the focus of our chapter is on agriculture and its supply chain, by including its role in job creation and in fueling economic growth, through ensuring a steady and plentiful supply of wage goods for a modernizing industrial and service economy, we emphasize the importance of complementary investments in public and curative health services. Indeed, as the current paradigm in terms of combatting malnutrition focuses on the first 1,000 days, from conception to 2 years of age, we also emphasize the role of investing in health infrastructure and promoting care behaviors, such as breastfeeding and appropriate weaning practices. In doing so, we stress that these investments are not divorced or in conflict with the structural transformation, both because of agriculture's role in job creation and economic growth, but also because women are at the heart of both processes—caring for and nurturing children, and in their roles as food producers and key workers along the food value chain. And furthermore, investing in the health and nutritional well-being of women and their children will have short- and long-term benefits, in terms of raising the productivity of the labor force and promoting economic growth.

References

Aker, J. C., and M. Fafchamps. 2010. "How Does Mobile Phone Coverage Affect Farm-Gate Prices? Evidence from West Africa." Unpublished draft, University of California, Berkeley.

Alston, J. M., G. W. Norton, and P. G. Pardey. 1995. *Science under Scarcity: Principles and Practice for Agricultural Research Evaluation and Priority Setting.* Ithaca, NY: Cornell University Press.

Ariga, J., and T. S. Jayne. 2010. "Fertilizer in Kenya: Factors Driving the Usage by Smallholder Farmers." In *Yes Africa Can: Success Stories from a Dynamic Continent*, edited by P. Chuhan-Pole, and M. Angwafo, pp. 269–288. Washington, DC: World Bank.

Arimond, M., and M. T. Ruel. 2004. "Dietary Diversity Is Associated with Child Nutritional Status: Evidence from 11 Demographic and Health Surveys." *Journal of Nutrition* 134 (10): pp. 2579–2585.

Asare-Marfo, D., E. Birol, C. Gonzalez, M. Moursi, S. Perez, J. Schwarz, and M. Zeller. 2013. "Prioritizing Countries for Biofortification Interventions Using Country-Level Data." HarvestPlus Working Paper No. 11, HarvestPlus, Washington, DC.

Atwood, D. A. 1990. "Land Registration in Africa: The Impact on Agricultural Production." *World Development* 18 (5): pp. 659–671.

Barrett, C. B., M. E. Bachke, M. F. Bellemare, H. C. Michelson, S. Narayanan, and T. F. Walker. 2011. "Smallholder Participation in Contract Farming: Comparative Evidence from Five Countries." *World Development* 40 (4): 715–730.

Barrett, C. B., and P. A. Dorosh. 1996. "Farmers' Welfare and Changing Food Prices: Nonparametric Evidence from Rice in Madagascar." *American Journal of Agricultural Economics* 78 (3): pp. 656–669.

Barrett, C. B., T. Reardon, and P. Webb. 2001. "Nonfarm Income Diversification and Household Livelihood Strategies in Rural Africa: Concepts, Dynamics, and Policy Implications. *Food Policy* 26 (4): pp. 315–331.

Behrman, J. R. 1998. "Intrahousehold Allocation of Nutrients in Rural India: Are Boys Favored? Do Parents Exhibit Inequality Aversion?" *Oxford Economic Papers* 40 (1): pp. 32–54.

Bernard, T., and D. Spielman. 2009. "Reaching the Rural Poor through Rural Producer Organizations? A Study of Agricultural Marketing Cooperatives in Ethiopia." *Food Policy* 34 (1): pp. 60–69.

Berti, P. R., J. Krasevec, and S. FitzGerald. 2004. "A Review of the Effectiveness of Agriculture Interventions in Improving Nutrition Outcomes." *Public Health Nutrition* 7 (5): pp. 599–609.

Binswanger-Mkhize, H., and A. F. McCalla. 2010. "The Changing Context and Prospects for Agricultural and Rural Development in Africa." In *Handbook of Agricultural Economics*, Vol. 4, edited by P. Pingali, and R. Evenson, 4th ed., pp. 3571–3712. Oxford: Elsevier B.V.

Black, R. E., L. H. Allen, Z. A. Bhutta, L. E. Caulfield, M. de Onis, M. Ezzati, C. Mathers, and J. Rivera, for the Maternal and Child Undernutrition Study Group. 2008. "Maternal and Child Undernutrition: Global and Regional Exposures and Health Consequences." *Lancet* 371 (9608): pp. 243–260.

Bliss, C. J., and N. H. Stern. 1982. *Palanpur: The Economy of an Indian Village.* Oxford: Clarendon Press and New York: Oxford University Press.

Bouis, H. E., and L. J. Haddad. 1992. "Are Estimates of Calorie-income Elasticities Too High?" *Journal of Development Economics* 39 (2): pp. 333–364.

Bouis, H. E., C. Hotz, B. McClafferty, J. V. Meenakshi, and W. H. Pfeiffer. 2011. "Biofortification: A New Tool to Reduce Micronutrient Malnutrition." *Food and Nutrition Bulletin* 32 (1 Suppl): pp. S31–40.

Carter, M. R., B. L. Barham, and D. Mesbah. 1996. "Agricultural Export Booms and the Rural Poor in Chile, Guatemala, and Panama." *Latin American Research Review* 31 (1): pp. 33–65.

Cercamondi, C. I., I. M. Egli, E. Mitchikpe, F. Tossou, C. Zeder, J. D. Hounhouigan, and R. F. Hurrell. 2013. "Total Iron Absorption by Young Women from Iron-biofortified Pearl Millet Composite Meals Is Double That from Regular Millet Meals but Less Than That from Post-harvest Iron-fortified Millet Meals." *Journal of Nutrition* 143 (9): pp. 1376–1382.

Coulter, J., and A. W. Shepherd. 1995. *Inventory Credit: An Approach to Developing Agricultural Markets.* FAO Agricultural Services Bulletin, Issue 120. Rome, Italy: Food and Agriculture Organization of the United Nations (FAO).

Dalberg. 2012. *Catalyzing Smallholder Agricultural Finance.* (September). Dalberg Global Development Advisors. <http://www.dalberg.com/documents/Catalyzing_Smallholder_Ag_Finance.pdf>.

Datt, G., and M. Ravallion. 1998. "Farm Productivity and Rural Poverty in India." *Journal of Development Studies* 34 (4): pp. 62–85.

Davis, K., E. Nkonya, E. Kato, D. A. Mekonnen, M. Odendo, R. Miiro, and J. Nkuba. 2012. "Impact of Farmer Field Schools on Agricultural Productivity and Poverty in East Africa." *World Development* 40 (2): pp. 402–413.

de Silva, H., and D. Ratnadiwakara. 2008. "Using ICT to Reduce Transaction Costs in Agriculture through Better Communication: A Case-Study from Sri Lanka." LIRNEasia, Colombo, Sri Lanka.

De Soto, H. 2000. *The Mystery of Capital: Why Capitalism Succeeds in the West and Fails Everywhere Else.* New York: Basic Books.

Dercon, S. 2002. "Income Risk, Coping Strategies and Safety Nets." *World Bank Research Observer* 17 (2): pp. 141–166.

Dolan, C. S., and K. Sorby. 2003. "Gender and Employment in High-Value Agriculture Industries." Agricultural and Rural Development Working Paper No. 7, World Bank, Washington, DC.

Dorjee, K., S. Broca, and P. Pingali. 2003. "Diversification in South Asian Agriculture: Trends and Constraints." ESA Working Paper No. 3-15, Agriculture and Development Economics Division, Food and Agricultural Organization of the United Nations (FAO), Rome, Italy.

Faber, M., V. Jogessar, and A. Benadé. 2001. "Nutritional Status and Dietary Intakes of Children Aged 2–5 Years and Their Caregivers in a Rural South African Community." *International Journal of Food Sciences and Nutrition* 52 (5): pp. 401–411.

Faber, M., and P. J. van Jaarsveld. 2007. "The Production of Provitamin A-rich Vegetables in Home-gardens as a Means of Addressing Vitamin A Deficiency in Rural African Communities." *Journal of the Science of Food and Agriculture* 87 (3): pp. 366–377.

Fafchamps, M. 2009. "Vulnerability, Risk Management, and Agricultural Development." Agriculture for Development Paper No. Afd-0904, Center of Evaluation for Global Action, University of California, Berkeley.

Fletschner, D. 2009. "Rural Women's Access to Credit: Market Imperfections and Intrahousehold Dynamics." *World Development* 37 (3): pp. 618–631.

Fletschner, D., and M. R. Carter. 2008. "Constructing and Reconstructing Gender: Reference Group Effects and Women's Demand for Entrepreneurial Capital." *Journal of Behavorial and Experimental Economics* (formerly *Journal of Socio-Economics*) 37 (2): pp. 672–693.

Fogel, Robert W. 1994. "Economic Growth, Population Theory, and Physiology: The Bearing of Long-Term Processes on the Making of Economic Policy." *American Economic Review* 84 (3): pp. 369–395.

Fogel, Robert W. 2004a. "Health, Nutrition, and Economic Growth." *Economic Development and Cultural Change* 52 (3): pp. 643–658.

Fogel, Robert W. 2004b. *The Escape from Hunger and Premature Death, 1700–2100: Europe, America, and the Third World*. Cambridge: Cambridge University Press.

Gladwin, C. H., K. L. Buhr, A. Goldman, C. Hiebsch, P. E. Hildebrand, G. Kidder, M. Langham, D. Lee, P. Nkedi-Kizza, and D. Williams. 1997. "Gender and Soil Fertility in Africa." In *Replenishing Soil Fertility in Africa*, SSSA Special Publication No. 51, edited by R. P. Buresh, P. A. Sanchez, and F. Calhoun, pp. 219–236. Madison, WI: Soil Science Society of America and American Society of Agronomy.

Gómez, M. I., C. B. Barrett, T. Raney, P. Pinstrup-Andersen, J. Meerman, A. Croppenstedt, B. Carisma, and B. Thompson. 2013. "Post-Green Revolution Food Systems and the Triple Burden of Malnutrition." *Food Policy* 42 (October): pp. 29–138.

Gómez, M. I., and K. D. Ricketts. 2013. "Food Value Chain Transformations in Developing Countries: Selected Hypotheses on Nutritional Implications." *Food Policy* 42 (October): pp. 139–150.

Gorton, M., J. Sauer, and P. Supatpongkul. 2011. "Wet Markets, Supermarkets and the 'Big Middle' for Food Retailing in Developing Countries: Evidence from Thailand." *World Development* 39 (9): pp. 1624–1637.

Grunert, K. G. 2005. "Food Quality and Safety: Consumers Perception and Demand." *European Review of Agricultural Economics* 32 (3): pp. 369–391 (as cited in Jabbar et al. 2010).

Hayami, Y., and R. W. Herdt. 1977. "Market Price Effects of Technological Change on Income Distribution in Semisubsistence Agriculture." *American Journal of Agricultural Economics* 59 (2): pp. 245–256.

Hoddinott, J., and Y. Yohannes. 2002. "Dietary Diversity as a Food Security Indicator." Discussion Paper No. 36, International Food Policy Research Institute (IFPRI), Washington, DC.

Hotz, C., C. Loechl, A. Lubowa, J. K. Tumwine, G. Ndeezi, A. Nandutu Masawi, R. Baingana, A. Carriquiry, A. de Brauw, J. V. Meenakshi, and D. O. Gilligan. 2012. "Introduction of β-Carotene-Rich Orange Sweet Potato in Rural Uganda Resulted in Increased Vitamin A Intakes among Children and Women and Improved Vitamin A Status among Children." *Journal of Nutrition* 142 (10): pp.1871–1880.

Humphrey, J. 2005. *Shaping Value Chains for Development: Global Value Chains in Agribusiness*. Eschborn: Deutsche Gesellschaft für Technische Zusammenarbeit (GTZ) GmbH.

IFPRI (International Food Policy Research Institute) and The World Bank. 2010. *Gender and Governance in Rural Services: Insights from India, Ghana and Ethiopia*. Washington, DC: World Bank.

Jabbar, M. A., D. Baker, and M. L. Fadiga, eds. 2010. "Demand for Livestock Products in Developing Countries with a Focus on Quality and Safety Attributes: Evidence from Case Studies." ILRI Research Report No. 24, International Livestock Research Institute, Nairobi, Kenya.

Jones, A. D., A. Shrinivas, and R. Bezner-Kerr. 2014. "Farm Production Diversity Is Associated with Greater Household Dietary Diversity in Malawi: Findings from Nationally Representative Data." *Food Policy* 46 (June): pp. 1–12.

Joshi, P., A. Gulati, P. S. Birthal, and L. Tewari. 2004. "Agriculture Diversification in South Asia: Patterns, Determinants and Policy Implications." *Economic and Political Weekly* 39 (24): pp. 2457–2467.

Kaitibie, S., A. Omore, K. Rich, and P. Kristjanson. 2010. "Kenyan Dairy Policy Change: Influence Pathways and Economic Impacts." *World Development* 38 (10): pp. 1494–1505.

Kaplinsky, R., and M. Morris. 2001. *A Handbook for Value Chain Analysis. Policy*. Ottawa: International Development Research Centre (IDRC).

Low, J. W., M. Arimond, N. Osman, B. Cunguara, F. Zano, and D. Tschirley. 2007. "A Food-Based Approach Introducing Orange-Fleshed Sweet Potatoes Increased Vitamin A Intake and Serum Retinol Concentrations in Young Children in Rural Mozambique." *Journal of Nutrition* 137 (5): pp. 1320–1327.

Minten, B. 2008. "The Food Retail Revolution in Poor Countries: Is It Coming or Is It Over?" *Economic Development and Cultural Change* 56 (4): pp. 767–789.

Morduch, J. 1994. "Poverty and Vulnerability." *American Economic Review* 84(2): pp. 221–225.

Narrod, C., D. Roy, J. Okello, B. Avendaño, K. Rich, and A. Thorat. 2009. "Public–Private Partnerships and Collective Action in High Value Fruit and Vegetable Supply Chains." *Food Policy* 34 (1): pp. 8–15.

Omore, A., and D. Baker. 2011. "Lessons Learned in Integrating Informal into the Formal Dairy Industry in Kenya through Training and Certification." In *Towards Priority Actions for Market Development for African Farmers: Proceedings of an International Conference, 13–15 May 2009, Nairobi, Kenya*. Nairobi: Alliance for a Green Revolution in Africa (AGRA) and International Livestock Reseach Institute (ILRI).

Pingali, P. 2004. "The Westernization of Asian Diets and the Transformation of Food Systems: Implications for Research and Policy." *Food Policy* 32 (3): pp. 281–298.

Pingali, P. 2010. "Agriculture Renaissance: Making 'Agriculture for Development' Work in the 21st Century." In *Handbooks in Economics*, Vol. 4, edited by P. Pingali, and R. Evenson, 4th edition, pp. 3867–3894. Oxford: Elsevier B.V.

Pingali, P. L. 2012. "Green Revolution: Impacts, Limits, and the Path Ahead." *Proceedings of the National Academy of Sciences of the United States of America* 109 (31): 12302–12308.

Pinstrup-Andersen, P., and E. Caicedo. 1978. "The Potential Impact of Changes in Income Distribution on Food Demand and Human Nutrition." *American Journal of Agricultural Economics* 60 (3): 402–415.

Quisumbing, A. R., and L. Pandolfelli. 2010. "Promising Approaches to Address the Needs of Poor Female Farmers: Resources, Constraints, and Interventions." *World Development* 38 (4): pp. 581–592.

Reardon, T., S. Henson, and A. Gulati. 2010. "Links between Supermarkets and Food Prices, Diet Diversity and Food Safety in Developing Countries." In *Trade, Food, Diet and Health: Perspectives and Policy Options*, edited by C. Hawkes, C. Blouin, S. Henson, N. Drager, and L. Dubé, pp. 111–130. Chichester: Wiley-Blackwell.

Reddy, G. P., M. R. K. Murthy, and P. C. Meena. 2010. "Value Chains and Retailing of Fresh Vegetables and Fruits, Andhra Pradesh." *Agricultural Economics Research Review* 23: pp. 455–460.

Ricketts, K., M. Gómez, and B. Mueller. 2013. "Privately-led Extension Models: Reviewing Current Approaches for Reaching Smallholders in the Coffee and Cocoa Sectors." Cornell University, Ithaca, NY.

Ruben, R., M. Slingerland, and H. Nijhoff. 2006. "Agro-Food Chains and Networks for Development: Issues, Approaches, and Strategies." In *The Agro-Food Chains and Networks for Development*, edited by R. Ruben, M. Slingerland, and H. Nijhoff, pp. 1–25. Dordecht: Springer.

Scobie, G. M., and R. Posada. 1978. "The Impact of Technical Change on Income Distribution: The Case of Rice in Colombia." *American Journal of Agricultural Economics* 60 (1): pp. 85–92.

Smith, A. (1776) 1960. *The Wealth of Nations*. Reprint, New York: Modern Library.

Stevenson, J. R., N. Villoria, D. Byerlee, T. Kelley, and M. Maredia. 2013. "Green Revolution Research Saved an Estimated 18 to 27 Million Hectares from Being Brought into Agricultural Production." *Proceedings of the National Academy of Sciences of the United States of America* 110 (21): pp. 8363–8368.

Timmer, B. C. P., and S. Akkus. 2008. "The Structural Transformation as a Pathway Out of Poverty: Analytics, Empirics and Politics." Working Paper No. 150, Center for Global Development, Washington, DC.

Torlesse, H., L. Kiess, and M. W. Bloem. 2003. "Community and International Nutrition Association of Household Rice Expenditure with Child Nutritional Status Indicates a Role for Macroeconomic Food Policy in Combating Malnutrition." *Journal of Nutrition* 133 (5): pp. 1320–1325.

Vanderpuye-Orgle, J., and C. B. Barrett. 2009. "Risk Management and Social Visibility in Ghana." *African Development Review* 21 (1): pp. 5–35.

Webb, P., and S. Block. 2012. "Support for Agriculture during Economic Transformation: Impacts on Poverty and Undernutrition." *Proceedings of the National Academy of Sciences of the United States of America* 109 (31): 12309–12314.

World Bank. 2007. *World Development Report 2008: Agriculture for Development*. Washington, DC: World Bank.

World Economic Forum. 2009. *The Next Billions: Business Strategies to Enhance Food Value Chains and Empower the Poor*. Boston, in collaboration with The Boston Consulting Group.

Zeller, M., A. Diagne, and C. Mataya. 1998. "Market Access by Smallholder Farmers in Malawi: Implications for Technology Adoption, Agricultural Productivity and Crop Income." *Agricultural Economics* 19 (1–2): pp. 219–229.

8

Is Small Farm-Led Development Still a Relevant Strategy for Africa and Asia?

Peter B. R. Hazell

Introduction

Small farm-led development has been the dominant agricultural development paradigm among agricultural economists since its remarkable success in driving Asia's Green Revolution during the 1960s and 1970s. The paradigm is based on several claimed advantages of small farms:

- Small farms are more efficient than large farms, as evidenced by an impressive body of empirical studies showing an inverse relationship between farm size and land productivity across Asia and Africa (Binswanger-Mkhize and McCalla 2010; Eastwood et al. 2010; Larson et al. 2014). Moreover, small farms typically achieve their higher land productivity using labor-intensive methods rather than capital-intensive machines. These are important efficiency advantages in poor countries where land and capital are scarce relative to labor.

- In poor, labor-abundant economies, not only are small farms more efficient, but because they also account for large shares of the rural poor, small farm development can be a "win-win" proposition for growth and poverty reduction. Asia's green revolution demonstrated how agricultural growth that reaches large numbers of small farms can transform rural economies and raise enormous numbers of people out of poverty (Rosegrant and Hazell 2000). Recent studies have also shown that a more egalitarian distribution of land not only leads to higher economic growth but also helps ensure that the growth that is achieved is more beneficial to the poor (World Bank 2007).

- Small farms also contribute to greater food security, both through feeding their own families and by supplying local markets with foods that may be less costly and less risky than alternative supplies, particularly in regions facing high transport costs. Because they produce more output per hectare than large farms, they also contribute to greater national food self-sufficiency in land-scarce countries.

- Small farm households with cash incomes also have more favorable expenditure patterns than large farms for promoting growth of the local non-farm economy, including rural towns. They spend higher shares of their incremental income on locally produced goods and services, many of which are labor intensive (Mellor 1976; Hazell and Roell 1983). These demand patterns generate additional income and jobs in the local non-farm economy, which can be beneficial to the poor.

Advocates of small farm development have long recognized that the efficiency advantages of small farms slowly disappear as countries develop. As per capita incomes rise, economies diversify, workers leave agriculture, rural wages go up, and land becomes cheaper relative to labor. It then becomes more efficient to have progressively larger and more mechanized farms. The result is a natural economic transition toward larger farms over the development process, but one that depends critically on the rate of rural–urban migration, and hence on the growth of the non-agricultural sector (Huang 1973; Eastwood et al. 2010).

Despite its proven success, the small farm development paradigm is widely challenged today, and there is considerable debate about its continuing relevance for Asia and Africa. Critics argue that because of rural population growth on a fixed land base, the onslaught of globalization and market liberalization policies, and the emergence of new types of farm technologies, the economic context for small-scale farming has substantially changed, and small may no longer be as beautiful as before. This chapter considers these arguments and their implications for agricultural development and small farm assistance strategies.

Patterns of Farm Size Transition and Their Consequences

Despite a chorus of small farm skeptics, small farms are proving surprisingly resilient and continue to increase in number. There are nearly 450 million farmers today who farm less than 2 hectares (ha) of land, and many more family farms larger than 2 ha who struggle to make an adequate living from farming. Small farms are predominantly concentrated in Asia and Africa and are home to some 2 billion people, including half the world's undernourished people and the majority of people living in absolute poverty (IFPRI 2005).

Average farm sizes continue to shrink across much of Asia and Africa. In India, for example, the average farm size about halved between 1971 and 2005–06, and the number of farms less than 2 ha doubled (Table 8.1). In China, the average farm size fell 30 percent between 1985 and 2000, but then bottomed out in 2000 and has shown a slight increase since then (Table 8.2). In Bangladesh, the average farm size shrunk from 1.4 ha in 1976–77 to 0.3 ha in 2005, and the percentage of farms smaller than 1 ha increased from half to about 90 percent (Otsuka 2013). In the Philippines, the average farm size fell from 3.6 ha in 1971 to 2.0 ha in 2002, and the share of small farms less than 1 ha increased from 13.6 to 40.1 percent. Indonesia and Thailand saw more modest declines of 15–20 percent in average farm sizes over similar periods and little change in the share of small farms less than 1 ha in size (Otsuka 2013).

African countries vary widely in their population densities, and an analysis of available census data shows that farm sizes are smaller in highly populated countries than in less populated countries—1.2 ha for highly populated African countries in the 2000s as compared to 2.9 ha in low-density Africa

Table 8.1. Farm size distribution, India

Census year	Average farm size (ha)	Number small farms less than 2 ha (millions)
1971	2.3	49.11
1991	1.6	84.48
1995–96	1.4	92.82
2001	1.3	98.10
2005–06	1.2	107.64

Source: Data from Otsuka (2013).

Table 8.2. Farm size distribution, China

	Cultivated land ha/household	% Net income from farming	% Net income from wage earnings	% Net income from other
1985	0.70	66.3	18.2	15.5
1990	0.67	50.2	20.2	29.6
1995	0.65	50.7	22.4	26.9
2000	0.55	37.0	31.2	31.8
2005	0.57	33.7	36.1	30.2
2010	0.60	29.1	41.1	29.8

Source: Data from Huang et al. (2012).

(Jayne et al. 2013). Farm sizes have also shrunk the most in the highly populated countries, from around 2.3 ha in the 1970s to 1.2 ha in the 2000s, compared to a decline from 3.0 to 2.9 ha in less densely populated countries (Jayne et al. 2013). In Kenya, the average farm size fell from 2.3 ha in 1997 to 1.9 ha in 2010, and in Rwanda, the size fell from 1.2 ha in 1984 to 0.7 ha in 2000 (Masters et al. 2013). The average farm size in Ethiopia declined from an estimated 1.4 ha per holding in 1977 to around 1.0 ha in 2001–02, though it appears to have stabilized since then (Headey et al. 2013). Based on repeat household surveys in eight African countries, Jirström et al. (2011) found that even over the six-year period 2002 to 2008, the average farm size declined by 15 percent in Ghana, 35 percent in Mozambique, 13 percent in Tanzania, and 10 percent in Zambia, but remained unchanged in Kenya and Malawi, and increased by 9 percent in Ethiopia and by 37 percent in Nigeria. The average change across the eight countries was a decline of 11 percent (from 2.4 to 2.2 ha per holding).

Small farms are also becoming more diversified into off-farm sources of income, often because they are now too small to provide an adequate living from farming. In China, non-farm income shares for farm households increased from 33.7 percent in 1985, to 63 percent in 2000, to 70.9 percent in 2010 (Huang et al. 2012). This is an extreme example, but non-farm income shares have reached 40 percent or more in many other Asian and sub-Saharan African countries and are often much higher for the smallest farms (Haggblade et al. 2007a). On average, this diversification is higher across Asia than Africa, but there is considerable variation within each continent.

Although there is a lot of country and regional variation, the overwhelming story in densely populated countries is one of more small farms, shrinking farm sizes, and increased income diversification. Despite growth—sometimes quite rapid growth—in national per capita incomes, there is little sign yet of any significant shift to the patterns of farm consolidation that occurred during the economic transformation of most of today's industrialized countries. Rather, the continuing shift toward ever smaller and more diversified farms might best be described as a "reverse transition." In some countries (e.g., Bangladesh, India, and the Philippines), even the total agricultural land area is becoming more concentrated among small farms, and it is the large farms that are being squeezed out.

There are many factors driving this reverse farm size transition. An important driver is rural population growth, especially growth in working age adults. Growth in rural working age adults, however, may reflect insufficient growth in urban jobs to enable faster rural–urban migration. Even relatively fast-growing countries like India have not generated sufficient growth in productive non-agricultural jobs to reduce the rural workforce. Bangladesh and China are two recent exceptions.

There are also a number of drivers that are more context-specific. These include negative factors, which work to trap people in rural areas:

- Constraints on rural–urban migration, such as language, racial, and cultural barriers; legal restrictions on resettlement (e.g., China).

- Inheritance systems that lead to subdivision of farms among multiple heirs.

- Restrictions on land market transactions, such as caps on farm size (India), or indigenous land rights systems that limit opportunities for land consolidation (Africa).

- An aging and immobile population of farmers. Farm exits tend to be an intergenerational phenomena; land is consolidated when farmers retire or die.

- Constraints on women's employment opportunities that keep them on the farm.

- Inadequate social security systems, so that farms are kept as a retirement hedge.

- Subsidies and other agricultural support policies that make small-scale farming more attractive than its real economic worth.

On the positive side, some drivers make it more attractive for workers to stay in rural areas:

- Dense rural settlement patterns that provide enough income-earning opportunities in the local non-farm economy, so that farm-based workers do not need to migrate to urban areas.

- Growing high-value opportunities in farming that create significant new employment opportunities in agriculture.

Many of these drivers are very powerful and seem unlikely to diminish in the near future. Rural populations are projected to nearly double by 2050 in Africa, so the pressure on land will keep growing. In contrast, rural population growth is slowing in much of Asia and is approaching a tipping point at which the rural workforce, and hence the pressure on the land base, begins to reverse. This has already happened in Bangladesh and China and may be happening more widely in dynamic regions with good market access within countries (Masters et al. 2013).

How fast these changes could happen will depend to a large extent on rates of national economic growth and the non-agricultural employment intensity of that growth. But rapid farm consolidation does not necessarily follow from economic growth because of some of the more context-specific constraints listed above. The earlier experiences of Japan, Taiwan, and South Korea suggest that the reverse farm size transition could continue until well into middle-income status (Otsuka 2013). In Japan, for example, the average farm size only bottomed out around 1960 at 1 ha and has since increased quite marginally to 1.2 ha in 1980 and 1.8 ha in 2005, while the percentage of farms less than 3 ha in size fell from 97.6 percent to 90.5 percent over the same period. China may finally have reached a tipping point in that the average farm size, which had fallen from 0.7 ha in 1985 to 0.55 ha in 2000, increased to 0.6 ha in 2010 (Table 8.2), but this is a very modest rate of farm consolidation considering the high rates of economic growth achieved in recent years.

Does the Reverse Farm Size Transition Matter?

From the perspective of economic efficiency or growth, it does not really matter that farms are getting smaller unless there are economies of scale in farming. On the production side, the available evidence still supports an inverse relationship between land productivity and farm size (see, for example, the recent paper by Larson et al. [2014]), but small farms are facing growing challenges in accessing modern inputs, credit, and high-value markets. Large farms seem able to capture economies of scale and scope in linking to value chains, so unless small farms are organized into marketing groups or contract farming arrangements, it is possible that they are becoming less efficient than large farms. If so, then the reverse transition does matter from an efficiency perspective. There are also concerns that some small farms, particularly in less favored areas, are degrading their resources through unsustainable farming practices, in which case it is hard to see how they could remain efficient farmers in the longer term.

Another concern, particularly in Africa and Latin America, is growing competition from corporate-sized farms that can exploit entirely new types of farming technologies—such as GPS-controlled precision farming, minimum tillage, genetically modified (GM) seed, and agrochemical packages—and back this with investments and political connections that give them privileged access to markets, modern inputs, insurance, and credit, all of which results in yields and cost structures that small farms simply may not be able to beat (Deininger and Byerlee 2011; Byerlee et al. 2012). A good example is the development model of Brazil's Cerrado region, which is being transplanted by private investors to parts of Africa (FAO and World Bank 2009). In some land surplus countries this development may be welcome and unstoppable, but unless carefully managed, it is a growing threat to small farmers in more populous countries.

Another efficiency concern is that as small farms get smaller, they may not have the kinds of cash income and expenditure patterns that help drive growth in the rural non-farm economy. During Asia's Green Revolution, for example, small farms generated significant marketed surpluses and cash incomes, much of which was spent locally on a range of agricultural inputs, consumer goods and services, and investment goods for their farm and household. These expenditure and investment patterns generated significant secondary rounds of employment-intensive growth in the rural non-farm economy— or large growth multipliers (see Haggblade et al. [2007b] for a review of the literature). Small farms today are less than half the size of the small farms of the Green Revolution era, and many are subsistence farms rather than market-oriented ones. Much may depend on how off-farm sources of income are spent, but the possibility arises that it is now the commercially oriented and medium-sized farms (what used to be called *small* farms) that are able to generate significant growth multipliers.

From a food security perspective, the reverse transition poses a difficult dilemma. Small farms provide for the food security of huge numbers of rural poor. Many small farms, however, are net buyers of food, and they generate relatively little of the food required to feed large urban populations. Urban population shares are projected to grow strongly across the developing world (UN 2011),[1] and feeding these populations will require rapid growth in marketed food supplies. For most foods, these supplies will need to come from larger farms and commercially oriented small farms that can generate net surpluses. It follows that a food security agenda needs two pillars. One pillar is to provide support to the many smallholders who farm largely to meet their own subsistence needs. The other pillar is to invest in large and medium-sized farms and commercially oriented smallholdings that can produce marketed surpluses for the cities.

From poverty and income equality perspectives, the reverse transition also poses difficult challenges. Although diversification into non-farm activities is a useful way of supplementing farm income, it may not be enough to maintain an adequate income, to escape poverty, or prevent widening rural–urban income gaps. Local diversification opportunities into high-value farming and non-farm activity are higher in fast-growing countries, and in dynamic and more densely populated rural areas. Small farms in such areas may be achieving adequate livelihoods despite having little land. In India and some other Asian countries, there appears to have been sufficient growth in remittances and rural non-farm income in recent years to enable farm households to successfully avoid any widening gap between rural and urban per capita incomes. Rural poverty rates have also declined in tandem with urban poverty rates (Binswanger-Mkhize 2012; Otsuka 2013).

Elsewhere, opportunities for diversifying into high-value farming or local non-farm opportunities are more limited, leaving many small farms trapped in subsistence-oriented farming and poverty. This is especially common in lagging regions, where most of Asia's rural poor now live (Ghani 2010). It is also common in many slowly growing African countries, where rural–urban income gaps are widening and rural poverty rates remain stubbornly high. The relatively slow growth of the agricultural sector and the generally sparser rural population densities in Africa also constrain growth in rural non-farm opportunities.

Evidence from Japan, South Korea, and Taiwan suggests that income diversification by small farms is not a long-term solution to the rural–urban income gap problem. In these countries, governments eventually had to introduce income support measures to narrow the income gap, and China and some other Asian countries are now beginning to follow suit (Otsuka 2013).

From an environmental perspective, more small and marginal farms can lead to mixed outcomes. Many small farms retain complex farming systems that are ecologically well balanced and serve to conserve in situ many underutilized and neglected foods and indigenous crop varieties and animal species. On the other hand, many highly intensified small farms are an important source of environmental pollution and zoonotic diseases. Many other small farms struggle to make a basic living and can become trapped in downward spirals of resource degradation and poverty (Cleaver and Schrieber 1994). Yet other small farms encroach into forests and are an important cause of deforestation. A larger number of small farms in a landscape also increases the difficulties of introducing knowledge-intensive Natural Resource Management (NRM) practices, and can make it more difficult to undertake the kinds of collective action needed to sustainably manage and improve watersheds and common properties. On the other hand, it needs to be noted that many large farms also cause significant environmental damage.

In sum, the reverse transition is not a uniformly good thing, creating new tensions and potential trade-offs between important economic, social, and environmental goals. Earlier assumptions that small farm growth is a winning proposition for growth, poverty alleviation, and food security can no longer be taken for granted, and the future outlook is for less complementary outcomes between these goals, which will pose more difficult choices for policymakers (Masters et al. 2013; Hazell and Rahman 2014).

The growing divergence between goals is most evident in the recent emergence of two very different agricultural agendas. On the one hand, recent increases in world food and energy prices have made agricultural growth an imperative for food security. Since most of the food-insecure households live in rural areas and mostly on farms, improving the productivity of subsistence-oriented farms has become a high priority for many governments and donors. On the other hand, higher agricultural and energy prices have turned agricultural growth into a "business" opportunity for producing food, raw materials, and biofuels, with significant growth in private agricultural investment by sovereign wealth funds and foreign and national corporate sector investors.

The business-oriented strategy does not have to be inconsistent with a pro-poor, food security approach, as long as it engages with large numbers of smallholders who are, or can become, commercially viable. Already, private sector investments along value chains are opening up new market opportunities for some smallholder farms, particularly for high-value products. However, it is also becoming apparent that many more smallholders are not only missing out on new high-value chains, but in some countries have also lost access to modern inputs, credit, and market outlets, even for their traditional food staples (Djurfeldt et al. 2011). There has also been growth in land grabbing and the development of corporate-sized farms, which threaten to displace smallholders from their land as well as their markets (Deininger and Byerlee 2011).

These challenges have led some to suggest that small farms have a limited future as farm businesses, and that it is better to encourage private investments in large-scale farm operations and to direct public assistance toward helping small farmers diversify out of agriculture, including helping more workers migrate and settle in urban areas (Maxwell et al. 2001; Collier 2009). The contrary view is that small farms can remain competitive in the market as full- or part-time businesses, as long as the public sector supports them by investing in the kinds of R&D and infrastructure that can make them more competitive, and by promoting farmer organizations to increase their bargaining power in the market (Hazell et al. 2007).

Given all the above, it is hard to disagree with Collier and Dercon (2014) that we need to move beyond the small vs. big farm debate, and think more about appropriate portfolios of small, medium, and large farms that are relevant to the resource endowments and stage of development of a country. We also need to recognize that large numbers of small farms are not going to make it as commercial businesses, especially asset-poor farmers in backward regions. Many of these kinds of farms are already diversifying their livelihoods out of farming, but there are many instances where this is not yet possible on the scale required, or where the returns to non-farm activities remain too low for them to escape poverty. Many are sinking into deeper poverty and subsistence modes of production because of higher food prices and reduced access to land, markets, and modern inputs.

What is the Right Strategy for Small Farms?

Small farms are a very diverse group, and they face varying prospects that depend on their own assets and aspirations, as well as on their country and regional context. Policies and investments to assist small farms need to take this diversity and context into account.

A number of farm typologies have been offered in the literature to help manage this diversity. Vorley (2002) distinguished between farmers operating in three rural worlds. In rural world 1, commercial farmers are globally competitive, linked to export markets, and use modern technologies; in rural world 2, farmers sell primarily in local, regional, and national markets and use intermediate technologies; in rural world 3, farmers are subsistence-oriented and use traditional technologies. The World Bank (2007) identified five smallholder groups: market-oriented, subsistence-oriented, off-farm labor-oriented, migration-oriented, and diversified households that combine multiple income sources. Berdegué and Escobar (2002) identified three groups of family farms based on regional context and household assets. The first category comprises family farms with good assets (land, labor, and/or access to capital) and locations in places with good agricultural potential and access to markets. These farmers are usually fully integrated in a market economy and make a substantial contribution to the production of food for domestic and international markets. The second category comprises family farms that have reasonable assets and agricultural potential but are constrained by being located in slow-moving regional economies with limited market access. The third category comprises resource-poor farmers located in places where conditions are adverse not only for agriculture, but often for non-farm activities. The majority of smallholders in this group are poor, subsistence-oriented, and may be diversified into low-productivity non-farm sources of income. Fan et al. (2013) differentiated small farms according to their profitability within the agricultural sector (subsistence farmers without profit potential, subsistence farmers with profit potential, and commercial smallholder farmers), and the different stages of economic transformation (agriculture-based, transforming, and transformed economies).

Key elements in these typologies are the characteristics of the region in which farmers live (especially its agricultural potential and access to markets) and the characteristics of the farm household themselves (assets, business orientation and acumen, and degree of diversification into off-farm sources of income). Drawing on this work, Hazell and Rahman (2014) classified smallholders into three groups for the purposes of targeting small farm assistance:

- *Commercial small farmers* who are already successfully linked to value chains, or who could link if given a little help. Commercially oriented small farms may be full- or part-time farmers.

- *Small farmers in transition*, who have or will soon have favorable off-farm opportunities and would do better if they were to either exit farming completely or obtain most of their income from off-farm sources. Most transition farmers are likely to leave farming, and it is just a question of when and how. Those that remain will farm part-time and may not be very market driven.

- *Subsistence-oriented small farmers* are marginalized for a variety of reasons that are hard to change, such as ethnic discrimination, affliction with HIV/AIDS, or living in remote areas with limited agricultural potential. Many of the same factors also prevent them from becoming transition farmers. Subsistence-oriented farmers frequently sell small amounts of produce at harvest to obtain cash income, but they are invariably net buyers of food over the entire year.

The relative importance of these three small farm groups varies widely from region to region. In a less favored region of a slow-growing country—the worst of all possible worlds, and a situation all too prevalent in Africa—there are relatively few market-oriented farms, but many subsistence-oriented small farmers, including those who are trying to transition out of farming but cannot because of a shortage of off-farm opportunities At the other extreme, in a dynamic region of a dynamic country—such as some of the coastal areas in China—many small farmers are producing lots of high-value products for the market, or are transitioning into better-paid opportunities in the industrial areas and in their local non-farm business economy. Relatively few subsistence-oriented farmers remain, and these are often the elderly or the infirm. Many other regions, of course, fall somewhere between these two extremes.

With economic growth and urbanization, significant numbers of commercially oriented small farms are likely to prosper through diversification into high-value agriculture. The most successful small farmers will tend to be located in areas with good agricultural potential and market access. Over time, some commercially oriented small farmers will become large farms, while others will eventually become transition farmers or successfully exit farming to the non-farm economy. Transition farmers will either have, or will be able to develop, suitable skills and assets for undertaking non-farm activity, and they are likely to live in well-connected areas with access to off-farm opportunities. Their farming activities are likely to be oriented towards their own consumption rather than the market. Subsistence-oriented farmers are more likely to persist in less-favored and tribal areas and to grow traditional food staples (both crop and livestock) for their own consumption.

Some Guiding Principles for Assisting Small Farms

Hazell and Rahman (2014) discussed the kinds of interventions that may be relevant for each of the three groups of small farms. Commercially oriented small farms need support as farm businesses. They need access to improved technologies and NRM practices, modern inputs, financial services, and markets, and secure access to land and water. Much of this assistance will need to be geared toward high-value production and provided on a business basis. Many smallholders will also require help acquiring the necessary knowledge and skills to become successful business entrepreneurs in today's value chains, especially women and other disempowered groups. Managing market and climate risk is a challenge for many small farms; and, in addition to insurance and access to safety nets, these farms need to develop resilient farming systems.

Transition farmers need help developing appropriate skills and assets to succeed in the non-farm economy, including, in many cases, assistance in developing small businesses. This can be especially important for women and other disempowered groups who have little experience working off-farm. The transition to the non-farm economy may also be facilitated by securing land rights and developing efficient land markets, so that transition farmers can more easily dispose of their farms. Since many transition farmers seem likely to continue to remain as part-time farmers, they can also benefit from improved technologies and NRM practices that improve their farm productivity.

Subsistence farmers are predominantly poor and will mostly need some form of social protection, often in the form of safety nets, food subsidies, or cash transfers. Interventions that help improve the productivity of their farms (e.g., better technologies and NRM practices) can make important contributions to their own food security, perhaps provide some cash income, and in many cases, may prove more cost-effective than some forms of social protection. Subsistence farmers have limited ability to pay for modern inputs or credit, however, so intermediate technologies that require few purchased inputs may be needed, or inputs will need to be heavily subsidized. Subsistence farmers are typically the most exposed and vulnerable to climate risks, and in addition to safety nets, they need help developing resilient farming systems.

Although the choice of assistance policies will need to be different for the three groups of small farms, not all interventions need to be as carefully targeted as others. If an intervention targeted at one group can benefit other groups at little or no additional cost beyond the cost of reaching the primary target group (e.g., some types of agricultural R&D), then the benefits captured by other groups can be viewed favorably as "spillover" benefits and careful targeting may not be required. However, if the benefits captured by other groups represent a diversion of benefits from the primary target group, then this must be viewed as a "leakage" that needs to be minimized through careful targeting. Cash transfers, food subsidies, and fertilizer vouchers intended for the poor typically fall into this category.

Further research is needed to develop and test the relevance of smallholder typologies and to assess the most effective interventions for each type of smallholder. This should also include analysis of the best ways to integrate agricultural interventions with complementary policies and investments, such as safety nets and assistance with migration and off-farm diversification. Another challenge is developing practical ways of identifying the different groups of farms on the ground. There has been a lot of recent work using Geographic Information Systems (GIS) and spatial analysis methods to identify target areas for rural development purposes. Most of this work focuses on mapping different regions in terms of their agroecology, market access, and rural population density (see, for example, Omamo et al. 2006), but, so far, there has been limited work on disaggregating further according to differences in farmer endowments, market orientation, and gender.

Conclusions

The case for smallholder development as a win-win strategy for achieving agricultural growth, poverty reduction, and food insecurity is less clear than it was during the Green Revolution era. The gathering forces of rapid urbanization, a reverse farm size transition toward ever smaller and more diversified farms, and an emerging corporate-driven business agenda in response to higher agricultural and energy prices are all creating a situation where policymakers need to differentiate more sharply between the needs of different types of small farms, and between growth, poverty, and food security goals.

Many smallholdings today are too small to provide adequate livelihoods, and their farm families have either begun a transition out of farming into the non-farm economy, or they are trapped in subsistence modes of farming, often in lagging regions. Both kinds of smallholders, transitional farmers and subsistence farmers, may need assistance developing new off-farm opportunities, and in overcoming poverty and food insecurity. These smallholders account for large shares of the total rural poor and food-insecure people in the developing world, and they are an important target group for international efforts to reduce poverty and food insecurity. However, transition and subsistence-oriented farms play a relatively minor role in producing marketed surpluses to drive economic growth and feed growing urban populations, and many are unlikely to successfully link to modern value chains. Interventions to improve on-farm productivity can be helpful to the food security of both groups, but will need to be complemented by other interventions that more directly alleviate poverty and facilitate off-farm transitions.

In contrast, there are also many small farmers who, because of their resource endowments, good location, or sheer entrepreneurial skill, are succeeding as commercial farm businesses, even if only on a part-time basis. These kinds of small farms are much more aligned with the new corporate-driven business agenda. As with small farms in the era of the Green Revolution, they can play important roles in driving economic growth and feeding urban populations. The greatest challenge facing these types of smallholders is accessing modern value chains. Private sector investments along value chains are opening up new market opportunities for some smallholder farms, particularly for high-value products, but it is also becoming apparent that many more commercially oriented smallholders are being left behind while larger farms are gaining market shares.

If more smallholder farms are to become commercially successful, policymakers will need to do more to support them. Key areas for support include improving the workings of markets for outputs, inputs, land, and financial services to overcome market failures that discriminate against small farms; investing in the kinds of R&D and rural infrastructure that small farmers need; helping to organize small farmers for the market; and incentivizing the private sector to link with more small farmers. The best way to achieve these is for government to work through private sector and civil society partners, creating an enabling policy and business environment, and scaling up proven successes.

Note

1. The United Nations (UN) projects that by 2050 urbanization will increase to 58 percent of the population in Africa and 64 percent in Asia (UN 2011).

References

Berdegué, J. A., and G. Escobar. 2002. "Rural Diversity, Agricultural Innovation Policies, and Poverty Reduction." AgREN Network Paper No. 122, Overseas Development Institute, London.

Binswanger-Mkhize, H. 2012. "India 1960–2010: Structural Change, the Rural Non-farm Sector, and the Prospects for Agriculture." Center on Food Security and the Environment, Stanford Symposium Series on Global Food Policy and Food Security in the 21st Century, Stanford University, Stanford, CA.

Binswanger-Mkhize, H., and A. F. McCalla. 2010. "The Changing Context and Prospects for Agricultural and Rural Development in Africa." In *Handbook of Agricultural Economics, Volume 4*, edited by Prabhu Pingali and Robert Evenson, pp. 3571–3712. Amsterdam: Elsevier.

Byerlee, D., A. Lissitsa, and P. Savanti. 2012. "Corporate Models of Broadacre Crop Farming: International Experience from Argentina and Ukraine." *Farm Policy Journal* 9 (2): pp. 13–15.

Cleaver, K., and G. Schrieber. 1994. *Reversing the Spiral: The Population, Agriculture, and Environment Nexus in Sub-Saharan Africa*. Washington, DC: World Bank.

Collier, P. 2009. "Africa's Organic Peasantry: Beyond Romanticism." *Harvard International Review* 31 (2) Summer: pp. 62–65.

Collier, P., and S. Dercon. 2014. "African Agriculture in 50 Years: Smallholders in a Rapidly Changing World?" *World Development* 63 (November): pp. 92–101.

Deininger, K., and D. Byerlee. 2011. "The Rise of Large Farms in Land Abundant Countries: Do They Have a Future?" Policy Research Working Paper 5588, World Bank, Washington, DC.

Djurfeldt, G., E. Aryeetey, and A. Isinika, eds. 2011. *African Smallholders: Food Crops, Markets and Policy*. Wallingford: CABI.

Eastwood, R., M. Lipton, and A. Newell. 2010. "Farm Size." In *Handbook of Agricultural Economics, Volume 4*, edited by Prabhu Pingali, and Robert Evenson, pp. 3323–3397. Amsterdam: Elsevier.

Fan, S., J. Brzeska, M. Keyzer, and A. Halsema. 2013. "From Subsistence to Profit: Transforming Smallholder Farms." Food Policy Report, International Food Policy Research Institute, Washington, DC.

FAO (Food and Agricultural Organization of the United Nations) and World Bank. 2009. *Awakening Africa's Sleeping Giant: Prospects for Commercial Agriculture in the Guinea Savannah Zone and Beyond*. Washington, DC: World Bank.

Ghani, E., ed. 2010. *The Poor Half Billion in South Asia: What Is Holding Back Lagging Regions?* New Delhi: Oxford University Press.

Haggblade, S., P. Hazell, and T. Reardon, eds. 2007a. *Transforming the Rural Nonfarm Economy*. Baltimore: Johns Hopkins University Press.

Haggblade, S., P. Hazell, and P. Dorosh. 2007b. "Sectoral Growth Linkages between Agriculture and the Rural Nonfarm Economy." In *Transforming the Rural Nonfarm Economy*, edited by S. Haggblade, P. Hazell, and T. Reardon, pp. 141–182. Baltimore: Johns Hopkins University Press.

Hazell, P., C. Poulton, S. Wiggins, and A. Dorward. 2007. "The Future of Small Farms for Poverty Reduction and Growth." 2020 Discussion Paper 42, International Food Policy Research Institute, Washington, DC.

Hazell, P., and A. Rahman, 2014. "Concluding Chapter: The Policy Agenda." In *New Directions for Smallholder Agriculture*, edited by P. Hazell, and A. Rahman, pp. 527–558. Oxford: Oxford University Press.

Hazell, P., and A. Roell. 1983. "Rural Growth Linkages: Household Expenditure Patterns in Malaysia and Nigeria." Research Report 41, International Food Policy Research Institute, Washington, DC.

Headey, D., M. Dereje, J. Ricker-Gilbert, A. Josephson, and A. S. Taffesse. 2013. "Land Constraints and Agricultural Intensification in Ethiopia." IFPRI Discussion Paper 01290, International Food Policy Research Institute, Washington, DC.

Huang, J., X. Wang, and H. Qui. 2012. "Small-scale Farmers in China in the Face of Modernisation and Globalisation." International Institute for Environment and Development (IIED)/Hivos, London and The Hague.

Huang, Y. 1973. "On Some Determinants of Farm Size across Countries." *American Journal of Agricultural Economics* 64 (1): pp. 89–92.

IFPRI. 2005. *The Future of Small Farms: Proceedings of a Research Workshop.* Wye, UK, June 26–29, 2005. Washington, DC: International Food Policy Research Institute.

Jayne, T. S., G. Anriquez, and E. Collier. 2013. "African Agriculture Toward 2030: Changes in Urbanization and Agricultural Land Dynamics and Their Implications for CGIAR Research." Paper prepared for the Independent Science and Partnership Council (ISPC) Foresight meeting, January 24–25, 2013, Boston, MA.

Jirström, M., A. Andersson, and G. Djurfeldt. 2011. "Smallholders Caught in Poverty—Flickering Signs of Agricultural Dynamism." In *African Smallholders: Food Crops, Markets and Policy,* edited by G. Djurfeldt, E. Aryeetey, and A. Isinika, pp. 74–106. Wallingford: CABI.

Larson, D., K. Otsuka, T. Matsumoto, and T. Kilic. 2014. "Should African Rural Development Strategies Depend on Smallholder Farms? An Exploration of the Inverse-Productivity Hypothesis." *Agricultural Economics* 45 (3): pp. 335–367.

Masters, W. A., A. Andersson Djurfeldt, C. De Haan, P. Hazell, T. Jayne, M. Jirström, and T. Reardon. 2013. "Urbanization and Farm Size in Asia and Africa: Implications for Food Security and Agricultural Research." *Global Food Security* 2 (3): pp. 156–165.

Maxwell, S., I. Urey, and C. Ashley. 2001. "Emerging Issues in Rural Development." An Issues Paper, Overseas Development Institute, London.

Mellor, J. W. 1976. *The New Economics of Growth: A Strategy for India and the Developing World.* Ithaca, NY: Cornell University Press.

Omamo, S. W., X. Diao, S. Wood, J. Chamberlin, L. You, S. Benin, U. Wood-Sichra, and A. Tatwangire. 2006. *Strategic Priorities for Agricultural Development in Eastern and Central Africa.* Washington, DC: International Food Policy Research Institute.

Otsuka, K. 2013. "Food Insecurity, Income Inequality, and the Changing Comparative Advantage in World Agriculture." *Agricultural Economics* 44 (s1): pp. 7–18.

Rosegrant, M., and P. Hazell. 2000. *Transforming the Rural Asian Economy: The Unfinished Revolution.* Hong Kong: Oxford University Press.

UN (United Nations). 2011. *World Urbanization Prospects: The 2011 Revision.* New York: Economic and Social Affairs, United Nations.

Vorley, Bill. 2002. "Sustaining Agriculture: Policy, Governance and the Future of Family Farming: A Synthesis Report of the Collaborative Research Project 'Policies that Work for Sustainable Agriculture and Regenerating Rural Livelihoods'." London: International Institute for Environment and Development (IIED).

World Bank. 2007. *World Development Report 2008: Agriculture for Development.* Washington, DC: The World Bank.

9

Agricultural R&D, Food Prices, Poverty, and Malnutrition Redux

Julian M. Alston and Philip G. Pardey

Introduction

Beginning in the early 1970s, Per Pinstrup-Andersen conducted pioneering work into the links between agricultural research and development (R&D) and its consequences for nutrition and health outcomes of the poor.[1] In this chapter, we revisit those links in the context of two 21st-century conundrums. First, while many of the world's poor remain undernourished, paradoxically, growing numbers of people from a very broad range of income and social strata are overweight or obese. Second, rates of investment in agricultural research are slowing in numerous (especially, rich) countries, despite continuing high social rates of return to the investments, a trend toward higher food prices, and slowing rates of farm productivity growth in many countries.

It is widely acknowledged that public agricultural R&D has been a crucial policy for creating the era of agricultural abundance that now appears to be in jeopardy.[2] To what extent is this abundance, which has saved and improved many millions of lives, also responsible for the rise of obesity? What is the nature of the trade-offs between health and nutrition problems arising from increasing food abundance (or rising incomes) versus health and nutrition problems arising from food scarcity (or poverty)? What are the implications for policy? Should we use agricultural R&D as an instrument of public health policy or other dimensions of social policy?

One view is that agricultural R&D should be revitalized and refocused to enhance farm productivity growth and make food more abundant and cheaper, thereby addressing problems of poverty and food security that are foreseen through to 2050 (Ravallion 2013). Some suggest that we should ramp up research on fruits and vegetables at the expense of research on cereals and livestock products, as a way of improving nutritional outcomes. Others propose that R&D should emphasize other dimensions of nutrition, such as developing staple foods that are richer in specific micronutrients. In this chapter, we explore these competing ideas. We present up-to-date evidence on trends in agricultural research investments, productivity, and prices, connecting them to patterns of human health outcomes around the world and drawing inferences for public R&D policy.

Economics and Politics of Agricultural R&D Policy

Since around the mid-19th century, the application of science to agriculture—increasingly by way of targeted investments in R&D—has released much labor and other (especially, land) resources from the production of food and other agricultural outputs (Ruttan 1982). In 1800, before this R&D-induced process of agricultural transformation was underway, the planet's population was around 980 million people, most of whom lived and worked in agriculture (an estimated 75–80 percent of the working population of the time earned its livelihood in agriculture; see Bairoch [1988]). Over two centuries later, in 2010, the world's population had increased sevenfold, and now—although a significant number of people still live a hand-to-mouth existence, growing much or all of the food they consume—more than half the world's population live in urban areas, while less than 40 percent of the working population earn their livelihoods from agriculture.[3] Land used in agriculture worldwide increased by much less than global population, such that in 2010, agriculture had to feed 1.41 persons per hectare compared with just under 1 person in 1800.

The fact that the Malthusian nightmare has been largely averted is attributable, in great part, to remarkable gains in agricultural productivity achieved through technological change.[4] Over the past 50 years, even though the world's population more than doubled and per capita incomes grew, compounding the growth in demand, the global food supply grew even faster. Real output from agriculture grew by 2.7 percent per year (equivalent to a 259 percent increase in real output from 1961 to 2010), and, in spite of the ever-tighter land constraint, agricultural output per person grew by 60.6 percent—from $209 per person in 1961 (2004–06 international prices) to $336 per person in 2010 (e.g., see Alston and Pardey [2014]). Consequently, between 1961 and 2010, real prices of cereals fell by roughly 60 percent. These increases in land and labor productivity were accomplished by intensifying the use of "modern" inputs—in particular, machinery, fertilizers, and irrigation—combined with improved genetic material and methods of production increasingly derived from organized scientific research (e.g., see Pardey et al. [2010]).

A great many studies have found consistently high rates of return to the investments in public and private agricultural R&D (e.g., see Hurley et al. [2014]). Double-digit benefit–cost ratios are typical. The benefits have accrued through enhanced farm incomes, lower costs of food production, reduced stress on the natural resource base, and the release of resources for other uses. The consequences can be seen in many measures of improved health and welfare, especially among the poor, though identifying the details of the complex pathways and attributing consequences among sources is challenging.

A Reversal of Fortune?

Recent trends are less salutary. By various measures, growth rates of agricultural productivity have systematically slowed for most countries and for the world as a whole since 1990, if not earlier—for example, since 1960 cereal yields have grown essentially linearly, which implies a progressive slowdown in proportional growth (Alston and Pardey 2014). This productivity slowdown—along with other factors—is reflected in prices (e.g., see Alston et al. [2009]).[5] Following the price spike of the early 1970s, over the years 1975 to 2000, the index of real prices for cereals declined relatively rapidly but at a progressively slower rate. And since 2000, prices have increased (Figure 9.1).

In the coming 50 years, significant growth in agricultural production will be necessary to meet both the increasing food demands of a growing and richer (as well as aging and urbanizing) world population and the ongoing, but likely less-pronounced, growth in the demand for bioenergy feedstocks (Pardey et al. 2014a). As in the past 50 years, much of this growth in production will have to come from increased productivity, given a tightening of the scope for expanding the agricultural use of land and water. Simply sustaining current (let alone, restoring the higher past) rates of productivity growth will, however, require greater effort in view of the emerging challenges of climate change and the attendant implications for changing abiotic (i.e., drought, temperature, and so on) and biotic (i.e., pest and disease) stresses on agricultural plants and animals (Pardey et al. 2014a).

The contemporary trends in science policy run contrary to these arguments. In spite of the adverse implications of slowing productivity growth (e.g., Alston et al. [2010a]), and even though rates of return to agricultural research are demonstrably very high, we have seen a slowdown in R&D spending growth and a diversion of funds away from farm productivity enhancement, especially in the richest countries (Pardey et al. 2013). China now spends more than the United States on public agricultural R&D, and the low- and middle-income countries are collectively outspending the

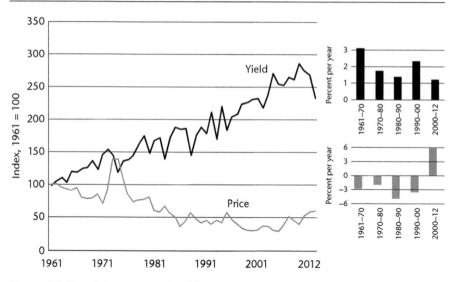

Figure 9.1 Trends in prices and yields of cereals, 1961–2012

Notes: All data pertain to the United States. The following commodities were included in the cereals average: barley, corn, oats, rice, rye, sorghum, and wheat. To estimate an average yield for cereals, we divided the sum of the quantity produced of each commodity by the corresponding sum of area harvested. To estimate a real price index for cereals, the respective annual series of commodity-specific nominal prices were first deflated by an index of prices received by farmers (base year 1961) developed by the authors using data from Gardner (2006) and USDA-NASS (2009, 2010, 2013b). An index of real cereal prices was then formed by using the commodity-specific value shares in the total value of cereal production as weights to aggregate the respective real price indexes for each of the included commodities.

Source: Yield data are from FAO (2013); price series are from USDA-NASS (2013a).

group of high-income countries. These patterns seem to indicate that in the high-income countries, at least, governments are not much concerned about agricultural productivity, despite evidence of very large benefits from farm-productivity enhancing agricultural R&D.

Why is this so? Commonly, policymakers in the high-income countries, in particular, appear to discount the evidence on the returns to research, which demonstrates a persistent gross underinvestment, or to misunderstand the implications—or perhaps they simply care more about other things. In the 1980s, some people said that investing in agricultural R&D was wasteful— at least in the high-income countries—because these countries were already overproducing farm commodities. This view reflected a misunderstanding of the fact that the important consequence of research has been to save resources on inframarginal production, and make food cheaper to produce, such that research is valuable even if a commodity is in surplus—which itself is an unusual (government-created) phenomenon. A more contemporary version of the same sentiment relates to obesity. Some say we already produce and consume too much of certain kinds of food—such as corn and other grains and livestock products—and we should cut back or cease undertaking R&D that enhances productivity of those foods in favor of R&D that promotes productivity in, and thus consumption of, foods such as fruits and vegetables that are perceived as being healthier and less fattening (e.g., Popkin [2010]). In this chapter, we seek to provide more clarity on the interpretation of traditional measures, along with some less traditional measures of the consequences of agricultural R&D for the poor.

What is Agricultural Productivity Worth Worldwide?

What might the world be like today if our forebears had opted not to make the research investments that enabled the Green Revolution and other changes in agriculture over the past 50 years? The counterfactual experiment of a world without the Green Revolution is hard to devise, even as a thought experiment—for example, what might the world be like if Norman Borlaug had become a professional wrestler (his early vocation) or a forester (his initial career choice) instead of a plant pathologist-cum-breeder?[6] One version of this idea is to consider the consequences today if we were to revert to the patterns of agricultural productivity that existed in 1961, holding current input use constant. In Table 9.1 the first column is the index of total factor productivity (TFP) in country j in 2009 ($TFP_{j,2009}$), given a base of $TFP_{j,1961} = 100$ in 1961, as estimated by Fuglie et al. (2012), which we take as read for this purpose. For the world as a whole, this index is 225, equivalent to cumulative growth of 1.7 percent per year over the 48-year period, while for Brazil it is much higher at 276 (2.1 percent per year) and for Nigeria it is much lower at 144 (0.7 percent per year). In Column 5 we report an approximate measure of benefits foregone if we reverted from 2009 to 1961 productivity levels—computed as $k_j * AgGDP_{j,2009}$—where $k_j = (TFP_{j,2009} - TFP_{j,1961})/TFP_{j,2009}$ and $AgGDP_{j,2009}$ (in Column 2) is a measure of agricultural GDP for 2009 from the World Bank (2012) measured in 2005 international (PPP) dollars. For the world as a whole, this total benefit is estimated to be $3,658 billion.[7] Arguably, at least half of this total can be attributed to public and private investments in agricultural R&D, though precise attribution is impossible, and the attributable share will vary among countries and regions.[8]

The benefits in Column 5 are distributed reasonably congruently with total population in Column 3—food is produced to a great extent within the countries and regions within which it is consumed—such that the benefits per capita in Column 6, which average $266 for the world as a whole, are reasonably comparable among regions once we set aside the very low measure for sub-Saharan Africa ($76). However, when we express these benefits per capita relative to GDP per capita from Column 5, in Column 6 we see that the benefits from agricultural productivity growth

Table 9.1 The value in 2009 of agricultural TFP growth since 1961

	TFP in 2009 1961 = 100	AgGDP	Population	GDP per capita	Total gain	Per capita benefits in 2009					Benefits as a share of GDP in 2009				
						All countries	Range excluding countries with negative TFP growth				All countries	Benefits as a share of GDP excluding countries with negative TFP growth			
							Mean	Median	Min.	Max.		Mean	Median	Min.	Max.
	(1)	(2)	(3)	(4)	(5)	(6)	(7)	(8)	(9)	(10)	(11)	(12)	(13)	(14)	(15)
	index	billion 2005 PPP$	million	2005 PPP$	billion 2005 PPP$	2005 PPP$					percent				
By region															
Asia & Pacific	211	1,978	3,557	4,171	1,042	293	245	212	17	909	7.0	7.8	7.0	0.4	22.6
EE & FSU	148	251	406	11,239	82	201	307	225	152	825	1.8	2.9	1.6	0.9	11.0
High Income	246	472	1,018	33,355	280	275	292	262	9	883	0.8	1.0	0.9	0.0	3.6
LAC	211	317	582	9,301	167	286	285	266	103	575	3.1	4.0	4.2	0.9	7.9
MENA	233	305	390	7,593	174	447	381	445	81	700	5.9	5.5	4.6	1.6	11.6
SSA	124	335	843	1,899	64	76	72	44	4	244	4.0	4.5	3.0	0.1	13.9
World	**198**	**3,658**	**6,796**	**9,317**	**1,809**	**266**	**239**	**200**	**4**	**909**	**2.9**	**4.0**	**2.6**	**0.03**	**22.6**
By income group															
High income	235	510	1,082	32,442	293	271	288	264	9	883	0.8	1.0	0.9	0.0	3.6
Upper middle	228	1,648	2,575	7,913	924	359	339	315	23	909	4.5	3.6	3.1	0.2	11.0
Lower middle	175	1,266	2,369	2,982	541	228	189	183	5	527	7.7	5.9	5.2	0.1	15.7
Low income	127	234	770	1,017	50	65	78	36	4	332	6.4	6.6	5.6	0.5	22.6

Note: All data and estimates pertain to the year 2009. We estimated the country-specific gain from TFP growth using the TFP index from Fuglie et al. (2012) and added these country-specific gains by region and income group. We then derived the TFP index implied by these gains for each region and income group. "High income" in the first part of the table (under gains from TFP growth by region) excludes the high-income countries that are part of EE & FSU, whereas "high income" in the second part includes all high-income countries as defined by the World Bank (2012).

Source: Authors' estimations based on TFP data from Fuglie et al. (2012), AgGDP and GDP data from World Bank (2012), and population data from UN (2013a).

are much more important as a share of income for lower-income countries, even if the benefits per capita per se may be smaller than in the high-income countries. These benefits represent only 0.8 percent of GDP for the high-income countries but a more significant 2.9 percent of GDP in 2009 for the world as a whole, and well over 5 percent of GDP for the middle-income countries, as a group, and the low-income countries. The ranking of countries now depends on both their growth rates of productivity and the country-specific relative importance of agriculture in the economy. Setting aside countries (mainly those in sub-Saharan Africa) where measured agricultural TFP failed to grow over the past half century, Figure 9.2 clearly illustrates how the relative economic importance of productivity growth in agriculture increases as per capita incomes decline.[9] This pattern showing the relative importance of gross benefits from agricultural productivity growth helps to account for the observation that policymakers in the high-income countries appear to be relatively unconcerned with farm productivity nowadays.

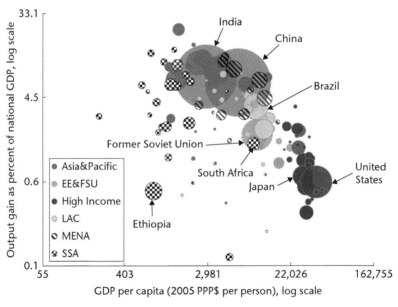

Figure 9.2 The comparative economic importance of agricultural productivity growth, 2009

Note: See Table 9.1. According to estimates from Fuglie et al. (2012), 24 countries had declining growth in TFP from 1961 to 2009. Those countries were excluded from this figure. For expositional reasons, we also excluded Singapore, Puerto Rico, Kuwait, and Qatar, countries where GDP per capita is comparatively large but output gain as a percent of GDP is exceptionally small. The size of the circles represents shares in global population.

Source: Authors' estimations based on TFP data from Fuglie et al. (2012), GDP and AgGDP data from World Bank (2012), and population data from UN (2013a).

The benefits from agricultural productivity growth are not distributed uniformly, of course, among households within a country—especially when we take into account that, through international commodity trade, productivity growth in one country can affect prices in another. Agricultural technology induces changes in the distribution of income among and within households, through a multitude of direct and indirect effects and the optimizing responses of the households. Even if agricultural technology has no direct effect on household incomes, it affects food security or poverty through its effects on the price of food. Benefits accrue to (farm) households both (a) through reductions in the costs of production (for those that adopt the technology), and (b) through reductions in the *net* costs of food purchases (the difference between their expenditure on food consumption and the value of their production) resulting from the fall in price. For food deficit households, the fall in price means a benefit; for food surplus households, it means a loss. In addition to these two direct sources of benefits, households may gain (or lose) indirectly from induced adjustments in factor markets in which they participate, as well as from broader, general equilibrium impacts (e.g., Alston et al. [2014]).

Figure 9.3 compares two stylized distributions of household income across households, conditional on the state of technology and a given draw of exogenous factors that gives rise to particular price outcomes (see Alston et al. [2014]). The income distribution across households, given technology τ_0, is denoted Y_0^e. Associated with this distribution, and defined by the corresponding prices is a "poverty line," reflecting the cost of a minimal quantity of food (or food calories) and other necessities, drawn at L_0^e. Under the alternative

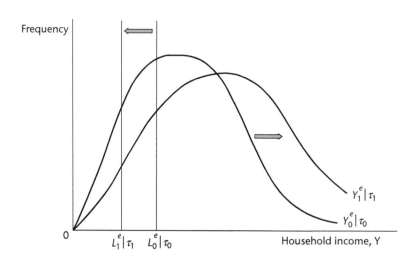

Figure 9.3 Agricultural technology and household income distributions
Source: Alston et al. (2014).

technology scenario, τ_1, but for the same draw of exogenous factors, food prices are lower and the poverty line is shifted to L_1^e, reducing the fraction of the population living in poverty for a given income distribution. This can be a big effect if we have a big change in the price of food, even with no direct changes in household incomes of the type that result from the effects of adoption of new technologies on reducing costs of production and the effects on household revenues induced by price changes. When the distribution of income shifts to the right from, say, Y_0^e to Y_1^e as a result of shifting from technology regime τ_0 to τ_1, the fraction of the population living in poverty is further reduced.[10]

A large and growing fraction of the world's poor are non-farm rural or urban dwellers whose only direct economic benefits from agricultural productivity growth will be through the impacts on food prices—whether as a result of changes in technology in their own country or elsewhere in the world. If we were to revert to 1961 farm productivity patterns today, other things held constant, farm commodity prices would be much higher than they were in 1961, given the much greater population and higher per capita incomes. For the very poor who are net buyers of farm products, the real income consequences of such an increase in prices would be very serious—devastating for many—as illustrated by the events following the commodity price spike in 2007.

To illustrate the regressive, negative real income consequences of an increase in food prices, Figure 9.4, Panel A arrays countries from lowest (Zimbabwe) to highest (Qatar) in terms of per capita income and reveals how the marginal dollar of income is spent across seven broad consumption categories. The low-income countries (to the left in the figure) spend an average of 47 percent of their marginal income on food, compared with just 13 percent on average by the rich countries. The shares of extra income spent on transportation and communication, as well as recreation and furniture, and housing and clothing, all increase as per capita incomes increase. Notably, while the share of marginal income devoted to food, beverages, and tobacco expenditures declines as per capita incomes increase, conversely, the marginal budget share of health and medically related expenditures increases (Figure 9.4, Panel B).[11]

Thus, the increase in real income from a fall in food commodity prices will have a much greater effect on the food budget, and thus, nutritional opportunity for the average person in a low-income country, who spends 47 percent of marginal income on food—having average per capita income of just $1,031 (2005 PPP prices) in 2010—compared with the average resident of a rich country, who spends only 13 percent of marginal income on food—having average per capita income of $33,112 in 2010.[12]

While we have abundant money-metric measures of the returns to agricultural research (such as benefit–cost ratios and internal rates of return), we have much less concrete evidence on the consequences for food security of

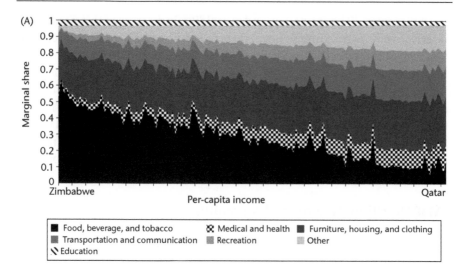

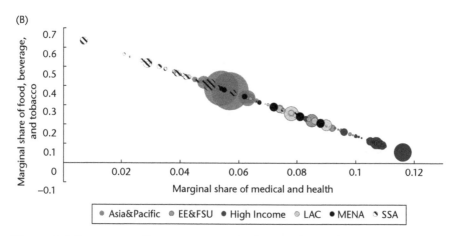

Figure 9.4 Country-specific average marginal expenditure shares by per capita income, 2005

Panel A: Marginal expenditure shares of per capita income

Panel B: Marginal expenditure shares of food beverages and tobacco versus medical and health purchases

Note: The sizes of the circles in Panel B indicate the respective countries' shares of global population.

Source: Marginal shares taken from Muhammad et al. (2011, Appendix Table 7); per capita incomes were computed by the authors using GDP data from World Bank (2012) and population data from UN (2013a).

the poor, or more generally, how the benefits from agricultural R&D are distributed among consumers, producers, agribusiness interests, and the like. More acutely lacking is a useful set of indicators of the extent to which agricultural R&D has affected nutrition and health outcomes, including infant mortality rates, life expectancy, and morbidity. Indicators of this nature may be effective in persuading policymakers to continue to invest in agricultural R&D when the standard money metric measures do not. Certainly, a claim that Norman Borlaug has saved a billion lives (as by Penn and Teller—see Jillette and Teller [2009]) captures the imagination more effectively than any claims about the dollar value of Borlaug's accomplishments. With this thought in mind, we next present some nutrition- and health-related indicators, followed by some exploratory assessments of the implications of realigning investments in agricultural R&D to target certain nutrition outcomes.

(Mal)Nutrition, Health, and Agriculture

Quantifying the relationship between R&D spending and agricultural productivity growth is tough enough. Clarifying the complex, cloudy, and sometimes confounding associations between agricultural production and productivity growth (and the commodity composition of that growth) and the human nutrition and health outcomes associated with food consumption is especially daunting, doubly so when drawing on aggregate data. Here we summarize some of the scholarship linking various anthropometric attributes to nutrition and other factors (from a broad historical perspective), complemented by some of the available empirical evidence on global poverty, malnutrition, and mortality. This provides a basis for beginning to build the conceptual and empirical bridges linking R&D, agricultural productivity, and anthropometric indicators to help calibrate thinking about the appropriate policies and priorities regarding agricultural R&D over the decades ahead.

Anthropometric Angles on Agriculture, Food, and Health

Cutler et al. (2006) critically assessed the reasonably extensive literature regarding the determinants of mortality, including its historical decline and the prevalence of premature death in today's poor countries. They singled out improvements in nutrition and public health along with urbanization, the avoidance of disease, and modern medical—especially therapeutic—treatments as putative factors accounting for the decline in mortality over time. Drawing on the work of Costa and Steckel (1997), Fogel (1997), and others, they concluded that the century of mortality decline in Europe (and presumably, in other places with similar incomes), that began in the middle of the 18th century, owed much to improvements in nutrition and economic growth.[13] This transitioned to a second phase, beginning in the late 19th century, in which "… improvements in public health [including sanitation, filtered and chlorinated water, and mass vaccinations] mattered more" (Cutler et al. 2006,

p. 106), followed by a third phase, from the 1930s onwards, in which medical treatments dealing with diseases and injuries became a primary driver of reduced mortality.

Diseases and Mortality

A host of anthropometric indicators are used to reveal different dimensions of human health, including height and weight (for age), body mass, and other under- and over-nourished related (e.g., obesity) metrics such as the prevalence of nutrition-related diseases, hypertension, diabetes, blindness, cognitive ability, and so on. One of the most prevalent, and arguably among the most compelling indicators, is average life expectancy at birth (Figure 9.5).[14] Using Johansson and Lindgren's (2013) compilation, the worldwide average life expectancy at birth in 1800 was just 31 years—ranging from 23 to

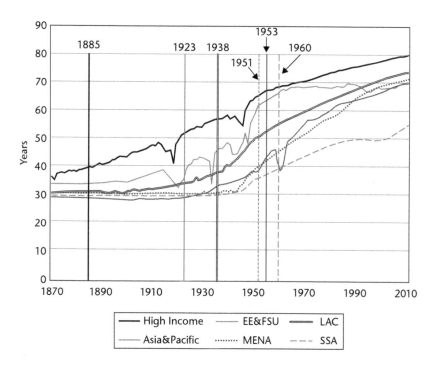

Figure 9.5 Average life expectancy at birth by world region, 1870–2010

Note: The regional average life expectancies plotted here were computed as weighted averages of the country-specific average life expectancies, where the weights were the respective population shares of countries within their regions. It took until 1885 for average life expectancy to reach 40 years in the high-income countries; 1923 for Eastern Europe and the former Soviet Union; 1938 for Latin America and the Caribbean; 1951 for the Middle East and North Africa; 1953 for Asia and Pacific; and 1960 for sub-Saharan Africa. Note the order of the regions shown, left to right, in the legend corresponds to the lines shown, top to bottom (at 1938 on x-axis), here in the figure.

Source: Developed by the authors using data from Johansson and Lindgren (2013).

219

25 years for Yemen, Sierra Leone, and Senegal to 39 to 40 years for the United States, Netherlands, and Belgium. By 2010, the global average had jumped to 70 years overall—ranging from 45 years for Sierra Leone and Haiti to 82 years for Switzerland, Hong Kong, and Japan. The regional pattern of increase is quite uneven. The rich countries reached an average life expectancy at birth of 40 years by 1885, but it took another 38 years until people in Eastern Europe and the former Soviet Union (EE and FSU) lived that long, on average. The sub-Saharan African region did not reach the 40-year threshold until 1960, by which time the average life expectancy at birth of people living in the rich countries had increased to 69 years.

The Johansson and Lindgren (2013) data indicate that, for the 201 countries around the world for which they developed estimates, all had an average life expectancy at birth in 2010 that was greater than the rich-country average of 40 years in 1885, the end of the first phase of mortality reduction in Cutler et al. (2006). Thus, most of the world's population is now living longer, and in many instances much longer, than did their rich-country counterparts in the late 19th century. Still, even as late as the middle of the 20th century, the regional (and country) spread in life expectancy was much greater than it was at the beginning of the 19th century. Over the past half-century, however, average life expectancies in most regions of the world have been closing in on the still-growing average life expectancy in the rich countries.[15]

The outlier is sub-Saharan Africa, where life expectancy at birth averaged 55 years in 2010, equivalent to the average life expectancy reached by today's rich countries in 1930. In sub-Saharan Africa, only 58 percent of the population has access to potable water, and just 31 percent has access to sanitation (and one-third of the population defecate out-of-doors, over 40 percent for those living in rural areas). In this region, average per capita income is just $1,074 (2005 PPP prices) per person (compared with a rich-country average of $33,112 per person); 69.2 percent of the population live on less than $2 per day, with food consumption of just 1,577 calories per person (versus 2,194 calories per person on average in rich countries); and there are just 0.16 physicians per 1,000 people (versus 2.9 per 1,000 in the rich countries).[16] All the factors that Cutler et al. (2006) associated with higher mortality rates are evident here.

An association between life expectancy and per capita income over the long term is revealed in Figure 9.6. The comparatively tight clustering of life expectancies in 1800 is once again evident in Figure 9.6, Panel A. This was an era when cross-country differences in per capita income were also muted, most of that income being earned in agriculture, and before the advent of modern sanitation, public health, and science-based medical services anywhere in the world.[17] Comparing Panel A with Panel B in Figure 9.6, over two centuries later in 2010, two key developments are evident. At any particular level of income, people live substantially longer than they did

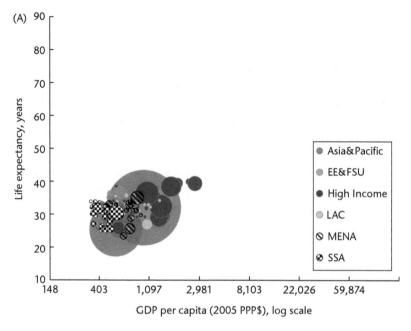

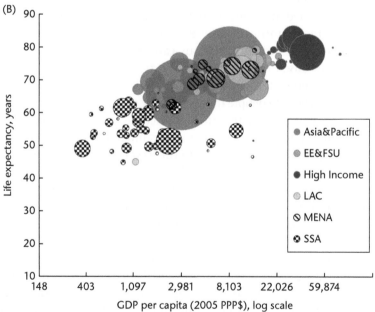

Figure 9.6 Per capita income and average life expectancy at birth, 1800 and 2010

Panel A: 1800

Panel B: 2010

Note: The sizes of the circles indicate the respective countries' shares of global population.

Source: Developed by the authors using data from Johansson and Lindgren (2013).

in the past. Second, the spread in life expectancies among countries is now more pronounced and appears to be positively, but not exclusively, related to per capita income. While per capita income affects food consumption along with access to and use of education, information, sanitation, medical, and other health-promoting goods and services, many of these factors affect life expectancy in different ways in different phases of a person's life (fetal, immediate post-natal, and later in life). These various and variable intertemporal effects linking per capita income over a lifetime both directly and indirectly to the timing of mortality thus confound the relationship between the data on average life expectancy at birth in a specific year and contemporaneous measures of average per capita income. Preston (1975, 1980, 1996), for example, estimates that increases in income alone account for only 20 percent of the increase in life expectancy.

Mortality affects us all, sooner or later. However, the notional causes of mortality vary across countries, and over time within countries. WHO (2011) data indicate that in 2008, a total of 50 million people died, and most (70 percent of the global total) of those deaths occurred in the middle-income countries. The generally older and smaller populations of the richer countries had a total of 7.2 million deaths (14 percent of their total), while 7.8 million people (15.5 percent) died in the increasingly populous but younger populations of the low-income countries. Figure 9.7 summarizes the numbers, shares, and rates of death according to various categories of diseases and injuries attributed as the cause of death. Death rates (i.e., the number of deaths per 100,000 people) generally increased as per capita incomes decreased, with 1,014 deaths per 100,000 people in low-income countries, 51 percent higher than the 672 deaths per 100,000 in high-income countries. Average death rates of upper-middle-income countries were similar to those of high-income countries, whereas average death rates in the lower-middle-income countries fell between the low- and upper-middle income averages.

Higher-income countries tend to have older populations, while the populations in lower-income countries are generally younger. Figure 9.8, Panels A–D stratifies countries into several per capita income and age cohorts. Cancers led to many more deaths in high- and upper-middle-income countries compared with the rest of the world, and most of those deaths involved the elderly. Most of the deaths attributed to cardiovascular diseases and diabetes also occurred in people over 60 years of age, but most of these deaths occurred in the middle-income countries. Around 81 percent of the worldwide deaths attributable to HIV, tuberculosis, and malaria occurred in the lower-middle- and low-income countries and largely afflicted those less than 14 years of age. The lower-middle- and low-income countries also accounted for 90 percent of the worldwide deaths attributed to maternal, perinatal, nutritional, and diarrheal diseases; and within the low-income countries, 19 percent of all deaths were associated with this group of

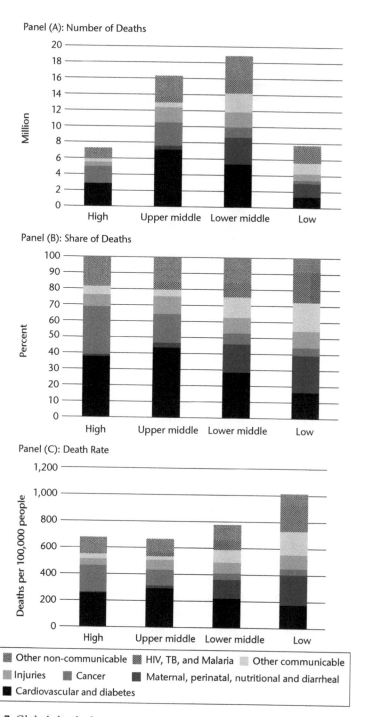

Figure 9.7 Global deaths by category of disease and injury, and by income class of country, 2008

Source: Developed by the authors with data from WHO (2011) and UN (2013a).

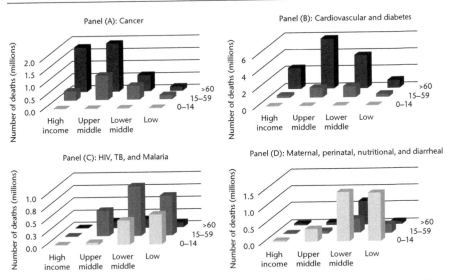

Figure 9.8 Number of deaths by category of disease, by age group, and by income class of country, 2008

Note: Countries grouped into income categories according to data from World Bank (2012). Age cohorts in years.

Source: Developed by the authors with data from WHO (2011) and UN (2013b).

diseases. Moreover, most of the deaths occurred among the young: 7.9 million children aged 14 years or less died from these diseases in lower-middle- and low-income countries, and 0.96 million children in the upper-middle- and high-income countries. A recent analysis by Black et al. (2013) estimated that in 2011, 3.1 million children under the age of 5 died from undernutrition, accounting for 45 percent of total child deaths worldwide in that year.

Figure 9.9, Panels A–C show the numbers of deaths associated with nutrition-related diseases in 2008. Most of those deaths occurred in middle-income countries (Panel A), but the more detailed causes of these deaths vary markedly across countries grouped by per capita income (Panel B). High- and upper-middle-income countries look similar on this score, where diseases associated most commonly with overnutrition (i.e., cerebrovascular, diabetes, and hypertensive heart disease) accounted for over 95 percent of the nutritionally related deaths in both groups of countries. In stark contrast, deaths from disease associated with contaminated food or undernutrition (i.e., diarrheal disease, prematurity and low birth weight, and "nutritional" diseases in WHO parlance) accounted for 31 percent and 48 percent of the deaths in lower-middle- and low-income countries, respectively. Over 63 percent of those "nutritional"-related deaths were associated with protein–energy malnutrition (Panels D and E).

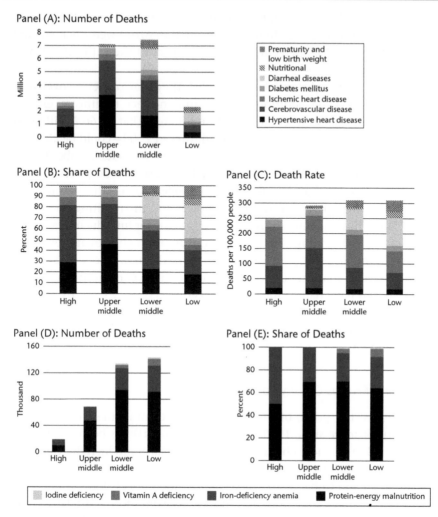

Figure 9.9 Deaths caused by nutrition-related diseases, by income class of country, 2008

Note: Panels D and E provide finer details on the "nutritional" causes of death identified in Panels A to C.

Source: Developed by authors with data from WHO (2011) and UN (2013a).

Obesity

The worldwide prevalence of obesity has increased rapidly, and the related health concerns are priority issues for governments and the medical community worldwide (e.g., see WHO [1997]; International Obesity Task Force [2005]). WHO (2013) data indicated that over one-fifth of the population in high-income countries was obese (BMI values of 30 kg/m2 or higher) in 2008.[18] The respective low- and middle-income shares were 3.2 and 10.1 percent, respectively, but these averages mask substantial regional differences.

For instance, only 4.2 percent of the people living in the Asia and Pacific region and only 7.6 percent living in sub-Saharan Africa were deemed obese, as compared with 23.6 percent of the population in the Latin America and Caribbean region.

In addition to the substantial personal costs they bear, obese and overweight people generate large additional direct and indirect healthcare expenses (for instance, MacEwan et al. (2014) estimated that $166.2 billion—or 15.2 percent of US public medical expenditures in 2009—could be attributed to obesity). However, the appropriate policy, if any, for reducing obesity is not clear. Some potential policies work through the use of food prices as incentives. Non-economists and economists alike appear to take the view that food prices should matter for consumption choices and the resulting obesity outcomes. Such thinking underpins various proposals for introducing tax or subsidy policies to discourage less healthy consumption choices and encourage healthier ones, and some such proposals work through prices of farm commodities used to make food. Economic studies have consistently found that farm subsidies have had negligible impacts on US obesity patterns; however, some have suggested that public agricultural research and development (R&D) may have contributed to obesity by making farm commodities cheaper and more abundant.[19]

Agricultural R&D as Obesity Policy

In real terms, the prices of major agricultural commodities have fallen by 50 percent or more since 1950, and agricultural R&D has been credited as a primary engine for those changes. In turn, these farm productivity gains have been reflected in lower prices of retail food products (e.g., Lakdawalla et al. [2005]; Miller and Coble [2007, 2008]). Lower food prices alone would be sufficient to encourage some increases in food consumption, but relative prices also moved in favor of the production and consumption of "unhealthy" foods that use field crops and livestock products as ingredients, potentially making matters worse.[20]

A reasonable question is whether society would have been served better by a different pattern of private and public investments in agricultural R&D and technologies.[21] A corollary question, looking forward, is whether the agricultural research portfolio should be tilted more in favor of healthy foods, and away from less healthy foods.[22] This is a complex question. Pertinent issues are (1) the extent to which it is possible to achieve public purposes related to obesity by changing the agricultural R&D portfolio; (2) the opportunity cost of conventional research benefits that must be foregone, through changing the mixture of research investments, in exchange for a given reduction in the prevalence of obesity; and (3) the extent to which these gains might be achieved at lower cost through the use of other policy instruments, more directly targeted at the problem of obesity (see Appendix A). Economic assessments consistently show remarkably high rates of return to public investments in agricultural research (e.g., Alston et al. [2011] report benefit–cost ratios in the range of 20:1 or 30:1 for the United States). These high benefit–cost ratios indicate that the total R&D portfolio is too small. An implication is that distorting that already too small portfolio with a view to achieving obesity objectives might impose very large social opportunity costs.

Recent empirical work supports that view in the case of the United States. Alston et al. (2013) investigated the effects of US public investment in agricultural R&D on food prices, per capita calorie consumption, adult body weight, obesity, public healthcare expenditures related to obesity, and social welfare. They used an econometric model to estimate the average effect of an incremental investment in agricultural R&D on the farm prices of 10 categories of farm commodities. Next, they used the econometric results in a simulation model to estimate the implied changes in prices and quantities consumed of nine categories of food for given changes in research expenditures. Finally, they estimated the corresponding changes in social welfare, including both the traditional measures of changes in economic surplus in markets for food and farm commodities, and changes in public healthcare expenditures associated with the predicted changes in food consumption, and hence, obesity.

Their results indicate that a 10 percent decrease in the stream of annual US public investment in agricultural (and food) R&D in the latter half of the 20th century would have caused a very modest decrease in average daily calorie consumption of American adults, resulting in small decreases in body weight (1.75 pounds per adult) and modest reductions in the external social costs of obesity ($3.8 billion in 2004). On the other hand, such a decrease in spending would have meant forgoing very substantial net national benefits, given the very large benefit–cost ratios for agricultural R&D ($28.7 billion in benefits forgone in 2004). Thus the net social (opportunity) cost was estimated to be $63 for a reduction of 1 pound of average US adult body weight. Similar results were found for other simulated changes in research spending. These measures suggest that changing agricultural R&D spending is an ineffective and very inefficient way to reduce obesity—perhaps more so, when we consider the R&D lags which mean that any change in policy today might not begin to substantially affect prices, consumption, and obesity for 20 or 30 years.

Other policies are likely to be more effective and efficient as obesity policies. These could include policies to reduce the distortions from insurance pools and free public healthcare, educational programs, and other policies to encourage and facilitate healthier individual choices about food and exercise, including taxes and subsidies.[23] Much has been written about the use of taxes on farm commodities (e.g., corn), particular nutrients (e.g., sugar, fats), or particular foods (e.g., sugar-sweetened beverages) to combat obesity, and some jurisdictions have enacted policies in this genre. Okrent and Alston (2012) evaluated such policies using the same model as used by Alston et al. (2013); hence, the findings are directly comparable. Okrent and Alston (2012) found that taxes on food, based on its fat content, sugar content, or total caloric content, would yield net social benefits. With these policies—unlike changing R&D spending to reduce obesity—the benefits from reduced excess healthcare spending costs would outweigh the reduction in private benefits from consumption and production of food. Specifically, they found that the tax policies they evaluated (unlike the research policies which would entail a social cost to reduce obesity) would yield a net social benefit per pound reduction in US average adult body weight (fat tax, $1.31 per pound of body weight; taxing all food, $1.54 per pound of body weight; sugar tax $1.73, per pound of body weight; caloric tax, $1.77 per pound of body weight). The greatest net benefit derives from a tax on total calories, which is to be expected since that tax more directly targets the source of the problem, an energy surplus. As the authors note, these results might understate the effectiveness of the tax instrument, since they did not allow for changes in food manufacturing to adapt to the taxes, and any such taxes would be regressive on the poor.

Alston et al. (2013) also simulated the effects of reverting, in 2004, to the agricultural productivity pattern implied by the agricultural knowledge stock of 1980. The implication was for a decrease in average US adult body weight in 2004 by 11 pounds, albeit at a very large social cost. While substantial, this represents only a fraction of the problem. In a broader economic context, Cutler et al. (2003) attributed the rise in obesity primarily to changes in technology—but not so much to changes in farming technology that contributed to the abundance of farm commodities used to make food, as to the development and adoption of labor-saving technology used to prepare food and the concomitant rise of mass-prepared food.[24] Other technological innovations—for example, those in telecommunications and public and private transportation—may also have contributed to obesity by encouraging reduced physical activity.

Would anyone seriously propose reverting to the 1970s technologies used at home and by industry in producing and preparing and processing food, and in every other aspect of our daily lives, with a view to saving the excess social costs attributed to the increase in prevalence of overweight and obesity among Americans? Perhaps some true zealots may state such a position, even if they choose not to reject all modern technologies in their personal lives. But such a policy would be extraordinarily expensive for the economy as a whole and would be regressive on the poor.

What is the appropriate policy? In light of the arguments and evidence presented here, it would seem to be appropriate to have an R&D policy that emphasized reducing distortions in research investments and worked towards maximizing net social benefits from research, and to use other instruments to tackle obesity—perhaps including some appropriately targeted food taxes as part of the policy set. Allowing for the presence of other economic distortions in the economy, as they influence the net social returns to different types of research investments, should not have large implications for the optimal research portfolio (see Alston et al. [1988], and Martin and Alston [1994]). Although we do not have detailed comparable empirical evidence of the same type related to the trade-offs involved in using agricultural research to achieve other types of social objectives, we suspect the findings will be similar in general—the rationale is conceptual, not empirical.

Conclusion

It is appropriate to be concerned with recent trends in agricultural R&D policy for several reasons. First, by all indications available to us, the world is spending too little on agricultural R&D in total and too little on certain types of agricultural R&D where institutions do not encourage private investment and governments have not sufficiently corrected the problem. As documented by Pardey et al. (2013), the world table is shifting with a rising role of the middle-income countries, a shrinking role of the high-income countries, and a continuing neglect in the poorest countries that may be the relevant focus of much of what we have discussed in this chapter. Second, the scarce resources that are being made available for public agricultural research are increasingly being asked to serve a multitude of masters for which they may be little suited. In many places, "agricultural" research resources are being diverted away from productivity-enhancing research in farming and food production to pursue environmental, nutritional, health, or income distributional targets. In many instances, agricultural research will be an ineffective instrument for pursuing the target in question and, even if effective, it will usually not be the least-cost means for the job.

In this chapter, we have sought to elucidate aspects of this situation. First, we have compiled a variety of measures that are suggestive of the view that agricultural R&D, directed at increasing the general abundance of food, generates a very large net social benefit *while* yielding great benefits for the health and well-being of the poor. Given the great and persistent under-investment in productivity-enhancing agricultural R&D, as in the Green Revolution, we can continue to do much good for the poor while doing well for the economy as a whole, simply by investing in those agricultural research areas where the total payoff will be highest. Second, as illustrated by the example of using agricultural R&D policy as obesity policy in the United States, the available empirical evidence indicates that it can be very counterproductive to seek to use public agricultural research as an instrument of social policy rather than using it as an instrument for correcting market failures in agricultural science.

Of course, the world is a much more complex place than our simple analytics can convey. In many places, even second-best solutions will be far beyond the reach of practical policy. In the political reality of agricultural science funding, it will continue to be better to accept funding conditional on it being used for a particular—lower payoff—purpose, if the alternative is to have an even worse problem of underinvestment in the total portfolio. Even so, having to compromise some of the time does not mean we should passively make the same kinds of choices when not constrained to do so, given that the research portfolio that maximizes total net benefits from the investment stands a good chance of being the one that also yields the greatest benefits for the poor, their health, and their life expectancies.

Appendix A: Agricultural R&D as an Instrument of Social Policy

Governments use a variety of policy instruments to pursue a range of social objectives related to human health and well-being, poverty, food security, the environment, and so on. Since agricultural R&D can have consequences for many of the human outcomes that are represented in this broad policy agenda, it seems natural for policymakers to want to consider these consequences in setting priorities for public agricultural R&D. Indeed, some propose to target agricultural R&D to achieve particular social objectives—such as healthier diets, better environmental outcomes, or reduced poverty—perhaps on the (mistaken) grounds that agricultural productivity is not a concern or that food is already abundant.

Such thinking suffers from several economic flaws. First, the fundamental economic rationale for public agricultural R&D is to correct market failures, mainly in the form of underinvestment arising from inadequate private property rights to inventions. Any diversion of public research spending away from the allocation that maximizes net social benefits necessarily compromises the primary purpose, and the social benefit from the investment necessarily falls. Moreover, since we are grossly underinvesting in agricultural R&D, in spite of extensive government intervention, the opportunity cost of diverting agricultural funds to other purposes will be very high. Second, public agricultural R&D is not the only policy instrument available to government. Other policies that are more closely targeted on particular social objectives are likely to be both more effective and more economically efficient than targeted agricultural R&D. Moreover, the economic relationships between research investments and social and economic outcomes are complicated and not transparently obvious.

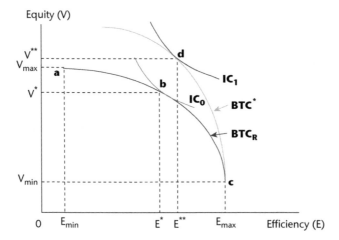

Figure A-9.1 Agricultural research trade-offs
Source: The authors, drawing on Alston et al. (1995, p. 90).

Indeed, it is conceivable that R&D targeted on a particular social objective may be less effective and less efficient and may contribute less to that purpose than non-targeted R&D would.

These ideas are illustrated in Figure A-9.1, which represents trade-offs between "efficiency" (E) measured by total benefits and "equity" (V) measured by benefits to a particular group as a share of the total. In this figure, BTC_R is the benefit-transformation curve for research that represents the combinations of efficiency and equity that could be attained by allocating different amounts of the total research budget to targeted research. Point **a** represents the attainable equity-efficiency combination that maximizes equity, and point **c** represents the attainable combination that maximizes efficiency. Policymakers perceiving a trade-off between these two objectives, as represented by the policy indifference curve, IC_0, might choose the combination at point **b** (E^*, V^*). However, if some other policy instrument could be used in conjunction with agricultural R&D, the higher benefit-transformation curve BTC^* would permit a greater quantity of both equity and efficiency, such as at point **d** (E^{**}, V^{**}) on IC_1. The optimal solution could involve none of the research being targeted to equity, depending on the efficacy of the non-research instruments.

Acknowledgments

The work for this project was partly supported by the University of California, Davis; the University of Minnesota; the HarvestChoice initiative, funded by the Bill & Melinda Gates Foundation; and the Giannini Foundation of Agricultural Economics. The authors gratefully acknowledge excellent research assistance provided by Connie Chan-Kang.

Notes

1. See, for example, Pinstrup-Andersen et al. (1976), Pinstrup-Andersen (2007), Herforth et al. (2012), and Pinstrup-Andersen (2013).
2. For example, Easterbrook (1997) concluded that, through his accomplishments in agricultural science, "Norman Borlaug has already saved more lives than any other person who ever lived." As Easterbrook (1997) explained, "Though barely known in the country of his birth, elsewhere in the world Norman Borlaug is widely considered to be among the leading Americans of our age. Perhaps more than anyone else, Borlaug is responsible for the fact that throughout the postwar era, except in sub-Saharan Africa, global food production has expanded faster than the human population, averting the mass starvations that were widely predicted—for example, in the 1967 best seller *Famine—1975!* The form of agriculture that Borlaug preaches may have prevented a billion deaths."
3. In fact, only 3.2 percent of the working population in high-income countries in 2010 was employed in agriculture, versus 64.5 percent of those in low-income countries (FAO 2013). See Pardey et al. (2014a), and the references quoted therein, for details of the sources for these and related data in this sub-section.
4. Concerns that human populations would grow faster than the capacity of the world to feed them, leading to widespread famine, are often associated with ideas from the late 18th- century writings of Thomas Malthus.
5. Jorgenson and Griliches (1967) showed that under certain conditions (constant returns to scale and perfect competition), the ratio of the price index for inputs to the price index for output (the inverse of what is sometimes referred to as the farmers' terms of trade) is exactly equal to the primal measure of total factor productivity, TFP (or more precisely, in practice, multi-factor productivity, MFP). See also Alston et al. (2010b, pp. 456–457).
6. See "Borlaug" at the University of Minnesota website (University of Minnesota 2014).
7. For comparison, in 2009, the world as a whole spent around $53 billion (2005 prices) on public and private agricultural and food R&D, roughly one-third of which was performed by private firms, and two-thirds was conducted in the public sector by national agricultural research agencies (Pardey et al. 2014b). In that year an additional $530 million (2005 prices) was invested in the international agricultural research centers of the CGIAR.
8. The use of such approximations to measure the benefits from innovation attributable to research-induced productivity growth can be traced back at least as far as Griliches (1958). This application has three elements of awkwardness. First, in principle, we would prefer to apply the "k" factor to the gross value of production (GVP), whereas AgGDP is a value-added measure. The discrepancy between AgGDP and GVP is likely to vary systematically with per capita incomes, with AgGDP representing a smaller share of GVP in the higher-income countries. Second, public and private agricultural R&D are responsible for only a fraction of the total growth in TFP, and this difference also will vary systematically among countries

depending on the stage of development. Third, the measures of TFP growth are likely to be more accurate for the higher-income countries, if only because they are more likely to have appropriately detailed data available in suitably long series.

9. Productivity estimates from Fuglie et al. (2012) indicate that 24 (out of 155) countries for which we have corresponding agricultural GDP estimates failed to sustain positive TFP growth in agriculture since 1961, and that 13 (55 percent) of those countries were in sub-Saharan Africa. In turn, these 13 countries had 2009 research intensity ratios (i.e., the share of agricultural R&D spending relative to AgGDP) of just 0.5 percent (compared with a global average of 1.0 percent), and one-third of these countries were spending less in inflation-adjusted terms on public agricultural R&D in 2009 than they were in 1961.

10. Even though some farmers will be made worse off (if, for instance, they are surplus producers and cannot adopt the new technology), the distribution generally shifts to the right, as drawn, reflecting the general improvement in incomes for households although some have shifted to the left within the distribution.

11. The specific linear relationship shown in Figure 9.4, Panel B follows directly from the functional form of the model applied by Muhammad et al. (2011), but the general pattern of a negative relationship is to be expected given the expected sizes of the elasticities of demand for food and healthcare with respect to total expenditure (or income).

12. Raw commodities represent a larger share of the total budget for the poor, partly because as incomes rise, consumers demand more services associated with food as well as other non-food items that also have larger elasticities of demand with respect to total expenditure. Thus, for the poor people in poor countries who typically eat less processed and more home-prepared foods, commodity costs represent a larger share of their food budget, which itself represents a comparatively large share of the total budget.

13. However, some dispute this view (e.g., see Feinstein [1998] and Easterlin [2004]). Moreover, citing work by Livi-Bacci (1991) and Harris (2004), Cutler et al. (2006, p. 101) noted that, "Another concern with the nutritional story is that, from the sixteenth to the eighteenth centuries, English aristocrats had no life expectancy advantage over the rest of the population, despite presumably better nutrition. Nor was mortality lower in well-fed populations of the same period, such as in the United States."

14. In the data we use here, life expectancy at birth in a given year is defined as "... the average number of years a newborn child would live if current mortality patterns were to stay the same" (Johansson and Lindgren 2011, p. 1)—measured as the average age of people who died in that year, or in other words, the average length of life to that point in time. A measure that reflects morbidity as well as mortality outcomes, such as disability-adjusted life years (DALYs), is an alternative anthropometric indicator (see, for example, Murray et al. [2012]).

15. The estimated national average life expectancy at birth in 1800 ranged from a maximum 40 years for Belgium down to 23 years for Yemen. In 2010, the spread was from 83 years for Japan down to 45 years for Sierra Leone.

16. The data on potable water and sanitation are from Banerjee and Morella (2011); the data on per capita income and physicians per capita are from World Bank (2013); the data on poverty are from Chen and Ravallion (2012); and the data on consumption are from FAO (2013). The water and sanitation data are for 2006, the poverty data for 2008, the physicians per capita data for 2009, and the rest for 2010.

17. The flush toilet was first popularized (initially in Britain and Europe) around the middle of the 19th century; the initial clinical application of penicillin in the early 1940s ushered in the modern era of antibiotics; and anti-retroviral treatments for HIV-infected people followed from scientific evidence on the viral dynamics of this disease in 1996.

18. BMI, or body mass index, is expressed as mass (in this instance, kilograms) per height (meters) squared.

19. For instance, see Cutler et al. (2003); Alston et al. (2006); Miller and Coble (2007); Alston et al. (2008); Okrent and Alston (2012); and Rickard et al. (2013).

20. Some authors have argued that this is because productivity gains for fruit and vegetable farm commodities have been somewhat slower than those for field crops and livestock (e.g., see Drewnowski and Specter [2004]; Drewnowski and Darmon [2005]; Popkin [2010]), but the detailed empirical analysis by Alston and Pardey (2008) does not support that view.

21. For example, Popkin (2010) attributes the rise in US obesity to a pervasive role of government in promoting the production and consumption of animal products, and a few grains and oilseeds, at the expense of other more healthy foods, both through direct subsidies and through public agricultural R&D. Many other writers on food and nutrition policy have echoed these sentiments. Like Popkin, these writers never clearly state the full details of the relevant counterfactual, however.

22. Some such policies have been initiated. In the 2008 Farm Bill, the US government introduced the Specialty Crops Research Initiative, mandating funding of $50 million per year for FY 2009–12 and authorizing additional annual appropriations of $100 million for a new program of competitive research grants. More recently, a report from the Institute of Medicine (Glickman et al. 2012) recommended that the American Congress and the Administration "should ensure that there is adequate public funding for agricultural research and extension so that the research agenda can include a greater focus on supporting the production of foods Americans need to consume in greater quantities according to the Dietary Guidelines for Americans" (p. 435). Such recommendations have also been echoed within the medical community (e.g., Grandi and Franck [2012]) and by policymakers (e.g., White House Taskforce on Childhood Obesity Report to the President [2010]).

23. Many of these policy options, like R&D, are not directly targeted at the economic distortion associated with obesity (mainly in excess costs of healthcare provision), and may be ineffective or inefficient for that reason. The issue becomes one of comparative effectiveness and efficiency of suboptimal policies in an nth-best world.

24. As shown by Alston et al. (2008), international differences in prices of food, as captured by the Big Mac index that reflects all of these factors, can account for some of the international differences in obesity prevalence.

References

Alston, J. M., M. A. Andersen, J. S. James, and P. G. Pardey. 2010a. *Persistence Pays: U.S. Agricultural Productivity Growth and the Benefits from Public R&D Spending*. New York: Springer Publishers.

Alston, J. M., M. A. Andersen, J. S. James, and P. G. Pardey. 2011. "The Economic Returns to U.S. Public Agricultural Research." *American Journal of Agricultural Economics* 93 (5): pp. 1257–1277.

Alston, J. M., B. A. Babcock, and P. G. Pardey. 2010b. "Shifting Patterns of Global Agricultural Productivity: Synthesis and Conclusion." In *The Shifting Patterns of Agricultural Production and Productivity Worldwide*, edited by J. M. Alston, B. A. Babcock, and P. G. Pardey, Chapter 15. CARD-MATRIC on-line volume, Ames, IA: Iowa State University.

Alston, J. M., J. M. Beddow, and P. G. Pardey. 2009. "Agricultural Research, Productivity and Food Prices in the Long Run." *Science* 325 (4): pp. 1209–1210.

Alston, J. M., G. W. Edwards, and J. W. Freebairn. 1988. "Market Distortions and the Benefits from Research." *American Journal of Agricultural Economics* 70 (2) (May): pp. 281–288.

Alston, J. M., W. J. Martin, and P. G. Pardey. 2014. "Influences of Agricultural Technology on the Size and Importance of Food Price Variability." In *Economics of Food Price Volatility*, edited by Jean-Paul Chavas, David Hummels, and Brian Wright. Chicago: University of Chicago Press.

Alston, J. M., G. W. Norton, and P. G. Pardey. 1995. *Science Under Scarcity: Principles and Practice for Agricultural Research Evaluation and Priority Setting*. Ithaca, NY: Cornell University Press.

Alston, J. M., A. M. Okrent, and J. C. Parks. 2013. "Effects of U.S. Public Agricultural R&D on U.S. Obesity and its Social Costs." Robert Mondavi Institute Center for Wine Economics Working Paper 1305, University of California, Davis. <http://vinecon.ucdavis.edu/publications/cwe1302.pdf>.

Alston, J. M., and P. G. Pardey. 2008. "Public Funding for Research into Specialty Crops." *HortScience* 43 (5): pp. 1461–1470.

Alston, J. M., and P. G. Pardey. 2014. "Agriculture in the Global Economy." *Journal of Economic Perspectives* 28 (1): pp. 121–146.

Alston, J. M., D. A. Sumner, and S. A. Vosti. 2006. "Are Agricultural Policies Making Us Fat? Likely Links between Agricultural Policies and Human Nutrition and Obesity, and Their Policy Implications." *Review of Agricultural Economics* 28 (3): pp. 313–322.

Alston, J. M., D. A. Sumner, and S. A. Vosti. 2008. "Farm Subsidies and Obesity in the United States: National Evidence and International Comparisons." *Food Policy* 33 (6) (December): pp. 470–479.

Bairoch, P. 1988. *Cities and Economic Development: From the Dawn of History to the Present*. Chicago: University of Chicago Press.

Banerjee, S. G., and E. Morella. 2011. *Africa's Water and Sanitation Infrastructure: Access, Affordability and Alternatives*. World Bank: Washington, DC.

Black, R. E., C. G Victora, S. P Walker, Z. A. Bhutta, P. Christian, M. de Onis, M. Ezzati, S. Grantham-McGregor, J. Katz, R. Martorell, and R. Uauy. 2013. "Maternal and Child Undernutrition and Overweight in Low-Income and Middle-Income Countries." *Lancet* 382 (9890): pp. 427–451.

Chen, S., and M. Ravallion. 2012. "More Relatively-Poor People in a Less Absolutely-Poor World." Policy Research Working Paper No. 6114, World Bank, Washington, DC.

Costa, D. L., and R. H. Steckel. 1997. "Long Term Trends in Health, Welfare, and Economic Growth in the United States." In *Health and Welfare During Industrialization*, edited by R. H. Steckel, and R. Floud, pp. 47–90. Chicago: University of Chicago Press.

Cutler, D., A. Deaton, and A. Lleras-Muney. 2006. "Determinants of Mortality." *Journal of Economic Perspectives* 20 (3) (Summer): pp. 97–120.

Cutler, D., E. Glaeser, and J. Shapiro. 2003. "Why Have Americans Become More Obese?" *Journal of Economic Perspectives* 17 (3) (Summer): pp. 93–118.

Drewnowski, A., and N. Darmon. 2005. "The Economics of Obesity: Dietary Energy Density and Energy Cost." *American Journal of Clinical Nutrition* 82 (1S): pp. 265S–273S.

Drewnowski, A. and S. Specter. 2004. "Poverty and Obesity: The Role of Energy Density and Energy Costs." *American Journal of Clinical Nutrition* 79 (1): pp. 6–16.

Easterbrook, G. 1997. "Forgotten Benefactor of Humanity." *The Atlantic Monthly* 279 (1) (January): pp. 75–82.

Easterlin, R. A. 2004. "How Beneficent is the Market? A Look at the Modern History of Mortality." In *The Reluctant Economist: Perspectives on Economics, Economic History, and Demography*, edited by R. A. Easterlin, pp. 101–140. Cambridge: Cambridge University Press.

FAO (Food and Agriculture Organization of the United Nations). 2013. FAOSTAT database. Retrieved January 2013 from <http://faostat.fao.org>.

Feinstein, C. H. 1998. "Pessimism Perpetuated: Real Wages and the Standard of Living in Britain During and After the Industrial Revolution." *Journal of Economic History* 58 (3): pp. 625–658.

Fogel, R. W. 1997. "New Findings on Secular Trends in Nutrition and Mortality: Some Implications for Population Theory." In *Handbook of Population and Family Economics*, edited by M. R. Rosenzweig, and O. Stark, pp. 433–481. New York: Elsevier Science, North Holland.

Fuglie, K. O., S. L. Wang, and W. E. Ball. 2012. *Productivity Growth in Agriculture: An International Perspective*. Wallingford: CAB International.

Gardner, B. L. 2006. "Prices Received and Paid by Farmers Indexes and Parity Ratio: 1909–1999, Series Da1337—1346." Table in *Historical Statistics of the United States, Earliest Times to Present: Millennial Edition*, edited by S. B. Carter, S. S. Gartner, M. R. Haines, A. L. Olmstead, R. Sutch, and G. Wright. New York: Cambridge University Press.

Glickman, D., L. Parker, L. J. Sim, H. Del Valle Cook, and E. A. Miller, eds. 2012. *Accelerating Progress in Obesity Prevention Solving the Weight of the Nation*. Committee on Accelerating Progress in Obesity Prevention, Food and Nutrition Board, Institute of Medicine of the National Academies. Washington, DC: The National Academies Press.

Grandi, S. M., and C. Franck. 2012. "Agricultural Subsidies: Are They a Contributing Factor to the American Obesity Epidemic?" *Archives of Internal Medicine* 172 (22): pp. 1754–1755.

Griliches, Z. 1958. "Research Costs and Social Returns: Hybrid Corn and Related Innovations." *Journal of Political Economy* 66 (5): pp. 419–431.

Harris, B. 2004. "Public Health, Nutrition, and the Decline of Mortality: The McKeown Thesis Revisited." *Social History of Medicine* 17 (3): pp. 379–407.

Herforth, A., A. Jones, and P. Pinstrup-Andersen. 2012. "Prioritizing Nutrition in Agriculture and Rural Development: Guiding Principles for Operational Investments." Health, Nutrition, and Population (HNP) Discussion Paper, World Bank, Washington, DC. <http://dyson.cornell.edu/faculty_sites/pinstrup/pdfs/HerforthJonesPPA.pdf>.

Hurley, T. M., X. Rao, and P. G. Pardey. 2014. "Re-examining the Reported Rates of Return to Food and Agricultural Research and Development." *American Journal of Agricultural Economics*. First published online: May 31, 2014. <http://ajae.oxfordjournals.org/content/early/2014/07/08/ajae.aau047>.

International Obesity Task Force. 2005. *EU Platform on Diet, Physical Activity and Health*. Brussels, International Obesity Task Force.

Jillette, P., and R. Teller. 2009. "Greatest Man to Ever Live: Norman Borlaug." <http://www.youtube.com/watch?v=cEBtO25xW-o>.

Johansson, K., and M. Lindgren. 2011. "Documentation for Life Expectancy at Birth (Years) for Countries and Territories, Version 4." Stockholm: Gapminder Foundation. <http://www.gapminder.org/documentation/documentation/gapdoc004_v7.pdf>.

Johansson, K., and M. Lindgren. 2013. "Life Expectancy at Birth (Years) for Countries and Territories, Version 6, data file." Stockholm: Gapminder Foundation. <http://www.gapminder.org/data/documentation/gd004/>.

Jorgenson, D. W., and Z. Griliches. 1967. "The Explanation of Productivity Change." *Review of Economic Studies*. 34 (3): pp. 249–283.

Lakdawalla, D., T. Philipson, and J. Bhattacharya. 2005. "Welfare-Enhancing Technological Change and the Growth of Obesity." *American Economic Review* (Papers and Proceedings) 92 (2): pp. 253–257.

Livi-Bacci, M. 1991. *Population and Nutrition: An Essay on European Demographic History*. Cambridge: Cambridge University Press.

MacEwan, J. P., J. M. Alston, and A. M. Okrent. 2014. "The Consequences of Obesity for the External Costs of Public Health Insurance in the United States." *Applied Economic Perspectives and Policy* 36 (4): pp. 696–716.

Martin, W., and J. M. Alston. 1994. "A Dual Approach to Evaluating Research Benefits in the Presence of Policy Distortions." *American Journal of Agricultural Economics* 76 (1)(February): pp. 26–35.

Miller, J. C., and K. H. Coble. 2007. "Cheap Food Policy: Fact or Rhetoric?" *Food Policy* 32 (1): pp. 98–111.

Miller, J. C., and K. H. Coble. 2008. "An International Comparison of the Effect of Government Agricultural Support on Food Budget Shares." *Journal of Agricultural and Applied Economics* 40 (2): pp. 551–558.

Muhammad, A. J., J. L. Seale, Jr., B. Meade, and A. Regmi. 2011 *International Evidence on Food Consumption Patterns An Update Using 2005 International Comparison Program Data*. ERS Technical Bulletin Nos. 1929.Washington, DC: United States Department of Agriculture.

Murray, C. J. L., et al. 2012. "Disability-adjusted Life Years (DALYs) for 291 Diseases and Injuries in 21 Regions, 1990–2010: A Systematic Analysis for the Global Burden of Disease Study 2010." *The Lancet* 380 (9859) (December): pp. 2197–2223.

Okrent, A. M., and J. M. Alston. 2012. "The Effects of Farm Commodity and Retail Food Policies on Obesity and Economic Welfare in the United States." *American Journal of Agricultural Economics* 94 (1): pp. 611–646.

Pardey, P. G., J. M. Alston, and C. Chan-Kang. 2013. "Public Agricultural R&D over the Past Half Century: An Emerging New World Order "*Agricultural Economics* 44 (s1) (November): pp. 103–113.

Pardey, P. G., J. M. Alston, and V. W. Ruttan. 2010. "The Economics of Innovation and Technical Change in Agriculture." In *Handbook of Economics of Innovation*, edited by B. H. Hall, and N. Rosenberg, Chapter 22, pp. 939–984. Amsterdam: Elsevier.

Pardey, P. G., J. M. Beddow, T. M. Hurley, T. K. M. Beatty, and V. R. Eidman. 2014a. "A Bounds Analysis of World Food Futures: Global Agriculture Through 2050." *Australian Journal of Agricultural and Resource Economics* 58 (4): pp. 571–589.

Pardey, P. G., C. Chan-Kang, S. Dehmer, J. M. Beddow, T. M. Hurley, X. Rao, and J. M. Alston. 2014b. "Investments in and the Economic Returns to Agricultural and Food R&D Worldwide." In *Encyclopedia of Agriculture and Food Systems*, edited by Neal K. Van Alfen, pp. 78–97. New York: Elsevier.

Pinstrup-Andersen, P. 2007. "Agricultural Research and Policy for Better Health and Nutrition in Developing Countries: A Food Systems Approach." *Agricultural Economics* 37 (S1) (December): pp. 187–198.

Pinstrup-Andersen, P. 2013. "Nutrition-Sensitive Food Systems: From Rhetoric to Action." *Lancet* 382 (9890) (August 3): pp. 375–376.

Pinstrup-Andersen, P., N. R. de Londono, and E. Hoover. 1976. "The Impact of Increasing Food Supply on Human Nutrition: Implications for Commodity Priorities in Agricultural Research Policy." *American Journal of Agricultural Economics* 58 (2) (May): pp. 131–142.

Popkin, B. 2010. *The World is Fat*. New York: Avery.

Preston, S. H. 1975. "The Changing Relation Between Mortality and Level of Economic Development." *Population Studies* 29 (2): pp. 231–248.

Preston, S. H. 1980. "Causes and Consequences of Mortality Declines in Less Developed Countries during the 20th Century." In *Population and Economic Change in Developing Countries*, edited by R. A. Easterlin, pp. 289–360. Chicago: University of Chicago Press for National Bureau of Economic Research.

Preston, S. H. 1996. "American Longevity: Past, Present, and Future." Paper No. 36, Center for Policy Research, Syracuse University, Syracuse, NY.

Ravallion, M. 2013. "How Long Will it Take to Lift One Billion People Out of Poverty?" *World Bank Research Observer* 28 (2) (August): pp. 139–158.

Rickard, B. J., A. M. Okrent, and J. M. Alston. 2013. "How Have Agricultural Policies Influenced Calorie Consumption and Obesity in the United States?" *Health Economics* 22 (3): pp. 316–339.

Ruttan, V. W. 1982. *Agricultural Research Policy*. Minneapolis: University of Minnesota Press.

University of Minnesota. 2014. "Borlaug." College of Food, Agricultural and Natural Resource Sciences (CFANS), St. Paul, MN. <http://borlaug.cfans.umn.edu/home/>.

United Nations. Department of Economic and Social Affairs, Population Division. 2013a. World Population Prospects: The 2012 Revision, Total Population Both Sexes data file. New York: United Nations. <http://esa.un.org/wpp/Excel-Data/population. htm>.

United Nations. Department of Economic and Social Affairs, Population Division. 2013b. World Population Prospects: The 2012 Revision, Population by Age Groups Both Sexes data file. New York: United Nations. <http://esa.un.org/wpp/Excel-Data/ population.htm>.

USDA-NASS (US Department of Agriculture, National Agricultural Statistics Service). 2013a. Crop Values 2012 Summary. Washington, DC, USDA, NASS.

USDA-NASS (US Department of Agriculture, National Agricultural Statistics Service). 2009, 2010, 2013b. All Farm Index: Prices Received and Prices Paid. Washington, DC, USDA, NASS. <http://www.nass.usda.gov/Charts_and_Maps/Agricultural_Prices/>.

White House Taskforce on Childhood Obesity Report to the President. 2010. *Solving the Problem of Childhood Obesity Within a Generation*. Executive Office of the President of the United States, Washington, DC.

WHO (World Health Organization). 1997. *Obesity, Preventing and Managing the Global Epidemic. Report of a WHO Consultation on Obesity*. Geneva: World Health Organization.

WHO (World Health Organization). 2011. Mortality and Burden of Disease Estimates for WHO Member States in 2008 (by sex). Geneva: WHO. April 2011. <http://www. who.int/healthinfo/global_burden_disease/estimates_country/en/index.html>.

WHO (World Health Organization). 2013.WHO Global Health Observatory Data Repository. <http://apps.who.int/gho/data/node.main.A897>.

World Bank. 2012. World Development Indicators. Washington, DC: World Bank. Accessed on December 3, 2013.

World Bank. 2013. *World Development Indicators*. Washington, DC: World Bank. Accessed on December 10, 2013.

10

Bioeconomy

Science and Technology Policy to Harmonize
Biologization of Economies with Food Security

Joachim von Braun

The Emerging Bioeconomy

In recent years numerous countries—mostly high-income countries and some emerging economies—have designed and adopted bioeconomy strategies and included them prominently in their science policy agendas (Table 10.1). Some developing countries have taken note of this trend and are also considering bioeconomy strategies. What are the drivers of this new strategic trend? And what are opportunities and risks for development and food and nutrition security? The answers to these questions in brief are: (1) the bioeconomy is driven by changed factor price structures and related price expectations, technological opportunities, and changed preferences; and (2) opportunities within the bioeconomy relate to income and job opportunities and investment incentives for agriculture worldwide on the one hand, while risks relate to accelerated scarcity of biomass as biomass-based products may compete with food availability and adversely impact on the poor, unless either new technologies are over-compensating the potential scarcities, or social protection measures are expanded.

These issues shall be elaborated in this chapter, and in particular, a science policy shall be considered that enhances the opportunities and prevents the risks of the bioeconomy for the poor.

Table 10.1 Bioeconomy age: New science and policy initiatives, 2009–13

Country	Initiatives
Australia	Bioenergy—Strategic Plan 2012–2015
Brazil	Biotechnology Development Policy (2007)
Denmark	Agreement on Green Growth (2009)
Germany	Nationale Forschungsstrategie BioÖkonomie 2030 (2010)
EU Commission	A Bioeconomy for Europe (2012)
Finland	National Resource Strategy and Sustainable Bio-Economy (2011)
Ireland	Delivering our Green Potential (2012)
Canada	Biorefining Conversions Network (2009)
Malaysia	Bioeconomy Initiative and National Biomass Strategy (2011)
Netherlands	Bio-based Economy 2010–2015
Russia	Bio-industry and Bio-resources—BioTech 2030 (2012)
Sweden	Research and Innovation Strategy for Bio-based Economy (2011)
UK	UK Bioenergy Strategy (2011)
USA	National Bioeconomy Blueprint (2012)

Definition of "Bioeconomy"

The term bioeconomy was probably first defined by Juan Enriquez-Cabot and Rodrigo Martinez in 1997 (Enriquez 1998). The concept had its breakthrough during a broad European Union (EU) consultation held in 2005: Experts from academia and industry were invited to contribute to a paper which outlined the perspectives of a bioeconomy within the next 20 years. The resulting so-called "Cologne Paper" was published on May 30, 2007, in Cologne at the conference "En Route to the Knowledge-Based Bio-Economy," hosted by the German Presidency of the Council of the European Union.[1]

Being a new concept, it should not be surprising that no generally accepted definition of "bioeconomy" emerged right away. The Bioeconomy Council of the German Government adopted a rather broad definition, stating: "Bioeconomy is the knowledge-based production and use of biological resources to provide products, processes and services in all economic sectors within the frame of a sustainable economic system" (Bioeconomy Council 2013). This definition of bioeconomy does not refer exclusively to biological resources acting as substitutes for other resources, but entails new products and processes as well. The European Commission (2012) defined it as: "The bioeconomy encompasses the production of renewable biological resources and their conversion into food, feed, bio-based products[2] and bioenergy."

The bioeconomy is a large cluster of sector elements comprising raw materials, new processes, and technologies cutting across sectors and penetrating the economy, not really a single "sector." The spectrum of sectors includes agriculture, forestry, fisheries, aquaculture, food industry, and partially chemical, pharmaceutical, cosmetic, pulp and paper, textile, and energy industries. New technology intervenes in bioeconomy advancements in all of the above sectors. These sectors have a strong innovation potential due to their use of a wide range of sciences (life sciences, agronomy, ecology, food science, and social sciences), enabling and industrial technologies (biotechnology, nanotechnology, information and communication technologies [ICT], and engineering), and local and tacit knowledge. This definition allows for an ecosystem-driven green economic and industrial vision of bioeconomy, that is, in which fossil fuels are replaced by bio-based substitutes, not only for energy, but also for material, clothing, plastic, chemical applications, and non-market services. The transition toward a bioeconomy, in this perspective, entails transition toward a sustainable use of waste and byproducts, contributing to new opportunities for the concerned sectors, reducing the potential harm to the environment, and taking into account the value of non-market services (Smeets et al. 2013).

Bioeconomy is both ancient and traditional (bread baking, beer brewing, food conservation, charcoal production), but also new and innovative (novel biomaterials; biopharmaceuticals; and biological food, feed, and cosmetic ingredients). Bioeconomy comprises both the above-mentioned classical sectors and industrial biotechnologies. It is a large cluster of activities in any economy; in fact, it is even the largest in some industrialized economies,

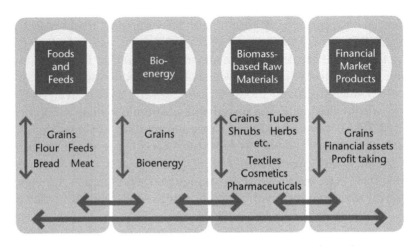

Figure 10.1 An interlinked value chain forming bioeconomy value webs
Source: The author.

in terms of its share in GDP and employment. The largest element of the bioeconomy, in terms of total output, employment, and so on, is typically agricultural and food production and processing. Bioeconomy, based on new biology, cuts across sectors and can be compared with ICT's penetration of the whole economy. Although bioeconomy draws on traditional biomass as a basic resource, biomass generation and refinement—for instance, in industrial biotechnology—is a critical part of bioeconomy, too. It is, therefore, not just a new mega value chain drawing on biomass, but it is rather an interlinked set of value chains forming the bioeconomy value web, even linked to financial markets as biomass products have become traded asset classes (Figure 10.1).

Theory of Bioeconomy and Conceptual Issues

The theoretical underpinnings of bioeconomy can be explored through a lens of economics of induced innovation (Hayami and Ruttan 1970), where innovation results from factor scarcities and related (expected) price changes (i.e., prices of land, water, carbon dioxide [CO_2], and energy). A normative approach would derive needed bioeconomy policy actions and investments from unsustainable resource use conditions and identify cost-minimal solutions, including related opportunities of technological change. Alternatively, taking a political economy perspective as a theoretical base would pinpoint demand for and supply of bioeconomy in political markets, including rent seeking. A helpful conceptual framework would provide a guide toward economic analysis of bioeconomy impacts, but it also would be useful to gain insights into actors' behaviors and political realities of allocation of innovation funding. Four analytical approaches may be promising.

First, an *economy-wide approach:* bioeconomy cannot be well captured merely as a sector of the economy; rather, it penetrates a host of sectors. Although the economic theory of bioeconomy can draw on economy-wide modeling concepts, its characteristic of cutting across sectors, however, poses practical and conceptual problems. There are difficulties to analyze the bioeconomy in established sector-disaggregated computable general equilibrium (CGE) models (Smeets et. al. 2014), and related attempts so far have been of limited use. The reasons are lack of data on the many newly created subsectors changed by bioeconomy; difficulties in depicting process innovations and recycling efficiencies, and technical change in production functions; and the fact that it is hard to capture new intermediary and end products. Still, it would be useful to embed bioeconomy in new economy-wide models after making an effort to tackle these data and conceptual complexities.

Second, via *tracking returns to investment in bioeconomy science and technology,* it would be productive to assess impacts on growth and distributional effects for sets of innovation examples of bioeconomy. This can, for instance, follow *partial equilibrium studies* or traditional rate of return studies, enriched by careful inclusion of environmental externalities.

Third, starting from *firms as strategic agents* is a useful unit of bioeconomy analysis. The implications for market performance are outcomes of critical interest. Yet that would require highly disaggregating supply and demand, and unless production processes are captured explicitly, a key aspect of efficiency gains would be neglected. Promising in that respect—also in view of the considerable involvement of government initiatives and new interlinkages among industries in competitive structures—may be a combination of partial equilibrium studies with *industrial organization* (IO) approaches, to guide business strategy and public policy (Schmalensee 1989). The traditional Structure-Conduct-Performance paradigm of IO (Bain 1959) can be the point of departure, where performance refers to the economic outcomes that result from the market structure and the firms' conduct. Joint innovation efforts across firms pursued recently in the pulp and paper industry seem to be a case in point (*The Economist* 2013). To be relevant, the traditional concept would, however, need adaptation regarding market boundaries, the basic assumptions that structure (concentration) is exogenous, and consideration of many differences between industries. To actually evaluate bioeconomic change for an industry's performance, the usual assessment criteria apply, that is, allocation efficiency, production efficiency, equity, and technological advancement.

Fourth, a *systems analysis approach* could be helpful, in which drivers of the bioeconomy would be related to change in systems components, and impacts on growth, distribution, and ecology can be derived in the context of policy interventions, including public investments. Competition among goals and complementarities of instruments should be explicitly modeled, and future scenarios could be developed. Such an approach would best include lifecycle analyses of inputs and outputs. However, the usual limitations of systems modeling apply—for instance, selective capture of causal relations, difficulties of systems boundary definition, and dynamics of technological change. Still, a systems approach to bioeconomy assessment may be appropriate compared to a more rigorous framework, such as the first option mentioned above, which constrains the desired flexibility and intersectoral linkages.

Combining all of the four approaches mentioned above with *innovation-storylines* may provide insights into the opportunities of the bioeconomy and highlight externalities (resource use, food security). In order to build the needed database for a flexible analytical approach, the EU is currently establishing a "bioeconomy observatory" with information on bioeconomy's sector components, technology innovations, research, and industry and processing elements (European Commission 2012).

The development of bioeconomy presents new challenges for the economics profession, such as going beyond the limitations of isolated value chain, sectoral, and commodity analyses toward learning more about a much broader set of relevant technologies and intermediate and final demands related to "agriculture." Moreover, there is a need to address the distributional effects related to the whole "agro-biomass" system in value webs with many externalities. The studies of resource use conflicts (land, water) and trade-offs need to be evaluated in a much broader context. There is also an urgent need for expanding our methods for tackling the challenges and opportunities in industrial organization research and mobilizing the whole agricultural economics toolbox, in much closer collaboration with other disciplines (nutrition, ecology, biotechnologies, biochemistry, etc.).

Strategic Relevance of Bioeconomy

Bioeconomy means making virtue out of necessity, that is, using more of what can sustainably grow on soils, with seed, sun, and water (including in ponds or tanks) and other inputs, and using those resources much more efficiently. And it entails producing bio-based materials even independently of soils. Bioeconomy, understood as "biologization" of the economy, is a societal and economic strategy involving producers and consumers. It addresses both the efficient use of biological routes in the production of materials, as a substitute for chemical reactions, and the use of biological raw materials instead of fossil carbon sources for industrial processes. It addresses concerns about the exploitative use of biological and other natural resources, especially water and soils.

Competitiveness in such a system will increasingly depend on innovations around bio-based products and processing technologies. They will be in demand worldwide if they are competitive in the market, and will also be perceived as better than non-bio-based products by consumers. This puts the bio-economy at the center of a new industrial strategy. While offering prospects of economic growth, the development of the bio-economy is expected to play an increasing role in addressing some of the big challenges faced by society:

- growing population and higher living standards, leading to increased demand for food, animal feed, fiber for clothing, material for housing, water, energy, and health services, including nutraceuticals and medical applications, contents of bioactive compounds, food crops with health benefits, biofortification, proteins, insulin, and blood substitutes, among others. Bioeconomic innovations can spread value chains, decrease water and fertilizer use, and improve fiber quality. They may also help in adaptation of crops to marginal growing conditions: heat, cold, drought, salinity, low nutrients, or concentration of toxic metals;

- declining resources—e.g., degraded ecosystems and loss of ecosystem services, including land degradation and unsustainable ocean fisheries, declining biodiversity—due to unsustainable management practices, and the effects of climate change on resources;

- adapting to limitation in fossil resources by providing a meaningful substitution of the consumption of such finite resources with the use of bio-based renewable resources, including modernized bioenergy (sugar-ethanol, dedicated lignocellulosic crops, etc.), enhanced use of vegetable oils in industrial applications, different fatty acid profiles (Amezaga et.al. 2013). Creating markets for "unused" biomass: carbon markets and eco-systems services;

- the need to move from production systems that entail waste that may be recycled, toward prevention of waste in the first place, that is, a zero waste strategy, where "waste" is designed to act as bio-resource for further biological processes in cascading relations. This is reflected in the system challenges and competing goals of sustainable production and the use of biomass, residues from various sources to produce goods and services, by reducing emission and waste on the value web along production, processing, and consumption of bio-based products (Figure 10.2).

A caveat here, however, is what are the consequences for the poor and their food security? Could an ill-designed strategic drive toward bioeconomy—as a strategy by the rich for the rich—accelerate the scarcity of food? A major concern is the transmission of changed price levels and price volatilities to food-insecure, low-income countries through international markets. On the other hand, bioeconomy investments in developing countries may also provide for agricultural growth, rural economic development, and employment and energy security.

The bio-energy component is only one element of bioeconomy, but an important one. The linkage between agriculture and energy arises from two major dimensions. First, the linkage arises from use of energy as a critical input in agricultural production. Modern agriculture is highly reliant on fossil resources, both directly as an input in production activity and indirectly as a raw material for production of agricultural inputs like fertilizers, pesticides, and machinery production, which has given rise to congruent food and fuel price increases, as well as agriculture contributing to greenhouse gas emission (Hertel and Beckman 2010; Woods et al. 2010). Second, another rapidly developing phenomenon is the bioenergy production from biological resources primarily supplied from agriculture, with energy production competing with

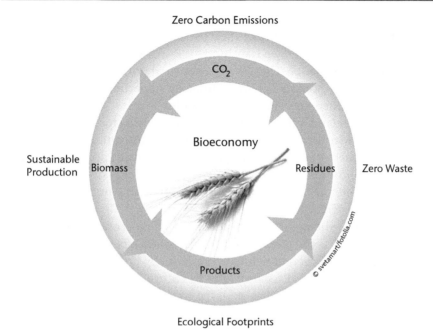

Zero Carbon Emissions

CO_2

Bioeconomy

Sustainable Production   Biomass   Residues   Zero Waste

Products

Ecological Footprints

Figure 10.2 System challenge and competing goals in bioeconomy
Source: The author.

food production for scarce resources (land, capital, and water), inducing increasing risks on agricultural productivity, especially in developing countries. Bioenergy generation can develop as a partial substitute for dwindling fossil-based energy, but the issue of competition with food production remains a concern. The "bioenergy–food price relation" was studied extensively in the recent literature. Hertel and Beckman (2010), investigating the relationship between energy and agricultural commodity markets, found that the rapid biofuel production and blending mandates reinforced the transmission of energy price volatility onto agricultural commodity price variation. Similarly, such strong impacts were identified by Tadesse et al. (2014).

Drivers of Bioeconomy

Several factors drive the development and wide-scale application of bioeconomy innovations. First, the growing demand due to global population and income growth requires substantial increases in food and feed production, applying more pressure and increasing the competition for land, water, and other scarce resources. On the other hand, non-renewable, fossil-based sources of energy remain scarce, leading to significant rises in their prices. Moreover, the environmental externalities of their use, such as emission of greenhouse gases, calls for more accelerated transition to cleaner sources of energy in order to mitigate climate change. Thus, the fundamental drivers of bioeconomy are (expected) resource scarcities, new technology opportunities, and changed preferences, the latter especially in rich countries.

The amount of land and water that is presently used for agricultural purposes cannot be substantially increased, as either cultivation makes no economic sense due to low potential yields, or expansion would negatively impact the environment and climate. The preferred way of increasing productivity is, therefore, to intensify farming sustainably on the land that is already used for agriculture, where, in many cases, water is the constraining factor. It is one of the main tasks of a sustainable bioeconomy to create the conditions in which the global provision of foodstuffs can be guaranteed. This includes further advances in crop varieties by breeding techniques, in addition to measures and technologies to reduce the considerable loss of produce from harvest to market observed today. Social and socioeconomic behavior must also be taken into consideration here to restrict excess consumption of biomass. However, the bioeconomy will not deliver its potential benefits quickly. It will probably move as slowly as agricultural research has in the past. Varietal crop innovations take typically a decade in plant breeding, and the various bioeconomy innovations will hardly be faster. World food consumption trends include more products that are rather biomass intensive, that is, animal products. A comprehensive integration of animal production into efficient value chains is an essential part of the bioeconomy. For instance, animal waste fat use for biodiesel generation through the process of ethyl ester blended with diesel may offer an option (Gürü et al. 2009).

Historically, biomass was the primary energy source. Also, for instance in Ethiopia today, biomass is still by far the dominant energy source, providing about 90 percent of primary energy. Here, the challenge is to make better use of biomass with new technologies, that is, a leapfrogging into a knowledge-based bioeconomy could be explored. The use of fossil fuels has been fundamental to economic growth and development since the Industrial Revolution. The fast growth in world biofuel production in recent years was initially driven by price expectations of fossil fuels and expectations of (low) bio-based raw material prices. Although bioenergy has some attractive features to substitute for fossil fuels in energy end uses (Nigam and Singh 2011), policies in support of and subsidies for this particular line of energy production have so far not comprehensively dealt with its negative externalities for food security and land use. Biofuel promotion policies need to be carefully evaluated in terms of their economic, social, and environmental sustainability. Subsidy, tax, and tariff instruments should be more carefully chosen and implemented, avoiding potential adverse effects (de Gorter and Just 2010).

The competitiveness of the bioeconomy in general and its various lines of production are determined by the expectations regarding long-term prices. Food and other biomass-related prices have been increasing to higher levels since 2008. Yet prices do not need to be taken as given. In the long run, the price dynamics mainly depend on the investments in innovation, not just on short-term supply and demand. R&D will be important in helping to reduce future shortages of biomass and will thereby influence price developments. Tapping the potentials of bioeconomy further depends on infrastructure and trade. Much of the biomass production potential in developing countries is in remote areas, where access to markets is impaired by limited infrastructure. The new price incentives for biomass production and utilization do not reach these areas, and that limits efficiency in the global bioeconomy. Infrastructure development and technology innovations may need to expand in sync, and processing facilities (including bio-refineries) may be best located close to biomass production bases.

Change in preferences tends to lead to more demand for bioeconomy products, but there are externalities. Hence the magnitude of the impact of preferences on the advent of bioeconomy is difficult to predict. The change in preferences for bio-based products is widespread in global middle classes, not just in rich countries. It probably relates to risk considerations and lifestyle perspectives. An empirical study on US bioenergy projects in southern Iowa and in northeastern Kentucky focused on farmers' perceptions and indicated that the development of the new bioeconomy may be hindered if local social and cultural contexts are not taken into account (Rossi and Hinrichs 2011). In developing countries, sociocultural values and acceptance can emerge as important barriers for biofuel development (Chin et. 2014). Externalities may be going significantly beyond the classical externalities of preferences, such as adverse attitudes toward genetically modified crops in rich countries, the latter in Europe, in particular. The externalities of these preferences for the poor and for food security have not been studied sufficiently.

Bioeconomy Innovations and Food Security

Technical and institutional innovations are key ingredients of sustainable bioeconomy development, as they may help to minimize the risks that may arise from trade-offs with food security through increasing efficiency and efficacy of resource use. Bioeconomy changes the world food equation on both the supply and demand side, and thereby may impact on food security.

Food and nutrition security depends upon the availability of food (through production and trade), access to food due to purchasing power, and the utilization of that food for human nutrition. Stability of the food system, especially of production and related markets, cuts across these three pillars of food and nutrition security. These concepts, however, need to be viewed in a dynamic context, where food and nutrition insecurity undermines the resilience of poor people especially in low-income countries, and thus, can erode both societal cohesion and the natural resource base of countries. The potential trade-off between bioeconomy-based sustainable economic growth and food security could raise ethical issues, if a trade-off between the two should occur (see Pinstrup-Andersen and Sandøe [2007] on such ethical issues).

Among the bioeconomic sectors, bioenergy production currently has the biggest potential impact on food security. There is an intense debate on the link between bioenergy development and food security (see von Braun and Pachauri [2006]; Naylor et al. [2007]; von Braun et al. [2008]; and Ewing and Msangi [2009], among others). The estimates of the share of bioenergy's contribution to the recent food price spikes in 2008 vary between 3 percent and 75 percent (Mitchell [2008] and Reuters [2008], both cited by Ciaian and Kancs [2011]). The proponents of bioenergy argue that the world has a significant under-utilized biomass resource potential, including biomass from agriculture and forestry residues (Slade et al. 2011). On the other hand, additional demand for biomass resources may increase pressures on agricultural land use, which incentivizes the conversion of natural land and affects the soil quality (Berndes et al. 2010; Edwards et al. 2010). The growing industrial demand for feedstock for bioenergy generation is also leading to increased land prices and land acquisitions (von Braun and Meinzen-Dick 2009; Cotula et al. 2011). The main challenge of bioenergy is manifested in the competitive use of natural resources and its trade-offs with food production. The trade-off is reflected in the higher food prices and the change in shadow prices of natural resources, which has significant economic, social, and livelihood implications.

Governments play important roles in shaping markets and the food systems (Pinstrup-Andersen and Watson 2011). Strategies for food and nutrition security need to take note of the fundamental changes that reposition food and nutrition in the context of the global and national bioeconomy. To the extent food security partly depends on the availability of food, which is part of biomass production and affected by new competitive uses of biomass for energy and industrial raw materials, new challenges will require a systemic approach identifying: (1) the consequences of substituting the consumption of finite resources by using biomass and other renewable resources; and (2) production systems that rely more on waste prevention, recycling, more efficient use of limited resources, and on an increased deployment of renewable resources.

The pros and cons of bioeconomy for food security need to be identified from at least two angles: first, competition in joint markets and related price formation, and second, synergies resulting from technology serving income generation among the poor. The search for efficiency in bioeconomy that would not be in competition with, but enhances food security, relates to:

- the development of new types of biomass-based production and new production techniques, and the creation and exploitation of synergies, for instance in fermentative production systems or bio-refineries;

- raising the resource efficiency of the newly interrelated value chains: from the production of biomass in agriculture and forestry at locations not suitable for food and feeds, to the use of wastes, to the efficiency of end products in the food sector, the energy sector, and areas of industry such as the chemical, textile, paper, or pharmaceutical sectors;

- new opportunities in the biochemical processes that can grow from the new science of fundamental processes within plants and microorganisms. Industrial biotechnology is a key element, for instance, in developing and using enzymes and whole cells for biotransformations and production processes, which are about to change the resource base of biochemical industries.

Reconciliation of food security goals and bioeconomy is thus largely a matter of technological and institutional innovations. Systematic research into the bioeconomy is still in its infancy and should be pursued to explore its perspectives. Implementation of measures will necessitate the active participation of all stakeholders in innovation:

- consumers as end users, because without their demand for bio-based products, opportunities remain limited;

- industry and enterprises will have to ensure that production and processing of materials is done using best technologies and management practices;

- governments will need to focus on wider sustainability issues with appropriate regulation and standard setting; innovation hurdles will need to be reduced, and an active science policy needs to be designed and pursued in the long run.

Advancement in bioscience and technological innovations may contribute to economic competitiveness of the bioeconomic sectors in numerous ways. First, higher yields and stress-resistant crop varieties increase land and water use efficiencies and improve food availability. Second, technologies for conversion of biomass waste and residue to bio-based materials increase use efficiency and productivity, and reduce pollution that arises, for instance, from dumping of municipal waste, widespread in the developing countries' megacities. Moreover, innovations create economic opportunities for enhanced use of byproducts, residue, and wastes as energy feedstock, contributing to reduced pressure on food security and stabilizing prices. On the other hand, significant technological innovation in the conversion of biomass to useful energy leads to the production of multipurpose bio-based products. In this context, a lack of technical capacity remains a constraint for the development of new bioeconomy sectors in most developing countries.

Another technical driver behind rapidly expanding bioeconomy is the evolution in information and communication technologies. The flow of information and dissemination of new findings on technical and other aspects of bioeconomy is critical for market functioning and effective coordination of the large number of actors in the bioeconomy's value webs. Among the key issues related to the innovations in bioeconomic value webs are transaction costs. These costs relate to public and private services, changing costs of access to natural resources, and to (venture) capital across the whole web. Improved internalization and capturing of externalities (negative and positive) in webs also entail costs. Prioritization of cost-cutting options should be guided by transparent environmental footprint measurements, web efficiency, and distributional effects (e.g., for the poor) across the bioeconomy web.

The complex nexus of bioenergy and food security with subsystem conflicts and complementarities depends on many factors such as resource abundance/scarcity, the local sociocultural values, preference and market situation, logistic and infrastructural facilities, economic condition, and government policy in a spectrum of sectors (agriculture, industrial, energy, etc.). In Ethiopia, it was found that large-scale biofuel investments might have a "win-win" outcome for improved smallholder productivity, food security, and incomes (Gebreegziabher et al. 2013). In Tanzania, Arndt et al. (2012) found that cassava-based biofuel generation is more productive and pro-poor than other feedstock alternatives. However, maximizing the impact of biofuel development on poverty reduction requires improving cassava productivity (Arndt et al. 2012). Even where biofuels can provide opportunities for job creation, poverty reduction, and income growth, their positive impacts may be constrained by weaknesses in property rights, particular land tenure security, and whether they reduce access to a common pool of natural resources by poor smallholders whose subsistence depends on these resources.

Climate change provides powerful incentives for investment in the bioeconomy in three ways: first, there is the need to establish a different energy base, including biomass; second, there exists the threat of declining crop productivity and production risks; and third, the emerging greenhouse gas (GHG) mitigation markets are increasing the incentives for biomass stocks (rather than flows, such as food production) for sequestration and recarbonizing the biosphere (Wheeler and von Braun 2013). Food security linkages do not just work via raw material markets, but also via land and water markets. The rapid expansion of investment in land acquisition to grow biofuels reflects the strong demand for biomass that has become an international issue. In the often unregulated land markets in which power rather than efficiency rules, the investment ventures need more policy attention to protect the rights of poor land users, especially small farmers and pastoralists.

Food security linkages with the bioeconomy need to consider the set of interlinked value chains, that is, the value web. For the bioeconomy to get into harmony with food security requires increased efficiency in this whole value web. Linkages to food security relate to how some of the key bioeconomy domains are actually evolving, both in terms of market development and in terms of technological progress. Here are some examples:

- *Biofuels:* Sugar- and corn-based ethanol will not be sufficient to achieve energy/climate goals; dedicated lignocellulosic crops to be converted into ethanol, or others with higher energy input/output ratio, are hoped for, but may emerge slowly at best. Plant breeding in this context is crucial in terms of lignin content and composition (amount of lignin present in cell walls) as is conversion technology with chemical innovations, such as catalytic conversion.

- *Fibers:* Cotton is the most common fiber, but there is now a need to spread the value chains to include fibers such as flax and hemp. These fibers are also a means to decrease water and fertilizer use (as compared to cotton). Breeding targets should aim to improve fiber quality by optimizing cell wall properties in relation to specific applications of fiber uses. Bio-based innovations in fibers include artificial spider fibers and milk protein-based fibers, already emerging with interesting properties for industrial uses (Bioeconomy Council 2014).

- *Oil crops:* Plant breeding to enhance use of vegetable oils in industrial applications, by introducing different fatty acid profiles in plants in order to simplify the refining or chemical modification of the oil, or by developing plants with new specialty fatty acids normally not present in food oil crops. Modern biotechnology is increasingly employed to achieve targets, such as reduced costs through higher seed yield, improved disease resistance, and use of byproducts.

- *Innovation in bioenergy generation* would significantly contribute to improved efficiency when it helps reduce wastage of biomass resources. Biomass is used in unprocessed form in many developing countries, poising health hazards and ecological problems. However, emerging technical innovation and food security issues have brought this to the forefront, with demand for better use of biomass. A third-generation biofuel generation has recently emerged which primarily uses algae, but many technologies remain at an early stage of development (Bentsen et al. 2014; Muller 2014). Opportunities also relate to the emerging bio-refinery sectors, that is, the processes of transforming biomass into a wide range of value-added products (chemicals, materials, food, and feed) or energy (biofuels, heat, or power).

- *Industrial biotechnology* is on a fast expansion track, for instance, with big investment in succinic acid plants[3] currently being pursued by many large chemical companies. This has the potential for establishing a changed resource base in chemical industries, without putting much pressure on scarce biomass.

- *Product innovations* may evolve at scale and are difficult to predict. Bioeconomy does not only consist of raw material substitution and upstream commodity processing, but very much entails new lines of end products at consumer level. These include new bioplastics, biomaterials for the car industry and for building construction, cosmetics products, bio-based synthetic meat, health products (e.g., biological anti-caries components in toothpaste), and graphene and its potential for many yet to be explored innovative applications in the bioeconomy.[4]

In sum, the emerging bioeconomy is changing the competition for food, land, and water. Food security-proof bioeconomy systems require new bio-mass types and cascading reuse systems, as well as end-product innovations, even unrelated to biomass. The emerging market for biomass and its agri-cultural underpinnings need sound institutional arrangements and codes of conduct beyond voluntary guidelines. The governance of the food system needs to pay renewed attention to property rights, especially land, including communal lands.

Science Policy for Reconciling Food Security and Bioeconomy

The linkages between science, technology, innovation, and food secu-rity are strong and positive (Pinstrup-Andersen 2007; Conway and Waage 2010), but the details of impacts in a bioeconomy context are less clear. Bioeconomy is redefining the demand for science related to agriculture and food. Essentially, it calls for overcoming commodity-focused research, moving toward systems innovations, that is, systems in which value chains interact in value webs. This challenges toolboxes in (agricultural) econom-ics. Science policy is understood here as the design of science landscapes; institutional arrangements for science funding, implementation, and partnerships; and the setting of goals and allocation of resources to science priorities. A traditional concept of agricultural research—while, of course, still important—with a focus on crops and animal production, emphasizing closing of "yield gaps" is, however, not sufficient in a bioeconomy age. The ingredients of science policy for innovation in the bioeconomy cut across many domains (land use and soils, water management, marine and terrestrial biodiversity genetic resources, plant and animal biotechnology, economics of interlinked value webs of the bioeconomic sectors, nutrition and health, recycling and energy conversion). In view of major constraints faced by low-income and emerging economies in the cluster of health, nutrition, human capital, food and agriculture, and natural resources management, the related sciences need particular attention. The context of this cluster is changing with the emerging bioeconomy, demanding a much stronger emphasis on basic science linked to applications. In this sense, science, technology, and innovation (STI) interact with resource use efficiency and productivity, processing system, and production of bio-based products (Figure 10.3).

Bioeconomy draws heavily on basic scientific research, which is lacking in developing countries. Current science funding is extremely limited in many low-income and emerging economies, and science policy

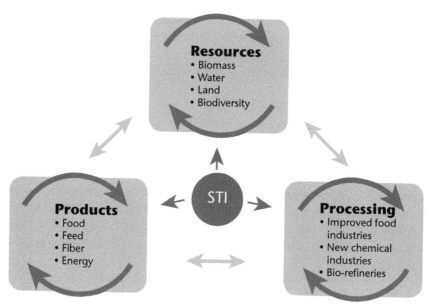

Figure 10.3 Bioeconomy: Cascading and feedbacks driven by science, technology, and innovation
Source: The author.

strategies are often not well informed by evidence. To take advantage of opportunities, emerging economies need to invest in building their analytical strength to prioritize science and technology investments. Low-income and emerging economies need to have access to basic science—which, being largely non-tradeable, is hard to buy from abroad—and connect to international science and knowledge-sharing systems. Science support needs to become a much stronger component in development cooperation policies, and rich countries need to open up access to their basic science capacities for emerging economies to facilitate domestic bioeconomy innovation (von Braun 2013).

Science policy in emerging economies may need to identify specific areas of focus for making the most effective contributions to development (Ruttan 1997), but doing so without becoming overly specialized in applied research that lacks the links to the broad benefits of basic science is a challenge. Economic growth models, which consider the importance of ideas and knowledge as engines for growth, originated in the early 1990s (see, for instance, Romer [1990]; Grossman and Helpman [1994]; Jones and Romer [2010]). One of the insights of these models is that new knowledge, which is typically a non-rival good (i.e., it can, in principle, be shared and used by several actors simultaneously without exhausting it), is increasing in the development and growth process. Network externalities in science systems may further accelerate these impacts of new knowledge in the development process. Cluster theory (Romer 1986, 1990; Porter 1990, 1998) argues for geographic proximity and agglomeration as being conducive for productivity, and this also can be relevant for the design of science landscapes. The new growth models are important to consider when bioeconomy science policy priorities are set.

In a bioeconomy age, the challenge of achieving food and nutrition security in its four dimensions (availability, access, utilization, and stability) needs the acceleration of science and technology investments that address all four dimensions (Figure 10.4). As the opportunities of bioeconomy depend upon complex science, the gap between the rich and the poor world may increase, unless improved science policy cooperation occurs. Bioeconomy policy needs the input from bioeconomy science, an input that can only take place if science targets the right needs, and scientific results are communicated efficiently (Furman et al. 2002; Ahn et al. 2010; Alberts 2010).

A number of low-income countries have designed suitable science policies but fail to implement them. The main reason is that these policies are not well integrated into the national development plans and budgets to facilitate and ensure appropriate levels of funding for implementation. Often, the resource constraints are too severe in two dimensions, finance and human resources

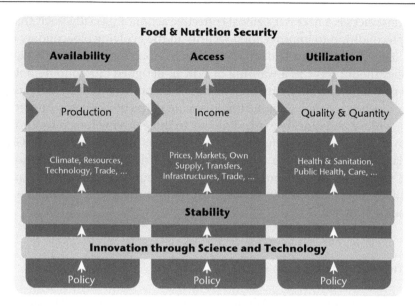

Figure 10.4 Science and technology serve food and nutrition security
Source: The author.

coming out of higher education (i.e., science spending per capita in rich countries is about 100 times what is often found in low-income countries), and in addition, science capacities must draw on higher education systems (i.e., the formation of human capital), and consider the interconnectedness of innovations (Alberts 2010).

Conclusion

Bioeconomy must ultimately be understood in a context of much larger societal, technological, and economic transformation toward a sustainable economic system. Bioeconomy is at the center of such transformation for economic and ecological sustainability. It is an opportunity and a challenge for governments, scientists, inventors, and small and large businesses, including farmers and social entrepreneurs. The essence of such transformational strategies are not only technological (new science) and behavioral (adjusted consumption), but the central issue may very well be institutional, that is, providing the regulatory framework and long-term incentives for industry and consumers, both at national and international levels. Bioeconomy will not unfold its transformational potentials if pursued in isolation by rich countries. Sharing new bioeconomy knowledge from the science systems of rich countries with developing countries and support for adaptation to local circumstances is a necessary global collective action. Especially, such sharing is a precondition to improve food security in the evolving bioeconomy context. The lessons from the disruption of global food markets by early biofuel policies should serve as a warning of how ill-designed bioeconomy policies may go wrong. It would, however, be misleading to view bioeconomy just as some bioenergy policy or biotechnology policy. The bioeconomy opportunities are broad and quickly expanding due to three driving forces: technology innovations, changed preferences, and resource price expectations. Given the large bio-resource base in developing countries, and the connection of large numbers of low-income farmers to it, an equitable and food security-oriented smart bioeconomy policy must involve them in a sustainable bioeconomy strategy.

Acknowledgments

Research assistance by Alisher Mirzabaev and Dawit Guta (both at ZEF) is gratefully acknowledged.

Notes

1. The "Cologne Paper" presents the findings of six workshops, which were held between January and March 2007. The participants discussed the following aspects: (1) Framework, (2) Food, (3) Biomaterials and Bioprocesses, (4) Bioenergy, (5) Biomedicine, and (6) New Concepts and Emerging Technologies (German Presidency of the Council of the European Union 2007).
2. Bio-based products are products that are wholly or partly derived from materials of biological origin, excluding materials embedded in geological formations and/ or fossilized.
3. Succinic acid is a diprotic, dicarboxylic acid with chemical formula $C_4H_6O_4$. More recently, succinic acid is being produced through the fermentation of glucose from renewable feedstock. As chemical industries transform from petro-based to environmentally sustainable materials, succinic acid is emerging as one of the competitive new bio-based chemicals.
4. Graphene is pure carbon in the form of a very thin, nearly transparent sheet, one atom thick. It is remarkably strong for its very low weight, and it conducts heat and electricity with great efficiency. Technically, graphene is a crystalline allotrope of carbon with two-dimensional properties <http://en.wikipedia.org/wiki/Graphene>. The Nobel Prize in Physics for 2010 was awarded jointly to Andre Geim and Konstantin Novoselov "for groundbreaking experiments regarding the two-dimensional material graphene" <http://www.nobelprize.org/nobel_prizes/physics/laureates/2010/>.

References

Ahn, M. J., M. Meeks, R. Bednarek, C. Ross, and S. Dalziel. 2010. "Towards High Performance Bioeconomy: Determining Cluster Priorities and Capabilities in New Zealand." *International Journal of Commerce and Management* 20 (4): pp. 308–330.

Alberts, B. 2010. "Policy-Making Needs Science." *Science* 330 (6009): p. 1287.

Amezaga, J., D. Bird, and J. Hazelton. 2013. "The Future of Bioenergy and Rural Development Policies in Africa and Asia." *Biomass and Bioenergy* 59 (December): pp. 137–141.

Arndt, C., K. Pauw, and J. Thurlow. 2012. "Biofuels and Economic Development: A Computable General Equilibrium Analysis for Tanzania." *Energy Economics* 34 (6): pp. 1922–1930.

Bain, J. S. 1959. *Industrial Organization: A Treatise*. [2nd ed 1968]. New York: John Wiley.

Bentsen, N., L. Felby, and B. Thorsen. 2014. "Agricultural Residue Production and Potentials for Energy and Materials Services." *Progress in Energy and Combustion Science*, 40 (February): pp. 59–73.

Berndes, G., B. Neil, and A. Cowie. 2010. "Bioenergy, Land Use Change and Climate Change Mitigation." IEA Bioenergy, Rotorua, New Zealand.

Bioeconomy Council of the German Government. 2013. "What is Bioeconomy?" Berlin. <http://biooekonomierat.de/home-en/bioeconomy.html>.

Bioeconomy Council of the German Government. 2014. Produktsammlung Bioökonomie. Berlin. <http://www.biooekonomierat.de/publikationen. html?tx_rsmpublications_pi1%5Bpublication%5D=27&tx_rsmpublications_ pi1%5Baction%5D=show&tx_rsmpublications_pi1%5Bcontroller%5D=Publica tion&cHash=c6532c528c088b63777608b2e787560e>.

Chin, H., W. Choong, S. Rafidah, W. Alwi, and A. Mohammed. 2014. "Issues of Social Acceptance on Biofuel Development." *Journal of Cleaner Production* 71 (May 15, 2014): pp. 1–10.

Ciaian, P., and D. A. Kancs. 2011. "Interdependencies in the Energy–Bioenergy–Food Price Systems: A Cointegration Analysis." *Resource and Energy Economics* 33 (1): pp. 326–348.

Conway, G., and J. Waage, J. 2010. *Science and Innovation for Development*. London: UK Collaborative on Developmental Sciences (UKCDS).

Cotula, L., L. Finnegan, and D. Macqueen. 2011. "Biomass Energy: Another Driver of Land Acquisition." IIED Briefing Paper, International Institute for Environment and Development, London. <http://pubs.iied.org/17098IIED.html>.

de Gorter, H., and Just, D. 2010. "The Social Costs and Benefits of Biofuels: The Intersection of Environmental, Energy and Agricultural Policy." *Applied Economic Perspectives and Policy* 32 (1): pp. 4–32.

The Economist. 2013. "The Paper Industry and Climate Change: Roll on the Green Revolution." November 30, 2013.

Edwards, R., D. Mulligan, and L. Marelli. 2010. "Indirect Land Use Change from Increased Biofuels Demand: Comparison of Models and Results for Marginal Biofuels Production from Different Feedstock." JRC Scientific and Technical Reports, European Union, Luxembourg.

Enriquez, J. 1998. "Genomics and the World Economy." *Science* 281 (5379): pp. 925–926.

European Commission. 2005. "New Perspectives on the Knowledge-Based Bio-Economy." Conference Report, Sixth Framework Programme, Brussels, September 15–16, 2005. <http://ec.europa.eu/research/conferences/2005/kbb/pdf/kbbe_conferencereport.pdf>.

European Commission. 2012. "Innovating for Sustainable Growth: A Bioeconomy for Europe." Communication from the Commission to the European Parliament, the Council, and the European Economic and Social Committee and the Committee of the Regions, February 13, 2012, Brussels. <http://ec.europa.eu/research/bioeconomy/pdf/201202_innovating_sustainable_growth.pdf>.

Ewing, M., and S. Msangi. 2009. "Biofuels Production in Developing Countries: Assessing Tradeoffs in Welfare and Food Security." *Environmental Science & Policy* 12 (4): pp. 520–528.

Furman, L., E. Porter, and S. Stern. 2002. "The Determinants of National Innovative Capacity." *Research Policy* 31 (6): pp. 899–933.

Gebreegziabher, Z., A. Mekonnen, T. Ferede, F. Guta, J. Levin, G. Köhlin, T. Alemu, and L. Bohlin. 2013. "The Distributive Effect and Food Security Implications of Biofuels Investment in 193 Ethiopia: A CGE Analysis." RFF Discussion Paper EfD DP 13-02, Environment for Development Discussion Paper Series, Resources for the Future, Washington, DC.

German Presidency of the Council of the European Union. 2007. Conference Report ("Cologne Paper"): "En Route to Knowledge-Based Bio-Economy" Conference, May 30, 2007, Cologne, Germany. <https://www.bmbf.de/pub/cp.pdf>.

Grossman, G. M., and E. Helpman. 1994. "Endogenous Innovation in the Theory of Growth." *Journal of Economic Perspectives* 8 (1): pp. 23–44.

Gürü, M., D. Artukoğlu, A. Keskin, and A. Kaco. 2009. "Biodiesel Production from Waste Animal Fat and Improvement of Its Characteristics by Synthesized Nickel and Magnesium Additive." *Energy Conversion and Management* 50 (3): pp. 498–502.

Hayami, Yujiro, and V. W. Ruttan. 1970. "Factor Prices and Technical Change in Agricultural Development: The United States and Japan, 1880–1860." *Journal of Political Economy* 78 (5): pp. 1115–1141.

Hertel, T. W., and J. Beckman. 2010. "Commodity Price Volatility in the Biofuel Era: An Examination of the Linkage between Energy and Agricultural Markets." GTAP Working Paper No. 60, Global Trade Analysis Project, Purdue University, West Lafayette, IN.

Jones, Charles I., and Paul M. Romer. 2010. "The New Kaldor Facts: Ideas, Institutions, Population, and Human Capital." *American Economic Journal: Macroeconomics* 2 (1): pp. 224–245.

Mitchell, D. 2008. "A Note on Rising Food Prices." Policy Research Working Paper 4682, The World Bank, Washington, DC.

Muller, A. 2014. "Sustainable Farming of Bioenergy Crops." In *Bioenergy Research: Advances and Applications*, edited by Vijai K. Gupta, Maria Tuohy, Christian P. Kubicek, and Jack Saddler, pp. 407–417. Amsterdam: Elsevier.

Naylor, R. L., A. J. Liska, M. B. Burke, W. P. Falcon, J. C. Gaskell, S. D. Rozelle, and K. G. Cassman. 2007. "The Ripple Effect: Biofuels, Food Security, and the Environment." *Environment: Science and Policy for Sustainable Development* 49 (9): pp. 30–43.

Nigam, P., and A. Singh. 2011. "Production of Liquid Biofuels from Renewable Resources." *Progress in Energy and Combustion Science* 37 (1): pp. 52–68.

Pinstrup-Andersen, P. 2007. "Agricultural Research and Policy for Better Health and Nutrition in Developing Countries: A Food Systems Approach." In *Contributions of Agricultural Economics to Critical Policy Issues*, edited by K. Otsuka and K. Kalirajan, pp. 187–198. Malden, MA: Blackwell.

Pinstrup-Andersen, P., and P. Sandøe, eds. 2007. *Ethics, Hunger and Globalization: In Search of Appropriate Policies.* Dordrecht: Springer-Verlag.

Pinstrup-Andersen, P., and Derrill D. Watson, II, eds. 2011. *Food Policy in Developing Countries: The Role of Government in Global, National, and Local Food Systems.* Ithaca, NY: Cornell University Press.

Porter, Michael E. 1990. *The Competitive Advantage of Nations.* New York: Free Press.

Porter, Michael E. 1998. "Clusters and the New Economics of Competition." *Harvard Business Review* 76 (6), Nov–Dec: pp. 77–90.

Reuters. 2008. "Bad Policy, Not Biofuel, Drive Food Prices: Merkel." Reuters, April 17, 2008. <http://www.reuters.com/article/idUSKRA45973520080424>.

Romer, P. 1986. "Increasing Returns and Long-run Growth." *Journal of Political Economy* 94 (51): pp. 1002–1037.

Romer, P. 1990. "Endogenous Technological Change." *Journal of Political Economy* 98 (5): pp. S71–S102.

Rossi, A., and C. Hinrichs. 2011. "Hope and Skepticism: Farmer and Local Community Views on the Socio-economic Benefits of Agricultural Bioenergy." *Biomass and Bioenergy* 35 (4): pp. 1418–1428

Ruttan, Vernon W. 1997. "Induced Innovation, Evolutionary Theory and Path Dependence: Sources of Technological Change." *The Economic Journal* 107 (444): pp. 1520–1529.

Schmalensee, R. 1989. "Inter-Industry Studies of Structure and Performance." In *Handbook of Industrial Organization*, vol. 2, edited by R. Schmalensee and R. Willig, pp. 951–1009. Amsterdam: Elsevier.

Slade, R., R. Saunders, R. Gross, and A. Bauen. 2011. "Energy from Biomass: The Size of the Global Resource." Imperial College Centre for Energy Policy and Technology and UK Energy Research Centre, London.

Smeets, Edward, Hannes Böttcher, Yannis Tsiropoulos, Martin Patel, Lauri Hetemäki, Marcus Lindner, Stefan Bringezu, Marleen Schouten, Franziska Junker, Martin Banse, and Siwa Msangi. 2013. "Systems Analysis Description of the Bioeconomy." WP 1 "Conceptual Model of Systems Analysis of the Bio-Based Economy" of the EU FP 7 SAT-BBE Project: Systems Analysis Tools Framework for the EU Bio-Based Economy Strategy. April 2, 2013.

Smeets, Edward, Myrna van Leeuwen, Hugo Valin, Yannis Tsiropoulos, Alexander Moiseyev, Marcus Lindner, Meghan O'Brien, Helmut Schütz, Marleen Schouten, Peter Verburg, Willem Verhagen, Franziska Junker, and Siwa Msangi. 2014. "Annotated Bibliography on Qualitative and Quantitative Models for Analysing the Bio-Based Economy." Working Paper D 2.3, WP2: "Tools for Evaluating and Monitoring of the EU FP 7 SAT-BBE Project: Systems Analysis Tools Framework for the EU Bio-Based Economy Strategy." Version 2. The Hague, The Netherlands, SAT-BBE.

Tadesse, G., B. Algieri, M. Kalkuhl, and J. von Braun. 2014. "Drivers and Triggers of International Food Price Spikes and Volatility." *Food Policy* 47: pp. 117–128.

von Braun, J., 2013. "International Co-operation for Agricultural Development and Food and Nutrition Security: New Institutional Arrangements for Related Public Goods." WIDER Working Paper, No. 2013/061, ISBN 978-92-9230-638-0, World Institute for Development Economics Research, Helsinki, Finland.

von Braun, J., A. Ahmed, K. Asenso-Okyere, S. Fan, A. Gulati, J. Hoddinott, L. Pandya-Lorch, M. Rosegrant, M. Ruel, M. Torero, T. van Rheenen, and K. von Grebmer. 2008. "High Food Prices: The What, Who, and How of Proposed Policy Actions." International Food Policy Research Institute (IFPRI), Washington, DC. <http://www.ifpri.org/publication/high-food-prices>.

von Braun, J., and R. Meinzen-Dick. 2009. "'Land Grabbing' for Foreign Investors in Developing Countries: Risks and Opportunities." IFPRI Policy Brief 13, International Food and Policy Research Institute, Washington, DC. <http://www.ifpri.org/publication/land-grabbing-foreign-investors-developing-countries>.

von Braun, J., and K. Pachauri. 2006. "The Promises and Challenges of Biofuels for the Poor in Developing Countries." IFPRI 2005–2006 Annual Report Essay, International Food Policy Research Institute, Washington DC.

Wheeler, T., and J. von Braun. 2013. "Climate Change Impacts on Global Food Security." *Science* 341 (6145): pp. 508–513.

Woods, J., A. Williams, J. Hughes, M. Black, and R. Murphy. 2010. "Energy and the Food System. *Philosophical Transactions of the Royal Society: Biological Science*, 365 (1554): pp. 2991–3006.

11

Global and Local Food Systems in the GM Labeling Campaign

Tina Andersen Huey

Introduction

Pinstrup-Andersen and Sandøe's *Ethics, Hunger and Globalization* (2007b) made an important contribution by casting food systems in an ethical light. Despite its surprising inattention to analyzing the ethics and responsibilities of multinational corporations in the global food system, the volume's reflections from thinkers in a variety of disciplines richly explored what ethics might mean in the context of global challenges. What do we do, though, once we have determined what can, or cannot, be expected from communities that share the planet? In contrast to health and ecological problems, it is very difficult to make global food security culturally relevant. It is also difficult to make it politically relevant, as other authors in this volume have argued, because key decisions are made at the national level, and global policies are hardly enforceable. It is ironic that even as international, research-based aid and development organizations have embraced participatory models in development practice, they still hew closely to an outdated science communication paradigm when it comes to GM food protests in rich countries, downgrading public fears (Juanillo 2001) to a problem of scientific literacy. This chapter argues that a strategy to employ communications theories and practices in the fight against hunger must include entering into the world view of food activists in the developed world, and that the labeling debate provides one window on it.

What is Labeling About? Why Should the Agricultural Development Community Care?

Among some economists, labeling of foods containing GMOs is seen as irrational, at best, and a detrimental contributor to higher food prices, at worst. Some consider the mere act of labeling to be an act of disinformation that draws meaningless and pernicious distinctions.

Communications scholars, drawing from anthropology and sociology, like to go into a loosely bounded field armed with both inductive and deductive reasoning, using what Glaser and Strauss called "grounded theory" (Glaser and Strauss 1967) to formulate hypotheses based upon constant comparison of data. Obviously, this is not a method that conforms to research paradigms in economics; but with this approach, a general question such as "What is labeling about?" allows unexpected frames and meanings to emerge. It allows the researcher to deconstruct, or unpack, the idea of labeling. Labeling campaigns are not approached as psychological questions about why people insist on knowing (or remaining ignorant about) something, but rather investigated for what they can tell us about the circulation of ideas. Sociological approaches pioneered by Howard Becker (1998) temper what otherwise can become a highly detailed semantic parsing. Becker encourages the operationalization of "why" questions as "how" questions. In the case of GM food labeling, one can operationalize the question as: "How is labeling used in a political context?"

A discursive approach reveals that what we often refer to as information contains a fair amount of storytelling, in contrast to science communication paradigms that too often see media messages as transparent vehicles for information transfer. Cultural studies approaches—which borrow from both anthropology and literary studies—argue that messages have an effect, but not necessarily in the way intended. For example, they can work to establish hegemony, which upholds political and economic structures that are weighted in favor of some and to the disadvantage of others. This is not an approach limited to cultural studies. Anthropology has employed literary "readings" since Clifford Geertz (1983) developed the idea of cultures as "texts" that could be deciphered. In food policy circles, an emphasis on narrative, or storytelling, has also been advocated by development anthropologists (Peel 1995; Richards 2007).

From popular books such as Michael Pollan's bestsellers[1] to the huge number of academic inquiries describing how identities are shaped through food consumption (see, e.g., Narayan [1995]; Zaman [2010]; Rich [2011]; Fajans [2012]; Pilcher [2012]; Bell and Valentine [2013]; Garth [2013]; and Cuadra [2013]), studying food requires all the analytical tools available, be they from economics, anthropology, sociology, cultural studies, or other disciplines.

Both symbolically and materially, "food is the quintessential test of our collective capacity to fashion sustainable communities" (Morgan et al. 2008, p. 197). Unfortunately, most monographs on "foodways" and identity ignore the fact that food also belongs squarely in what Crang, Dwyer, and Jackson call commodity culture, and studying it requires a "reconnection between the study of cultural representations and the exploration of structures of inequality" (Crang et al. 2003, p. 444). Many economic- and technology-focused analyses of food systems, too, give scant attention to these structures of inequality.

The methodological discussion is important in the context of this volume, which not only celebrates past work in agricultural development economics but also asks important questions about the future of food systems. As Candace Slater points out in her analysis of news coverage of the "Lost Tribe" of the Amazon, there is a policy/interpretive divide on global sustainability questions (Slater 2010). Slater argues that narratives that seem objective are always cultural texts—a view that is extensively developed in the large body of literature on the social construction of science, too (see, e.g., the work of Kuhn [1962], Feyerabend [1975], and Barnes et al. [1996]; as well as Fleck [1979], and Golinski [2005]). Indeed, it is not appropriate to view GM food protests as a problem of science communication. Cultural studies and interpretive approaches can help elucidate new ways to find common ground in the context of a dizzyingly expanding public sphere and extremely dynamic institutional change.

In the fall of 2013, the thorny question of labeling gained unprecedented traction in Connecticut, which passed the first bill in the United States requiring labeling of GM food. Maine has since enacted similar legislation. On its face, labeling is a demand to know what is in a product. But if the GM or GMO label reifies a category of crops and foods that are not actually different (Herring 2007), perhaps it is worth asking how the demand for labeling is used to tell a story about what is new and what is old.

This approach reveals numerous strands of discontent related to modernity that cannot be disentangled using the comb of science literacy.

Consumption as Political Action

In 2013, 18 states in the US were pursuing legislation mandating labeling of food containing genetically modified ingredients. In July 2013, Connecticut became the first state in the US to pass a bill requiring labels on any product containing GMOs. Through purposive snowball sampling[2] that began in my local food co-op [full disclosure: I am an active working member of the co-op], I determined that the central activist organization in this campaign was called GMO Free, and its Connecticut division is GMO Free CT.

I looked at interviews with the founder of GMO Free CT, the websites of related organizations, more than 100 newsletters, and Twitter archives using the archival search service Topsy.

What emerges is that the labeling campaign was driven by concerns about power relations as much as, or more than, any documentable health or environmental risks. In an interview, the leader of GMO Free CT, Tara Cook-Littman, states: "GMO labeling is also a symbol of taking back our government from corporate interests. It's about people taking back power and getting lawmakers to take action in the interests of the people and not corporations" (Cook-Littman 2013).

Indeed, the relationship between corporations and government are a recurring subtext in activist discourse. In 2012, the organization "Just Label It" urged recipients of its mailing list to contact their representatives regarding the 2013 Agriculture Appropriations Bill, in particular, the so-called Farmer Assurance Provision. The campaign director of Just Label It used three bullet points to explain what was at stake:

This policy rider would:

- eliminate fundamental and constitutional safeguards of our judicial review system
- undermine the USDA's oversight and approval process, and weaken protections for consumers
- allow powerful chemical companies to dodge reasonable safeguards against potentially hazardous GE crops

The mailing continues to state that, "without the appropriate supervision and safeguards, large corporations will continue to control our food safety, with a high cost to both our health and environment" (Just Label It [Center for Food Safety], personal communication, June 26, 2012). As this message shows, labeling campaigns were a big tent. In this case, the message of Just Label It was not merely a demand for personal choice; the demand for transparency on the box of food was part of a demand for transparency and accountability more broadly.

The success of the labeling movement in Connecticut was ascribed by the leader of GMO Free CT to the effective creation of a coalition and the use of social media. Indeed, communication tools and messages highlighted common interests while eliding any differences in agendas. They kept it simple, sending another email urging recipients to call Connecticut's senators in Washington and the speaker of the state house, and providing the recipients with all the necessary contact details. The message here was simple, as recipients were urged to "state the following: 'I am calling to ask that you please support our right to know what is in our food.'" GMO Free CT, driven by an entrepreneurial leader whose primary concern was allergens, nonetheless promoted the idea of choice first, and concerns about food safety second.

The message of GMO Free and allied activist organizations was sometimes plain: labeling equals choice. Food safety and environmental risk were downplayed, in favor of the question of choice. In making the individual voter conscious of his or her choice, GMO Free, like other social movements, emphasized the importance of autonomy and democratic processes. As will be discussed later, these were local or national in scope, as most democratic processes are, no matter how global other systems become.

In anti-biotechnology protests, genetically modified organisms play an important symbolic role, representing unequal knowledge distribution and economic power in the global food system, even though such a system is only partially theorized by the public (Huey 2005a). The importance of recognizing this symbolic role of biotechnology cannot be overstated, yet many scientists appear to shake their heads in wonder that anybody could be opposed to something when no health risks have been demonstrated. Many agricultural research scientists would agree with science blogger Kevin Bonham's (2013) analogy that "you don't blame crop dusting on airplanes," and his call for better education of the public so that they may grasp the scientific facts of biotechnology. Bonham, rare for a science writer, brings in a wider definition of "risk":

> Yes, market forces have spoken, but I think a lot of the concern (a concern I share) is that there aren't sufficient regulations in place (or at least, enforcement of those regulations) to prevent really terrible outcomes. It's easy to see how many actors all working in their own self interest could cause serious problems w/r/t food security, the environment etc. (Bonham 2013, #comment-477)

While the assertion of "terrible outcomes" is subject to empirical risk assessment, and the question of what regulations can and cannot accomplish is up for debate, the main thrust of this post is the lack of coordination and transparency inherent in "actors all working in their own self interest."

The observation has been made that democratic control, and not the rearrangement of DNA, is perceived as the main risk of biotechnology (Lassen et al. 2002). However, it is important to take this one step further and observe that democracy and accountability are two distinct phenomena (Fox 2007). Labeling campaigns may focus on securing democratic rights (choice), but underlying the campaigns is a demand for accountability. The desire for strengthened regulations is one indication of this. At the same time, activists assert that political institutions are corrupted by vested interests that spend billions of dollars to lobby legislators. Perhaps this helps explain why these concerns are played out in the sphere of food consumption. If the regulatory system is portrayed as being in the pockets of the biotechnology industry, then the only influence individuals have is *qua* consumers.

Consumers are the warriors, supermarkets the battlefield, and choice (operationalized as labeling) an indispensable weapon. This may be a uniquely American approach dating back to pre-Revolutionary War colonists banding together as consumers against British goods and economic domination (Breen 2005). Indeed, it appears that political "food fights," at least in the US, primarily target the consumption arena, even though the history of anti-biotech movements shows that the movement targets GM technology, including research, as a whole (Frewer et al. 1997; Thackray 1998; Purdue 2000; Bauer and Gaskell 2002). Whereas in other countries activists might seek moratoria on biotechnology research—for example, working through the political system to influence the allocation of funding to such research—the current emphasis on labeling, at least in the United States, strongly suggests that activists expect more success as consumers than as citizens. The sentiment is captured well in the following post:

> Monsanto may be able to screw up elections, but it can't stop me from voting with my dollars. (Silenus7 posting on Bonham 2013, #comment-545. <http://blogs. scientificamerican.com/food-matters/2013/11/11/gmo-labeling-debate-follow-up/#comment-545>)

To be sure, pursuing labeling laws requires political action. But once the laws are in place, the story goes that the rest will be determined at the checkout counter. But does (democratic) choice lead to accountability?

Because accountability is the real goal, the choice frame is almost always accompanied by a corporate depredations frame.[3] Naturally, one might ask if the choice and corporate depredations frames reflect genuine concern, or whether they were taken up as a kind of deliberate strategy, based upon market testing showing that these arguments hold up better than health risk arguments. That is a question for further research. But the extent to which the corporate depredations frame is present in anti-biotechnology messaging—indeed dominates it—is interesting. It is inconclusive whether labeling campaigners themselves are driven by unease with the distribution of power more than by concerns about health risks, but the storytelling of their campaigns certainly is. Moreover, the movement coalesces around the question of power.

In Connecticut, the labeling campaign gained traction from a farmer interest group, which also employed the corporate depredations frame. Farmers especially were an important interest group in this issue, on both sides. NOFA, the Northeast Organic Farming Association, recruited farmers to a rally at the Hartford Capitol, encouraging them to "bring a farm sign" (NOFA email, May 20, 2013), demonstrating savoir faire with regard to media practices. As with the consumer-oriented labeling movement, NOFA used the negative history of corporations to rally their supporters. The supporters were told:

You should be at this rally if you have concerns about putting our food supply in the hands of the folks who brought us PCBs, Agent Orange, Astroturf, Roundup, lead in gasoline, and CFCs. (This labeling legislation is an important step in fighting the money and power that Monsanto and Dupont wield to keep us ignorant).

The email continues to state that, "... you don't need to attend this rally if you don't care about the corporate takeover of the food system" (NOFA, email communication, May 20, 2013).

The broader coalition consisted primarily of the Northeast Organic Farmers Association of Connecticut, Sierra Club, Food Democracy Now, the Institute for Responsible Technology, Organic Consumers Association, Alliance for Natural Health, and Center for Food Safety. Also called to participate in this coalition were chefs and restaurateurs. They were asked by NOFA to bring food samples, because there would be tables and tablecloths set up outside the Capitol. Chefs and restaurateurs were told that "even if you cannot bring food to taste, let's all be there in solidarity (in our chef whites) to take back control of our ingredients from Big Food!" (NOFA, email communication, May 20, 2013). Interest groups in other parts of the country were also part of the network. The Farm-to-Consumer Legal Defense Fund, which states its purpose as defending "... the rights and broaden[ing] the freedoms of family farms and artisan food producers while protecting consumer access to raw milk and nutrient-dense foods" <http://www.farmtoconsumer.org/mission-statement.html>, and which is based in the Midwest, shared its mailing list by forwarding an announcement about Occupy Monsanto, the two-day event at Monsanto headquarters (see <http://occupy-monsanto.com/occupy-monsanto-gmo-free-midwest/>).

The Boundaries of Concern

Did this apparent preoccupation with "big food" imply an awareness of the global food system, with its diverse stakeholders? What were the boundaries of the non-local awareness? A look at another labeling campaign offers some clues.

The labeling bill being prepared in Washington State at the same time as the bill in Connecticut (and which ultimately failed in November 2013), also focused on the simple message of the right to know. In a video advertisement sent to Connecticut activists, the Washington group, "YES on 522," focused strictly on the sound bite of the right to know. Visually, however, the b-roll footage focused on apples and salmon, two major exports from Washington State, and one brief sound bite featured a man standing by a fishing boat, stating, "We already label farm-raised fish. If salmon is genetically engineered the label should say so too" ("Yes on 522" 2013).

Given their iconic use in this ad, salmon and apples seem to discursively represent Washingtonian identity. What is certain is that these are huge crops in Washington, but they are not big industries in Connecticut. Yet in the fall of 2013, as the Washington State bill came up for a vote, GMO Free CT encouraged its mailing list members to change their Facebook and Twitter profile pictures to an image they provided, which stated, "Connecticut supports 522." The Washington and NOFA part of the Connecticut movement created what could be called an axis of activism in the labeling campaign, out of a recognition that state-level legislative change would be required if federal change were to be achieved. Thus, in the case of this campaign, the boundary of concern was the United States—not the entire global food system.

Anti-GM activism increasingly uses globalization as the main risk frame (Heller 2001). In my earlier work, I noted that elements of globalization, food safety, and environment are ever more tightly bound together, discursively (Huey 2005a). Now it appears as though the "submerged networks" (Melucci 1989), which existed separately on each of these topics, may have been precursors to a new social movement centered not only on participation but also on accountability. The dynamics of globalization have exacerbated the difficulties of participation and accountability, but the role of the consumer in stoking political action is as old as the American Revolution (Breen 2005). An important question is whether the focus on consumption, as a center of political action, encourages or inhibits solutions to the problem of global food insecurity.

Perhaps social media (and digital media, more broadly), have created the conditions for broadening the sphere of concern, as the Washington–Connecticut axis of activism, described above, suggests. At least one study of website linking patterns, however, suggests that organizations do not exploit the promise of digital media to expand the sphere of concern to populations outside the political realm of influence (Huey 2005b). Indeed, there is a disparity between global rhetoric and local engagement in civil society. The "globals" don't go local, and the locals don't go global. In anti-GM campaigns, the real farmer or consumer in other parts of the world rarely appears as anything but a shadow of concern—even when concepts referring to farmers in distant poor countries are taken up, as in the following use, by NOFA, of Via Campesina's idea of "food sovereignty" in their communications:

> Food sovereignty is a rapidly emerging hot topic globally. On May 25, tens of thousands of activists around the world will "March Against Monsanto." Marches are planned on six continents, in 36 countries, totaling events in over 250 cities, and in the US, events are slated to occur simultaneously at 11 a.m. Pacific in 47 states. (NOFA, email communication, May 20, 2013)

Any sense of a global food system, as well as the arguments for considering consumers and producers in other parts of the food system, are conspicuously missing in anti-GM campaigns, with one exception: discourse about Monsanto's domination. For example, GMO-Free Midwest, organizers of the 2012 Occupy Monsanto day, promised that the event would offer education about, among other things, "the use of GMOs to dominate the global food production" (GMO-Free Midwest 2012). If there is global solidarity in new food movements, it appears to be solidarity against Monsanto. It does not matter that Monsanto is not the entity accountable to label food; it nonetheless figured prominently in the food labeling campaign. Why is this so? Perhaps it is because Monsanto, with its tens of millions of dollars spent to advertise against labeling bills and propositions, continues to provide a convenient antagonist in this drama.

Knowledge and Accountability

The concept of agricultural deskilling (Stone 2007) has currency in the development episteme, although there is disagreement on whether, where, or when transgenic crops contribute to deskilling. Despite this disagreement on the particulars, the concept of deskilling is relevant to rich countries, and specifically, to consumers; consumer movements for labeling resist the unintelligibility of food biotechnology (Huey 2005a). The plot of the GM food story is that not only are consumers at the mercy of a multinational, unaccountable conglomerate, but they are also at the mercy of unintelligible forms of knowledge. Biotechnology is discursively set up as abstract, remote, and vested, in contrast to farmers' knowledge (specific, local, and diverse), or consumers' knowledge (autonomous). Genetic engineering, like any advanced technology, sharpens the divide between insiders and outsiders on the basis of comprehension. The social and practical consequences of the "concentration of knowledge in biotechnology" (Lewontin 2000) spurs labeling campaigners. "Why should we as the consumer need an advanced degree in identifying GMOs?" asked Tara Cook-Littman, in testimony given to the general assembly of the CT state legislature in 2012 (Connecticut General Assembly 2012).

Thompson's observation that the consumer "… is likely to be much more capable of assessing evidence on whether the insiders are forthright and well intentioned than on whether they are knowledgeable" (Thompson 2007, p. 230) is supported by decades of empirical communications research into social influence and attitude formation. When critics of labeling laws claim that labeling will simply add confusion or even worsen the public's misunderstanding of genetic engineering, they fail to understand that labels may have the benefit of contributing to the perception that food manufacturers are "forthright and well-intentioned." Moreover, they fail to see labeling as a rational attempt to address significant information asymmetries not only regarding biotechnology (von Braun and Mengistu 2007), but also the endeavors of corporations, governments, and international agencies.

Because of these asymmetries, aretaic ethics[4] are a key concern when it comes to food (Thompson 2007), and they permeate contemporary food movements. In an interesting twist, when Monsanto introduced its sweet corn in 2012, Food & Water Watch began a campaign focused not on labeling, but rather on pressuring Walmart to reject the corn. Walmart, as is well-known by now, has tremendous market sway on everything from prices to content (as in music, for instance). Food & Water Watch found its political pressure point on the market jugular, exploiting the PR chink in the corporate armor that makes direct-to-consumer retailers more vulnerable than a business-to-business company such as Monsanto, which has proved itself impervious to such strategies precisely because its products go through several middlemen before reaching the consumer, dissipating the force of leverage available. Thus, the introduction of genetically engineered sweet corn for human consumption provided an unusual opportunity for activists. Indeed, Walmart and Monsanto were cast as a celebrity love match, as "Walsanto," in a campaign designed to drive traffic to Food &Water Watch's social media platforms (see <http://www.foodandwaterwatch.org/food/walsanto/>).

Surely this is a stunning example of aretaic ethics at work in the food wars (Thompson 2007). Thompson's observation that the consumer "… is likely to be much more capable of assessing evidence on whether the insiders are forthright and well intentioned than on whether they are knowledgeable" (Thompson 2007, p. 230) is also supported by political communications research (see, for example, Downs [1957]; Popkin [1993]) and echoes Aristotle's observation that, "we believe good men more readily and fully than others; this is true generally whatever the question is, and absolutely true where exact certainty is impossible and opinions are divided" (Aristotle, trans. 1984, I, p. 1356a).

In another example (see <http://www.cornucopia.org/2012/08/prop37>), one nationally influential food co-op produced a poster with the Cornucopia Institute that they distributed to all co-ops on their mailing list. The poster lists food companies either as "organic heroes" or "corporate charlatans"—all based on whether or not the company in question was supporting the 2012 California Proposition 37, a ballot initiative for mandatory labeling of genetically-engineered food (Cornucopia Institute 2012).

Like the attempted shaming of Walmart, this effort attempts to shame any companies that donated to advertising against Proposition 37, but this message adds another twist. In order to make the honor roll of organic heroes, a company had to actively support Proposition 37 in favor of labeling. In other words, organic food manufacturers could not be content with producing GM-free food; rather, they were expected to enter into the political fray around labeling—and their ethics were questioned if they did not. The creator of the graphic explained that:

> The organic industry, and cooperatives, inextricably married, have always been values-based movements. The fact that many cooperatives, and organic companies for that matter, are financially successful is because we have always promoted and maintained an ethical alternative approach to food production and marketing. (Mark Kastel, Cornucopia.org, email communication, September 6, 2012)

In the message above, there is no room for dissent about what it means to be organic, but moreover, there is no room for dissent on the topic of labeling—a very hard stance indeed, given the lack of discussion about the scientific evidence and the potential merits of employing transgenic technology in some scenarios.

This kind of messaging does not appear to fit into the paradigm that casts opponents to transgenics as deficient in their understanding of science or confused about the difference between risk and uncertainty. The examples here suggest that, rather than focusing on science and scientific risk communication, development organizations and researchers would do well to consider the role of fairness judgments, including the growing social psychology literature on the role of fairness judgments in situations of uncertainty (Van den Bos and Lind 2002), especially in problems associated with social interdependence and socially based identity processes (e.g., Kelley and Thibaut [1978]; Tyler and Lind [1992]; Lind [2001]), a category of "problem" into which food certainly falls.[5]

Discussion

While science-centered rhetoric emphasizes universality, movements to label GM food embrace the rhetoric of particularity and contingency—and work within national political structures—as demonstrated by the Connecticut and Washington labeling campaigns. In movement discourse, ethical food production goes beyond the science, to changing the business models and power of Monsanto, Walmart, and other large corporations, whose business practices are portrayed as unaccountable to the public. Labeling functions as a way to mitigate the perception of information asymmetries and unfairness. As such, it falls in the realm of governance, not science.

The ethics of labeling cannot be evaluated on the basis of scientific risk assessment. Pinstrup-Andersen and Sandøe (2007a) argue that ethics can bring out the assumptions in policy options. Yet "ethics" cannot be used as a general term describing externalities. To use ethics successfully requires entering into the "other's" ethics. To be sure, movements to place moratoria on research, and other cultural trends toward putting the brakes on technology, raise serious ethical dilemmas. In the context of acute malnutrition, hunger, and starvation in the world, it seems incredibly amoral to exhort slowness. The question is passionately posed as some version of "would you let people die while the world catches up to what we already know?" If indeed "trusted knowledge" derives from "slow, deliberate accumulation of environmental and social learning" (Scoones 2007, p. 93), then there is a terrible impasse, and one that is exemplified by the explosive GMO controversy. Globalization has brought new channels of diffusion and a new public sphere. For this reason, the consumer in wealthy countries must enter into any analysis of food systems. Unfortunately, critics view the anti-GM movement through a narrow lens, seeing activists as either scientifically illiterate or as Luddites.[6]

As labeling campaigns suggest, it is critical to devote attention to increased transparency of scientific research and to social and market innovations. Researchers in agricultural development organizations have huge political capital and credibility. Yet there is almost complete silence from them on the question of patents, ecological "lumping" in the form of monoculture, and whether food production can be sustainably pursued side-by-side with the exigencies of quarterly profit statements to shareholders.

Calling out opponents of transgenic agriculture as Luddites, or romantics, or urban delusionals, or residents of rich countries who therefore should have nothing to say about it—does nothing to usher in the "intuitive complementarity" (Herring 2007, p. 24) between ecologically dressed agriculture, including organics, and new methods of crop breeding, including transgenics. Though driven by risk perception that appears at odds with science, food-related social (or consumer) movements should be considered allies of international food research organizations and be included in their "epistemic communities" (Haas 1992). Activism on behalf of greater transparency of channels of financing, production, and distribution can only benefit the cause of hunger and poverty alleviation. Greater attention to these issues by influential development researchers would go a long way toward engaging consumer and farmer activists in rich countries on behalf of technologically inclusive sustainable agricultural development in poor countries.

Notes

1. See, e.g., *The Omnivore's Dilemma* (2006); *In Defense of Food: An Eater's Manifesto* (2008); and *Cooked* (2013). Pollan's essays and interviews are frequently published in influential outlets, including, for example, *The New York Times*, National Public Radio (NPR), the radio program *Democracy Now,* and on the television program *Bill Moyers Journal* on Public Broadcasting Service (PBS).

2. Snowball sampling is an ethnographic method that begins with a small pool of participants (informants) who provide additional participants in their networks who themselves provide additional participants that may be eligible for study. It is sometimes called "chain sampling" or "chain-referral sampling."

3. In mass communications research, one concept of "framing," first developed by Erving Goffman (1974), is used to describe narrative elements that emphasize a given interpretation of events while excluding competing interpretations (for research on the framing of controversial social issues, see, e.g., Gamson and Modigliani [1987]). A different strand, equivalence framing theory, best known from the work of Kahneman et al. (1982) on heuristics and biases in decision-making, relates to variations in how the same information (stimulus) is presented, and the cognitive processes and choices that result.

4. Aretaic ethics are also known as virtue ethics. As applied to food production and food systems, aretaic ethics might interpret production and consumption choices as indicative of moral character.

5. Although the organic food industry is becoming big business, the story told about it remains that it is the ethical alternative to big food. If the campaign for labeling is a call for greater transparency of markets and supply chains, then organic food is positioned as one area of transparency. The consumer of locally produced, GMO-free food is posited as a re-embedded bulwark (Starr 2010) against the food corporation's "ability to partition and distantiate itself from the natural and organic geographies for which it is responsible" (Morgan et al. 2008, p. 69): i.e., a fairness judgment.

6. The instructive irony of this term is, of course, that the Luddites of the late 18th century destroyed large factory machines, but not smaller ones. The mill workers were not against technology, but rather the deployment of capitalism (Hobsbawm 1952) at the expense of labor. It is these questions of fairness and accountability that are often ignored in the heat of defending new agricultural technologies.

References

Aristotle. 1984. "Rhetoric." Translated by W. Rhys Roberts. In *The Rhetoric and the Poetics of Aristotle,* Modern Library College Edition. New York: Random House.

Barnes, B., D. Bloor, and J. Henry. 1996. *Scientific Knowledge: A Sociological Analysis.* London: Bloomsbury Academic.

Bauer, M., and G. Gaskell, eds. 2002. *Biotechnology: The Making of a Global Controversy.* Cambridge: Cambridge University Press.

Becker, H. 1998. *Tricks of the Trade: How to Think about Your Research While You're Doing It.* Chicago: University of Chicago Press.

Bell, D., and G. Valentine. 2013. *Consuming Geographies: We Are Where We Eat.* New York: Taylor and Francis.

Bonham, Kevin. 2013. "GMO Labeling Debate Follow-Up." Food Matters Blog. *Scientific American,* November 11, 2013. <http://blogs.scientificamerican.com/food-matters/2013/11/11/gmo-labeling-debate-follow-up/>.

Breen, T. H. 2005. *The Marketplace of Revolution: How Consumer Politics Shaped American Independence.* Oxford: Oxford University Press.

Connecticut General Assembly. 2012. Testimony for GMO Labeling. <http://www.cga.ct.gov/2012/ENVdata/Tmy/2012HB-05117-R000222-Tara%20Cook-Littman-TMY.PDF>.

Cook-Littman, Tara. 2013. "How to Pass a State GMO Labeling Bill." <http://www.non-gmoreport.com/.../how-to-pass-state-gmo-labeling-bill.php>.

The Cornucopia Institute. 2012. "Breaking News: Corporations Stab Organic Consumers in the Back—Familiar Brands Funding Attack and Consumers Right to GMO Labeling." August 16, 2012, Updated November 6, 2012. <http://www.cornucopia.org/2012/08/prop37/>.

Crang, P., C. Dwyer, and P. Jackson. 2003. "Transnationalism and the Spaces of Commodity Culture." *Progress in Human Geography* 27 (4): pp. 438–456.

Cuadra, C. M. 2013. *Eating Puerto Rico: A History of Food, Culture, and Identity.* Chapel Hill, NC: University of North Carolina Press.

Downs, A. 1957. *An Economic Theory of Democracy.* New York: Harper Collins.

Fajans, J. 2012. *Brazilian Food: Race, Class and Identity in Regional Cuisines.* London: Berg.

Feyerabend, P. 1975. *Against Method.* London: Verso.

Fleck, L. 1979. *The Genesis and Development of Scientific Fact.* Chicago: University of Chicago Press.

Food & Water Watch. 2012. "Walsanto—Follow the Love Affair." <http://www.foodandwaterwatch.org/food/walsanto/>.

Fox, J. 2007. *Accountability Politics: Power and Voice in Rural Mexico.* Oxford: Oxford University Press.

Frewer, J., C. Howard, and R. Shepherd. 1997. "Public Concerns in the United Kingdom about General and Specific Applications of Genetic Engineering: Risk, Benefit and Ethics." *Science, Technology and Human Values* 22 (1): pp. 98–124.

Gamson, W. A. and Modigliani, A. 1987. "The Changing Culture of Affirmative Action." In *Research in Political Sociology, 3,* edited by R. G. Braungart, and M. M. Braungart, pp. 137–177. Greenwich, CT: JAI Press.

Garth, H. 2013. *Food and Identity in the Caribbean.* London: Bloomsbury.

Geertz, C. 1983. *Local Knowledge: Further Essays in Interpretive Anthropology.* New York: Basic Books.

Glaser, B., and A. Strauss. 1967. *The Discovery of Grounded Theory: Strategies for Qualitative Research.* New York: Aldine de Gruyter.

GMO-Free Midwest. 2012. Occupy Monsanto Flyer. <http://occupy-monsanto.com/occupy-monsanto-gmo-free-midwest/>.

Goffman, E. 1974. *Frame Analysis: An Essay on the Organization of Experience.* New York: Harper and Row.

Golinski, J. 2005. *Making Natural Knowledge: Constructivism and the History of Science.* Chicago: University of Chicago Press.

Haas, P. 1992. "Epistemic Communities and International Policy Coordination." *International Organization* 46 (1): pp. 1–35.

Heller, C. 2001. "From Risk to Globalizations: Discursive Shifts in the French Debate About GMOs." *Medical Anthropology Quarterly* 15 (1): pp. 25–28.

Herring, R. 2007. "The Genomics Revolution and Development Studies: Science, Poverty and Politics." *Journal of Development Studies* 43 (1): pp. 1–30.

Hobsbawm, E. J. 1952. "The Machine Breakers." *Past and Present* 1 (1): pp. 57–70.

Huey, T. 2005a. *The Legitimization of Knowledge in Discourse About Genetically Modified Food*. Dissertation. Ann Arbor, MI: ProQuest/UMI.

Huey, T. 2005b. "Thinking Globally, Eating Locally: Website Linking and the Performance of Solidarity in Global and Local Food Movements." *Social Movement Studies* 4 (2): pp. 123–137.

Juanillo, N. 2001. "The Risks and Benefits of Agricultural Biotechnology: Can Scientific and Public Talk Meet?" *American Behavioral Scientist* 44 (8): pp. 1246–1266.

Kahneman, D., P. Slovic, and A. Tversky, eds. 1982. *Judgment under Uncertainty: Heuristics and Biases*. New York: Cambridge University Press.

Kelley, H. H., and J. W. Thibaut. 1978. *Interpersonal Relations: A Theory of Interdependence*. New York: Wiley.

Kuhn, Thomas. 1962. *The Structure of Scientific Revolutions*. Chicago: University of Chicago Press.

Lassen, J., K. H. Madsen, and P. Sandøe. 2002. "Ethics and Genetic Engineering: Lessons to be Learned from GM Foods." *Bioprocess Biosystems Engineering* 24 (5): pp. 263–271.

Lewontin, R. 2000. *It Ain't Necessarily So: the Dream of the Human Genome and Other Illusions*. New York: New York Review of Books.

Lind, E. A. 2001. "Fairness Heuristic Theory: Justice Judgments as Pivotal Cognitions in Organizational Relations." *Advances in Organizational Justice*, edited by Jerald Greenberg and Russell Cropanzano, pp. 56–88. Stanford, CA: Stanford University Press.

Melucci, A. 1989. *Nomads of the Present: Social Movements and Individual Needs in Contemporary Society*. London: Hutchinson.

Morgan, K., T. Marsden, and J. Murdoch. 2008. *Worlds of Food: Place, Power, and Provenance in the Food Chain*. Oxford: Oxford University Press.

Narayan, U. 1995. "Eating Cultures: Incorporation, Identity and Indian Food." *Social Identities* 1 (1), pp. 63–86.

Peel, J. D. Y. 1995. "For Who Hath Despised the Day of Small Things? Missionary Narratives and Historical Anthropology." *Comparative Studies in Society and History* 37 (3): pp. 581–607.

Pilcher, J. 2012. *Planet Taco: A Global History of Mexican Food*. Oxford: Oxford University Press.

Pinstrup-Andersen, P., and P. Sandøe. 2007a. "Introduction and Summary." In *Ethics, Hunger and Globalization: In Search of Appropriate Policies*, edited by P. Pinstrup-Andersen, and P. Sandøe, pp. 1–13. Dordrecht: Springer.

Pinstrup-Andersen, P., and P. Sandøe, eds. 2007b. *Ethics, Hunger and Globalization: In Search of Appropriate Policies*. Dordrecht: Springer.

Popkin, S. I. 1993. "Information Shortcuts and the Reasoning Voter." In *Information, Participation, and Choice: An Economic Theory of Democracy in Perspective*, edited by Bernard Grofman, Chap. 1, pp. 17–35. Ann Arbor, MI: University of Michigan Press.

Purdue, D. A. 2000. *Anti-GenetiX: The Emergence of the Anti-GM Movement*. Aldershot: Ashgate.

Rich, R. 2011. *Bourgeois Consumption: Food, Space and Identity in London and Paris, 1850–1914*. Manchester: Manchester University Press.

Richards, P. 2007. "How Does Participation Work? Deliberation and Performance in African Food Security." *IDS Bulletin* 38 (5): pp. 21–35.

Scoones, I. 2007. Comments to Stone, G. D., "Agricultural Deskilling and the Spread of Genetically Modified Cotton in Warangal." *Current Anthropology* 48(1): pp. 67–99.

Slater, Candace. 2010. "Metaphors and Myths in News Reports of an Amazonian 'Lost Tribe': Society, Environment and Literary Analysis." In *Environmental Social Sciences: Methods and Research Design*, edited by I. S. Vaccaro, E. A. Smith, and S. Aswani, pp. 157–187. Cambridge: Cambridge University Press.

Starr, A. 2010. "Local Food: A Social Movement?" *Cultural Studies <-> Critical Methodologies* 10 (6): pp. 479–490.

Stone, Glenn Davis. 2007. "Agricultural Deskilling and the Spread of Genetically Modified Cotton in Warangal." *Current Anthropology* 48 (1): pp. 67–99.

Thackray, A., ed. 1998. *Private Science: Biotechnology and the Rise of the Molecular Sciences*. Philadelphia: University of Pennsylvania Press.

Thompson, P. 2007. "Ethics, Hunger, and the Case for Genetically Modified (GM) Crops." In *Ethics, Hunger and Globalization: In Search of Appropriate Policies*, edited by P. Pinstrup-Andersen, and P. Sandøe, pp. 215–235. Dordrecht: Springer.

Tyler, R., and E. A. Lind. 1992. "A Relational Model of Authority in Groups." *Advances in Experimental Social Psychology* 25: pp. 115–191.

Van den Bos, K., and E. A. Lind. 2002. "Uncertainty Management by Means of Fairness Judgments." *Advances in Experimental Social Psychology* 34: pp. 1–60.

von Braun, J., and T. Mengistu. 2007. "On the Ethics and Economics of Changing Behavior." In *Ethics, Hunger and Globalization: In Search of Appropriate Policies*, edited by P. Pinstrup-Andersen, and P. Sandøe, pp. 181–200. Dordrecht: Springer.

Yes on 522. 2013. "Washingtonians." Official Campaign Advertisement (Video). <https://www.youtube.com/watch?v=0lPFkesAKRU>.

Zaman, T. 2010. *Food, Identity and Symbolic Metaphors in the Bengali-Canadian Community*. Saarbrücken: Lambert Academic Publishing.

12

Population Increases and Agricultural Productivity

Barbara Boyle Torrey and E. Fuller Torrey, MD

Introduction

The race between agricultural productivity and population increases began in the Middle East approximately 11,000 years ago. Agriculture made the supply of food more plentiful and secure; it also increased the demand for food by increasing the fertility rates of the Neolithic farmers. On the other hand, mortality rates later began to increase because of zoonotic and other infectious diseases associated with growing human settlements and the domestication of animals. Though agriculture had mixed influences on Neolithic population dynamics—increased fertility, increased mortality, and increased settlement—the net effect led inexorably to an increasing world population.

Agriculture caused the earliest demographic transition; industrialization later caused another wave of transitions. In the 19th century, fertility and mortality rates in industrializing countries began to fall, and today the rates have stabilized at very low rates. It was only in the 1960s that the demographic transition began in the non-industrial countries. These transitions were unfolding in societies that had a much larger population base than the initial Neolithic or even industrial societies. And, therefore, the race between agriculture and people in the developing countries has been understandably most intense. The Green Revolution after World War II improved agriculture in many developing countries, so that less than 20 percent of people around the world today have insufficient food (FAO 2013). Many of these people, however, are concentrated in sub-Saharan Africa, where more than 31 percent have inadequate food today. Therefore, although the race between increasing population size and agricultural productivity began in the Middle East 11 millennia ago, it is a race that is still being run in Africa today.

This chapter will briefly describe the earliest demographic transition in the Neolithic era; it will then describe the later transitions in the 19th and 20th centuries. It will concentrate on describing the varieties of sub-Saharan Africa's demographic transitions and the stall in a number of them. This chapter does not proscribe solutions to the demographic stall, but it does note several implications of an incomplete transition and why future efforts to address hunger and malnutrition must focus on Africa.

The Agricultural Revolution and the Neolithic Population Transition

The shift from foraging to farming began in the Neolithic Age in Iran's Zagros Mountains about the same time as it began in Jericho, northern Syria, and southeastern Turkey (Willcox 2013). Anthropological research suggests that the transition to agriculture was a result of local population pressures, technological innovations, and climate changes (Rosenberg 1998). Recent research has also shown that the transition to agriculture had important effects on Neolithic population dynamics.

Analyses of 133 ancient cemeteries suggest that the early agricultural societies significantly increased their population fertility relative to foraging societies (Bocquet-Appel 2002, 2011). This was because the agricultural transition resulted in an increased per capita consumption of high-calorie grains (such as wheat, lentils, and maize) and high-protein milk from domesticated animals (Pennington 1996). The richer food increased the energy balance of women of reproductive age, thereby shortening their birth intervals and increasing their fertility rates. The result was an estimated increase of 2 children per woman in agricultural groups relative to the previous foraging groups in the same area. This is the same initial phenomenon that occurs today when the nutrition of undernourished women improves (Martorell 1995).

The increase in fertility rates leveled off about 1,000 years after the introduction of agriculture at a time when mortality rates were increasing (Bocquet-Appel 2011). The increased consumption of carbohydrates, which humans metabolize into sugars, led to increases in dental caries and other chronic diseases. In addition, the increased density of the agricultural settlements created reservoirs that both maintained and spread infectious diseases (Larsen 2006).

Of course, humans were never free from infectious diseases. These ancient diseases, now called heirloom infections, were caused by microbes that were passed from our primate ancestors to early hominids. If the Garden of Eden existed, Adam may have had herpes cold sores, Eve may have had hepatitis, the mosquitoes circling around them may have been carrying the malaria parasite, and the snake was almost certainly carrying salmonella bacteria. Each animal, including humans, harbor their own microbes. Therefore,

Table 12.1. Illustrative population estimates from the Neolithic period to the present

	Population (in millions)	Births per 1,000	Births between benchmarks (in billions)
8,000 BC	5	80	1.1
1 AD	300	80	48
1200	450	60	26.6
1650	500	60	12.8
1750	795	50	3.2
1850	1,300	40	4
1900	1,700	40	2.9
1950	2,500	31–38	3.4
1995	5,800	31	5.4
2011	7,000	23	2.1

Source: Based on a more detailed table from Haub (2011).

when hominids began hunting animals, the animals' microbes began hunting the hominids. Most microbes are harmless to other species. But some are not and can cause disease and death in humans (Torrey and Yolken 2005).

The domestication of animals in the Middle East during the Neolithic period also led to a new range of infectious zoonotic diseases in the farmers. Domesticated cows gave us rhinoviruses, which still cause our common cold, and measles. Cows and goats gave us tuberculosis; ticks gave us African spotted fever. And sheep are the leading animal candidate for the origin of human *Helicobacter pylori*, which causes stomach ulcers (Torrey 2005). Today over 60 percent of the microbes that cause human diseases come from animals. If we consider all the microbes that came originally from animals and continued to evolve in humans, then at least three-quarters of all human infections today are zoonotic.

The increase in mortality in Neolithic farmers followed the increase in fertility closely, but fertility increased a little faster (Bocquet-Appel 2002). The growth rate over the period from 10,000 years ago to 2,000 years ago is estimated to be only 0.05 percent a year (Haub 2011). People continued to settle in villages, and with larger settlements came irrigation and increases in food. And increases in food, in turn, supported the small but inexorably growing population. Eight thousand years later the world's population had increased 60-fold to 300 million and was gaining momentum. See Table 12.1.

The Industrial Revolution and the Later Demographic Transitions

It took all of human history to get to the first billion people by 1800. And just as agriculture had caused the earliest demographic transition in the Neolithic era, industrialization and urbanization of the 19th and 20th centuries caused the later transitions. In the countries that were industrializing in the 19th century, there were improvements in both food supply and in public health that caused the death rates to drop. Fertility rates then began to decline with higher child survival rates, and the improving status of women. For example, US birth rates declined from 55 per 1,000 women (of reproductive age) in 1820 to 32.3 in 1900. By 1940, the birth rate had reached 19.4 (US Bureau of the Census 1975). By and large, these early transitions had been confined to industrializing nations. It was only in the 1960s that the transition from high birth and death rates to lower rates began in the developing countries.

Despite the rapid drop in the birth rates in the 19th and 20th centuries, the absolute numbers of people kept increasing rapidly. At the beginning of the Industrial Revolution, Thomas Malthus sounded an alarm about the future population disaster (Malthus 1798). Despite his warning, the world's population grew to 2 billion in just 130 years. And it took only another 30 years for world population to add the next billion. Although many people starved between Malthus' first warning and 1960, the vast majority of people survived to reproductive age and continued having children.

Many scholars in the 20th century, who were worried about the limited carrying capacity of the land, echoed Mathus' refrain. Many others, however, realized that, with increasing amounts of experience and scientific inputs, agriculture would not only keep up with population growth, but it could improve the supply of food per capita (Boserup 1965). Despite unprecedented population growth, agricultural production gains from the Green Revolution did mostly keep up with population growth in the developing world. Today much of the world has completed the demographic transition from high birth and death rates to lower rates and has reached or is approaching replacement rate fertility (total fertility rate of the world's population today is now 2.5 children per woman). However, the one continent that has just begun the population transition is Africa, and it now faces the biggest challenge in the struggle between food security and growing populations.

The Future Sub-Saharan African Demographic Transition and Dividend

World hunger is increasingly concentrated in Africa (Watson and Pinstrup-Andersen 2010). Africa also has the least productive agriculture and the highest prevalence of undernutrition in the world (FAO 2006). Although food inadequacy in Africa has declined from 41 percent of the population in 1990–92, it is still too high—at 31 percent—today (FAO 2013). This current food inadequacy problem in Africa is exacerbated by the continent having the highest population growth rates in the world.

Sub-Saharan Africa today has the highest total fertility rates (TFR) in the world, with an average of 5.1 children per woman. Because of its high fertility rates, it also has the highest annual population growth rates anywhere in the world (2.5 percent per year). And, the growth in the next 40 years means that sub-Saharan Africa will more than double its population by 2050 (PRB 2013). Ironically, sub-Saharan Africa likely grows enough food today to supply its current population with its biological caloric requirements; and with the increase in international trade in the last half-century, what food is not available domestically might be available from abroad. The presence of so much undernutrition, however, means that the food is not efficiently distributed, either spatially or temporally. In the next 40 years, the African population will not only increase 150 percent, but it will also be older than the current population and more urban. Older populations require more food than children, and urban populations demand more food than rural ones. Therefore, the demands on agricultural productivity to adequately feed Africa's future population may more than double (Torrey 2010).

Many studies have shown that African farmers can double their yields using current technologies. In order to do so, however, small farmers need better infrastructure, research and development, and improved government institutions and policies (Pinstrup-Andersen 1988, 2010; Pinstrup-Andersen and Schiøle 2000; Pinstrup-Andersen and Pandya-Lorch 2001; Wiebe et al. 2001; Koning and Pinstrup Andersen 2007; Pinstrup-Andersen and Sandøe 2007; and Pinstrup-Andersen and Watson 2011). Although in the last two decades total agricultural factor productivity has increased over 2 percent annually in developing countries, in general, it has been below 1 percent in Africa (Fuglie and Wang 2012).

Some countries have done much better than others who are neighbors with similar climates and conditions. For instance, the estimate of food inadequacy in Rwanda is 38 percent, while in neighboring Burundi it is 77 percent (FAO 2013). In Ethiopia the food inadequacy has been reduced from 78 percent 20 years ago to 44 percent today. During the same period in Eritrea, food adequacy has declined from 82 percent to 72 percent. It will require significantly higher public and private investments, especially in research and development, to increase agricultural productivity. Fortunately, "Africa knows what is needed for food security" (Pinstrup-Andersen 2012).

Current Fertility Trends

The challenge is to increase the supply of food and decrease the future demand for it simultaneously, by slowing population growth rates. The most important way to decrease population growth rates is to reduce total fertility rates. Most African fertility rates began to decline in the 1980s, a generation later than in most other developing countries. But today in sub-Saharan Africa, the number of children per woman is estimated at 5.1, which is 2.5 times higher than what is needed for a stable replacement rate. In fact, there are 31 countries in the world with fertility rates higher than 5 children per woman. Twenty-nine of those countries are in sub-Saharan Africa (UN 2013).

Of course, the fertility trends for sub-Saharan Africa vary by region (UN 2013). For example, Southern Africa began its demographic transition earlier than the rest of sub-Saharan Africa (in the 1960s), and today the region has the lowest average fertility rates on the continent (2.5 children per woman). Eastern Africa, on the other hand, started its transition to lower fertility in the late 1980s, and today it is estimated to have a fertility rate of 4.9. Western Africa started its fertility transition about the same time as Eastern Africa but has not gone as far, with a rate today of 5.6. And Central Africa started its fertility transition in the late 1990s and has the highest fertility rates in sub-Saharan Africa today (5.7).

There is also considerable variation in fertility transitions even within regions and between neighboring countries. The fertility rate in Swaziland is 47 percent higher than in its neighbor South Africa. In Eastern Africa, Rwanda has an estimated fertility rate of 4.6, whereas its neighbor, Burundi has a rate of 6.1. In Central Africa, the Congo has a fertility rate that is 2 children higher than Chad (4.4 vs. 6.3). In Western Africa, Niger has the highest fertility rate of 7.6, while its southern neighbor Benin has a rate of 4.9.

The variation is not only among regions and between neighbors, but it is also within countries. A recent study of 15 sub-Saharan African countries shows that urban–rural differences in malnutrition exist in each of these countries (Fotso 2007). Recently, the differences have narrowed, however, because of the increase in malnutrition in the urban slums. The study also found that people of similar social and economic status (SES) have similar levels of malnutrition, regardless of where they live. Another study of several African countries showed the outcomes of the malnutrition in child mortality rates (Gunther 2012). The highest child mortality rates were found in the rural areas where malnutrition was highest and the SES lowest; it was lowest in the formal settlements in urban areas, and in the informal urban slums, the mortality rate was in between.

Influences on Fertility Rates

There are a number of factors that affect the fertility of African women. Female education, economic development, urbanization, contraception prevalence, ideal family size, and infant mortality are all correlated with decreasing fertility rates around the world, and they are also correlated with each other.

As would be expected, the level of education positively affects the other variables and remains significant after controlling for them (Bongaarts 2010).

Sub-Saharan African countries are different from other developing countries, because at every education level, the ideal number of children is higher than in other countries at the same level of education and same time in the demographic transition (Martin 1995). Even though Africa's ideal number of children was higher than in other parts of the world, education does reduce the African ideal. African countries with a higher level of education in the mid-1970s had an earlier onset of fertility decline. The level of education, however, did not strongly affect the speed of the transition once it had started (Garenne 2012).

Fortunately, female education is increasing in Africa (Lutz 2013). The current average years of schooling in Africa is 5.8 and is projected to be between 9.7 and 11 years by 2050. Africa is also continuing to urbanize, and both trends—increasing education for women and urbanization of the population—will help lower future fertility rates (Garenne 2012). These trends, however, will not be enough to rapidly reach stable populations, given the demographic momentum that already exists in Africa. The United Nations now projects that sub-Saharan African will be still growing strongly at the end of this century (UN 2013).

An Estimated Stall in Fertility Rates

It has taken sub-Saharan Africa two decades to reduce fertility rates from 6.1 to 5.1 children per woman. At that rate of change, it would take 60 more years to reach a replacement rate of 2.1 children per woman. A more concerning trend is that the decline in African fertility rates may have stalled. And in some countries, African fertility may have even started to increase again (Bongaarts and Casterline 2013; UN 2013).

The United Nations publishes country-level population projections every 2 years, which are based on data from demographic surveys, censuses, and other health information. Although these data are better than many economists think, they are considerably less precise than statistics in developed countries. The most important assumptions used for estimating future populations are the estimated current population and the projected future total fertility rate. These assumptions are adjusted every 2 years, based on new data and methodologies.

The *2012 United Nations World Prospects* projections for sub-Saharan Africa showed a slight downward adjustment for the 2010 population, based on recent census and survey information (UN 2013). More concerning, however, was an upward adjustment in the total fertility rate for the year 2010 that was 0.3 children larger than had been previously assumed in the 2010 projections. In 15 African countries with high fertility rates, the estimated average number of children has been adjusted upward by more than 5 percent over 2010 assumptions (Wilmoth 2013). Since two of these countries have the largest populations in Africa, the effect on the future size of the sub-Saharan African population is especially concerning. The 2012 changes in current and future fertility rates increase the previous estimates for future sub-Saharan African population by over 100 million in 2050 and by over 500 million in 2100 population projections. That means that the race to provide adequate food for future populations is now harder than people had thought even 2 years ago. See Table 12.2.

Of course, the changes in fertility assumptions by region are the net effects of changes both up and down. In Southern Africa, which has the lowest fertility rates on the continent, the assumed fertility rate did not change. In Eastern Africa, however, the increase in UN fertility assumptions of 0.3 children per woman is the net result of five countries' fertility assumptions increasing, six remaining the same, and six small countries' assumptions declining. (Rwanda had the largest decline in its TFR estimate between 2010 and 2012, from 5.4 to 5.1).

In Western Africa, the average increase of the fertility rate of 0.2 children is the net result of UN estimates increasing for 10 countries, staying the same for three, and decreasing for two. Central Africa had the biggest increase in the assumed 2010 fertility rate. Between 2010 and 2012, the UN increased their estimated fertility rate by 0.5. All of the Central African countries' estimated rates increased except for the Central African Republic and Equatorial Guinea.

Table 12.2. Sub-Saharan African population and total fertility rate projections UN 2010 and 2012 Prospects medium variant

| | Population (in millions) | | |
	2010	2012	Difference
2010 estimate	856	831	−25
2020	1,088	1,077	−11
2030	1,354	1,368	14
2040	1,647	1,704	57
2050	1,960	2,074	114
2100	3,358	3,816	458
	Total fertility rates		
	Children per woman		
2010–2015	4.78	5.11	0.33
2020–2025	4.13	4.45	0.32
2030–2035	3.58	3.88	0.3
2040–2045	3.16	3.42	0.26
2050–2055	2.85	3.04	0.19

Source: Author's table based on data from UN (2013, 2011).

The Demographic Dividend

One of the implications of a slow or stalled fertility decline in sub-Saharan Africa is that it may compromise the expected future demographic dividend, such as both Asian and Latin American countries experienced after rapid decreases in fertility rates. This dividend refers to the accelerated economic growth that occurs when the ratio of the labor force population to the dependent population (primarily children in developing countries) increases rapidly. This rapid age structure change means that households have fewer dependents at home, can save more of their earnings, and invest more in each one of their children.

These increases in both investments and human capital tend to accelerate economic growth above its long-term trend line, as happened in East Asia. Between 25 to 40 percent of the major economic growth in East Asian countries in the late 20th century may be attributed to their demographic dividend that was precipitated by rapid drops in fertility rates (Bloom 2011).

The demographic dividend does not last forever, because one of the long-term consequences of rapid fertility declines is an aging of the population. Initially, an aging population primarily affects the median age of the labor force population. An aging population, however, eventually increases the number of dependents, which include both children and the elderly. If the economic growth from the demographic dividend is used well, though, the country is likely to be strong enough to manage its new aged dependents in the future.

One of the key factors in the demographic dividend is a rapidly growing labor force. And the labor force age group (aged 15–64 years old) in sub-Saharan African countries is growing faster than in most countries in the world. In fact, Africa's labor force population is likely to be larger than in China or India by 2040 (Olajide 2013). In addition, many of the economies in Africa are growing more rapidly than they have in the past, which is likely to increase the education and training for the rapidly growing labor forces. Indeed, Africa has some of the fastest-growing economies in the world today, even before the full force of the demographic dividend appears.

Despite strong economic growth, the ratio of the labor force-aged population to the younger and older populations, which determines the size of the demographic dividend, is only slowly changing because of the persistently high fertility rates. Experts believe that Africa has not reduced its fertility rates enough to optimize the demographic dividend (Olajide 2013). Even in Ethiopia where there has been a substantial decrease in fertility and an increase in economic growth, the demographic dividend, such as East Asia experienced, is estimated to be more than two decades away (Gribble and

Bremner 2012). In fact, because sub-Saharan Africa has not followed the traditional demographic transition patterns of the rest of the world, it may also not experience the same kind of demographic dividend.

Improvements in Health

One of the demographic areas in which Africa is making good progress is health. Between 1990 and 2010, the African infant mortality rate decreased 31 percent, and maternal mortality rates decreased 44 percent (Olajide 2013). Africa has also made good progress against the mortality rates due to the AIDS epidemic. The epidemic was a stark reminder that zoonotic diseases that increased the mortality rates in the Neolithic period can still have devastating effects on human populations today. Sub-Saharan Africa was the hardest-hit area of the world. Fortunately, development of new medications has made AIDS a chronic disease rather than a deadly one for those who have access to them (Torrey 2005). The UN's projections assume that Africa's mortality rates will continue to decline as healthcare improves and infant and child mortality, in particular, declines.

The reason that improvements in mortality are so important is because historically they have been highly correlated with future decreases in fertility around the world. The ideal family size of African women is less than their ultimate family size because of the unpredictability of high infant and child mortality rates. When the improvements in health, especially reproductive health, and decreases in mortality become dependable, there is likely to be further decreases in ideal number of children and in fertility, as has recently happened in Rwanda.

Conclusion

Sub-Saharan Africa's persistent population growth will complicate future attempts to improve the food sufficiency of the continent. The agricultural sciences have been successful in feeding the nearly 10 billion people who were born in the 20th century. Future research now must be directed toward Africa in the 21st century. Africa's challenge is to improve its agricultural productivity faster than its future rapidly growing population. Sub-Saharan governments have the examples of the other developing countries around the world that are finishing their demographic transitions. And they have the incentive that if they can slow their population increases sufficiently, they can realize their future demographic dividend that will accelerate their growth and development.

References

Bloom, David. 2011. "Seven Billion and Counting." *Science* 333 (6042): pp. 562–569.

Bocquet-Appel, Jean-Pierre, 2002. "Paleoanthropological Traces of a Neolithic Demographic Transition." *Current Anthropology* 43 (4): pp. 637–650.

Bocquet-Appel, Jean-Pierre, 2011. "When the World's Population Took Off: The Springboard of the Neolithic Demographic Transition." *Science* 333 (6042): pp. 560–561.

Bongaarts, John, 2010. "Poverty, Gender, and Youth: The Causes of Educational Differences in Fertility in Sub-Saharan Africa." Working Paper No. 20, Population Council, New York.

Bongaarts, John, and John Casterline. 2013. "Fertility Transition: Is Sub-Saharan Africa Different?" *Population and Development Review* 38 (s1) (Population and Public Policy: Essays in Honor of Paul Demeny): pp. 153–168.

Boserup, E. 1965. *The Condition of Agricultural Growth: The Economics of Agrarian Change under Population Pressure*. Chicago: Aldine Press.

FAO (Food and Agricultural Organization). 2006. *State of Food Insecurity in the World*. Rome: Food and Agricultural Organization of the United Nations.

FAO (Food and Agricultural Organization). 2013. *The State of Food Insecurity in the World*. Rome: Food and Agricultural Organization of the United Nations. Table V7-4 Prevalence of Food Inadequacy. Metadata. <http://www.fao.org/economic/ess/ess-fs/ess-fadata/en/#.VQiHZWTF81Q>.

Fotso, Jean-Christophe. 2007. "Urban–Rural Differentials in Child Malnutrition: Trends and Socioeconomic Correlates in Sub-Saharan Africa." *Health and Place* 13 (1): pp. 205–223.

Fuglie, Keith O., and Sun Ling Wang. 2012. "New Evidence Points to Robust but Uneven Productivity Growth in Global Agriculture." US Department of Agriculture, Economic Research Service. *Amber Waves* 10 (3).

Garenne, Michel. 2012. *Education and Fertility in Sub-Saharan Africa: A Longitudinal Perspective*. DHS Analytical Studies No. 33. Calverton, MD: ICF International.

Gribble, J. N., and J. Bremner. 2012. "Achieving a Demographic Dividend." *Population Reference Bureau Bulletin* 67 (2) (December).

Gunther, Isabel, and Kenneth Harttgen. 2012. "Deadly Cities? Spatial Inequities in Mortality in Sub-Saharan Africa." *Population and Development Review* 38 (3): pp. 469–486.

Haub, Carl, 2011. "How Many People Have Ever Lived on Earth?" <http://www.prb.org/Publications/Articles/2002/HowManyPeopleHaveEverLivedonEarth.aspx>.

Koning, Niek, and Per Pinstrup-Andersen. 2007. *Agricultural Trade Liberalization and the Least Developed Countries*. Dordrecht: Springer.

Larsen, Clark Spencer. 2006. "The Agricultural Revolution as Environmental Catastrophe: Implications for Health and Lifestyle in the Holocene." *Quaternary International* 150 (1): pp. 12–20.

Lutz, Wolfgang, ed. 2013. "Global Human Capital Projections form the Human Core of New IPCC SSP Scenarios." Table 2. *Popnet* Winter 2012/13.

Malthus, Thomas R., 1798. *An Essay on the Principle of Population*. Reprinted in Oxford World Classics. Oxford: Oxford University Press, 1999.

Martin, Teresa Castro. 1995. "Women's Education and Fertility: Results from 26 Demographic and Health Surveys." *Studies in Family Planning* 26 (4): pp. 187–202.

Martorell, R. 1995. "Results and Implications of the INCAP Follow-Up Study." *Journal of Nutrition* 125 (4 Supplement): pp. 1127S–1138S.

Olajide, Ademola, 2013. "Demographic Dividend for Africa's Development Transformation." Presentation at the African Regional Conference on Population and Development Beyond 2014: "Harnessing the Demographic Dividend: The Future We Want for Africa." African Union and United Nations Economic Commission for Africa, September 30–October 4, 2013, Addis Ababa, Ethiopia.

Pennington, Renee L., 1996. "Causes of Early Human Population Growth." *American Journal of Physical Anthropology* 99 (2): pp. 259–274.

Pinstrup-Andersen, Per, ed. 1988. *Food Subsidies in Developing Countries: Costs, Benefits and Policy Options.* Baltimore: Johns Hopkins University Press.

Pinstrup-Andersen, Per, ed. 2010. *The African Food System and its Interaction with Human Health and Nutrition.* Ithaca, NY: Cornell University Press.

Pinstrup-Andersen, Per. 2012. "Africa Knows What is Needed for Food Security." *Business Daily Africa*, posted September 6, 2012. <http://www.businessdailyafrica.com/ Opinion+++Analysis/Africa+knows+what+is+needed+for+food+security/-/539548/ 1498428/-/12ufayh/-/index.html>.

Pinstrup-Andersen, Per, and Rajul Pandya-Lorch, eds. 2001. *The Unfinished Agenda: Perspectives on Overcoming Hunger, Poverty, and Environmental Degradation.* Washington, DC: International Food Policy Research Institute.

Pinstrup-Andersen, Per, and Peter Sandøe, eds. 2007. *Ethics, Hunger and Globalization: In Search of Appropriate Policies.* Dordrecht: Springer.

Pinstrup-Andersen, Per, and Ebbe Schiøler. 2000. *Seeds of Contention: World Hunger and the Global Controversy over GM Crops.* Baltimore and London: Johns Hopkins University Press.

Pinstrup-Andersen, P., and Derrill D. Watson, II. 2011. *Food Policy for Developing Countries: The Role of Government in Global, National, and Local Food Systems.* Ithaca, NY, and London: Cornell University Press.

PRB (Population Reference Bureau). 2013. World Population Data Sheet 2013, Population Reference Bureau, Washington, DC. <http://www.prb.org/Publications/ Datasheets/2013/2013-world-population-data-sheet/data-sheet.aspx>.

Rosenberg, Michael, 1998. "Cheating at Musical Chairs: Territoriality and Sedentism in an Evolutionary Context." *Current Anthropology* 39 (5): pp. 653–681.

Torrey, Barbara Boyle. 2010. "Population Dynamics and Future Food Requirements." In *The African Food System and its Interaction with Human Health and Nutrition,* edited by Per Pinstrup-Andersen, pp. 182–198. Ithaca, NY: Cornell University Press.

Torrey, E. Fuller, and Robert H. Yolken, 2005. *Beasts of the Earth: Animals, Humans and Disease.* New Brunswick, NJ, and London: Rutgers University Press.

UN (United Nations). 2013. *World Population Prospects: The 2012 Revision.* Population Division of the United Nations Department of Economic and Social Affairs of the United Nations Secretariat, New York.

UN (United Nations). 2011. *World Population Prospects: The 2010 Revision*. Population Division of the United Nations Department of Economic and Social Affairs of the United Nations Secretariat, New York.

US Bureau of the Census. 1975. *Historical Statistics of the United States, Colonial Times to 1970*. Bicentennial Edition, Part 1, p. 49. Washington, DC.

Watson, Derrill, II, and Per Pinstrup-Andersen, 2010. "The Nutrition Situation in Sub-Saharan Africa." In *The African Food System and its Interaction with Human Health and Nutrition*, edited by Per Pinstrup-Andersen, pp. 14–33. Ithaca, NY: Cornell University Press.

Wiebe, Keith, Nicole Ballenger, and Per Pinstrup-Andersen, eds. 2001. *Who Will be Fed in the 21st Century? Challenges for Science and Policy*. International Food Policy Research Institute, Economic Research Service of the U.S. Department of Agriculture, and American Agricultural Economics Association. Baltimore: Johns Hopkins Press.

Willcox, George, 2013. "The Roots of Cultivation in Southwestern Asia." *Science* 341 (6141): pp. 39–40.

Wilmoth, John, 2013. Director of the Population Division, UN Department of Economic and Social Affairs, as Quoted in the UN Press Release, June 13, 2013: "World Population Projected to Reach 9.6 billion by 2050 with Most Growth in Developing Regions, Especially Africa—says UN." United Nations, New York.

Part III
Globalization and Political Economy

13

Ending Hunger and Undernutrition by 2025

Accelerating the Pace

Shenggen Fan, Tolulope Olofinbiyi, and Sinafikeh Gemessa

Introduction

Tremendous progress has been made toward the Millennium Development Goals (MDGs), but progress has been largely uneven, both across regions and across goals. Although the global target of halving the proportion of people living in extreme poverty has been achieved, the target of halving the proportion of people who suffer from hunger is not on track. About 805 million people worldwide still suffer from chronic hunger (FAO et al. 2014).

As the 2015 deadline draws close, discussions on how to accelerate progress toward meeting the MDGs and beyond have gained much momentum. The post-2015 development agenda represents a framework for developing the new Sustainable Development Goals (SDGs), which will advance what began with the MDGs. Based on a series of consultations in 2013, the UN Secretary General's High-level Panel of eminent persons on the Post-2015 Development Agenda proposed new goals and targets to guide the agenda.

Building on this initial effort, an intergovernmental Open Working Group on Sustainable Development Goals developed an updated proposal for the SDGs for resolution at the UN General Assembly in September 2014. While progress has been made, there is still a lack of consensus on food security and nutrition goals, and more work is needed before a coherent and holistic post-2015 framework is achieved.

The post-2015 agenda, which puts sustainable development at the center, considers the goal of eliminating extreme poverty to a zero level by 2030 as its top priority. Although this is commendable and ambitious, we argue that the goal of eliminating hunger and undernutrition is equally important and calls for more urgent action. This goal needs to be prioritized correspondingly, and we should aim to achieve it by 2025.[1]

Environmental sustainability is certainly a must on the path to ending hunger and undernutrition, but it is crucial to continuously keep in focus the people whom the SDGs are intended to benefit. The post-2015 agenda should not pursue environmental sustainability goals at the expense of food security and nutrition goals and the well-being of poor and hungry people. Instead, the framework should focus on developing sustainable people-focused goals with clear targets and timelines for ending hunger and undernutrition by 2025.

Hunger and undernutrition should be eliminated for both economic and ethical reasons. It would be difficult to break out of poverty or sustain economic development in countries where large numbers of the population still lack the food security and nutrition needed to lead healthy and productive lives (Black et al. 2013). Research evidence shows that undernutrition, for example, has negative impacts on human capital formation and productivity, thus leading to large global economic losses (Horton and Steckel 2013). In addition to these economic reasons, eliminating hunger and undernutrition should be considered a global ethical task that deserves top priority.

Although ending hunger and undernutrition by 2025 is a huge task, it is not beyond reach. To achieve this goal, governments and donors should allocate sufficient resources and pursue appropriate policies and investments. The experiences of countries such as Brazil, China, Thailand, and Vietnam in reducing hunger and undernutrition suggest that it is realistic to strive for this goal, if the pace of reduction is accelerated. There are several lessons to be learned from the experiences of these countries in charting out pathways to even greater success. As progress is not linear, technological, policy, and institutional innovations to date put us in a better position to spur even greater successes in reducing hunger and undernutrition. It is important to note, however, that achieving the goal may still leave about 5 percent of the population suffering from residual hunger and undernutrition.[2]

The structure of the chapter is as follows. It begins by highlighting evidence on why it pays off to equally prioritize the elimination of hunger and undernutrition. Next, the chapter focuses on the experiences of successful countries to show why the global community should aspire to end hunger and undernutrition by 2025. Further, key lessons that can be learned from the experiences of these countries and others are discussed. It concludes with a discussion of some salient approaches that can provide future directions toward accelerating the pace of hunger and undernutrition reduction.

Ending Hunger and Undernutrition Pays Off

Hunger in this chapter means food intake that is insufficient to meet the dietary energy requirements of an active and healthy life (FAO 2013). Specifically, it refers to the consumption of fewer than about 1,800 kilocalories per day. Hunger can lead to undernutrition, which refers to the outcome of prolonged inadequate intake of macronutrients (such as calories, proteins, and fats) and micronutrients (such as vitamins and minerals). The World Health Organization (WHO) estimated that more than 2 billion people suffer from these vitamin and mineral deficiencies, also known as hidden hunger (WHO 2013a). Vitamin A, iron, iodine, and zinc deficiencies are the most common (Hoddinott et al. 2013a).

Undernutrition usually takes the form of micronutrient deficiencies, child stunting (low height-for-age), child underweight (low weight-for-age), or child wasting (low weight-for-height). Stunting or linear growth failure is the most critical form of undernutrition, which is associated with adverse outcomes related to slow physical and cognitive development (Hoddinott et al. 2013b). It arises due to inhibited skeletal growth and reduced accumulation of muscle mass and fat (Hoddinott et al. 2013a).

Stunting is also linked to negative neurological outcomes. This occurs due to damages to the chemical processes associated with spatial navigation, memory formation, and memory consolidation. A major outcome of neurological damages is low cognitive development with both short- and long-term consequences, such as low schooling attainment and lifetime earning potential (Hoddinott et al. 2013a). Globally, it is estimated that 162 million (or 25 percent) children under 5 years of age are stunted (UNICEF 2013). In sub-Saharan Africa and South Asia, the prevalence of stunting remains particularly high—approximately 38 percent in both regions.

Hunger and undernutrition cause and perpetuate poverty and have detrimental effects on human health (Behrman et al. 2004). Thus, poverty, hunger, and undernutrition are interrelated in a vicious cycle where one leads to the other. To break this cycle, elimination of hunger and undernutrition should be clearly prioritized, as both impose huge social and economic costs.

The costs and burdens of hunger and undernutrition can be felt at individual, household, and societal levels. Growth failure in early life is likely to be passed to the next generation. Women affected by stunting are more likely to have their first child at younger ages, have more children, and live in poor households as adults (Hoddinott et al. 2013a).

Productivity losses and direct healthcare costs caused by hunger and undernutrition also have adverse economy-wide effects. According to the Food and Agricultural Organization of the UN (FAO), these costs are equivalent to

US$1.4–2.1 trillion per year, or 2–3 percent of global GDP (FAO 2013). Horton and Steckel (2013) estimated this loss to be 8 percent of world GDP over the 20th century, but only declining to 6 percent in the first half of the 21st century. Recent country-level cost estimates range from 2 percent of GDP in Egypt and Panama to over 10 percent in Ethiopia and Guatemala (Martínez and Fernández 2008; AU et al. 2013a, 2013b).

The economic returns to eliminating hunger and undernutrition can be very high. Bhutta et al. (2013) estimated that globally it may be possible to reduce of the deaths of children under 5 years of age by 15 percent, with $10 billion a year spent on 10 core nutrition interventions. This is less than 1 percent of the cost of hunger and undernutrition. Country-level evidence also shows large economic returns (Hoddinott et al. 2013b). In India, for example, every dollar spent on interventions to reduce stunting is estimated to generate about US$34 in economic returns. In Ethiopia and Nigeria, the returns are about US$12 and US$27, respectively.

Aspiration to End Hunger and Undernutrition by 2025 is Achievable

Successful country experiences suggest that the global community should aspire to eliminate hunger and undernutrition by 2025. The strategies employed by successful countries such as Brazil, China, Thailand, and Vietnam, as discussed in this chapter, differ and can be broadly classified as agricultural growth-led or social protection and nutrition intervention-led, or a combination of both. In China and Vietnam, for example, success may have primarily been driven by an agricultural growth-led strategy. In Brazil, success may be seen as resulting mainly from a strategy that targeted social protection and nutrition interventions to those in need of it the most. Success in Thailand, on the other hand, has likely been facilitated by a combination of these two main strategies.

Experiences of these countries present other developing nations with lessons and insights, as they design and implement successful context-specific strategies that are targeted effectively to address hunger and undernutrition. In what follows, trends of relevant indicators in countries that had successes in reducing hunger and undernutrition are discussed, in addition to a brief overview of the main elements of the strategies employed (see also Table 13.1).

Agricultural Growth-Led Strategies

CHINA

China is on track to eliminate undernutrition by 2025 and will be close to eliminating hunger if it continues on its current rate of reduction based on

Table 13.1. Undernourishment and child stunting for successful countries by strategies adopted

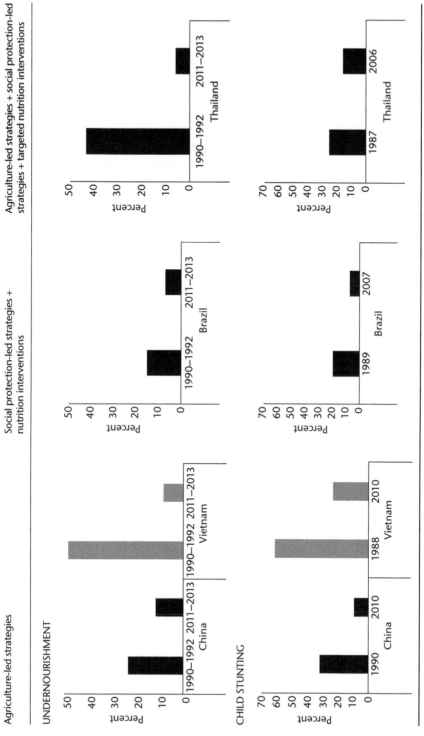

Source: FAO (2013) and World Bank (2013a).

our cutoff point of 5 percent prevalence for both indicators.[3] Between 1990 and 2010, China reduced the prevalence of undernourishment by half from roughly 23 to 11 percent. More impressively, the prevalence of child stunting was reduced by more than two-thirds from 32 to 9 percent between 1987 and 2010.

As Fan et al. (2007) pointed out, China's success was catalyzed by the decollectivization of agriculture, in particular, the introduction of the Household Responsibility System for securing land rights; pro-market reforms and the dismantling of state planning and monopolies; and the implementation of policies that supported human capital development and rural non-farm economic growth. These reforms, which began in the late 1970s, had a strong initial emphasis on agricultural growth—stimulated by improved incentives in smallholder agriculture—and rural development.

These changes led to significantly higher incomes among rural dwellers, where levels of poverty and hunger were initially the highest, and to increased access to food at affordable prices (Ravallion and Chen 2007).[4] In addition, social programs—including interventions in nutrition, health, and family planning—were implemented on a large scale (von Braun et al. 2008). To complement these interventions, investments in education, clean water, and good sanitation were also expanded.

Despite the strong potential of social protection policies to promote inclusive growth, such policies were not at the forefront of China's strategies during the reform period. China could likely have achieved much greater success if well-targeted social protection programs had been launched and scaled up earlier. Instead, enterprise-based social security was the standard in urban areas despite major economic transformation, including rising unemployment and labor mobility (Ravallion 2009). In recent years, however, the government of China launched its main social protection program, the Minimum Livelihood Guarantee Scheme[5] (widely known as *Dibao*).

Overall, careful experimentation was vital for the design, sequencing, and implementation of successful reforms in China (Fan et al. 2007). To facilitate the flow of information for policymaking, China established a strong monitoring and evaluation system, including an effective data collection strategy (von Braun et al. 2008). In addition, the reforms profited from other factors such as good initial conditions in rural infrastructure, agricultural research and extension services, and institutional capacity.

VIETNAM

At the current rate of reduction, Vietnam can eliminate hunger by 2025, but is not likely to eliminate stunting. Between 1990 and 2013, the prevalence of undernourishment fell substantially from approximately 48 to 8 percent. The prevalence of child stunting was also reduced from a very high 61 percent in

1988 to 23 percent in 2010. While the prevalence of child stunting remains high, it can still be eliminated by 2025 if the right policies and strategies are implemented.

Similar to China, early success in Vietnam was likely largely driven by growth in agriculture, complemented by targeted nutrition and health programs (World Bank 2012).[6] In the late 1980s, the government of Vietnam introduced the *Doi Moi* reforms, which consisted of four main elements—equitable land reform; liberalization of agricultural marketing and trade; pragmatic and sequenced liberalization for attracting and benefiting from foreign direct investment; and sustained investment in human development (Vandemoortele and Bird 2011).

The implementation of Resolution 10 in 1988 (recognition that the household is the basic production unit of the rural economy) drastically improved agricultural incentives (World Bank 2012). The 1993 Land Law that was established also allowed for the issuance of land use certificates to all rural households, thereby enabling them to inherit, transfer, exchange, lease, and mortgage land rights (Klump 2007). Both Resolution 10 and the 1993 Land Law played a critical role in enhancing agricultural growth in the 1990s, enabling Vietnam to become one of the major rice-exporting countries. Rapid agricultural growth contributed to higher rural incomes and also to the movement of labor into non-agricultural sectors.

Public expenditure targeted at improving nutrition and health outcomes was also large. A comprehensive nutrition policy to improve dietary diversity and programs to increase micronutrient supplementation were implemented. Further, Vietnam established child health and family planning programs, maintained national health coverage, and provided health subsidies to poor people (von Braun et al. 2008). It is notable that the implementation of these reforms occurred with a focus on promoting equity while improving living standards (Vandemoortele and Bird 2011).

In recent years, however, inequality has been rising, for example, between the north and the south regions and between urban and rural areas, as poor and vulnerable groups have become hard to reach (Klump 2007). The agricultural sector is likely to continue to play a critical role in stimulating more pro-poor growth in Vietnam, as a majority of its poor continue to earn 75 percent of their income from the sector (World Bank 2012).

More inclusive growth can be further promoted through important measures such as improved access to markets, rural infrastructure, and basic services, as well as further development of the private sector both within and outside of agriculture (Klump 2007). The implementation of the new Enterprise Law in 2000, for example, has set in motion a move toward private sector growth. Effective social protection policies will also be crucial, as Vietnam continues to experience economic transformation (World Bank 2012).

Social Protection-Led Strategies and Targeted Nutrition Interventions

BRAZIL

Brazil has already eliminated undernutrition and is close to ending hunger. The prevalence of undernourishment declined from 15 to 7 percent between 1990 and 2013. The prevalence of child stunting fell between 1989 and 2007 from around 19 percent to 7 percent, and this figure is expected to be lower for the past few years.

New macroeconomic and trade policy reforms, introduced in the mid-1990s in Brazil, together with pro-poor social spending, arguably have spurred this success. Social protection reforms, which have played an important role since the late 1990s, involved the expansion and better targeting of social assistance and social security programs. As part of the reforms, existing transfer programs were consolidated under Brazil's flagship social program, popularly known as *Bolsa Família* (Holmes et al. 2011).[7] The program, which promotes improved education and healthcare for beneficiaries, is now the largest conditional cash transfer program in the world to date. Essential to the success of *Bolsa Família* is the integrated approach with other social programs and social policies for food and nutrition security (de Souza 2009).

To support social protection programs, key social legislation and policies—particularly, the 1988 statutory right of every citizen to social security, the 2003 Zero Hunger strategy, and the 2004 basic income law—were put in place by the government of Brazil (Holmes et al. 2011). Public investments in education, healthcare, clean water, and good sanitation were also scaled up, as von Braun et al. (2008) indicated.

The high initial level of inequality in Brazil, coupled with policy distortions that promoted inequality, seemed to have hampered progress (Ravallion 2009). In more recent years, declining inequality, observed in the background of higher macroeconomic stability and more progressive social policies, has created room for accelerated progress.

Agriculture-Led Strategies Plus Social Protection-Led Strategies and Targeted Nutrition Interventions

THAILAND

Thailand is close to eliminating hunger and is showing slower but good progress toward ending undernutrition. The country dramatically reduced the prevalence of undernourishment from approximately 43 to 6 percent between 1990 and 2013. Progress toward reducing the prevalence of child stunting has been slower, but also significant, falling from about 25 percent to 16 percent between 1987 and 2006. If implementation of the appropriate strategies is accelerated in Thailand, the elimination of undernutrition is likely.

Agriculture was the driving force of pro-poor growth in Thailand in the 1960s and 1970s (Cherdchuchai and Otsuka 2006). Growth benefited from strong public expenditure in rural infrastructure, macroeconomic stability, more secure land rights, and the world commodity boom that occurred between 1972 and 1974. Fast-paced agricultural growth in this period contributed to higher rural incomes and reduced poverty.

From the mid-1980s, pro-poor growth in Thailand was led mainly by the development of the non-rural sector and a structural shift of household income from farm to non-farm activity (Cherdchuchai and Otsuka 2006). In the 1990s, however, government policies refocused on agriculture (FAO 2006). Thailand's agricultural sector became characterized by a market-oriented approach—with well-developed marketing chains, and interaction between smallholders and private companies, as well as high diversification and specialization of products, encouraged by public expenditures on agricultural research and extension. This contributed to increased incentives for agricultural production, which enabled Thailand to become one of the largest global exporters of rice (Leturque and Wiggins 2010).

Remarkably, Thailand adopted an integrated and community-based approach to improving nutrition and health outcomes, beginning in the early 1980s (Kachondham et al. 1992). During this time, Thailand introduced the 2nd National Health and Nutrition Policy, which focused on targeted nutrition interventions (particularly to underdeveloped areas, children, and pregnant and lactating women) to tackle undernutrition (von Braun et al. 2008). Nutrition programs were not implemented in isolation, but were instead integrated within the National Economic and Social Development Plan, and clear linkages between agriculture and nutrition were established to ensure sustainability of impact.

In addition, the 2nd National Health and Nutrition Policy concentrated on behavior change and communication to prevent undernutrition. By utilizing social mobilization, the policy leveraged community-based primary healthcare as a delivery system for nutrition and health interventions (von Braun et al. 2008).

Barrientos (2010) noted that such integrated approaches and local participation continued to improve in the 1990s and led to the introduction of the Universal Health Coverage Scheme in 2002. The scheme is fully financed by the government of Thailand and entitles every citizen to free basic healthcare. More recently, the government has also extended social protection programs that go beyond healthcare to cover, among others, death and old age benefits to workers both in the formal and informal sectors (UNESCAP 2011).

Lessons Learned

As the experiences of the successful countries discussed in this chapter show, the pathway to ending hunger and undernutrition is likely to include a mix of agricultural growth, nutrition, and social protection strategies. Lessons learned from these success stories and beyond are useful to inform the design and implementation of context-specific strategies to address hunger and undernutrition in other developing regions, particularly in sub-Saharan Africa and South Asia.

Type of Growth Matters

Agricultural growth, as part of overall economic growth, contributes directly to the reduction of hunger and undernutrition. This impact occurs mainly through increases in the ability of farm households to purchase and produce more nutritious foods, lower food prices for poor consumers, and higher demand for rural labor (Diao et al. 2007; Fan and Brzeska 2012).

The experiences of China and Vietnam in the 1980s clearly show that smallholder-focused growth strategies in agriculturally predominant economies, such as those in sub-Saharan Africa, offer the largest impacts on hunger and undernutrition reduction. Strong growth linkages between agriculture and the rest of the economy will be important to achieve such impacts (Johnston and Mellor 1961; Mellor 1976).

As Ligon and Sadoulet (2011) demonstrated, agricultural income growth has a higher and positive effect on the expenditures of the poorest households compared to non-agricultural income growth. Most of these poor households tend to be employed in the agriculture sector. Similarly, Headey (2011) suggested through a cross-country study that agricultural growth has a significant effect on calorie intake, although the effect on dietary diversity is marginal. With the exception of India, the author also finds that growth in the agricultural sector is particularly associated with improved nutrition through reduced underweight and stunting in more food-insecure countries.

Just as sectoral growth patterns matter for reduction in poverty, hunger, and undernutrition, sub-sectoral growth patterns also matter. As Fan and Brzeska (2012) articulated, whether growth in a subsector will be pro-poor and pro-nutrition depends on the subsector's: (1) linkages with the rest of the economy, (2) initial size and geographic concentration, (3) growth potential, and (4) market opportunities. Even though staple crop growth, for example, has been shown to reduce calorie deficiency (see Figure 13.1), Pauw and Thurlow (2010) found that it did not have much impact on nutrition in Tanzania. This is because growth came mainly from crops that were not grown by the poor and hungry.

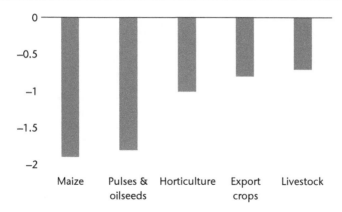

Figure 13.1 Calorie deficiency-growth elasticities by sub-sector in Tanzania (2000–07)
Source: Data on elasticities from Pauw and Thurlow (2010).

Agriculture's significant role in an economy can also be gradually replaced by the manufacturing and service sector, while poverty, hunger, and undernutrition remain largely a rural phenomenon (Fan et al. 2013). This is largely happening in the transforming economies of Asia, North Africa, and the Middle East. In these economies, growth in agriculture and the rural nonfarm economy is important for hunger and undernutrition reduction.

Agriculture's contribution to growth could further be reduced while, at the same time, urban poverty begins to exceed rural poverty. This is happening in the transformed economies of Eastern Europe and Latin America. In these economies, agriculture functions in the same way as other competitive sectors, such as manufacturing, though it will most likely remain predominant in some areas (World Bank 2008; Fan et al. 2013). The elimination of hunger and undernutrition in these countries would rely more heavily on targeted nutrition and social protection programs.

Integrated Approaches Are Key

Ruel and Alderman (2013) emphasized that accelerating progress in the reduction of undernutrition requires greater effort in integrating nutrition-specific interventions (which address the immediate causes of undernutrition such as inadequate food and nutrient intake, feeding and care practices, and low burden of infectious diseases) with nutrition sensitive-programs (which address the underlying causes of undernutrition such as food insecurity, inadequate caregiving resources, and insufficient access to health, water, and sanitation services). See Figure 13.2.

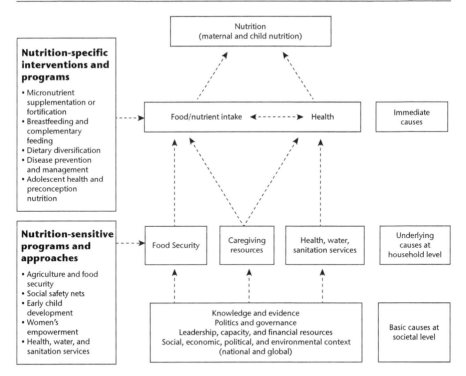

Figure 13.2 Conceptual framework for action to achieve optimum nutrition outcomes
Source: Adapted from von Grebmer et al. (2010) and Black et al. (2013).

Thailand's experience shows that well-targeted nutrition interventions, implemented using an integrated approach, are crucial to accelerate progress in nutrition. Thailand is one of the few countries to prioritize nutrition in the early 1980s by targeting necessary healthcare and nutritious food supplementation to people affected by hunger and undernutrition (Fritschel 2013).

The effectiveness, coverage, and scale of nutrition-specific interventions (such as micronutrient supplementation and optimum breastfeeding practices) can be improved immensely when nutrition-sensitive programs (such as agriculture and early child development programs) are leveraged as delivery platforms (Bhutta et al. 2013; Ruel and Alderman 2013). Furthermore, the nutrition sensitivity of programs can be increased through, for example, improved targeting of interventions, use of conditions, integrated nutrition goals and actions, and focus on improvements in women's empowerment.

Social protection strategies that are well-designed and implemented are also important, as growth alone is not sufficient to eliminate hunger and undernutrition. The experience of Brazil suggests that social protection programs together with nutrition interventions, if properly targeted, offer much promise to effectively tackle poverty, hunger, and undernutrition, as well as inequality.

Social safety nets, such as conditional cash transfers, can contribute to growth (and food security and nutrition) by building assets and protecting them from shocks; reducing inequality; facilitating structural reform of the economy; and increasing the effective allocation of resources (Alderman and Hoddinott 2009). The effectiveness and impacts of social protection programs, however, depends on proper design and implementation. As Alderman and Hoddinott (2009) pinpointed, effective safety nets should have a clear objective; feasible means of targeting beneficiaries; reliable mode of resource transfer; sound monitoring and evaluation system; and transparency in operation.

Country-Led Strategies Lead to Large Successes

As past experiences show, the greatest successes in fighting hunger and under-nutrition have been primarily country-driven or catalyzed by country-led strategies (Spielman and Pandya-Lorch 2009). This type of approach leads to a great degree of national ownership over the strategies employed, thereby contributing to success. For example, China's land reforms in the late 1970s to support exit from collective agriculture and similar reforms in Vietnam in the late 1980s were country-led. Brazil and Thailand also led carefully designed and targeted social service provision programs that were well integrated into their national strategies.

Adopting a country-led approach, in many cases, has also meant implementation of unorthodox but necessary policies that were well adapted to the local context. Partial and sequenced liberalization of markets pursued in China and the similar two-track approach pursued in Vietnam, involving the protection of some sectors and liberalization of others, are examples of such policies.

Country-led approaches extend beyond government-led action. Successful reforms have not only been country-driven, but also driven by a bottom-up approach. Community involvement has the potential to act as a successful driving force in efforts to eliminate hunger and undernutrition, as Thailand's experience demonstrates.

Evidenced-Based Policymaking and Policy Experimentation are Crucial

National policies and strategies aimed at ending hunger and undernutrition in developing countries are more likely to be successful when driven by evidence and much less by theory or ideology. Testing and careful experimentation in the form of pilot projects and policy experiments can improve policymaking by providing decision-makers with information on what investments and processes work before scaling up successful policies and programs.

Policies aimed at ending hunger and undernutrition in developing countries must be repeatedly tried, tested, adjusted, and tried again before being scaled up. Experimentation offers vital information on the proper design, sequencing, and implementation of reforms. Policymakers must foster a culture that values adaptation and change by creating the legal and political space for local experimentation. They also need to design appropriate frameworks for evaluating experiments, allow for impartial monitoring of these experiments, and rapidly transform lessons learned into large-scale reforms.

In China, for example, under the collectivized system, rewards were not easily matched to individual efforts, and farmers had little incentive to increase productivity (Lin 1992). When local authorities in the poor Anhui Province experimented with contracting land to individual households, the individual teams brought in yields that were far larger than the collectivized teams. Faced with such strong evidence, central authorities eventually conceded the benefits of the new system of contracting land. The system became known as the Household Responsibility System (Fan 2010).

Although experimentation can improve the success rate of reforms, as successful pilot projects are scaled up and unsuccessful policy options are eliminated, it should be noted that reforms can take time to mature and have lasting impacts.

Environmental Sustainability Must Be People-Focused

Today, agricultural and food systems are increasingly threatened by a mix of factors, including higher demand for food, feed, fiber, and fuel; scarcity and degradation of natural resources such as land and water; and climate change leading to growing incidence and intensity of extreme weather events. Business as usual will not be enough to end hunger and undernutrition by 2025, and environmental sustainability must be taken seriously.

Certainly, previous strategies to reduce hunger and undernutrition have not paid adequate attention to environmental sustainability. China's impressive achievement, for example, came with a costly environmental burden. Up to a quarter of the country's cultivated land is suffering from declining productivity as a result of land degradation, and as much as half of the water used in agriculture is being lost due to inefficient irrigation (Bai and Dent 2009; NBS 2013; World Bank 2013b). In Thailand, per capita carbon emissions and fresh water withdrawals have become significantly higher than regional averages, partly due to intensified agricultural production (World Bank 2014).

Moving forward, sustainable agriculture and food systems should be leveraged to end hunger and undernutrition by 2025. Agricultural growth strategies must promote resource-use efficiency and adaptation to climate change. One approach to increasing sustainable growth in agricultural productivity is known as sustainable agricultural intensification. This approach places significant emphasis on the need to make agriculture and food systems more efficient and has played a central role in the post-2015 agenda discussions.

A key step in this direction will be to provide farmers with a favorable environment that will ensure sustainable agricultural growth, including the reversal of increasingly popular water and energy subsidies that encourage unsustainable use of natural resources. It is also equally important to encourage farmers to adopt specific agricultural technologies that increase agricultural productivity and enhance environmental sustainability. Large-scale adoption of these technologies should stimulate increased food production and reduced food prices, as well as improved food security and nutrition (for more details, see Ringler et al. [2014]).

Environmental sustainability should, however, not undermine poor people's food security and nutrition. As each of these goals is critical to achieve the other, win-win strategies that promote synergies and manage trade-offs between environmental sustainability, food security, and improved nutrition must be pursued.

The elimination of agricultural subsidies, for example, to reduce unsustainable natural resource use can cause food prices to increase, as the environmental costs of agricultural production are fully internalized. This has negative implications for poor producers who are net buyers of food and for poor consumers who spend most of their income on food. To properly address this trade-off, better targeted, more productive, and flexible social safety nets should be provided to poor and vulnerable groups. This will help to minimize the potential negative impacts of reducing inefficient subsidies in the short term for the poor and vulnerable, and also offer long-term opportunities for them to escape poverty and food insecurity.

Better and Timelier Measurement of Hunger and Undernutrition is Vital

In order to measure progress toward ending hunger and undernutrition, a plurality of indicators that together can capture the multidimensional nature of both phenomena is important. Thus, at the global level, this chapter recommends tracking indicators used to measure such conditions as stunting, underweight, and wasting. In addition, it is important that individual, household, and institutional factors that influence these indicators are continuously examined and monitored. It is also crucial at this time that discussions on the post-2015 agenda culminate in a consensus on methodologically sound indicators that are cost-effective and practical. In the following, these input and outcome indicators are discussed, as well as ways to improve their usefulness.

Input-Side Indicators: Calorie Deficiency and Diet Diversity

Calorie deficiency is measured by the widely used FAO prevalence of undernourishment indicator (see Table 13.2). This indicator does not capture imbalances in the consumption of macro- and micronutrients, access by individual household members, variation within countries, and short-lived or within-year variations in food security (FAO et al. 2012; Headey and Ecker 2013). Additionally, evidence gathered in different contexts shows that calorie consumption is a weak, indirect predictor of nutrition outcomes (see, for example, Pelletier et al. [1995]; Deaton and Drèze [2009]; Jensen and Miller [2010]).

The construct of the FAO undernourishment indicator should make better use of representative household surveys, and the distribution framework of calories must be more regularly updated (de Haen 2011; Carletto et al. 2013). The indicator should be complemented with information on the other dimensions of undernutrition, such as dietary quality.

Research suggests that dietary diversity indicators are better measures of hunger and undernutrition, as compared to calorie deficiency (Hoddinott and Yohannes 2002; Arimond and Ruel 2004; Arimond et al. 2010). Further, dietary diversity indicators are more sensitive to macro- and micronutrient intake, shocks that affect food and nutrition security, and seasonal variations. Potential dietary diversity indicators are presented in Table 13.2. Frequent measurements of dietary diversity are essential to evaluate the nutritional implications of interventions and to help guide future policies and programs. Dietary diversity indicators that sufficiently capture local contexts while facilitating comparability within and between countries must be further developed and promoted.

While dietary diversity indicators are good predictors of the likelihood of adequacy in micronutrient intakes, these indicators may not consistently predict specific micronutrient deficiencies across different contexts (Arimond et al. 2010; Headey and Ecker 2013). Direct measures of deficiency in essential micronutrients such as iron, vitamin A, and zinc, or outcomes of a lack of dietary diversity should also be tracked on a regular basis, particularly in countries where these deficiencies are severe.

Outcome-Side Indicators: Stunting, Underweight, and Wasting

Anthropometric measures that gauge the nutritional status of individuals, particularly stunting (low height-for-age) should be measured frequently. Studies by Victora et al. (2008) and Haddad (2013), for example, argue that stunting is increasingly recognized as a better indicator of chronic undernutrition because of its greater specificity in measurement compared to other

Table 13.2. Select indicators for measuring hunger

Measure	Approach	Origin	Availability	Proposed changes
Input-side indicators				
Calorie deficiency indicator				
Prevalence of undernourishment	Calculated using estimates of country food availability, distribution, and calorie requirements to ascertain the proportion of the population that falls below the minimum dietary energy requirement level. Those individuals are considered undernourished. It uses data on national food balance sheets and occasional household surveys	Food and Agriculture Organization	Reported as a 3-year average	• Indicator should be reported yearly at national and sub-national levels using representative household surveys • Distribution framework of calories should be regularly updated
Dietary diversity indicators				
Food Consumption Score	Calculated using the frequency-weighted consumption of 8 food groups by a household in the past 7-days before the survey. Greater weight is assigned to food groups with higher nutritional value such as meat and fish	World Food Programme	Collected mostly for independent research and programs	• Indicator should be reported yearly at national and sub-national levels • Scores should be computed at individual level and be comparable over time and space
		OR		
Household Dietary Diversity Score	Calculated by summing the number of food groups consumed by members of the household over a 24-hour recall period. Twelve food groups are used, making the indicator a number between 0 and 12	United States Agency for International Development	Collected mostly for independent research and programs	• Indicator should be reported yearly at national and sub-national levels • Indicator should consider the type and frequency of food consumed beyond 24 hours, differentiate weights by the nutrient content of food groups, and be comparable over time and space

(*Continued*)

Table 13.2. Continued

Measure	Approach	Origin	Availability	Proposed changes
Anthropometric indicators				
		Outcome-side indicators		
Prevalence of stunting	Calculates the proportion of children whose height-for-age is less than 2 standard deviations below the median height-for-age of the international reference population. The international reference population represents the well-nourished population	World Health Organization	Varies by country	• Indicator should be reported yearly at national and sub-national levels
Prevalence of underweight	Calculates the proportion of children whose weight-for-age is less than 2 standard deviations below the median height-for-age of the international reference population	World Health Organization	Varies by country	• Indicator should be reported at national and subnational levels in hunger hotspot areas • Frequency of data collection should be determined by specific context, e.g., frequency and intensity of weather shocks such as droughts
Prevalence of wasting	Calculates the proportion of children whose weight-for-height is less than 2 standard deviations below the median height-for-age of the international reference population	World Health Organization	Varies by country	• Indicator should be reported at national and subnational levels in hunger hotspot areas • Frequency of data collection should be determined by specific context e.g. frequency and intensity of weather shocks such as droughts

Note: Data for all the indicators should be collected collaboratively by international organizations and national and regional governments.

Source: Authors' own construct and compilation based on Swindale and Bilinsky (2006); WFP (2008); de Haen et al. (2011); FAO et al. (2012); Carletto et al. (2013); Headey and Ecker (2013); and WHO (2013b).

indicators such as underweight (low weight-for-age). However, underweight and wasting indicators should also be measured frequently to assess the relatively short-term impacts of undernutrition.

The challenge with using anthropometric indicators is parceling out the causality of these outcomes. Stunting, for example, may be an outcome of undernutrition, or it may be associated with non-food factors such as poor sanitation, lack of access to safe drinking water, and inadequate care practices.[8] In using anthropometric indicators to assess hunger and undernutrition, greater effort is required to control for such confounding factors (Olsen 1999).

Improving Measurement through Capacity Building and Innovations

The reliance of indicators, such as diet diversity scores and anthropometric measures, on relatively expensive household or individual surveys makes their regular update a challenge (Arimond et al. 2010; Ruel et al. 2010). The lack of capacity in developing countries to collect reliable and timely data, due to shortages in statistical infrastructure and human capital, exacerbates the problem. Increased investments aimed at building the capacity of developing countries to collect sound data are essential inputs to designing and implementing evidence-based policies and programs that make the goal of eliminating hunger and undernutrition possible.

Investments in innovative tools, such as information and communication technologies that reduce the cost and time to collect data and publish the findings while improving the quality of the data collected, are equally essential (Headey and Ecker 2013). Cell phone-based and computer-assisted personal interviewing, for example, hold great potential to conduct household surveys in a cost-effective manner, among their other benefits (Caeyers et al. 2012; Ballivian and Azevdeo 2013). Additionally, innovations that increase accurate accounting of citizens in developing countries, such as biometric identification, should be further promoted (Crook 2013; Gelb and Clark 2013).

Accelerating the Pace of Hunger and Undernutrition Reduction

Concrete and integrated actions by all key stakeholders, including national governments, donors, civil society, and the private sector are required to eliminate hunger and undernutrition by 2025. Countries such as Brazil, China, Thailand, and Vietnam offer success stories, but sub-Saharan Africa and South Asia remain home to around 62 percent of the world's undernourished people (FAO et al. 2013). The positive experiences of successful countries suggest that we can aspire to end global hunger and undernutrition, if sufficient resources are allocated and appropriate policies and investments are pursued.

The post-2015 agenda should be facilitated by a global and inclusive partnership and also be grounded in a multisectoral approach. This partnership should be characterized by clearly defined roles and responsibilities in order to increase accountability and avoid duplication of efforts. The SDGs that will eventually be agreed upon should be ambitious, pragmatic, and time-bound, and have clear objectives. Strategies to achieve environmental sustainability within the post-2015 agenda must be people-focused. The agenda should work to achieve the goals of environmental sustainability, food security, and improved nutrition by promoting win-win strategies that maximize synergies while managing trade-offs between the goals.

Policies aimed at ending hunger and undernutrition must be country-led in order to be more effective, efficient, and sustainable, as well as better adapted to the local context. The international community should refrain from promoting "one-size-fits-all" policies and programs and should support the design and implementation of country-led strategies. Most critically, national governments must build bottom-up support for their policies and allocate adequate budgets to strategies that support more inclusive growth, including growth in viable smallholder agriculture; well-targeted social protection programs linked to improved food security and nutrition outcomes; and specialized nutrition interventions.

The ability of countries to implement innovative policy responses must be increased by strengthening institutions and capacity. The International Food Policy Research Institute (IFPRI), for example, supports the Africa-owned and Africa-led Comprehensive Africa Agriculture Development Programme (CAADP) through its Regional Strategic Analysis and Knowledge Support System by providing high-quality analyses and knowledge products to improve policymaking and implementation under the CAADP framework.

The successful engagement of key actors, including emerging economy donors, the private sector, and philanthropic organizations is also a crucial element for advancing progress toward ending hunger and undernutrition by 2025. The opportunities presented by these actors must be fully harnessed, given their growing role in the global sphere.

Between 2009 and 2012, China, for example, trained approximately 3,000 agricultural experts and built five new agricultural technology demonstration centers in Africa (FOCAC 2012). Brazil has also increased its support for agricultural growth in Africa and has assisted in establishing social protection programs on the continent. These emerging donors and others should enhance their knowledge sharing and transfer with other developing countries. In addition, partnerships between emerging donors and other developing countries must be made more transparent, better coordinated, and strategic.

The private sector, with the right incentives, can provide effective and sustainable investment and innovation, which is critical to ending hunger and undernutrition by 2025. Governments in developing countries must provide enabling environments for the private sector initiatives to flourish. To achieve this, improvement of the regulatory landscape, including reducing the hurdles to doing business and sound intellectual property rights laws, are crucial. Incentives such as temporary tax concessions should be explored.

Public–private partnerships should be leveraged in activities such as agricultural research and technology dissemination, as they present the opportunity for public and private sectors to capitalize on each other's competencies and increase efficiency and results by sharing resources, risk, costs, and benefits (Spielman and Zambrano 2013). For example, PepsiCo partnered with the Ethiopian government, The World Food Programme (WFP), and United States Agency for International Development (USAID) in a pilot project to scale up chickpea production and fight undernutrition in Ethiopia (WFP 2012).

Public–private partnerships and private sector initiatives must be monitored and evaluated to ensure that investments toward the fight against hunger and undernutrition are socially and environmentally responsible. For this, research organizations, including CGIAR, have an important role to play.

Philanthropic organizations also play an important role in the fight against hunger and undernutrition, and the opportunities they present should be further harnessed. For example, the Bill & Melinda Gates Foundation funds programs aimed at increasing small farmers' productivity and the nutrition outcomes of hungry people, among others (BMGF 2013). The Bangladesh Rural Advancement Committee (BRAC) also works to achieve similar results by employing a holistic approach to poverty and hunger alleviation, including through empowerment of vulnerable groups (BRAC 2013). Philanthropic activity, however, must be better coordinated to avoid inefficiencies, including duplication of effort.

Reliable and timely data, including that on relevant indicators of hunger and undernutrition, at all levels is urgently needed to support evidence-based policymaking for accelerated progress. This should be a collaborative effort by international organizations and national and regional governments. Data collection and analytical capacities in developing countries (particularly in terms of statistical infrastructure and human capital) should be improved significantly in order to support the collaborative effort.

Finally, ending hunger and undernutrition by 2025 should be given top priority in the post-2015 development agenda. This makes economic sense and should be considered as a global ethical duty. Concerted and results-based efforts that are grounded in multisector, multi-actor approaches have great potential to help us achieve the goals of food security, improved nutrition, and environmental sustainability.

Acknowledgment

The authors would like to thank Erica Smith for valuable research assistance.

Notes

1. The World Health Assembly calls for a 40 percent reduction in the number of children under 5 years of age that are stunted—this is not ambitious enough. We should aim to eliminate child stunting by 2025. While more progress has been achieved in recent years, the data on child stunting remains outdated. Increased efforts by donors, global institutions, and developing countries will further accelerate progress.
2. In Europe, for example: "There are now more than 18 million people receiving EU-funded food aid, 43 million who do not get enough to eat each day, and 120 million who are at risk of poverty in countries covered by Eurostat" (IFRC 2013, p. 9). This suggests that the level of hunger in Europe is about 6 percent.
3. To determine whether countries are able to eliminate hunger and undernutrition, we calculated the average annual rate of reduction in the past for the prevalence of undernourishment and stunting and used it to project what the levels would be by 2025.
4. Growth in the rural economy accounted for most of China's success since 1980. Agricultural growth had about four times the impact of growth in non-agricultural sectors. For details, see Ravallion and Chen (2007).
5. The objective of the program is to guarantee a minimum income in urban areas, by filling the gap between actual income and a "*Dibao* line" that is set locally.
6. In 1992, 80 percent of Vietnam's population resided in rural areas, 75 percent of the labor force depended on agriculture as the primary source of livelihood, and agriculture contributed to a little over 40 percent of GDP. Further, the contribution of agriculture to GDP had fallen to 20 percent as of 2010, and the share of the total labor force in agriculture had dropped to less than 50 percent in 2012.
7. For impacts of *Bolsa Família*, see de Brauw et al. (2014).
8. In addition to these confounding factors, while there is better consensus on the indicators used for children under 5 years of age, there is less agreement on the indicators for adolescents and adults. For adolescents, for example, their physical development can vary significantly, depending on the effects and onset of puberty, making it hard to define "normal development" (FAO 2005). In such cases, diet diversity scores and direct measures of macro- and micronutrient deficiency are better indicators of nutritional status.

References

Alderman, H., and J. Hoddinott. 2009. "Growth Promoting Social Safety Nets. In *The Poorest and Hungry: Assessments, Analyses, and Actions*, edited by J. von Braun, R. Vargas Hill, and R. Pandya-Lorch, pp. 279–286. Washington, DC: International Food Policy Research Institute.

Arimond, M., and M. T. Ruel. 2004. "Dietary Diversity Is Associated with Child Nutritional Status: Evidence from 11 Demographic and Health Surveys." *Journal of Nutrition* 134 (10): pp. 2579–2585.

Arimond, M., D. Wiesmann, E. Becquey, A. Carriquiry, M. C. Daniels, M. Deitchler, N. Fanou-Fogny, M. L. Joseph, G. Kennedy, Y. Martin-Prevel, and L. E. Torheim. 2010. "Simple Food Group Diversity Indicators Predict Micronutrient Adequacy of Women's Diets in 5 Diverse, Resource-Poor Settings." *Journal of Nutrition* 140 (11): pp. 2059–2069.

AU (African Union), NEPAD (the New Partnership for Africa's Development), UNECA (United Nations Economic Commission for Africa), and the WFP (World Food Programme). 2013a. *The Cost of Hunger in Egypt: Implications of Child Undernutrition on the Social and Economic Development of Egypt*. World Food Programme and the Government of Egypt.

AU (African Union), NEPAD (the New Partnership for Africa's Development), UNECA (United Nations Economic Commission for Africa), and the WFP (World Food Programme). 2013b. *The Cost of Hunger in Ethiopia: Implications for the Growth and Transformation of Ethiopia*. World Food Programme and Government of Ethiopia.

Bai, Z., and D. Dent. 2009. "Recent Land Degradation and Improvement in China." *Ambio* 38 (3): pp. 150–156.

Ballivian, A., and J. P. Azevedo. 2013. "Listening to LAC: Using Mobile Phones for High Frequency Data Collection." Final Report, World Bank, Washington, DC.

Barrientos, A. 2010. "Social Protection and Poverty." Social Policy and Development Programme Paper 42, United Nations Research Institute for Social Development, Geneva, Switzerland.

Behrman, J. R., H. Alderman, and J. Hoddinott. 2004. "Hunger and Malnutrition." In *Global Crises, Global Solutions*, edited by B. Lomborg, pp. 305–333. Cambridge: Cambridge University Press.

Bhutta, Z., J. Das, A. Rizvi, M. Gaffey, N. Walker, S. Horton, P. Webb, A. Lartey, and R. Black. 2013. "Evidenced-Based Interventions for Improvement of Maternal and Child Nutrition: What Can Be Done and At What Cost?" *Lancet* 382 (9890): pp. 452–477.

Black, R. E., H. Alderman, Z. A. Bhutta, S. Gillespie, L. Haddad, S. Horton, A. Lartey, V. Mannar, M. Ruel, C. G. Victora, S. P. Walker, and P. Webb. 2013. "Maternal and Child Undernutrition: Building Momentum for Impact." *Lancet* 382 (9890): pp. 372–375.

BMGF (Bill & Melinda Gates Foundation). 2013. Foundation Fact Sheet. <http://www.gatesfoundation.org/Who-We-Are/General-Information/Foundation-Factsheet>.

BRAC (Bangladesh Rural Advancement Committee). 2013. BRAC Overview. <http://brac.net/courageintheheart/bracoverview>.

Caeyers, B., N. Chalmers, and J. De Weerdt. 2012. "Improving Consumption Measurement and Other Survey Data through CAPI: Evidence from a Randomized Experiment." *Journal of Development Economics* 98 (1): pp. 19–33.

Carletto, C., A. Zezza, and R. Banerjee. 2013. "Towards Better Measurement of Household Food Security: Harmonizing Indicators and the Role of Household Surveys." *Global Food Security* 2 (1): pp. 30–40.

Cherdchuchai, S., and K. Otsuka. 2006. "Rural Income Dynamic and Poverty Reduction in Thai Villages from 1987 to 2004." *Agricultural Economics* 35 (Supplement s3): pp. 409–423.

Crook, C. 2013. "India's Biometric IDs Put Its Poorest on the Map." *BloombergView*, August 23, 2013. <http://www.bloomberg.com/news/2013-04-23/india-s-biom etric-ids-put-its-poorest-on-the-map.html>.

de Brauw, A., D. O. Gilligan, J. Hoddinott, and S. Roy. 2014. "The Impact of *Bolsa Família* on Women's Decision-Making Power." *World Development* 59 (July): pp. 487–504.

de Haen, H., S. Klasen, and M. Qaim. 2011. "What Do We Really Know? Metrics for Food Insecurity and Undernutrition." *Food Policy* 36 (6): pp. 760–769.

de Souza, P. A. 2009. "The Fight against Poverty and Hunger in Brazil." In *The Poorest and Hungry: Assessments, Analyses, and Actions*, edited by J. von Braun, R. Vargas Hill, and R. Pandya-Lorch, pp. 383–386. Washington, DC: International Food Policy Research Institute.

Deaton, A., and J. Drèze. 2009. "Nutrition in India: Facts and Interpretations." *Economic and Political Weekly* 44 (7): pp. 42–65.

Diao, X., S. Fan, S. Kanyarukiga, and Y. Bingxin. 2007. *Agricultural Growth and Investment Options for Poverty Reduction in Rwanda*. Washington, DC: International Food Policy Research Institute.

Fan, S. 2010. *Halving Hunger: Meeting the First Millennium Development Goal through Business as Unusual*. Washington, DC: International Food Policy Research Institute.

Fan, S., and J. Brzeska. 2012. "The Nexus between Agriculture and Nutrition: Do Growth Patterns and Conditional Factors Matter?" In *Reshaping Agriculture for Nutrition and Health*, edited by S. Fan, and R. Pandya-Lorch, pp. 31–38. Washington, DC: International Food Policy Research Institute.

Fan, S., J. Brzeska, M. Keyzer, and A. Halsema. 2013. *From Subsistence to Profit: Transforming Smallholder Farms*. Washington, DC: International Food Policy Research Institute.

Fan, S., A. Gulati, and S. Dalafi. 2007. "Overview of Reforms and Developments in China and India." In *The Dragon and the Elephant: Agricultural and Rural Reforms in China and India*, edited by A. Gulati, and S. Fan, pp. 10–44. Baltimore: The Johns Hopkins University Press, published for the International Food Policy Research Institute.

FAO (Food and Agriculture Organization). 2005. "Assessing the Contribution of Aquaculture to Food Security: A Survey of Methodologies." FAO Fisheries Circular 1010, Food and Agriculture Organization, Rome, Italy.

FAO (Food and Agriculture Organization). 2006. "Rapid Growth of Selected Asian Economies. Lessons and Implications for Agriculture and Food Security. Republic of Korea, Thailand and Viet Nam." Food and Agriculture Organization, Rome, Italy.

FAO (Food and Agriculture Organization). 2013. *The State of Food and Agriculture 2013*. Rome: Food and Agriculture Organization.

FAO (Food and Agriculture Organization), WFP (World Food Programme), and IFAD (International Fund for Agriculture Development). 2012. *The State of Food Insecurity in the World 2012. Economic Growth Is Necessary but not Sufficient to Accelerate Reduction of Hunger and Malnutrition*. Rome: Food and Agriculture Organization.

FAO (Food and Agriculture Organization), WFP (World Food Programme), and IFAD (International Fund for Agriculture Development). 2013. *The State of Food Insecurity in the World 2013. The Multiple Dimensions of Food Security*. Rome: Food and Agriculture Organization.

FAO (Food and Agriculture Organization), WFP (World Food Programme), and IFAD (International Fund for Agriculture Development). 2014. *The State of Food Insecurity in the World 2014. Strengthening the Enabling Environment for Food Security and Nutrition*. Rome: Food and Agriculture Organization.

FOCAC (Forum on China–Africa Cooperation). 2012. Implementation of the Follow-Up Actions of the Fourth Ministerial Conference of the Forum on China-Africa Cooperation. <http://www.focac.org/eng/dwjbzjjhys/t952532.htm>.

Fritschel, H. 2013. "What's Politics Got to Do with It?" IFPRI *Insights* Magazine, November 20, 2013, International Food Policy Research Institute, Washington, DC.

Gelb, A., and J. Clark. 2013. "Identification for Development: The Biometrics Revolution," CGD Working Paper 315, Center for Global Development, Washington, DC.

Haddad, L. 2013. "How Should Nutrition Be Positioned in the Post-2015 Agenda?" *Food Policy* 43 (December): pp. 341–352.

Headey, D. 2011. "Turning Economic Growth into Nutrition-Sensitive Growth." Paper Presented at the International Food Policy Research Institute Conference on "Leveraging Agriculture for Improving Nutrition and Health," New Delhi, India, February 10–12, 2011.

Headey, D., and O. Ecker. 2013. "Rethinking the Measurement of Food Security: From First Principles to Best Practice." *Food Security* 5 (3): pp. 327–343.

Hoddinott, J., R. Behrman, J. A. Maluccio, P. Melgar, A. R, Quisumbing, M. Ramirez-Zea, A. D. Stein, K. M. Yount, and R. Martorell. 2013a. "Adult Consequences of Growth Failure in Early Childhood." *American Journal of Clinical Nutrition* 98 (5): pp. 1170–1178

Hoddinott, J., H. Alderman, J. R. Behrman, L. Haddad, and S. Horton. 2013b. "The Economic Rationale for Investing in Stunting Reduction." *Maternal and Child Nutrition* 9 (Suppl. S2): pp. 69–82.

Hoddinott, J., and Y. Yohannes. 2002. "Dietary Diversity as a Food Security Indicator." Food Consumption and Nutrition Division Discussion Paper 136, International Food Policy Research Institute, Washington, DC.

Holmes, R., J. Hagen-Zanker, and M. Vandemoortele. 2011. "Social Protection in Brazil: Impacts on Poverty, Inequality and Growth." Overseas Development Institute, London, UK.

Horton, S., and R. H. Steckel. 2013. "Malnutrition: Global Economic Losses Attributable to Malnutrition 1990–2000 and Projects to 2050." In *How Much Have Global Problems*

Cost the World? A Scorecard from 1990 to 2050, edited by B. Lombard, pp. 247–272. Cambridge: Cambridge University Press.

IFRC (International Federation of Red Cross and Red Crescent Societies). 2013. "Think Differently: Humanitarian Impacts of the Economic Crisis in Europe." International Federation of Red Cross and Red Crescent Societies, Geneva.

Johnston, D. G., and J. W. Mellor. 1961. "The Role of Agriculture in Economic Development." *American Economic Review* 51 (4): pp. 566–593.

Jensen, R. T., and N. H. Miller. 2010. "A Revealed Preference Approach to Measuring Undernutrition and Poverty Using Calorie Shares," NBER Working Paper No. 16555, National Bureau of Economic Research, Cambridge, MA.

Kachondham, Y., P. Winichagoon, and K. Tontisirin. 1992. "Nutrition and Health in Thailand: Trends and Actions." United Nations Institute of Nutrition and Mahidol University, Bangkok and Nakhon Pathom, Thailand.

Klump, R. 2007. "Pro-Poor Growth in Vietnam: Miracle or Model?" In *Delivering on the Promise of Pro-Poor Growth: Insights and Lessons from Country Experiences,* edited by T. Besley, and L. J. Cord, pp. 119–146. Washington, DC, and Basingstoke: World Bank and Palgrave Macmillan.

Leturque, H., and S. Wiggins. 2010. "Thailand's Progress in Agriculture: Transition and Sustained Productivity Growth." Overseas Development Institute, London, UK.

Ligon, E. A., and E. Sadoulet. 2011. "Estimating the Effects of Aggregate Agricultural Gowth on the Distribution of Expenditures." CUDARE Working Paper 1115, Department of Agricultural and Resource Economics, University of California-Berkeley, Berkeley, California.

Lin, J. 1992. "Rural Reforms and Agricultural Growth in China." *American Economic Review* 82 (1): pp. 34–51.

Martínez R., and A. Fernández. 2008. *The Cost of Hunger: Social and Economic Impact of Child Undernutrition in Central America and the Dominican Republic.* Santiago, Chile: United Nations.

Mellor, J. W. 1976. *The New Economics of Growth: A Strategy for India and the Developing World.* Ithaca, NY, and London: Cornell University Press.

NBS (National Bureau of Statistics China). 2013. *China Statistical Yearbook 2013.* Beijing: China Statics Press.

Olsen, C. M. 1999. "Nutrition and Health Outcomes Associated with Food Insecurity and Hunger. *Journal of Nutrition* 129 (2): pp. 5215–5245.

Pauw, K., and J. Thurlow. 2010. "Agricultural Growth, Poverty, and Nutrition in Tanzania." IFPRI Discussion Paper 947, International Food Policy Research Institute, Washington, DC.

Pelletier, D. L., K. Deneke, Y. Kidane, B. Haile, and F. Negussie. 1995. "The Food-First Bias and Nutrition Policy: Lessons from Ethiopia." *Food Policy* 20 (4): pp. 279–298.

Ravallion, M. 2009. "A Comparative Perspective on Poverty Reduction in Brazil, China, and India." World Bank Policy Research Working Paper 5080, World Bank, Washington, DC.

Ravallion, M., and S. Chen. 2007. "China's (Uneven) Progress Against Poverty." *Journal of Development Economics* 82 (1): pp. 1–42.

Ringler, C., N. Cenacchi, J. Koo, R. Robertson, M. Fisher, C. Cox, N. Perez, K. Garrett, and M. Rosegrant. 2014. "Sustainable Agricultural Intensification: The Promise of Innovative Farming Practices." In *2013 Global Food Policy Report*. Washington, DC: International Food Policy Research Institute.

Ruel, M. T., and H. Alderman. 2013. "Nutrition-Sensitive Interventions and Programmes: How Can They Help to Accelerate Progress in Improving Maternal and Child Nutrition?" *Lancet* 382 (9891): pp. 536–551.

Ruel, M. T., M. Deitchler, and M. Arimond. 2010. "Developing Simple Measures of Women's Diet Quality in Developing Countries: Overview." *Journal of Nutrition* 140 (11): pp. 2048–2050.

Spielman, D. J., and R. Pandya-Lorch, eds. 2009. *Proven Successes in Agricultural Development: A Technical Compendium to Millions Fed*. Washington, DC: International Food Policy Research Institute.

Spielman, D. J., and P. Zambrano. 2013. "Policy, Investment, and Partnerships for Agricultural Biotechnology Research in Africa: Emerging Evidence." In *Genetically Modified Crops in Africa: Economic and Policy Lessons from Countries South of the Sahara*, edited by J. Falck-Zepeda, G. P. Gruère, and I. Sithole-Niang, pp. 183–205. Washington, DC: International Food Policy Research Institute.

Swindale A., and P. Bilinsky. 2006. *Household Dietary Diversity Score (HDDS) for Measurement of Household Food Access: Indicator Guide,* Version 2. Washington, DC: FHI 360/Food and Nutrition Technical Assistance Project (FANTA).

UNESCAP (United Nations Economic and Social Commission for Asia and the Pacific). 2011. "The Promise of Protection: Social Protection and Development in Asia and the Pacific." United Nations Economic and Social Commission for Asia and the Pacific, Bangkok, Thailand.

UNICEF (United Nations Children's Fund). 2013. Eastern and Southern Africa. Nutrition. <http://www.unicef.org/esaro/5479_nutrition.html>.

Vandemoortele, M., and K. Bird. 2011. "Vietnam's Progress on Economic Growth and Poverty Reduction: Impressive Improvements." Overseas Development Institute, London, UK.

Victora, C. G., L. Adair, C. Fall, P. C. Hallal, R. Martorell, L. Richter, and H. S. Sachdev. 2008. "Maternal and Child Undernutrition: Consequences for Adult Health and Human Capital." *Lancet* 371 (9609): pp. 340–357.

von Braun, J., M. Ruel, and A. Gulati. 2008. "Accelerating Progress toward Reducing Child Malnutrition in India: A Concept for Action." IFPRI Research Brief 12, International Food Policy Research Institute, Washington, DC.

von Grebmer, K., M. Ruel, P. Menon, B. Nestorova, T. Olofinbiyi, H. Fritschel, Y. Yohannes, C. von Oppeln, O. Towey, K. Golden, and J. Thompson. 2010. *2010 Global Hunger Index: The Challenge of Hunger: Focus on the Crisis of Child Undernutrition*. Bonn, Washington, DC, and Dublin: Deutsche Welthungerhilfe, International Food Policy Research Institute, and Concern Worldwide.

WFP (World Food Programme). 2008. *Food Consumption Analysis: Calculation and Use of the Food Consumption Score in Food Security Analysis*. Rome: World Food Programme, Vulnerability Analysis and Mapping (VAM).

WFP (World Food Programme) 2012. World Food Program's Private Sector Partnership and Fundraising Strategy: An Evaluation,Vol. 1. Office of Evaluation Report OE/2012/010, World Food Programme.

WHO (World Health Organization). 2013a. Nutrition: Micronutrients. <http://www.who.int/nutrition/topics/micronutrients/en/index.html>.

WHO (World Health Organization). 2013b. Global Database on Child Growth and Malnutrition: The Database. <http://www.who.int/nutgrowthdb/database/en/>.

World Bank. 2008. *World Development Report: Agriculture for Development*. Washington, DC: World Bank.

World Bank. 2012. *Well Begun, Not Yet Done: Vietnam's Remarkable Progress on Poverty Reduction and the Emerging Challenges*. Hanoi: World Bank.

World Bank. 2013a. World Development Indicators. <http://data.worldbank.org/data-catalog/world-development-indicators>.

World Bank. 2013b. *China 2030: Building a Modern, Harmonious, and Creative Society*. Washington DC: World Bank.

World Bank. 2014. Environment in East Asia and Pacific: Thailand Environment. <http://go.worldbank.org/5XB27I9200>.

14

The Present Pattern of Growth, Inequality, and Poverty in Sub-Saharan Africa

Erik Thorbecke

Introduction

The main objective of this chapter is to review and analyze the present economic growth spell in sub-Saharan Africa (SSA). The next section presents evidence relating to the growth, inequality, and poverty performance within SSA, as a whole, and at the country level during the period 1990–2012. The main findings are that (1) a quantum jump in GDP growth per capita occurred around 2000; (2) income inequality remained stubbornly very high; and (3) absolute poverty has declined significantly since 2000. The following section is devoted to a conceptual analysis of the interrelationship among growth, inequality, and poverty. Such an analysis is necessary in order to understand the anatomy of growth. A major implication of this analysis for SSA is that high inequality acts like a filter in the capacity of growth to reduce poverty.

Next, I argue that the two most important elements of a development strategy, focused on achieving a broad-based and inclusive growth pattern within the present context of SSA, are the reduction of inequality and the creation of productive jobs. Then, I attempt to answer the question of whether the recent structural transformation process has become more effective in contributing to inclusive growth in the African subcontinent. The tentative answer, based on an examination of the structural transformation in a sample of SSA countries before and subsequent to the present growth spell, is in the affirmative. It appears that workers moving out of agriculture during the current growth spell were generally better able to find more productive jobs in non-agricultural sectors. Lastly, I address the issue of how the structural transformation can be further accelerated to facilitate intersectoral labor flows, and especially, rural–urban migration. Two key interventions are highlighted: investment in infrastructure and integrated rural development to improve small farmers' productivity. The final section concludes.

Growth, Inequality, and Poverty Performance within Sub-Saharan Africa, 1990–2012

First, we explore the growth, inequality, and poverty trends at the level of the whole SSA region before focusing on country trends. Since the beginning of this millennium, economic growth in SSA has been remarkable. It accelerated from essentially a zero (0.14 percent) per capita annual growth rate of GDP for the subcontinent, as a whole, between 1960 and 2000, to around 3 percent between 2000 and 2012. One can safely characterize this evolution as a quantum jump. Of the 10 fastest growing economies in the world during the last decade, six were in SSA.

The high pace of growth has led to a significant reduction in poverty. For the whole SSA region, the poverty headcount ratio at the $1.25/day poverty line (the proportion of the population below that poverty line) fell from 58 percent in 1999 to 48.5 percent in 2010. Yet, pushed by still-strong demographic trends, the estimated number of poor continued to rise from 377 million to 414 million over the same period.[1]

The only aggregate estimate of the change in income inequality in Africa (African Development Bank 2012) that I could find indicates a slight increase in inequality—with the Gini coefficient rising from 0.43 in 2000–04 to 0.46 in 2005–09. In general, inequality is relatively very high in SSA, with six of the most uneven countries in the world being in Africa (South Africa's Gini coefficient in 2008 was 0.63).

Turning next to the more disaggregated picture and focusing on the country-level performance, Table 14.1 shows the annual growth rates of per capita GDP income (at constant 2005 dollars) for four periods: 1980–90, 1990–2000, 2000–10, and 2010–12 for 37 SSA countries. The following observations can be inferred from Table 14.1. First, the quantum acceleration in growth, in many instances from negative growth or stagnation in the 1990s to high positive growth since 2000, is no less than a dramatic phenomenon. For example, between the 1990s and the recent 2000–10 period, Angola went from a –2 percent annual growth rate to 10.4 percent; Chad went from –1 percent to 7.2 percent; Ethiopia from –0.5 percent to 7 percent; Liberia from –0.6 percent to almost 7 percent; Mozambique from 2.6 percent to 6.2 percent. Other noteworthy discrete growth jumps included Nigeria from 0.2 percent to 4.3 percent; Rwanda, from –1.1 percent to 6.7 percent; Sierra Leone from –2.5 percent to 3.4 percent, and Tanzania from 0.1 percent to 4.8 percent.

Table 14.1. Annual growth rate of per capita GDP for selected sub-Saharan African countries*

Country	1980–90	1990–2000	2000–10	2010–12
Angola (earliest data: 1985)	0.57%	−2.00%	10.38%	2.12%
Benin	0.22%	1.20%	0.72%	1.62%
Botswana	10.25%	3.75%	3.63%	4.05%
Burkina Faso	0.94%	2.74%	3.33%	4.13%
Burundi	1.38%	−3.12%	0.03%	0.79%
Cameroon	0.26%	−1.32%	0.68%	1.80%
Central African Republic	−1.35%	−1.01%	−0.73%	1.58%
Chad	2.61%	−1.02%	7.23%	0.23%
Congo, Dem. Rep.	−1.76%	−5.82%	2.21%	4.20%
Congo, Rep.	2.07%	−1.22%	1.97%	0.89%
Côte d'Ivoire	−2.67%	−0.57%	−0.54%	−0.11%
Ethiopia (earliest data: 1981)	−0.90%	−0.45%	6.95%	5.27%
Gabon	−0.82%	−0.89%	−0.41%	4.11%
Ghana	−0.86%	1.84%	3.69%	9.36%
Guinea (earliest data: 1986)	0.79%	0.10%	0.41%	1.29%
Guinea–Bissau	3.07%	−1.64%	0.26%	−0.35%
Kenya	0.34%	−0.98%	1.48%	1.70%
Lesotho	1.88%	2.53%	3.75%	2.80%
Liberia	−7.20%	−0.58%	4.55%	7.28%
Madagascar	−2.02%	−1.29%	−0.37%	−0.35%
Malawi	−1.79%	1.70%	1.66%	0.17%
Mali	−1.02%	1.53%	3.11%	−2.21%
Mauritania	−1.07%	−0.06%	2.21%	3.16%
Mozambique	−0.92%	2.62%	6.15%	4.81%
Namibia	−1.91%	1.25%	3.59%	3.51%
Niger	−2.56%	−1.58%	−0.84%	2.69%
Nigeria	−1.43%	0.23%	4.33%	4.10%
Rwanda	−1.29%	−1.07%	6.72%	5.27%
Senegal	−0.43%	0.32%	1.34%	0.20%
Sierra Leone	−1.41%	−2.46%	3.41%	8.77%
South Africa	−0.90%	−0.42%	2.45%	1.81%
Sudan	−0.52%	3.13%	3.63%	3.28%
Swaziland	6.95%	0.85%	1.17%	−2.12%
Tanzania (earliest data: 1988)	2.16%	0.12%	4.84%	3.54%
Togo	−2.02%	−0.33%	−0.45%	2.54%
Uganda (earliest data: 1982)	−0.11%	3.58%	4.64%	1.56%
Zambia	−1.73%	−1.70%	3.20%	3.83%

* The table reports average annual growth rate of per capita GDP (at constant 2005 international dollars) during four periods: 1980–90, 1990–2000, 2000–10, and 2010–12. GDP data is from World Bank Indicators.

Out of the sample of 37 countries in Table 14.1, 32 countries reported higher growth rates in the present decade than in the preceding one,[2] three countries showed essentially no change,[3] and only two countries showed worsening growth performance (Benin and Togo). Although 20 countries in the 1990s suffered from negative GDP growth, only five stagnated in the 2000s (Central African Republic, Côte d'Ivoire, Gabon, Niger, and Togo). Figure A-14.1 in the Appendix shows the country trends over time for GDP per capita growth. It reveals that in most SSA countries an acceleration of growth occurred after 2000.

Table 14.2. Poverty headcount ratio and poverty gap for selected sub-Saharan African countries*

Country	Headcount (%)			Poverty Gap (%)		
	1990	1999	2010	1990	1999	2010
Angola	46.7	54.3	43.7	24.8	29.9	16.6
Benin	42.1	45.4	44.2	13.2	14.8	14.2
Botswana	25.9	26.4	13.4	8.8	9.1	3.3
Burkina Faso	72.2	66.7	44.6	35.7	27.5	14.7
Burundi	84.9	86.2	79.8	41	46.5	34.7
Cameroon	15.3	14.9	9.3	3.2	3.2	1.1
Central African Republic	80.5	65.9	62.3	54.2	36.2	30.9
Chad	69.1	71.3	46.4	30.7	32.4	16.6
Congo, Dem. Rep.	56.3	87.2	85	23.4	51.9	48.9
Congo, Rep.	51.7	60.1	48.4	21.3	26.9	19.2
Côte d'Ivoire	17	23.7	22.7	3.9	6.7	7.1
Ethiopia	62.1	55.2	30.7	21.9	16	8.2
Gabon	2.4	7.1	0.5	0.4	1.4	0.1
Ghana	50.5	38	22.2	17.9	13.8	7.2
Guinea	92.3	60.2	38.3	62.9	25	12.5
Guinea-Bissau	42.3	49.8	46.5	22.3	18	15.4
Kenya	36.2	24.1	39.9	14.2	7.2	15.1
Liberia	68.5	80	82.6	28.2	37.1	39.7
Madagascar	74.1	82.3	81.3	38.8	44.3	43.3
Malawi	89	80.5	64.4	53.9	42.5	28.1
Mali	85.4	73.6	50.4	52.1	36.3	16.4
Mauritania	43.2	21.7	24	16.8	6	7
Mozambique	81.3	67.6	61.2	41.9	29.7	26.2
Namibia	50	40.8	28.7	25.3	16.4	7.8
Niger	66.4	72	43.5	25.2	33.4	12.4
Nigeria	60.4	70	68	28.7	33.4	33.7
Rwanda	67.4	73.9	63.2	25.8	35.8	26.6
Senegal	65.5	47.3	30.3	34.1	15.9	9.4
Sierra Leone	62.2	73.3	51.7	43.7	40.1	16.6
South Africa	22.1	25.6	13.8	5.9	7.8	2.3
Sudan	56.2	40.3	19	21.3	13.7	5.2
Swaziland	83.9	72.1	40.6	54	38	16
Tanzania	69.8	80.1	62.5	27.7	38	24.6
Togo	35.6	36.5	29.5	10.1	10.5	9
Uganda	68.7	60.5	34	31.9	24.5	10.4
Zambia	54.4	53.7	74.5	35.5	24.5	41.9

* This table is produced by the World Bank PovcalNet and rearranged by the author to report the headcount ratio and poverty gap for selected sub-Saharan African countries (37 countries in total) in three selected years: 1990, 1999 (since data for 2000 is not available), and 2010. Poverty line of $1.25/day is used.

Table 14.2 gives the poverty headcount ratio and the poverty gap[4] for the same sample of SSA countries for 1990, 1999, and 2010. Based on a comparison of the headcount ratio in 1999 and 2010, the incidence of poverty fell in 27 countries, remained essentially the same in seven countries, and rose in only three countries (Kenya,[5] Mauritania, and Zambia). Again, there are some examples of large reductions in poverty between 1999 and 2010, such as Burkina Faso from 67 percent to 45 percent, Ethiopia from 55 percent to 31 percent, Senegal from 47 percent to 30 percent, and Uganda from

61 percent to 34 percent. In general, the poverty gap measure of poverty tracks fairly closely the headcount ratio measure for most countries. The poverty reduction performance of some of the largest SSA countries remains mixed, with essentially no progress in Nigeria and the Democratic Republic of the Congo, but remarkable progress in Ethiopia, Tanzania, and South Africa.

The information on income inequality across African countries over time is very incomplete. It relies on household surveys that are only spasmodically run and are subject to changing survey methodologies that make comparisons over time questionable. Only a few SSA countries run surveys at regular intervals. For all these reasons, information on income inequality has to be looked at very critically. Table 14.3 summarizes the information available in the form of Gini coefficients given for the specific survey years, which vary from one country to another. The first observation that comes to mind in scrutinizing Table 14.3 is that inequality is still very high in many SSA countries. Out of the 26 countries for which there were at least two observations from around 2000 and the late 2000s, nine countries revealed rising inequality, eight countries reported no significant change, and nine indicated lower inequality. The same mixed picture appears when one focuses on the most populated countries. Inequality appears to have gone up in Ethiopia, South Africa, and Tanzania, and down in Nigeria.

Human development and well-being are highly multidimensional concepts that can only be captured imperfectly by monetary measures. The Human Development Index (UNDP 2014) does, in a limited way, incorporate different dimensions of well-being such as education and health, in addition to income. The most recent Human Development Index (HDI) reported that out of the 14 best performers in terms of the annual growth rate of HDI between 2000 and 2013, no fewer than 11 were from SSA. A number of African countries enjoyed major improvements in education and in the reduction of infant mortality.

To summarize the evidence above, one can conclude that: (1) most of the African subcontinent has undergone a remarkable acceleration in GDP growth that can be characterized, at least for the time being, as a quantum jump; (2) this high economic growth has contributed to a significant reduction in absolute poverty ($1.25/day poverty line) in the majority of SSA countries; (3) income inequality remains very high in much of SSA, and there is no convincing evidence that the growth pattern has led to a general reduction in inequality, as inequality appears to be rising in as many countries as it is falling; and (4) a number of SSA countries have undergone significant improvements in human development, albeit from very low levels.

To understand how the structure (pattern) of growth influences the distribution of income and poverty, it is essential to analyze the interrelationship among growth, inequality, and poverty at the conceptual level. This analysis is undertaken in the next section.

Table 14.3. Gini coefficients of inequality in selected sub-Saharan countries

Country	Survey year	Gini index
Angola	2008.5	42.7
	2000	58.6
Benin	2003	38.6
Botswana	1993.9	61.0
	1985.5	54.2
Burkina Faso	2009	39.8
	2003	39.6
	1998	46.9
	1994	50.7
Burundi	2006	33.3
	1998	42.4
	1992	33.3
Cameroon	2007	38.9
	2001	40.4
	1996	40.7
Central African Republic	2008	56.3
	2003	43.6
	1992.4	61.3
Chad	2002.5	39.8
Congo, Dem. Rep.	2005.5	44.4
Congo, Rep.	2005	47.3
Côte d'Ivoire	2008	41.5
	2002	48.4
	1998	43.8
	1995	36.7
	1993	36.9
	1988	36.9
	1987	40.4
	1986	38.6
	1985	41.2
Ethiopia	2010.5	33.6
	2005	29.8
	1999.5	30.0
	1995	40.0
	1981.5	32.4
Gabon	2005	41.5
Ghana	2005.5	42.8
	1998.3	40.8
	1991.5	38.1
	1988.5	36.0
	1987.5	35.4
Guinea	2007	39.4
	2003	40.3
	1994	44.9
	1991	46.8
Guinea-Bissau	2002	35.5
	1993	47.8
	1991	n/a

(*Continued*)

Table 14.3. Continued

Country	Survey year	Gini index
Kenya	2005.4	47.7
	1997	42.5
	1994	42.1
	1992	57.5
Lesotho	2002.5	52.5
	1994.4	63.2
	1993	57.9
	1986.5	56.0
Liberia	2007	38.2
Madagascar	2010	44.1
	2005	47.2
	2001	47.5
	1999	41.8
	1997	39.2
	1993	46.1
	1980	46.9
Malawi	2010	43.9
	2004.3	39.0
	1997.5	50.3
Mali	2010	33.0
	2006	39.0
	2001	40.0
	1994	50.6
Mauritania	2008	40.5
	2004	41.3
	2000	39.0
	1995.5	37.3
	1993	50.1
	1987	43.9
Mozambique	2007.5	45.7
	2002.5	47.1
	1996.2	44.5
Namibia	2003.7	63.9
	1993	74.3
Niger	2007.5	34.6
	2005	43.9
	1994.4	41.5
	1992	36.1
Nigeria	2011	39.7
	2009.8	48.8
	2003.7	42.9
	1996.3	46.5
	1992.3	45.0
	1985.5	38.7
Rwanda	2010.8	50.8
	2005.8	53.1
	2000	51.5
	1984.5	28.9

(Continued)

Table 14.3. Continued

Country	Survey year	Gini index
Senegal	2011	40.3
	2005	39.2
	2001	41.3
	1994.4	41.4
	1991	54.1
Sierra Leone	2011	35.4
	2003	42.5
	1989.5	n/a
South Africa	2008.7	63.1
	2005.7	67.4
	2000	57.8
	1995	56.6
	1993	59.3
Sudan	2009	35.3
Swaziland	2009.5	51.5
	2000.5	50.7
	1994.5	60.7
Tanzania	2007	37.6
	2000.4	34.6
	1991.9	33.8
Togo	2011	39.3
	2006	34.4
Uganda	2009.3	44.3
	2005.5	42.6
	2002	45.8
	1999	43.1
	1996.2	37.1
	1992	42.6
	1989	44.4
Zambia	2010	57.5
	2006	54.6
	2004.3	50.7
	2002.8	42.1
	1998	53.4
	1996	49.8
	1993	52.6
	1991	n/a

Source: PovcalNet: the on-line tool for poverty measurement developed by the Development Research Group of the World Bank. <http://iresearch. worldbank.org/PovcalNet/index.htm>3.

The Interrelationship Linking Growth, Inequality, and Poverty[6]

The economy of any nation or region is influenced, *inter alia*, by the process of globalization, which is largely exogenous (outside the control of the national state), and by the national development strategy, which includes the set of policies followed by the government and the existing institutions and is, at least partially, endogenous (under the limited control of the government).

By globalization, we mean here greater economic integration within the world economy manifested through increased openness. The major channels through which globalization affects the economy of any given country are trade, foreign investment, technology transfer, and labor migration (see Nissanke and Thorbecke [2010] for a detailed discussion of the various globalization transmission mechanisms). Thus, for example, an increase in Uganda's exports of horticultural products contributes to GDP growth, and because horticultural products are labor-intensive, their production contributes also to poverty reduction through increased employment of unskilled workers. In contrast, foreign direct investment in oil exploration and oil wells, likewise, contributes to output but creates few jobs—and may lead to more inequality in income distribution—because oil exploration and drilling relies on capital-intensive technologies. Skilled labor migration from poor countries deprives them of human capital, which is partially compensated by a flow of return remittances to family members back home. The point is that the various globalization channels at work influence the structure of growth differently in different settings. In order to understand the full (general equilibrium) effects of both globalization and the development strategy adopted by a given country on its economy, one needs to unveil the interrelationships among growth, inequality, and poverty.

Figure 14.1 illustrates schematically how globalization and a given development strategy affect the structure of growth, inequality, and poverty (abstracting from a number of feedback loops originating with poverty reduction

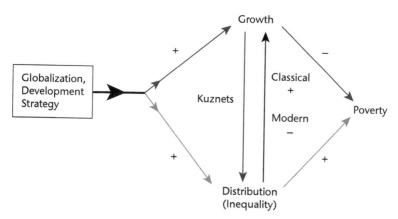

Figure 14.1 Globalization and development strategy and interrelationships among growth, inequality, and poverty
Source: Author's drawing.

back to growth and inequality that are discussed subsequently). In general, globalization and the country-specific development policies and institutions will contribute to growth (the upper left arrow in Figure 14.1) and have a more indeterminate effect on income distribution (the lower left arrow). In turn, these last two channels—the growth and distribution channels—interact dynamically to produce a growth–inequality–poverty triangular relationship (the triangle on the right side in Figure 14.1). The latter is referred to as Bourguignon's Triangle (Bourguignon 2004).

A key and controversial link in this triangle is that from income (and wealth) inequality to growth. This relationship is characterized by two conflicting theories. The classical theory argues that income inequality is required for growth, as the rich have a higher marginal propensity to save than the poor. Hence a more unequal income distribution, for the same level of aggregate income, will generate a larger total flow of savings, leading to more investment and higher growth (Kaldor 1956). In contrast, the modern "New Political Economy of Development" makes a strong case that greater income inequality is likely to dampen growth through a variety of channels, such as the diffusion of political and social instability, unproductive rent-seeking activities, and increased insecurity of property rights (Perotti 1993; Thorbecke and Charumilind 2002; Devereux and Sabates-Wheeler 2007). Still another link in the growth–inequality–poverty nexus is from growth to inequality. The Kuznets' law—that held that, at an early stage of development, growth would bring about a worsening of the income distribution up to a threshold level of per capita income and reduce inequality beyond this threshold—has essentially been dethroned.

In summary, the pattern of growth—that is shaped by the forces of globalization and the national development strategy—determines the state of the income distribution and of poverty. Each link of the causal chain in the growth–inequality–poverty nexus plays its role in contributing to the developmental outcome in any given country. Inequality acts as a filter between growth and poverty alleviation.

Based on the Bourguignon Triangle, Bourguignon (2004) formulated an extended growth–inequality–poverty model expressed in a reduced form equation. This "identity" model is derived on an approximation to an assumed log-normal income distribution which allows us to more comprehensively explain the heterogeneity of the nexus across countries and time periods. The full Bourguignon model expresses the growth in the poverty rate as a function of income growth, the initial Gini inequality coefficient, the growth of the Gini coefficient, the ratio of the poverty line to income, and some interacting terms.

Fosu (2012) tested this model using a sample of 23 SSA countries' data covering the period 1981–2007. His main findings were that the progress in poverty reduction between the mid-1990s and mid-2000s was considerable and essentially similar to that of South Asia and India. Furthermore, "income growth was on average the main engine for poverty reduction in SSA since the mid-1990s. In certain countries, though, inequality was crucial. This inequality role is in two parts: (1) declining inequality tended to decrease poverty, though not necessarily in very low low-income countries, and (2) lower initial inequality raised the rate at which growth was transformed to poverty reduction. The former role may be impeded, however, by low income levels as well as by the high levels of initial inequality" (Fosu 2012, p. 10). Viewed within a global context, the relatively low levels of income in most SSA countries and high inequality were major constraints to poverty reduction. A final noteworthy finding is the considerable heterogeneity of conditions across Africa.

We conclude this section with two robust observations. First, inequality is the filter between growth and poverty reduction. High inequality acts in two ways to dampen the impact of growth on poverty alleviation: (1) by impeding (and, at the limit, blocking) the transmission of growth to benefit the poor households; and (2) by fostering social and political conflicts that can retard subsequent growth. Secondly, the high variety of initial conditions across SSA means that generalizations need to be qualified and that appropriate national development strategies can only be formulated within the specific context of the prevailing initial conditions (see Nissanke and Thorbecke [2010]).

In the last decade or so, the development community has broadened from its focus on the narrower concept of poverty reduction per se to include human development for all. Building on the foundations of Sen's functioning and capabilities approach, human development has taken over center stage as the ultimate goal of development. Human development consists of a plethora of dimensions and aspects as they relate to health, education, nutrition, shelter, access to information, participation, nature of regime (degree of democracy and liberty), and many others. The evolution in the conception of development climaxed with the present paradigm of inclusive growth, which has been widely adopted by the development community.

The next section attempts, first, to define the meaning of inclusive growth within the context of SSA and, secondly, to determine the extent to which the present growth spell is inclusive.

Major and Distinct Features of Inclusive Growth within the Present Context of SSA: Reducing Inequality and Creating Productive Jobs

In the last half-dozen years, a rich literature on inclusive growth has flourished.[7] Although there appears to be a substantial degree of agreement among different authors and agencies regarding the main features of inclusive growth, no unique definition has been adopted by the development community. Perhaps the most comprehensive and concise definition of inclusive growth is that of the Indian Planning Commission (2011): "growth that reduces poverty and creates employment opportunities, access to essential services in health and education, especially for the poor, equality of opportunity, empowerment through education and skill development, environmental sustainability, recognition of women's agency and good governance" (p. 2). In turn, the African Development Bank (2012) defines inclusive growth as, "economic growth that results in a wider access to sustainable socio-economic opportunities for a broader number of people, regions or countries, while protecting the vulnerable, all being done in an environment of fairness, equal justice, and political plurality" (p. 2).

A case can be made that the major differences between the conventional approach to inclusive growth (as exemplified by the World Bank and the Asian Development Bank) and the African vision that would be appropriate to the distinct setting of SSA, reside in the (1) treatment of inequality; (2) the critical importance of creating stable, productive jobs; and (3) a successful structural transformation.

The first issue is whether in a subcontinent where poverty incidence and income inequality are still endemic and the highest in the world, a *fall* in income inequality should be an inherent feature of inclusive growth. In a nutshell, the question should be: how pro-poor should the pattern of growth be? There are two definitions of pro-poor growth. The *relative* definition is that the poor benefit proportionately more than the non-poor from the prevailing growth, which implies a fall in income inequality. The *absolute* definition only requires that the poor benefit from growth.[8] Ianchovichina and Lundstrom (2009) and the World Bank adopt the absolute definition, while the African view appears more sympathetic to the relative definition as the following quotation suggests: "Long-term sustainable high economic growth rates are necessary to reduce poverty and must be accompanied by growing productive employment to reduce inequality" (African Development Bank 2012, p. 2). Note the emphasis on *employment* in the above quotation—a point we return to shortly.

Reduction in Inequality

The main argument in favor of the absolute definition can be illustrated by an example drawn from Ianchovichina and Lundstrom (2009):

> For example, a society attempting to achieve pro-poor growth under the relative definition would favor an outcome characterized by average income growth of 2 percent where the income of poor households grew by 3 percent,

over an outcome where average growth was 6 percent, but the incomes of poor households grew by only 4 percent. While the distributional pattern of growth favors poor households in the first scenario, both poor and non-poor households are better off in the second scenario.

Two key assumptions are implicit in the above causal argument. First, any possible reverse effects from income inequality to the pace and pattern of growth are ignored (such as the presumed dampening effects of inequality on growth proposed by the "New Political Economy of Development" discussed earlier in the previous section). Secondly, no welfare value is attached to less inequality in the income distribution as a development objective in its own right. Even recognizing that a certain degree of income inequality is required to provide entrepreneurs the necessary incentives for growth to occur, society, in its social welfare function, might value greater equity as an end in itself.

Given the extremely high and, in some instances, still growing income inequality prevailing in many SSA countries, it makes sense to incorporate a reduction in income inequality as an essential part of an inclusive growth strategy in the African context.

Creation of Productive Jobs

The creation of productive jobs is absolutely essential in an environment characterized by: (1) extremely high unemployment and underemployment; (2) demographic trends that keep on adding more and more individuals to the productive age groups; (3) the general absence of social security schemes and weakening family social solidarity ties; and (4) the fact that a large share of the population resides in rural areas and depends on agriculture for its livelihood. As the influential McKinsey Report on *Africa at Work: Job Creation and Inclusive Growth* concludes: "For growth to be inclusive, African workers need to be employed. Employment income is the only sustainable mechanism for most of the population to share in the proceeds of growth" (McKinsey 2012, p. 11).

Traditionally, analysts have distinguished between informal and formal jobs. A somewhat more transparent and operational distinction is between vulnerable and stable jobs. Stable jobs are those held by employers (business owners) and employees (contract workers entitling them to basic remunerations), whereas vulnerable jobs include own-account workers who are self-employed mainly in subsistence agriculture or informal urban activities and family workers who work without a formal wage for other family members (McKinsey 2012). The great majority of the labor force in Africa is employed in vulnerable jobs (63 percent in 2010); only 28 percent were in stable jobs, and 9 percent were classified as unemployed. Between 2000 and 2010, Africa added 52 million new "vulnerable jobs" and 37 million new "stable jobs" (the annual growth rate of stable jobs during this period was 3.9 percent, which was considerably above the growth rate of the productive age group).

For growth to be truly inclusive, this trend has to continue with stable employment growing faster than vulnerable employment. Presently, about half of the African labor force is still employed in (largely small-scale) agriculture, and stable jobs in manufacturing, retail and hospitality (tourism), and construction (particularly, infrastructure) will have to be created to facilitate the migration out of agriculture and the rural areas. The potential rural migrants need to find productive jobs outside of agriculture. This is particularly essential as the African continent is about to reap a demographic dividend, "courtesy of its young and rapidly growing workforce and declining dependency ratio" (McKinsey 2012, p. 2). The good news is that Africa will have the lowest dependency burden in the world and a very large potential for future growth in the form of a labor force that in 20 years' time is estimated to become larger than that of either China or India. But, of course, to take advantage of this potential demographic dividend, a very large number of new (hopefully) productive jobs will need to be created.

The sectors with the greatest potential for generating stable jobs are: agriculture, retail and hospitality (tourism), manufacturing, construction, transport and communications, and government. Given the diversity of initial conditions and stages of development within SSA, the appropriate employment strategy will need to be tailored to the existing structure of the economy. One possible classification was proposed by Thorbecke (2014b) and derived on the basis of four hierarchical criteria. The first discriminating criterion is the *ex post* quality of institutions and governance that allows a breakdown between failed states and functioning states. The second criterion breaks down functioning states based on the prevailing structure of production and the importance of agriculture in overall growth and poverty reduction. This leads to a further distinction between those economies that are essentially agriculture-based and those in which agriculture has become a relatively minor sector (called "transforming economies," such as South Africa's). The third discriminating criterion separates countries according to their resource endowment (particularly oil and mineral resources) into resource-rich and resource-scarce groups, and on whether the agricultural environment is favorable or not. The final bifurcating criterion is the influence of geography and whether a given country is coastal or landlocked. The above taxonomic scheme yields a typology consisting of six relatively distinct categories of SSA countries: (1) Failed States; (2) South African Region; (3) Coastal, Resource-Scarce, "More Favorable Agricultural Potential" countries; (4) Landlocked, Resource-Scarce, "More Favorable Agricultural Potential" countries; (5) Resource-Rich, "More Favorable Agricultural Potential" countries; and (6) Countries with Less Favorable Agricultural Potential.

Has the Recent Structural Transformation Become More Effective in Contributing to Inclusive Growth in SSA?

We shall focus on the poorer countries at an early stage of development, that is, Category 3 above (including on the West Coast: Senegal, Ghana, Benin, Gambia, Togo, and Guinea-Bissau; and on the East Coast: Kenya, Tanzania, and Mozambique); and Category 4 above (e.g., Uganda and Ethiopia). For these countries, the role of agriculture is crucial. These countries are still largely agricultural—characterized by the bulk of the labor force employed in agriculture and a high proportion of GDP originating in that sector. Most of the producers are smallholders and subsistence farmers using traditional technology. In order to understand the anatomy of the growth process in such economies, one has to turn to the structural transformation—one of the best-known dynamic regularities affecting the composition of output over time.

As the structural transformation proceeds, both the share of agricultural output to total output and the share of agriculture in the labor force decline. However, the share of the latter remains continuously larger than the former, reflecting lower labor productivity in agriculture than in the rest of the economy and presumably greater poverty. The international cross-sectional regression line shows an amazing regularity underlying the structural transformation. Gradually as countries grow, and per capita income increases, the labor force shed from agriculture is absorbed productively in sectors outside agriculture. Although most Asian countries followed the normal growth pattern represented by the international cross-sectional regression line (Figure 14.2, upper left panel), the majority of SSA countries between 1960 and 2000 underwent a flawed structural transformation characterized by a stagnating per capita income and a dramatic fall in the share of agriculture in the labor force (Figure 14.2, lower left panel). This meant that the migration that occurred was not pulled by rising incomes outside agriculture but pushed by lack of income opportunities within agriculture, resulting in stagnant rural incomes (de Janvry and Sadoulet 2010). In the few SSA countries where the structural transformation pattern followed the "normal" pattern (such as Burkina Faso and Uganda), this appeared to have been linked to episodes of GDP growth (Figure 14.2, lower right panel).

The influential World Development Report, *Agriculture for Development* (World Bank 2008), makes a strong and convincing case that agriculture is the only possible engine of growth in many poor SSA countries. The key question is whether the sector, which was Africa's Achilles' heel for so long and tended to be unmercifully exploited by politicians who were motivated by short-term gains, is contributing to the present growth spell. More specifically, has there been acceleration in the growth of agricultural output since 2000, and how inclusive has it been?

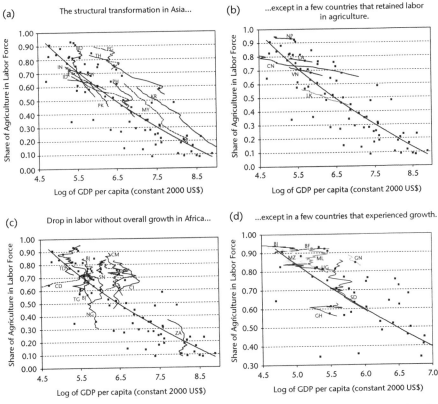

Figure 14.2 Structural transformation: Deviations from the normal pattern for the share of agriculture in the labor force in Asia and Africa

Source: Provided by Elisabeth Sadoulet and Alain de Janvry. Data from World Bank, World Development Indicators.

The evidence suggests that a changing policy environment and increased attention to agriculture has had a significant effect on overall productivity growth based on technical efficiency gains (Fuglie and Rada 2011). Although the *resource-based growth* has been very modest, enabling agricultural production to grow by about 2 percent annually since 1960, agricultural productivity from the mid-1980s onward has shown gradual improvements. This *productivity-based growth* raised average farm output per unit of input by another percentage point, resulting in average growth of about 3 percent per year between 1986 and 2011. In spite of recent progress, agricultural productivity in SSA still lags far behind other regions of the world (Fuglie and Rada 2013).

While the observed growth in agricultural production appears to have been modest since the beginning of the new millennium, there is some evidence that the structural transformation has followed a more "normal" course and is less "flawed" than before 2000. In another paper (Thorbecke 2014a),

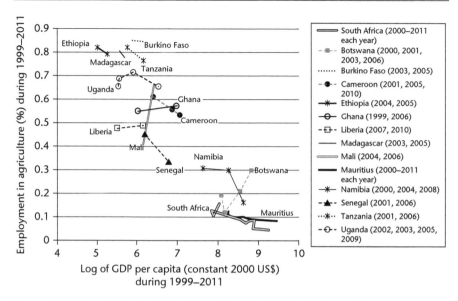

Figure 14.3 Recent structural transformation in selective SSA countries

Source: Thorbecke (2014a). This figure is reproduced here with acknowledgment of UNU-WIDER in Helsinki, who commissioned the original research.

I gathered the most recent observations on the share of employment in agriculture and constant per capita GDP available for any sub-period from 2000 forward.[9]

I found only 14 SSA countries for which at least two annual observations were available from 2000 onward.[10] As can be seen from Figure 14.3, the number of observations and timespans vary from country to country, and therefore, the figure has to be interpreted carefully. However, in general, Figure 14.3 suggests that, for the sample of countries included, the structural transformation during the present growth spell appears to be closer to "normal" with a few exceptions.[11] Based on this limited information, our tentative conclusion is that the structural transformation in the present growth spell has generally been inclusive insofar as it reflects a more orderly rural–urban migration process and workers being pulled out of agriculture into more productive non-agricultural jobs rather than pushed out.

Structural Transformation, Rural–Urban Migration, and Job Creation

A key question at this stage is how the structural transformation process can be accelerated and made more effective in facilitating intersectoral labor mobility, and especially, rural–urban migration. As agricultural labor productivity improves, workers are released and have to find employment outside the sector. In addition, high fertility rates ensure new workers are added to the labor force. The workers shed from agriculture will search for jobs in rural off-farm activities or in urban areas. This migration can be made easier and smoother through a number of policy interventions.

Infrastructure Investment

First, infrastructure investment is a crucial ingredient for inclusive growth. Rural roads reduce transaction costs (particularly transportation costs) for small farmers in bringing their products from farm to markets. Rural roads also facilitate the movement of workers out of agriculture into non-agricultural activities and thereby help accelerate the structural transformation.

One particular group that would be positively affected by the building of schools and clinics is girls and young women. In fact, Rauniyar and Kanbur (2010) argue that the focus on investing in infrastructure projects targeted towards inclusive development will have to be complemented by policies which improve the *utilization* of the infrastructure by disadvantaged groups. In addition, well-designed public work programs, including rural road construction, offer employment opportunities to unskilled informal workers—yet another vulnerable group. These programs need not be considered just as short-term social protection schemes to reduce poverty; they can be productive in their own right.

There are a number of channels through which infrastructure investment can promote inclusive growth by, among others: (1) creating new jobs; (2) reducing production costs; (3) expanding overall production capacity; (4) providing better connections to markets; and (5) improving access to key facilities (such as schools, clinics, and water sources) (Asian Development Bank 2012). Finally, improving the transportation network can contribute to a smoother and less disruptive urbanization process in Africa.

Integrated Rural Development and Rural Education and Training

Secondly, an important lesson learned from the successful experience of East Asia, and more particularly South Korea and Taiwan, is the emphasis on integrated rural development at an early stage of development. This process relied on a combination of research into more productive technologies, providing small farmers with inputs (e.g., seeds and fertilizer), credit, and extension services, and promoting multipurpose institutions such as farmers' cooperatives. One of the effects of a strategy of increasing productivity in small-scale agriculture was to raise farmers' incomes, accelerating and facilitating the labor migration out of agriculture into rural off-farm activities as well as rural–urban migration. A key ingredient in this strategy consisted of investment in rural (often vocational) education, which provided the migrants with desirable skills that were valuable in off-farm activities and in urban industrial endeavors and reduced the transaction costs of moving.

Given how notoriously poor the educational system is throughout most of SSA, a revamping of this system to better prepare children in rural areas for the kinds of skills (often vocational) required to perform the jobs opening up in such sectors as labor-intensive manufacturing, tourism, finance, and business services is essential to a successful structural transformation.

Summary and Conclusions

The empirical evidence reviewed earlier in this chapter indicates that most of sub-Saharan Africa has enjoyed an unprecedented acceleration in the growth of GDP per capita since 2000 that can be considered a quantum jump. High growth rates of GDP, in turn, have contributed to a significant fall in poverty and improvements in human development. The main cloud in what would otherwise be a blue sky and rosy outlook is the continuing high amount of income inequality that prevails in most SSA countries.

The nature of the interrelationships among growth, inequality, and poverty, as discussed earlier, is a crucial determinant of the pattern of growth and how inclusive that pattern is. High inequality acts in at least two ways to dampen the effect of growth on poverty reduction: first, by impeding the transmission of the benefits of growth to poor households and, second, by fostering social and political conflicts that can retard future growth.

The concept of inclusive growth, which is the latest paradigm adopted by the development community, was reviewed earlier in the section entitled "Major and Distinct Features of Inclusive Growth within the Present Context of SSA." Within the context of the African subcontinent where, notwithstanding recent progress, severe poverty and high inequality are still endemic, the reduction of inequality and the creation of productive and stable jobs need to be the two key pillars of an inclusive growth strategy.

Posing the question, "Has the recent structural transformation become more effective in contributing to inclusive growth in SSA?" in the next section, a case was made that the structural transformation in SSA has become more inclusive in the last decade. After a long period, prior to the new millennium, during which the structural transformation was flawed and characterized by workers being pushed out of agriculture into often even less productive jobs, there is some evidence that, since around 2000, agricultural workers were able to be pulled into more productive non-agricultural employment.

Finally, we explored how the structural transformation can be speeded up and made more effective by facilitating the rural–urban migration process.

Appropriate infrastructure investment in rural roads, among other strategies, can act as a lubricant to the migration process. In addition, integrated rural development is crucial to raising the productivity of small-scale farm households, thereby allowing the release of labor no longer required. The promotion of rural (vocational) education and training may be another measure, facilitating a more effective migration by providing rural workers with the necessary and desirable skills to fill productive jobs outside of agriculture.

Appendix

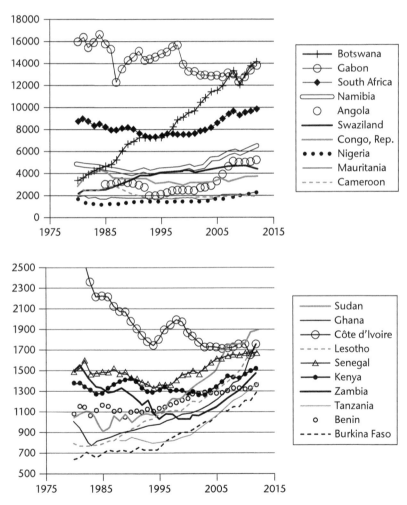

Appendix Figure A-14.1 Trends in GDP per capita (constant 2005 int'l $) for sub-Saharan African countries during 1980–2012

Source: Data from World Bank, World Development Indicators (downloaded on November 20, 2013).

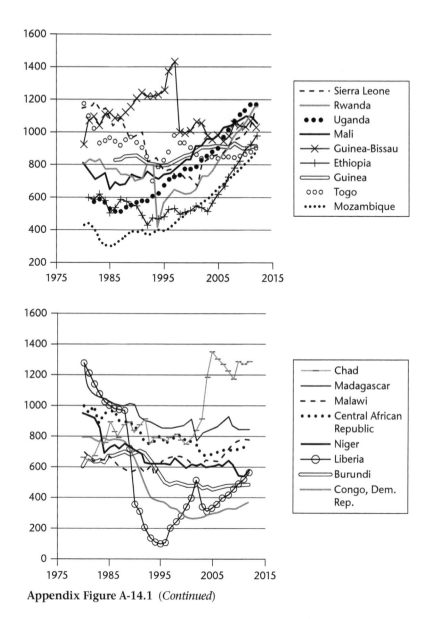

Appendix Figure A-14.1 (*Continued*)

Notes

1. As I warned in Thorbecke (2013): "In the process of scrutinizing and analyzing poverty and inequality trends, it is essential to confront the data problem. The World Bank's "PovcalNet" data set used here is based on official statistics provided by the statistical offices of the member countries. Even though it is the most comprehensive and internally consistent data set available on poverty and inequality, at the country level, it is particularly incomplete in its coverage of SSA and the World Bank apparently undertakes only a minimum of quality control." It could be argued even more strongly that, given the state of national income accounts in most SSA countries, GDP statistics are subject to high measurement errors. Furthermore, changing national income accounts' and surveys' methodologies (which occurs relatively often in SSA) affect the accuracy of comparisons over time.

2. Or lower negative growth rates.

3. *Changes* in growth rates of 5 percent above or below the prevailing level in the first period were considered as no change.

4. The poverty gap indicates the share of total GDP that would be required to bring all the poor in the population up to the poverty line. In other words, the poverty gap represents the share of GDP needed to eliminate poverty assuming perfect targeting was possible.

5. I am suspicious of the reported headcount ratio for Kenya. The World Bank's "PovcalNet" shows that the latter rose from 24.1 percent in 1999 to 39.9 percent in 2010, in spite of a growth rate of GDP per capita of about 1.5 percent annually in the 2000s. It is true that the impact of this modest growth on poverty reduction was mitigated by a worsening income distribution—the Gini coefficient rising from 42.5 in 1997 to 47.7 in 2005 (the last survey year available; see Table 14.3).

6. This section is based on Thorbecke (2013).

7. The discussion of inequality and its impact on pro-poor growth in the first part of this section relies extensively on Thorbecke (2014b).

8. Thus an extreme case where the average income of the poor increases by only 1 percent following a GDP growth spell of 8 percent would be considered pro-poor according to the absolute definition.

9. The data set (time series) used by de Janvry and Sadoulet (2010) to derive Figure 14.2 was not kept up in recent years. Instead of using the share of agriculture in the labor force, which is apparently no longer available, we had to rely on the share of agriculture in total employment. Although these two concepts are not analogous, their movements over time tend to coincide.

10. Most, but not all, of the 14 countries shown in Figure 14.3 belong to the two categories (i.e., Category 3: Coastal, Resource-Scarce, "More Favorable Agricultural Potential"; and Category 4: Landlocked, Resource-Scarce, "More Favorable Agricultural Potential") that we are focusing on.

11. Mali is the only country in the sample that appears to suffer from a flawed transformation, with a large (and unexplainable) fall in the agricultural share of employment combined with a fall in GDP per capita. Given the very short

time span (2004–06), a measurement error cannot be ruled out. In turn, Ghana, Botswana, and Liberia report rising shares of agricultural employment together with significant GDP growth. This could reflect increasing productivity in agriculture.

References

African Development Bank. 2012. "Briefing Notes for AfDB's Long-Term Strategy." Briefing Note No 6: Inclusive Growth Agenda, April 10, 2012.

Asian Development Bank. 2012. *Infrastructure for Supporting Inclusive Growth and Poverty Reduction in Asia*. Mandaluyong City, Philippines: Asian Development Bank.

Bourguignon, F. 2004. "The Poverty–Growth–Inequality Triangle." Paper presented at the Indian Council for Research on International Economic Relations, New Delhi, February 4, 2004.

de Janvry, A., and E. Sadoulet. 2010. "Agricultural Growth and Poverty Reduction: Additional Evidence." *World Bank Research Observer* 25 (1): pp. 1–20.

Devereux, S., and R. Sabates-Wheeler. 2007. "Editorial Introduction: Debating Social Protection." *Institute of Development Studies: IDS Bulletin* 38 (3): pp. 1–7.

Fosu, A. 2012. "Growth, Inequality, and Poverty in Sub-Saharan Africa: Recent Progress in a Global Context." (Paper prepared for the African Economic Research Consortium Plenary Session, Nairobi, December 4, 2011, revised version).

Fuglie, K., and N. Rada. 2011. "Policies and Productivity Growth in African Agriculture." ASTI/IFPRI-FARA Conference Working Paper 19, International Food Policy Research Institute, Washington, DC, and Forum for Agricultural Research, Accra, Ghana. <http://www.ifpri.org/sites/default/files/publications/fuglie.pdf>.

Fuglie, K., and N. Rada. 2013. "Research Raises Agricultural Productivity in Sub-Saharan Africa." United States Department of Agriculture: Economic Research Service.

Ianchovichina, E., and S. Lundstrom. 2009. "What is Inclusive Growth?" Note prepared for the Diagnostic Facility for Shared Growth. World Bank.

Indian Planning Commission. 2011. *Inclusive Growth: Vision and Strategy*. New Delhi, India.

Kaldor, N. 1956. "Alternative Theories of Distribution." *Review of Economic Studies* 23 (2): pp. 83–100.

McKinsey Global Institute. 2012. *Africa at Work: Job Creation and Inclusive Growth*. McKinsey & Company.

Nissanke, M., and E. Thorbecke. 2010. *The Poor Under Globalization in Asia, Latin America, and Africa*. Oxford: Oxford University Press.

Perotti, R. 1993. "Political Equilibrium, Income Distribution, and Growth." *Review of Economic Studies* 60 (4): pp. 755–776.

Rauniyar, G., and R. Kanbur. 2010. "Inclusive Development: Two Papers on Conceptualization, Application, and the ADB Perspective." January Draft, Independent Evaluation Department, Asian Development Bank.

Thorbecke, E. 2013. "The Interrelationship Linking Growth, Inequality and Poverty in Sub-Saharan Africa." *Journal of African Economies* 22 (suppl 1): pp. i15–i48.

Thorbecke, E. 2014a. "The Anatomy and Institutional Architecture of Inclusive Growth in Sub-Saharan Africa." UNU/WIDER Working Paper 2014/041, UNU-WIDER, Helsinki, Finland.

Thorbecke, E. 2014b. "The Anatomy of Growth in Sub-Saharan Africa." In *Economic Growth and Poverty Reduction in Sub-Saharan Africa: Current and Emerging Issues*, edited by Andy McKay, and Erik Thorbecke, Oxford University Press, forthcoming.

Thorbecke, E., and C. Charumilind. 2002. "Economic Inequality and Its Socioeconomic Impact." *World Development* 30 (9): pp. 1477–1495.

UNDP (United Nations Development Programme). 2014. *Human Development Report 2014*. New York: UNDP.

World Bank. 2008. *World Development Report 2008: Agriculture for Development*. Washington, DC: World Bank.

15

Social Mobilization and Food Security

The Contribution of Organized Civil Society to Hunger
Reduction Policies in Latin America

Marygold Walsh-Dilley and Wendy Wolford

Introduction

With the food and financial crises of 2008–11, concerns over global food
security have become increasingly pronounced (Barrett 2013). A his-
toric 1 billion people were hungry in 2008—roughly 1 in 7 of the world's
population—raising questions about how to feed a population of 9.6 billion
people in 2050. Concerns about population growth, peak oil and the search
for alternatives, resource degradation, and climate change have infused new
energy into discussions of agriculture and food security, although much
of the current discussion still focuses on food supplies. Notwithstanding
Amartya Sen's early work (see, for example, Sen [1976, 1981]) on the importance of entitlements, there is a strong focus internationally on whether it is
possible to produce enough food for all, given a fixed resource base. In the
contemporary literature, therefore, Per Pinstrup-Andersen's work stands out.
He forces us to look at access to food, particularly by the poor, arguing that
the key food security question relates not to productive capacity and supply,
but to how available food is distributed and whether or not it is produced
sustainably (Pinstrup-Andersen and Herforth 2008). He agrees that there is
significant cause for concern, but suggests that the problems of food insecurity, both today and in the future, can be solved with careful multisectoral
strategies oriented toward reducing rural poverty—a significant cause of environmental degradation—as well as connecting rural farmers to the market
and ensuring that food is distributed to those who need it. Contemporary

markets often fail to function adequately in accordance with societal ethics and goals, meaning that governments have an essential role to play in making up for market failure (Pinstrup-Andersen 2007, 2013; Pinstrup-Andersen and Watson 2011). Pinstrup-Andersen has been a chief proponent of the important role of government policies and programs in constructing global, national, and local food systems.

Building on the contributions of Pinstrup-Andersen and others about the importance of governance in addressing food insecurity, we examine the production of *good* governance in improving food security. We argue that relations between the state and civil society are central to understanding governance outcomes for food security. We suggest that civil society actors, particularly social movements invested in rural production or consumption issues, play a significant role in ensuring political commitment to hunger and food security. This argument calls upon a particular conception of the state, and we draw on recent work that conceptualizes the state as a set of relationships rather than a set of institutions (Alvarez 1998; Alvarez et al. 2008). These state–society relationships shape the nature of institutions and produce political cultures (Wolford 2010) that influence the ability and willingness of actors across the political arena to engage in anti-hunger work (Masset 2010).

Classical theories of the state (see, for example, Tilly [1978]; Tarrow [1994]; de Janvry et al. [2002]) tend to conceptualize the state as a coherent governing body that stands apart from—and usually above—its citizens (Ferguson and Gupta 2002). Objections to this theoretical distinction date back to the 1970s with Philip Abrams' "Notes on the Difficulty of Studying the State" (1988) (see also, Mitchell [1999]). Many scholars have since taken up the charge to open up "the black box" of the state, analyzing "every day forms of state formation" (Joseph and Nugent 1994), corruption (Gupta 2005), political cultures in state agencies (Alvarez 2009; Wolford 2010, forthcoming), and more. A growing literature on state–society relations emphasizes the mutual constitution and transformation of state and society (Fox 1993, 1996; Evans 1995; Migdal 2001).

At the most basic level in a democracy, civil society elects their representatives and potentially has significant influence over the nature of campaign promises. Beyond elections, civil society actors interact regularly with state institutions and agents, and it can be difficult to draw a hard line between state and society in practice. By recognizing the borders of state institutions as porous rather than solid, we are able to see the ways in which policies are influenced by banal interactions between civil society and state actors over space and time—over dinners at home, in the shopping mall, and on the street, and over the life of individuals who work for the government one year and for a civil society organization the next (or both simultaneously).

This perspective is particularly necessary for understanding food security policies in Latin America, where state–society relations have shifted dramatically over the past two decades. In the span of 20 or 30 years, military dictatorships across the region were overturned by popular protests that ushered in the so-called Third Wave of Democracy (Hagopian and Mainwaring 2005). New democracies from Argentina and Brazil to Bolivia strove to respond to popular demands for inclusion, even as they struggled with the legacies of Import-Substitution Industrialization and the burden of global economic crisis. The Third Wave of Democracy became the neo-liberal wave, as governments implemented radical policies for privatization, trade liberalization, and austerity. Resistance against these policies ushered in a new wave of progressive governments (referred to in the media as the "pink tide") that promised to attend to popular demands for inclusion, representation, and distribution. Throughout this tumultuous period, new social movements have organized to pressure their governments for greater access and recognition.

Although some of these movements retain the revolutionary or oppositional ideology and rhetoric of the 1970s and early '80s, many more have been incorporated into formal governance structures, whether directly through elected and appointed positions, or indirectly through consultation, mobilization, and organization. This incorporation results from what Evelina Dagnino calls the "perverse confluence" of democracy and neo-liberalism, where electoral participation combined with decentralization and growing disillusion to create both the potential and the demand for an active civil society (Dagnino 2003; Postero 2010).[1] As civil society organizations have grown stronger, they have taken on more of the everyday work of governing; charitable organizations provide services once associated with the state, and social movements are vested with the authority to distribute state resources, enact state policies, and garner political support. Thus, the move toward participation and the incorporation of formerly radical elements into the state (both directly and indirectly) in Latin America has forced scholars to appreciate the messy, fuzzy, soft nature of the boundaries between state and society.

In this chapter, we first outline the potential contribution that a state–society perspective makes to understanding and addressing food security issues. We suggest there are at least seven ways in which civil society influences—indeed improves—food security governance and state commitments toward hunger and malnutrition reduction. We then present macro-level data on political commitment to food security, demonstrating that Latin America has a particularly high commitment to hunger issues. We suggest that this is, in good part, due to the forms of state–society interaction in the region. We then turn to evidence from four countries: Peru, Bolivia, Brazil, and Guatemala. We focus specifically on the role of civil society in the formation and implementation of nutrition and anti-hunger policies; such efforts are both integral to a food security program and are comparable across countries. We have chosen these countries because they represent a range of experiences and state–society relationships. These four countries have all put significant effort into developing a strong nutrition policy, but have had differential involvement by civil society with varying degrees of success. In Peru, strong civil society incorporation has strengthened both the commitment to and implementation of nutritional and anti-hunger programs; in Bolivia, civil society is incorporated into government on paper but the depth of true participation is weak and anti-hunger programming has stalled; in Brazil, a radical social movement has retained its oppositional stance, even as it works with government officials to construct and implement a far-reaching set of programs to combat hunger, malnutrition, and rural poverty; and in Guatemala, levels of food insecurity are high, but the country is making significant progress, in large part due to participatory collaboration between the national state, key civil society groups and movements, and other stakeholders. Although these case studies demonstrate that social mobilization and participation do not always improve food security, they do show that attention to the relations between state and society are necessary to understand state commitments and programs to address food security. To conclude, we draw out a set of lessons from the case studies and broader literature on Latin America for fruitful forms of state–society relations.

State Commitment to Hunger Reduction and the Contribution of Social Movements

Beginning in 1974, with the first World Food Conference convened in Rome by the UN's Food and Agricultural Organization (FAO), global agreements to reduce hunger and malnutrition have been affirmed repeatedly in international forums. Yet, the progress made falls short of agreed-upon goals. Although, on one hand, we have more evidence that identifies the types of food policies that work (Pinstrup-Andersen and Pandya-Lorch 2001; Pinstrup-Andersen and Watson 2011), political struggles and governance failures get in the way of successful policy construction to address hunger and food insecurity. Food policy is influenced by a large range of stakeholders and must account for many different interests, but powerful stakeholder groups, such as agribusiness leaders, large farmers, and elite actors with divergent interests, have more access to and influence over policymakers than the poor and malnourished (Pinstrup-Andersen 2013). As a result, a significant frustration is that developing country governments give low priority to action aimed at reducing hunger and malnutrition (Pinstrup-Andersen and Watson 2011). Even with a commitment to addressing food insecurity, hunger reduction is a highly political and contentious process (Gillespie et al. 2013), and disagreements over interventions and strategies are an almost universal feature of related policy discussions (Pelletier et al. 2011). Governments often lack the technical or financial capacity to implement strategies, regardless of how they are reached (Abers and Keck 2009). These conditions have hampered successful policies and programs that target hunger and malnutrition, resulting in significantly less progress on hunger reduction than was widely agreed to in the Millennium Development Goals and other targets.

Recognizing the politics of hunger and malnutrition reduction, recent work asks how enabling environments and processes that build and sustain political momentum and the capacity to address food security might be cultivated (Pelletier et al. 2011; Mejía Acosta and Fanzo 2012; Gillespie et al. 2013; Hoey and Pelletier 2013). Three overlapping domains emerge as important in this research, and Gillespie et al. (2013) argue they can each be developed and sustained through deliberative action (see also Pelletier et al. [2011]).

The first domain relates to forging widespread recognition of the problem of hunger—creating knowledge about the existence, causes, and consequences of malnutrition—and articulating narratives that compel widespread commitment and action. The timeliness, credibility, and persuasiveness of evidence are important both for convincing a broader audience and for designing effective programming to combat food insecurity. Developing a single, compelling narrative that frames nutrition as part of the national development agenda is particularly effective (Mejía Acosta and Fanzo 2012). Ultimately, these communication and framing processes are important, since they are what generate both the political will among political leaders and policymakers, and the broader stakeholder buy-in necessary to translate this commitment into effective programs. There are, of course, feedback loops between these two components—an invested stakeholder set will also pressure policymakers to take action as well as facilitate the programs that are in effect.

The second set of factors contributing to hunger reduction efforts relates to governance and politics: how state mechanisms work to both champion hunger issues, as well as to coordinate effective and efficient action. The approaches that are best able to reduce hunger and malnutrition are multisectorial (De Schutter 2012), but coordination between ministries and at different scales is often difficult to achieve (Hoey and Pelletier 2013). Establishing a body to coordinate action, distribute funding effectively, incorporate various stakeholders, and monitor progress is an important factor in developing effective hunger programming, but only if these bodies have real power (Mejía Acosta and Fanzo 2012). The direct involvement of the president or prime minister can be a powerful tool; the successes in countries that have been best able to address hunger through policy are often traced back to the direct involvement and commitment of the state executive (Sanchez-Montero et al. 2010; De Schutter 2012; Mejía Acosta and Fanzo 2012).

The third important domain for hunger reduction relates to capacity and resources for the implementation of interventions. There is a wide range of interventions necessary at multiple scales, from national trade policy to science and technology development and targeted poverty-relief, education, and healthcare programs (Pinstrup-Andersen and Herforth 2008). Successful delivery of services at the local level tends to work best in countries where there is a sense of ownership over local programs and where governance structures are adequately decentralized (Mejía Acosta and Fanzo 2012).

Increasingly, a fourth factor is identified as instrumental for improving governance for food security and hunger reduction: the participation and empowerment of civil society (Sanchez-Montero et al. 2010; De Schutter 2012; Gillespie et al. 2012; Mejía Acosta and Fanzo 2012). Civil society groups, in this account, are important to ensure accountability and to generate pressure to ensure the sustainability of programs over time. We do not dispute this, but here we suggest that rather than a fourth element, social mobilization and civil society groups are integral to each of the three stages of governance outlined above.

Civil society organizations (CSOs)—including, but not limited to, social movements—shape the governance mechanisms above in seven key ways: through state formation, voice, framing, pressure, targeting, oversight or accountability and, in some cases, implementation (see Table 15.1 below). In what follows, we address each of these in more detail.

State Formation

Civil society contributes to state formation in ways that influence food security through a number of avenues. Social movements, in particular, were elemental in the rise of progressive governments across Latin America, and this core constituency influences the types of political promises and strategies that elected leaders pursue. The political ideologies of these new executives reflect the growing discontent with inequality and pervasive poverty that social movements have mobilized around. But even beyond the election of executives, civil society pressure and mobilization can influence how various institutions of the state relate to each other, contributing to or detracting from cultures of vertical and horizontal coordination, for example.

Voice

CSOs provide a key mechanism for articulating concerns about hunger to broader audiences and generating wider commitment and action. They give *voice* to the poorest and most vulnerable, raising their concerns in the

Table 15.1 Civil society contributions to state policy

Areas of contribution	Specific mechanisms
State formation	• Election of executive • Shape of class relations in state • Use of force versus consent • Incorporation of societal demands in state agenda
Voice	• Speaking for the poor, marginal, and excluded • Aggregating demands • Articulating demands in an intelligible political language
Framing	• Presentation of issue to entire nation, to global community, and to political leaders • Situating theme within broader "moral economy" of norms and common sense understandings of social justice
Pressure	• Organization of bodies in the street • Tactical maneuvers—using local, national, and international media, blockades, hunger strikes, international standards or law • Shaming (bodies versus political power)
Targeting	• Identifying the most needy • Establishing the networks and infrastructure to reach these audiences; disseminating information to target audience • Assisting target audience in accessing services
Oversight	• Continued pressure during implementation phase • Self-selection of beneficiaries • Threat of exit and opposition if project/policy/program fail • "Legs on the ground" provide feedback
Implementation	• Service delivery—assistance or assumption of task • Participatory design, evaluation, and execution

Source: Authors.

local, national, and international spheres. Providing voice is a considerable service for populations too busy and poor to take the time or figure out how to make demands. Social movements and civil society organizations provide a link between populations most vulnerable to food insecurity and the people and institutions with power to do something about it. They make policymakers aware of and concerned about the problem of food insecurity, its causes and consequences, and in that way, urge governments to take action (Masset 2010). CSOs can serve as brokers between political representations and everyday people suffering the negative effects of exclusion.

Framing

CSOs can work to frame the issue of food security in ways that resonate with the public, policymakers, and legal frameworks. They also create narratives around food security that provide opportunities for new means of addressing food insecurity, such as through the framework of human rights (Jha 2009;

Mander 2012). Two recent examples of transnational framing around food are the Right to Food campaign led by the FAO, and its affirmation of the right to be a peasant that is based on the demands for food sovereignty, both of which rely crucially on state support.

Pressure

CSOs bring together and coordinate stakeholder groups in ways that *pressure* policymakers to take the voices and needs of the most vulnerable into account. Social movement participants take to the streets, occupy public buildings, and erect blockades that choke off critical flows of goods or people. Pressure tactics are often most effective when state representatives are provided with a low-threat potential response—distributing food baskets or raising the minimum salary, as opposed to conducting full-scale land reform or raising taxes. The pressure that mobilization campaigns generate, along with that of the press and opposition parties, makes ignoring the problem too costly politically, keeping policymakers in check and on task (Masset 2010).

Targeting

Identifying and bringing targeted populations into and generating buy-in for policy programs is not always an easy task. The most needy populations are not always aware of the services available to aid them, and these people frequently lack the skills and resources required to access services. Social movements and other civil society groups often have linkages to such populations, or have the capacity to build infrastructures to reach them. They are also potentially better equipped to understand the constraints such populations face in accessing services and are able to help develop the resources to overcome them. Thus, CSOs not only represent the poorest and most vulnerable people to the state, but these organizations also serve as representatives of the state to these groups within the population.

Oversight

Many studies of civil society and the state stop short of oversight, arguing that civil society is necessary to pressure the government but do not identify evaluation of the capacity of government to make good on its promises as among its important contributions. Yet, particularly in the context of "weak states" that either lack key competencies or feel little social obligation to follow through on promises, continued oversight by CSOs or social movements can be crucial. Social movements and civic organizations provide important technical capacities (Dagnino 2003; Abers and Keck

2009), *targeting* support toward appropriate beneficiaries and *overseeing* the implementation and evaluation of programs to ensure government accountability. They also build public buy-in and local ownership of programs, which in one study Mejía Acosta and Fanzo (2012) found contributed to effective nutrition programming.

Implementation

There are situations in which CSOs or social movements may be called upon to actually take the place of the state in implementing food security programs. If the state is unresponsive or incapable of providing the resources, the responsibility for executing a program may be deliberately outsourced (often to a private third-party contractor) or unintentionally assumed (often by a social movement displeased by the state's efforts). In this case, the civil society actor may govern in ways that allow the program to be disseminated, even in the absence of sufficient state capacity.

Social scientists in and of Latin America have worked on the conditions that help to shape the productive integration of the state and social movements, and some key elements stand out (see, for example, Dagnino [2003]). Social movements are most effective when: (1) they are truly representative of populations in need, with resources to legitimate their participation, whether those resources are social capital, organization, financial reserves, etc.; (2) they possess members with technical capacity equal to the tasks they have taken on; and (3) social movement activists and members choose to collaborate with government actors or entities but retain the right and capacity to step outside the partnership and protest if efforts are not productive.

Of course, not all mobilization or protest contributes to responsible governance around hunger reduction or food security outcomes. In fact, one form of spontaneous protest that was seen during the recent food crisis—food riots—might have actually contributed to the development of policies that lowered food prices for the urban poor, but at the expense of smallholder agriculture and the rural sector, where most of the world's poorest people are located (Pinstrup-Andersen and Herforth 2008).

There are certainly other negative cases of popular mobilization—indeed, many feared that social movements threatened the delicate return to democracy in Latin America in the 1980s and argued that support for such movements would reignite a backlash among conservative forces, such as the agrarian elite and military. Movements such as the Shining Path in Peru and the FARC (The Revolutionary Armed Forces of Colombia or *Fuerzas Armadas Revolucionarias de Colombia*) in Colombia certainly did little for regional food security, and so we need to be able to assess the state–society interactions that give rise to socially productive movements and unproductive ones. Based on our brief overview of the possible contributions of civil society and social movements, we argue that the ability of both to positively contribute to food security depends as much on the nature of state–society relations as on the characteristics of the movement itself.

Thus, in this chapter, we suggest that hunger and malnutrition reduction strategies benefit from a particular kind of state–society relation—one in which society is not an external force motivating good governance, but rather is central to processes whereby problems are identified and policies to address them are formed and implemented. That is, civil society is not an external entity that contributes to good governance by leveraging the state; rather, governance emerges out of the state–society relations. We focus on the Latin American experience to draw out each of these roles that social movements can play in building food security. We focus, in particular, on hunger and malnutrition reduction strategies, comparing the experiences of four countries: Brazil, Guatemala, Peru, and Bolivia. We examine state–society interactions in the framing, formulation, and implementation of policies, drawing out lessons from both their successes and difficulties.

More and more, advocates point to the importance of political will to improve food security. They suggest that the ability to reduce hunger is not simply a matter of economic growth, but rather that hunger issues need to be prioritized and addressed through state programs and policies. Masset (2010), for instance, has developed a basic theory of change, starting with political will and ending in hunger outcomes. In this chapter, we suggest that we cannot start with political will as an independent variable influencing hunger outcomes. Rather, we posit that political will itself is a dependent category, and we suggest that social mobilization is a key factor influencing the level of political commitment toward hunger reduction around the world.

The Political Commitment to Food Security

There are a number of indices that measure hunger and food security outcomes, from poverty measures and measures of caloric intake to anthropomorphic measures of childhood stunting (see Masset [2010] for a review). Yet, these measures fail to tell us about the processes that influence hunger or the determinants of hunger eradication. Improvements in hunger outcomes require political will, and addressing hunger is, in large part, a matter of political priorities (Masset 2010; te Lintelo et al. 2011; FAO 2012). Two different ways that this commitment has been measured are through the Right to Food measures of the FAO (Vidar 2006; Knuth and Vidar 2011) and the Hunger and Nutrition Commitment Index (te Lintelo et al. 2011, 2013). Both indicate that Latin America, as a region, has particularly high levels of commitment to address food security. This commitment has had tangible results, and Latin America is the only region where the absolute number of undernourished people has fallen over the past two decades (FAO 2009, 2011).

The FAO Right to Food data keep track of the degree of legal protection of the right to food afforded in constitutions and the associated framework laws that lay out the general principles and obligations of the state with regard to food (FAO 2011). Constitutional protection is an important litmus test for the commitment to hunger reduction, because it supersedes all acts of legislation contrary to it (Knuth and Vidar 2011). There are different degrees of constitutional protection of the right to food. Twenty-three countries in the world explicitly recognize the right to food as a human right (14 in Latin America), but only nine of these countries recognize it as a separate and stand-alone right. Of these nine countries, six are in Latin America: Bolivia, Brazil, Ecuador, Haiti, Guyana, and Nicaragua (Knuth and Vidar 2011). Similarly, of the 10 countries that have already adopted framework laws on food security, nine are Latin American: Argentina, Bolivia, Brazil, Ecuador, El Salvador, Guatemala, Nicaragua, Peru, and Venezuela[2] (Knuth and Vidar 2011). As of 2011, framework laws are being drafted in an additional nine countries, including three in Latin America: Honduras, Mexico, and Paraguay[3] (Knuth and Vidar 2011).

The FAO Right to Food data do reflect an element of government commitment to reduce hunger, but fail to capture the ways in which this legislative or constitutional commitment is actually leading to a change in policy or programming. The Hunger and Nutrition Commitment Index (HANCI) seeks to do just that. The HANCI uses secondary data to measure state commitment to food security across three areas of government action (legal frameworks, policies and programs, and public expenditures) and ranks countries on the basis of these measurements (te Lintelo et al. 2011, 2013). This measure recognizes that hunger and malnutrition reduction requires multisectoral action and includes measures on a range of components, including access to resources like land, water, and sanitation; extension coverage; gender parity and rights; government expenditures on health, agriculture, and nutrition; and policies and programs such as vitamin A coverage and the promotion of complementary feeding. Although it is rather simple, it is quite broad in its approach to capturing the commitment to hunger reduction.[4]

The first round of the HANCI covers 45 developing countries, with a focus on Africa. Only three Latin American countries are included at this stage: Guatemala, Peru, and Brazil. Not surprisingly, given what we know about the strength of right to food commitments in Latin America, these three countries all are ranked in the top five of the HANCI, and Guatemala is the top-ranked country of the index (see Appendix Table A-15.1). Guatemala performs particularly well on the nutrition commitment index. This is encouraging, as Guatemala is rated as having an "alarming" hunger situation in the Global Hunger Index, and it has one of the world's highest rates of child stunting (te Lintelo et al. 2013).

The HANCI findings indicate that the commitment to address hunger and malnutrition is not determined by economic growth or national income (te Lintelo et al. 2013). For instance, Malawi's gross national income of $871 per capita is much lower than either Guinea-Bissau's ($1,240) or Angola's ($5,230), and Malawi has a slower rate of growth than both countries as well. But Malawi ranks second on the HANCI, whereas Angola and Guinea-Bissau rank relatively low on the HANCI ratings (see Appendix Table A-15.1). An important question that should be addressed concerns the factors that contribute to building such a commitment to hunger and malnutrition reduction. It is this question that motivates the present work.

The Role of Social Mobilization in Food Security: Examining the Cases

In this section, we analyze the politics behind the hunger reduction programs in four countries: Peru, Brazil, Bolivia, and Guatemala. We pay particular attention to the role of civil society and social movements. These case studies illustrate the importance of state–society interactions, and we draw out the avenues through which civil society influences state commitment and governance using the seven arenas of influence identified above (state formation, voice, framing, pressure, targeting, oversight, and implementation).

Peru: State and Civil Society Working Together

Peru has been very successful at addressing hunger and malnutrition over the past decade. Following a significant change in policy in 2005, previously stagnant malnutrition rates fell from 22.9 to 17.9 percent by 2010, with reductions occurring mainly in rural areas (De Schutter 2012). This success is attributed to a new strategy of horizontal integration, involving the promotion of effective coordination across different government sectors and multiple stakeholders; vertical integration involving the implementation of the strategy across different scales; and financial and budgetary coordination across all levels (Mejía Acosta 2011). Integral to these efforts—indeed, recognized as the key ingredient prompting these changes—was the Child Nutrition Initiative (CNI), an advocacy coalition made up of civil society representatives, international NGOs, cooperation agencies, and research institutions. CNI was led by CARE Peru, but included several agencies: Action Against Hunger, ADRA (Adventist Development and Relief Agency) Peru, Caritas Peru,

United Nations' Children's Fund (UNICEF), UN Population Fund, Future Generations, Institute of Nutrition Research, the Mesa de Concertacíon para la Lucha Contra la Pobreza (MCLCP),[5] FAO, Pan American Health Organization, Plan International, Prisma, World Food Programme (WFP), and the United States Agency for International Development (USAID). This coalition allowed member organizations and agencies to overcome the fragmented approach that had been pursued by the Peruvian government up to that point (Mejía Acosta 2011). It also was inclusive, attracting private sector investment in poverty and malnutrition alleviation and increasing the influence of smaller NGOs (Mejía Acosta 2011), as well as providing a platform through which international funders could reliably support hunger reduction in Peru. The CNI played multiple roles: advocating for making nutrition the central component in the government's fight against poverty; providing a coordination mechanism to channel technical and financial distributions from different cooperating agencies; and serving as a public platform to disseminate and review government efforts and to secure future political commitments from elected politicians (Mejía Acosta 2011). It worked to frame hunger reduction as a central element of Peruvian national development, exerted pressure both before and after elections in ways that forced candidates to commit to hunger reduction, and later ensured that the elected leaders followed through on their promises.

The CNI made a series of well-known interventions into Peruvian politics that were integral to making nutrition a national priority. First, they developed a comprehensive framework for understanding the causes and consequences of malnutrition in Peru and its essential role in national development, and generated narratives around how best to approach malnutrition reduction. Second, the CNI was instrumental in generating buy-in from key political stakeholders, first at the national level and later at the regional level. One of the key events that publicized the advocacy work of the CNI was its campaign to secure commitments from political candidates. In 2006, the CNI obtained the signatures of all 10 presidential candidates on the "5 by 5 by 5" commitment—a pledge to reduce chronic child malnutrition by 5 percent in children under 5 years of age in the 5 years until 2011, and also to focus on rural malnutrition and close the rural–urban gap.

Upon the election of Alan García, the CNI maintained political pressure to make sure that he fulfilled his campaign promise. One element of this was a draft policy document, outlining actions for the first 100 days of government. This provided President García with a roadmap for living up to the "5 by 5 by 5" commitment, and in fact, his government actually increased the target to 9 percent. The CNI used this successful strategy to secure commitments of regional officials and the candidates in the subsequent presidential election, which resulted in the election of Ollanta Humala in 2011. The activities of the CNI ensured a degree of continuity, despite the fact that these presidents came from different parties (Mejía Acosta and Fanzo 2012).

The case of Peru, and in particular the important role played by the Child Nutrition Initiative, demonstrates how civil society organizations can be critical for good food security governance. The CNI played multiple roles in the areas of advocacy, coordination, and technical capacity. The civil society, social movement, and donor agencies that the CNI brought together were integral for generating widespread stakeholder buy-in through their work to *frame* hunger in ways that mobilized action, contributed to *state formation and the creation of state priorities*, and channeled technical capacities in ways that allowed the state to *implement* programs that were potentially beyond its resources. While program implementation is always difficult, the pressure of civil society groups in Peru ensured the sustained commitment of the President's Office, which played an important role in coordinating efforts across sectors as well as raising the profile of nutrition issues in the public more broadly—thereby ensuring greater buy-in at local and regional levels. In Peru, the CNI also pressured regional and local leaders, which contributed to better vertical integration of nutrition programs as well. Finally, CNI contributed important technical assistance as nutrition policies were formulated in Peru.

Brazil: Radical Opposition Within and Outside the State

Brazil is widely lauded for its explicit attention to food security and hunger issues, its creative and forward-thinking programs and projects, and its relationship between state and civil society. Eradicating hunger and fighting poverty have become key objectives in the domestic policy agenda, and as a result, Brazil has managed to meet the first Millennium Development Goal early by reducing extreme poverty by half well in advance of the 2015 deadline (da Silva et al. 2011). This new attention to hunger and poverty is, in part, a response to extreme inequality that has limited the ability of the rapid increase in Brazilian agricultural output and productivity over the past 30 years. Brazil is now the world leader in several key commodities, including livestock, fruits, and grains, but this impressive increase in productivity has not been evenly distributed. Brazil has the second highest level of inequality in land ownership in the world (second only to Paraguay); farms over 500 hectares make up only 2 percent of the country's total but cover 56 percent of arable land, and these farms have historically captured the majority of public support. In 2006, family farms supplied more than 70 percent of the domestic food consumption, but received only 25 percent of total agricultural credits. This inequality has manifested in the creation of two separate ministries—one for agribusiness, essentially, and one for agrarian development, or the rural poor and small family farmers that were left out of the commodities boom.

In 2002, Luiz Inácio Lula da Silva was elected president of Brazil. During his administration (2003–10), Brazil implemented a host of social protection policies to address hunger, malnutrition, and poverty. Lula had close ties to social movements in Brazil, particularly the largest grassroots social movement in the world, the Movement of Rural Landless Workers (MST). The MST has historically been very important for raising the profile of the small farm sector and the issue of land inequality, and has pressured the government to enact agrarian reforms that promote and support small and family farm production. The MST threw the full weight of its membership (estimated at 1.5 million) behind Lula's campaigns for the presidency, and has worked closely with Lula to develop a series of measures aimed at developing and supporting progressive policies oriented toward food security and sovereignty (Wolford and Nehring 2013). One significant element of both the Lula campaign and his subsequent administration is the *Fome Zero* (Zero Hunger) program. This program was launched in 2001, when Lula was a candidate for presidency, and then in 2003 it became the main governmental strategy guiding economic and social policies in Brazil (da Silva et al. 2011).

Fome Zero, which was developed through a collaboration between civil society leaders, technical experts, and politicians (including Lula, of course), is a national poverty alleviation and food security strategy; it is an explicitly multisectoral program that targets the structural causes of poverty and hunger. Over the past 10 years, *Fome Zero* has led to a reduction in hunger and poverty throughout Brazil, improving access to food, contributing to income generation and rural employment, supporting family agriculture, and encouraging social inclusion and participatory democracy. Between 2003 and 2008, the number of people in poverty decreased by 27 percent (from 15.4 million to 11.3 million), and Brazil's extremely poor fell by nearly half (Wolford and Nehring 2013).

One important element of this strategy was the Federal Law for Food and Nutrition Security, a framework law on food security that recognizes food as a basic human right (FAO 2011). This law created the institutional framework for addressing hunger and malnutrition in Brazil, including re-establishing the National Council on Food and Nutritional Security (CONSEA), along with an inter-ministerial coordination mechanism (FAO 2011). CONSEA is composed of governmental actors, such as the National Secretariat for Food Security, and numerous civil society actors, such as indigenous organizations and social movements, including the very strong presence of the MST. The council has played a large role in bringing together advocates for agrarian reform, the right to food, agroecology, and other environmental concerns and communicating those concerns to the president of Brazil. The National

Food and Nutritional Security Plan (PNSAN), which was created under Lula, provides the coordinating mechanism, linking the various programs and initiatives across sectors to promote the human right to adequate food. PNSAN is specifically designed to link hunger reduction and food assistance to family farm production and sustainable agroecological systems, emphasizing the role of the family farm in feeding the country (the backbone of the *Fome Zero* framework). PNSAN has actively promoted respect for social movement goals such as food sovereignty and the guarantee of the human right to adequate food, including access to water, as a state policy and in international negotiations and cooperation (Wolford and Nehring 2013).

None of this would have been possible without social movement and CSO contributions on many levels. Social movements, particularly the MST, were instrumental to the rise of Lula, who has centralized the Zero Hunger program in his administration's social and economic policy. Civil society groups were also involved in the design and development of the program, and later continued to exert pressure to ensure that the program was implemented, as well as having overseen the execution of various aspects in order to ensure accountability. The MST employs a variety of tactics at multiple levels of governance, from the municipality to the federal level, to ensure that programs are actually carried out, tactics that carry with them the threat—and opportunity—of both opposition and collaboration (Wolford and Nehring 2013). Other CSOs have been important to monitoring and reporting the violations of the human right to food, helping to bring violations to the courts or other arbiters (FAO 2011).

Wolford and Nehring (2013) illustrate the role of social movements and civil society organization in ensuring access to food for some of the most vulnerable groups in Brazil. They point, in particular, to the role of the MST in providing food for landless poor who are involved in land occupations. Land occupations are technically illegal, but, in practice, these actions are supported by state officials who have come to see the occupations as a normal part of the process. These land occupations are increasingly governed through official state mechanisms, forms, and negotiators. Indeed, civil society actors look to the National Institute for Colonization and Agrarian Reform (INCRA) to have the land occupation demands heard and to provide supplies—including food—to maintain the encampment (Wolford and Nehring 2013).

In the case of Brazil, civil society—and especially, highly visible and active social movements—have had a significant role in how the state has addressed hunger and malnutrition reduction. Central to processes of *state formation*, these movements and organizations have also played an important representational role on behalf of the most poor and vulnerable, applying steady *pressure* on even sympathetic state officials and authorities to ensure the demands of the poor were met. They have also had an important role in the *implementation* of government interventions, targeting needy populations and funneling resources to the most poor and vulnerable.

Bolivia: The Surprisingly Limited Influence of Civil Society

Food security and food sovereignty issues have been central to Bolivia's development agenda since the election of President Evo Morales in 2005, and also make a strong showing in the newly drafted constitution that was drawn up through a constituent assembly in a highly contentious process (Samdup 2011; Cuesta et al. 2013). These commitments are linked to efforts to radically reform politics, in response to sustained protest by indigenous and other social movements in Bolivia (Postero 2010), but implementation of programs to enforce these new guarantees has been limited (Samdup 2011). Nonetheless, Bolivia has developed a food security strategy that takes a multisectoral approach and incorporates no fewer than 13 projects and programs, including agriculture, health, education, and finance and trade sectors.[6]

Bolivia's difficulty implementing effective food security projects is not due to lack of funding. Due to the nationalization of the hydrocarbon sector, government revenues from natural gas extraction have generated resources that the state has used to address poverty in the country (Postero 2010). Indeed, absorbing these new revenues has proven difficult, particularly at the municipal level where local governments sometimes fail to spend their full budgets (Samdup 2011). Rather, success in implementing hunger and malnutrition reduction programming is limited by coordination issues, in terms of both horizontal and vertical coordination, and lack of technical capacity. These failures are accompanied by a notably limited involvement of civil society organizations in hunger and nutrition policy and programming. Elsewhere in Latin America, linkages between state and civil society has allowed CSOs to fill some of these coordinating and technical roles, while at the same time facilitating civil society pressure on governments in ways that ensure sustained commitment and action. This did not happen in the Bolivian case.

The Zero Malnutrition (ZM) Program provides a good example of these difficulties (see the detailed study of the initial phases of ZM by Hoey and Pelletier [2013], and also Samdup [2011]). The program was initiated in 2003 but floundered until 2006, when the Morales administration made malnutrition reduction a core goal of the 2006–10 National Development Plan. After a period of uncertainty (Hoey and Pelletier 2013), the ZM Program was formally launched by Morales in July 2007.

The overarching goal of the Zero Malnutrition Program is eradication of malnutrition among children, with an emphasis on children under 2 years of age. It takes a multisectoral and decentralized approach, involving 10 ministries. Despite its multisectoral intentions, coordination between ministries has been a challenge. Whereas in other countries, one significant element of successful nutrition efforts has been the direct involvement of the president and the executive office particularly to coordinate efforts (Mejía Acosta and Fanzo 2012), in Bolivia, President Morales was relatively uninvolved in the formulation and implementation of the ZM policy aside from the launch and the later public signing of major donor contributions to ZM (Hoey and Pelletier 2013). Thus, although Morales' mandate to reduce poverty and inequality propelled nutrition into the National Development Plan, the process of policy formulation and implementation has not benefited from the coordination of the presidency, as in Peru.

Nonetheless, ZM has benefited from charismatic "nutrition champions" that have pushed the program forward, particularly in the Ministry of Health, and to a lesser extent, in the Ministry of Education (Samdup 2011; Hoey and Pelletier 2013; Vidal n.d.). The problem was, however, that few of the initial ZM initiatives required collaboration across sectors, and there was relatively little buy-in from the non-health and education ministries. There was significant confusion about why and how these sectors should be involved and what their roles and responsibilities were, and there was some pushback in these ministries against ZM-related interventions and delegates (Samdup 2011; Hoey and Pelletier 2013). What was lacking was strong horizontal cooperation between ministries and a way to build commitment across these sectors.

There was also an issue with vertical coordination between state, departmental, and municipal levels. While the initial vision was to set up food and nutrition councils at the departmental and municipal level, the Municipal Food and Nutrition Councils formed but never functioned, were confused as to their role, or became obsolete (Hoey and Pelletier 2013). Although there were ministry-led ZM interventions underway in the target municipalities by 2008, there was little buy-in at the municipal level, where ultimately much of the nutrition work needed to be done (Samdup 2011; Hoey and Pelletier 2013). This was due to lack of awareness, along with confusion over how the funds needed to be spent; and some regulations even limited what municipalities could do. Indeed, Samdup (2011) reports that municipal authorities, when informed about ZM, were not well briefed about the rules concerning the dispersal of funding under decentralization laws and were also concerned about new corruption laws. Samdup (2011) also reports a lack of technical expertise within municipalities, which were not allowed to hire consultants to provide this expertise.

Perhaps surprisingly, given the role of social movements in bringing the leftist administration of Evo Morales into power, there has been very limited inclusion of civil society groups or even any other non-government stakeholders in the initial stages of the ZM Program. By 2008, NGOs, donors, and civil society organizations, frustrated by the lack of progress, began to push back against their own exclusion from the ZM policy formation and implementation, ultimately forcing ZM coordinators to change strategies (Hoey and Pelletier 2013). Indeed, some of the latter successes of the ZM Program were related to state–society linkages. For instance, a partnership between the National Council on Food and Nutrition, which oversees the implementation of the ZM, and the Association of Female Mayors and Municipal Councilwomen (ACOBOL) provided training to municipal-level leaders which helped generate the technical capacity, political will, and momentum necessary for the program to take root at the local level (Samdup 2011).

Part of the problem in Bolivia has to do with the form that its state–society linkage has taken under Morales. Social movements have had a big impact on the Morales government, particularly in its initial years, but they have been kept very close as well and given privileged preference in appointments, access, and participation in the policy process. This has generated a steadfast loyalty among a core group who counterprotest any competing claims by movements seeking to pressure Morales' government (Silva 2013). Thus, there has been little ability of social movements and other civil society groups to step outside of the state and protest against or exert pressure on the Morales administration, which limits the potential for a productive state–society relationship.

Thus, despite the fact that social movements have had considerable influence in terms of state formation, they have not retained the independence to step outside of that relationship with the state in order to fulfill the roles that we argued, earlier in the chapter, contribute to effective state–society interaction around food security and hunger reduction.

Guatemala: A Regional Model for Inclusive Food Security Governance

Learning the lessons from other countries and from its own lackluster initial attempts to address hunger and malnutrition, Guatemala has recently developed a program that explicitly brings in civil society and seeks to mobilize the population at large around both the importance of hunger reduction and the impact that each citizen can make. Indeed, Guatemala's re-established National Food Security and Nutrition System is widely recognized as a model for multisector, multistakeholder coordination (te Lintelo et al. 2013), and it holds the very top spot on the Hunger and Nutrition Commitment Index.

The initial legal framework for Guatemala's National System of Food and Nutrition Security (SINESAN) was actually laid out in 2005. This law, along with the adoption of a state food policy, was an important step symbolizing the elevation of hunger and malnutrition as a priority for national development. However, the law was never fully implemented for lack of widespread awareness, buy-in, and commitment on the part of both political and civil society (FAO 2011). In 2012, hunger reduction was identified as a central component of President Otto Pérez Molina's "National Agenda for Change" (te Lintelo et al. 2013), and the resulting Zero Hunger Pact (*Pacto Hambre Cero*) became a national priority, framed as "the basis for the integral development of the entire Guatemalan population" (Gobierno de Guatemala, n.d.). The Zero Hunger Pact has two goals: the reduction of chronic child malnutrition by 10 percent between 2012 and 2015, and the mitigation of seasonal hunger and prevention of associated deaths due to acute malnutrition.

Learning from the earlier failure to transfer the legal commitment to hunger reduction into a sustained program to do so, in Guatemala's Zero Hunger Pact community, citizen, and CSO participation are central to success, and is emphasized at multiple scales and across each component of the plan. Emphasizing citizen participation as one of six cross-cutting themes, the plan calls for a social mobilization of the people, seeking to initiate strategies to encourage them to care about hunger issues and to get involved in hunger reduction efforts. It stipulates: "We need to move forward and awaken, so that ALL Guatemalan men and women can change from indifference to indignation and then move into action" (Gobierno de Guatemala n.d.). Citizens are called upon to monitor and support the actions of the government through social media and other means. One initiative highlighted in the plan is "#Guate sin Hambre" (Guatemala without Hunger), a social media and youth movement seeking to raise awareness about malnutrition and promoting a model of public–private participation where everyone feels that they have something to contribute (Gobierno de Guatemala n.d.). The plan also calls upon community, national, and international leaders to give voice to and mobilize these social movements.

Civil society groups and social movements are written into the plan at all scales. For instance, there are five civil society representatives on the Council for Food and National Security (CONESAN), the entity ultimately responsible for the Zero Hunger Pact. And civil society is identified as playing an important support role in the execution of the plan at the departmental, municipal, and community levels, and supported as a means for ensuring the long-term viability of the plan.

In the Guatemala case, we can see how the state is seeking to build a strong state–society relationship in order to conquer food insecurity. They explicitly draw upon the potential of a mobilized citizenry to give voice to the problem of hunger and malnutrition, frame it through narratives that resonate with the public more broadly, and monitor government actions in order to keep the pressure on to ensure continued commitment to hunger reduction.

Conclusions

In this chapter, we try to make the case for paying attention to state–society linkages when discussing food security. Increasingly, there is widespread agreement on the importance of political will for addressing hunger and malnutrition: food security is highly political. But, we suggest that we cannot simply treat political commitment to food security as an independent factor. Instead, we suggest that scholarly work is needed to address how such commitment is generated. We argue that social mobilization plays an important role in generating, sustaining, and translating this commitment into effective action. We argue, in particular, that the state—understood as a set of state–society relations—relies upon civil society organizations in multiple arenas, including state formation, giving voice to excluded and vulnerable groups, framing, targeting, oversight, pressure, and project implementation.

Effective state–society relations that are able to positively influence food security do not simply reflect favorable structural characteristics within countries, such as homogeneity of the population or low levels of inequality. It could be argued that such societies are more likely to have pro-poor policies in general, and civil society can thus be regarded as a symptom rather than cause of commitments to reduce hunger and malnutrition. But this clearly is not the case in Latin America, where countries are highly stratified, with diverse populations and long histories of marginalization and exclusion. Indeed, the shift to the left is generally connected to widespread protests at the high inequality and political exclusion of diverse segments of the population. Further, we argue that in Latin America, state–society interactions are not always harmonious, but require the ability of civil society actors to step far enough outside of the relationship to exert pressure by making credible threats to state actors. Civil society has to be visible (Scott 1998) in order to be heard.

Appendix

Appendix Table A-15.1. HANCI 2012 Hunger and Nutrition Commitment Index and ranking

	Hunger Reduction Commitment Ranks	Nutrition Commitment Ranks	Hunger and Nutrition Commitment Ranks
Guatemala	1	1	1
Malawi	2	5	2
Madagascar	8	9	3
Peru	2	11	4

(Continued)

Appendix Table A-15.1. Continued

	Hunger Reduction Commitment Ranks	Nutrition Commitment Ranks	Hunger and Nutrition Commitment Ranks
Brazil	10	7	4
Philippines	9	11	6
Indonesia	14	7	7
Gambia	24	2	8
Tanzania	13	10	8
Burkina Faso	5	16	10
Ghana	12	13	10
Bangladesh	21	6	12
Mozambique	26	4	13
Vietnam	18	17	14
Rwanda	14	21	14
Mali	5	29	16
Zambia	21	14	17
Nepal	34	3	18
Cambodia	17	22	18
Uganda	19	19	20
Senegal	16	26	21
China	7	33	22
South Africa	2	36	23
Niger	23	20	24
Ethiopia	10	34	25
Sierra Leone	31	22	26
Pakistan	30	25	26
Benin	33	17	26
India	27	30	29
Nigeria	32	27	30
Côte d'Ivoire	39	24	31
Togo	20	42	32
Cameroon	36	28	33
Kenya	38	32	34
Liberia	28	40	35
Lesotho	25	43	36
Afghanistan	45	15	36
Mauritania	35	37	38
Yemen	42	31	39
Sudan	29	45	40
Myanmar	43	35	41
Burundi	40	38	42
Angola	36	44	43
Congo, DR	41	40	44
Guinea-Bissau	44	39	45

Source: Compiled by authors with data from HANCI (2014).

Notes

1. These movements are a departure from the militarized guerilla movements based in Marxist ideologies of class warfare that motivated struggles for social change in the 1970s (Alvarez et al. 1998; Postero and Zamosc 2004). These guerilla movements emerged out of a particular form of state–society relations, and in the 1970s democratic inclusion was frequently sought through violent means. The extreme reaction

of the state in response to such movements prompted more widespread demands for democratic deepening, leading to the Third Wave of Democracy in the 1980s.

2. Indonesia is the only additional country to adopt a framework law on food security.

3. Draft laws are also being developed in India, Malawi, Mozambique, South Africa, Tanzania, and Uganda.

4. See te Lintelo et al. (2013) and HANCI (2014) for an overview of the specific elements included in this measurement.

5. Designated as a space for state and civil society actors to work together to coordinate poverty reduction initiatives, the MCLCP was a response to interim President Paniagua's call for a state policy that involved the participation of private and public sectors, as well as civil society, in the design, implementation, and monitoring of policy (Mejía Acosta 2011). The MCLCP is made up of representatives from the Ministries of Health, the Presidency, Education, Agriculture, Women and Social Development, Work and Social Promotion, Transport and Communication, Housing and Construction, Economy and Finance, Justice, Energy and Mines, and Production, along with five representatives from civil society organizations, two representatives from NGOs, three representatives from municipalities, two representatives from religious institutions, two representatives from cooperating organizations, and one representative from business (MCLCP 2014).

6. These projects and programs include: National Plan for Land Titling; National Plan for Land Distribution and Human Settlement; Planting the Right for Food (SEMBRAR); Creation of Rural Food Initiatives (CRIAR); Organized Enterprises for Development (EMPODERAR); Renewal of the Role of State in Rural Food Business (RECREAR); Development of Territorial, Integration, and Cross-Sectoral Production Complex; Sustainable Use of Natural Resources (SUSTENAR); Conservation of Natural and Environmental Quality (CONSERVAR); Food Security Support Program (PASA); Multisectoral Program of Zero Malnutrition; School Breakfast and Lunch Program (Cuesta et al. 2013).

References

Abers, Rebecca Naera, and Margaret E. Keck. 2009. "Mobilizing the State: The Erratic Partner in Brazil's Participatory Water Policy." *Politics & Society* 37 (2): pp. 289–314.

Abrams, Philip. 1988. "Notes on the Difficulty of Studying the State (1977)." *Journal of Historical Sociology* 1 (1): pp. 58–89.

Alvarez, Sonia E. 1998. "Latin American Feminisms 'Go Global': Trends of the 1990s and Challenges for the New Millennium." In *Cultures of Politics/Politics of Cultures: Re-Visioning Latin American Social Movements*, edited by Sonia E. Alvarez, Evelina Dagnino, and Arturo Escobar, pp. 293–324. Boulder, CO: Westview Press.

Alvarez, Sonia E. 2009. "Beyond NGO-ization?: Reflections from Latin America." *Development* 52 (2): pp. 175–184.

Alvarez, Sonia E. et al. 2008. "Social Movements and 21st Century Cultural-Political Transformations: An Inter-University Consortium on the Americas in Comparative and Transnational Perspective." Coordinated by the Center for Latin American,

Caribbean, and Latino Studies (CLACLS); University of Massachusetts, Amherst (UMass); and the Democracy and Global Transformation Program, Universidad Nacional General San Marcos, Lima, Perú. <http://www.umass.edu/civsoc/Project_Summary_files/Project_Summary_Sept_2008_W03_English.pdf>.

Alvarez, Sonia E., Evalina Dagnino, and Arturo Escobar. 1998. *Cultures of Politics/Politics of Cultures: Re-visioning Latin American Social Movements*. Boulder, CO: Westview Press.

Barrett, Christopher B., ed. 2013. *Food Security & Sociopolitical Stability*. Oxford: Oxford University Press.

Cuesta, Jose, Svetlana Edmeades, and Lucia Madrigal. 2013. "Food Security and Public Agricultural Spending in Bolivia: Putting Money Where Your Mouth Is?" *Food Policy* 40: pp. 1–13.

da Silva, José Graziano, Maoro Eduardo Del Grossi, and Calo Galváo de Fraca, eds. 2011. *The* Fome Zero *(Zero Hunger) Program: The Brazilian Experience*. Brasilia: Ministry of Agrarian Development.

Dagnino, Evelyn. 2003. "Citizenship in Latin America: An Introduction." *Latin American Perspectives* 30 (2): pp. 3–17.

de Janvry, Alain, Elisabeth Sadoulet, and Rinku Murgai. 2002. "Rural Development and Rural Policy." In *Handbook of Agricultural Economics*, Vol. 2, edited by Bruce L. Gardner and Gordon C. Rausser, pp. 1593–1658. Amsterdam: Elsevier.

De Schutter, Olivier. 2012. "The Contribution of the Right to Food to Global Food Security: A Tool not a Symbol." *Asian Development Bank Gender Network Newsletter* 6 (2): pp. 1–4.

Evans, Peter B. 1995. *Embedded Autonomy: States and Industrial Transformation*. Princeton, NJ: Princeton University Press.

FAO. 2009. *Guide on Legislating for the Right to Food*. Rome: Food and Agriculture Organization of the UN.

FAO. 2011. *Right to Food: Making it Happen—Progress and Lessons Learned through Implementation*. Rome: Food and Agriculture Organization of the UN.

FAO. 2012. *The State of Food Insecurity in the World 2012*. Rome: Food and Agriculture Organization of the UN.

Ferguson, James, and Akhil Gupta. 2002. "Spatializing States: Toward an Ethnography of Neoliberal Governmentality." *American Ethnologist* 29 (4): pp. 981–1002.

Fox, Jonathan. 1993. *The Politics of Food in Mexico: State Power and Social Mobilization*. Ithaca, NY: Cornell University Press.

Fox, Jonathan. 1996. "How Does Civil Society Thicken? The Political Construction of Social Capital in Rural Mexico." *World Development* 24 (6): pp. 1089–1103.

Gillespie, Stuart, Lawrence Haddad, Venkatesh Mannar, Purnima Menon, and Nicholas Nisbett. 2013. "The Politics of Reducing Malnutrition: Building Commitment and Accelerating Progress." *Lancet* 382 (9891): pp. 552–569.

Gobierno de Guatemala. n.d. *The Plan for the Zero Hunger Pact*. <http://www.sesan.gob.gt/index.php/descargas/22-zero-hunger-pact/file>.

Gupta, Akhil. 2005. "Narratives of Corruption: Anthropological and Fictional Accounts of the Indian State." *Ethnography* 6 (1): pp. 5–34.

Hagopian, Frances, and Scott Mainwaring. 2005. *The Third Wave of Democratization in Latin America: Advances and Setbacks*. Cambridge: Cambridge University Press.

HANCI (Hunger and Nutrition Commitment Index). 2014. Institute of Development Studies, Brighton, UK. <http://www.hancindex.org>.

Hoey, Lesli, and David L. Pelletier. 2013. "Bolivia's Multisectoral Zero Malnutrition Program: Insights on Commitment, Collaboration, and Capacities." *Food and Nutrition Bulletin* 32 (2): pp. S70–S81.

Jha, Manish K. 2009. "Food Security in Perspective: The Significance of Social Action." *Community Development Journal* 44 (3): pp. 351–366.

Joseph, Gilbert M., and Daniel Nugent. 1994. *Everyday Forms of State Formation: Revolution and the Negotiation of Rule in Modern Mexico*. Durham, NC: Duke University Press.

Knuth, Lidija, and Margaret Vidar. 2011. *Constitutional and Legal Protection of the Right to Food around the World*. Rome: Food and Agriculture Organization of the UN.

Mander, Harsh. 2012. "Food from the Courts: The Indian Experience." *IDS Bulletin* 43 (S1): pp. 15–24.

Masset, Edoardo. 2010. "A Review of Hunger Indices and Methods to Monitor Country Commitment to Fighting Hunger." *Food Policy* 36 (S1): S102–S108.

MCLCP (Mesa de Concertacíon para la Lucha Contra la Pobreza). 2014. Lima, Peru. <http://www.mesadeconcertacion.org.pe/>.

Mejía Acosta, A., and Jessica Fanzo. 2012. "Fighting Maternal and Child Malnutrition: Analysing the Political and Institutional Determinants of Delivering a National Multisectoral Response in Six Countries." Synthesis Paper, Institute of Development Studies, Brighton, UK.

Mejía Acosta, Andrés. 2011. "Analysing Success in the Fight against Malnutrition in Peru." IDS Working Paper #367, Institute of Development Studies, Brighton, UK.

Migdal, Joel. 2001. *State in Society: Studying How States and Society Transform and Constitute One Another*. Cambridge: Cambridge University Press.

Mitchell, Timothy. 1999. "State, Economy, and the State Effect." In *State/Culture: State-formation after the Cultural Turn*, edited by George Steinmetz, pp. 76–97. Ithaca, NY: Cornell University Press.

Pelletier, David L., Purnima Menon, Tien Ngo, Edward A. Frongillo, and Dominic Frongillo. 2011. "The Nutrition Policy Process: The Role of Strategic Capacity in Advancing National Nutrition Agendas." *Food and Nutrition Bulletin* 32 (2 Suppl): pp. S59–69.

Pinstrup-Andersen, Per. 2007. "Agricultural Research and Policy for Better Health and Nutrition in Developing Countries: A Food Systems Approach." *Agricultural Economics* 37 (S1): pp. 187–198.

Pinstrup-Andersen, Per. 2013. "Nutrition-Sensitive Food Systems: From Rhetoric to Action." *Lancet* 382 (9890): pp. 375–376.

Pinstrup-Andersen, Per, and Anna Herforth. 2008. "Food Security: Achieving the Potential." *Environment* 50 (5): pp. 48–62.

Pinstrup-Andersen, Per, and Rajul Pandya-Lorch. 2001. *The Unfinished Agenda: Perspectives on Overcoming Hunger, Poverty, and Environmental Degradation*. Washington, DC: IFPRI.

Pinstrup-Andersen, Per, and Derrill Watson, II. 2011. *Food Policy for Developing Countries*. Ithaca, NY: Cornell University Press.

Postero, Nancy. 2010. "The Struggle to Create a Radical Democracy in Bolivia." *Latin American Research Review* 45 (S): pp. 59–78.

Postero, Nancy, and Leon Zamosc. 2004. *The Struggle for Indigenous Rights in Latin America*. Brighton: Sussex Academic Press.

Samdup, Carole. 2011. *The Human Right to Food in Bolivia: Mission Report*. Quebec: International Centre for Human Rights and Democratic Development.

Sanchez-Montero, Manuel, Núria Salse Ubach, and Morwenna Sullivan. 2010. *Undernutrition: What Works? A Review of Policy and Practice*. Action Against Hunger International and Tripode. <http://www.medbox.org/food-security-nutrition/undernutrition-what-works/preview>.

Scott, James. 1998. *Seeing Like a State: How Certain Schemes to Improve the Human Condition Have Failed*. New Haven, CT: Yale University Press.

Sen, Amartya. 1976. "Famines as Failures of Exchange Entitlements." *Economic and Political Weekly* 11 (31–33): pp. 1273–1280.

Sen, Amartya. 1981. *Poverty and Famines: An Essay on Entitlement and Deprivation*. Oxford: Clarendon Press.

Silva, Eduardo. 2013. "Social Movements, Policy, and Conflict in Post-Neoliberal Latin America: Bolivia in the Time of Evo Morales." *Research in Political Sociology* 21: pp. 51–76.

Tarrow, Sidney G. 1994. *Power in Movement: Social Movements, Collective Action, and Politics*. Cambridge: Cambridge University Press.

te Lintelo, Dolf, Lawrence Haddad, Rajith Lakshman, and Karine Gattelier. 2013. *The Hunger and Nutrition Commitment Index (HANCI 2012): Measuring the Political Commitment to Reduce Hunger and Undernutrition in Developing Countries*. Brighton: Institute of Development Studies.

te Lintelo, Dolf, Lawrence Haddad, Jennifer Leavy, Edoardo Masset, and Alan Stanley. 2011. *Measuring the Commitment to Reduce Hunger: The Hunger Reduction Commitment Index*. Brighton: Institute of Development Studies.

Tilly, Charles. 1978. *From Mobilization to Revolution*. New York: Addison-Wesley.

Vidal, Raul. n.d. "The Zero Malnutrition Program: A Multisectoral and Decentralized Approach." <http://www.be-causehealth.be/media/15057/Bolivia%20-%20PDC%20Because%20Health%20-%20Main%20Vidal.pdf>.

Vidar, Margret. 2006. "State Recognition of the Right to Food at the National Level." WIDER Research Paper No. 2006/61, United Nations University–World Institute for Development Economics Research (UNU–WIDER), Helsinki, Finland.

Wolford, Wendy. 2010. "Participatory Democracy by Default: Land Reform, Social Movements and the State in Northeastern Brazil." *Journal of Peasant Studies* 37 (1): pp. 91–109.

Wolford, Wendy. Forthcoming. "From Mosquitos to Marx: The Changing Dynamic of State and Social Mobilization for Land in Brazil." *Latin American Research Review*.

Wolford, Wendy, and Ryan Nehring. 2013. "Moral Economies of Food Security and Protest in Latin America." In *Food Security and Sociopolitical Instability*, edited by Christopher B. Barrett, pp. 302–323. Oxford: Oxford University Press.

16

Distributional Impacts of the 2008 Global Food Price Spike in Vietnam

Andy McKay and Finn Tarp

Introduction

The point of departure of this chapter is that the global economy is passing through a period of profound change (Addison et al. 2011). The global economy is still recovering from the global financial crisis, which originated among rich countries. Poorer countries have been affected in a variety of ways, including reduced export demand and reduced private financial flows. In the background, climate change remains unchecked, potentially threatening to undermine development progress achieved over the past few decades. In addition, the world prices of food and fuel have increased substantially, particularly in 2008, but sustained since then. Assuming the restoration of global economic growth, this is likely to lead to a continuation of the increase in food and energy prices, which are now structurally linked in new ways.

This has led to suggestions that malnutrition, hunger, and poverty have increased as a result. But did this actually happen? In this chapter we study how consumers and producers fared in one specific country case, Vietnam, with a focus on a critically important crop—namely, rice. As a key part of this, we analyze how the Vietnamese government responded to the crisis. This underlines the importance of understanding how increased food prices are transmitted to consumers and producers, and how they respond.

Vietnam is a populous Southeast Asian economy with a particular economic and political history in the middle of a dynamic Asian development experience. Following the *Doi Moi* policy reforms in 1986, gross domestic product (GDP) grew steadily at 7.6 percent a year for around 5 years. Growth accelerated to 9.8 percent in the early 1990s until 1998, when it leveled off to

7 percent following the Asian crisis. Shortly afterward this higher growth was re-established, but then dropped again following the world financial crisis in 2008. Despite these fluctuations, the annual average growth rate has been at 7 percent or above for nearly 25 years. When a country grows at 7 percent a year, income is doubled in about 10 years; over a period of 25 years, people become five times richer. So the average Vietnamese person who was earning US$1.25 a day in 1990 is now earning around US$6, assuming that growth has been equally distributed.

More than two-thirds of the Vietnamese population was born after 1975, and the younger generation is living in a radically different Vietnam from the country that was reunited in 1975. One of the most remarkable changes is a substantial decrease in absolute poverty. Vietnam has seen the sharpest drop of the share of the population living in absolute poverty in the world. Some observers have erroneously concluded that poverty has increased more recently. They overlook the fact that the latest poverty assessment, suggesting that poverty is around 20 percent of the population, is based on a poverty line of US$2.25 per day. This is almost double the poverty line used in previous poverty assessments. Without doubt, Vietnam has reduced poverty at rates that even surpass those of China.

Debate about the drivers behind Vietnam's economic success and its sustainability continues. There is widespread agreement that high savings and investment has played a key role. In contrast, the role of technical progress has tended to be discounted. However, Abbott et al. (2011) estimated that a significant share of the difference between GDP and employment growth is due to technical change, including technical progress in agriculture.

These factors have also helped underpin rapid growth in the agricultural sector. The key crop for Vietnam is rice, which is grown by smallholders throughout Vietnam and plays a central role in ensuring national food security. This is an overriding policy concern, following the traumatic experience of the early 1980s, when major food shortages were experienced. In fact, it is difficult to overstate the economic and political importance of rice to the Vietnamese economy and the development experience. Since the 1980s, though, substantial progress has been achieved, with Vietnam moving from being a net importer of rice to a major world exporter in 1989. Reflecting the critical food security concerns, the government restricts farmers to growing rice on specific land areas, and a major share of land continues to be allocated to growing rice. Increasingly, these restrictions are also motivated by export targets established within the national planning framework (Markussen et al. 2011).

A previous study by Vu and Glewwe (2011) analyzed the welfare effects of the relatively slow food price increase until 2006. In contrast, we focus here on how the much larger increases in the rice price from 2006 to 2012 impacted consumers and producers in Vietnam, and try to assess distributional impact. As an integral part of this, we also analyze and assess government policies related to rice production and prices. This provides a critical lens for understanding agricultural policies in Vietnam and other low and lower middle-income countries, for which agriculture is a critical sector (Hai and Talbot 2013). In this analysis, we are fortunate to be able to draw not only on generally available macroeconomic data but also on a unique panel data set in rural Vietnam covering the period 2006–12, the Vietnam Access to Resources Household Survey (VARHS), as well as the national Vietnam Household Living Standards Survey (VHLSS).

This chapter is structured in the following way. In the next section we summarize the extensive literature looking at the welfare impact of food price changes, in particular the large volume of literature that followed the 2008 crisis. Next, we discuss the data used, and then we provide further information on the policymaking framework, as well as contextual background on the nature of livelihoods and production in rural Vietnam. We identify a number of the factors which are important influences on rice production and consumption. We then present empirical evidence on the nature and impact of rice price changes, and finally, interpretation and conclusions.

Literature Review

The question of the impact of a price change on producers and consumers is a core and widely studied question in economics; the price changes may be a consequence of many factors such as tax changes or, as here, changes in the world price of a traded commodity. A wide body of consumer and producer theory, as well as a range of applied general equilibrium approaches, have been used to analyze this question. In a developing country context, this has commonly been pursued in terms of an agricultural household model. A classic example is the study by Deaton (1989), which looked at the welfare and other impacts of a change in the rice price in Thailand and recognized the key distinction between net consumers (who lose from food price increases) and net producers (who gain). In a similar analysis in Bangladesh, Ravallion (1990) highlighted the importance of taking into account the labor position of the household. Many other empirical studies have looked at the impact of food price increases; for instance, Barrett and Dorosh (1996) found that in Madagascar the beneficial effects of a rice price increase were highly concentrated among wealthier farmers. Jensen et al. (2010) demonstrated the intricacies of measuring price incentives in an economy-wide general equilibrium context.

The impact of changes in prices on consumers and producers depends on the extent to which they are transmitted to the poor (Winters et al. 2004).

In the 1980s, it was regularly argued that getting the prices right meant complete liberalization, with a view to having full pass through and being fully aligned with world prices. The analytic basis for this position has since been questioned. First, it is far from clear that governments should abstain from stabilizing prices to some extent. Second, given real world departures from the perfectly competitive model, such as transport and transactions costs, full pass through is unlikely to ever happen. Intervention is often a second best policy measure in the context of exceptional price changes (Abbott 2011; Martin and Anderson 2011).

Viewed from a slightly different perspective, there were very widely expressed concerns, at the time of the 2008 price spike, about its likely impacts on poverty, malnutrition, and mortality. Although a blog by the Chief Economist for Africa of the World Bank suggested the possibility of 700,000 excess deaths, a study by Friedman and Schady (2009) predicted much lower numbers of 30,000 to 50,000 (with a differential effect on girls). UNICEF, the World Food Programme (WFP), and others issued warnings about the potentially severe impact of the food price increase, and the international media followed suit.

There was also a succession of quick-response empirical studies carried out at this time. Many of these were published in a supplement issue of *Agricultural Economics* in late 2008. In this issue, a study by Ivanic and Martin (2008), based on surveys in 10 countries, predicted a global rise of poverty of around 3 percentage points. This estimate was higher in urban than rural areas, though the impact was marginally lower (around 2.7 percent) when estimated wage responses were taken into account.

The same journal issue included many country studies, which almost all recognized the net consumer/net producer distinction. For instance, in Thailand a general equilibrium analysis suggested that the negative effect on consumers dominated the positive impact on net suppliers (Warr 2008); in Mozambique the impact of the fuel price increase dominated any food price impact (Arndt et al. 2008); in Hunan Province in China, no adverse nutritional effect was found because of substitution to cheaper food sources (Jensen and Miller 2008); and in Uganda the impact of food price increases was limited because of the extent of dependence on consumption from own production (Benson et al. 2008).

Although the World Bank study of Ivanic and Martin (2008) expressed concerns about large poverty impacts (and similar concerns were raised at the time on the World Bank website), the empirical studies show a diversity of experience, mostly identifying adverse effects—noting that some of this analysis did not adequately capture government responses and general economy-wide equilibrium effects.

A general equilibrium study for Vietnam (Coxhead et al. 2008) showed limited transmission of the price increase, but also highlighted the importance of the labor market as a moderating influence. In a later study for Vietnam, Vu and Glewwe (2011), applying Deaton's (1989) approach, found a net positive welfare effect of the food price increase up to 2006; the average decrease in welfare for those made worse off was more than offset by the average increase in welfare for those that gained. In addition, Abbott et al. (2012) showed wide sectoral variation and imperfect price transmission from world prices to domestic markets in Vietnam from 1999–2008. Thurlow et al. (2011) developed a dynamic computable general equilibrium to decompose impacts of the global commodity and financial crisis. These results indicated that the 2008 commodity price increased employment and reduced poverty by favoring labor-intensive exports, especially agriculture.

Government measures taken in a number of countries to reduce the transmission of the price spike to domestic markets included export restrictions, removal of import tariffs, releasing buffer stocks, introducing subsidies, fiscal policy, and expanding safety nets. Some countries pursued these policies more actively and more effectively than others. Elleby and Hansen (2014) find that Vietnam was the only one of eight Asian rice-producing countries that managed to effectively limit the extent to which world food price instability was transmitted to the domestic price.

This evidence raises the challenging question of why some countries are able to define and implement these policies more effectively than others. A recent important contribution in this regard is the political-economy analysis, *Food Price Policy in an Era of Market Instability*, spearheaded by Per Pinstrup-Andersen, and forthcoming as an Oxford University Press book volume in the series of WIDER Studies in Development Economics. This included 14 country case studies,[1] with conclusions drawn based on a synthesis of these.

Data

In this chapter we rely on aggregate time series on rice prices available from a variety of international sources, but predominantly on two key sets of household surveys: (1) the VHLSS national household survey, collected by the General Statistics Office of Vietnam (GSO), with the support of the World Bank; and (2) a specialist in-depth survey of rural Vietnam, referred to as VARHS, which also provides the key source of contextual information for much of the discussion in the next section. From the VHLSS, we use data on consumption and production of rice as a basis to identify net consumers and net producers; we also use these data to compute average purchase and sale prices at the household level.[2]

The VARHS was conducted in the rural areas of 12 provinces, by the University of Copenhagen in conjunction with the Central Institute for Economic Management (CIEM), the Institute for Labour Science and Social Affairs (ILSSA), and the Centre for Agricultural Policy of the Institute for Policy and Strategy for Agriculture and Rural Development (CAP/IPSARD). The 12 provinces were selected to facilitate the use of the survey as an evaluation tool for Danida-supported development programs in Vietnam. Seven of the 12 provinces are covered by the Danida business sector support program (BSPS), and five are covered by the agricultural and rural development (ARD) program. The provinces supported by the agricultural support program are located in the Northwest and Central Highlands, so these relatively poor and sparsely populated regions are oversampled. The sample is statistically representative at the provincial level, but not at the national level.

VARHS was conducted as a panel survey in 2006, 2008, 2010, and 2012, with 2,080 households included in all four waves, with larger numbers of households available for shorter periods. The survey collected detailed, plot-level information on land transactions, property rights, mode and time of acquisition, and other plot characteristics. It also provided detailed information at the household level on agricultural inputs, outputs, and investment, in addition to general information about individuals and households (CIEM 2007, 2009, 2011, 2013).

Context

Levels of rice production and productivity in Vietnam were very low and declining in the early years of the newly unified country in 1975, especially in the north (Pingali and Xuan 1992). In this period rice was still cultivated on a collective basis, but in 1981, Vietnam moved to an individual contract system of production, requiring a fixed amount of rice to be sold to the state at a fixed price, while allowing the farmer to sell any surplus, similar to the household responsibility system established in China in 1979. In Vietnam, the introduction of this system of production resulted in important increases in productivity over the following years (Pingali and Xuan 1992).

Significant further reforms were introduced in a series of measures following from the initiation of the *Doi Moi* reform process in 1986, with land reforms playing a major role. The reforms of 1987, implemented in 1988, provided households with increased tenure security in relation to use rights for land; this was confirmed in a further reform in 1993, which initiated the process of issuing farmers Land Use Certificates (or "red books"), giving them among other things the right to buy and sell land (subject to land ceilings).

The 1988 reforms decentralized input supplies and privatized output markets, such that farmers were no longer required to supply the state, but could sell to private traders. In addition, the 1988 and 1993 reforms nominally gave farmers the ability to make decisions over their cultivation and the use of their land. Yet in implementing the land policies, the government was concerned about the impact on rice production and marketing, and so revisions were made in 1998 and 2001 that made it clear that any change of use within rice growing areas was only allowed within the existing physical planning framework of central and local government (Vasavakul 2006; Markussen et al. 2011). The implication of the revisions is that farmers are obliged to grow rice on at least 35 percent of total agricultural land, and these restrictions are particularly enforced in the Red River and Mekong Deltas, the main rice growing areas. These restrictions are made clear in the red books, which specify for which purposes land is to be used.

Markussen et al. (2011, p. 840) summarized the more recent situation as follows:

> Twenty four years after the introduction of the Doi Moi reform process ... Households sell their production output to private buyers, trade land, and sell labor on the private market. At the same time the state ... retains a hugely important role in economic life. The state intervenes actively in the land market, supplies many inputs in agricultural production, strongly dominates formal markets for financial services, and plays a key role in a large number of local organizational activities. More specifically, authorities intervene heavily in farmers' choice of crops, and while the land law gives households the right to sell, rent, exchange, mortgage, and bequeath their land, many farmers do not have the right to decide how to use their plots.

The VARHS data they analyzed showed that half the plots in the survey faced restrictions, even if 74 percent had a Land Use Certificate. It is also notable that in the 2008 data they used, farmers did not have a Land Use Certificate for 26 percent of their plots.

The 25 years since the implementation of the reforms in 1988 have seen many important changes in rural Vietnam, but the importance of rice remains in 2013. In 1988, agriculture was the dominant activity, with rice being crucially important. Household survey data for 1993 demonstrated that nearly two-thirds of income came from agriculture (Niimi et al. 2003). In 2000, nearly 10 percent of Vietnamese value added came from rice (Tarp et al. 2002).

It is certainly the case that livelihoods are now much more diversified in rural Vietnam, with large numbers of households engaged in non-farm activities; at the same time, the large majority of households still farm, and most of them grow rice.

Analysis of the VARHS data provides important insights in relation to land, rice cultivation, and marketing. As a direct result of the egalitarian land allocation process in the 1980s and 1990s, land fragmentation is widespread in Vietnam, especially in the northern plains area. The mean farm size is less than a hectare, and households on average have around five plots, more in the north. Often these are at some distance from the home. Most plots operated by households were allocated by the state, most households have never participated in the land sales market, and the share of households participating in the rental market is small, even if the relative importance of markets is rising (Khai et al. 2013).

The data also confirm that most households cultivated rice, even if only just over half of them sold rice in 2006. By 2008 and 2010, both the proportion of households selling and the share of their output sold had increased (Cazzuffi et al. 2011). In most areas households sell to traders, though some sell to individuals. Some households sell consistently, but many only sell from time to time; those with larger land areas or more irrigated land are more likely to sell; poorer households and those headed by ethnic minorities are less likely to sell.

The panel data collected by VARHS have been used to assess the dynamics of welfare in rural Vietnam (McKay and Tarp 2013). The results show significant progress on average in terms of each of the welfare measures they consider (food consumption, income, and assets). At the same time, they also show quite a lot of diversity, with a significant minority of households becoming worse off over this period. Ethnic minorities show significantly less progress than the majority Kinh population, and there are important geographic variations, with some provinces showing very little progress. Households in which one or more younger person has left progress significantly better than those without such migrations. The extent to which households are engaged in agriculture, though, is not significantly associated with welfare progress: households with a high reliance on agriculture, and those with a low reliance on agriculture, both number among those who advanced over the period and those who fell back.

Empirical Evidence on the Rice Price Changes and their Distributional Impact

To analyze the impact of the rice price increase, we start by looking at aggregate price data to document the magnitude and timing of the shock, and then use the VHLSS data to identify net producers and consumers. We also rely on these data to study trends in consumer and producer prices at the regional and consumption quintile levels, and subsequently, on VARHS to do a detailed analysis of production response and sales.

Patterns of Price Changes

As a backdrop to the analysis, the evolution of the world rice price since 2000 is presented in Figure 16.1. This shows very clearly the very large price spike in 2008, but equally clear is the underlying increasing trend since at least 2000. The average US$ price of rice increased by a factor of 2.13 between 2006 and 2008, and most of this increase happened between 2007 and 2008, when the world price almost doubled. It fell by about a quarter from 2008 and 2010, and then continued to increase at the underlying trend. The reasons for the 2008 food price spike have been widely discussed; the focus here is on the impact of these price variations in Vietnam, a country where almost everyone consumes rice and where around half of the national population and approximately 80 percent of the rural population produce it.

As the exchange rate of the Vietnamese Dong (VND) against the US$ changed little over the 2006–08 period, the border price of rice changed in a similar way to the world price. But the pattern of change of the domestic retail and producer prices is somewhat different (Figure 16.2). Each of these three prices more or less doubled between 2006 and 2010, but the world price was much more volatile over this period, as well as over the longer 2000–11 period. The standard deviation of the percentage change in the border price is 46.9 percent over the period 2006–10, compared to 26.0 percent and 20.7 percent in the case of the domestic retail and producer prices,

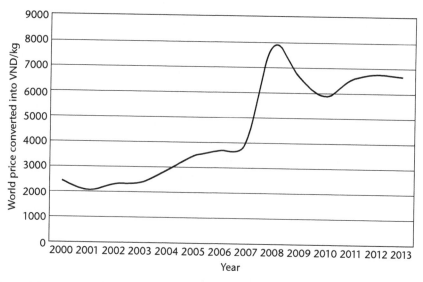

Figure 16.1 World price of rice

Source: Authors' calculations and construction based on World Bank (2013).

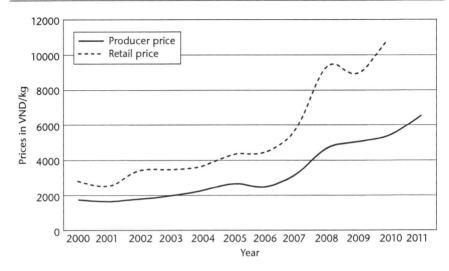

Figure 16.2 Prices of rice in Vietnam

Source: Authors' calculations and construction based on FAO (2014) and IRRI (2014).

respectively; and there is a sharp spike in the border price between 2007 and 2008, whereas in the case of the other prices, the increase is much more gradually spread out.

Market forces now play a very important role in the determination of the producer and retail prices in Vietnam, given that almost all rice sales are made to private traders and that rice is bought by consumers in the market. However, this does not mean that policy interventions do not influence prices, and especially in exceptional circumstances. It is illustrative that in response to the 2007–08 shock, the government of Vietnam introduced an export ban and public procurement and stock management policies to smooth out price developments. According to Government Decree No 75/2008/ND-CP, signed by the prime minister in 2008, rice is characterized as a good that is subject to price stabilization policies. Among 27 policy responses to food price changes between 2001 and 2010, 23 were focused on influencing long-term price developments, whereas four measures were focused on short-term price stabilization (including rice export control and procurement and stocking policies). Hai and Talbot (2013) discussed this in more detail, including detailed timing on the specific interventions (see their Figure 9, p. 15). These interventions explain why domestic prices changed much more smoothly over the 2006–10 period, compared to world prices.

The developments shown by the aggregate rice price data are confirmed by the survey data. The VHLSS survey data can also be used to compute the evolution of the prices paid by consumers. The price for ordinary rice was VND4,990 per kilogram in 2006, increasing to VND8,580 in 2008 (an increase of 72.1 percent), and VND10,840 in 2010 (an increase of 26.3 percent compared to 2008) per kilogram of ordinary rice bought. These data are based on prices actually paid by individual consumers and computed in order to be nationally representative; the survey data suggest a smaller increase in consumer prices between 2006 and 2008 than the aggregate price series, though a slightly larger one between 2008 and 2010.

Both VHLSS and VARHS enable estimates to be made of the prices received by farmers selling rice. According to VHLSS, the average producer price was VND2,470 per kilogram in 2006, VND4,050 in 2008 (an increase of 63.8 percent), and VND4,930 in 2010 (a 21.8 percent increase compared to 2008); according to VARHS, the figures are VND2,600 in 2006, VND4,200 in 2008, VND5,530 in 2010, and VND6,050 in 2012.

Although there are some small differences between VHLSS and VARHS in relation to the magnitude of increase in producer prices, the survey data actually suggest smaller magnitudes of increase in both consumer and producer prices than the aggregate price series. These survey data probably give a more accurate measure of the prices paid by consumers or received by farmers than the aggregate time series data. This said, the differences can also reflect quality adjustments on the part of consumers or monopsony power on the part of traders not passing on the full benefit of price increases to producers. It is clear that whichever source of data is chosen, there were substantial increases in both the retail and producer price of rice in Vietnam between 2006 and 2008. The more credible survey data suggest that both consumer and producer prices increased less than border prices.

The survey data can also be used to consider differences in prices paid or received between different categories of households. The retail price paid consistently increased with the consumption quintile, which might be considered an indication of quality. There is not a consistent pattern of geographic variation, although the retail price does tend to be slightly higher in the Red River Delta region than elsewhere. Producer prices tended to be higher each year in the northern half of the country than in the south, but here there is no consistent pattern of variation with consumption quintiles.

Producers, Net Producers, and Net Consumers of Rice

A sharp increase in the price of rice will have an adverse effect on net consumers of rice and a positive impact on net producers, other things being equal. The VHLSS surveys collected information on both consumption and production of rice, both with a 12-month reference period, and are therefore quite a good basis to identify net consumers and net producers. Table 16.1 shows the number of households producing rice in the three VHLSS survey years,

Table 16.1. Shares of net producers and net consumers of rice in Vietnam

	2006			2008			2010		
	% producing rice	Of which		% producing rice	Of which		% producing rice	Of which	
		Net producers	Net consumers		Net producers	Net consumers		Net producers	Net consumers
By quintile:									
Lowest	75.6	68.5	7.1	73.0	62.9	10.1	63.6	60.2	3.4
2nd	70.3	66.5	3.8	68.0	63.4	4.6	55.8	53.5	2.3
3rd	61.4	59.0	2.4	55.6	53.0	2.5	48.6	46.9	1.7
4th	41.7	40.1	1.6	40.7	39.1	1.6	35.5	34.9	0.7
Highest	13.9	13.4	0.5	16.1	15.8	0.3	17.0	16.6	0.4
By region:									
Red River Delta	64.8	62.7	2.2	63.2	60.8	2.5	58.5	57.7	0.8
Northeast	70.3	66.4	4.0	68.7	62.9	5.8	68.9	67.3	1.6
Northwest	72.8	59.0	13.9	73.6	50.3	23.3	69.3	64.8	4.5
North Central Coast	68.7	64.2	4.5	64.9	58.6	6.3	65.8	62.6	3.3
South Central Coast	57.6	54.1	3.5	55.7	52.4	3.2	46.9	45.0	1.9
Central Highlands	39.2	33.5	5.6	38.7	32.9	5.7	29.7	27.7	2.1
Southeast	12.4	11.0	1.4	11.0	10.5	0.6	4.6	3.8	0.7
Mekong Delta	37.4	36.7	0.7	36.5	35.5	1.0	32.2	30.1	2.2
Total	50.6	47.7	2.9	48.7	45.2	3.5	44.1	42.4	1.7

Source: Authors' calculations based on VHLSS Surveys (2006, 2008, and 2010).

and among these, the number who were net producers and net consumers, disaggregated by consumption quintile and geographic region.

According to VHLSS, 51 percent of households in the entire country grew rice in 2006, and 49 percent did so in 2008. The proportion for 2010 is slightly lower, at 44 percent, probably reflecting the different sampling frame. In any case, it is clear that in all of these years a significant majority of rural households grow rice. In all years, the percentage of households growing rice is much higher in the northern regions, compared to the south and is highest of all in the northeast and northwest. Closely related to this, the percentage of rice growers decreased significantly with the quintile; but even in 2010 almost 64 percent of those in the lowest quintile grew rice.

A large majority of these rice producers produce in excess of their consumption requirements of rice, and only small numbers of rice-producing households are net rice consumers. The proportion of households that were net consumers increased to a small extent between 2006–08, when the rice price increased most, but even in 2008 only a small minority of rice producers were net rice consumers. Given this, most producing households should in theory benefit if they sell and receive a higher producer price.

Net consumers are a minority among rice producers in all regions and all quintiles, but there are significant variations. The incidence of net consumers is highest in the first quintile (net consumers tend on average to be poorer, much more highly represented in the bottom quintile in all years) and in the northwest. In the northwest, nearly a third of rice producers (23.3/73.6) were net consumers in 2008, strikingly higher than in the other years. They are likely to have been adversely affected by the 2008 rice price increase, not yet having had the time to adjust. Non-producing consumers of rice clearly suffer from the rice price increase. On average this group, a significant proportion of which is urban, are much better off than those who produce rice.

Table 16.2 compares the average per capita real total consumption of rice producers with non-producers, and among rice-producing households, contrasts net consumers with net producers. The mean consumption of households producing rice is less than half that of non-producers, taking into account all the differences in relative prices. In other words, rice producers, that is, smallholders, are much poorer. This is not to say that there are not some poor households among the non-producing group; 9.6 percent of these households were in the first quintile in 2006 (and so 90.4 percent were not). Poor non-producing households are more likely to be in the North Central Coastal region or the Central Highlands.

Among rice producers, the net consumers have a significantly lower average total consumption level than that of net producers, and this differential widened in 2008. Among rice producers, net consumers were poorer to start with in 2006 and were significantly harder hit by the rice price increase. As

Table 16.2. Average total real per capita consumption

	2006		2008		2010	
	Mean	Median	Mean	Median	Mean	Median
Net producers	4487.4	4011.7	6316.4	5451.5	11647.1	10126.8
Net consumers	3730.9	3162.7	4654.2	4159.7	8474.6	7271.6
Non-producers	8805.7	6919.7	11382.8	8944.7	21303.1	16482.2

Note: 2010 data in 2010 prices; others are in 2006 prices; in thousands of Vietnamese Dong.

Source: Authors' calculations based on VHLSS Surveys (2006, 2008, and 2010).

already seen, and especially in 2008, many of these net consumers were in the northwest, where the proportion of ethnic minorities in the population is high. In other words, the losers from the price shock would appear, in particular, to be poorer households in this region. This potentially explains, in part, the results already discussed above from the welfare dynamics analysis using VARHS.

In summary, rice producers tend to be the poorer households in Vietnam. The very large majority are producing in excess of their consumption requirements. These households benefited from the rice price increases. Non-producing consumers certainly suffer; but the vast majority of these households are non-poor. These are the main headlines, but it is important not to neglect other facts. The relatively few rice producers that are net rice consumers tend to be very poor, and some non-producing consumers are also very poor.

Accordingly, the impact of the rice price shock in 2008 no doubt made significant numbers of households better off, while at the same time making smaller numbers worse off. We also note that the share of net consumers significantly reduced between 2008 and 2010, and we now turn to analyzing the production response.

The Production Response

How then did farmers respond to the higher price? The VARHS collects detailed information on household production and constitutes a panel of 2,080 households, covering the years 2006, 2008, 2010, and 2012. Table 16.3 provides summary information to assess the changes in production behavior over this period. Some 77 percent of these households grew rice in 2006; the number declined marginally over the following 6 years (this finding is also confirmed by VHLSS). This coincides with the time in which the number of households required to grow rice by restrictions imposed by the commune authorities was generally reduced. The output of rice increased consistently

Table 16.3. Production characteristics for VARHS sample households

	% growing rice	Average output	% selling	% using improved seeds	% subject to crop restrictions	Average sales price (1000 VND/kg)
2006	76.9	2308	38.4	38.2	57.5	2.60
2008	73.5	2349	56.1	35.2	39.4	4.20
2010	70.9	2416	40.2	55.8	26.0	5.53
2012	68.8	2760	40.1	47.7	35.4	6.05

Source: Authors' calculations based on VARHS Surveys (2006, 2008, 2010, and 2012), as summarized in CIEM (2007, 2009, 2011, 2013), respectively.

over this period. This is so, even taking into account the slightly smaller number of households farming in later years. In other words, production has certainly increased. Particularly striking in 2008 was the sharp increase in the number of households selling rice compared to 2006, no doubt incentivized by the higher rice price, as well as a good harvest in that year. The extent of selling fell off a bit in later years, but remains higher than 2006. In terms of production technique, by 2010, significantly more farmers were using improved varieties of seeds, and this remained higher in 2012 than it was in 2008.

It seems clear that rice-producing households have indeed adjusted and responded to the increased rice price, by producing more and selling more on average. As expected, the strongest and most consistent response is observed in the southern high-production province of Long An, where markets are more highly developed.

Conclusion

The spike in the international rice price in 2007–08 was indeed exceptional, with the price doubling in a year. Looked at over the period from 2000 to date, it appears much more as a large but temporary deviation around a long-term upward trend. In any case, it was a major issue of policy concern at the time, both nationally and internationally, with UNICEF, the World Bank, and the World Food Programme all predicting dramatic adverse consequences. Internationally, calls were made for action to alleviate expected poverty and malnutrition consequences, with little attention given to providing an overall balanced assessment of the situation.

As the world's second largest rice exporter, Vietnam stood to benefit in aggregate from this, but, maybe surprisingly, reduced its export quota and later imposed an export ban. These steps were widely discussed and subjected to severe criticism at the time, both within and outside Vietnam, with some arguing that this contributed to undermining the global rice market and deprived producers of higher incomes as a result. Our somewhat different assessment is that the Vietnamese government took these steps because it was primarily concerned with ensuring national food security in these exceptional times. In particular, early 2008 crop predictions emerging from the national planning system suggested a poor harvest, and food stocks were running down.

Throughout the past two decades, the government of Vietnam has sought to assure a steady increase in producer prices, rather than allowing prices to vary substantially in response to short-term market fluctuations. In addition, the government sought to alleviate price impacts by granting exemptions from taxes on consumers (VAT) and producers (CIT). The combined effect of these actions, among others, has been to limit the increase of both the consumer price and producer price of rice, while keeping their relative levels reasonably constant. Although producer prices did increase slightly less than consumer prices over this period, several other compensatory actions were subsequently taken to support producers, including exemption from land taxes, increased extension support, and increased credit.

The government also announced in late 2009 that it would implement a US$3.3-billion stimulus package for agriculture and rural development. The producer price continued to increase in 2009–10, even though the world price fell in this period. In other words, the government smoothed out the increase in the price received by producers over this period, while keeping a keen eye on food security and consumer prices. In addition, during the same period, the prime minister ordered business to buy paddy rice at a floor price, to ensure 30 percent profits for farmers.

As the very large majority of rice producers in Vietnam produce in excess of their consumption requirements, they benefitted from these policies, increased their production levels, and in time became more likely to adopt improved seeds. Non-producing households did lose out, but they tended to be much better off, on average. In addition there was a small minority of producers who were net consumers, and who also lost out. These households were disproportionately likely to live in the northwest, to be poor, and to be comprised of ethnic minorities.

Overall, this analysis suggests that the Vietnamese government acted relatively effectively in extremely difficult circumstances. Indeed, Elleby and Hansen (2014) suggest that it acted more effectively than many other countries in responding to extraordinary price fluctuations. Moreover, our analysis shows that, by and large, poorer households, being net producers, were the beneficiaries while the losers tended mostly to be relatively wealthy, non-producing consumers.

Acknowledgments

We are grateful to Chiara Cazzuffi for research assistance, to David Sahn and Patricia Mason for editorial guidance, and to comments from participants in the conference "New Directions in the Fight against Hunger and Malnutrition: A Festschrift in Honor of Per Pinstrup-Andersen," December 13–14, 2013. Suggestions made at the Nordic Conference on Development Economics held in Helsinki in mid-June 2014 are also acknowledged, and we are grateful for the constructive comments of an anonymous reviewer on an earlier draft of this study. Special thanks are due to staff from the Central Institute of Economic Management (CIEM) and the Institute for Labour Studies and Social Affairs (ILSSA) in Vietnam for continued collaboration in data collection and analysis. The usual caveats apply.

Notes

1. Chapoto (2012); Ghoneim (2012); Kirsten (2012); Mueller and Mueller (2012); Admassie (2013); Babu (2013); Baltzer (2013); Bryan (2013); Chirwa and Chinsinga (2013); Ganguly and Gulati (2013); Hai and Talbot (2013); Huang et al. (2013); Nhate et al. (2013); Nzuma (2013); Olomola (2013); Raihan (2013); Rausser and de Gorter (2013); Resnick (2013); Swinnen et al. (2013); Watson, II (2013).
2. VHLSS used the same sampling frame for its rounds between 2002 and 2008, before changing to a new sample frame from 2010. In this study we use it to compare between 2006 and 2010 on a cross-sectional basis.

References

Abbott, P. C. 2011. "Export Restrictions as Stabilization Responses to Food Crises." *American Journal of Agricultural Economics* 94 (2): pp. 428–434.

Abbott, P., F. Tarp, and C. Wu. 2011. "Structural Transformation, Biased Technological Change, and Employment in Vietnam." Unpublished draft.

Abbott, P., F. Tarp, and C. Wu. 2012. "Transmission of World Prices to the Domestic Market in Vietnam." Unpublished draft.

Addison, T., C. Arndt, and F. Tarp. 2011. "The Triple Crisis and the Global Aid Architecture." *African Development Review* 23 (4): pp. 461–478.

Admassie, A. 2013. "The Political Economy of Food Price: The Case of Ethiopia." WIDER Working Paper No. 2013/001, UNU-WIDER, Helsinki, Finland.

Arndt, C., R. Benfica, N. Maxiliano, A. M. D. Nucifero, and J. T. Thurlow. 2008. "Higher Fuel and Food Prices: Impacts and Responses for Mozambique." *Agricultural Economics* 39 (Suppl. s1): pp. 497–511.

Babu, S. C. 2013. "Policy Process and Food Price Crisis: A Framework for Analysis and Lessons from Country Studies." WIDER Working Paper No. 2013/070, UNU-WIDER, Helsinki, Finland.

Baltzer, K. 2013. "International to Domestic Price Transmission in Fourteen Developing Countries during the 2007–08 Food Crisis." WIDER Working Paper No. 2013/031, UNU-WIDER, Helsinki, Finland.

Barrett, C. B., and P. A. Dorosh. 1996. "Farmers' Welfare and Changing Food Prices: Non-Parametric Evidence from Rice in Madagascar." *American Journal of Agricultural Economics* 78 (3): pp. 656–669.

Benson, T., S. Mugarura, and K. Wanda. 2008. "Impacts in Uganda of Rising Food Prices: The Role of Diversified Staples and Limited Price Transmission." *Agricultural Economics* 39 (Suppl. s1): pp. 513–524.

Bryan, S. 2013. "A Cacophony of Policy Responses: Evidence from Fourteen Countries during the 2007/08 Food Price Crisis." WIDER Working Paper No. 2013/029, UNU-WIDER, Helsinki, Finland.

Cazzuffi, C., A. McKay, Luu Duc Khai, Nguyen The Long, and Thuy Do Minh. 2011. "Constraints to Market Participation in Agriculture in Vietnam." CIEM Working Paper, Central Institute for Economic Management (CIEM), Hanoi.

Chapoto, A. 2012. "The Political Economy of Food Price Policy: The Case of Zambia." WIDER Working Paper No. 2012/100, UNU-WIDER, Helsinki, Finland.

Chirwa, E., and B. Chinsinga. 2013. "Dealing with the 2007/08 Global Food Price Crisis: The Political Economy of Food Price Policy in Malawi." WIDER Working Paper No. 2013/30, UNU-WIDER, Helsinki, Finland.

CIEM. 2007. "Vietnam Access to Resources Household Survey Characteristics of the Vietnamese Rural Economy: 2006 Survey." Central Institute for Economic Management (CIEM), Hanoi.

CIEM. 2009. "Vietnam Access to Resources Household Survey Characteristics of the Vietnamese Rural Economy: 2008 Survey." Central Institute for Economic Management (CIEM), Hanoi.

CIEM. 2011. "Vietnam Access to Resources Household Survey Characteristics of the Vietnamese Rural Economy: 2010 Survey." Central Institute for Economic Management (CIEM), Hanoi.

CIEM. 2013. "Vietnam Access to Resources Household Survey Characteristics of the Vietnamese Rural Economy: 2012 Survey." Central Institute for Economic Management (CIEM), Hanoi.

Coxhead, I., Vu Hoang Linh, and Le Dong Tam. 2008. "Global Market Shocks and Poverty in Vietnam: The Case of Rice." *Agricultural Economics* 43 (5): pp. 575–592.

Deaton, A. 1989. "Rice Prices and Income Distribution in Thailand: A Non-Parametric Analysis." *Economic Journal* 99 (395): pp. 1–37.

Elleby, C., and H. Hansen. 2014. "Domestic Food Prices in Asia and the Rice Crisis." Unpublished manuscript, Department of Food and Resource Economics, University of Copenhagen.

FAO. 2014. FAOSTAT. Food and Agricultural Organization of the United Nations, Rome. <http://faostat3.fao.org/faostat-gateway/go/to/home/E>.

Friedman, J., and N. Schady. 2009. "How Many More Infants Are Likely to Die in Africa as a Result of the Global Financial Crisis?" Policy Research Working Paper WPS 5023, World Bank, Washington, DC.

Ganguly, K., and A. Gulati. 2013. "The Political Economy of Food Price Policy: The Case Study of India." WIDER Working Paper No. 2013/034, UNU-WIDER, Helsinki, Finland.

Ghoneim, A. F. 2012. "The Political Economy of Food Price Policy in Egypt." WIDER Working Paper No. 2012/096, UNU-WIDER, Helsinki, Finland.

Hai, N. M., and T. Talbot. 2013. "The Political Economy of Food Price Policy: The Case of Rice in Vietnam." WIDER Working Paper No. 2013/035, UNU-WIDER, Helsinki, Finland.

Huang, J., J. Yang, and S. Rozelle. 2013. "The Political Economy of Food Pricing Policy in China." WIDER Working Paper No. 2013/038, UNU-WIDER, Helsinki, Finland.

IRRI (International Rice Research Institute). 2014. "World Rice Statistics." <http://ricestat.irri.org:8080/wrs2/entrypoint.htm>.

Ivanic, M., and W. Martin. 2008. "Implications of Higher Global Food Prices for Poverty in Low Income Countries." *Agricultural Economics* 39 (Suppl. s1): pp. 405–416.

Jensen, H. T., S. Robinson, and F. Tarp. 2010. "General Equilibrium Measures of Agricultural Bias in Fifteen Developing Countries." *American Journal of Agricultural Economics* 92 (4): pp. 1136–1148.

Jensen, R. T., and N. H. Miller. 2008. "The Impact of Food Price Increases on Caloric Intake in China." *Agricultural Economics* 39 (Suppl. s1): pp. 465–476.

Kirsten, J. F. 2012. "The Political Economy of Food Price Policy in South Africa." WIDER Working Paper No. 2012/102, UNU-WIDER, Helsinki, Finland.

Khai, Luu Duc, T. Markussen, S. McCoy, and F. Tarp. 2013. "Access to Land: Market and Non-Market Land Transactions in Rural Vietnam." In *Land Tenure Reform in Asia and Africa: Assessing Impacts on Poverty and Natural Resource Management*, edited by S. Holden, K. Otsuka, and K. Deininger, pp. 162–186. New York: Palgrave Macmillan.

Markussen, T., K. van den Broeck, and F. Tarp. 2011. "The Forgotten Property Rights: Evidence on Land Use Rights in Vietnam." *World Development* 39 (5): pp. 839–850.

Martin, W., and K. Anderson. 2011. "Export Restrictions and Price Insulation during Commodity Price Booms." *American Journal of Agricultural Economics* 94 (2): pp. 422–427.

McKay, A., and F. Tarp. 2013. "Diversity among Rapid Transformation: Welfare Dynamics in Rural Vietnam, 2006 to 2012." In-Depth Studies. CIEM-DANIDA Project, Central Institute for Economic Management (CIEM), Hanoi.

Mueller, B., and C. Mueller. 2012. "The Impact of the 2007–08 Food Price Crisis in a Major Commodity Exporter." WIDER Working Paper No. 2012/095, UNU-WIDER, Helsinki, Finland.

Nhate, V., C. Massingarela, and V. Salvucci. 2013. "The Political Economy of Food Price Policy: Country Case Study of Mozambique." WIDER Working Paper No. 2013/037, UNU-WIDER, Helsinki, Finland.

Niimi, Y., P. Vasaduva-Dutta, and L. A. Winters. 2003. "Trade Liberalisation and Poverty in Vietnam." PRUS Working Paper No. 17, Poverty Research Unit at Sussex (PRUS), University of Sussex, Brighton, UK.

Nzuma, J. M. 2013. "The Political Economy of Food Price Policy: The Case of Kenya." WIDER Working Paper No. 2013/026, UNU-WIDER, Helsinki, Finland.

Olomola, A. S. 2013. "The Political Economy of Food Price Policy in Nigeria." WIDER Working Paper No. 2013/016, UNU-WIDER, Helsinki, Finland.

Pingali, P., and V. T. Xuan. 1992. "Vietnam: Decollectivization and Rice Productivity Growth." *Economic Development and Cultural Change* 40 (4): pp. 697–718.

Raihan, S. 2013. "The Political Economy of Food Price Policy: The Case of Bangladesh." WIDER Working Paper No. 2013/002, UNU-WIDER, Helsinki, Finland.

Rausser, G. C., and H. de Gorter. 2013. "US Policy Contributions to Agricultural Commodity Price Fluctuations, 2006–12." WIDER Working Paper No. 2013/033, UNU-WIDER, Helsinki, Finland.

Ravallion, M. 1990. "Rural Welfare Effects of Food Price Changes under Induced Wage Responses: Theory and Evidence for Bangladesh." *Oxford Economic Papers* 42 (3): pp. 574–585.

Resnick, D. 2013. "Personalistic Policy-Making in a Vibrant Democracy: Senegal's Fragmented Response to the 2007/08 Food Price Crisis." WIDER Working Paper No. 2013/015, UNU-WIDER, Helsinki, Finland.

Swinnen, J., L. Knops, and K. van Herck. 2013. "Food Price Volatility and EU Policies." WIDER Working Paper No. 2013/032, UNU-WIDER, Helsinki, Finland.

Tarp, F., D. Roland-Holst, and J. Rand. 2002. "Trade and Income Growth in Vietnam: Estimates from a New Social accounting Matrix." *Economic Systems Research* 14 (2): pp. 157–184.

Thurlow, J., F. Tarp, S. McCoy, N. M. Hai, C. Breisinger, and C. Arndt. 2011. "The Impact of the Global Commodity and Financial Crises on Poverty in Vietnam." *Journal of Globalization and Development* 2 (1): pp. 1–31.

Vasavakul, T. 2006. "Agricultural Land Management under Doi Moi: Policy Makers' Views." In *Agricultural Development and Land Policy in Vietnam*, edited by S. P. Marsh, T. G. MacAuley, and P. V. Hung, pp. 221–232. Sydney: Australian Centre for International Agricultural Research.

Vu, L., and P. Glewwe. 2011. "Impacts of Rising Food Prices on Poverty and Welfare in Vietnam." *Journal of Agriculture and Resource Economics* 36 (1): pp. 14–27.

Warr, P. 2008. "World Food Prices and Poverty Incidence in a Food Exporting Country: A Multihousehold General Equilibrium Analysis for Thailand." *Agricultural Economics* 39 (Suppl. s1): pp. 525–537.

Watson, II, D. D. 2013. "Political Economy Synthesis: The Food Policy Crisis." WIDER Working Paper No. 2013/050, UNU-WIDER, Helsinki, Finland.

Winters, L. A., N. McCulloch, and A. McKay. 2004. "Trade Liberalization and Poverty: The Evidence So Far." *Journal of Economic Literature* 42 (1): pp. 72–115.

World Bank. 2013. "Commodity Markets Outlook." Volume 2, Global Economic Prospects 2013/07. Washington, DC: World Bank. <http://siteresources.worldbank.org/INTPROSPECTS/Resources/334934-1304428586133/CommodityMarketsOutlook_July2013.pdf>.

17

Independence or Influence

Trade-offs in Development Policy Research

Roger Slade and Mitch Renkow

> *Most policy research on African agriculture is irrelevant to agricultural and overall economic policy in Africa.*
> —Steve Were Omamo (2003, p. ix)

Introduction

In the social sciences, policy-based research is generally understood to mean research that is explicitly designed to inform and usually to change public policy.[1] As a "discipline," in both developed and developing countries, it has been much studied. In the field of development, there is a vast literature on the conceptual basis of policy research and on how to design it, how to do it, how to evaluate it, and on the tools, drawn from many branches of the social sciences, that should be deployed in doing so (ODI 2004; Global Development Network 2013). Within this literature, much is said about maximizing the influence of policy research by ensuring that it is relevant.[2]

But how is relevance best secured? And to whom is it relevant? Some commentators emphasize the value of conducting research in a patron–client relationship, whereby the researcher delivers answers to questions posed by the government or some other public agency. This, for example, is the process followed by the International Growth Centre (IGC). Others advocate generating policy results and lessons that have wide international relevance—international public goods (IPGs)—that enable policy consumers to make more informed choices. This is the approach used by many research centers with large geographic mandates, including the International Food Policy Research Institute (IFPRI) and some other member institutions of the Consultative Group on International Agricultural Research (CGIAR). Others, notably think tanks, organizations like the Food and Agricultural Organization (FAO), and contract research institutions in the Organisation for Economic Co-operation and Development (OECD) countries, pursue a more normative approach and undertake research in the quest for more and better knowledge, paying scant attention to whether it is applicable beyond a specific circumstance.[3] Major donors, such as the World Bank, seek policy relevance by directly supporting policy research in public institutions, as well as by conducting their own evidence-based policy research. Yet others seek to identify gaps in public policy knowledge that are amenable to investigation and thus, when filled, are likely to be relevant to specific situations.[4] The Bill & Melinda Gates Foundation (BMGF) has funded several attempts to do this.[5]

In writing about these alternative approaches, few, if any, commentators have addressed the advantages and disadvantages of different ways of organizing policy research in order to maximize relevance. Thus, it is difficult to discern whether experience to date suggests that one way is better than another or that a particular organizational model is optimal. While few commentators fail to mention the critical role played by collaboration between the producers and consumers of policy research,[6] the absence of a comprehensive analysis of the efficacy of organizational forms[7] also means that the risks of collaboration tend to be under-researched.[8]

What are these risks? In collaborative, objective policy research centered on proximity to decision-makers, the key risk is that of "capture."[9] Capture will be used in this chapter as shorthand to denote a situation in which consumers of policy research unduly distort the conduct of independent analysis by researchers and, by extension, the setting of institutional research priorities. Such distortions may take the form of constraints imposed on the identification of relevant researchable topics; on the acquisition of necessary data; on the use of certain analytical methods; or on the dissemination of scientific results and policy findings.

By this definition, capture is a matter of degree. We also postulate that the degree to which an institution is captured matters: the greater the extent of capture, the lower the likelihood that research will generate first-best solutions to policy problems and, correspondingly, the greater the likelihood of delivering sub-optimal policy advice. This risk may become very serious in situations where the openness of the policy arena is constrained and the freedom of expression restricted by a prevailing political or economic ideology. In such situations, there are explicit trade-offs to be made that balance the goal of objectively identifying first-best outcomes against political judgments about relevance, influence, and priority. First-best solutions are sometimes simply impossible without, *inter alia*, a supporting institutional structure. In Ethiopia, IFPRI's focus on creating institutions may be seen as an indirect route to increasing the chances that first-best solutions might ultimately be attainable.

In this chapter, we consider these issues associated with the efficacy of collaborative policy research through the lens of IFPRI's experience conducting policy research in Ethiopia between 1995 and 2010.[10] From 1995 to 2004, nearly all of IFPRI's Ethiopia work was undertaken by Washington-based research teams, working on specific themes under various "global research programs." This changed in 2004 with the establishment of IFPRI's Ethiopia Strategy Support Program (ESSP). The ESSP was set up to provide direct support to the government of Ethiopia in the design and implementation of its national agricultural development strategy.

We compare both the design and influence of IFPRI's research activities under these two distinct approaches to policy research. We find that the establishment of the ESSP rendered IFPRI much more of an "insider" in Ethiopia's policymaking process than had previously been the case. This had profound effects on the composition and influence of IFPRI's research. We argue that the ESSP enhanced the relevance of IFPRI's work—particularly its contribution to institutional change in Ethiopia—but at the cost of partial capture by a government whose prevailing ideological position is inimical to the use of free markets as a means of allocating resources, particularly in agriculture and rural development. We note further that the partial capture of the ESSP is likely to be an inevitable "cost of doing business" within Ethiopia's policymaking milieu, and that the effectiveness of the ESSP has depended to a large degree on the idiosyncratic efforts of ESSP program directors.

IFPRI's Approach to Policy Research

IFPRI was incorporated as a tax-exempt corporation in Washington, DC, in 1975.[11] In 1980, it began its association with the CGIAR, becoming a full member in 1984. Its initial mandate focused its work on the policies needed to increase food production in developing countries, as well as trade and aid in foodstuffs. With time, this mandate has been expanded to allow coverage of most aspects of rural development and the relations between agricultural and rural development policy and macroeconomic policy, although there has been a relative decline in the emphasis on trade and aid. Early on, there was also a clear emphasis on building policy research capacity in developing countries through collaborative activity.

During its first decade of operation, even as its staff grew in number and diversity, IFPRI's primary modus operandi was via research projects anchored in Washington, DC, with some short-term deployment of staff to countries where empirical work was undertaken. When the leadership changed in 1992 (Per Pinstrup-Andersen replaced John Mellor), the search for international public goods (IPGs) became an explicit objective of IFPRI's research.[12] The search for IPGs was based on similar and simultaneous forms of investigation in several countries, in the hope that there would be strong commonalities in the findings and policy conclusions, such that their value to others would be self-evident and widespread.[13] The earliest long-term assignments of IFPRI staff to outposts throughout the world also took place at about this time, and networks of policy researchers and policy users were built to further foster the cross-country exchange of policy knowledge.[14] These approaches (the search for IPGs and networking) have since dominated IFPRI's research, although there seems to have been a reduction in the emphasis on the search for IPGs in recent years.[15] These changes were accompanied by an increase in targeted policy support to selected nations, particularly in Africa.

By the end of Pinstrup-Andersen's tenure as director-general in 2002, IFPRI's thinking had developed to the point where explicit plans for supporting policy development in specific countries were being articulated.[16] These plans included multiple studies intended to help countries devise coherent policy frameworks and well-considered strategies for rural poverty reduction and increased agricultural production. This approach was fully consistent with the strong push by the donor community (in the light of the Millennium Development Goals), to get each developing country to prepare its own comprehensive Poverty Reduction Strategy Program (PRSP).

IFPRI also decided to launch a series of Strategy Support Programs (SSPs) that would help selected countries improve their rural policy frameworks and their capacity to undertake their own policy research.[17] The SSPs were to be collaborative in nature and would involve posting IFPRI staff to work alongside local researchers and research institutions in the selected countries. They were also intended to have finite lives—"to have worked themselves out of a job," in the words of one IFPRI researcher. In this way, work in a given country could be scaled down and eventually ended, while a new SSP was built in another country. The first of the SSPs turned out to be Ethiopia, where an IFPRI policy research unit was established in 2004.[18]

IFPRI's Policy Research Experience in Ethiopia

As one of the poorest, most populous, and largest countries in Africa, Ethiopia's development challenges—and the policies pursued to address those challenges—have long been the focus of attention by researchers, development policy analysts, and donors. From 1995 to 2004, almost all of IFPRI's work in Ethiopia was undertaken by Washington-based research teams, pursuing specific themes under various "global research programs." In each case, Ethiopia was just one of several countries in a larger multi-country study. This was in line with IFPRI's prevailing modus operandi of pursuing rigorous empirical research capable of contributing to a broader understanding of economic development processes. The IPGs generated in this way included peer-reviewed published outputs (books, monographs, journal articles, and discussion papers); collaborative research with both domestic and international researchers; and the building of national capacity for policy research through workshops, formal training programs, and knowledge networks.

IFPRI entered into a different kind of relationship with Ethiopia in 2004, when the Ethiopia Strategy Support Program (ESSP) was set up to provide well-researched policy advice to support the government of Ethiopia (GoE) in the design and implementation of its national agricultural development strategy, as well as advice on other agricultural and rural development (ARD) policy matters.[19] The ESSP involved placing a small team of IFPRI researchers in Addis Ababa to work with the Ethiopian Development Research Institute (EDRI) and other national counterparts on policy analysis, capacity development, and communications. However, the Addis Ababa-based ESSP team was, and continues to be, backstopped by researchers based in Washington, DC.

The ESSP was designed with the explicit intent of increasing the influence and impact of IFPRI's policy research, without sacrificing the analytical rigor and intellectual independence of the investigators. The research agenda was to be collaboratively determined. The key distinguishing features of the ESSP model, compared with IFPRI's prior mode of operation in Ethiopia, was the posting of a core of researchers to Addis Ababa who were to work very closely with domestic partners in the local policy establishment—government officials, academics, and quasi-independent researchers—on the design and conduct of the research. The resulting "demand-led" research produced by the ESSP was expected to enhance the relevance and impact of its outputs, increase domestic research capacity, and lead to greater policy relevance and impact.

An Ideological Divide

Throughout the period considered here, there has existed an ideological divide between the government of Ethiopia (GoE) and key donors, a divide that has an important bearing on the research that "outsiders" (like IFPRI) could undertake if they wished to influence policy decisions.[20] Throughout our period of review, the GoE maintained a distinctive ideological position reflecting its antecedents in the Tigrayan People's Liberation Front, a movement that had Marxist foundations and drew heavily on Leninist and Stalinist thinking. With time the prevailing political and economic ideology in Ethiopia took on a more purely African form, the roots of which can be traced to the 1967 Arusha Declaration. That declaration argued that in order to ensure economic justice, the state must have effective control over the principal means of production; and that it is the responsibility of the state to intervene actively in the economic life of the nation to prevent the exploitation of one person by another or one group by another (Nyerere 1968, p. 391). Thinking of this kind is widely said to have informed the policy positions of the late Prime Minister Meles Zenawi, Ethiopia's prime minister throughout the period covered by this study and the driver of government policy in all spheres, especially the economic.

In the agricultural sector, this thinking, according to several informed commentators, finds its clearest expression in a deep suspicion of free markets on the grounds that they are both exploitative and corrupt—a belief graphically described by one commentator as "traders are thieves." This viewpoint has led to a policy bias in favor of state-sanctioned or state-owned marketing bodies, among which cooperatives are the long-standing favorites and the very recent Ethiopian Commodity Exchange the most visible. It has also led to the neglect of policy reform in domestic input and output markets for agriculture. For many years the GoE, in its dialogue with donors, has proven to be very sensitive to any change that seemed to promote private sector commercial expansion—despite "agricultural development-led industrialisation" having been the GoE's stated objective for two or more decades. Competition has and continues to be moderated, if not resisted, at every opportunity.

These comments should not, however, be taken to imply that that Meles Zenawi's government has been unsuccessful. From the beginning, the government and the prime minister have advocated "pro-poor" domestic policies and have emphasized social inclusion and equity. According to the World Bank, the Ethiopian government ranks first in Africa on spending as a share of GDP going to pro-poor sectors. The administration has also sought to decentralize and to devolve power, creating self-governing regional development organizations. Even though Zenawi's administration inherited one of the worst-performing economies in the world, Ethiopia's economy grew steadily throughout his time in office. Over much of the past decade, Ethiopia's GDP is said to have grown about 9 percent per year, reflecting broadly successful "structural policies" and improving public sector management and institutions.

Nevertheless, the ideological leanings of the GoE during the years spanned by this study may be fairly characterized as being highly suspicious of—even hostile to—letting markets work as a means of allocating resources. This ethos is diametrically opposed to the core idea of neoclassical economics that reliance on sensibly regulated but essentially free markets is the best means of promoting allocative efficiency and maximizing material well-being among the largest number of people. Also, there seem to be clear limits to the GoE's acceptance of policy messages (and the research that underpins them) that are based on "first-best," free-market solutions.

Most governments (and hence most donors) reflect some underlying ideology of either the left or the right. Thus, the GoE's left-leaning position is not unusual among developing countries, although it seems to have been held more consistently than in many others.[21] In contrast, and despite the fact that IFPRI's work in Ethiopia and elsewhere reflects a more heterodox approach to finding middle ground between state-centered and market-based policies than might be adopted by many other institutions within the donor community (e.g., the World Bank), the great bulk of IFPRI research (and the training of its research staff) is rooted in neoclassical economics. The upshot is that a significant share of IFPRI's research in Ethiopia may be fairly characterized as seeking (second-best) solutions to problems created by market failures, while another large share is directed toward the creation and operation of institutions as a possible means of delivering and implementing first-best solutions.

In addition, and perhaps as a consequence of this ideological mismatch, Ethiopian policymakers seem to display a resistance to "outside advice" from independent domestic sources such as the Economic Policy Research Institute (EPRI)[22] and from the donor community that is greater than in most other places.[23] This view was expressed by a broad range of knowledgeable informants interviewed during this study. These informants cogently argued that this resistance has had several very important effects on the influence of IFPRI's research (and economic research in Ethiopia more generally) and on how that research influences policy. First, it greatly lengthens the gestation period during which research-based policy ideas are transformed into specific policy changes. Some see these lags as being the result of key policymakers buying time to consider what is being offered—time during which the origins of the advice may become obscured. Thus, outright rejection of clear and convincing policy advice is rare, and in some cases change does (eventually) come. Second, and paradoxically, the GoE has an additional tendency to become "overly exuberant" with some policy changes. Third, it renders more difficult than usual the attribution of specific policy changes to specific research outputs.

The net result is a policy arena in which both the determination of research issues and the delivery of research findings are matters requiring unusual delicacy on the part of IFPRI researchers. This attentiveness to the politics of policymaking is highly relevant to our interests insofar as it affects both research design and the presentation of research results.

Outputs and Outcomes

In this section we summarize the influences that IFPRI's research efforts have had on the way agricultural policies are determined in Ethiopia. The pathway whereby a policy research institution such as IFPRI can produce positive impacts is often characterized as follows (Gardner 2008): a policy problem or issue justifies the outlay of money and manpower on a set of research activities. This leads to *outputs* (research papers, etc.) that are ingredients in an interactive (and iterative) process involving many stakeholders that, in turn, produces *outcomes* in the form of a consensus for change and the legal steps, institutional steps, or both necessary to give effect to the new or changed policy. Last, those outcomes deliver *impact* in the form of net welfare gains—both to a defined population of beneficiaries and to non-targeted groups (in the form of knowledge or welfare spillovers).

The immediacy in this simple model is not always found in practice. In particular, the process whereby policy-research outputs contribute to policy outcomes may depend on a host of variables, including the formation and effectiveness of "advocacy coalitions" around a particular policy issue (Weible et al. 2009). In Ethiopia, however, such coalitions, especially those involving civil society organizations, have been only weakly present since the Civil War (1974–91). By far the strongest agent of policy change has been the prime minister's office.[24]

In Ethiopia, decision-making is highly concentrated, and if policy research by an institution like IFPRI is persuasive, consequent policy change may be directly attributable to its work. However, such influence is not likely to be openly acknowledged in Ethiopia. Moreover, deficits in local capacity for both policy interpretation and implementation may require substantial efforts to first be directed at augmenting human capital and *then* enhancing (or creating) the local institutions within which that human capital is employed. For this reason and others, there may well be long time gaps in the final stages of delivering policy change and achieving welfare gains. With this as a backdrop, we next briefly summarize the outputs, outcomes, and influences of IFPRI's policy research in Ethiopia.

Outputs

IFPRI's research in Ethiopia since 1995 has addressed four main research themes: (1) Market Development; (2) Poverty and Food Security; (3) Public Investment; and (4) Sustainable Land Management (SLM). Taken as a whole, IFPRI's research output in Ethiopia has been prodigious—324 publications

No. of
Publications

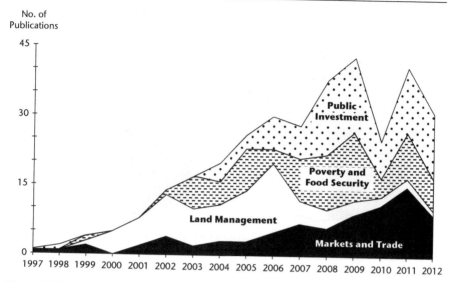

Figure 17.1 Number of publications annually by subject area, 1997–2012

Note: For each year, these are the total number of publications (broken down by subject area) reported in Google Scholar as of September 2012.

Source: Renkow and Slade (2013).

since 1995. Approximately one-fifth of these (62) were peer-reviewed journal articles; and an additional 47 were externally reviewed books, book chapters, and research monographs (Renkow and Slade 2013).

Figure 17.1 shows the number of publications by thematic area produced annually by IFPRI research in Ethiopia over the period of analysis (there were no reported publications prior to 1997).[25] Two trends stand out: first, the annual output of publications has grown steadily with time, peaking in 2009 when 43 papers were released; and second, the composition of the research has changed substantially since 1997. Between 1997 and 2006, the largest share of published output was in the area of land management. Subsequently, the salience of land management declined, and other subjects became more prominent.

Over the entire period considered, the distribution of published outputs across research themes was quite balanced (Figure 17.2 and Table 17.1). However, research on land management, and on poverty and food security was cited about twice as much as the other two thematic areas of research (public investment, markets and trade). To some extent citations are indicative of possible spillover effects on other research—that is, the extent to which initial research may have generated or contributed to international public goods (IPGs).

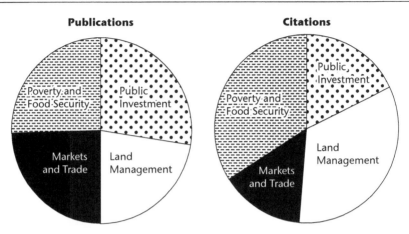

Figure 17.2 Total publications and citations by research theme
Source: Renkow and Slade (2013).

Outcomes

The most important outcomes attributable to IFPRI's work in Ethiopia lie in the establishment and operation of institutions. These include fundamental contributions to three important and highly visible organizations—the Productive Safety Net Programme (PSNP), the Ethiopian Commodity Exchange (ECX), and the Agricultural Transformation Agency (ATA)—as well as to three "intellectual institutions"—the Ethiopian Rural Household Survey (ERHS), the Ethiopian computable general equilibrium (CGE) model, and a series of spatial analyses published as atlases. In Ethiopia, as in many countries, institutional change is a necessary precondition of improvement in many dimensions of agricultural policy. In Ethiopia, it may also be a way of bridging the ideological gap between the suppliers and consumers of policy research.

Table 17.1 summarizes by thematic area the key outcomes to which IFPRI research made fundamental contributions. These are briefly described below:

- *Productive Safety Net Programme (PSNP)*—Begun in 2005, the PSNP is the second largest social safety net program in Africa. It was established to replace Ethiopia's near chronic reliance on ad hoc international food assistance with a more systematic set of continuing interventions to improve livelihood outcomes in areas with perennial food deficits. IFPRI's role has been to monitor and evaluate program effectiveness, including the identification of efficacious improvements. As a result, IFPRI enjoys nearly universal acclaim (from the GoE and donors alike) for its contributions to the program's success.

Table 17.1. Key outcomes associated with IFPRI research in Ethiopia

Research theme	Outcomes	Impact pathway
Food security and poverty	Productive Safety Net Program (2005–present)	Monitor and improve targeting efficiency of program operations
	Ethiopian Rural Household Survey (1989–present)	Longest-duration household-level panel data set in sub-Saharan Africa; IPGs generation
Land management	—	
Public investment	Ethiopian CGE Model (2006–present)	Policy analysis tool (applications include exchange rate policy, food price inflation strategy, climate change planning, urban planning)
	Atlas of the Rural Economy (2006–present)	Spatial analysis capability
Markets and trade	Ethiopian Commodity Exchange (2008–present)	Institutionalize, integrate agricultural markets
	Agricultural Transformation Agency (2010–present)	Institutionalize, integrate agricultural R&D, input distribution, and extension systems
ESSP	Ethiopian Commodity Exchange; Ethiopian CGE Model; *Atlas of the Rural Economy*	

- *Ethiopian Rural Household Survey (ERHS)*—The ERHS is the centerpiece of IFPRI's research on poverty in Ethiopia. Begun in 1989, this longitudinal survey has been collected in seven rounds—making it the longest duration panel data set of its kind in sub-Saharan Africa. It has been widely used by researchers, both within and outside of Ethiopia, in a variety of investigations into the dynamics of household poverty.[26]

- *Ethiopian Computable General Equilibrium Model (ECGE)*—The ECGE was developed by ESSP staff (in collaboration with local partners) to support *ex ante* analyses of a variety of macroeconomic policy options. These include: (a) quantifying the implications for economic growth of alternative public investment allocations; (b) developing strategies for reducing food price inflation; (c) assessing the growth and distributional effects of foreign exchange rationing; and (d) examining the potential impacts of global climate change on Ethiopia.

- *Atlases of the Ethiopian Rural Economy*—Working with the GoE's Central Statistical Agency (CSA), ESSP staff produced several national atlases that compiled spatially disaggregated information on the biophysical environment, access to services, demographic characteristics of the population, and crop and livestock production. The training of CSA staff in Geographic Information Systems (GIS) methodology has enabled the CSA to independently produce additional regional atlases.

- *Ethiopian Commodity Exchange (ECX)*—The ECX is the most visible outcome of IFPRI's policy research in Ethiopia. Eleni Gabre-Madhin, the first head of the ESSP, was the prime mover in the establishment of the ECX and subsequently became its founding director. Her research, along with other ESSP research, argued strongly for Ethiopia to set up a commodity exchange for grains (see, for example, Gabre-Madhin [2005]); Gabre-Madhin and Goggin [2005]). This argument was predicated on observations that the existing market structure was highly fragmented, that transport-adjusted prices varied widely across the country, that there were numerous informal impediments to inter-regional trade in grain, that the law of contracts was ignored or only weakly enforced (so that contractual defaults were frequent), and that non-local price information was hard for traders to obtain. The culminating outcome of this research was the acceptance by the GoE that the ECX should be established.

- *Agricultural Transformation Agency (ATA)*—Funded by the Bill & Melinda Gates Foundation, the ATA was established to refine and guide policy changes required to address systemic bottlenecks within Ethiopia's agricultural economy. IFPRI's involvement in a set of diagnostic studies played an instrumental role in the establishment of the ATA; and very recently, IFPRI has been contracted to provide research-backstopping services for the fledgling ATA. The ATA is tackling very large problems—for example, reforming the seed and fertilizer sectors; developing soil maps for the entire country using state-of-the-art satellite-imaging technology; and pursuing a plan to rapidly and dramatically scale up teff production by disseminating improved technologies that rely on novel, but untested, planting techniques. Each of these may yield remarkable breakthroughs. They may also yield spectacular (and highly visible) failures.

- *ESSP Outputs and Outcomes*—The ESSP's outputs span a large part of the ARD spectrum.[27] They include six journal articles, 55 working and discussion papers, 16 research notes, and a number of other papers, research reports, atlases, and books (Renkow and Slade 2013). More than 80 percent of ESSP's publications were not externally peer reviewed, and therefore, there is little independent evidence of quality. In the absence of an effective results-focused research monitoring system, there are few ways of tracking whether these outputs (publications) produced both outcomes (policy change) and impact (welfare change) or contributed in some less obvious way toward policy thinking about ARD in Ethiopia. In sum, few of the wide range of ESSP outputs appear to have produced tangible outcomes in Ethiopia. The most notable exception is the research that led to the creation of the Ethiopian Commodity Exchange.[28] ESSP contributions to the ability of Ethiopian partners to create, process, and analyze information themselves—most notably through collaboration and training activities associated with the CGE model and the GIS-based *Atlases of the Ethiopian Economy*—represent other less visible outcomes that may produce substantial benefits over the long run.

Finally, conspicuously absent from Table 17.1 is any evidence of substantive outcomes of IFPRI's research on Sustainable Land Management (SLM)—research which preceded the organization of the ESSP. That work generated an impressive array of (widely cited) refereed publications, but little in the way of sustained policy influence. For example, a 2007 review of IFPRI's research on SLM issues in Ethiopia, conducted as part of a broader evaluation of IFPRI's global research program on less-favored areas, found that while the research succeeded in bringing information to policy debates surrounding poverty issues in less-favored areas, there was no tangible evidence of influence on policy outcomes (English and Renkow 2007). Six years later, we found little to add to these assessments (Renkow and Slade 2013). Very few interlocutors had strong memories of the SLM program of research. Individuals with direct connections to that work recalled that it contributed to the policy debate on land management and environmental sustainability over the years; but in no case was a specific new government policy or policy modification attributed to that research. This betokens a program of research that, for all its successes in producing a large number of well-cited publications, seems to have run counter to GoE ideology and failed to produce traceable policy change.

IFPRI's Influence on Policy Formation

As the preceding section indicates, IFPRI's activities in Ethiopia have generated a steady stream of high-quality research output across a number of ARD subjects. Significant benefits flow from the knowledge generated. It has produced evidence-based policy recommendations. It has contributed through other research projects inside and outside of Ethiopia to the generation of IPGs. It has played a key role in underpinning the formation and operation of a number of important Ethiopian organizations—most notably the PSNP, the ECX, and the ATA. IFPRI has also been instrumental in producing "intellectual institutions"—for example the ERHS, the GIS-based *Atlases of the Ethiopian Economy*, and the Ethiopian CGE model—that have expanded knowledge and enabled further research. In addition, several informants asserted that

IFPRI has raised the level of debate about ARD policy and strategy by creating an environment of evidence-based discussion. An increase in openness and transparency in framing policy is a valuable, if unquantifiable, benefit.

But how, if at all, has IFPRI influenced ARD policy formation within Ethiopia? The somewhat depressing answer is very little. Before the advent of the ESSP, and despite the impressive quantity of published output, the authors were unable to trace with confidence any clear-cut case of attributable *policy influence*, notwithstanding the PSNP.[29] And, after the advent of the ESSP, the evidence is also scant. It is certainly reasonable to attribute the major change in marketing policy represented by the ECX to IFPRI's unflinching efforts, but even here it is hard to say whether there has been any positive and lasting welfare change. What is known is that the ECX is yet to meaningfully address the marketing issues it was originally set up to resolve, namely the multiple shortcomings in domestic grain markets.[30]

Overall, there are few examples of policy influence or welfare changes plausibly attributable to the ESSP's research. This lack of clear influence and impact is almost certainly explained, at least in part, by the GoE's ideological stance that has delayed or curtailed policy actions on agricultural input and output markets (the ECX notwithstanding) and land reform.[31] These observations are fully consistent with the claims in the literature that the nature and influence of a research organization's work depend to a large extent on the political context and governance system in which it operates (see Keijzer et al. [2011], for example).[32] In Ethiopia, however, other forces—in particular, the way in which the research agenda is set, research priorities are established, and research results disseminated—also contributed. We take these up in the remainder of this section.

Idiosyncrasy

IFPRI's ability to be part of the policy dialogue in Ethiopia—as well as its visibility as a "player" in policy debates—took a quantum leap forward with the institution of the ESSP. However, the ESSP's research agenda has not been framed using formal priority-setting techniques—that is, a rigorous and systematic examination of existing policy to identify policy gaps and to determine which gaps, if filled, are likely to have the biggest payoffs within the prevailing political economy.

Rather, the process has been much more idiosyncratic in that topics have emerged largely in response to the particular interests of individual staff (particularly of the program directors) and the availability of particular analytical skills or constructs. However, analyses of some key issues, such as agricultural input markets and price transmission, have languished without inspiring action, reflecting the ideological barriers mentioned earlier. Moreover, it was explained to the authors by one of the prime minister's closest advisors that allowing IFPRI to set up the ESSP in Ethiopia provided the GoE with effective protection against pressures for policy analysis and reform from Ethiopia's major donors.

To a striking extent, the ESSP has depended on the idiosyncratic skills, relationships, and institutional connections to Ethiopia's policy milieu of some of its staff. This has, by and large, worked to the advantage of the ESSP thus far.[33] Nonetheless, the important role played by idiosyncrasy in the choosing of research questions pursued by the ESSP has also created organizational vulnerability to changes in the leadership of both the ESSP *and* the GoE.

Capture

An organization like the ESSP faces the risk of being captured by the host government. Given its clear success in advocating some policy and institutional changes, it is unlikely that the ESSP was ever fully captured by the GoE. However, the failure to take a more determined stand on certain controversial areas of policy—for example, land issues, the value of direct GoE involvement in the operation of the ECX, or the reform of input markets and agricultural supply side issues—suggest that the ESSP was heavily influenced by the GoE's bias against markets. Hence, it is hard to avoid the conclusion that the ESSP has been at least partially captured.

The threat of capture and the delicate efforts required to avoid it have been characterized by some IFPRI insiders as the unavoidable "price of doing business" in Ethiopia. Ultimately, this is an issue of balance. But because intellectual independence—as well as the *perception* of intellectual independence—is vital to IFPRI's effectiveness over the long run, this issue merits continued careful monitoring.

Nevertheless, the very close connections of key ESSP staff to the politically powerful in Addis Ababa has resulted in important institutional changes, and by some accounts, a gradually increasing willingness by the GoE to listen carefully to evidence-based policy arguments on some topics that initially met with unyielding resistance.[34]

Advocacy

The literature on policy research is replete with abundant discourse on the importance of advocacy in achieving policy influence and change (see, for example, Weiss [2001]). In Ethiopia there was little evidence that IFPRI or the ESSP had fully grasped this importance. In general, research findings were not well explained, and only simple efforts such as policy briefs (often more concerned with method than findings) and infrequent workshops and conferences were used to deliver policy messages. There was no identifiable use of lobbying techniques or advocacy coalitions,[35] nor, seemingly, was the political economy of reform in Ethiopia systematically explored.[36] Key policymakers were not targeted except through the idiosyncratic method noted above. A more strategic and instrumental approach to advocacy may have yielded a greater measure of policy influence.[37]

Summation

At the outset of this chapter, we posed some basic questions: How did IFPRI ensure the relevance of its policy research in Ethiopia? Was relevance enhanced or diminished by the sharp increase in the degree of collaboration provided by the ESSP?[38] As a result, to what extent did IFPRI positively influence ARD policy reform in Ethiopia and thereby produce discernable welfare gains for Ethiopia's smallholders?

Drawing on the evidence and findings outlined in this chapter, it is fair to argue that IFPRI's policy research in Ethiopia was indeed relevant to the country's main agricultural development challenges. There can be no doubt that IFPRI's Washington-led policy research on sustainable land management, household poverty and food security, agricultural markets, and public investment—both prior to and after the establishment of the ESSP—addressed a number of key issues faced by Ethiopia's multitudinous, impoverished smallholders laboring under gross market imperfections for both inputs and outputs.

The advent of the ESSP intensified the process of collaboration between IFPRI researchers and the GoE, and thereby increased the relevance of IFPRI's in-country research. We have argued that it did so via the strong idiosyncratic links of key ESSP staff to important policymakers in Ethiopia—notably the prime minister and his chief economic advisor. The work supporting the establishment of the commodity exchange, as well as consultative analyses of macroeconomic policy options (using the Ethiopian CGE model) are the clearest examples. This work helped to build IFPRI's credibility in Ethiopia, first with the government (who acknowledge IFPRI's contributions to improving the quality of policy discussion) and second among donors. The goodwill thus generated helped to cement IFPRI's highly praised programmatic work on the evaluation of the PSNP (work that has always been led from Washington). It remains debatable, however, whether or not the ESSP would have added measurably to the relevance of IFPRI's policy work in the absence of these idiosyncratic links.[39]

Additionally, it is probable that the ESSP increased the likelihood of capture or partial capture, the idiosyncratic links being something of a two-way street in this context. Proximity is a precondition of capture. As argued at the outset of this chapter, however, capture does not necessarily imply that policy research is irrelevant or lacking in first-best solutions. In the case of Ethiopia, partial capture and the ideological divide mostly operated to restrict the ESSP research agenda (thus limiting relevance) and to greatly handicap the speedy adoption of reforms—hence the absence of discernable welfare change attributable to the ESSP.[40]

To conclude, it is worth posing a final question. Could the risk of capture have been foreseen at the outset and could it have been mitigated? It is certain that the ideological divide (as we have called it) was present when the ESSP was established in 2004 and well understood in donor circles. Thus, it is unlikely that IFPRI set up the ESSP in ignorance of this problem. On the other hand, one or two key policy advisors to Meles Zenawi seemed, at the time, to offer a large welcome mat to the incoming IFPRI researchers—a welcome mat that concealed an implacable resistance to donor pressure for policy change and a distaste for market-driven resource allocation.

Acknowledgments

This chapter represents an extension of an assessment of the impact of IFPRI's research activities in Ethiopia from 1995 to 2010 (Renkow and Slade 2013). IFPRI's financial support for that research is gratefully acknowledged.

Notes

1. According to Broadbent (2012), the use of research has a political nature, and political context is key to understanding the role of research-based evidence in African policy debates. In examining what is meant by such research-based policy, she also presents a critique of the largely unexamined nature of the concept. For the purposes of this chapter, "policy" is taken to mean an action or set of actions intended to make practical a strategy, plan, or other defined objective(s).
2. Relevance in this context is understood to mean that "the research is more likely to contribute to policy if: the evidence fits within the political and institutional limits and pressures of policymakers and resonates with their assumptions or sufficient pressure is exerted to challenge these assumptions, the evidence is credible and convincing, provides practical solutions to pressing policy problems, and is packaged to attract policymakers' interest, and if researchers and policymakers share common networks, trust each other, and communicate effectively" (Harris 2012, p.2, citing Court and Young 2006). The Overseas Development Institute (ODI) emphasizes that policy influence is affected by topical relevance and the operational usefulness of an idea (ODI 2004).
3. This raises concerns about the relevance of such research and the ease of access to the results (ODI 2004).

4. Most of these approaches seek to comply with the Weberian injunction that researchers in the social sciences should avoid imposing their own value judgments. Other ways of conducting policy research may sidestep this challenge less easily. See Kolavalli et al. (2013).

5. The extensive donor support of policy-based research in developing countries (around US$3 billion annually) is a direct response to a severe market failure in most developing counties (see Jones and Young [2007]; Stone [2009]). Extensive donor support, however, also affects the ownership of policy recommendations (ODI 2004; Ohemeng 2005; Keijzer et al. 2011).

6. Various authors consider the role of collaboration through distant—commonly virtual—means or through close physical proximity (Hovland 2003; Ryan and Garrett 2003). Others emphasize that collaboration should be for the long term (Saxena 2005). National and international networks of researchers, and to a lesser degree policy users, intended to foster collaboration and mutual understanding have risen in importance in the last two decades, although their effectiveness as genuinely collaborative mechanisms in the production of research-based policy knowledge has been mixed (Hearn and Mendizabal 2011; Mendizabal et al. 2011).

7. A clear case for such research was made by Court and Young (2003).

8. For example, in a long and otherwise comprehensive paper (including some 12 detailed country case studies) on influencing policy processes at the national level, FAO fails to address this issue (Maetz and Balié 2008).

9. It is interesting to note that this issue was a concern at the time decisions were made about the location of IFPRI. Some influential players argued that Washington, DC, posed the risk that major donors would exercise undue influence over the work of the fledgling institute.

10. At the behest of one former IFPRI director general, we also considered going beyond our mandated period and examining the antecedents of IFPRI's research in Ethiopia stretching back to the 1980s. Eventually, we rejected this proposition on the grounds that evidence of attributable policy outcomes is extremely slight, and also because of the acute difficulty of identifying people who could accurately recall these long-past activities.

11. "IFPRI's roots, and arguments about its purposes and function, reach back [to the 1960s]. The problem of dealing with global food policy issues was a matter of concern, and even of controversy, both before and during the discussions that led to the creation of the CGIAR in 1971…" (Farrar 2000).

12. This search for IPGs was paralleled by a prize-winning international effort to disseminate IFPRI's work on all aspects of food policy worldwide—the 2020 Vision Initiative.

13. For evidence of this, see Renkow and Byerlee (2010).

14. A recent example of these IFPRI networks is the Regional Strategic Analysis and Knowledge Support System (ReSAKSS), established in 2006, to provide readily available analysis, data, and tools of the highest quality to encourage evidence-based decision-making, improve awareness of the role of agriculture for development in Africa, fill knowledge gaps, promote dialogue, and facilitate the benchmarking and review processes associated with the Comprehensive Africa Agriculture

Development Program (IFPRI 2013). However, the ways in which the ReSAKSS would deliver these ambitions remained ill-defined, leading to concerns in a 2007 external review by IFPRI's Development Strategy and Governance Division (the responsible division) that its role and functions should be reconsidered (Bromley and Thompson 2007).

15. This thinking was well summarized by Bromley and Thompson (2007, p. 7):

> In ... the absence of clarity about why development has stalled in particular countries, and then what strategies seem most efficacious in getting development underway in the light of those impediments... [i]t is doubtful that this issue can be comprehensively addressed by conducting cross-country studies of what has "worked" and what has "not worked" in a group of countries. The difficulty lies in the contested causal structure in such studies. That is, econometric analysis of such relations cannot reveal the causal processes in the development arena. This means that *ex post* econometric research must be complemented by careful diagnostics if research is to provide widely disparate countries with plausible strategies for development.

16. This thinking was greatly influenced by the widely acknowledged success of an ad hoc IFPRI research team stationed in Dhaka, Bangladesh, from 1989–94, that undertook highly influential research on wheat and rice markets, food rationing, and other aspects of food policy.

17. From the outset, the SSPs were intended to have a direct impact on poverty and food security in selected countries by (a) strengthening applied policy research on a broad range of food policy and development strategy issues; (b) enhancing the national capacity to undertake policy research; (c) strengthening the policy dialogue by providing better information and communication; (d) providing an institutional framework within which IFPRI's research teams could undertake country case study research as part of their international research portfolios; and (e) providing a listening and learning environment in relation to national food policy issues for IFPRI staff (IFPRI internal memorandum 2006).

18. A regional technical assistance unit based in Costa Rica was set up in 2005, as well as a long distance (non-resident) program with China. Other SSPs were set up in Ghana, Nigeria, and Uganda shortly thereafter.

19. Taken at face value, IFPRI was invited into Ethiopia by the GoE. However, IFPRI had already surveyed the scene and noted that the infrastructure for public information and policy analysis was quite rudimentary, and that policy debates in particular were not keenly sought either by public or public sector authorities (Rahmato 2008).

20. This situation is not unique to Ethiopia. An antithetical political culture has long been cited as a barrier to the influence of policy research (Kingdon 1984; Court and Young 2003), as well as to the growth and power of civil society organizations of all types (Rahmato 2008).

21. According to Rahmato (2008, p. 2), "... the close of the 1980s saw the emergence of what were called a 'new generation' of African leaders who promised to renounce the tradition of authoritarian rule, and who committed themselves to responsible government and free elections. Uganda, Congo, Ethiopia, Malawi, and even Zimbabwe were included in this category. However, it was not long before these promises were conveniently ignored, and progress towards democratic

government was stalled or altogether derailed. At present, in many of these countries, the authoritarian tradition is once again making itself strongly felt, and there is disregard for the rule of law, massive corruption, and lack of administrative accountability."

22. EPRI is the research arm of the Ethiopian Economic Association (a professional society).

23. According to Rahmato (2008, p. 9), "...the policy-making tradition in Ethiopia has not been friendly to independent opinion and the decision-making process remains essentially closed to public scrutiny. Parliament has always been a pliant institution and traditionally rubber-stamps the government's initiatives. Policy is commonly drafted by a small group of trusted individuals who are often close to the power-holders. There is no attempt to consult stakeholders or professionals outside government, or to solicit public opinion. ... Quite frequently, policy planners are inaccessible to the public and their efforts are shrouded in secrecy."

24. In Ethiopia, decision-making authority is concentrated within the executive branch of the government, overwhelmingly in the prime minister's office. Inputs from the parliament and other ministries (with the partial exception of the Ministry of Finance) are modest at best, and institutions capable of informed and effective policy implementation at the local, regional, and national levels are largely absent under the current political system.

25. These data were compiled, based on Google Scholar searches for specific IFPRI staff members who did research in Ethiopia, using Harzing's Publish or Perish software that retrieves and analyzes academic citations. No allowance was made for "quality"—an unpublished working paper is counted the same as a peer-reviewed journal article. Nor is allowance made for multiple outputs resulting from the same research effort (for example, a working paper that evolves into a journal article); all are included. Nevertheless, these data provide a rough indication of the overall research effort, the quantity of output, and changes in the overall portfolio of IFPRI's research in Ethiopia with the passage of time. The data include works published through early 2012, that mainly reflect research conducted through 2010. Finally, the reported figures do not include papers on famine and food aid conducted by Patrick Webb and Joachim von Braun (see, for instance, Webb and von Braun [1994]), as that research mostly preceded the period of this review.

26. Google Scholar lists 303 publications that have used the data set, and these publications in turn have been cited nearly 5,000 times.

27. Subjects include cooperatives and rural producer organizations, market development, spatial analysis, agricultural growth, infrastructure investment, land rights and management, macroeconomic issues, urbanization, crop production, insurance and climate change, poverty, hunger and nutrition, input markets and microcredit, technology adoption, livestock, extension, gender, and food price inflation.

28. Our review revealed a remarkably wide array of opinions about the ECX's impacts on traders and farmers—some sanguine, others not. However, because the ECX has not been subject to a comprehensive external review, judgment about these

competing claims—not to mention evaluation of the overall impact of the ECX on traders and farmers—is currently impossible.

29. The effectiveness of the PSNP has been measurably improved by IFPRI, but these improvements do not constitute policy change other than in the narrow sense of internal policy adjustments to the program.

30. The ECX's original attempts to address these weaknesses failed badly, and the ECX was "rescued" (less than 2 years after its launch) by a government decision to give it a near monopoly of coffee marketing, despite there being an already functioning, if imperfect, coffee marketing system.

31. There is a possibility that the lack of engagement on land reform is at least partly attributable to a prevailing (if unofficial) institutional "rule" within IFPRI—said to have been initiated by John Mellor, IFPRI's director-general at the time—that IFPRI would not engage in research closely related to land reform.

32. There is also the obvious possibility that IFPRI's policy research led to the avoidance of an intended but misguided policy. Krugman (2004) believes that the avoidance of policy errors is the single largest gain attributable to policy research. However, we found no evidence to support this contention in IFPRI's work in Ethiopia.

33. It is worth noting that idiosyncratic priority setting *may* be consistent with more formal priority setting methods, but this cannot be predicted *ex ante*. For example, it is likely that the ECX, the CGE, and spatial modeling would have been high on any list of formally determined policy needs. And other topics, such as land and livestock issues, may yet prove to have been prescient choices.

34. This finding seemingly runs counter to the prevailing view in the literature that doing "my" research usually leads to the neglect of creating a more enabling environment for evidence-based discussion (Broadbent 2012).

35. In fairness to IFPRI, such activity is difficult in Ethiopia where "... independent governance and advocacy institutions... are of recent origin and have been operating under difficult circumstances. It was only in the last decade or so that independent policy institutions or institutions undertaking broadly similar functions began to make their appearance in this country. They have in other words a short history and an uncertain future" (Rahmato 2008, p. 1).

36. There is a considerable literature on this subject, much of which questions the traditional assumption of linearity in the research to policy nexus in favor of more multicentered and overlapping structures. See, for example, the several publications that resulted from ODI's Research & Policy in Development (RAPID) <http://www.odi.org.uk/programmes/rapid>.

37. Some commentators on ways to maximize the impact of policy research argue for comprehensive information and communication strategies to be designed at the outset (e.g., Harris [2012]).

38. Following Court and Young (2003), relevance means topicality, operational usefulness, and credibility.

39. Indeed, it seems reasonable to posit a counterfactual in which some outcomes attributable to IFPRI's research would have emerged absent the ESSP. For example, much of IFPRI's research supporting the formation of the Agricultural Transformation Agency was organized from Washington, DC. Note also that while IFPRI was a key

player in the creation of the ATA, it was not the only one. McKinsey and Co. was also instrumental, and the drive for change was greatly aided by the power and persuasiveness of the BMGF.

40. It has been posited by one reviewer that the absence of discernable impact from IFPRI's research may be the result of the relevant impacts being captured by others. This study found little evidence, however, of substantive policy research in ARD by others (notwithstanding the work on pastoralism by Tufts University and the persuasive contributions of the World Bank to the reform of agricultural input and output markets). Moreover, in extensive discussions on Ethiopian ARD, none of the major donors referred to influential policy research organizations other than IFPRI.

References

Broadbent, E. 2012. "The Politics of Research-Based Evidence in African Policy Debates: Synthesis of Case Study Findings." Evidence-Based Policy in Development Network (EBPDA)/Mwananchi, London.

Bromley, D., and K. Thompson. 2007. "A Center Commissioned External Review of IFPRI's Development Strategy and Governance Division (DGSD)." International Food Policy Research Institute, Washington, DC.

Court, J., and J. Young. 2003. "Bridging Research and Policy: Insights from 50 Case Studies." ODI Working Paper 213, Overseas Development Institute, London.

Court, J. and J. Young. 2006 "Bridging Research and Policy in International Development: An Analytical and Practical Framework." *Development in Practice* 16 (1): pp. 85–90.

English, J., and M. Renkow. 2007. "The Impacts of IFPRI's Global Research Program on the Sustainable Development of Less Favored Areas." Impact Assessment Discussion Paper 26. International Food Policy Research Institute, Washington, DC.

Farrar, C. 2000. *IFPRI's First Ten Years*. Washington, DC: International Food Policy Research Institute.

Gabre-Madhin, E. 2005. "Getting Markets Right." Paper presented at the Workshop "Managing Food Price Instability in Low-Income Countries," Washington, DC, February 28–March 1.

Gabre-Madhin, E. Z., and I. Goggin. 2005. "Does Ethiopia Need a Commodity Exchange? An Integrated Approach to Market Development." EDRI-ESSP Policy Working Paper 4, International Food Policy Research Institute, Addis Ababa, Ethiopia.

Gardner, B. L. 2008. "Methods of Assessing Policy-Oriented Research: A Review." In *Impact Assessment of Policy-Oriented Research in the CGIAR: Evidence and Insights from Case Studies*, edited by CGIAR Science Council. Study Commissioned by the Science Council Standing Panel on Impact Assessment. Rome, Italy: CGIAR Science Council Secretariat.

Global Development Network. 2013. "Research Within the Policy Process." <http://www.politicsandideas.org/?p=1921>.

Harris. R. 2012. "The Impact of Research on Development Policy and Practice: An Introduction to the Review of Literature." Research to Action website. <http://www.

researchtoaction.org/2013/07/the-impact-of-research-on-development-policy-and
-practice/>.

Hearn, S., and E. Mendizabal. 2011. "Not Everything That Connects Is a Network."
ODI Background Note, Overseas Development Institute, London. <http://www.odi.
org.uk/sites/odi.org.uk/files/odi-assets/publications-opinion-files/6313.pdf>.

Hovland, I. 2003. "Knowledge Management and Organisational Learning: An
International Development Perspective. An Annotated Bibliography." ODI Working
Paper 224, Overseas Development Institute, London.

IFPRI. 2013. "Regional Strategic Analysis and Knowledge Support System (ReSAKSS)."
International Food Policy Research Institute website. <http://www.ifpri.org/book-5308/
ourwork/program/regional-strategic-analysis-and-knowledge-support-system-resakss>.

Jones, N., and J. Young. 2007. "Setting The Scene: Situating DFID's Research Funding
Policy and Practice in an International Comparative Perspective." Scoping Study
Commissioned by DFID Central Research Department, Overseas Development
Institute, London.

Keijzer, N., E. Spierings, and J. Heirman. 2011. "Research for Development? The Role of
Southern Research Organizations in Promoting Democratic Ownership: A Literature
Review." ECDPM Discussion Paper No. 106, European Centre for Development
Policy Management, Maastricht, the Netherlands.

Kingdon, J. W. 1984. *Agendas, Alternatives, and Public Policies*. Boston, MA: Little,
Brown, and Co.

Kolavalli, S., M. Keefe, and R. Birner. 2013. "Reflections on Influencing Country
Policies and Strategies: The Toy Story." GSSP Discussion Note No. 23, Ghana Strategy
Support Program, International Food Policy Research Institute, Accra, Ghana.

Krugman, P. 2004. "Assessing the Benefits of Economics Research: What Are the
Problems?" In *What's Economics Worth? Valuing Policy Research*, edited by P. G. Pardey
and V. H. Smith, pp. 69–86. Published for the International Food Policy Research
Institute. Baltimore and London: Johns Hopkins University Press.

Maetz, M., and J. Balié. 2008. *Influencing Policy Processes: Lessons from Experience*.
Rome: Food and Agricultural Organization (FAO).

Mendizabal, E., A. Datta, and J. Young. 2011. "Developing Capacities for Better Research
Uptake: The Experience of ODI's Research and Policy in Development Programme."
Background Note, Overseas Development Institute (ODI), London, December.

Nyerere, J. K. 1968. *Freedom and Socialism*. Dar es Salaam: Oxford University Press.

ODI (Overseas Development Institute). 2004. "Bridging Research and Policy in International
Development: An Analytical and Practical Framework. ODI Briefing Paper, London.

Ohemeng, F. L. K. 2005. "Getting the State Right: Think Tanks and the Dissemination
of New Public Management Ideas in Ghana." *Journal of Modern African Studies* 43 (3):
pp. 443–465.

Omamo, S. W. 2003. "Policy Research On African Agriculture: Trends, Gaps and
Challenges." ISNAR Research Report No. 21, International Service for National
Agricultural Research.

Rahmato, D. 2008. "Policy Research Institutions and Democratization: Recent
Experience and Future Challenges." Paper Presented on the Occasion of the Tenth
Anniversary of the Forum for Social Studies. Addis Ababa.

Renkow, M., and D. Byerlee. 2010. "The Impacts of CGIAR Research: A Review of Recent Evidence." *Food Policy* 35 (5): pp. 391–402.

Renkow, M., and R. Slade. 2013. "An Assessment of IFPRI'S Work in Ethiopia 1995–2010: Ideology, Influence, and Idiosyncrasy." Independent Impact Assessment Report No. 36, International Food Policy Research Institute, Washington, DC.

Ryan, J. G., and J. L. Garrett. 2003. "The Impact of Economic Policy Research: Lessons on Attribution and Evaluation from IFPRI." Impact Assessment Discussion Paper No. 20. International Food Policy Research Institute, Washington, DC.

Saxena, N. 2005. "Bridging Research and Policy in India." *International Development* 17 (6): pp. 737–746.

Stone. D. 2009. "Rapid Knowledge; 'Bridging research and policy' at the Overseas Development Institute." *Public Administration and Development* 29 (4): pp. 303–315.

Webb, P., and J. von Braun. 1994. *Famine and Food Security in Ethiopia: Lessons for Africa.* Chichester: John Wiley and Sons.

Weible, C. M., P. Sabatier, and K. McQueen. 2009. "Themes and Variations: Taking Stock of the Advocacy Coalition Framework." *Policy Studies Journal* 37 (1): pp. 121–140.

Weiss, C. 2001. "Policy Research as Advocacy: Pro and Con" *Knowledge and Policy* 4 (1): pp. 37–56.

18

Who Makes Global Food Policy?

Robert Paarlberg

Introduction

For better or worse, we do not yet have a single, centrally governed world food system. The world is better understood as one broken into many relatively separate national food systems. This should not be too surprising; separate sovereign nation states (or their empires) have been the dominant actors in international politics at least since the 1648 European Peace of Westphalia. Food and farming, to the present day, remain firmly governed within this fractured Westphalian world.

Since national governments are suspicious of others and jealous of their own authority, most have never wanted to be part of a "global" food system. These governments typically set in place policies with a strong bias against imports of staple foods, so that international markets today still supply only a small portion of the world's primary food consumption. Even for heavily traded crops like wheat, imports currently satisfy only slightly more than 20 percent of total consumption worldwide. For rice, it is just 5 percent, and for packaged foods, about 10 percent. The rest of the world's food is produced, processed, and consumed entirely within the borders of separate nation states, under the separate and exclusive jurisdiction of the governments of those states. This pattern persists despite today's much lower transportation costs, because most national governments do not want to depend on other countries for their basic food supply. Even if they have significant unsatisfied food needs within their own borders, they will still set in place import restrictions intended to preserve national "self-sufficiency" in food. India, the country that is home to the largest number of undernourished people on earth, still imposes an average 50 percent tariff on imports of food and farm products, and as a consequence, in most years it accepts virtually zero commercial imports of wheat or rice (Hertel and Keeny 2006).

The Foundations of National Control

National governments remain the dominant actors in food and farming because of the exclusive legal jurisdiction they enjoy, as sovereign states, over the farms and food markets trapped within their borders. Farming systems are uniquely tied to the land, which is a physical resource that cannot be transferred electronically offshore. By determining who owns the land, and by maintaining restrictions over food exports and imports at the border, state authorities have most of the tools they need to reduce external control over their own domestic food markets.

Sovereign states have an array of policy instruments at their disposal to employ in governing their food and farm sectors. Prosperous and productive farm sectors in rich countries not only are protected from imports at the border, but they also receive lavish producer income and insurance subsidies behind the border. In rich countries, it is not unusual to find a significant share of total farm income dependent on these national policy interventions (in the European Union, 19 percent of farm income was derived from such government measures in 2012, and 65 percent in Japan) (OECD 2013). Food systems in rich countries are also heavily shaped by national tax and competition policies, plus the presence (or absence) of strong national regulations for food safety, animal welfare, and environmental protection.

Meanwhile in poor countries, state interventions in the agricultural production and marketing sector are just as powerful, but less likely to be pro-farmer; they are traditionally consumer-biased ("urban-biased"), rather than farmer-biased. Some developing countries in Asia have long asserted control over the food and farming sector through the centralized regulation of river valley irrigation systems. In other cases, national programs governing the ownership and distribution of agricultural land (including periodic efforts at redistribution under the slogan of "land reform") have also been powerful governmental prerogatives. State subsidies for fertilizers and pesticides, or electricity for irrigation pumps, can provide benefits to some farmers, even while counterpoised macroeconomic policies, such as overvalued exchange rates, are placing a net burden on others. State-run monopolies over farm input supplies, or over commodity purchases, frequently put a price squeeze on growers. Public sector food distribution systems are also maintained to deliver cheap commodities to urban constituencies, often including the middle class and the poor.

Public budget spending by national governments is also decisive in determining outcomes in the food and farming sector. India had a green revolution in the farm sector in the 1960s and 1970s, in part, because the central government dedicated more than 20 percent of its public budget to agricultural development (Hazell 2009). A green revolution has been slow to come to Africa, in part, because public spending levels on that continent are far lower, typically only 5 percent of the budget, and in some cases, less than that.

This dominant influence that is exercised over food and farming systems by national governments is, by itself, neither good nor bad; different states have used their authority in dramatically different ways and with dramatically divergent effects. Consider North and South Korea, states on the same peninsula that share a common language, culture, and national history, and both with a history of powerful central policy guidance. Yet, since the 1950s, with entirely different food and farming policies in North versus South Korea, the South today is awash in food abundance, while the North has struggled since the 1990s with the specter of famine. Or, consider the record of China. When the government of China experimented with fully collectivized farming during Mao's Great Leap Forward in 1959–61, production collapsed, and a needless famine claimed 30 million lives. Then after Mao's death, far more enlightened Chinese leaders chose a new policy direction that extended land rights and marketing privileges to small farmers, triggering an agricultural boom that lifted hundreds of millions out of poverty and provides, to the present day, a foundation for broadly based industrial growth in China.

The Relative Weakness of Global Governance Institutions

Because separate national governments so often select policies that are self-serving and at times harmful to their neighbors, policy reformers have long championed the creation of "global governance" institutions above the level of the nation state. Particularly since World War II, and most explicitly within the new United Nations system, a number of supranational institutions have now been created to provide improved global governance over food and farming. The resources controlled by these institutions remain meager, however, and the jurisdictions where they seek to act remain almost entirely under sovereign national control.

Today's global system is cluttered with intergovernmental organizations, but most have limited means to influence core activities within national-level food and farming sectors. For example, when food prices spiked on the international market in 2008, the secretary-general of the United Nations set up the High Level Task Force on the Global Food Security Crisis, purportedly to produce an "action plan" for an appropriate global response. From the language the Task Force used, it might have seemed that the United Nations was taking charge of the crisis. Yet, upon a closer look, no new authority and no new funding had been granted by national governments to this UN Task Force, so it posed no threat to national governmental control, and in the end, it had no measurable impact on any food production or consumption. The Task Force held meetings and commissioned reports, but little more. To an extent, this was a repeat of what had happened during a much earlier world food crisis in 1974, when the UN created a comparably toothless Committee on World Food Security (CFS), which also lacked the independent authority needed to influence events.

The more significant reactions to the 2008 price spike came not from the global governance institutions of the UN system, but instead from the national governments of the major economic powers, partly coordinated through international groupings of governments such as the Group of 8 (G8) or the Group of 20 (G20). The G20, which includes emerging and transitional economic powers such as Brazil, China, India, Indonesia, South Africa, and Turkey, was established in 1999, in the wake of the East Asian financial crisis, as a means to broaden international consultations beyond the older and smaller G8. Both the G8 and the G20 now meet on a regular basis at the head of state (or "summit") level, and these meetings have become settings in which significant national policy changes can be pledged or pursued. For example, after the food price spike of 2008, at a G8 summit meeting in Italy in July 2009, the world's leading powers concluded a financially significant "L'Aquila pledge" to increase their spending for agricultural development assistance. Such G8 meetings can sometimes help national governments act by forging an expectation that others will act as well, but it will always be separate national governmental actions that are at stake in the process.

The purpose of G8 and G20 meetings is to facilitate cooperation among separate sovereign nation states, not to replace or override those states. Efforts to override state preferences at these international meetings regularly fail. When President Nicolas Sarkozy of France attempted, in 2011, to use his temporary chairmanship of a G20 Summit to impose reforms over commodity futures trading policies, to reduce subsidies for biofuels, and to discipline commodity export restraints, he was effectively blocked by the other major economic powers, including the United States, the United Kingdom, Brazil, and Russia (Paarlberg 2011).

Groupings of national governments can act only if the individual national governments agree, and the same can usually be said of organizations of national governments (so-called intergovernmental organizations, or IGOs). These IGOs may have secretariats of their own, but their budgets are typically dependent on national government contributions, and their authority is still constrained by state power and the nation state sovereignty norm. One example of an IGO is the World Trade Organization (WTO), originally created as the General Agreement on Tariffs and Trade (GATT) at an international conference in Bretton Woods, New Hampshire, in 1944. The WTO offers its Geneva headquarters as a venue where national governments can negotiate agreements on trade, including agricultural trade, but if the national governments fail to reach an agreement—as when the 2001 Doha Round of negotiations was suspended without a result in 2008—there is nothing the WTO secretariat in Geneva can do about it. The WTO does have a Dispute Settlement Body (DSB) to adjudicate claims by member governments regarding non-compliance with existing international agreements. Governments can defy this body, however, if they wish. For example, in 2005, the United States was told by the WTO Dispute Settlement Body that elements of its cotton subsidy program were illegal under the 1993 Agreement on Agriculture, but the US refused at first either to change its policies adequately or to pay compensation. In 2008, the US Congress even passed a new farm bill explicitly preserving some of the policies the DSB had found to be illegal. Brazil, which had brought the complaint against the United States, eventually threatened retaliation in 2010, at which point the US responded, not by changing its cotton policy, but instead by offering compensation payments to cotton growers in Brazil. The outcome was an ironic double violation of free trade principles: US taxpayers were now paying for trade-distorting cotton subsidies in two countries rather than just one (Schnepf 2011).

The International Monetary Fund (IMF) and the World Bank (IBRD) are two additional international institutions created at the Bretton Woods Conference in 1944. Both have been criticized for bullying national governments into unwelcome stabilization and structural adjustment agreements, and although these institutions do have influence over smaller states, they exercise that influence mostly on behalf of the larger states. Both the IMF and the World Bank are largely funded by the world's wealthiest countries, and their senior leadership is appointed by those countries, so they most often do the bidding of those countries (Wade 2002). They are the agents of the major economic powers that originally created them and continue to pay to sustain their activities.

Moreover, like the WTO, these international financial institutions are often unable to control the governments that challenge their guidance. Even the poorest governments have a long history of defying the Bank and the Fund. In 1994, the World Bank completed a study of 29 governments in sub-Saharan Africa that had undergone structural adjustment and found that 17 of those 29 had reduced the overall tax burden they placed on farming, but some, because of persistently overvalued exchange rates, had actually increased that burden. Only four of the 29 had eliminated parastatal marketing boards for major export crops, and none of the 29 had set in place both agricultural and macroeconomic policies that measured up to World Bank standards (World Bank 2004). Later, the International Food Policy Research Institute (IFPRI) found that many of the reforms undertaken in response to World Bank pressures were reversed when conditions changed, or in response to subsequent external shocks (Kherallah et al. 2002). The World Bank, in any case, reduced its influence over developing world agriculture following the 1980s, when it began to cut the total value of its assistance work in the sector. Between 1978 and 2006, the agricultural share of total World Bank lending fell from 30 percent to only 8 percent, and in 2005, World Bank President Paul Wolfowitz even admitted in an offhand comment, "My institution's largely gotten out of the business of agriculture" (Hitt 2005).

Within the United Nations System, there are three "Rome institutions" with specific responsibilities in food and agriculture: the International Fund for Agricultural Development (IFAD), the UN World Food Programme (WFP), and the Food and Agriculture Organization (FAO). The youngest of these is IFAD, established in 1977 to finance development projects focused specifically on food production and rural poverty alleviation. Ideologically, IFAD is less constrained than the Bank or the Fund by a market-oriented "Washington Consensus," but for this reason, in part, it has been given fewer lending resources by the major economic powers. A second Rome-based organization, the UN World Food Programme (WFP), was established in 1961 to manage the delivery of humanitarian food assistance to poor countries and refugee populations. Individual national governments are still the source of nearly all international food aid, but more than half is now at least channeled to its destination by the WFP. The WFP has a proven record of preventing famine, as in the case of the 1991–92 and 2001–02 droughts in Southern Africa, but the WFP does not have the authority or resources to overcome national governments that object to its presence (for example, the government of North Korea), or armed groups (for example, the al Shabaab militia in southern Somalia) that prefer to keeps its operations away.

The oldest and most prominent Rome-based UN institution is the FAO. Founded in 1945, the FAO devotes most of its energy to gathering and distributing information about food and farming around the world. It also provides a forum for nations to meet to set goals, share expertise, and negotiate agreements on agricultural policy. The FAO itself controls few financial resources and exercises little or no political authority. Periodic UN "Food Summit" meetings at the FAO produce only bland unfunded resolutions. In some cases, the resolutions are negotiated by junior officials, before the actual meeting gets underway (this was the case for the 2009 Summit). The FAO data collection activities are of considerable value, and the FAO's technical advice has been world class in some niche areas (such as integrated pest management or

IPM). The FAO's operations are heavily dominated, however, by an oversized central bureaucracy. The FAO has had lethargic leadership over the years from a string of non-accountable officials, many who hold their positions because of their political friends rather than their professional competence. As a UN agency, the FAO operates on a "one country–one vote" model of governance, which gives a great deal of influence to the so-called "G-77" group of poor countries that tends to vote as a bloc. The rich countries, that are understandably mistrustful of this outcome, respond by limiting the financial contributions they make to the FAO, further weakening the organization (Center for Global Development 2013). Reviews of the FAO also criticize the fact that more than half of the staff and budget spending remains at headquarters in Rome, rather than in the field where actual needs exist (FAO 2007).

In the area of agricultural technology development and research, the most important international institution is the Consultative Group on International Agricultural Research (CGIAR), a network of 15 separate research centers created in 1971 and chaired by the World Bank. The multiple centers of the CGIAR have had a four-decade history of success in developing useful new farm technologies for the developing world. The improved rice varieties originally developed by the International Rice Research Institute (IRRI) have now been released in more than 77 countries, allowing the world to more than double total rice production since 1965. Two-thirds of the developing world's total area planted in wheat are now planted with varieties that contain improvements developed by the CGIAR's International Maize and Wheat Improvement Center (CIMMYT). Yet the CGIAR depends heavily on national governments for its funding, and since the 1990s, it has struggled to sustain this support. In addition, the CGIAR is disadvantaged in reaching poor farmers, because it typically operates at a distance from national-level research, extension, and policymaking institutions in the developing world. It is these national-level institutions that enjoy the jurisdictional access needed to move innovations into farmers' fields.

By itself, the CGIAR can do little to address agricultural science deficits in regions such as sub-Saharan Africa, because national government leadership is essential and most national governments in Africa have long been underinvesting in agricultural science. According to a study by Beintema and Stads (2006), between 1991 and 2000, the annual rate of growth of agricultural research spending in all of sub-Saharan Africa (excluding Nigeria and the Republic of South Africa) was actually a *negative* 3/10ths of 1 percent. Since 2000, there has been scant improvement. Africa's own governments (through the New Partnership for Africa's Development (NEPAD), a technical body of the African Union) have established an investment "target" for R&D spending of 1 percent of agricultural GDP, but as of 2006–08, only five countries, out of 11 for which data was available, had met this "research intensity" target, and many were actually going in the wrong direction. In fact, according to data from Pardey et al. (2012), out of 43 countries in sub-Saharan Africa in 2009, 20 actually had a lower research intensity for agriculture than in 1980. All agricultural science must eventually be local, so if separate national governments fail in this manner to take a local lead, there may be little an international research organization such as CGIAR can accomplish.

The Limited Power of Multinational Corporations

Activists, and quite a few academics, like to argue that national governments enjoy less control over global food and farming outcomes than private multinational corporations. The power of these corporations, it is said, comes in part from their monopoly position in private markets but also from the corrupting influence they exercise over national governments. In fact, some intergovernmental organizations such as the WTO, the IMF, and the World Bank are routinely described by these same critics as little more than subordinate agents, operating on behalf of their global corporate masters.[1]

Assertions of corporate monopoly in the food sector often begin with claims that 90 percent of international grain trade goes through the hands of just four private companies: Archer Daniels Midland, Bunge, Cargill, and Louis Dreyfus—known collectively as the ABCD traders. A 2012 study commissioned by the NGO Oxfam described the control of these companies as far-reaching:

> Through their roles in biofuels investment, large-scale land acquisition, and the financialization of agricultural commodity markets, the ABCDs are at the forefront of the transformation that is determining where money in agriculture is invested, where agricultural production is located, where the produce is shipped, and how the world's population shares (or fails to share) the bounty of each harvest. (Murphy et al. 2012)

Such assertions are often made, but it is important to remember that less than 20 percent of world food production ever enters international trade, so there are strict limits on the global "control" over food that is available to any company that specializes in international trade. Moreover, despite market concentration, the four large trading companies do compete with each other, ensuring that a measure of control resides with consumers. Finally, it is telling that those who claim to see corporate control over grain markets seldom make consistent arguments regarding the impact of that control. Some say the companies conspire to make international grain prices artificially low (through a "dumping" of surplus production into poor countries), but others blame the companies for driving grain prices artificially high. In reality, grain-trading companies make money whether international prices are low or high, but they do so by skillfully responding to price and supply changes in the market rather than by controlling those changes.

Corporate control is also said to derive from seed patents, such as those registered by companies like Monsanto. The chief limitation to this argument is that in most countries, including nearly all developing countries, national laws prohibit local patent claims on seeds. Because the national governments of most developing countries do not recognize intellectual property claims on seeds, patent claims made by Monsanto in the United States or in Canada are worthless within these countries. Out of the 71 countries that have promised to enforce at least some intellectual property rights claims on seeds, by becoming party to the International Union for the Protection of New Varieties of Plants, only two are from Africa—Kenya and the Republic of South Africa—and neither of these two has joined the 1991 Act of the Convention that promises to recognize patent claims (UPOV 2012). The other governments of Africa, and most in Asia, have simply opted not to recognize such claims.

In addition, seed companies are not yet in a position to control farming in these countries, because so many developing world farmers still replant seeds saved from their own harvest. In the Indian Punjab, 74 percent of farmers still plant their own saved seeds, and when Indian farmers do buy seeds, they have 500 private Indian seed companies to turn to, not just the big multinationals like Pioneer or Monsanto. The weak influence of Monsanto over farming in the developing world is also revealed by the fact that the national governments of most developing countries have not yet made it legal for farmers to plant any of Monsanto's genetically engineered seeds. Among all of the developing countries of sub-Saharan Africa, only one—Burkina Faso—has legalized the planting of any genetically modified (GM) seeds, and the only such crop approved in Burkina is cotton, an industrial crop rather than a food crop. Globally, in fact, national governments nearly everywhere continue to block the planting of GMO food staple crops, such as wheat, rice, or potato. When it comes to country-by-country approvals for GMO food crops, the supposedly powerful Monsanto company has been blocked nearly everywhere by the policies of national governments.

Critics of biotechnology seed companies also underestimate the extent to which these companies compete with each other. For example, when Monsanto tried to market a new corn seed variety in the United States called "Smartstax" in 2010, it overpriced the product and lost market shares to a competitor seed company, Pioneer-DuPont. In the end, Monsanto had to reduce its price premium by 67 percent in order to win back customers, and even then it failed to recover market share.

The allegation that private food and agribusiness companies exercise influence over national governments by paying bribes does have some foundation. In one sensational case in 2012, investigators learned that a subsidiary of Wal-Mart in Mexico had bribed local and national officials to make possible the building of 19 large new stores, in some cases without construction permits. Wal-Mart paid nearly $1 million in bribes for some of these individual stores. The limit to Wal-Mart's influence was dramatically illustrated in 2013, however, when the company gave up a 6-year effort to open multi-brand stores in India, because the government had imposed a local purchase requirement on this foreign company that it was not imposing on India's own firms (Rajiv 2013). Wal-Mart could not accept this discrimination and had to walk away.

In a similar vein, Monsanto was required to pay a $1.5 million fine (to the US Justice Department) for having bribed an Indonesian official in 2002, hoping to get around an environmental impact study on its cotton seeds. Yet, in this case the bribe was unsuccessful, because the requirement for the study was never officially waived, and Monsanto's cotton seeds are still not legal to plant in Indonesia. Even in countries where bribery is common, then, the final result may not always reflect corporate control.

Are NGOs Challenging National Governments for Control?

International non-governmental organizations (INGOs) have become influential players within food and the farming sectors, especially in the developing world. Some of these INGOs exercise influence through projects on the ground. For example, Heifer International operates roughly 900 projects in 53 different countries to promote food self-reliance through gifts of livestock and training. Other INGOs work almost exclusively through social mobilization and advocacy. One example is La Via Campesina, an organization founded at a meeting in Belgium in 1993, which calls for organized action on behalf of small farmers to weaken the influence of globalized agribusiness. Via Campesina comprises about 150 local and national organizations in 70 countries, and it champions an agrarian vision of local control that it calls "Food Sovereignty." Greenpeace, an environmental advocacy organization based in Amsterdam, also campaigns against globalization and agribusiness, and particularly against genetically engineered crops. Greenpeace claims 2.8 million members worldwide. Consumers International, a global federation of more than 240 advocacy organizations in 120 different countries, promotes consumer food safety.

In areas such as food safety and farm technology, NGO advocacy does sometimes succeed in blocking or restricting corporate behavior. In the

1970s, a network of NGOs accused the Nestlé company of promoting infant formula products through unethical methods, such as giving away free samples in maternity wards. An NGO-led boycott of Nestlé products—animated by the sensational slogan that "Nestlé Kills Babies"—eventually led to a new International Code of Marketing of Breast-milk Substitutes, which Nestlé pledged to follow in 1984 (Boyd 2012). Also in the 1980s, an international NGO advocacy campaign led by the Pesticide Action Network (PAN) managed to produce an International Code of Conduct on the Distribution and Use of Pesticides, and later a binding international agreement, the Rotterdam Convention. In the 1990s, European-based NGOs spread alarms about genetically engineered crops that led to a virtual ban on the planting of those crops in Europe in only a few years, plus regulatory blockage in most of the rest of the world as well. In 2013, an activist from the United Kingdom who had participated in the early anti-GMO campaigns (but who later changed his mind about the technology and apologized), admitted that, "This was the most successful campaign I have ever been involved in" (Lynas 2013).

Not all NGO advocacy works to block things. In the area of food security, some groups like Bread for the World use information and advocacy campaigns to promote food aid and agricultural development. Others, like Oxfam, combine research and policy advocacy with actual development projects on the ground (Oxfam calls itself a "do tank"). Still others, like Catholic Relief Services, work almost exclusively delivering humanitarian relief. In the area of agricultural development, however, there are limits to what NGOs from the outside can accomplish on their own. They deliver excellent training and services but are less able to provide the expensive investments in road construction, electricity, irrigation, and agricultural research needed in many of the poorest countries. National governments in the developing world, often supported by donor agencies with still more taxpayer-derived resources, must take the lead here.

Among NGOs, independently endowed philanthropic foundations such as the Rockefeller Foundation and the Ford Foundation built an early record of influence in agricultural development, helping to launch Asia's original green revolution in the 1960s and 1970s. Today, it is the Bill & Melinda Gates Foundation that does the most to promote the green revolution cause. The Ford Foundation in New York, with roughly $10 billion in assets, has now moved away from promoting science-dependent approaches to farming, and the Rockefeller Foundation, with assets only one-third the size of Ford, cannot do the task by itself. In 2006, however, the Bill & Melinda Gates Foundation, which had $37 billion in assets, moved decisively into grant making in agricultural development (adopting the Rockefeller Foundation as a junior partner). This work began with a $150 million joint venture called the Alliance for a Green Revolution in Africa (AGRA), chaired by former UN

Secretary-General Kofi Annan. This initiative centers on an effort to improve the varieties of seed available to small farmers for staple food crops in Africa. By 2012, the Gates Foundation had made grants for agricultural development totaling more than $2 billion.

This is a significant resource commitment, but without stronger fiscal and institutional support from national governments in Africa, the AGRA program will struggle to reach scale, and so far, national government commitments from Africa have been weak. At an African Union summit meeting in Maputo in 2003, Africa's heads of government pledged to spend at least 10 percent of their budgets on agriculture by 2008, but as of 2009 only six countries had met that target, while 39 had not, and in many of those 39, the share of spending going to agriculture had actually declined between 2003 and 2009. In 2013, the ONE campaign did an updated review of the spending patterns of 19 African countries and found that only four of the 19 had met the 10 percent target. Meanwhile, seven countries were "seriously off track," with *less* than 5 percent of their expenditures going to agriculture (ONE Campaign 2013). If national governments do not act, the efforts of philanthropic foundations will fail to accomplish the task.

Conclusion

This review of the current influence over global food and farming by national governments, intergovernmental organizations, multinational corporations, and transnational NGOs leads to a single unavoidable conclusion: Despite globalization, it is still national governments that have the most to say about final outcomes in the food and farming sector. In his long career as a food policy analyst and advocate, Per Pinstrup-Andersen never lost sight of this reality. In fact, in Pinstrup-Andersen's most recent project, a review of the political economy of national policy responses to the international food price spikes of 2008 and 2010–11, he provides us with yet another major scholarly contribution, precisely because it emphasizes this reality of national governmental control. At a time when far too many policy analysts, not to mention nearly all journalists, were inferring from higher international prices that poor consumers everywhere must be facing a new "food crisis," Pinstrup-Andersen organized a research project that focused on actual price fluctuations within national markets, country by country. He and his team found, in many cases, weak price transmission from international to national markets, due to high transport costs (especially in poor land-locked countries) and also because of deliberate trade and procurement policy actions taken by national governments to stabilize domestic prices (even when this meant fiscal losses and a further destabilization of international prices). In some cases price instability persisted at the national level, but it was completely out of phase with international price fluctuations (Pinstrup-Andersen 2014).

It was within separate markets at the national level that most world citizens confronted the "food crisis" of 2008, and the great strength of Pinstrup-Andersen's most recent research project is precisely its focus on those separate national markets, and the separate national political systems that continue to manage (or mismanage) them (Pinstrup-Andersen 2014). By resisting the seduction of global market models, and opting instead for a careful review and comparison of descriptive statistics, and a timeline tracing of policy decisions and decision processes inside more than a dozen different national governments, Pinstrup-Andersen's most recent work has captured the real world of food and agricultural policy, far better than the work of those who are perhaps more recently trained, but far less experienced, and not as attuned to the demanding imperatives of policy-relevant basic research. For those of us who work in the field of international food policy, Pinstrup-Andersen's work has always been attuned to the political realities facing individual national governments, driven by an awareness that this is where both the policy problems and the potential policy payoffs can be found.

Note

1. An example of this line of thinking would be the book by David C. Korten (2001), endorsed by the World Economic Forum, titled *When Corporations Rule the World* (Berrett-Koehler Publishers).

References

Beintema, N. M., and G.-J. Stads. 2006. "Agricultural R&D in Sub-Saharan Africa: An Era of Stagnation." Agricultural Science and Technology Indicators (ASTI) Initiative. Background Report, International Food Policy Research Institute, Washington, DC. <http://www.asti.cgiar.org/pdf/AfricaRpt_200608.pdf>.

Boyd, Colin. 2012. "The Nestlé Infant Formula Controversy and a Strange Web of Subsequent Business Scandals." *Journal of Business Ethics* 106 (3): pp. 283–293.

Center for Global Development. 2013. "Time for FAO to Shift to a Higher Gear." A Report of the CGD Working Group on Food Security, Center for Global Development, Washington, DC.

FAO (Food and Agricultural Organization). 2007. "FAO: A Challenge of Renewal." Submitted to the Council Committee for the Independent External Evaluation of FAO (September). <http://www.fao.org/unfao/bodies/IEE-Working-Draft-Report/K0489E.pdf>.

Hazell, Peter B. R. 2009. "The Asian Green Revolution." IFPRI Discussion Paper 00911, November. International Food Policy Research Institute, Washington, DC.

Hertel, T. W., and R. Keeny. 2006. "What Is at Stake: The Relative Importance of Import Barriers, Export Subsidies, and Domestic Support." In *Agricultural Trade Report and the Doha Development Agenda*, edited by Kym Anderson and Will Martin, pp. 37–62. Washington, DC: World Bank.

Hitt, G. 2005. "A Kinder, Gentler Wolfowitz at World Bank?" *The Wall Street Journal*, September 22.

Kherallah, M., C. Delgado, E. Gabre-Madhin, N. Minot, and M. Johnson. 2002. *Reforming Agricultural Markets in Africa*. Published for the International Food Research Policy Institute. Baltimore and London: The Johns Hopkins University Press. <http://www.ifpri.org/publication/reforming-agricultural-markets-africa>.

Korten, David C. 2001. *When Corporations Rule the World*. 2nd ed. San Francisco, CA: Berrett-Koehler Publishers.

Lynas, Mark. 2013. "Lecture to Oxford Farming Conference, 3 January 2013." <http://www.marklynas.org/2013/01/lecture-to-oxford-farming-conference-3-january-2013/>.

Murphy, Sophia, David Burch, and Jennifer Clapp. 2012. *Cereal Secrets: The World's Largest Grain Traders and Global Agriculture*. Oxfam Research Reports, August. <https://www.oxfam.org/sites/www.oxfam.org/files/rr-cereal-secrets-grain-traders-agriculture-30082012-en.pdf>.

OECD StatExtracts Database. 2013. Monitoring and Evaluation. Reference Tables: Producer Support Estimate by Country. Paris: Organisation for Economic Co-operation and Development. Last updated September 2013. <http://stats.oecd.org/Index.aspx?QueryId=50477>.

ONE Campaign. 2013. "Data Report: A Growing Opportunity: Measuring Investments in African Agriculture." <http://www.one.org/us/policy/a-growing-opportunity/>.

Paarlberg, Robert. 2011. "An Action Plan on Food Price Volatility and Agriculture: What to Expect from the G-20 Summit," Chicago Council on Global Affairs, Issue Brief Series, September 30. <http://www.thechicagocouncil.org/publication/action-plan-food-price-volatility-and-agriculture-what-expect-g-20-summit>.

Pardey, Philip G., Julian Alston, and Connie Chan-Kang. 2012. "Agricultural Production, Productivity and R&D over the Past Half Century: An Emerging New World Order." International Association of Agricultural Economists Conference, August 18–24, 2012, Foz do Iguaçu, Brazil.

Pinstrup-Andersen, Per, ed. 2014. *Food Price Policy in an Era of Market Instability: A Political Economy Analysis*. WIDER Studies in Development Economics. November. New York: Oxford University Press.

Rajiv, Theodore. 2013. "Walmart-Bharti Call It Quits in India." *The American Bazaar,* October 9. <http://www.americanbazaaronline.com/2013/10/09/walmart-bharti-call-quits-india/>.

Schnepf, Randy. 2011. "Brazil's WTO Case Against the U.S. Cotton Program." CRS Report for Congress, 7-5700, June 21, Congressional Research Service, Washington, DC.

UPOV (International Union for the Protection of New Varieties of Plants). 2012. Members of the International Union for the Protection of New Varieties of Plants. <http://www.upov.int/export/sites/upov/members/en/pdf/pub423.pdf>.

Wade, Robert H. 2002. "U.S. Hegemony and the World Bank: The Fight Over People and Ideas." *Review of International Political Economy* 9 (2): pp. 215–243.

World Bank. 2004. *Adjustment in Africa: Reforms, Results, and the Road Ahead.* A World Bank Policy Research Report. Washington, DC: World Bank.

19

The Implications of a Changing Climate on Global Nutrition Security

Andrew D. Jones and Sivan Yosef

Introduction

On November 8, 2013, a 600-kilometer wide typhoon tore across the central Philippines with wind speeds peaking well above 300 kilometers per hour. One of the strongest storms in recorded history, Typhoon Haiyan killed thousands and displaced hundreds of thousands more. In 2012, a devastating drought in the United States swept over nearly two-thirds of the country, affecting crop production and river commerce. It was widely considered the worst drought incident since the Dust Bowl of the 1930s. In July 2010, unusually heavy monsoon rains submerged one-fifth of Pakistan, inundating hundreds of thousands of hectares of agricultural land, killing 2,000 people and 1.2 million livestock, and causing $10 billion in damages (Thomas Reuters Foundation 2013). In that same year, hundreds of wildfires broke out across Russia on the heels of the hottest recorded summer in Russian history. The fires caused billions of dollars in damages.

Though it is difficult to directly attribute the cause of these events to the phenomenon of rising global temperatures commonly referred to as climate change, events like these may become increasingly common on a hotter planet. Beginning primarily during the industrial era, anthropogenic emissions from the burning of fossil fuels have driven increases in atmospheric concentrations of greenhouse gases (GHGs), which have in turn led to positive radiative forcing (i.e., a positive net change in the Earth's energy balance) and an increase in global mean temperatures (Figure 19.1) (IPCC 2013). The statement made by the Intergovernmental Panel on Climate Change (IPCC) in its most recent working group report (AR5) that the "warming of the climate

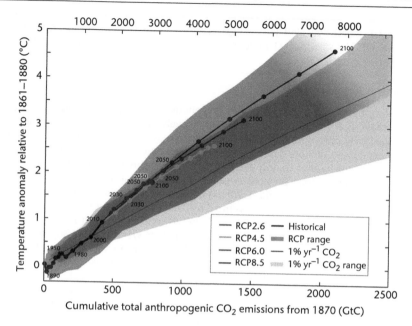

Figure 19.1 Anthropogenic CO_2 emissions and global temperature anomalies (1890–2100)

Note: Since the beginning of human civilization until the start of the industrial era, the atmospheric concentration of CO_2 was approximately 275 parts per million (ppm). Current atmospheric concentrations of CO_2 are approximately 400 ppm and rising by approximately 2 ppm per year.

Source: Reprinted with permission from: IPCC (2013). [IPCC (Intergovernmental Panel on Climate Change). 2013. *Climate Change 2013: The Physical Science Basis*. Geneva, Switzerland: IPCC.]

is unequivocal" (IPCC 2013, p. 2) is perhaps the most trivial statement in a gamut of bleak observations and predictions made by climate scientists (see Box 19.1). Among the four future climate scenarios, or Representative Concentration Pathways (RCPs) identified by the working group, the most severe, RCP8.5, represents continued high global greenhouse gas (GHG) emissions. Under this scenario, the predicted change in global mean surface temperatures will likely exceed 2°C above the pre-industrial climate by the end of the century, and this could result in temperature increases more than double that. Hansen et al. (2007) estimated that warming even above 1.7°C relative to the pre-industrial era could result in potentially irreversible ice sheet and species loss.

The changes in surface and ocean temperatures, extreme weather events, precipitation patterns, and sea levels that are occurring and are predicted to intensify in coming decades will pose significant challenges to global development efforts to improve the health and well-being of human populations. Improving and safeguarding the nutritional status of populations is arguably the cornerstone of such efforts.

Box 19.1 PRINCIPAL FINDINGS FROM THE WORKING GROUP I CONTRIBUTION TO THE FIFTH ASSESSMENT REPORT OF THE INTERGOVERNMENTAL PANEL ON CLIMATE CHANGE (IPCC)

What Has Already Changed?

1) Atmospheric concentrations of the greenhouse gases carbon dioxide (CO_2) and methane (CH_4) now exceed pre-industrial levels by 40 percent and 150 percent, respectively (391 ppm and 1803 ppb, respectively); mean rates of increase in the concentrations of these gases is unprecedented in the previous 22,000 years.
2) Surface temperatures during each of the previous three decades have been successively warmer than previous decades; a mean warming of 0.85°C (90 percent confidence interval (CI): 0.65–1.06) has occurred at land and ocean surfaces.
3) The upper ocean (0–75 m) has warmed by 0.11°C (90 percent CI: 0.09–0.13), and it is likely that lower depths (700 to 2000 m) warmed as well from 1957 to 2009.
4) The extent of Arctic sea ice has decreased, glaciers worldwide are shrinking, and the polar ice sheets are rapidly losing mass (e.g., the mean rate of ice loss from the Greenland ice sheet increased from 34 gigatons (Gt) year^{-1} (90 percent CI: –6–74) to 215 Gt year^{-1} (90 percent CI: 157–274) from the period 1992 to 2011).
5) The rate of sea level rise is more rapid than the mean rate of the previous two millennia; global average sea level rise was 1.7 mm year^{-1} (90 percent CI: 1.5–1.9] between 1901 and 2010 and 3.2 mm year^{-1} [2.8–3.6] between 1993 and 2010.
6) The pH of ocean surface water has decreased by 0.1 from the pre-industrial era.

What Changes Are Expected?

1) Increases in global mean surface temperatures for 2081–2100 relative to 1986–2005 will be in the range of 0.3°C to 1.7°C under the strongest GHG emission mitigation scenario (RCP2.6), and as high as 2.6°C to 4.8°C under a scenario of continued high GHG emissions (RCP8.5).
2) Extreme precipitation events will become more intense and frequent over mid-latitude land masses and tropical regions.
3) Surface ocean warming is estimated to be in the range of 0.6°C to 2.0°C, with more pronounced warming in tropical and northern subtropical regions.
4) A nearly ice-free Arctic Ocean in September is likely by mid-century under a scenario of continued high GHG emissions (RCP8.5).
5) Global mean sea level rise for 2081–2100 will likely range from 0.26 m to 0.82 m relative to 1986–2005, under varying GHG emission mitigation scenarios.

Source: IPCC (2013). Working Group Contribution to the Fifth Assessment Report of the IPCC.

In September 2000, a summit of world leaders committed to a set of eight Millennium Development Goals (MDGs) aimed at achieving broad progress by 2015 across a number of development sectors, including health, education, and the environment. Nutrition was explicitly recognized in the first of these MDGs and was strongly interwoven with several of the other goals. Although considerable progress has been achieved, the goal to reduce, by half, the proportion of people who suffer from hunger has not yet been met, and there are considerable disparities in the distribution of hunger throughout the globe.

Recent estimates indicate that one in eight people, or 842 million individuals, were unable to meet their dietary energy requirements in 2011–13 (FAO 2013a). The large majority of these people live in low-income countries. In sub-Saharan Africa, in particular, one in four individuals is not able to meet energy requirements (FAO 2013a). Chronic undernourishment is especially detrimental to the development of young children. In 2011, 165 million children worldwide younger than 5 years of age were stunted (Black et al. 2013). Child stunting is caused in part by chronic nutritional deficiencies and can lead to deficits in cognitive development, work and reproductive capacity, and susceptibility to adult chronic disease (Kuklina et al. 2006; Walker et al. 2011). At the same time, in 2008, 1.4 billion adults were overweight and 500 million obese, more than double the prevalence in 1980 (WHO 2013c). Child overweight has also increased by 54 percent since 1990, with 43 million children younger than 5 years of age overweight in 2011 (UNICEF et al. 2012). The basic causes of these varying manifestations of malnutrition are rooted in disparities in sustainable access to productive resources including information, technology, capital, institutions, and most notably, natural resources (UNICEF 1990; Lakerveld et al. 2012). The far-reaching influence of climate change on Earth's underlying biological and physical systems has the potential to directly or indirectly affect access to all of these resources, and therefore, the health and nutrition of the global population. It is critical then, to understand the potential pathways by which climate change will impact global public health and nutrition, and the possible avenues of action that might be pursued to mitigate harmful effects and successfully adapt to the changing global environment.

In this chapter, we aim to identify the principal linkages between climate change and nutrition, and to elaborate mitigation and adaptation options for addressing the threat of climate change to nutrition security. We highlight the following three pathways that encompass the upstream systems that climate change will impact and the downstream outcomes that may directly or indirectly affect nutrition outcomes: (1) agricultural production and food security; (2) the stability of natural ecosystems, human livelihoods, and regional security; and (3) disease vectors and human health and nutrition. Figure 19.2 summarizes each of these pathways. It is important to emphasize that these pathways are purposefully broadly defined. As we will explore, given the global scale at which positive radiative forcing operates, any given climate-related event or exposure may influence nutrition through multiple, simultaneous pathways. Pathways may also interact such that additive, or more likely, synergistic nutritional impacts will emerge (e.g., increased distribution and survival of disease vectors may exacerbate

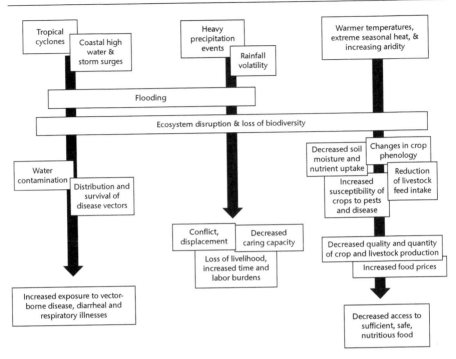

Figure 19.2 A conceptual framework of the pathways of influence from climate change to the underlying determinants of poor nutrition
Source: Authors.

the severity of the nutritional consequences that stem from increased food insecurity). Therefore, these pathways should be viewed as guideposts toward understanding the potential impacts of climate change on nutrition rather than as a strictly prescribed causal framework.

Climate Change Consequences and their Pathways of Impact on Human Nutrition

Agricultural Production and Food Security

Food security is a multi-faceted concept that encompasses the availability of, access to, and utilization of food, as well as the stability of these factors over time. Though food security is commonly used to refer only to access to sufficient quantities of food, the definition of the term explicitly states that access to safe and nutritious food is a necessary criterion for achieving food security (FAO 1996). Our use of the term, therefore, refers to access to sufficient quantities of food, as well as the nutritional quality of diets. Food security, clearly, is intimately connected to the global system of food production.

Agricultural production depends on predictable local temperatures and patterns of precipitation. To the extent that changes in climate introduce volatility into these patterns, or alter the biophysical conditions to which crops are adapted, agricultural production—and therefore food security—may be impacted. We discuss below the potential impacts of climate change on crop and livestock production and the pathways by which these impacts may affect food security.

WARMING SURFACE TEMPERATURES

Global surface temperatures have warmed across all major crop-growing regions (e.g., maize, wheat, rice, soybean) over the past 30 years (Figure 19.3) (Lobell et al. 2011). This change in climate has the potential to impact agricultural production in several different ways, with varying impacts across world regions. Warmer temperatures alter the rate of plant development by reducing critical growth periods. Though crop phenology responds approximately linearly to temperature changes (Gate and Brisson 2010), exceeding certain temperature limits could result in more precipitous, non-linear shortening of developmental stages (Schär et al. 2004). Accelerated crop ripening and shorter periods for grain filling can decrease yields (Craufurd and Wheeler 2009). Heat stress can also damage plant reproductive tissues and increase pollen sterility (Thornton and Cramer 2012). Warming temperatures may also promote plant disease and pest outbreaks (Alig et al. 2002; Gan 2004; Tubiello et al. 2007), increasing both insect pest numbers and their range (CCSP 2008). Changes in crop phenology associated with warmer temperatures may allow increased pest damage to crops at sensitive early stages of crop development (Rosenzweig et al. 2001). Globally, and at mid- to high latitudes, crop productivity will likely increase slightly under increases in temperatures of 1°C to 3°C (IPCC 2007), due in part to lengthened growing seasons, reduced frost damage, and enlarged root surface areas under warmer soil temperatures that may facilitate increased nutrient uptake (St. Clair and Lynch 2010). In mountainous areas such as the Andes, less severe frosts and warming temperatures at higher elevations may allow for expanded production of previously uncultivated fields (Haverkort and Verhagen 2008). However, these relationships show threshold effects. Temperature increases above 3°C would have negative impacts on crop production even at high latitudes (IPCC 2007). In seasonally dry and tropical regions at lower latitudes, even small increases in local temperatures are projected to deleteriously affect crop productivity (IPCC 2007).

Warmer mean global surface temperatures are projected to have heterogeneous impacts on crop productivity across latitudes and staple crops. Rice, wheat, and maize provide nearly one-third of all food calories consumed by

(A)

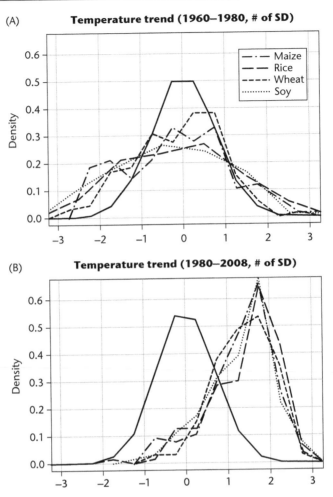

Figure 19.3 Frequency distributions of country-level growing season temperature trends for the periods 1960–80 (A) and 1980–2008 (B) for maize, rice, wheat, and soy

Notes: Trends are expressed as the total trend for the period (e.g., °C per 29 years), divided by the historical standard deviation for the period 1960–2000.

The distribution of temperature trends across regions for 1980–2008 is right-shifted from the null distribution, such that trends are often two or more times the historical standard deviation.

Source: From: D. B. Lobell, W. Schlenker, and J. Costa-Roberts. 2011. "Climate Trends and Global Crop Production since 1980." *Science* 333 (6042): pp. 616–620. Reprinted with permission from The American Association for the Advancement of Science (AAAS).

the more than 4.5 billion people in the Global South (Thornton and Cramer 2012). It is estimated that warming temperatures will result in declines in wheat and maize yields, though declines in wheat may be less severe than declines in maize. Deryng et al. (2011) predicted that between 2000 and 2050 wheat and maize yields will decline by 14–25 percent and 19–34 percent,

respectively, under warming conditions of 2.2°C to 3.2°C above pre-industrial temperatures with no adaptation. Under a more favorable emissions scenario (i.e., Special Report on Emissions Scenarios [SRES] A1B), gains in wheat
yields of 1.6 percent (95 percent probability interval (PI): –4.1 percent, 6.7
percent) have been estimated, while maize yields are expected to decline by
14.1 percent (95 percent PI: –28 percent, –4.3 percent) (Tebaldi and Lobell
2008). Again, these impacts may be felt differently across regions. In a
meta-analysis of the mean change in crop yields across a range of general circulation models, mean yield changes of –17 percent (no variance
parameter reported) by 2050 were calculated for wheat in Africa, though
no significant changes in wheat yields were found in South Asia (Knox et
al. 2012). Mean declines in maize yields were calculated at –11 percent, –7
percent, –13 percent, and –18 percent in Southern Africa, West Africa, the
Sahel, and South Asia, respectively. There is less evidence on the effects
of global climate change on horticultural crops (Peet and Wolfe 2000).
Vegetables and fruits are vulnerable to environmental extremes, such as
high temperatures, limited water availability, and associated low soil moisture and salinity (de la Peña and Hughes 2007). Climate change is therefore expected to impact yields of these crops and may influence farmers to
adopt or abandon horticulture as an adaptation strategy; however, more
research is needed to understand these dynamics (Seo and Mendelsohn
2007; Kurukulasuriya 2008).

Livestock are similarly affected by warming temperatures and extreme
heat. Animals reduce feed intake at high temperatures (by greater than
25–30 percent, depending on the animal species) to maintain their body
temperature (Thornton and Cramer 2012). These reductions in intake may
result in substantial productivity losses (Parsons et al. 2001). Furthermore,
although warmer surface temperatures may actually increase pasture productivity in highland areas, higher temperatures can reduce water availability and negatively affect pasture biomass production (Tubiello et al. 2007).
Climate change could also facilitate the spread of animal diseases and pests
(e.g., warmer winters may increase the range of livestock diseases such as
bluetongue virus), as well as increase livestock mortality, especially under
drought conditions (IPCC 2007).

DROUGHT AND PRECIPITATION
The effect of warmer surface temperatures on crop yields depends in part
on existing soil moisture and precipitation. Therefore, in addition to surface temperatures, aridity is an important concern when examining the
potential impact of climate change on crop yields. As aridity increases, both
soil nitrogen (N) and soil organic carbon (C) concentrations may decline,
becoming uncoupled from soil phosphorus (P), which could constrain plant

and microbial activity and negatively affect organic matter decomposition (Delgado-Baquerizo et al. 2013). Temperature-driven soil moisture deficits can also decrease nutrient acquisition, reduce biological nitrogen fixation, and disrupt nutrient cycling (St. Clair and Lynch 2010). Combined, these changes would yield a net negative impact on the mineral nutrition of crops far exceeding any potential beneficial effects of warming temperatures (St. Clair and Lynch 2010). The impacts of surface warming on crop productivity then could be exacerbated under drought conditions. Lobell et al. (2011) calculated that for each degree-day spent above 30°C between 1980 and 2008, maize yields in Africa were reduced by 1 percent under optimal rain-fed conditions and by 1.7 percent under drought conditions (median impact of climate change trends on global maize yields [1980–2008]: –3.8 percent; 95 percent CI: –5.8 percent, –1.9 percent).

More frequent and more severe droughts are a serious concern under future climate change scenarios. These may be meteorological droughts caused by long-term declines in precipitation, hydrological droughts resulting from long-term declines in surface runoff and groundwater levels, or agronomic droughts evidenced by reductions in soil moisture availability during the crop growing season (St. Clair and Lynch 2010). Warming of the lower atmosphere strengthens the hydrologic cycle (i.e., warm air holds more water vapor than cool air), causing dry regions to become drier and wet regions to become wetter (Trenberth 2011; World Bank 2012). In dry regions, droughts may be intensified by enhanced surface drying through increased evaporation, and evapotranspiration accompanies warming temperatures (Trenberth 2011). Given that millions of smallholder farmers around the world are already farming on rain-fed marginal lands, especially drylands, and that future gains in food production will rely increasingly on expansion of production onto drylands (Reynolds et al. 2007), drought intensification under climate change scenarios poses considerable challenges to future food production and food security. Even farmers with access to irrigation may face increasing challenges managing water stress (i.e., the ratio of irrigation withdrawals to renewable water resources). Irrigation water requirements are likely to substantially increase under most climate change scenarios, perhaps disproportionately in Southeast Asia and the Middle East (Döll 2002; Fischer et al. 2007).

At the opposing end of the spectrum, wet regions may experience amplified precipitation under increased atmospheric water vapor loading (World Bank 2012). The IPCC (2013) predicts that extreme precipitation events over mid-latitude land masses and wet tropical regions will intensify and become more frequent in the coming decades. Increases in annual runoff, though, may be unevenly distributed across seasons such that during the rainy season, excessive precipitation leads to flooding, while water stress during the low-flow season is not abated (World Bank 2012). Excessive precipitation can reduce crop yields, erode sloped soils, contribute to soil nutrient loss, and, in poorly drained soils that become waterlogged, create conditions of hypoxia that promote elemental toxicities, impaired root growth, and reduced nutrient uptake (Kawano et al. 2009; St. Clair and Lynch 2010; Zougmoré et al. 2013). These extreme conditions, together with volatility in the onset and the ending of rains that may disrupt germination and require farmers to sow crops multiple times (Mary and Majule 2009), present challenges to agricultural production, even in regions where water stress is not a common concern.

A potential benefit of increased atmospheric concentrations of CO_2 on crop yields is a phenomenon known as "CO_2 fertilization." CO_2 fertilization refers to the sequestration of CO_2 by photosynthetic plants under conditions of increased ambient CO_2 concentrations such that plant growth is actually enhanced. However, the potential for this phenomenon to occur outside of controlled settings is uncertain. A recent review of so-called FACE (Free Air CO_2 Enrichment) experiments revealed that grain crop yields, especially C4 species (e.g., maize), increased far less than anticipated under elevated CO_2 concentrations (Ainsworth and Long 2005). Even if the CO_2 fertilization effect were to yield benefits to crop yields in controlled settings, in actual farmers' fields, the potential for this phenomenon to yield production gains would be determined by the presence of other potentially limiting soil nutrients such as phosphorus and nitrogen (World Bank 2012). As noted earlier, under arid conditions and conditions of low soil moisture, which may be common under warming surface temperatures, it is not at all clear whether these nutrients would be sufficiently available.

FOOD SECURITY CONSEQUENCES OF CHANGES IN AGRICULTURAL PRODUCTION

Taken together, the manifestations of climate change described above—including warmer surface temperatures, more frequent extreme temperatures, increasing droughts in some regions, and extreme precipitation in other regions—present serious challenges to the stability of global food supplies and food security. The populations of low-income countries will disproportionately bear the burden of food insecurity brought about by these climatic changes (Wheeler and von Braun 2013). Food insecurity is already widespread in low-income countries. The Food and Agricultural Organization of the United Nations (FAO) estimates that the total number of undernourished individuals in high-income and low-income countries in the period 2011–13 was 16 million and 830 million, respectively (FAO 2013a). As we have seen, the negative consequences of climate change on agricultural production may be greatest in the low-latitude tropical regions of the globe, precisely where the vast majority of the world's poor already live. With so many individuals already enduring seasonal or chronic food insecurity in low-income countries, and many more balancing on the edge of that precipice, the potential is great that warming temperatures and climate-related shocks will deepen food insecurity to levels from which it may be difficult to rebound. This situation could have clear negative effects for the nutritional status of populations, especially vulnerable groups like young children. Perhaps not surprisingly, the overwhelming majority of the world's stunted children live in these same low-income countries where the prevalence of food insecurity is highest (Black et al. 2008). Even accounting for economic growth, climate change may increase the prevalence of severe stunting in sub-Saharan Africa and South Asia by one-quarter and nearly two-thirds, respectively (Lloyd et al. 2011).

For poor subsistence households whose consumption depends in large part on their own agricultural production, climate change-induced declines in agricultural productivity may have direct negative consequences on food availability and access. Yet, food prices are also of critical importance to these households. Global cereal prices are expected to increase under most climate change scenarios, even those that account for farmer adaptation (Rosenzweig and Parry 1994; Parry et al. 2004). Recent events highlight the effect of major weather events on food prices. The 2010–11 droughts in Russia and China, for example, compounded by market speculation and reactionary policies, may have contributed to a doubling of international wheat prices (Wegren 2013). Growing urban populations with increasing incomes and demand for food, combined with climate-related reductions in crop productivity, may cause real agricultural prices to rise between 2010 and 2050, even under a perfect mitigation scenario (Nelson et al. 2010).

An increase in food price volatility is far more certain than any absolute increase in prices, however. The volatility of global rice and wheat prices doubled from the period 1980–2006 to 2007–10, with the world most recently facing two major food price crises (Minot 2013). Evidence is mixed on the extent to which this global volatility has transmitted to various regions and countries. A recent study of 67 staple foods in Africa, for example, showed that the average volatility of African grain prices was high (with a coefficient of variation of 0.12, compared to 0.06–0.08 for global volatility), while another study of the Middle East estimated that a 1 percent increase in world prices translated into average domestic price increases of 0.2–0.4 percent (Lanchovichina et al. 2012; Minot 2013). Depending on the transmission of prices from global to regional and local markets, then, higher prices for agricultural commodities produced by poor farmers could be a boon for these households. Agricultural income may be spent on more nutritious and diverse foods, as well as non-food expenditures that can improve nutritional status, such as investments in health and education. Agricultural income may also be saved, instead of consumed immediately, allowing households to accumulate assets such as land, livestock, and durable goods, which may help them to cope with subsequent weather-related shocks (Hoddinott 2011).

However, most poor households, in both urban and rural areas, are net purchasers of food (Byerlee et al. 2006; Ivanic and Martin 2008), commonly devoting more than half of their income to food (56–78 percent) (Banerjee and Duflo 2007). Increases in food prices, then, will disproportionately affect the poor, decreasing access to sufficient quantities of food (WFP 2008), as well as high-quality diets (i.e., adequate micronutrient intakes) (Iannotti et al. 2012). Climate change-related increases in food prices linked to reductions in agricultural productivity may not only affect current earnings of vulnerable families, but for agricultural households, this may be in addition to the potential adverse consequences to long-term earning potential from climate change-related degradation of underlying farm assets (e.g., livestock, soil, and water). Reduced investments in health, nutrition, and education from this double burden on current and future earnings could have irreversible, intergenerational consequences on nutrition (Alderman 2010). Coping strategies that many poor households already employ (e.g., utilizing asset or cash savings, informal and formal borrowing, social safety nets, and livelihood diversification) could conceivably play a role in sustaining their nutrition and health in the face of climate change. These types of strategies, however, may not be well suited to deal with systemic shocks that can affect entire communities, countries, or regions (Ceballos and Robles 2014).

Declines in agricultural productivity resulting from warming global temperatures and population-driven increases in food demand certainly have the potential to negatively impact food sufficiency, one component of food security. Food security, though, encompasses not only access to sufficient quantities of food, but also food that is safe and nutritious. Climate change may have direct negative consequences on the nutritional quality of food crops (e.g., reduced grain filling capacity, impaired soil nutrient acquisition), and may indirectly affect diet quality at a macro scale by reinforcing historical emphases on staple crop production. The technological advances of the Green Revolution propelled massive increases in the yields of staples like maize, wheat, and rice (Hafner 2003). Much less investment has been targeted at improving production of pulse crops, fruits, and vegetables, all of which provide incredibly important complementary nutrients and phytochemicals to diets. As a result, for the past five decades, cereal grain and oilseed production has far outpaced global production of pulses, fruits, and vegetables (FAO 2013b). Though output of fruits and vegetables has increased in recent years (FAO 2013b), with production of cereal grains and oilseed crops threatened by warming temperatures, it is possible that agricultural research efforts will be redoubled toward further enhancing production of these crops at the expense of pulses, fruits, and vegetables.

Providing diverse, nutrient-dense diets is clearly important for preventing and alleviating chronic undernutrition. However, it is also of paramount importance for addressing the rising global burden of overweight and non-communicable diseases. Especially among the poor, overconsumption of calories is often achieved by consuming energy-dense, nutrient-poor foods. These foods may be the most economically accessible. Perhaps not surprisingly, then, micronutrient deficiencies are in fact common among overweight and obese individuals (Garcia et al. 2009). Maintaining production diversity under a changing climate, then, alongside efforts to improve yields of staple grains, is an important goal for addressing the entire spectrum of malnutrition. Overall, the evidence supporting these plausible impacts of climate change on the nutritional quality of food crops and the consumption patterns of households is limited, and more research is required to clearly elucidate these pathways.

Food safety, another component of food security, may also be threatened by climate change. Though many food safety-related concerns may be exacerbated with warming temperatures (e.g., warming seas may contribute to increases in human shellfish and reef fish poisoning and salmonellosis) (Schmidhuber and Tubiello 2007), the threat of mycotoxins stands out because of the scale at which it may affect populations. It is estimated that mycotoxins, the toxic secondary metabolites of fungi from the genera *Aspergillus, Fusarium,* and *Penicillium,* may contaminate as much as one-quarter of all agricultural crops worldwide (Smith et al. 1994). This proportion would likely climb under climate change scenarios. Many staple crops, including maize and groundnut, but also nuts and fruits, are susceptible to colonization and infection by mycotoxins (Fung and Clark 2004). *Aspergillus* may infect crops before harvest and during storage, especially under conditions of prolonged exposure to high humidity or drought—precisely the kinds of extreme conditions that warming global temperatures may exacerbate. Aflatoxins, a group of mycotoxins produced by *Aspergillus flavus* and *Aspergillus parasiticus,* are potent carcinogens (Fung and Clark 2004) and are associated with child growth stunting (Gong et al. 2002; 2004). Contamination of food supplies by aflatoxins and other mycotoxins is of particular concern in rural areas of low-income countries, where screening and food safety controls are often absent (Lewis et al. 2005). These are the same regions, especially in sub-Saharan Africa, which may be especially vulnerable to the effects of warmer surface temperatures. Prolonged periods of high temperatures (>30°C) and drought stress could leave crops considerably more prone to mycotoxin contamination (Paterson and Lima 2010; Magan et al. 2011; Van der Fels-Klerx et al. 2013). Increasing mean temperatures could also expand the range of latitudes at which mycotoxin-producing fungi are able to compete (Tirado et al. 2010).

The Stability of Natural Ecosystems, Human Livelihoods, and Regional Security

Human livelihoods, directly or indirectly, rely on the multitude of ecosystem services provided by the natural environment. These include provisioning services (i.e., food, fresh water, fuelwood, fiber, biochemical, and genetic resources), regulating services (e.g., regulation of air quality, water regulation and purification, and pollination), and other supporting services (e.g., soil formation, nutrient cycling, and primary production) (UNEP 2003). Though the potential impact of climate change on terrestrial and marine ecosystems will likely be heterogeneous across regions, warming temperatures, especially those predicted under continued high GHG emissions (i.e., RCP8.5), will alter ecosystem function across all global regions to some extent.

Biological diversity is strongly linked to ecosystem productivity and resilience (Chapin et al. 2000; Tilman et al. 2001). Destructive changes in ecosystems associated with warming global temperatures will therefore have far-reaching consequences for biodiversity. Ecosystem functioning and service provision are expected to change dramatically under warming global temperatures. Examples of these changes include: (1) widespread forest retreat and transition to lower biomass, drier ecosystems; (2) more frequent and intense forest fires from heat stress, increasing aridity, and changes in human land use; (3) expansion of ocean hypoxic zones and declines in nutrient availability to phytoplankton under warming ocean temperatures; (4) erosion or destruction of coral reefs from ocean acidification, and increased frequency and intensity of tropical cyclones; and (5) loss of mangroves from rising sea levels and increasing atmospheric CO_2 concentrations (World Bank 2012). Furthermore, biome shifts and migration of species toward the poles and toward higher elevations could disrupt predator–prey relationships and traditional food sources (World Bank 2010). As greater increases in temperatures lead to increasingly severe changes in ecosystems, thresholds—or tipping points—are possible whereby irreversible loss of ecosystems will occur beyond certain temperature limits. Global mean temperature increases greater than 2°C will put 20 to 30 percent of plant and animal species at risk of extinction (IPCC 2007). Temperature increases beyond 4°C could lead to more profound species loss, associated with the permanent dieback of rainforests (see, for example, Lenton et al. [2008]).

The degradation of ecosystem services and accompanying loss of biodiversity could have widespread impacts on human livelihoods. As already discussed, warming surface temperatures could lead to declines in crop and animal productivity, especially in the tropics, via several different pathways (e.g., changes in crop phenology, increased susceptibility to pests and disease, increasingly volatile and extreme rainfall events, less access to water for irrigation, and reduction in livestock feed intake). In coastal regions, rising sea levels, strong storm surges, and saltwater intrusion on coastal agricultural land will also likely make that land unusable (Wheeler and von Braun 2013). For the 80 percent of rural poor households who depend on agriculture as a source of livelihood, these changes could have a substantial impact on nutrition outcomes (IFAD 2010). Income earned from agriculture may be used not only to purchase food, but also for health, education, and hygiene inputs. Loss of income for any of these purchases could negatively impact nutrition outcomes in the short-term, especially for women and children, by affecting diet quality and household health, sanitation, and hygiene environments. Early nutrition deficits, lost educational opportunities, and intergenerational stunting can also translate into long-term losses in productivity, health, and nutrition (Martorell and Zongrone 2012). Especially in tropical regions, households that depend on fisheries for livelihood may be negatively affected by declining fish stocks—whether from the poleward migration of fish away from warming waters or the degradation of fish habitat from acidifying oceans and increased hypoxic zones (World Bank 2012). Households dependent on forest products for food or livelihood would face similar pressures from loss of forest habitat or the transformations of forest habitat into less biodiverse, lower biomass, more arid ecosystems. Biodiversity is also important for the discovery of new medicines (Bernstein and Ludwig 2008), as well as the formulation of traditional medicines, which are estimated to be used by 60 percent of the world's population (WHO 2013a). Ecosystem degradation and biodiversity loss could then also have direct impacts on human health and nutrition. The pace of these changes—and the challenge of disentangling causal effects among many potentially confounding factors—have meant that the empirical evidence directly linking natural resource degradation and biodiversity loss to nutrition outcomes is limited. More research is needed to understand the nutritional consequences of ecosystem disruption as these environmental changes accelerate in the coming decades.

Lost or diminished livelihoods resulting from degradation of natural resources and ecosystem services under climate change may threaten economic stability and exacerbate societal inequalities. Conflict could then result as individuals compete for the allocation of increasingly scarce resources, or act out grievances over economic disparities. Food riots in response to rising food prices are one example of this phenomenon (Barrett 2013). Hsiang et al. (2013) observed that 1 standard deviation increase in a location's temperature is associated with a 13.2 percent increase in the rate of intergroup conflict. Similarly, in Somalia, 1 standard deviation (within region) increase in temperature anomalies and drought length was associated with a 62 percent increase in the likelihood of conflict (Maystadt and Ecker 2014). Indeed, the effect of increasing temperatures on conflict is especially strong in regions that are temperate or warm—precisely the regions where the largest increases in mean temperature are predicted, that have the lowest inter-annual temperature variability, and that are already the most food insecure (Hsiang et al. 2013). Given that conflict further disrupts livelihoods (Goodhand 2001), health systems, public institutions, and infrastructure, as well as degrades productive resources and exacerbates food insecurity, nutrition outcomes are likely to be profoundly negatively impacted via multiple pathways from climate change-induced conflicts.

Disease Vectors and Human Health and Nutrition

The synergistic relationship between infection and malnutrition has been recognized for decades (Scrimshaw et al. 1968). Nutrient deficiencies can impair resistance to infection (Scrimshaw and SanGiovanni 1997), and infection can impair absorption of nutrients. In low-income regions, a vicious circle is often present, wherein lack of access to improved water and sanitation coincides with poor diets, food insecurity, and poor access to health services, thus exacerbating both malnutrition and disease. Many studies in diverse contexts have demonstrated that access to improved water and sanitation yields benefits for the health, growth, and development of children (Esrey and Hebert 1985; Habicht 1986; Checkley et al. 2004). Access to these resources may improve the nutritional status of children by reducing the incidence of diarrhea (Checkley et al. 2008), or by preventing or ameliorating environmental enteric dysfunction (Humphrey 2009). Climate change could have direct negative impacts on water and sanitation, especially for poor populations that already lack adequate access to these resources.

WATER, SANITATION, AND HYGIENE

Climate change may deleteriously affect water quality, sanitation, and hygiene in several important ways. Short-term, seasonal, and cyclic multi-year warming trends may lead to increased episodes of diarrhea in adults and children (Checkley et al. 2000; Singh et al. 2001; Lama et al. 2004; Alexander et al. 2013). One explanation for this trend is the warming ocean waters that are associated with warmer temperatures during the El Niño-Southern Oscillation (ENSO), which may stimulate populations of *Vibrio cholera*, the gram-negative bacteria that cause cholera (Salazar-Lindo et al. 1997). Reliance on stagnated or otherwise contaminated secondary water sources during droughts, or increases in the population density or activity of flies that carry diarrheal disease-causing organisms during periods of high temperature, are other plausible mechanisms by which diarrhea may be associated with warmer temperatures (Alexander et al. 2013). To the extent that extreme rainfall events, stronger storm surges, and more frequent flooding accompany climate change, increased runoff could transfer pathogens from environmental reservoirs to ground and surface water, thereby increasing incident diarrhea cases (Medina et al. 2007). More frequent and intense high tides and wave damage associated with climate change could also threaten the water supplies of island communities through the intrusion of saltwater into underground freshwater reserves (Singh et al. 2001) or coastal aquifers (Antonellini et al. 2008). Perhaps not surprisingly, outbreaks of water-borne diseases will likely be most severe in regions that are already environmentally degraded and lack public infrastructure for sanitation and hygiene (Schmidhuber and Tubiello 2007).

VECTOR-BORNE DISEASES

Climate change may also influence the distribution and survival of other disease vectors, including mosquitoes. Mosquitoes may carry five different species of the *Plasmodium* parasite that causes malaria and are also responsible for the transmission of viruses that cause various forms of encephalitis, yellow fever, and dengue fever. The reach of these viruses is expected to expand under climate change (Hales et al. 2002), though the spread of malaria is perhaps of most concern, given the high mortality burden associated with it. There were approximately 219 million cases of malaria in 2010, causing 660,000 deaths, mostly African children (WHO 2013b). Malnourished children may have as much as a two-fold higher risk of dying from malaria than non-malnourished children (Muller et al. 2003), and malaria may lead to acute weight loss (McGregor 1982), stunting in young children (Nyakeriga et al. 2004), and intrauterine growth restriction among fetuses of infected mothers (Landis et al. 2009). There is evidence that warming temperatures are allowing mosquito populations to expand into highland regions where they previously were never observed (Epstein et al. 2013). In parts of East and Southern Africa, new species of mosquitoes are establishing populations (Peterson 2009; World Bank 2012), with one study suggesting that by 2050 more than 200 million additional individuals will be at risk for malaria because of warming temperatures (Béguin et al. 2011). Stagnant water from extreme rain events and flooding under climate change may provide additional habitat for mosquitoes. Changes in temperature, precipitation, and humidity that accompany climate change will likely also influence the distribution and survival of other disease vectors, including those that cause leishmaniasis, Lyme disease, and schistosomiasis (World Bank 2012).

Strategies for Reducing the Potential Harmful Impacts of Climate Change on Nutrition

Strategies for reducing the potential harmful impacts of climate change on nutrition fall under two broad categories: mitigation and adaptation. Mitigation refers to the reduction of GHG emissions to prevent greater increases in global mean temperatures than are already expected. Past and current GHG emissions are already substantial enough, though, that even under the most robust mitigation scenario (RCP2.6), global mean temperatures will likely still rise by 2°C (van Vurren et al. 2011). Adaptation, therefore, will be required in addition to mitigation to confront the consequences of warming temperatures that are already occurring and that will continue into the future.

Mitigation

The increase in atmospheric concentrations of CO_2, CH_4, and nitrous oxide (N_2O) has occurred primarily because of human activity (IPCC 2013). Therefore, mitigation will necessarily require reducing anthropogenic emissions of these GHGs, as well as capturing and storing carbon. In 2012, 84 percent of global energy consumption came from non-renewable liquids, natural gas, and coal (US Energy Information Administration 2013). This percentage is predicted to decline only marginally to 78.5 percent by 2040, but with a 42 percent increase in total energy consumption from all of these sources (authors' calculations) (US Energy Information Administration 2013). If these predictions hold true, it seems unlikely that achieving the emission levels predicted by conservative emissions scenarios will be feasible.

While the burning of fossil fuels for electricity and heat is the single largest source of global GHG emissions (26 percent), deforestation and land clearing for agriculture, as well as other agriculture-related emissions (e.g., management of agricultural soils, livestock, rice production, and biomass burning), together contribute nearly a third of all emissions (31 percent) (IPCC 2007). Therefore, perhaps more than in any other sector, changes in agriculture have the potential to contribute substantially to climate change mitigation, and, in turn, may also have the greatest potential to mitigate the negative impacts on nutrition outcomes that are predicted from climate change. Changes that result in greater, more efficient, or more equitable food production could yield nutritional benefits via the food security and livelihood pathways outlined above. However, given the enormous ecological footprint of agriculture—especially animal agriculture—on water and forest resources, and ecosystem services more broadly, changes to agricultural production systems that work to mitigate GHG emissions could also facilitate improvements in nutrition and health outcomes by reducing ecosystem disruptions, stabilizing livelihoods, and reducing vulnerability to vector-borne illnesses. We therefore limit our discussion of mitigation and adaptation strategies primarily to the agriculture sector (including food, fiber, and fuel production).

Various strategies for mitigating the emissions of GHGs from the agriculture sector have been proposed. These include: (1) adopting cropping systems with reduced reliance on inorganic fertilizers and pesticides (e.g., using legumes in crop rotations and providing temporary vegetative cover between successive crops); (2) improving nitrogen (N) use efficiency to reduce N_2O emissions; (3) adopting reduced- or no-till agriculture to reduce soil carbon losses; (4) increasing the use, efficiency, and effectiveness of irrigation to enhance carbon storage in soils (though CO_2 costs associated with water delivery would need to be minimized); and (5) using agro-forestry to increase soil carbon sequestration by planting trees on the same land used for food and livestock production (IPCC 2007). In general, reducing fossil fuel use overall by improving energy efficiency in agriculture could result in a decrease of 770 megatonnes (Mt) CO_2-eq/year by 2030 (Smith et al. 2008). Furthermore, allowing sections of agricultural land to revert to native vegetation, or creating grassed waterways or shelterbelts, are other effective ways of increasing carbon storage and mitigating GHG emissions from agriculture (IPCC 2007). For poor farmers, however, who may already be cultivating small plots on marginal lands, this may not be a feasible option.

Two agricultural transformations in particular could provide multiple wins for food production and access, GHG emissions mitigation, and sustainable development: (1) reducing food waste, and (2) reducing consumption of animal-source foods (ASF). If achieved, these approaches would lessen the need for intensification of food production. However, they require overcoming enormous societal inertia from population pressures, changing preferences, and price incentives, as well as weighing the imperative of addressing the immediate food security needs of vulnerable populations.

Approximately one-third of all food produced globally for human consumption is lost or wasted (Stuart 2009). In low-income countries, these losses tend to occur close to the source of production in the form of post-harvest losses or spoilage between farm and market. In higher-income countries, food waste is most prevalent among households, restaurants, and the food service industry. Cheap food prices are a strong incentive for food waste in high-income countries where higher income consumers spend a much lower proportion of their income on food than the poor in low-income countries. While healthy, edible food is often discarded along production lines because of perceived cosmetic imperfections, and fully stocked supermarket shelves mean that foods close to expiration are ignored by shoppers, high-income countries mainly waste food because they can afford to (Swedish Environmental Protection Agency 2009). Per capita food waste by consumers in Europe and North America is estimated to be 95–115 kg/year, and only 6–11 kg/year in sub-Saharan Africa and Asia (Gustavsson et al. 2011). In low-income countries, premature harvesting, poor storage facilities, food safety issues, lack of infrastructure to transport food efficiently and effectively, lack of processing facilities, and unsanitary storage and sales conditions are responsible for most food losses (Gustavsson et al. 2011). Reducing global food loss and waste would lessen the overall need for increased food production and could, therefore, limit the need for agricultural intensification, preventing, in part, the GHG emissions from that intensification. Investing in rural infrastructure and markets in these countries, then, is a high priority for reducing food waste, as well as improving rural livelihoods more generally.

Reducing consumption of ASFs, similar to reducing loss and waste in our food system, is a strategy with enormous potential to mitigate climate change, but one that requires swimming upstream against equally powerful demographic currents, especially in emerging economies. Demand for ASFs has rapidly increased as the global population has grown and become increasingly urban and wealthy (Delgado et al. 1999). Global meat consumption increased by at least 50 percent in the latter half of the 20th century and is projected to increase by another 24 percent by 2030 (WHO 2013c). Global meat production has likewise risen to meet the increased demand—production has tripled over the last four decades (Chang 2011) and is projected to more than double by 2050 from 2000 production levels (FAO 2006a). Increases in meat consumption, associated with increased urbanization and rising levels of wealth, will likely be the principal driver of increased global food demand in the coming decades, more so than population growth (Tilman et al. 2011). Though livestock production is an especially important component of the livelihoods of the poor, it also has far-reaching negative consequences for global food production potential, environmental sustainability, and climate change. Livestock production: (1) uses more land than any other single human activity; (2) has led to massive deforestation (70 percent of previously forested land in the Amazon is now animal pasture and agricultural land for feed crops) and therefore, reductions in biodiversity; (3) contributes to soil erosion and land degradation associated with overgrazing; (4) is responsible for 9 percent, 37 percent, and 65 percent of anthropogenic CO_2, CH_4, and N_2O emissions, respectively; (5) accounts for over 8 percent of all human water use, mainly from irrigation of crops that are fed to livestock; and (6) contributes greatly to water pollution from animal wastes, antibiotics and hormones, sediments from eroded pastures, and fertilizer and pesticides used for feed crops (FAO 2006b). Shifting diets toward plant-based food like cereals and grain legumes, which are much more efficient at converting energy into protein, or even transitioning consumption from beef to poultry or from grain-fed to pasture-fed beef would work to lessen these impacts (Tscharntke et al. 2012). In addition to the nutrition impacts that may occur via the climate change pathways described earlier, intensive animal production and consumption of ASFs, red meat in particular, could have direct health consequences. Prospective cohort studies have demonstrated that consumption of red meat is associated with an increased risk of total mortality, cancer mortality, and Type 2 diabetes (Yip et al. 2013). Furthermore, consumption of dairy products likely increases the likelihood or severity of prostate cancer (though it may be protective against colorectal cancer) (Ludwig and Willett 2013). At the same time, however, ASFs are rich in highly bioavailable nutrients such as iron, zinc, and vitamin A that are often lacking in the diets of undernourished children and women in low-income settings. ASFs have been shown to improve early growth in infants and children (Neumann et al. 2003) and are critical for preventing and mitigating nutritional anemia among young children and women of childbearing age (WHO 2013d). Therefore, the consumption of ASFs is certainly important, especially for the poor. However, in low- and middle-income countries undergoing the nutrition transition and facing a simultaneous burden of micronutrient malnutrition and nutrition-associated chronic disease (Caballero 2005), the calculus of managing ASF production and consumption for the promotion of both sustainable agricultural production and optimal human nutrition may not be straightforward. The type of meat or dairy product, the amount produced and consumed, and the life stage at which it is consumed, are all important considerations.

One promising approach to creating greater efficiencies and mitigating climate change within the livestock production sector, as well as other agricultural sectors, is payment for ecosystem services (PES). The costs associated with the depletion of natural resource stocks and the degradation of ecosystem services are not currently reflected in the pricing of almost any goods and services, though they may contribute directly to such depletion and degradation. There are, in fact, real costs associated with the provision and protection of ecosystem services; however, these services are complex and poorly understood (Farley and Costanza 2010). Therefore, the correct price for a service, its potential effectiveness, and possible negative consequences are not always clear. Payments for carbon sequestration are one example of this, wherein eucalyptus plantations that sequester carbon unfortunately also degrade biodiversity, disrupt water provision, and limit nutrient cycling (Lohman 2006; Farley and Costanza 2010). Nonetheless, full costing—that is, pricing goods and services such that environmental "externalities" are reflected in the price paid by consumers—will help to prevent long-term degradation of ecosystem services (Pinstrup-Andersen 2013). Removing subsidies that promote overexploitation of natural resources and securing property rights for commons and waste sinks are also important (FAO 2006b).

The RCP2.6 emissions scenario assumes not only a substantial reduction in GHG emissions (i.e., a reduction of 70 percent compared to a "business-as-usual" baseline scenario), but also assumes widespread use of bioenergy and reforestation measures (van Vurren et al. 2011). Carbon capture and storage (CCS), wherein CO_2 emissions from large carbon point sources such as coal- and gas-fired electric power generation facilities are captured, transported off-site, and injected into geological formations for long-term storage, is seen as a transition technology that may require several decades to peak (IPCC 2005). GHG emissions from facilities incorporating CCS could be reduced by as much as 80–90 percent, though challenges associated with the cost of retrofitting existing facilities, distance from sequestration sites, and increased fuel needs and costs of energy production at plants, all suggest that this technology may be limited in its mitigation potential in the near term (IPCC 2005). Bioenergy and carbon capture and storage (BECCS) is an approach that substitutes production of bioenergy from biomass sources for traditional fuels in combination with CCS (Rhodes and Keith 2008). This approach has the potential to yield negative emissions, though limits to the scale of biomass production and the negative impacts of displacing food production with bioenergy production, especially in tropical regions where much of the expansion would likely need to occur, presents serious logistical and ethical concerns to this approach being adopted on a large scale (Rhodes and Keith 2008). More ambitious geoengineering approaches (e.g., ocean fertilization) for actively removing carbon dioxide from the atmosphere to achieve net negative emissions remain controversial and unproven with unknown side effects (IPCC 2005).

Mitigation has the potential to positively impact nutrition outcomes by reducing the harmful environmental costs associated with future increases in global temperatures. To the extent that these same strategies increase households' production and consumption of diverse foods, increase incomes through more resilient farming practices and livelihoods, and/or directly incentivize shifts in diets toward healthier patterns, they may also have direct, positive nutritional impacts.

Adaptation

The negative effects of climate change, including lost agricultural productivity, ecosystem degradation, biodiversity loss, and the expansion and intensification of vector-borne diseases, will be felt most strongly by those populations who are already bearing the burdens of food insecurity, livelihood insecurity, environmental decline, conflict, malnutrition, and ill health.

The actions needed to adapt to climate change, therefore, are largely the same as those needed for sustainable development broadly. These include: improving rural transportation and communications infrastructure, expanding educational opportunities, strengthening the capacity of institutions, providing greater access to information, income-earning opportunities, and productive resources, and ensuring equity in access to the benefits that accrue from these improvements (Smit 2001). Efforts to achieve these improvements are ongoing, though climate change will make achieving success more elusive.

Agroecological intensification (AEI) is one approach within the agriculture sector to attempt to achieve these sustainable development goals, while at the same time increasing the capacity of rural communities to adapt to climate change. AEI encompasses a set of agricultural practices rooted in agroecological principles and a reliance on inexpensive information rather than inexpensive fossil fuels to increase productivity in agriculture, while also enhancing ecological resilience and ecosystem service provision (Dobermann and Nelson 2013). These practices are often adapted to local and regional contexts and may include selecting well-adapted, hybrid, or high-yielding seeds, planting and harvesting at suitable times, employing integrated pest management, increasing the efficiency of fertilizer and water use, applying integrated soil and nutrient management, and leveraging agro-forestry and recycling of agricultural by-products (Dobermann and Nelson 2013).

Other technologies and services in addition to those encompassed by AEI will also contribute substantively to climate change adaptation efforts. Within the agriculture sector, for example, breeding or developing crops with enhanced traits (e.g., tolerance to heat, drought, and salinity; pest and disease resistance; biological nitrogen fixation; early maturing varieties) may allow for improved yields (or a blunted decline in yields) in regions experiencing increasingly frequent or severe droughts, warm spells, or deficits in soil nutrients (Lybbert and Sumner 2010). Low-cost insurance products, such as index-based micro-insurance, are other instruments that may be leveraged to assist poor farmers in particular in adapting to a more volatile climate (Barrett et al. 2007). In the energy sector, advances in renewable fuels (solar, wind, hydro, artificial photosynthesis) could have wide-ranging impacts, reducing fossil fuel consumption across all sectors and decreasing reliance on biofuels (Harris 2013). With respect to water consumption, water desalination plants already provide clean drinking water to millions of people in arid regions throughout the world, and these plants are expected to proliferate in the coming decades to meet the increased demand for water by a growing and urbanizing population amidst increasing droughts (Henthorne 2011). These technologies and other similar approaches will constitute an important component of climate adaptation strategies that will strengthen food security, livelihoods, and human health. However, these strategies are not "silver bullet" solutions and will need to be combined with conservation efforts and integrated management approaches. In Israel, for example, approximately 35 percent of drinking-quality water comes from desalination (anticipated to be 70 percent by 2050); however, the country also recycles nearly 90 percent of its wastewater for agricultural use (AP 2014). Similarly, use of drought-resistant crops does not obviate the need to sustainably manage the micronutrient and soil organic matter content of soils in the long term.

If successful in strengthening the resilience of the natural resource base, AEI practices, combined with investments in technologies, could certainly positively impact household food and livelihood security, with subsequent benefits for nutrition. Direct nutrition actions, however, are also a necessary component of an adaptive climate-sensitive nutrition strategy. Not surprisingly perhaps, this strategy will require doing "more of the same, and better" (Crahay et al. 2010). These nutrition actions include: scaling up coverage of nutrition-specific actions (e.g., food and vitamin supplementation, breastfeeding promotion, disease prevention and management) (Bhutta et al. 2013);

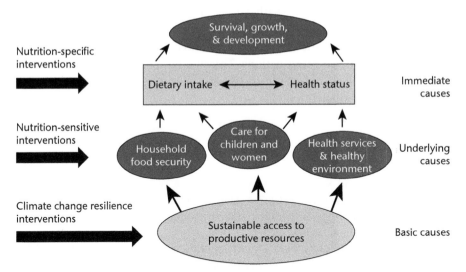

Figure 19.4 Entry points for nutrition-specific, nutrition-sensitive, and climate change resilience interventions within the UNICEF Conceptual Framework of the Determinants of Malnutrition

Source: Adapted from: UNICEF (1990).

Note: The basic causes of poor child growth, development, and survival are rooted in disparities in sustainable access to productive resources. Nutrition-specific interventions address the most proximal determinants of poor nutrition, while nutrition-sensitive interventions often address the underlying causes of household food insecurity ("food"), poor hygiene and sanitation ("health"), and insufficient care for women and children ("care"). Climate change adaptation strategies for improved nutrition will require incorporating climate change resilience actions into nutrition-sensitive investments such that access to food, health, and care resources are achieved through sustainable, climate-sensitive approaches.

incorporating climate change resilience actions into nutrition-sensitive investments (e.g., agriculture, education, and social safety net programs) (Ruel and Alderman 2013); and strengthening health systems, and disproportionately increasing women's access to resources, education, and opportunities (Figure 19.4).

Conclusion

The contrasting burdens of undernutrition and obesity, which currently afflict billions of people around the globe, are a testament to the great strides that still must be made in achieving equity in our food systems, health systems, and global economy. Climate change will perhaps be the most transformative force in shaping the trajectory of these efforts. Though nutrition may seem like a distant outcome, in contrast to the more proximal threats to global ecosystems posed by climate change, protecting the nutrition and health of populations must be a concurrent priority if human communities are to have the capacity to weather the coming storm. Similarly, efforts by the nutrition community to ensure the healthy growth and development of mothers, children, adolescents, the elderly, and all populations, must work to incorporate climate-sensitive actions. This will require explicitly considering ecological and social contexts in the design, planning, and implementation of programs and policies.

References

Ainsworth, E. A., and S. P. Long. 2005. "What Have We Learned from 15 Years of Free-Air CO2 Enrichment (FACE)? A Meta-Analytic Review of the Responses of Photosynthesis, Canopy Properties and Plant Production to Rising CO2." *The New Phytologist* 165 (2): pp. 351–371.

Alderman, H. 2010. "Safety Nets Can Help Address the Risks to Nutrition from Increasing Climate Variability." *Journal of Nutrition* 140 (1): pp. 148S–152S.

Alexander, K. A., M. Carzolio, D. Goodin, and E. Vance. 2013. "Climate Change is Likely to Worsen the Public Health Threat of Diarrheal Disease in Botswana." *International Journal of Environmental Research and Public Health* 10 (4): pp. 1202–1230.

Alig, R. J., D. M. Adams, and B. A. McCarl. 2002. "Projecting Impacts of Global Climate Change on the U.S. Forest and Agriculture Sectors and Carbon Budgets." *Forest Ecology and Management* 169 (1–2): pp. 3–14.

Antonellini, M., P. Mollema, B. Giambastiani, K. Bishop, L. Caruso, A. Minchio, L. Pellegrini, M. Sabia, E. Ulazzi, and G. Gabbianelli. 2008. "Salt Water Intrusion in the Coastal Aquifer of the Southern Po Plain, Italy." *Hydrogeology Journal* 16 (8): pp. 1541–1556.

AP (Associated Press). 2014. "Israel's Desalination Program Averts Future Water Crises." *Haaretz*. May 31. <http://www.haaretz.com/life/nature-environment/1.596270>.

Banerjee, A. V., and E. Duflo. 2007. "The Economic Lives of the Poor." *Journal of Economic Perspectives* 21 (1): pp. 141–168.

Barrett, C., ed. 2013. *Food Security and Sociopolitical Stability*. New York: Oxford University Press.

Barrett, C. B., B. J. Barnett, M. R. Carter, S. Chantarat, J. W. Hansen, A. G. Mude, D. E. Osgood, J. R. Skees, C. G. Turvey, and M. N. Ward. 2007. "Poverty Traps and Climate Risk: Limitations and Opportunities of Index-Based Risk Financing." IRI Technical Report No. 07-03, International Research Institute for Climate and Society, Earth Institute, Columbia University, Palisades, NY. <http://iri.columbia.edu/docs/publications/Poverty_WordFmt%20c6%20Dec%202007%20CBB%20Revision-1.pdf>.

Béguin, A., S. Hales, J. Rocklov, C. Astrom, V. R. Louis, and R. Sauerborn. 2011. "The Opposing Effects of Climate Change and Socio-Economic Development on the Global Distribution of Malaria." *Global Environmental Change* 21 (4): pp. 1209–1214.

Bernstein, A. S., and D. S. Ludwig. 2008. "The Importance of Biodiversity to Medicine." *JAMA* 300 (19): pp. 2297–2299.

Bhutta, Z. A., J. K. Das, A. Rizvi, M. F. Gaffey, N. Walker, S. Horton, P. Webb, A. Lartey, Robert E. Black, the Lancet Nutrition Interventions Review Group, and the Maternal and Child Nutrition Study Group. 2013. "Evidence-Based Interventions for Improvement of Maternal and Child Nutrition: What Can Be Done and at What Cost?" *Lancet* 382 (9890): pp. 452–477.

Black, R. E., L. H. Allen, Z. A. Bhutta, L. E. Caulfield, M. de Onis, M. Ezzati, M., C. Mathers, J. Rivera, and Maternal and Child Undernutrition Study Group. 2008. "Maternal and Child Undernutrition: Global and Regional Exposures and Health Consequences." *Lancet* 371 (9608): pp. 243–260.

Black, R. E., C. G. Victora, S. P. Walker, Z. A. Bhutta, P. Christian, M. de Onis, M. Ezzati, S. Grantham-McGregor, J. Katz, R. Martorell, R. Uauy, and the Maternal and Child Nutrition Study Group. 2013. "Maternal and Child Undernutrition and Overweight in Low-Income and Middle-Income Countries." *Lancet* 382 (9890): pp. 427–451.

Byerlee, D., T. S. Jayne, and R. J. Myers. 2006. "Managing Food Price Risks and Instability in a Liberalizing Market Environment: Overview and Policy Options." *Food Policy* 31 (4): pp. 275–287.

Caballero, B. 2005. "A Nutrition Paradox—Underweight and Obesity in Developing Countries." *New England Journal of Medicine* 352 (15): pp. 1514–1516.

CCSP (US Climate Change Science Program). 2008. *The Effects of Climate Change on Agriculture, Land Resources, Water Resources and Biodiversity in the United States*. A Report by the US Climate Change Science Program and the Subcommittee on Global Change Research. Washington, DC: US Environmental Protection Agency.

Ceballos, F., and M. Robles. 2014. "Weather Risks and Insurance Opportunities for the Rural Poor." 2020 Conference Brief 10, International Food Policy Research Institute, Washington, DC.

Chang, J. 2011. "Meat Production and Consumption Continue to Grow." Vital Signs Online, Worldwatch Institute, Washington, DC. <http://vitalsigns.worldwatch.org/vs-trend/meat-production-and-consumption-continue-grow-0>.

Chapin, F. S., III, E. S. Zavaleta, V. T. Eviner, R. L. Naylor, P. M. Vitousek, H. L. Reynolds, D. U. Hooper, S. Lavorel, O. E. Sala, S. E. Hobbie, M. C. Mack, and S. Díaz. 2000. "Consequences of Changing Biodiversity." *Nature* 405 (6783): pp. 234–242.

Checkley, W., G. Buckley, R. H. Gilman, A. Assis, R. L. Guerrant, S. S. Morris, K. Mølbak, P. Valentiner-Branth, C. F. Lanata, and R. E. Black. 2008. "Multi-country Analysis of the Effects of Diarrhoea on Childhood Stunting." *International Journal of Epidemiology* 37 (4): pp. 816–830.

Checkley, W., L. D. Epstein, R. H. Gilman, D. Figueroa, R. I. Cama, J. A. Patz, and R. E. Black. 2000. "Effect of El Niño and Ambient Temperature on Hospital Admissions for Diarrhoeal Diseases in Peruvian Children." *Lancet* 355 (9202): pp. 442–450.

Checkley, W., R. H. Gilman, R. E. Black, L. D. Epstein, L. Cabrera, C. R. Sterling, and L. H. Moulton. 2004. "Effect of Water and Sanitation on Childhood Health in a Poor Peruvian Peri-Urban Community." *Lancet* 363 (9403): pp. 112–118.

Crahay, P., A. Mitchell, A. Gomez, A.-D. Israël, C. Salpeteur, H. Mattinen, H. Deret, J. Lapegue, L. Grosjean, M. A. Aissa, R. Brown, S. H. Swan, S. Pietzsch, and C. Dufour. 2010. "The Threats of Climate Change on Undernutrition—A Neglected Issue That Requires Further Analysis and Urgent Actions." UN Standing Committee on Nutrition. *SCN News* 38: pp. 4–10.

Craufurd, P. Q., and T. R. Wheeler. 2009. "Climate Change and the Flowering Time of Annual Crops." *Journal of Experimental Botany* 60 (9): pp. 2529–2539.

de la Peña, R., and J. Hughes. 2007. "Improving Vegetable Productivity in a Variable and Changing Climate." ICRISAT (International Crops Research Institute for the Semi-Arid Tropics). *SAT* e-journal 4 (1).

Delgado, C., M. W. Rosegrant, H. Steinfeld, S. Ehui, and C. Courbois. 1999. "Livestock to 2020: The Next Food Revolution." Food, Agriculture, and the Environment Discussion Paper 28, International Food Policy Research Institute, Food and Agricultural Organization of the United Nations, International Livestock Research Institute.

Delgado-Baquerizo, M., F. T. Maestre, A. Gallardo, M. A. Bowker, M. D. Wallenstein, J. L. Quero, V. Ochoa, B. Gozalo, M. García-Gómez, S. Soliveres, P. García-Palacios, M. Berdugo, E. Valencia, C. Escolar, T. Arredondo, C. Barraza-Zepeda, D. Bran, J. A. Carreira, M. Chaieb, A. A. Conceição, M. Derak, D. J. Eldridge, A, Escudero, C. I. Espinosa, and J. Gaitán et al. 2013. "Decoupling of Soil Nutrient Cycles as a Function of Aridity in Global Drylands." *Nature* 502 (7473): pp. 672–676.

Deryng, D., W. J. Sacks, C. C. Barford, and N. Ramankutty. 2011. "Simulating the Effects of Climate and Agricultural Management Practices on Global Crop Yield." *Global Biogeochemical Cycles* 25 (2). doi: 10.1029/2009GB003765.

Dobermann, A., and R. Nelson. 2013. "Opportunities and Solutions for Sustainable Food Production." Background Research Paper for the High-Level Panel of Eminent Persons on the Post-2015 Development Agenda, Sustainable Development Solutions Network of the United Nations.

Döll, P. 2002. "Impact of Climate Change and Variability on Irrigation Requirements: A Global Perspective." *Climatic Change* 54 (3): pp. 269–293.

Epstein, P. R., H. F. Diaz, S. Elias, G. Grabherr, N. E. Graham, W. J. M. Martens, E. Mosley-Thompson, and J. Susskind. 2013. "Biological and Physical Signs of

Climate Change: Focus on Mosquito-Borne Diseases." *Bulletin of the American Meteorological Society* 79 (3): pp. 409–417.

Esrey, S. A., and J.-P. Habicht. 1986. "Epidemiologic Evidence for Health Benefits from Improved Water and Sanitation in Developing Countries." *Epidemiologic Reviews* 8: pp. 117–128.

FAO (Food and Agriculture Organization). 1996. *Rome Declaration on World Food Security and World Food Summit Plan of Action.* Rome, Italy: Food and Agriculture Organization of the United Nations.

FAO (Food and Agriculture Organization). 2006a. *World Agriculture: Towards 2030/2050.* Rome, Italy: Food and Agriculture Organization of the United Nations.

FAO (Food and Agriculture Organization). 2006b. *Livestock's Long Shadow: Environmental Issues and Options.* Rome, Italy: Food and Agriculture Organization of the United Nations.

FAO (Food and Agriculture Organization). 2013a. *The State of Food Insecurity in the World: The Multiple Dimensions of Food Security.* Rome, Italy: Food and Agriculture Organization of the United Nations.

FAO (Food and Agriculture Organization). 2013b. FAOSTAT. Food and Agriculture Organization of the United Nations, Rome, Italy. <http://faostat.fao.org>.

Farley, J., and R. Costanza. 2010. "Payments for Ecosystem Services: From Local to Global." *Ecological Economics* 69 (11): pp. 2060–2068.

Fischer, G., F. N. Tubiello, H. van Velthuizen, and D. A. Wiberg. 2007. "Climate Change Impacts on Irrigation Water Requirements: Effects of Mitigation, 1990–2080." *Technological Forecasting and Social Change* 74 (7): pp. 1083–1107.

Fung, F., and R. F. Clark. 2004. "Health Effects of Mycotoxins: A Toxicological Overview." *Journal of Toxicology: Clinical Toxicology* 42 (2): pp. 217–234.

Gan, J. 2004. "Risk and Damage of Southern Pine Beetle Outbreaks under Global Climate Change." *Forest Ecology and Management* 191 (1–3): pp. 61–71.

Garcia, O. P., K. Z. Long, and J. L. Rosado. 2009. "Impact of Micronutrient Deficiencies on Obesity." *Nutrition Reviews* 67 (10): pp. 559–572.

Gate, P., and N. Brisson. 2010. "Advancement of Phenological Stages and Shortening of Phases." In *Climate Change, Agriculture and Forests in France: Simulations of the Impacts on the Main Species*, edited by N. Brisson, and F. Levrault, pp. 65–78. Angers, France: ADEME.

Gong, Y. Y., K. Cardwell, A. Hounsa, S. Egal, P. C. Turner, A. J. Hall, and C. P. Wild. 2002. "Dietary Aflatoxin Exposure and Impaired Growth in Young Children from Benin and Togo: Cross Sectional Study." *BMJ* (Clinical Research ed.) 325 (7354): pp. 20–21.

Gong, Y., A. Hounsa, S. Egal, P. C. Turner, A. E. Sutcliffe, A. J. Hall, K. Cardwell, and C. P. Wild. 2004. "Postweaning Exposure to Aflatoxin Results in Impaired Child Growth: A Longitudinal Study in Benin, West Africa." *Environmental Health Perspectives* 112 (13): pp. 1334–1338.

Goodhand, J. 2001. "Violent Conflict, Poverty and Chronic Poverty." CPRC Working Paper, No. 6, Chronic Poverty Research Centre, UK.

Gustavsson, J., C. Cederberg, U. Sonesson, R. van Otterdijk, and A. Meybeck. 2011. *Global Food Losses and Food Waste: Extent, Causes and Prevention.* Rome: Food and Agriculture Organization of the United Nations.

Hafner, S. 2003. "Trends in Maize, Rice, and Wheat Yields for 188 Nations over the Past 40 Years: A Prevalence of Linear Growth." *Agriculture, Ecosystems and Environment* 97 (1–3): pp. 275–283.

Hales, S., N. de Wet, J. Maindonald, and A. Woodward, 2002. "Potential Effect of Population and Climate Changes on Global Distribution of Dengue Fever: An Empirical Model." *Lancet* 360 (9336): pp. 830–834.

Hansen, J., M. Sato, R. Ruedy, P. Kharecha, A. Lacis, R. Miller et al. 2007. "Dangerous Human-Made Interference with Climate: A GISS ModelE Study." *Atmospheric Chemistry and Physics* 7 (9): pp. 2287–2312.

Harris, R. 2013. "Could An 'Artificial Leaf' Fuel Your Car?" National Public Radio (NPR), April 10. <http://www.npr.org/2013/04/23/176790800/could-an-artificial-leaf-fuel-your-car>.

Haverkort A. J., and A. Verhagen. 2008. "Climate Change and Its Repercussions for the Potato Supply Chain." *Potato Research* 51: pp. 223–237.

Hebert, J. R. 1985. "Effects of Water Quality and Water Quantity on Nutritional Status: Findings from a South Indian Community." *Bulletin of the World Health Organization* 63 (1): pp. 145–155.

Henthorne, L. 2011. "The Current State of Desalination 2011." IDA (International Desalination Association) World Congress on Desalination and Water Reuse, September 4–9, Perth, Australia.

Hoddinott, J. 2011. "Agriculture, Health, and Nutrition: Toward Conceptualizing the Linkages." 2020 Conference Paper 2, International Food Policy Research Institute, Washington, DC.

Hsiang, S. M., M. Burke, and E. Miguel. 2013. "Quantifying the Influence of Climate on Human Conflict." *Science* 341 (6151): doi: 10.1126/science.1235367.

Humphrey, J. H. 2009. "Child Undernutrition, Tropical Enteropathy, Toilets, and Handwashing." *Lancet* 374 (9694): pp. 1032–1035.

Iannotti, L. L., M. Robles, H. Pachon, and C. Chiarella. 2012. "Food Prices and Poverty Negatively Affect Micronutrient Intakes in Guatemala." *Journal of Nutrition* 142 (8): pp. 1568–1576.

IFAD (International Fund for Agricultural Development). 2010. *Rural Poverty Report 2011*. Rome: International Fund for Agricultural Development.

IPCC (Intergovernmental Panel on Climate Change). 2005. *IPCC Special Report on Carbon Dioxide Capture and Storage*. (B. Metz, O. Davidson, H. C. de Coninck, M. Loos, and L. A. Meyer, eds.). Cambridge, and New York, NY: Cambridge University Press.

IPCC (Intergovernmental Panel on Climate Change). 2007. *Contribution of Working Groups I, II and III to the Fourth Assessment Report of the Intergovernmental Panel on Climate Change*. Geneva, Switzerland: IPCC.

IPCC (Intergovernmental Panel on Climate Change). 2013. *Climate Change 2013: The Physical Science Basis*. Geneva, Switzerland: IPCC.

Ivanic, M., and W. Martin. 2008. "Implications of Higher Global Food Prices for Poverty in Low-Income Countries." Policy Research Working Paper 4594, World Bank, Washington, DC.

Kawano, N., O. Ito, and J.-I. Sakagami. 2009. "Morphological and Physiological Responses of Rice Seedlings to Complete Submergence (Flash Flooding)." *Annals of Botany* 103 (2): pp. 161–169.

Knox, J., T. Hess, A. Daccache, and T. Wheeler. 2012. "Climate Change Impacts on Crop Productivity in Africa and South Asia." *Environmental Research Letters* 7 (3): 034032. doi:10.1088/1748-9326/7/3/034032.

Kuklina, E. V., U. Ramakrishnan, A. D. Stein, H. H. Barnhart, and R. Martorell. 2006. "Early Childhood Growth and Development in Rural Guatemala." *Early Human Development* 82 (7): pp. 425–433.

Kurukulasuriya, P. 2008. "Crop Switching as a Strategy for Adapting to Climate Change." *African Journal of Agricultural and Resource Economics* 2 (1): pp. 1–23.

Lakerveld, J., J. Brug, S. Bot, P. J. Teixeira, H. Rutter, E. Woodward, O. Samdal, L. Stockley, I. De Bourdeaudhuij, P. van Assema, A. Robertson, T. Lobstein, J.-M. Oppert, R. Ádány, and G. Nijpels, on behalf of the SPOTLIGHT consortium. 2012. "Sustainable Prevention of Obesity through Integrated Strategies: The SPOTLIGHT Project's Conceptual Framework and Design." *BMC Public Health* 12: 793.

Lama, J. R., C. R. Seas, R. Leon-Barua, E. Gotuzzo, and R. B. Sack. 2004. "Environmental Temperature, Cholera, and Acute Diarrhoea in Adults in Lima, Peru." *Journal of Health, Population, and Nutrition* 22 (4): pp. 399–403.

Lanchovichina, E., J. Loening, and C. Wood. 2012. "How Vulnerable Are Arab Countries to Global Food Price Shocks?" Policy Research Working Paper 6018, World Bank, Washington, DC.

Landis, S. H., V. Lokomba, C. V. Ananth, J. Atibu, R. W. Ryder, K. E. Hartmann, J. M. Thorp, A. Tshefu, and S. R. Meshnick. 2009. "Impact of Maternal Malaria and Under-Nutrition on Intrauterine Growth Restriction: A Prospective Ultrasound Study in Democratic Republic of Congo." *Epidemiology and Infection* 137 (2): pp. 294–304.

Lenton, T. M., H. Held, E. Kriegler, J. W. Hall, W. Lucht, S. Rahmstorf, and H. J. Schellnhuber. 2008. "Tipping Elements in the Earth's Climate System." *Proceedings of the National Academy of Sciences* 105 (6): pp. 1786–1793.

Lewis, L., M. Onsongo, H. Njapau, H. Schurz-Rogers, G. Luber, S. Kieszak, J. Nyamongo, L. Backer, A. M. Dahiye, A. Misore, K. DeCock, C. Rubin, and the Kenya Aflatoxicosis Investigation Group. 2005. "Aflatoxin Contamination of Commercial Maize Products during an Outbreak of Acute Aflatoxicosis in Eastern and Central Kenya." *Environmental Health Perspectives* 113 (12): pp. 1763–1767.

Lloyd, S. J., R. S. Kovats, and Z. Chalabi. 2011. "Climate Change, Crop Yields, and Undernutrition: Development of a Model to Quantify the Impact of Climate Scenarios on Child Undernutrition." *Environmental Health Perspectives* 119 (12): pp. 1817–1823.

Lobell, D. B., W. Schlenker, and J. Costa-Roberts. 2011. "Climate Trends and Global Crop Production since 1980." *Science* 333 (6042): pp. 616–620.

Lohman, L., ed. 2006. *Carbon Trading: A Critical Conversation on Climate Change, Privatisation and Power.* Uppsala, Sweden: Dag Hammarskjold Foundation, Durban Group for Climate Justice and the Corner House.

Ludwig, D. S., and W. C. Willett. 2013. "Three Daily Servings of Reduced-Fat Milk: An Evidence-Based Recommendation?" *JAMA Pediatrics* 167 (9): pp. 788–789.

Lybbert, T., and D. Sumner. 2010. "Agricultural Technologies for Climate Change Mitigation and Adaptation in Developing Countries: Policy Options for Innovation and Technology Diffusion." Issue Brief No. 6, International Centre for Trade

461

and Sustainable Development, Geneva, Switzerland, and International Food & Agricultural Trade Policy Council, Washington, DC.

Magan, N., A. Medina, and D. Aldred. 2011. "Possible Climate-Change Effects on Mycotoxin Contamination of Food Crops Pre- and Postharvest." *Plant Pathology* 60 (1): pp. 150–163.

Martorell, R., and A. Zongrone. 2012. "Intergenerational Influences on Child Growth and Undernutrition." *Paediatric and Perinatal Epidemiology* 26 (Suppl 1): pp. 302–314.

Mary, A. L., and A. E. Majule. 2009. "Impacts of Climate Change, Variability and Adaptation Strategies on Agriculture in Semi Arid Areas of Tanzania: The Case of Manyoni District in Singida Region, Tanzania." *African Journal of Environmental Science and Technology* 3 (8): pp. 206–218.

Maystadt, J.-F., and O. Ecker. 2014. "Extreme Weather and Civil War: Does Drought Fuel Conflict in Somalia through Livestock Price Shocks?" *American Journal of Agricultural Economics* doi: 10.1093/ajae/aau010. March 25. <http://ajae.oxfordjournals.org/content/early/2014/03/25/ajae.aau010.full.pdf+html>.

McGregor, I. A. 1982. "Malaria: Nutritional Implications." *Reviews of Infectious Diseases* 4 (4): pp. 798–804.

Medina, D. C., S. E. Findley, B. Guindo, and S. Doumbia. 2007. "Forecasting Non-Stationary Diarrhea, Acute Respiratory Infection, and Malaria Time-Series in Niono, Mali." *PLoS ONE* 2 (11): e1181.

Minot, N. 2013. "How Volatile Are African Food Prices?" Research Brief 19, International Food Policy Research Institute, Washington, DC.

Muller, O., M. Garenne, B. Kouyate, and H. Becher. 2003. "The Association between Protein-Energy Malnutrition, Malaria Morbidity and All-Cause Mortality in West African Children." *Tropical Medicine and International Health* 8 (6): pp. 507–511.

Nelson, G. C., M. W. Rosegrant, A. Palazzo, I. Gray, C. Ingersoll, R. Robertson, S. Tokgoz, T. Zhu, T. B. Sulser, C. Ringler, S. Msangi, and L. You. 2010. *Food Security, Farming, and Climate Change to 2050: Scenarios, Results, Policy Options.* Washington, DC: International Food Policy Research Institute.

Neumann, C. G., N. O. Bwibo, S. P. Murphy, M. Sigman, S. Whaley, L. H. Allen, D. Guthrie, R. E. Weiss, and M. W. Demment. 2003. "Animal Source Foods Improve Dietary Quality, Micronutrient Status, Growth and Cognitive Function in Kenyan School Children: Background, Study Design and Baseline Findings." *Journal of Nutrition* 133 (11 Suppl 2): pp. 3941S–3949S.

Nyakeriga, A. M., M. Troye-Blomberg, A. K. Chemtai, K. Marsh, and T. N. Williams. 2004. "Malaria and Nutritional Status in Children Living on the Coast of Kenya." *American Journal of Clinical Nutrition* 80 (6): pp. 1604–1610.

Parry, M. L., C. Rosenzweig, A. Iglesias, M. Livermore, and G. Fischer. 2004. "Effects of Climate Change on Global Food Production under SRES Emissions and Socio-economic Scenarios." *Global Environmental Change* 14 (1): pp. 53–67.

Parsons, D. J., A. C. Armstrong, J. R. Turnpenny, A. M. Matthews, K. Cooper, and J. A. Clark. 2001. "Integrated Models of Livestock Systems for Climate Change Studies. 1. Grazing Systems." *Global Change Biology* 7 (1): pp. 93–112.

Paterson, R. R. M., and N. Lima. 2010. "How Will Climate Change Affect Mycotoxins in Food?" *Food Research International* 43 (7): pp. 1902–1914.

Peet, M. M., and D. W. Wolfe. 2000. "Crop Ecosystem Responses to Climatic Change: Vegetable Crops." In *Climate Change and Global Crop Productivity*, edited by K. R. Reddy, and H. F. Hodges, pp. 213–243. Wallingford: CAB International.

Peterson, A. T. 2009. "Shifting Suitability for Malaria Vectors across Africa with Warming Climates." *BMC Infectious Diseases* 9:59. doi:10.1186/1471-2334-9-59.

Pinstrup-Andersen, P. 2013. "Contemporary Food Policy Challenges and Opportunities." *Australian Journal of Agricultural and Resource Economics*. doi: 10.1111/1467-8489.12019.

Reynolds, J. F., D. M. S. Smith, E. F. Lambin, B. L. Turner, II, M. Mortimore, S. P. J. Batterbury, T. E. Downing, H. Dowlatabadi, R. J. Fernández, J. E. Herrick, E. Huber-Sannwald, H. Jiang, R. Leemans, T. Lynam, F. T. Maestre, M. Ayarza, and B. Walker. 2007. "Global Desertification: Building a Science for Dryland Development." *Science* 316 (5826): pp. 847–851.

Rhodes, J., and D. Keith. 2008. "Biomass with Capture: Negative Emissions within Social and Environmental Constraints: An Editorial Comment." *Climatic Change* 87 (3–4): pp. 321–328.

Rosenzweig, C., A. Iglesias, X. B. Yang, P. Epstein, and E. Chivian. 2001. "Climate Change and Extreme Weather Events: Implications for Food Production, Plant Diseases, and Pests." *Global Change and Human Health* 2 (2): pp. 90–104.

Rosenzweig, C., and M. L. Parry. 1994. "Potential Impact of Climate Change on World Food Supply." *Nature* 367 (6459): pp. 133–138.

Ruel, M. T., and H. Alderman. 2013. "Nutrition-Sensitive Interventions and Programmes: How Can They Help to Accelerate Progress in Improving Maternal and Child Nutrition?" *Lancet* 382 (9891): pp. 536–551.

Salazar-Lindo, E., P. Pinell-Salles, A. Maruy, and E. Chea-Woo. 1997. "El Niño and Diarrhoea and Dehydration in Lima, Peru." *Lancet* 350 (9091): pp. 1597–1598.

Schär, C., P. L. Vidale, D. Lüthi, C. Frei, C. Häberli, M. A. Liniger, and C. Appenzeller. 2004. "The Role of Increasing Temperature Variability in European Summer Heatwaves." *Nature* 427 (6972): pp. 332–336.

Schmidhuber, J., and F. N. Tubiello. 2007. "Global Food Security under Climate Change." *Proceedings of the National Academy of Sciences* 104 (50): pp. 19703–19708.

Scrimshaw, N. S., and J. P. SanGiovanni. 1997. "Synergism of Nutrition, Infection, and Immunity: An Overview." *American Journal of Clinical Nutrition* 66 (2): pp. 464S–477S.

Scrimshaw, N. S., C. E. Taylor, and J. E. Gorden. 1968. "Interactions of Nutrition and Infection." Monograph Series No. 57, World Health Organization, Geneva, Switzerland.

Seo, N., and R. Mendelsohn. 2007. "An Analysis of Crop Choice: Adapting to Climate Change in South American Farms." WPS4152, World Bank, Washington, DC.

Singh, R. B., S. Hales, N. de Wet, R. Raj, M. Hearnden, and P. Weinstein. 2001. "The Influence of Climate Variation and Change on Diarrheal Disease in the Pacific Islands." *Environmental Health Perspectives* 109 (2): pp. 155–159.

Smit, B. 2001. "Adaptation to Climate Change in the Context of Sustainable Development and Equity." In *Climate Change 2001: Impacts, Adaptation and Vulnerability. Contribution of Working Group II to the Third Assessment Report of the Intergovernmental Panel on Climate Change*, edited by J. J. McCarthy, O. F. Canziani,

N. A. Leary, D. J. Dokken, and K. S. White, pp. 817–912. Cambridge: Cambridge University Press.

Smith, J. E., G. L. Solomons, C. W. Lewis, and J. G. Anderson. 1994. *Mycotoxins in Human Nutrition and Health*. Brussels, Belgium: European Commission CG XII.

Smith, P., D. Martino, Z. Cai, D. Gwary, H. Janzen, P. Kumar, B. McCarl, S. Ogle, F. O'Mara, C. Rice, B. Scholes, O. Sirotenko, M. Howden, T. McAllister, G. Pan, V. Romanenkov, U. Schneider, S. Towprayoon, M. Wattenbach, and J. Smith. 2008. "Greenhouse Gas Mitigation in Agriculture." *Philosophical Transactions of the Royal Society B: Biological Sciences* 363 (1492): pp. 789–813.

St. Clair, S. B., and J. P. Lynch. 2010. "The Opening of Pandora's Box: Climate Change Impacts on Soil Fertility and Crop Nutrition in Developing Countries." *Plant and Soil* 335 (1–2): pp. 101–115.

Stuart, T. 2009. *Waste: Uncovering the Global Food Scandal*. New York: W.W. Norton and Company, Inc.

Swedish Environmental Protection Agency. 2009. *Minskat svinn av livsmedel I skolkök–erfarenheter och framgångsfaktorer*. Stockholm: Swedish Environmental Protection Agency (SEPA).

Tebaldi, C., and D. B. Lobell. 2008. "Towards Probabilistic Projections of Climate Change Impacts on Global Crop Yields." *Geophysical Research Letters* 35 (8). doi:10.1029/2008GL033423.

Thomas Reuters Foundation. 2013 "Pakistan Floods." April 8. Thomas Reuters Foundation. <http://www.trust.org/spotlight/pakistan-floods-2010/>.

Thornton, P., and L. Cramer, eds. 2012. "Impacts of Climate Change on the Agricultural and Aquatic Systems and Natural Resources within the CGIAR's Mandate." CCAFS Working Paper 23, CGIAR Research Program on Climate Change, Agriculture and Food Security (CCAFS), Copenhagen, Denmark. <https://cgspace.cgiar.org/handle/10568/21226>.

Tilman, D., C. Balzer, J. Hill, and B. L. Befort. 2011. "Global Food Demand and the Sustainable Intensification of Agriculture." *Proceedings of the National Academy of Sciences* 108 (50): pp. 20260–20264.

Tilman, D., P. B. Reich, J. Knops, D. Wedin, T. Mielke, and C. Lehman. 2001. "Diversity and Productivity in a Long-Term Grassland Experiment." *Science* 294 (5543): pp. 843–845.

Tirado, M. C., R. Clarke, L. A. Jaykus, A. McQuatters-Gollop, and J. M. Frank. 2010. "Climate Change and Food Safety: A Review." *Food Research International* 43 (7): pp. 1745–1765.

Trenberth, K. E. 2011. "Changes in Precipitation with Climate Change." *Climate Research* 47 (1–2): pp. 123–138.

Tscharntke, T., Y. Clough, T. C. Wanger, L. Jackson, I. Motzke, I. Perfecto, J. Vandermeer, and A. Whitbread. 2012. "Global Food Security, Biodiversity Conservation and the Future of Agricultural Intensification." *Biological Conservation* 151 (1): pp. 53–59.

Tubiello, F. N., J.-F. Soussana, and S. M. Howden. 2007. "Crop and Pasture Response to Climate Change." *Proceedings of the National Academy of Sciences* 104 (50): pp. 19686–19690.

UNEP (United Nations Environment Programme). 2003. *Millennium Ecosystem Assessment: Ecosystems and Human Well-being*. Washington, DC: Island Press.

UNICEF (United Nations Children's Fund). 1990. "Strategy for Improved Nutrition of Children and Women in Developing Countries." UNICEF Policy Review, United Nations Children's Fund, New York.

UNICEF (United Nations Children's Fund), WHO (World Health Organization), and The World Bank. 2012. "UNICEF-WHO-The World Bank Joint Child Malnutrition Estimates." UNICEF, New York; WHO, Geneva; The World Bank, Washington, DC.

US Energy Information Administration. 2013. *International Energy Outlook 2013*. Washington, DC: U.S. Energy Information Administration.

Van der Fels-Klerx, H. J., E. D. van Asselt, M. S. Madsen, and J. E. Olesen. 2013. "Impact of Climate Change Effects on Contamination of Cereal Grains with Deoxynivalenol." *PLoS ONE* 8 (9): e73602.

van Vurren, D. P., E. Stehfest, M. G. J. den Elzen, T. Kram, J. van Vliet, S. Deetman, M. Isaac, K. K. Goldewijk, A. Hof, A. M. Beltran, R. Oostenrijk, and B. van Ruijven. 2011. "RCP2.6: Exploring the Possibility to Keep Global Mean Temperature Increase Below 2°C." *Climate Change* 109 (1–2): pp. 95–116.

Walker, S. P., T. D. Wachs, S. Grantham-McGregor, M. M. Black, C. A. Nelson, S. L. Huffman, H. Baker-Henningham, S. M. Chang, J. D. Hamadani, B. Lozoff, J. M. Meeks Gardner, C. A. Powell, A. Rahman, and L. Richter. 2011. "Inequality in Early Childhood: Risk and Protective Factors for Early Child Development." *Lancet* 378 (9799), pp. 1325–1338.

Wegren, S. K. 2013. "Food Security and Russia's 2010 Drought." *Eurasian Geography and Economics* 52 (1): pp. 140–156.

WFP (World Food Programme). 2008. Summary of Price Impact Assessment Findings. WFP, Rome, Italy.

Wheeler, T. R., and J. von Braun. 2013. "Climate Change Impacts on Global Food Security." *Science* 341 (6145): pp. 508–513.

WHO (World Health Organization). 2013a. Climate Change and Human Health: Biodiversity. World Health Organization. <http://www.who.int/globalchange/ecosystems/biodiversity/en/>.

WHO (World Health Organization). 2013b. Media Centre: Malaria. Fact Sheet. World Health Organization. <http://www.who.int/mediacentre/factsheets/fs094/en/>.

WHO (World Health Organization). 2013c. Nutrition: Global and Regional Food Consumption Patterns and Trends. World Health Organization. <http://www.who.int/nutrition/topics/3_foodconsumption/en/index4.html>.

WHO (World Health Organization). 2013d. Nutrition: Micronutrient Deficiencies: Iron Deficiency Anaemia. World Health Organization. from <http://www.who.int/nutrition/topics/ida/en/>.

World Bank. 2010. World Development Report 2010: Development and Climate Change. World Bank, Washington, DC.

World Bank. 2012. "Turn Down the Heat: Why a 4°C Warmer World Must Be Avoided." A Report for the World Bank by the Potsdam Institute for Climate Impact Research and Climate Analytics, World Bank, Washington, DC.

Yip, C. S. C., G. Crane, and J. Karnon. 2013. "Systematic Review of Reducing Population Meat Consumption to Reduce Greenhouse Gas Emissions and Obtain Health Benefits: Effectiveness and Models Assessments." *International Journal of Public Health* 58 (5): pp. 683–693.

Zougmoré, R., A. Mando, and L. Stroosnijder. 2013. "Soil Nutrient and Sediment Loss as Affected By Erosion Barriers and Nutrient Source in Semi-Arid Burkina Faso." *Arid Land Research and Management* 23 (1): pp. 85–101.

Index

Index

Africa (*Cont.*)
structural transformation 10, 176, 179, 186, 337–41
stunting 39, 41, 63, 79, 144, 297, 435, 442
survey data 24, 195, 285, 327, 344, 403
transfer programs 39, 49, 50
undernourishment 9, 64, 69, 165, 313
urbanization 67, 69, 205, 285, 340
women, primary food producers 166
zinc–deficient soils 78
see also individual African countries
African Development Bank 334
African Union 428
Agricultural Transformation Agency (ATA) 126, 402, 403, 404, 405, 413–14
agriculture:
and bioeconomy 8, 240–54
and climate change 13, 238, 308–9, 432–50, 453–4
commercial systems 166, 171–2, 201
deskilling 271
and economic growth 171, 175–7, 199, 216–17, 304–5, 316
emissions 449–50
employment 4, 165, 169, 186, 196, 209, 232, 240, 323, 335–6, 339, 344–5, 361, 446
and fertilizer use 75
and food security 7, 140, 143, 146, 169, 172–3, 199, 254–7, 347, 432–4
GDP share 167–8, 170, 172, 212–14, 316
Green Revolution 72, 186, 192, 212, 279, 282, 419
and health 172, 186, 218–25
high–value 202
income from 10, 165, 169, 174, 175, 181, 215, 379, 442–3, 446
as instrument of social policy 230–1
and labor 10, 169, 316, 337–8
link to energy sector 246–8, 252–4
low–productive systems 166, 168, 170–1, 174–9
modernizing systems 166, 168, 171, 179–85, 186
Neolithic 279, 280–1
no–till 13, 450
and nutrition 144, 149, 156, 165–86
and obesity 225–9
output growth 209, 398
pathways linking with nutrition 166, 172–4
policies 113, 123, 172, 174–9, 183, 204, 314–6, 375, 388, 393, 395, 400, 422
and population growth 9, 279–88
private sector interests 177, 182–3, 315, 424, 427–8
production 126, 338, 418, 435, 436–7, 441–4
productivity 9, 11, 167–71, 175–7, 209–18, 232–3, 279–88, 338, 345, 443, 454

public sector interest 177, 182–3, 315, 357, 420, 428
R&D 8, 208–35, 254–5
R&D indicators 217–18
rates of return 210, 216
reasons for poor performance 167
rural development 340, 378, 388, 395–7, 410
and rural women 165, 177–8
structural transformation 186, 337–9
stunting 165, 168
in sub–Saharan Africa 282–8
subsistence 7, 201–2
system typologies 170–2, 201
technology 2, 8, 79, 170, 174, 197, 215, 374, 423–4
transgenic 271–4, 425
agriculture–led strategies 171, 299–304
agroecological intensification (AEI) 454–55
Aker, J. 49, 50, 182
Akresh, R. 41, 42, 54
Alderman, H. xix, 4–5, 36–60, 305, 306, 307, 443, 456
Alliance for a Green Revolution in Africa (AGRA) 427–8
Alston, J. M. xix, 8, 180, 208–39
Amarante, V. 44
anemia 5, 39, 45, 46, 51, 52, 61, 63, 180, 225, 452
Angola 324, 325, 326, 328, 342, 358, 368
animal diseases 73, 281, 439
Annan, K. 428
Archer Daniels Midland 424
Argentina 41, 94, 349, 357
aridity 436, 439–41, 445–6, 454
Ariga, J. 176
Aristotle 272
Arndt, C. 252, 376
Asia 186, 304, 337
agriculture 7, 166, 171, 175, 179–81, 186, 192–205, 210, 213, 214, 217, 300, 301, 303–5, 308, 316, 378–9, 388, 419
animal–source food 183
crop yield 7, 175, 439
data sets 24, 26, 375, 377–8
demographic dividend 287
economic growth 2, 287, 337, 374
environmental sustainability 308, 373, 437–9
fertility 287
financial crisis 374, 377, 420
food access 147, 165
food crisis 116–24, 127–8, 373–4
food waste 451
FSNM systems 120, 121–2, 123–4, 127, 128–9
GDP 214, 221, 374
Green Revolution 7, 166, 175–6, 186, 192, 198, 419, 427